THE

SACRED BOOKS

OF THE

HINDUS

TRANSLATED BY

VARIOUS SANSKRIT SCHOLARS.

EDITED BY

Major B. D. Basu, I. M. S. (Retired).

VOLUME XXVI. Part 3.

THE SRIMAD DEVI BHAGAVTAM.
TRANSLATED BY

SWAMI VIJNANANDA.

THIRD EDITION.

PUBLISHED BY

Sudhindranatha Vasu at the Panini Office, Bhuvaneswari

Asrama, Bahadurganj, Allahabad.

Printed by Manzur Ahmad at the Modern Printing Works, Allahabad.

CONTENTS.

THE NINTH BOOK.

THE TENTH BOOK.

THE ELEVENTH BOOK.

THE TWELFTH BOOK.

THE END.

FOREWORD.

Śrî Bhagavân Veda Vyâsa first composed one Purâṇam only. From this, the three disciples of his, Lomaharṣaṇa and two others, compiled the three other Saṃhitâs. So at first these four Purâṇas were extant. From these four Purâṇas, the eighteen Mahâ Purâṇas were written. And long after this many other Upa-Purâṇas came into appearance. That the Purâṇas were collected and compiled from the original Âdi Purâṇa Samhitâ can easily be traced if each Purâṇam be read attentively. Lots of proofs can be obtained. If one reads the orders of creation in the Viṣṇu, Matsya, Brahmâṇḍa, Padma and other Purâṇas, one will find that all the Purâṇas are treating of one and the same thing, the same subject ; so much so, that, at some places, the verses are the same. In some places, some verses are more similar and, in some Purâṇas, some verses are less similar. This is all the difference. The ideal is one and the same in all the Purâṇas. Hence so great and striking are the similarities and resemblances witnessed in verses and descriptions. If there were different Purâṇas in their originals before, many in number, and if the Purâṇas at present extant were written from those different Purâṇas, then so many striking similarities and resemblances, seen at present, would never have occurred.

The following eighteen Purâṇas are mentioned in due order in the Viṣṇu Purâṇam. First, the Brahma ; second, the Padma ; third, the Viṣṇu Purâṇam ; fourth, the Śaiva ; fifth, the Bhâgavata ; sixth, the Nâradîya ; seventh, the Mârkaṇḍeya ; eighth, the Âgneya ; ninth, the Bhaviṣya ; tenth, the Brahma Vaivarta ; eleventh, the Linga ; twelfth, the Varâha ; thirteenth, the Skanda ; fourteenth, the Vâmana ; fifteenth, the Kûrma ; sixteenth, the Matsya ; seventeenth, the Garuḍa ; and eighteenth, the Brahmâṇḍa Purâṇam. In one and all of these Purâṇams are described duly the (1) Sarga (creation), (2) Pratisarga (the secondary creation), (3) Vams'a (lineage of kings), (4) Manvantara (duration of the Manu periods) and (5) Vams'ânucharitams (histories of the several lines and their descendants). " O Maitreya ! The Purâṇam that I am describing to you is the Viṣṇu Purâṇam. This has been composed after the Padma Purâṇam." From the above statement of the Viṣṇu Purâṇam, it is seen that the eighteen Purâṇas were not composed and compiled at one and the same time. First the Brahma Purâṇam was written ; next, the Padma Purâṇam was written ; next, the Viṣṇu Purâṇam and so forth. Gradually, one after another, the eighteen Purâṇas were composed, written and published.

According to Dr. H. H. Wilson, the several Purâṇas were composed from the ninth century A. D. to the sixteenth century A. D. Many savants of the west and Bâbu Akṣaya Kumâra Datta, and several others of the east agree with Dr. H. H. Wilson.

The above learned men declare that the Skanda Purâṇam is very recent. But other savants of India are not ready to admit or accept this. Lately Mahâ Mahopâdhyâya Hara Prasâd Śâstrî has got one Puthi (manuscript) of the Nandikes'vara Mâhâtmya of the Skanda Purâṇam from Nepal that clearly belongs to the seventh century A. D. In the Calcutta University there exists one Puthi containing the Kâs'i Khaṇḍa of the Skanda Purâṇam, handwritten in 933 Saka Era. Owing to these reasons, the original Skanda Purâṇam, now extant, cannot be considered so recent. That the Skanda Purâṇam had been quite in vogue even before the seventh century A. D. is beyond any doubt. Besides the extracts by Śamkarâchârya from the Mârkaṇḍeya Purâṇam, the collections by Vâṇa in the 7th century A. D. of his materials from the Devî Mâhâtmya in the Mârkaṇḍeya Purâṇam and his mentioning the Pavanaprokta Purâṇam, the collections of details of the Sûrya Śatakam from the Saura Purâṇam by his contemporary Mayûrabhaṭṭa, the compilation at that time of the Brahma Siddhânta from the chief source Viṣṇudharmottara Purâṇam, the collecting of proofs by Alberouni in the eleventh century A. D. from the Âditya, Vâyu, Matsya and Viṣṇu and Viṣṇudharmottara Purâṇas, from the gifts made by Ballâla Sen, the king of Bengal, mentioning the Brahma, Matsya, Mârkaṇḍeya, Agni, Bhaviṣya, Varâha, Kûrma, and Viṣṇudharmottara Purâṇas, and Âdya, Kâlikâ, Nandi, Nâra Simha, and Śâmba Upapurâṇas we can safely reject the opinions held by Dr. H. H. Wilson, and Akṣaya Kumâra Datta and others.

That the eighteen Purâṇas were extant before the period of Śaukarâchârya, Vâṇa Bhaṭṭa and others, there is no doubt. If the order of sequence of events be seen, as far as the origins of various personages and dynasties, etc., are concerned, then it may be safely admitted that the original first nine (9) Purâṇas were composed and written before the Âpastamba Dharma Sûtras were written. Thus the composition period of the chief Purâṇas comes just after the Vaidik period. Now the eighteen (18) Purâṇas, that we see current in their present forms now, were not so in the previous times. We may conclude that the Âdi Viṣṇu Purâṇam was written in the time of Parîkṣit; the Garuḍa Purâṇam was written in the time of Janamejaya, the son of Parîkṣit, and that the Matsya and Brahmâṇda Purâṇas were composed in the time of the grandson of Janamejaya, named Adhîsîma Kriṣṇa.

The description of Bhaviṣya Râja Vaṃsa, the dynasties to come, was added afterwards.

Amongst the five characteristics, the recitation of the Bhaviṣya Râja Vaṃsa, the dynasties to come, does not seem to be a principal element of the Purâṇas. The meaning of Vamsânncharita is the recitation of the characters of the famous kings and their descendants that lived and died; not that of the future dynasties of kings (as coming after the time of the writing of the Purâṇas) and so is not settled in the more ancient Purâṇas, the Viṣṇu, Matsya or Brahma Purâṇas. In the later Śrî Mad Bhâgavata, the descriptions of the past, present and future lines of kings were meant and so written out. But it should be remembered that to write of the present and the past is one thing and to write of the future is a different thing. Though we do not find in the Jâvâ Dvîpa edition of the Brahmâṇḍa Purâṇam, of the fifth century A. D. anything about the future dynasties, yet since that period they began to be inserted gradually in the different Purâṇas. This can be proved from the Tantra vârtik of the famous Kumârila Bhaṭṭa. Bhaṭṭa Kumârila writes in one place :—The divisions of the earth, the chronology of the dynasties, the measurements of countries and their periods of existences, the future events, etc., are the subjects to be dealt with in the Purâṇas.

The different Purâṇas treated by the different sects have assumed, as it were, the aspect of the pure gold mixed with various alloys. Now to extract the pure gold by burning and smelting the ore has, indeed, become a very difficult task. What the eighteen Purâṇas were in their first pure stage can be somewhat made out on seeing the Matsya Purâṇam.

The famous Pundit Akṣaya Kumâr Dutt writes :—"In the Purâṇas, the creations both primary and secondary, the description of the dynasties and the lives of the famous persons of the dynasties form the subject matter. To advise on the religious rites and ceremonies is not the object. But in the Purâṇas, and then in the Upa-Purâṇas, now extant, the recitations of the glories of the Devas and the Devîs, their worship, their festivities and the Vratas and Niyamas form the greater part. The aforesaid five characteristics form here, as it were, the appendages merely. If to give instructions on Dharma were the object of the older Purâṇas, as is now the theme of the present Purâṇas, then it would not have been spoken by the Sûta caste people ;it would then have been one of the duties of the Ṣaṭ Karmas'âlî Brâhmaṇas, performing duly the six Karmas. To instruct the Riṣis, Munis, and other ordinary Brâhmaṇas would not have been the duty of the inferior Sûta (carpenter) caste.

These Purâṇas form, as it were, the different centres of the different religious sects in promulgating the superiority of their own tenets. The Ävatâra-Vâda is one of the chief features of the Purâṇas. In the Purâṇas dwelling on the glories of Śiva, many Avatâras of Śiva are described. So, in the Vaiṣṇava Purâṇas, many Avatâras of Viṣṇu are dwelt upon. The theory of re-incarnation is not of the latest periods as most people imagine from the ten Avatâras. It goes far back into the oldest treatises of the Vedas. The Matsya incarnation is treated in the Śatapatha Brâhmaṇa (1-8-1-2,10) ; the Kûrma incarnation in the Taittirîya Âraṇyaka (1-23-1) and in Śatapatha Brâhmaṇa (7-4-3-5) ; the Varâha incarnation is mentioned in the Taittirîya Samhitâ, in the Taittirîya Brâhmaṇa (1-1-3-5) and in Śatapatha Brâhmaṇa (14-1-2-11); the Vâmana incarnation in the Rik-Samhitâ (1-22-17) and in Śatapatha Brâhmaṇa (1-2-5-1,7) ; the Râma Bhârgava incarnation in Aitareya Brâhmaṇa ; the Kriṣṇa incarnation, the son of Devakî, in the Chhândogya Upaniṣada (3-17) and the Vâsudeva Śrî Kriṣṇa is dwelt with in the Taittirîya Âraṇyaka (10-1-6). According to a major part of the Vedic books, the incarnations of Kûrma and Varâha, etc, are the incarnations of Brahmâ. But in the Vaiṣṇavic Purâṇas, those very same are regarded as the Avatâras of Viṣṇu.

So in the Brahmâṇḍa and other Śaiva Purâṇas various incarnations of Śiva are acknowledged. So the incarnations of the Sun are also mentioned in the Bhaviṣya and Saura Purâṇas, etc. As, on the one hand, the devotees of Brahmâ, Viṣṇu, Śiva, and the Sun dwelt upon the glories of their own Iṣṭa Deities in their various incarnations, so, on the other hand, the Riṣî Mârkaṇḍeya and the other sages sang the glories of the Devî Bhagavatî in their Śâkta Purâṇas. Brahmâ is mentioned in various places in the Vedas as the oldest Deity to be worshipped. It is not on that account to be thought that the worships of Viṣṇu, Śiva and the other Devas are very latest. In the Rik Samhitâ, in various places, hundreds of Viṣṇu mantras are found. So in the Sâma, Yajus, and Âtharva Vedas. Mahâ Deva is known as Rudra in the Rik Samhitâ. In the four Vedas, the hymns are sung of the Rudra Deva. The most famous of these is the Rudrâdhyâya in the Yajur Vedas.

Though the modern Pundits shew their reluctance in acknowledging the identity of the Vaidik Rudra and Mahâ Deva, yet we do not hesitate to admit of the above identity when we find in the Vâjasaneya Śata Rudrî the names of Śiva, Girîs'a, Pas'upati, Nîlagrîva, Sitikaṇṭha, Bhava, Sarbba, Mahâ Deva, etc. Especially in the Atharva Samhitâ, when we see the names Mahâ Deva (9-7-7), Bhava (6-9-3-1), Pas'upati (9-2-5), etc., we do not entertain any doubt. When we study the origin of Śiva in the Śata patha Brâhmaṇa (6-1-3-7/19) and in the Śamkṣyâyana Brâhmaṇa (6-1-3-7/19) we do not find any great difference between the above and what are mentioned in the Mârkaṇḍeya Purâṇa and in the Viṣṇu Purâṇa. So the worship of the Sun is also very ancient in the Vedas.

Now we come to the topic of Śakti in the Vedas. Those persons who on merely hearing the names of Śivâ, Durgâ, consider them as of a very recent period, ought to know that the worship of Durgâ or Śakti is not, really speaking, of a very late origin. When we read in the Vâjasaneya Samhitâ "Ambikâ" (3-57) and "Śivâ" (16-1), in the Talavakâra Upaniṣad (3-11,12; 4-1,2) Umâ Haimavatî as Brahma Vidyâ Incarnate, and in the Taittrîya Âraṇyaka (10 Pra) "Kanyâ Kumârî," "Kâtyâyanî," Durgâ, etc, we remember the same Durgâ, the consort of Śiva. From those very olden times, the worship of the Âdyâ Śakti, the Brahma incarnate, is extant. These can be very well seen if we study the Vedas.

What is indicated in the germ form, rather commenced in the Vedic treatises, that very thing is expanded and matured in the Purâṇas. Seeing this dilation as if of a story, we may take the Purâṇas, as if of a very late origin. The Pûrvapakṣins believe that what is reflected in the Vedas, that same thing is twisted and tortured fully and fabricated into a huge body in the Purâṇas. Take the Rik of the Rik Samhitâ "Idam Viṣṇur vichakrame tredhâ nidâdhe padaṃ, samu ḍhâmasya pâṃsure" (1-22-17) and Triṇî padâ vichakrame Viṣṇur gopâ adâbhyah, ato dharmâṇi dhârayan "(1-22-18)," Viṣṇu strode his three steps in this world. The whole universe is pervaded with the dust of His feet." "Viṣṇu, bold and dauntless, difficult to be overcome, and the Preserver of the whole world put his three steps on the earth, etc., for the preservation of the Dharma." But the Paurâṇikâs have rendered it as the Vâmana's act of overcoming Vali, and so on. What is stated very concisely in the Vedas with an object, distant in view, that same thing is expanded in the Purâṇas in the form of a big narrative. Therefore we see some distortions and differences in the Purâṇas, rendering the anecdotes in the Purâṇas assume a somewhat separate and independent aspect. But for this reason merely, we cannot reject the Purâṇic descriptions as if of a very strange, fanciful character or as of a very recent and worthless production.

From the very earliest times there have sprung up different worshippers of the different Devas and Devîs. Worshippers of the different Deities would consciously or unconsciously give rise to different religious sects. This will be seen, if we study the religious and moral histories of the people. Now it is quite natural for the Riṣi who had got his desired end by worshipping a particular Deva, that he would pay his devotion to that Deva, love him with his heart and soul and expect earnestly that others, too, pay similar deep love and devotion to his Deity and thereby derive the highest bliss and get their desired ends. From this tendency of love and devotion and a desire that others may also taste of the sweetness thereof, the different Devas have come to be worshipped by the different Riṣis and the different peoples. Again from the disciples of these Deva Bhakta Riṣis, many different religious sects have cropped up in this world.

The Veda is not the general property of all. The Ritvigs, Hotâs, Udgâtâs and various Yâjñiks, claim the Veda as their own property. But the Itihâsas and the Purâṇas are not so; they are the general property of all men and women. To advise and give instructions on various religious, moral, social, industrial, technical, and other cognate subjects, the Purâṇas were composed. Therefore it is written in the Brahmâṇḍa Purâṇam that that Brâhmaṇa who has studied even the four Vedas with their Angas and the Upaniṣadas and yet has not studied the Purâṇas, cannot be clear-sighted, wise, and skilful. For it is the Vedas that are enlarged, expanded, and explained in the Itihâsas and in the Purâṇas. Hence the persons void of the knowledge of the Purâṇas, are afraid of the Vedas, for they are verily the persons that insult the Vedas. The Purâṇas are very ancient and they explain the Vedas; hence they are named the Purâṇas. Those who know these Purâṇas are freed of all their sins.

The Viṣṇu Bhâgavat was written after the Itihâsas and the other Purâṇas were composed, and written. And then Śrî Vyâsa Deva found his full satisfaction. Hence this treatise is known as the Pañchametara Purâṇa. Some hold the opinion that this Śrî Mad Bhâgavat was written by Bopa Deva, the great grammarian of Bengal. There are the ten characteristics of the Purâṇas:—(1) Sarga, (2) Visarga, (3) Samsthâ, (4) Rakṣâ, (5) Manvantara, (6) Vaṃs'a kathana, (7) Vaṃs'ânucharita, (8) Pralaya, (9) Hetu and, (10) Apâs'raya. Whereas some others consider the five characteristics as the angas of the Purâṇas to be dwelt upon. Those that are characterised by the ten qualities are denominated as Mahâ Purâṇas and those of five qualities are known as the Upa-Purâṇas or the Alpa Purâṇas.

The creations of Mahat, Ahamkâra, the Sthûla and Sûkṣma indriyas and the gross creations are known as the Sarga. From the inherent tendencies and desires, the vîjas, as it were, the creation of all these moveables and non-moveables is known as Visarga or the secondary creation. The ways and means of living of all the Chara Bhûtas and men are known as Samsthâ or Sthiti. The Avatâras of Nârâyaṇa for the preservation of the Devas, Tiryakas, men, and the Riṣis are known as the Rakṣâ. The periods of the Aṃsâvatâras are known as the Manvantaras. The descriptions of the histories or stories, past, present, and future of the several holy kings born of Brahmâ are known as Vaṃs'akathana; and the descriptions of the characters of their descendants are known as Vaṃs'ânukathana. The four different Layas Naimittika, Prâkritik, Nitya and Âtyantika are known as the Pralayas. Describing the Jîvas as the cause of the origin, creation, preservation, and destruction of this vis'va is known as Hetu. And Apâs'raya is the Great Refuge of All, the Great Solace of all, the Great Witness of the three states Jâgrat, Svapna and Suṣupti. The five characteristics of the Upa Purâṇas are Sarga, Pratisarga, Vams'a, Manvantara and Vaṃs'ânucharita. If we consider the five characteristics, this Devî Bhâgavata is reckoned as one of the Mahâ Purâṇas. There are three hundred and eighteen Adhyâyas in the Devî Bhâgavatam whereas in the Bhâgavatam there are three hundred and thirty-two Adhyâyas. So some discrepancy arises here as far as the Adhyâyas are concerned. Ṡrî Viṣṇu Bhâgavat is mainly philosophical, following the Dars'anas. Whereas the Ṡrî Mad Devî Bhâgavatam follows the Tantras. Therefore in the treatises on Devî Yâmala, etc., the superiority of this Devî Bhâgavata is maintained. By no means, therefore, anyone is to consider this Devî Bhâgavatam as of a very recent date. It is now proved that in the first century A. D. the Tantras were widely current. The worship of Râdhâ is the effect of the Tântrik influence. In the Viṣṇu Bhâgavat no mention is made of Râdhâ. Owing to these various reasons, though some portions of Śrî Devî Bhâgavatam were more ancient than Viṣṇu Bhâgavatam, yet the present treatise got its present bearing and form between the (9th) ninth and (11th) eleventh century. A. D. And Nilakaṇṭha and Swâmî are the two commentators of this Devî Bhâgavatam.

From various considerations : it may be seen that in very ancient times there was only one Bhâgavatam and that was respected by the Bhâgavatas. Then on account of the Bauddhik influence, when the Brâhmaṇya Dharma declined. that old Bhâgavatam was on the point of dying out. Next when the Brâhminism revived, the Vaiṣṇavas and various other sects became powerful, the Vaiṣnavas composed their Śrî Bhâgavat and the Śâktas composed their Devî Bhâgavatam. In conclusion, we assert also that on account of the anecdotes of Mangala Chaṇḍi, Ṣaṣṭhi and Manasâ and other Devîs occurring in the Devî Bhâgavataṃ, we hesitate much to accept the treatise in the ranks of the ancient Purâṇas and we are very much inclined to think that there had been many interpolations of a recent character and that, too, from Bengal.

OM TAT SAT.

ŚRÎ MAD DEVÎ BHÂGAVATAM.

THE NINTH BOOK.

CHAPTER I.

1. Śrî Nârâyaṇa said :—This (Highest) Prakriti is recognised as five-fold. When She is engaged in the work of Creation, She appears as :—

(1) Durgâ, the Mother of Gaṇes'a (2) Râdhâ, (3) Lakṣmî, (4) Sarasvatî and (5) Sâvitrî.

2-3. Nârada replied :—O Thou, the Best of Jñânins ! Who is this Prakriti ? (Whether She is of the the nature of Intelligence or of matter?) Why did She manifest Herself and then again why did She reveal Herself in these five forms ? And what are Her characteristics ? Now Thou oughtest to describe the lives of all, the different modes of their worship, and the fruits that are accrued thereby. Please also inform me which Forms of them manifested themselves in which different places. Dost Thou please narrate to me all these.

4-18. Nârâyaṇa said :—" O Child ! Who is there in this world that can describe fully the characteristics of Prakriti ! However I will describe to you that much which I heard from my own father, Dharma. Hear. The prefix " Pra" in the word Prakṛiti means exalted, superior, excellent ; and the affix " Kṛiti" denotes creation. So the Goddess, the Devî Who is the most excellent in the work of creation is known as the Devî Prakṛiti. To come closer :—" Pra" signifies the Sattva Guṇa, the most exalted quality, " Kṛi" denotes the Rajo Guṇa and " Ti" denotes the Tamo Guṇa. (The Sattva Guṇa is considered as the Highest as it is perfectly clear and free from any impurities whatsoever ; the Rajo Guṇa is considered intermediate as it has this defect:— that it spreads a veil over the reality of things, so as not to allow men to understand the True Reality, while the Tamo Guṇa is considered worst as it completely hides the Real Knowledge).

So when this Intelligence of the nature of Brahma, beyond the three attributes, gets tinged with the above three Guṇas and becomes omnipotent, then She is superior (Pradhânâ) in the work of creation. Hence She is styled as Prakriti.

O Child Nârada! The state just preceding that of creation is denoted by "Pra"; and "Kri" signifies creation. So the Great Devî that exists before creation is called Prakriti after creation. The Paramâtmâ by His Yoga (*i.e.*, Mâyâ Śakti, the Holy Ghost) divided Himself into two parts; the right side of which was male and the left side was the female Prakriti. (*Note*:—The Holy Ghost is the principle of Conception and Emanation, Creation). So the Prakriti is of the nature of Brahma. She is Eternal. As the fire and its burning power are not different, so there is no separate distinction between Âtman and His Śakti, between Puruṣa and Prakriti. Therefore those that are foremost and the highest of the Yogis do not recognise any difference between a male and a female. All is Brâhman. He is everywhere as male and female for ever. There is nothing in this world that can exist for a moment even without this Brahman consisting of male and female. (*i.e.* they are Brahman with Mâyâ manifested). Out of the Will of Śrî Kriṣṇa, to create the world Whose Will is all in all, came out at once the Mûlâ Prakriti, the Great Devî Îs'varî, (the Lady Controller of the Universe) Brahma with Mâyâ in a state of equilibriums). By Her Command came out five Forms from Her, either for the purpose of creation or for bestowing Favour and Grace to the Bhaktas (devotees). Durgâ the Mother of Gaṇes'a, comes, as the first, the most auspicious, loved by Śiva. She is Nârâyaṇî, Viṣṇu Mâyâ, and of the nature of Pûrṇa Brahma (the Supreme Brahma). This eternal, all auspicious Devî is the Presiding Deity of all the Devas and is, therefore, worshipped and praised by Brahmâ and the other Devas, Munis, and Manus. This Bhagavatî Durgâ Devî, (when She gets pleased) destroys all the sorrows, pains and troubles of the Bhaktas that have taken Her refuge, and gives them Dharma, everlasting name and fame, all auspicious things and bliss and all the happiness, nay, the Final Liberation! She is the Greatest Refuge of these Bhaktas that come to Her wholly for protection and are in great distress, whom She saves from all their dangers and calamities. In fact, know this Durgâ Devî as, verily, the Presiding Deity of the heart of Kriṣṇa and as His Highest Śakti, of the nature of the Holy Fire and the Holy Light. She is Omnipotent and resides always with Kriṣṇa, the Great God. She is worshipped by all the Siddha Puruṣas (those that have attained success); the (eighteen) Siddhis all go to Her and when pleased She gives whatever Siddhis (success) that Her Bhaktas want.

19-40. This Great Devî is the intelligence, sleep, hunger, thirst, shadow, drowsiness, fatigue, kindness, memory, caste, forbearance, errors, peace, beauty, and consciousness, contentment, nourishment, prosperity, and fortitude, She is sung in the Vedas and in other S'âstras

as the Mahâ Mâyâ, of the nature of the Universe. In reality, She is the
All-Śakti of the Universe and She is the Śakti of Kṛiṣṇa. All these
qualities are also mentioned in the Vedas. What is mentioned here is a
tithe merely, in comparison to that of the Vedas. She has infinite
qualities. Now hear of other Śaktis. The second Śakti of the Paramâtman is named Padmâ (Lakṣmî). She is of the nature of Śuddha Sattva
(Higher than Sattva Guṇa) and is Kṛiṣṇa's Presiding Deity of all wealth
and prosperity. This very beautiful Lakṣmî Devî is the complete master
of the senses ; She is of a very peaceful temper, of good mood and all-auspicious. She is free from greed, delusion, lust, anger, vanity and egoism.
She is devoted to Her husband and to Her Bhaktas ; Her
words are very sweet and She is very dear to Her husband, indeed, the
Life and Soul of Him. This Devî is residing in all the grains and vegetables and so She is the Source of Life of all the beings. She is residing in
Vaikuṇṭha as Mahâ Lakṣmî, chaste and always in the service of her
husband. She is the Heavenly Lakṣmî, residing in the Heavens and the
royal Lakṣmî in palaces and the Griha Lakṣmî in the several families of
several householders. O Nârada ! All the lovely beauty that you see in
all the living beings and all the things, it is She ; She is the glory and
fame of those that have done good and pious works and it is She that is the
prowess of the powerful Kings. She is the trade of merchants, the mercy
of the saints, engaged in doing good to others and the seed of dissensions in
those sinful and viscious persons as approved of in the Vedas. She is
worshipped by all, reverenced by all. Now I will describe to you about the
third Śakti of the Great God who is the Presiding Deity of knowledge
speech, intelligence, and learning. This third Śakti is named Sarasvatî.
She is all the learning of this endless Universe and She resides as medhâ
(intelligence) in the hearts of all the human beings ; She is the power in
composing poetry ; She is the memory and She is the great wit, light,
Splendour and inventive Genius. She gives the power to understand the
real meaning of the various difficult Siddhânta works ; She explains and
makes us understand the difficult passages and She is the remover of all
doubts and difficulties. She acts when we write books, when we argue
and judge, when we sing songs of music ; She is the time or measure in
music ; She holds balance and union in vocal and instrumental music.
She is the Goddess of speech ; She is Presiding Deity in the knowledge of
various subjects ; in argumentations and disputations. In fact all the
beings earn their livelihood by taking recourse to Her. She is peaceful and
holds in her hands Viṇâ (lute) and books. Her nature is purely Sâttvic
(Śuddha Sattva), modest and very loving to Śrî Hari. Her colour is
white like ice clad mountains, like that of the white sandal, like that of the
Kunda flower, like that of the Moon, or white lotus. She always repeats

the name of Paramâtmâ Śrî Krişņa while She turns Her bead composed of jewels. Her nature is ascetic; She is the bestower of the fruits of the asceticism of the ascetics; She is the Siddhi and Vidyâ of all; She grants always success to all. Were She not here, the whole host of Brâhmiņs would always remain speechless like the dead cluster of persons. What is recited in the Vedas as the Third Devî is the Holy Word, the Third Śakti, Sarasvatî. Thus I have described Her. Now hear the glories of the other Devîs in accordance with the Vedas. She is the mother of the four colours (castes), the origin of the (six) Vedâmgas (the limbs of the Vedas and all the Chhandas, the Seed of all the mantrams of Sandhyâ vandanam and the Root, the Seed of the Tantras; She Herself is versed in all the subjects. Herself an ascetic, She is the Tapas of the Brâhmiņs; She is the Tejas (Fire) and the caste of the Brâhmiņ caste and embodies in Herself all sorts of Samskâras (tendencies; inclinations); She is the Japam. Pure, known by the names of Sâvitrî and Gâyatrî, She resides always in the Brahma Loka (the Sphere of Brahmâ) and is such as all the sacred places of pilgrimages want Her touch for their purification.

41-47. Her colour is perfectly white like the pure crystal. She is purely Śuddha Sattva, of the nature of the Highest Bliss; She is eternal and superior to all. She is of the nature of Para Brahma and is the bestower of Mokşa. She is the Fiery S'akti and the Presiding Deity of the Brahma Teja (the fiery spirit of Brahma, and the Brâhmaņas). The whole world is purified by the touch of Whose Feet, this Sâvitrî Devî is the Fourth Śakti. O Child Nârada! Now I will describe to you about the Fifth Śakti, the Devî Râdhikâ. Hear. She is the Presiding Deity of the five Prâņas; She Herself is the Life of all; dearer than life even to Śrî Krişņa; and She is highly more beautiful and superior to all the other Prakriti Devîs. She dwells in everything; She is very proud of Her good fortune (Saubhâgyam); Her glory is infinite; and She is the wife, the left body, as it were, of Śrî Krişņa and She is not in any way inferior to Him, either in quality or in the Tejas (fiery Spirit) or in any other thing. She is Higher than the Highest; the Essence of all, infinitely superior, the First of all, Eternal, of the nature of the Highest Bliss, fortunate, highly respected, and worshipped by all. She is, the Presiding Devî of the Râsa Lîlâ of Śrî Krişņa. From Her has sprung the Râsa maņḍalam and She is the Grace and the Ornament of the Râsa maņḍalam (the dance in a circle in Râsa).

Note:—Extracts from a paper on Creation as explained by Hon'ble Justice Sir G. Woodroffe.

The Lecturer commenced by pointing out that an examination of any doctrine of creation reveals two fundamental concepts: Those of Being

(Kuṭastha) and Becoming (Bhava); Changelessness and Change; the one and Many. The Brahman or Spirit in its own nature (Svarupa) is and never becomes. It is the evolutes derived from the Principle of Becoming (Mûlâ prakriti) which constitute what is called Nature. The latter principle is essentially Movement. The world is displayed by consciousness (chit) in association with Mûlâ prakriti in cosmic vibration (spandana). Recent Western hypotheses have made scientific "matter" into Mâyâ in the sense that it is but the varied appearances produced in our mind by vibration of and in the single substance ether. The doctrine of vibration (Spandana) is however in India an ancient inheritance. The whole world is born from the varied forms of the initial movement in Mûlâ Prakriti. The problem is how does such multiplicity exist without derogation to the essential unit of its efficient cause, the spirit? The lecturer then made a rapid survey of the Sânkhya philosophy on this point, which assumed two real and independent principles of Being and Becoming which it calls Puruṣa and Prakriti and passed from this the easiest dualistic answer to the pure monism of Sankara which asserted that there was but one Principle of Being, the Sadvastu and Mâyâ, whether considered as a Śakti of Îs'vara or as the product of such Śakti was Avastu or nothing. He then pointed out that the Tântrik doctrine with which he dealt occupied a middle position between these two points of view. Śiva in the Kulârnava Tantra says "Some desire Monism (Advaitavâda), others Dualism (Dvaitavâda). Such, however, know not My Truth which is neither Monism nor Dualism (Dvaitâdvaita vivarjita). Tantra is not Dvaitavâda for it does not recognise Prakriti as an independent unconscious principle (Achit). It differs from Śaṇkara's Advaitavâda in holding that Prakriti as a conscious principle of Becoming, that is as Śakti, is not not Avastu, though its displayed picture, the world is Mâyâ. It effects a synthesis of the Śânkhya dualism by the conversion of the twin principles of Puruṣa and Prakriti into the unity which is the Ardhanârîs'vara Śiva Śakti.

As regards other matters it adopts the notions of the Sânkhya such as the concepts of Mûlâ prakriti with the three Guṇas, vibration (spandana), evolution (Pariṇâma) of the Vikritis and the order of emanation of the Tattvas. Śakti which effects this exists and is Herself never unconscious (Achit) though It has the power to make the Jîva think It is such. If this were understood one would not hear such nonsense as that the Śâktas (whose religion is one of the oldest in the world) worship material force or gross matter (Jaḍa).

The lecturer then shortly explained the nature of Śakti (Śakti Tattva), a term which derived from the root "Śak" meant the Divine Power whereby the world was created, manifested and destroyed. In Tantra the power and the Lord who wields it (Śaktimân) are one and the same, Śiva and Śakti are one and the same, Śiva is Brahman, Śakti is Brahman. The first is the transcendent, the second the immanent aspect of the one Brahman, Who is both Śiva and Śakti. The Mother creates (Kâryavibhâvinî). The Father wills what She does (Karya-Vibhâvaka). From their union creation comes. Śakti is not like the diminutive female figure which is seen on the lap of some Indian images, to which is assigned the subordinate position which some persons consider a Hindu wife should occupy. She is not a handmaid of the Lord but the Lord Himself in Her aspect as Mother of the worlds. This Śakti is both Nirguṇa and Saguṇa that is Chit S'akti and Mâyâ Śakti.

After this defining The nature of Śakti by which the world was created, the lecturer commenced an account of its manifestation as the universe, following in the main the Śâradâ Tilaka written in the eleventh century by Lakṣmanâchârya. the Guru of the celebrated Kashmirian Tântrik, Abhinava Gupta. The following is a very abbreviated summary of this, the main portion of the paper. The lecturer first referred to the Aghanâvasthâ state which was that Niṣkala Śiva and touching upon the question why Śiva became Sakala (associated with Kalâ) and creative explained the term Kalâ and the theory of Adriṣṭasriṣṭi taught by the Tantra as by other Śâstras. The former is according to Sânkhya, Mûlâprakriti ; according to Vedânta, Avidyâ and according to the Śiva Tantra, Śakti. The latter is the doctrine that the impulse to creation is proximately caused by the Karma of the Jîvas. It is the seed of Karma which contains the germ of Cosmic will to life. When Karma becomes ripe, there arises the state called Îkṣaṇa and other names indicative of creative desire and will. There then takes place a development which is peculiar to the Tantra called Sadris'a Pariṇâma, which is a kind of Vivartta. The development is only apparent for there is no real change in the Ânandamaya Koṣa. Śakti which exists in Sakala Śiva in a purely potential state is said to issue from Him. This is the first Kinetic aspect of Śakti in which Sattaguṇa is displayed. This is the Paramâkâṣâvasthâ. Nâda (Sound, Word) then appears. Śakti becomes further Kinetic through the enlivening of the Rajo Guṇa. This the Akṣarâvasthâ. Then under the influence of Tamas, Îṣvara becomes Ghanibhûta and what is called the Parâvindu. This is the Avyaktâvasthâ. Thus the Supreme Vindu men call by different names, Mahâ Viṣṇu, Brahma purûṣa, or Devî. It is compared to a grain of gram which under its sheath contains two seeds in undivided union. These are Śiva Śakti and their encircling sheath is Mâyâ. This Vindu unfolds and displays itself, in the threefold aspect of Vindu, Vîja, Nâda ; or Śiva, Śakti, and Śiva Śakti ; the three Śaktis of will, knowledge and action. This is the mysterious Kâma Kalâ which is the root of all Mantras. These seven :—Sakala Siva, Śakti, Nâda, Parâvindu, Vindu, Vija, Nâda are all aspects of Śakti which are the seven divisions of the Mantra Om and constitute what is called the creation of Parâ sound in the Îs'vara creation.

The lecturer having explained the nature of these Śaktis which formed part of the sound (Śabda), Sadriṣa Pariṇâma, referred to the form or meaning (Artha) creation in the same development by the appearance of the six Śivas from Śambhu to Brahmâ which were aggregate (Samaṣṭi) sound powers. It was he said, on the differentiation of the Parâvindu that there existed the completed causal Śabda which is the Hidden Word. The causal body or Parâ Śabda and Artha being complete, there then appeared the Displayed word or Śabdârtha. This is a composite like the Greek Logos. The Śabda Brahman or Brahman as cause of Śabda is the Chaitanya in all beings. The Śabdârtha in the Vedantin Nâmarûpa or world of name and form of this Śabdârtha the subtle and gross bodies are constituted, the Śaktis of which are the Hiraṇyagarbha sound, called Madhyamâ and the Virâṭ sound Vaikharî. By Śabda is not meant merely physical sound which as a quality of atomic ether is evolved from Tâmasik Ahamkâra.

The lecturer then pointed out that there had been Adriṣṭa Sriṣṭi up to the appearance of Śakti and Vivartta development up to the completion of the "Word" or causal sound. There then takes place real evolution (Pariṇâma) in which the Tattvas (or elements discovered as a result of psychological analysis of our worldly experience) are said to emanate according to the Sânkhya and not the Vedântic scheme, though there were some peculiarities in the Tântrik exposition which the lecturer noted. Finally Yogika Sriṣṭi was accepted in so far as it was the elements which in varied combinations made up the gross world.

In conclusion the lecturer pointed out that Indian Śâstra was a mutually connected whole. Such peculiarities as existed in any particular Śâstra were due to variety of standpoint or purpose in view. The main point in this connection to be remembered was that the Tantra was practical Sâdhanâ Śâstra. Whilst Śankara dealt with the subject from the standpoint of Jñânakâṇḍa, the Tantra treated it from the point of view of worship (Upâsanâkâṇḍa) the Tântrik doctrine is compounded of various elements some of which it shared with other Śâstras, some of which are its own, the whole being set forth according to a method and terminology which is peculiar to itself.

48-70. She is the Lady of the Râsa Lîlâ, the Foremost of the Jovial, humourous (witty) persons and dwells always in Râsa. Her abode is in Goloka and from Her have come out all the Gopîkâs. Râsa—The circular dance of Krisna and the cow-herdesses of Vrindâvana. Her nature is the Highest Bliss, the Highest Contenment, and Excessive Joy; She transcends the three Sattva, Rajo and Tamo Guṇas and is Nirâkâra (without any particular form); but She dwells everywhere but unconnected with any. She is the soul of all. She is without any effort to do anything and void of Ahamkâra. She assumes forms only to show Her favour to Her Bhaktas. The intelligent learned men (Pundits) read Her Mahimâ (glories) in meditating on Her according to the Vedas. The chief of the Devas and the Munis could never see Her; Her clothings are fire proofs and She is decorated with many ornaments all over Her body. Her body looks as if the crores of moons have risen all at once; She is the Giver of Bhakti (devotion) towards Krisna, service towards Krisna; and She bestows all wealth and prosperity. In Varâha Kalpa *i. e.*, when the Varâha incarnation took place, She incarnated Herself as the daughter of one Gopa (cowherd), named Vrisabhânu. And Earth was blessed by the touch of Her feet. She is such as Brahmâ and the other Devas could never perceive Her by any of their senses, yet every one at Vrindâvan saw Her very easily. She is the Gem amongst women. And when She is seen on the breast of Krisna, it seems that lightenings flash in the blue mass of clouds in the sky. In days gone by, Brahmâ practised several austerities for sixty thousand years to purify Himself by seeing the nails of Her toes; but far from seeing that, He could not have that even in His dreams. At last He succeeded in seeing Her at Vrindâvana and became blessed. O child Nârada! This is the fifth Prakriti and she is denominated as Râdhâ. Every female in every Universe is sprung from a part of Śrî Râdhâ or part of a part. O Nârada! Thus I have described to you the five Highest Prakritis Durgâ and others. Now I am going to describe those that are parts of these Prakritis. Hear. The Gânges, Gangâ has sprung from the lotus feet of Visnu; Her form is fluidlike; She is eternal. And She is the veritable burning Fire to burn away the sins of the sinners. She is sweet to touch in taking baths and in drinking; She gives final liberation to the Jîvas, and leads easily to the Goloka Abode. She is the holiest amongst the places of pilgrimages and is the first of the running rivers. She is the rows of pearls in the clotted hairs of Mahâdeva's head and She is the Tapasyâ (asceticism) incarnate of the Tapasvîs (ascetics) of the Bhârata Varsa. This Ganges purifies the three worlds and is the part of Mûlâ Prakriti; She shines like the Full Moon, is white like white lotus and like milk; She is pure S'uddha Sattva, clear, free from any Ahamkâra, chaste and beloved of Nârâyaṇa. The Tulasî Devî is the consort of Viṣṇu. She is the ornament of Nârâyaṇa, and dwells always at the lotus feet of Nârâyaṇa. By Her are performed all the acts of worship, all austerities, and all Sankalaps (resolves). She is the chief of all the flowers, holy and able to give merits (Puṇyam) to others. At Her sight and touch, Nirvâṇa can be obtained ; and, were it not for Her, there could be no other fire in this Kali Yuga to burn the sins. She Herself is of the nature of Fire and at the touch of Whose lotus-feet, the earth is purified ; all the Tîrthas desire to have Her sight and touch for purification and without Her all acts in this world become fruitless. She bestows Mokṣa (liberation) to those who want final liberation, grants all sorts of desires to several people, Who Herself is like a Kalpa Vrikṣa, Who is the Presiding Deity of all the trees in Bhârata and Who has come here to grant satisfaction to the ladies of Bhârata Varṣa and She is considered very superior throughout all parts of India. This Tulasî Devî is the chief factor of Mûlâ Prakṛiti.

71-95. Then comes the Manasâ Devî, the daughter of Kas'yapa. She is the dear disciple of Śankara and is therefore very learned in matters of S'âstras. She is the daughter of Ananta Deva, the Lord of Snakes and is respected very much by all the Nâgas. She Herself is very beautiful, the Lady of the Nâgas, the mother of the Nâgas and is carried by them. She is decorated with ornaments of the Snakes ; She is respected by the Nâgendras and She sleeps on the bed of Snakes. She is Siddha Yoginî, the devotee of Viṣṇu and always ready in the worship of Viṣṇu; She is the Tapas and the bestower of the fruits of Tapas. Herself an ascetic, She spent three lakh years (according to the Deva measure) and has become the foremost of the ascetics in Bhâratvarṣa. She is the Presiding Deity of all the mantras ; Her whole body shines with Brahmateja (the Holy Fire of Brahma). Herself of the nature of Brahma, She again meditates on Brahman. She is sprung from a part of Śrî Kriṣṇa and the chaste wife of Jarat Kâru Muni, the mother of Âstika, the great Muni ; She is the part of Mûlâ Prakriti. O Child Nârada ! Now comes the S'aṣṭhî Devî, the Mother of Devasenâ. She is the most superior amongst the Gaurî and the other sixteen Mâtrikâs. This chaste woman is the giver of sons and grandsons in the three worlds and the nurse, the foster mother of all. She is the sixth part of Mûlâ Prakriti and is hence known by the name of Śaṣṭhî. She lives near to every child as an aged Yoginî. Her worship is everywhere prevalent in the twelve months Vais'âkha, etc. When the child gets born, on the sixth day Her worship is done in the lying-in-chamber and again on the 21st day (after twenty days have passed away) the most auspicious worshipful ceremony of Her is performed. The Munis bow down to Her with reverence and want to visit Her daily.

She protects all children always with a mother's affectionate heart. This Ṣaṣṭhî Devî is again the part of Mûlâ Prakṛiti. Then appears the Devî Mangala Chaṇḍikâ. She goes from one house to another, on land or through water or in air, doing great good to them ; She has come out of the face of the Prakṛiti Devî and is doing always all sorts of good to this world. Her name is Mangala Chaṇḍî because She is all auspicious at the time of creation and assumes very furious angry appearance at the time of destruction. So the Pundits say. On every Tuesday in all the worlds Her worship is done ; and She, when pleased, gives to women sons, grandsons, wealth, prosperity, fame and good of all sorts and grants all desires. This Mangala Chaṇḍî is again the part of Mûlâ Prakriti. Now come the lotus-eyed Mâhes'varî Kâlî who when angry can destroy all this universe in a moment, who sprang from the forehead of the Mûlâ Prakriti, Dûrgâ to slay the two Demons Śumbha and Nis'umbha. She is the half-portion of Dûrgâ and qualified like Her, fiery and energetic. The beauty and splendour of whose body make one think as if the millions of suns have arisen simultaneously. Who is the foremost of all the Śaktis and is more powerful than any of them, Who grants success to all the persons, Who is superior to all and is of Yogic nature, Who is exceedingly devoted to Kriṣṇa and like Him fiery, well-qualified, and valorous, Whose body has become black by the constant meditation of S'rî Kriṣṇa, Who can destroy in one breath this whole Brahmâṇḍa, Who was engaged in fighting with the Daityas simply for sport and instruction to the people and Who, when pleased in worship can grant the four fruits Dharma, Artha, Kâma and Mokṣa. This Kâlî is also the part of Prakriti. The Devî Basundharâ (Earth) is again the part of Mûlâ Prakriti. Brahmâ and the other Devas, all the Muni maṇḍalams (the spheres of Munis), fourteen Manus and all men sing hymns to Her. She is the support of all and filled with all sorts of grains. She is the source of all gems and jewels, She bears in Her womb all the precious metals. All sorts of best things issue from Her. She is the Refuge of all. The subjects and kings worship Her always and chant hymns to Her. All the Jîvas live through Her and She bestows all sorts of wealth and prosperity. Without Her, all this, moving or non moving, become void of any substratum. Where to rest on!

96-143. O Child Nârada! Now hear about them who are issued again from the parts of Mûlâ Prakriti as well as the names of their wives. I will now narrate duly. The Devî "Svâhâ" is the wife of Agni (Fire), and the whole Universe worships Her. Without Her, the Devî can never take any oblations. Dakṣiṇâ and Dîkṣâ are both the wives of Yajna (Sacrifice). They are honoured everywhere. So much so that without Dakṣiṇâ (the fees given at the end of the Sacrifice) no sacrificial ceremonies can be complete and fructifying. The Devî "Svadhâ" is the wife of the Pitris. All worship this Devî "Svadhâ" whether they are Munis, Manus, or men If this mantra "Svadhâ" be not uttered while making an offering to the Pitris, all turn out useless. The Devî "Svasti" is the wife of the Vâyu Deva; She is honoured everywhere in the Universe. Without this "Svasti" Devî no giving nor taking nor any action can be fructifying and useful. "Puṣṭî" (nourishment) is the wife of Gaṇapatî. All in this world worship this Puṣṭî Devî. Without this "Puṣṭî", women or men alike all become weaker and weaker. Tuṣṭî (satisfaction, contentment) is the wife of Ananta Deva. She is praised and worshipped everywhere in this world. Without Her no one anywhere in the world can be happy. "Sampattî" is the wife of Îsâna Deva. The Suras, the men all alike worship Her. Were it not for Her, all in this world would be oppressed with dire poverty. The Devî "Dhritî" is the wife of Kapila Deva. She is honoured equally in all places. Were it not for Her, all the people in this world would have become impatient. The "Satî" Devî is the wife of Satya Deva. (Truth.) She is endearing to the whole world. The liberated ones worship Her always. Were it not for the truth loving Satî, the whole world would have lost the treasure in friendship. Dayâ "Mercy" endearing to the whole world is the chaste wife of "Mohâ Deva". She is liked by all. Were it not for Her, all the world would have become hopeless. The Devî "Pratiṣṭhâ" (fame, celebrity) is the wife of Puṇya Deva (merit). She gives merits to persons according as they worship Her. Were it not for Her, all the persons would remain dead while living. The Devî "Kîrti" (fame) is the wife of Sukarma (good works). Herself a Siddha (one who has acquired the result of one's success), all the blessed people honour Her with great reverence. Were it not for Her, all the persons in this world would have been dead, devoid of any fame. Kriyâ (work-efforts, action, doing) is the wife of "Udyoga" (enthusiasm). All honour Her greatly. O Muni Nârâda! Were it not for Her, the whole people would be void of any rules and regulations. Falsehood is the wife of Adharma (unrighteousness) She is honoured greatly by all the cheats that are extant in this world. Were she not liked by them, then all the cheats would become extinct. She did not fall in the sight of any body in the Satya Yuga. Her subtle form became visible in the Tretâ Yuga. When the Dvâpara Yuga came, She became half developed. And at last when the Kali Yuga has come, She is fully developed and there is no second to Her whether in bold confidence and shamelessness or in talking much and pervading everywhere. With her brother Deceitfulness She roams from one house to another. Peace and modesty and (shame) are both the wives of good behaviour. Were they not existent, all in this world would have turned out deluded and mad. Intelligence, genius and fortitude, these three are the wives of Jñâna (knowledge). Had they not lived, every one would become stupid and insane. Mûrti is the wife of Dharma Deva. She is of the nature of Beauty to all and very charming. Were it not for Her, Paramâtmân would not get any resting place; and the whole universe would have become Nirâlamba (without anything to rest). This Chaste Mûrti Devî is of the nature of splendour, loveliness and Lakşmî. She is everywhere respected, worshipped and reverenced. 'Sleep', the Siddha Yoginî, is the wife of Rudra Deva, who is of the nature of Kâlâgni (the universal conflagration at the break-up of the world). All the Jîvas spend their nights with Her. The twilights, night and day are the wives of Kâla (Time.) If they were not, the Creator even would not be able to reckon time. Hunger and thirst are the wives of Lobha (covetuousness). They are thanked, respected and worshipped by the whole world. Had they not lived, the whole world would have merged ever in an ocean of anxieties. Splendour and burning capacity are the wives of Tejas (fire). Without these, the Lord of the world could never have created and established order in this universe. Death and old age are the daughters of the Kâla, and the dear wives of Jvarâ (the disease). Without these, all the creation would come to an end. The Tandrâ (drowsiness,, lassitude) and Prîti (satisfaction) are the daughters of Nidrâ (sleep). And they are the dear wives of Sukha (pleasure). They are present everywhere in this world. O Best of Munis! Śraddhâ (faith) and Bhakti (devotion) are the wives of Vairâgyam (dispassion). For then all the persons can become liberated while living (Jîvanmuktas). Besides these there is Aditi, the Mother of the Gods, Surabhi, mother of cows; Diti, the mother of the Daityas; Kadru, the mother of the Nâgas (serpents); Vinatâ, the mother of Gaduda, the prince of birds; and Danu, the mother of the Dânavas. All are very useful for the purpose of creation. But these all are parts of Mûlâ Prakriti. Now I will mention some of the other parts of Prakriti. Hear. Rohiņî, the wife of the Moon, Sanjñâ, the wife of the Sun; Śatarûpâ, the wife of Manu; Śachî, the wife of Indra; Târâ, the wife of Brihaspati; Arundhatî, the wife of Vas'iştha; Anasûyâ, the wife of Atri; Devahûtî, the wife of Kardama; Prasûti, the wife of Dakşa; Menakâ, the mind born daughter of the Pitris and the mother of Ambikâ, Lopâmudrâ, Kuntî, the wife of Kuvera, the wife of Varuņa, Bindhyâvalî, the wife of the King Bali; Damayantî, Yas'odâ, Devakî, Gândhârî, Draupadî, Śaivyâ, Satyavatî, the chaste and noble wife of Brişabhânu and the mother of Râdhâ; Mandodarî; Kaus'alyâ, Kauravî; Subhadrâ; Revatî, Satyabhâmâ, Kâlindî, Lakşmaņâ; Jâmbavatî; Nâgnajiti, Mitrabindâ,

Laksaṇâ, Rukmiṇî, Sîtâ, the Lakṣmî incarnate; Kâlî, Yojana gandhâ, the chaste mother of Vyâsa, Ûṣâ, the daughter of Vâṇa, her companion Chitralekhâ; Prabhâvatî, Bhânumatî, the Satî Mâyâvatî, Reṇukâ, the mother of Paras'urâma; Rohiṇî, the mother of Balarâma, Ekanandâ and the sister of Śrî Kriṣṇa, Satî Durgâ and many other ladies are the parts of Prakriti. The village Deities are also the parts of Prakriti and all the female sexes, everywhere in the Universe are all come from the parts of Prakriti. So to insult any woman is to insult the Prakriti. If one worships a chaste Brahmin woman, who has her husband and son living, with clothings, ornaments, and sandal paste, etc., one worships, as it were, Prakriti. If any Vipra worships a virgin girl, eight years old, with clothings, ornaments and sandalpaste, know that he has worshipped the Prakriti Devî. The best, middling, and worst are all sprung from Prakriti. Those women that are sprung from Sattva Guṇa are all very good natured and chaste; those that are sprung from Rajo Guṇa are middling and very much attached to worldly enjoyments and do their selfish ends and those that are sprung from Tamo Guṇas are recognised as worst and belonging to the unknown families. They are very scurrilous, cheats, ruining their families, fond of their own free ways, quarrelsome and no seconds are found equal to them. Such women become prostitutes in this world and Apsarâs in the Heavens. The Hermaphrodites are parts of Prakriti but they are of the nature of Tamo Guṇas.

144-159. Thus I have described to you the nature of Prakriti. So in this Puṇyabhûmi Bhârata Varṣa, to worship the Devî is by all means desirable. In days past by, the King Suratha worshipbed the Mûlâ Prakriti Durgâ, the Destructrix of all evils. Then again Śrî Râma Chandra worshipped Her when he wanted to kill Râvaṇa. Since then Her worship is extant in the three worlds. She was first born as the honourable daughter of Dakṣa. She destroyed the whole hosts of Daityas and Dânavas. It was She who, hearing the abusive words uttered against Her husband at the Yajña by Dakṣa, Her father, gave up Her body and took up again Her birth. She took Her birth in the womb of Menakâ and got again Pas'upati as Her husband. And of the two sons, Kârtika and Gaṇes'a, born to Her, Kârtika was the Aṇsa (part) of Nârâyaṇa and Gaṇapati was Śrî Kriṣṇa Himself, the Lord of Râdhâ. O Devarṣi! After the two sons, Lakṣmî Devî came out of Durgâ. Mangala Râja, the King Mars first worshipped Her. Since then, all in the three worlds began to worship Her, whether they are Devas or men. The King As'vapati first worshipped Sâvitrî Devî; and since then the Devas, Munis, all began to worship Her. When the Devî Sarasvatî was born, the Bhagavân Brahmâ first worshipped Her; next the greatest Munis, Devas all began to worship Her. On the full moon night of the month of Kârtik, it was Bhagavân Śrî Krişņa, the Highest Spirit, that worshipped, first of all, the Devî Râdhâ within the Râsa Maņḍalam. the enclosure, within which the Râsa-lîlâ was performed (the circular dance) in the region Goloka. Then under the command of Śrî Krişņa, all the Gopas (cowherds), Gopîs, all the boys, girls, Surabhî, the queen of the race of the cows, and the other cows worshipped Her. So since Her worship by the inhabitants of Goloka, by Brahmâ and the the other Devas and the Munis, all began to worship ever Śrî Râdhâ with devotion and incense, light and various other offerings. On earth She was first worshipped by Suyajña, in the the sacred field of Bhâratvarşa, under the direction of Bhagavân Mahâdeva. Subsequently, under the command of the Bhagavân Śrî Krişņa, the Highest Spirit, the inhabitants of the three worlds began to worship Her. The Munis with great devotion, with incense, flowers and various other offerings worship always the Devî Radhâ. O Child Nârada! Besides these, all the other Devîs that have issued from Prakriti Devi are all worshipped. So much so that in the villages, the village Deities, in the forests, the forest Deities and in the cities, the city Deities are worshipped. Thus I have described to you all according to the Śâstras the glorious lives of the Devî Prakriti and Her parts. What more do you want to hear?

Here ends the First Chapter on the Description of Prakriti in the Ninth Book of the Mahâpurâņam Śrî Mad Devi Bhâgavatam of 18,000 verses by Maharşi Veda Vyâsa.

CHAPTER II.

1-4. Nârada said :—O Lord! I have heard all that you said in brief about the Prakriti Devî. Now describe in detail. Why the Mûlâ Prakriti Âdyâ Śakti (the Prime Force) was created at the very beginning before the creation of this world of five elements. How did She, being of the nature of the three Guņas, come to be divided into five parts? I desire to hear all this in detail. Now kindly describe their auspicious births, methods of worship, their meditation, their stotras, (praises) Kavachas (the mystic syllables considered as a preservation like armour) glory and power in detail.

5-26. Nârâyaņa spoke :—" O Devarşi! The Mûlâ Prakriti, of the nature of Mâyâ of Para Brahman is an eternal entity (Nitya padârtha) just as the Âtman, the celestial space (the nabho maņḍal); Time (Kâla), the ten quarters, the Universe Egg, the Goloka and, lower than this, the Vaikuņtha dhâma all are eternal things. Âtman and Prakriti are in inseparable union with each other as Fire and its burning capacity, the Moon and her beauty, the lotus and its splendour, the Sun and his rays are inseparably united with each other. As the goldsmith cannot prepare golden ornaments without gold and as the potter cannot make earthen pots without earth, so the Âtman cannot do any work without the help of this omnipotent Prakriti. The letter "Sa" indicates "Ais'yaryam" prosperity, the divine powers; and "Kti", denotes might, strength; and in as much as She is the Bestower of the above two, the Mûlâ Prakriti is named "Śakti". "Bhaga" is indicative of knowledge, prosperity, wealth, fame; and in as much as Mûlâ Prakriti has all these powers, She is also called "Bhagavatî." And Âtman "is always in union with this Bhagavatî Who is all powers, so He is called "Bhagavân." The Bhagavân is therefore sometimes with form; and sometimes He is without form. *Note*:—When Prakriti becomes latent, God is without form; with Prakriti manifest, God is with form.) The Yogis always think of the Luminous Form of the Formless Bhagavân and declare Him to be all blissful Para Brahma, the God. Though He is invisible, the Witness of all, Omniscient, the Cause of all, the Giver of everything and of every form, yet the Vaiṣṇavas do not say so. The Vaiṣṇavas declare how can fire, strength and energy come when there is no fiery, strong, energetic Person behind it? Therefore He who shines in the centre of this fiery sphere is the Para Brahma; He is the Fiery Person; He is Higher than the Highest. He is All Will; He is All-Form, the Cause of all causes and His Form is Very Beautiful. He is Young; He looks very peaceful and loved by all. He is the Highest; and His Blue Body shines like new rain-clouds. His two eyes defy the beauty of the autumn lotuses in the mid-day; His exquisitely nice rows of teeth put all the series of pearls in the dark back-ground. The peacock's feather is seen on His crown; the garland of Mâlatî flowers is suspended from His neck; His nose is exceedingly beautiful; the sweet smile is always seen on His lips. There is no second like Him in showing favour to the Bhaktas. He wears yellow clothings, as if the burning fire is emanating all round; the flute is seen on both His hands, reaching to the knees. His body is decorated all over with jewels. He is the Sole Refuge of this Universe; the Lord of all, omnipotent and omnipresent. No trace of deficiency can be seen in Him; He is Himself a Siddha (perfect) Puruṣa; and the foremost of all Siddha Puruṣas; bestows Siddhis to all. The Vaiṣṇavas meditate always That Eternal Śrî Kriṣṇa, the Deva of the Devas. He takes away fully all the fears of birth, death, old age, and all ills and sorrows. The age of Brahmâ is the twinkling of His eye. That Highest Self, the Para Brahma is denominated as Kriṣṇa. The word "Kriṣ" denotes Bhakti to Śrî Kriṣṇa and the letter "ṇa" signifies devotion to His service. So He is the Bestower of Bhakti and devotion to His Service. Again "Kriṣ" denotes all; everything; and "ṇa" signifies the root. So He Who is the Root and Creator of all, is Śrî Kriṣṇa. When He desired, in the very beginning, to create this Universe, there was nothing then except Śrî Kriṣṇa; and at last, impelled by Kâla, (His Own Creation) He became ready, in His part, to do the work of creation.

27-61. The Lord, who is All Will, willed and divided Himself into two parts, His Left part becoming female and His Right part becoming male. Then that Eternal One, Who is greatly loving, looked at the female, His left part, the Sole Receptacle to hold all the contents of love, very lovely to the eyes, and looking like the beautiful lotus. The loins of this woman defy the Moon; Her thighs put the plantain trees quite in the background; Her breasts are mistaken for the beautiful Bel fruits; flowers are scattered as Her Hairs on the head; Her middle part is very slender, very beautiful to behold! Exceedingly lovely; appearance very calm; sweet smile reigning in Her lips; side long glances with Her; Her clothing is purified by fire; all over Her body decorated with gems. Her eyes, also, like the Chakora bird (Greek partridge) began to drink incessantly with joy the moon beams from the face of Śrî Kriṣṇa, defying, as it were, the ten millions of moons. On Her forehead there was the dot of vermilion (red-lead); over that the dot of white sandal paste and over that was placed the musk. The fillets or braids of hair on Her head are slightly curved; this was decorated with Mâlatî garlands; on Her neck was suspended the necklace of gems and jewels and She is always very amorous towards Her husband. On looking at Her face, it seems that ten millions of moons have arisen at once; when She walks, her gait puts (humiliates) those of ganders and elephants in shade. O Muni! Śrî Kriṣṇa, the Lord of the Râsa Dance, and the Person of Taste in the Râsa Sport, looked askance at Her for a while and then catching hold of Her by Her hand went to the Râsamaṇḍalam and began to play the Râsa sport, (the amorous pastime). It seemed then the Lord of amorous pastimes had become incarnate there and had been enjoying the various pleasures of amorous passions and desires. So much, that Brahma's one day passed away in that sport. The Father of the Universe, then becoming tired, impregnated in an auspicious moment in Her womb who was born of His left portion. The Prakriti Devî was also tired of the embraces of S'rî Kriṣṇa; so after the intercourse, she began to perspire and breathe frequently. Her perspiration turned into water and deluged the whole universe, with water; and Her breath turned into air and became the life of all the beings. The female that sprung from the left side of Vâyu became his wife and out of their contact orginated Prâṇa, Apâna,

Samâna, Udâna and Vyâna, the five sons. These are the five vital Vâyus of all the beings. Besides these from the womb of the Vâyu's wife came out Nâga and the other four lower Vâyus. The water that came out from perspiration, Varuṇa Deva became the presiding Deity of that; and the female, sprung out of the left side of Varuṇa Deva, became the wife of Varuṇa, called Varuṇânî. On the other hand, the S'akti, of the nature of knowledge of S'rî Krisṇa, remained pregnant for one hundred manvantaras. Her body became effulgent with Brahma-teja (the fire of Brahma). Krisṇa was her life and She again was dearer to Krisṇa than his life even. She remained always with S'rî Krisṇa; so much so that She constantly rested on His breast. When one hundred Manvantaras passed away, that Beautiful One gave birth to a Golden Egg. That egg was the repository of the whole universe. The Beloved of Krisṇa became very sorry to see the egg and out of anger, threw that within the water collected in the centre the Universe. Seeing this, Śrî Krisṇa raised a great cry and immediately cursed Her duly and said:—"O Angry One! O Cruel One! When you have forsaken out of anger this son just born of you, I say then that you become from to-day bereft of any issue. Besides, let all those godly women that will spring out of your parts, they also be deprived of having any issue or sons and they will remain ever constant in their youth. O Muni! While S'rî Krisṇa was thus cursing, suddenly came out from the tongue of the beloved of Krisṇa, a beautiful daughter, of a white colour. Her clothings were all white, in her hands there were lute and book and all Her body was decorated with ornaments made of gems and jewels. She was the presiding Deity of all the S'âstras. Some time later the Mûla Prakriti, the Beloved of Krisṇa divided into two parts. Out of Her left portion came Kamalâ and out of her right portion came Râdhikâ. In the meantime S'rî Krisṇa divided himself into two parts. From his right side appeared a form two-handed; and from left side appeared a form four-handed. The S'rî Krisṇa addressed the Goddess Speech, holding flute in her hand, "O Devî! You follow this four-handed Person as his wife" and then spoke to Râdhâ:—"O Râdhe! You are a sensitive, proud lady; let you be My wife; so it will do you good." S'rî Krisṇa also told Lakṣmî gladly to become the wife of the four-handed Nârâyaṇa. Then Nârâyaṇa, the Lord of the world, took both Lakṣmî and Sarasvatî to the abode Vaikuṇtha. O Muni! Both Lakṣmî and Sarsvatî became issueless, being born of Râdhâ. From the body of Nârâyaṇa arose his attendants, all four-handed. They were all equal to him in appearance, in qualifications; in spirit and in age. On the other hand, from the body of Kamalâ arose millions and millions of female attandants all equal to Her in form and qualifications. Then arose innumerable Gopas (cow-herds) from the pores of S'rî Krişņa. They were all equal to the Lord of Goloka in form, Guņas, power and age; they were all dear to Him as if they were His life.

62-88. From the pores of Râdhikâ came out the Gopa Kanyâs (cow-herdesses). They were all equal to Râdhâ and all were Her attendants and were sweet-speaking. Their bodies were all decorated with ornaments of jewels, and their youth was constant, they were all issueless as S'rî Krişņa cursed them thus. O Best of Brâhmaņas! On the other hand, suddenly arose Durgâ, the Mâyâ of Vişņu (The Highest Self) eternal and whose Deity was Krişņa.

(*N. B.*) Durgâ was the Avatâra of Mûla Prakriti not the Avatâra of Râdhâ as Lakşmî and Sarasvatî were.) She is Nârâyanî; She is Îs'ânî; She is the Śakti of all and She is the Presiding Deity of the intelligence of S'rî Krişņa. From Her have come out many other Devis; She is Mûla Prakriti and she is Îs'varî; no failings or insufficiencies are seen in Her. She is the Tejas (of the nature of Fire) and She is of the nature of the three Guņas. Her colour is bright like the molten gold; Her lustre looks as if ten millions of Suns have simultaneously arisen. She looks gracious always with sweet smile on Her lips, Her hands are one thousand in number. Various weapons are in all Her hands. The clothings of the three-eyed one are bright and purified by Fire. She is decorated with ornaments all of jewels. All the women who are the jewels are sprung from Her parts and parts of parts and by the power of Her Mâyâ, all the people of the world are enchanted. She bestows all the wealth that a householder wants; She bestows on Krişņa's devotees, the devotion towards Krişņa; nay, She is the Vaişņavî Sakti of the Vaişņavas. She gives final liberation to those that want such and gives happiness to those that want happiness. She is the Lakşmî of the Heavens; as well She is the Lakşmî of every household. She is the Tapas of the ascetics, the beauty of the kingdoms of the kings, the burning power of fire, the brilliancy of the Sun, the tender beauty of the Moon, the lovely beauty of the lotus and the S'akti of S'rî Krişņa the Highest Self. The Self, the world all are powerful by Her Śakti; without Her everything would be a dreary dead mass. O Nârada! She is the seed of this Tree of World; She is eternal; Śhe is the Stay, She is Intelligence fruits, hunger, thirst, mercy, sleep, drowsiness, forgiveness, fortitude, peace, bashfulness, nourishment, contentment and lustre. The Mûla Prakriti praising Śrî Krişņa stood before Him. The Lord of Râdhikâ then gave Her a throne to sit. O Great Muni! At this moment sprang from the navel lotus the four—faced Brahmâ, with his wife Sâvitrî, an exceedingly beautiful woman. No sooner the fourfaced Brahmâ, the foremost of the Jñânins, fond of asceticism and holding Kamaṇḍalu in His hand came into being than He began to praise Srî Kriṣṇa by His four mouths. On the other hand the Devî Sâvitrî, with a beauty of one hundred moons, born with great ease, wearing apparel purified by fire and decorated with various ornaments praised Kriṣṇa, the One and Only Cause of the Universe and then took Her seat gladly with Her husband in the throne made of jewels. At that time Kriṣṇa divided Himself into two parts; His left side turned into the form of Mahâdeva; and his right side turned into the Lord of Gopikâs (cow-herdesses). The colour and splendour of the body of Mahâdeva is pure white like white crystal; as if one hundred suns have arisen simultaneously. In His hands there are the trident Trisûl and sharp-edged spear Pattiśa; His wearing is a tiger skin; on His heads matted hair Jaṭâ of a tawny hue like molten gold; His body was besmeared all over with ashes, smile reigning in His face and on His forehead, the semi-moon. He has no wearing on his loins; so He is called Digambara the quarters of the Sky being His clothing; His neck is of a blue colour; the serpent being the ornaments on His body and on His right hand the nice bead of jewels well purified. Who is always repeating with His five faces the Eternal Light of Brahmâ, and Who has conquerred Death by praising Śrî Kriṣṇa, Who is of the nature of Truth, the Highest Self, the God Incarnate, the material cause of all things and the All auspicious of all that is good and favourable, and the Destroyer of the fear of birth, death, old age and disease and Who has been named Mrityunjaya (the conqueror of Death). This Mahâdeva took His seat on a throne made of jewels (diamonds, emeralds, etc.)

Here ends the Second chapter of the Ninth Book on the origin of Prakriti and Puruṣa in the Mahâpurâṇam Śrî Mad Devî Bhâgavatam of 18,000 verses by Maharṣi Veda Vyâsa.

CHAPTER III.

1-34. Nârâyaṇa said:—"O Devarṣi! The egg (born of Mûla Prakriti) that was floating in the waters for a period equal to the life period of Brahmâ, now in the fulness of time, separated into two parts. Within that egg there was a powerful Child, lustrous like one thousand millions of suns. This child could not suck mother's milk, as it was forsaken by Her. So being tired of hunger, the child for a moment cried repeatedly. The child that will become the Lord of countless Brahmâṇḍas (universes), now an orphan having no father nor mother began to look upwards from the waters. This boy came to be denominated afterwards by the name of Mahâ Virâṭ, when he became gross and grosser. As there is nothing finer than radium so there is nothing grosser than Mahâ Virâṭ. The power of this Mahâ Virâṭ one-sixteenth of that of S'rî Kriṣṇa, the Highest Self. But this boy, born of the Prakriti Râdhâ is the Sole Stay of all this Universe and he is denominated by the name "Mahâ-Viṣṇu". In his every pore countless universes are existing. So much so that even Śrî Kriṣṇa could not count them. If it were possible to count the number of the lust particles, it is impossible to count the number of the Universes. So there are endless Brahmâs, Viṣṇus, and Mahes'varas. In every Brahmâṇḍa, there is Brahmâ Viṣṇu, and Maheṣa. Each Brahmâṇḍa extends from Pâtâla to the Brahmaloka. The abode of Vaikuṇṭha is higher than that (i. e. it is situated outside of Brahmâṇḍa), again the abode of Goloka is fifty koṭi yojanas (50 × 10 × 4 × 2 million miles) higher than Vaikuṇṭha. This Goloka Dhâma is eternal and real as Śrî Kriṣṇa is eternal and real. This world composed of the seven islands is surrounded by the seven oceans. Forty-nine Upa Dvîpas (smaller islands adjacent to them) are existing here. • Besides there are countless mountains, and forests. Higher than this earth is the Brahmaloka with seven heavens and below this are the seven Pâtâlas. This is the bounding limit of Brahmâṇḍa. Just above this earth there is the Bhûrloka; above is Bhuvarloka; then Svarloka, then Janaloka, then Taparloka, then Satyaloka, and above that is Brahmaloka. The splendour of Brahmaloka is like that of molten gold. But all the substances whether outside or inside this Brahmaloka, are transient. When this Brahmâṇḍa (cosmos) dissolves, everything dissolves and is destroyed. All are temporary like bubbles of water. Only Goloka and Vaikuṇṭha are eternal. In every pore of this Mahâ Virâṭ is existing one Brahamâṇḍa (cosmos). What to speak of others even Kriṣṇa cannot count the number of these Brahmâṇḍas. In every Brahmâṇḍa there is Brahmâ, Viṣṇu and Mahes'a. O Child Nârada! In every Brahmâṇḍa, the number of the gods is three koṭis or 30 millions. Some of them are the Dikpatis (the Regents of the quarters); some are the Dikpâlas (the Rulers of the Quarters), some are asterisms, and some planets. In the Bhûrloka, there are four Varṇas (Brâhmiṇs, etc.,) and in the Pâtâlas there are Nâgas. Thus the Universe exists composed of moveable and non-moveable things (this is Brahmâṇḍa Vivriti). O Nârada! Now the Virâṭ Puruṣa began to look up to the skies again and again but He could not see anything within that egg except the void. Then distressed with hunger he cried out repeatedly and became merged in anxiety. Next moment getting back his consciousness, he began to think of Kriṣṇa, the Highest Person and saw there at once the eternal light of Brahma. He saw there His form as deep blue like new rain-cloud;

with two hands, garment of a yellow colour, sweet smile on His face, flute in His hand and He seemed to be very anxious to show His Grace to Devotees. Looking at the Lord, His Father, the boy became glad and smiled. The Lord, the Bestower of boon granted him boons appropriate for that moment "O Child! Let you possess knowledge like Me; let your hunger and thirst vanish; let you be the holder of innumerable Brahmâṇḍas till the time of Pralaya (the universal dissolution). Be without any selfishness, be fearless and the bestower of boons to all. Let not old age, death, disease, sorrow nor any other ailings afflict thee. Thus saying He repeated thrice on his ear the six-lettered great Mantra "Om Krisṇâya Svâhâ" worshipped by the Vedas with their Amgas, the Giver of desires and the destroyer of all troubles and calamities. O Brahmâ's Son! Thus giving the mantra, Śrî Krisṇa arranged for his fooding thus:— In every universe, whatever offerings will be given to S'rî Krisṇa, one sixteenth of that will go to Nârâyaṇa. the Lord of Vaikuṇṭha and fifteen-sixteenth is to go to this boy, the Virâṭ. S'rî Krisṇa did not allot any share for Himself. Himself transcending all the Guṇas, and Full, He is always satisfied with Himself. What necessity is there for any further offerings? Whatever the people offer with devotion, the Lord of Lakṣmî, the Virâṭ eats all these. Bhagavân S'rî Krisṇa giving thus to the Virâṭ the boon and the Mantra said:— "O Child! Say what more you desire; I will give you that instantly. The Virâṭ boy, hearing thus the words of Śrî Krisṇa, spoke:— "O Thou Omnipresent! I have got no desires whatsoever, save this that as long as I live, whether for a short time or for a long time, let me have pure Bhakti towards Thy lotus feet

35-41. In this world he is Jivanmukta (liberated whilst living) who is your Bhakta; and that bewildered fool is dead while living who is devoid of any Bhakti to Thee. What needs he to perform Japam, asceticism, sacrifice, worship, holding fasts and observances, going to sacred places of pilgrimages and other virtuous acts if he be without any bhakti to S'rî Krisṇa? Vain is his life who is devoid of any devotion to S'rî Krisṇa, under Whose Grace he has obtained his life and Whom he does not now pay homage and worship. He is endowed with S'akti as long as Âtmâ (Self) resides in his body; no sooner the Âtma departs from his body all the S'aktis accompany him. O Great One! And thou art the Universal Âtman (soul) who transcends Prakriti, Who is All will, the Primeval Person and of the nature of the Highest Light. O Child! Thus saying, the Virâṭ boy remained silent. Śrî Krisṇa then, spoke in sweet words:— "O Child! Let you remain as fresh as ever like Me. You will not have any fall even if innumerable Brahmâs pass away.

42-57. Let you divide yourself in parts and turn into smaller Virâṭs in every universe. Brahmâ will spring from your navel and will create the cosmos. From the forehead of that Brahmâ will spring eleven Rudras for the destruction of the creation. But they will all be parts of S'iva. The Rudra named Kâlâgni, of these eleven Rudras, will be the destroyer of all this Vis'vas (cosmos). Besides, from each of your sub-divisions, the Viṣṇu will orignate and that Bhagavân Viṣṇu will be the Preserver of this Vis'vu world. I say that under my favour you will always be full of Bhakti towards Me and no sooner you meditate on Me, you will be able to see My lovely form. There is no doubt in this; and your Mother, Who resides in My breast, will not be difficult for you to see. Let you remain here in ease and comfort. I now go to Goloka. Saying thus S'rî Kriṣṇa, the Lord of world disappeared. Going to His own abode He spoke instantly to Brahmâ and S'ankara, skilled in the works of creation and destruction:— "O Child Brahmâ! Go quickly and be born in parts from the navels of each of the smaller Virâṭs that will arise from the pores of the Great Virâṭ. O Child Mahâdeva! Go and be born in parts from the forehead of each Brahmâ in every universe for the destruction of the creation; (but be careful that you not forget) and perform austerities for a long, long time. O Son of the Creator Brahmâ! Thus saying, the Lord of the Universe remained silent. Brahmâ and Śiva, the auspicious, bowing to the Lord, went to their own duties. On the other hand, the Great Virâṭ that lay floating in the waters of the Brahmâṇḍa sphere, created from his every pore each smaller Virâṭ. That youth Janârdan of the form of the Great Cosmos, wearing yellow garment of the bluish-green colour of the Durba grass, lay sleeping pervading everywhere. Brahmâ took his birth in His navel. He, then, after his birth, began to travel in that navel-lotus and in the stem of the lotus for one lakh yugas. But he could not find out the place whence the lotus or its stem had sprung up. O Nârada! Then your father became very anxious and came back to his former place and began to meditate the lotus feet of Śrî Kriṣṇa. Then, in meditation, with his intro pective eye, he first saw the small Virâṭ, then the endless great Viraṭ lying on the watery bed, in whose pores the universes are existing and then he saw the God S'rî Kriṣṇa in Goloka with Gopas and Gopis. He then began to praise the Lord of Goloka when He granted boons to your father, and he began to do the work of creation.

58-62. From the mind of your father, were born first Sanaka and other brothers and then from his forehead eleven Rudras sprang. Then from the left side of that small Virâṭ lying on the bed of waters, the four-handed Viṣṇu Bhagavân, the Preserver of the Universe, came. He went to Śvetadvîpa, where he remained. Then your father became engaged in creating this Universe, moveable and non-moveable, composed of three worlds, heaven, earth and Pâtâla, in the navel of that small Virâṭ Puruṣa. O Nârada! Thus from the pores of that great Virâṭ each universe has sprung and in every universe there is one small Virâṭ, one Brahmâ, one Viṣṇu and one S'iva and S'anaka and others. O Best of twice born! Thus I have described the glories of Kriṣṇa, that give exceeding pleasure and Mokṣa. Now say what more you want to hear?

Here ends the Third Chapter of the Ninth Book on the Origin of Brahmâ, Viṣṇu and Mahes'a and others in the Mahâ Purâṇam S'rî Mad Devî Bhâgavatam of 18,000 verses by Maharṣi Veda Vyâsa.

CHAPTER IV.

1-3. Nârada said:— By your Grace I have heard everything very sweet like nectar, of the origin of things. Now may I ask you which Devî of these five Prakritis has been worshipped by what Mantra? and by whom? How has each of them been praised? and by whom? How has the worship of their Mûrtis (form) become prevalent in this world? What are the Stotram (hymn of praise), the Dhyân (meditation) glory and life of these? Also what sort of boon do each of the Devîs grant? and to whom? Kindly describe all these in detail.

4-12. Nârâyaṇa said:— "O Child! Durgâ, the mother of Gaṇes'a, Râdhâ, Lakṣmî, Sarsavati and Sâvitrî, these are the five Prakritis sprung directly from Mûla Prakriti. The methods of their worship, wonderful glorious acts, excellent stotrams, and their lives, inculcating good to all, and sweet like nectar are all widely written in the Vedas, Purâṇas, Tantras and other S'âstras. So there is no need to describe them here again. Now I am describing in detail the auspicious characters of these that are sprung from the parts and Kalâs of the Prakriti. Hear attentively. Kâlî, Vasundharâ, Gangâ, Ṣaṣṭhî, Mangal Chaṇḍikâ, Tulasî, Manasâ, Nidrâ, Svadhâ, Svâhâ, and Dakṣiṇâ, these are the parts of Prakriti. By and by I will describe, briefly, the merit-giving characters, and pleasant to hear. Along with these I will describe the Karmas of the Jîvas, and the great exalted lives of Durgâ and Râdhâ. I am now describing Sarasvatî's character. Hear, O Muni! S'rî Kriṣṇa introduced first in this Bhârata, the worship of the Devî Sarasvatî, the holder of Vîṇâ in Her hands, under whose influence, the hearts of illiterate stupid persons become illumined with knowledge. The amorous Devî Sarasvatî sprang from the end of the lips of Râdhâ and so she desired to marry Kriṣṇa out of amorous feelings. S'rî Kriṣṇa, the controller of the hearts of all, knew it instantly and addressed the Mother of the people in true words proper to Her and beneficial to Her in the end. O Chaste One! The four-armed Nârâyaṇa is born from My parts; He is young, of good features and endowed with all qualifications; so much so, he is like Me. He is a Knower of amorous sentiments of women and He fulfils those desires; what to speak of His beauty, ten millions of the God of love are playing in His body. O Beloved! And if you desire to marry and remain with Me, that will not be of any good to you. For Râdhâ is near to Me; She is more powerful than you. If a man be stronger than another, he can rescue one who takes his shelter; but if he be weaker, how can he then, himself weak, protect his dependant from others. Though I am the Lord of all, and rule all, yet I cannot control Râdhâ. For She is equal to me in power, in beauty, in qualifications, equal to Me in every respect. Again it is impossible for Me to quit Râdhâ for She is the presiding Deity of My life. Who can relinquish life? Though a son is very dear to his father, still it may be questioned, is he dearer than his father's life? So, O Auspicious One! Go to the abode Vaikuṇṭha; you will get your desires fulfilled there. You will get for your husband the Lord of Vaikuṇṭha and you will live ever in peace and enjoy happiness Though Lakṣmî is residing there yet like you she is not under the control of lust, anger, greed, delusion and vanity. She is also equal to you in beauty, qualities, and power. So you will live with her in great delight and Hari, the Lord of Vaikuṇṭha, will treat both of you equally. Moreover, I say this in particular that in every universe, on the fifth day of the bright fortnight of the month of Mâgha, every year, the day when the learning is commenced, a great festival will be held and men, Manus, Devas, and the Munis desirous of liberation, Vasus, Yogis, Nâgas, Siddhas, Gandarbhas, Râkṣasas, all will perform your worship with devotion in every Kalpa till the time of Mahâ Pralaya comes. All are required to be Jitendriya (having their senses under control) and Samyami (concentrating his mind, and with a religious vow) and they will invoke Thee on a jar or on books and then meditate according to what is stated in the Kaṇva Śâkhâ of Yajurdeva and then worship and sing hymns to Thee. Thy Kavacha (an armour; a mystical syllable हूं considered as a preservative like armour) is written on the bark of the Bhûrja tree and then with eight kinds of scents mingled with it is placed within a golden nut or ring named Mâduli) and then held on the neck or on the right arm. The learned should recite Thy Stotras during worship. Thus saying, the Puraṇ Brahma S'rî Kriṣṇa Himself worshipped the Devî Sarasvatî. Since then, Brahmâ, Viṣṇu, Mahes'a, Ananta Deva, Dharma, Sanaka and other Munindras, all the Devas, Munis, all the kings and all the human beings are worshipping the Devî Sarasvatî. O Nârada! Thus the worship of the Eternal Devî is made extant in the three worlds.

30-31. Nârada said:— "O Chief of the Knowers of the Vedas! Now describe to me the methods of worship, Dhyân, Kavacham, hymns, the appropriate offerings of the Pûjâ flowers, sandalpaste and other good things necessary in these worships and which are so sweet to hear. I am ever very eager and anxious to hear these.

32-59. Nârâyaṇa said:— "O Nârada! I am now stating the method of worship of the Devî Sarasvati, the Mother of the Worlds, according to Kaṇva S'âkhâ of the Yajurveda. Hear. On the day previous to the fifth day of the bright fortnight of the month of Mâgh or the day of commencement of education, the devotee should control his senses, concentrate his mind and take his bath. Then he is to perform his daily duties and instal the jar (Ghaṭa) with devotion and according to the Mantras of the Kaṇva Śâkhâ or the Tantra, as the case may be. He is to worship first on that Ghaṭa (jar) Gaṇapati (Gaṇes'a), then meditate the Devî Sarasvatî as described below, invoke Her and again read the Dhyân and then worship with Ṣoḍas'opachâra (sixteen good articles offered in the worship). O Good One! Now I am speaking, according to my knowledge, about the offerings as ordained in the Vedas or Tantras. Hear. Fresh butter, curd, thickened milk, rice freed from the husk by frying, sweetmeats (Til Laddu) prepared of Til, sugar cane, sugarcane juice, nice Guḍ (molasses), honey, svastik, sugar, rice (not broken) out of white Dhân, chipiṭak of table rice (Âlo châl), white Modak, Harbiṣyânna prepared of boiled rice with clarified butter and salt, Piṣṭaka of jaoâ or wheaten flour, Paramânna with ghee, nectar like sweetmeats, cocoanut, cocoanut water, Svastik Piṣṭaka, Svastik and ripe plantain Piṣṭaka, Kaseru (root), Mûlâ, ginger, ripe plantains, excellent Bel fruit, the jujube fruit, and other appropriate white purified fruits of the season and peculiar to the place are to be offered in the Poojâ. O Nârada! White flowers of good scent, white sandalpaste of good scent, new white clothes, nice conchshell, nice garlands of white flowers, nice white necklaces, and beautiful ornaments are to be given to the Devî. I say now the Dhyânam sweet to hear, of the Devî Sarasvatî according to the Vedas, capable to remove errors! Hear. I hereby bow down to the Devî Sarasvatî, of a white colour, of a smiling countenence and exceedingly beautiful, the lustre of whose body overpowers that of the ten millions of Moons, whose garment is purified by fire, in whose hands there are Vîṇa and books, who is decorated with new excellent ornaments of jewels and pearls and whom Brahmâ, Viṣṇu, Mahes'vara and the other Devas Munis, Manus and men constantly worship. Thus meditating the Devî, the intelligent persons should offer all articles, after pronouncing the root Mantra. Then he is to hymn and hold Kavacha and make Sâṣṭâṅga praṇâms before the Devî. O Muni! Those whose Devî Sarasvatî is the presiding Deity, are not to be spoken of at all (*i. e.* they will naturally do all these things and with a greater fervour). Besides all should worship the Devî Sarasvatî on the day of commencement of education and every year on the Śûkla Panchamî day of the mouth of Mâgh. The eight-lettered Mantra, as mentioned in the Vedas is the root Mantra of Sarasvatî. (Aim Klîm Sarasvatyai namaḥ). Or the Mantra to which each worshipper is initiated is his Mûlmantra (not Mantra). Or uttering the Mantra "Śrîm Hrîm Sarasvatyai Svâhâ," one is to offer everything to the Devî Sarasvatî. This Mantra is the Kalpa Vrikṣa (*i. e*, the tree which yields all desires). Nârâyaṇa, the ocean of mercy, gave in ancient times, this very Mantra to Vâlmikî in the holy land Bhârata Varṣa on the banks of the Ganges; next Bhrîgu gave this Mantra on the occasion of solar eclipse to Maharṣi Sukrâcharya on the Puṣkara Tîrtha; Mârîcha gave to Brihaspati on a lunar eclipse; Brahmâ gave to Bhrigu in the Vadarikâ Âs'rama; Jaratkâru gave to Âstika on the shore of the Kṣiroda ocean; Bibhâṇḍaka gave this to the intelligent Riṣyasringa on the Sumeru mountain, Śiva gave this to Kaṇâda and Gotama. Sûrya gave to Yâjnavalkya and Kâtyâyana, Ananta Deva gave to Pâṇini, to the intelligent Bhâradvâja and to Śâkaṭâyana in Bali's assembly in the Pâtâla. If this Mantra be repeated four lakhs of times, all men attain success. And when they become Siddhas with this Mantra, they become powerful like Brihaspati. In past times, the Creator Brahmâ gave a Kavacha named Vis'vajaya to Bhrigu on the Gandhamâdana Mountain. I now speak of that. Hear.

60-61. Once on a time Bhrigu asked Brahmâ the Lord of all, and adored by all, thus:—"O Brahman! Thou art the foremost of those that know the Vedas; there is none equal to thee in matters regarding the knowledge of the Vedas; (so much so that there is nothing that is not known to thee; for all these have sprung from thee). Now say about the Vis'vajaya Kavacha of the Devi Sarasvatî, that is excellent, without any faults and embodying in it all the properties of all the Mantras.

62-91. Brahmâ' said:—"O Child! What you have asked about the Kavacha of Sarasvatî that is sweet to hear, ordained and worshipped by the Vedas, and the giver of all desired fruits, now hear of that. In the very beginning, the all-pervading Śrî Kriṣṇa, the Lord of the Râsa circle, mentioned this Kavacha to me in the holy Brindâvana forest in the abode Goloka at the time of Râsa in Râsa Maṇḍala. This is very secret; it is full of holy unheard, wonderful Mantras. Reading this Kavacha and holding it (on one's arm) Brihaspati has become foremost in matters of intelligence; by the force of this Kavacha Śukrâchârya has got his ascendancy over the Daityas; the foremost Muni Vâlmikî has become eloquent and skilled in language and has become Kavîndra and Svâyambhuva Manu; holding this Kavacha he has become honoured everywhere. Kaṇâda, Gotama, Kaṇva, Paṇini, Śakaṭâyana, Dakṣa, and Kâtyâyana all have become great authors by virtue of this Kavacha; Kriṣṇa Dvaipâyana Veda Vyâsa made the classification of the Vedas and composed the eighteen Purâṇas. Śâtâtapa, Samvarta, Vas'iṣṭha, Parâsara and Yâjnavalkya had become authors by holding and reading this Sarasvatî Kavacha. Riṣyas'riṇga, Bhâradvâja, Âstika, Devala, Jaigiṣavya, and Yâyâti all were honoured everywhere by virtue of this Kavacha. O Dvija! The Prajâpati Himself is the Riṣi of this Kavacha; Brihatî is its Chhaṇḍa; and Śâradâ Ambikâ is its presiding Deity. Its application (Viniyoga) is in the acquisition of spiritual knowlege, in the fruition of any desires or necessities, in composing poems or anywhere wheresoever success is required. May Śrîm Hrîm Sarasvatyai Svâhâ protect fully my head; Śrîm Vâgdevatâyai Svâhâ, my forehead; Om Hrîm Sarasvatyai Svâhâ, my ears always Om Śrîm Hrîm Bhagabatyai Sarasvatyai Svâhâ always my eyes; Aim Hrîm Vâgvâdinyai Svâhâ, always my nose; Om Hrîm Vidyâdhiṣṭhâtrî Devyai Svâhâ, my lips always; Om Śrîm Hrîm Brâhmyai Svâhâ my rows of teeth; Aim, this single letter protect my neck; Om S'rîm Hrîm my throat; S'rîm, my shoulders, Om Hrîm Vidyâdhiṣṭhâtrî Devyai Svâhâ, always my chest; Om Hrîm Vidyâdhi svarûpâyai Svâhâ my navel; Om Hrîm Klîm Vâṇyai Svâhâ my hands; Om Svarva vârnatmî Kâyai Svâhâ my feet; and let Om Vâgadhiṣṭhâtridevyai Svâhâ protect all my body. Let "Om Sarvakanṭhavâsinyai Svâhâ protect my east; Let Om Svarvajihbâgra vâsinyai Svâhâ, the South-east; Om Aim Hrîm S'rîm Klîm Sarasvatyai budhajananyai Svâhâ, my South; Aim Hrîm S'rîm, this three-lettered Mantra my South-west; Om Aim Jhibbâgravâsinyai Svâhâ, my West; Om Svarvâm bikâyai Svâhâ, my North west; Om Aim S'rîm Klîm Gadyavâsinyai Svâhâ my North; Aim Sarvas'âstra vâsinyai Svâhâ, my North-east; Om Hrîm Sarvapûjitâyai Svâhâ, my top; Hrîm Pustakavâsinyai Svâhâ my below and let "Om Grantha vîjasvarupâyai Svâhâ protect all my sides. O Nârada! This Vis'vajaya Kavacha of the nature of Brahma and its embodied Mantra I have now spoken to you. I heard this before from the mouth of Dharma Deva in the Gandhâmâdana mountain. Now I speak this to you out of my great affection for you. But never divulge this to anybody. One is to worship one's spiritual Teacher (Guru Deva) according to due rites and ceremonies with clothings, ornaments, and sandalpaste and then fall down prostrate to him and then hold this Kavacha. Repeating this five lakhs of times, one gets success and becomes a Siddha. The holder of this Kavacha becomes intelligent like Brihaspati, eloquent, Kavîndras, and the conqueror of the three worlds, no sooner one becomes a Siddha in this. In fact, he can conquer everything by virtue of this Kavacha. O Muni! Thus I have described to you this Kavacha according to Kâṇva Śâkhâ. Now I am speaking about the method of worship, Dhyâna and the praise of this Kavacha. Hear.

Here ends the Fourth Chapter of the Ninth Book on the hymn, worship and Kavacha of Sarasvatî Devî in Śrî Mad Devî Bhâgavatam of 18,000 verses by Maharṣi Veda Vyâsa.

CHAPTER V.

1-5 Nârâyaṇa said:—"O Nârada! I now describe the Stotra (hymn) of Sarasvatî Devî, yielding all desires that Yâjñavalkya, the best of the Riṣis recited in days of yore to Her. The Muni Yâjñavalkya forgot all the Vedas out of the curse of Guru and with a very sad heart went to the Sun, the great merit-giving place. There he practised austerities for a time when the Lolâkhya Sun became visible to him, when, being overpowered by great sorrow, he began to cry repeatedly; and then he sang hymns to him. Then Bhagavân Sûrya Deva became pleased and taught him all the Vedas with their Amgas (limbs) and said:—"O Child! Now sing hymns to Sarasvatî Devî that you get back your memory." Thus saying, the Sun disappeared. The Muni Yâjñavalkya finished his bath and with his heart full of devotion began to sing hymns to the Vâg Devî, the Goddess of Speech.

6-32. Yâjñavalkya said:—"Mother! Have mercy on me. By Guru's curse, my memory is lost; I am now void of learning and have become powerless; my sorrow knows no bounds. Give me knowlege, learning, memory, power to impart knowlege to disciples, power to compose books, and also good disciples endowed with genius and Pratibhâ (ready wit). So that in the council of good and learned men my intelligence and power of argument and judgment be fully known. Whatever I lost by my bad luck, let all that come back to my heart and be renewed as if the sprouts come again out of the heaps of ashes. O Mother! Thou art of the nature of Brahma, superior to all; Thou art of the nature of Light, Eternal; Thou art the presiding Deity of all the branches of learning. So I bow down again and again to Thee. O Mother! The letters Anusvâra, Viṣarga: and Chandravindu that are affixed, Thou art those letters. So obeisance to Thee! O Mother! Thou art the exposition (Vyâkhyâ) of the Śâstras; Thou art the presiding Deity of all the expositions and annotations. Without Thee no mathematician can count anything. So Thou art the numbers to count time ; Thou art the Śakti by which Siddhântas (definite conclusions) are arrived at ; Thus Thou dost remove the errors of men. So again and again obeisance to Thee. O Mother! Thou art the Śakti, memory, knowledge, intelligence, Pratibhâ, and imagination (Kalpanâ). So I bow down again and again to Thee. Sanatkumâra fell into error and asked Brahmâ for solution. He became unable to solve the difficulties and remained speechless like a dumb person. Then Śrî Krişņa, the Highest Self arriving there, said :—"O Prajâpati! Better praise and sing hymns to the Goddess of speech ; then your desires will be fulfilled. Then the four-faced Brahmâ advised by the Lord, praised the Devî Sarasvatî ; and, by Her grace, arrived at a very nice Siddhânta (conclusion). One day the goddess Earth questioned one doubt of Her to Ananta Deva, when He being unable to answer, remained silent like a dumb person. At last He became afraid ; and advised by Kas'yapa, praised Thee when He resolved the doubt and came to a definite conclusion. Veda Vyâsa once went to Vâlmîki and asked him about some Sûtras of the Purâņas when the Muni Vâlmîki got confounded and remembered Thee, the Mother of the world. When by Thy Grace, the Light flashed within him and his error vanished. Thereby he became able to solve the question. Then Vyâsadeva, born of the parts of Śrî Krişņa, heard about the Purâņa Sûtras from Vâlmîki's mouth and came to know about Thy glory. He then went to Puşkara Tîrtha and became engaged in worshipping Thee, the Giver of Peace, for one hundred years. Then Thou didst become pleased and grant him the boon when he ascended to the rank of the Kavîndra (Indra amongst the poets). He then made the classification of the Vedas and composed the eighteen Purâņas. When Sadâ Śiva was questioned on some spiritual knowledge, by Mahendra, He thought of Thee for a moment and then answered. Once Indra asked Brihaspati, the Guru of the Devas, about Śabda Śâstra (Scriptures on sound). He became unable to give any answer. So he went to Puşkara Tîrtha and worshipped Thee for a thousand years according to the Deva Measure and he became afterwards able to give instructions on Śabda Śâstra for one thousand divine years to Mahendra. O Sures'varî! Those Munis that give education to their disciples or those that commence their own studies remember Thee before they commence their works respectively. The Munîndras, Manus, men, Daityendras, and Immortals, Brahmâ, Vişņu and Maheşa all worship Thee and sing hymns to Thee. Vişņu ultimately becomes inert when He goes on praising Thee by His thousand mouths. So Mahâ Deva becomes when he praises by His five mouths; and so Brahmâ by His four mouths. When great personages so desist, then what to speak of me, who is an ordinary mortal having one mouth only! Thus saying, the Maharṣi Yâjñavalkya, who had observed fasting, bowed down to the Devî Sarasvatî with great devotion and began to cry frequently. Then the Mahâmâyâ Sarasvatî, of the nature of Light could not hide Herself away. She became visible to him and said "O Child! You be good Kavîndra (Indra of the poets)." Granting him this boon, She went to Vaikuṇṭha. He becomes a good poet, eloquent, and intelligent like Brihaspati who reads this stotra of Sarasvatî by Yâjñavalkya. Even if a great illiterate reads this Sarasvatî stotra for one year, he becomes easily a good Pundit, intelligent, and a good poet.

Here ends the Fifth Chapter of the Ninth Book on Sarasvatî stotra by Yâjañvalkya in Śri Mad Devî Bhâgavatam of 18,000 verses by Maharṣi Veda Vyâsa.

CHAPTER VI.

1-10 Nârâyaṇa said:—"O Nârada! Sarasvatî lives always in Vaikuṇṭha close to Nârada. One day a quarrel arose with Gangâ, and by Her curse, Sarasvatî came in parts as a river here in this Bhârata. She is reckoned in Bhârata as a great sanctifying holy and merit-giving river. The good persons serve Her always, residing on Her banks. She is the Tapasyâ and the fruit thereof of the ascetics. She is like the burning fire to the sins of the sinners. Those that die in Bhârata on the Sarasvatî waters with their full consciousness, live for ever in Vaikuṇṭha in the council of Hari. Those that bathe in the Sarasvatî waters, after committing sins, become easily freed of them and live for a long, long time in Viṣṇu-Loka. If one bathes even once in the Sarasvatî waters, during Châturmâsya (a vow that lasts four months), in full moon time, in Akṣayâ or when the day ends, in Vyatîpâta Yoga, in the time of eclipse or on any other holy day or through any other concomitant cause or even without any faith and out of sheer disregard, one is able to go to Vaikuṇṭha and get the nature of Śrî Hari. If one repeats the Sarasvatî Mantra, residing on the banks of the Sarasvatî, for one month, a great illiterate can become a great poet. There is no doubt in this. Once shaving one's head, if one resides on the banks of the Sarasvatî, daily bathes in it, one will have not to meet with the pain of being again born in the womb. O Nârada! Thus I have described a little of the unbounded glories of Bhârata that give happiness and the fruits of all desires.

11. Sûta said :—" O Saunaka ! The Muni Nârada hearing thus, asked again at that very moment to solve his doubts. I am now speaking of that. Hear.

12-15. Nârada said :— " O Lord ! How did the Devî Sarasvatî quarrel with the Devî Gangâ and how did she by Her curse turn out in India, into a holy river in giving virtues. I am becoming more and more eager and impatient to hear about this critical incident. I do not find satiety in drinking your nectar-like words. Who finds satiety in getting his good weal ? Why did Gangâ curse Sarasvatî, worshipped everywhere. Gangâ is also full of Sattva Guṇas. She always bestows good and virtue to all. Both of them are fiery and it is pleasant to hear the cause of quarrels between these two. These are very rarely found in the Purâṇas. So you ought to describe that to me.

16-21. Nârâyaṇa said :— " Hear, O Nârada ! I will now describe that incident, the hearing of which removes all the sins. Lakṣmî, Sarasvatî and Gangâ, the three wives of Hari and all equally loved, remain always close to Hari. One day Gangâ cast side-long glances frequently towards Nârâyaṇa and was eagerly looking at Him, with smile on Her lips. Seeing this, the Lord Nârâyaṇa, startled and looked at Gangâ and smiled also. Lakṣmî saw that, but she did not take any offence. But Sarasvatî became very angry. Padmâ (Lakṣmî) who was of Sattva Guṇa, began to console in various ways the wrathful Sarasvatî ; but she could not be appeased by any means. Rather Her face became red out of anger ; she began to tremble out of her feelings (passion) ; Her lips quivered ; and She began to speak to Her husband.

22-38. The husband that is good, religious, and well qualified looks on his all the wives equally ; but it is just the opposite with him who is a cheat. O Gadâdhara ! You are partial to Gangâ ; and so is the case with Lakṣmî. I am the only one that is deprived of your love. It is, therefore, that Gangâ and Padmâ are in love with each other ; for you love Padmâ. So why shall not Padmâ bear this contrary thing ! I am only unfortunate. What use is there in holding my life ? Her life is useless, who is deprived of her husband's love. Those that declare you, of Sattva Guṇas, ought not to be ever called Pundits. They are quite illiterate ; they have not the least knowledge of the Vedas. They are quite impotent to understand the nature of your mind. O Nârada ! Hearing Sarasvatî's words and knowing that she had become very angry, Nârâyaṇa thought for a moment and then went away from the Zenana outside. When Nârâyaṇa had thus gone away, Sarasvatî became fearless and began to abuse Gangâ downright out of anger in an abusive language, hard to hear ;—" O Shameless One ! O Passionate One ! What pride do you feel for your husband ? Do you like to show that your husband loves you much ? I will destroy your pride to-day. I will see to-day, it will be seen by others also, what your Hari can do for you ? Saying thus Sarasvatî rose up to catch hold of Gangâ by Her hairs violently. Padmâ intervened to stop this. Sarasvatî became very violent and cursed Lakṣmî :—" No doubt you will be turned into a tree and into a river. In as much as seeing this undue behaviour of Gangâ, you do not step forward to speak anything in this assembly, as if you are a tree or a river. Padmâ did not become at all angry, even when she heard of the above curse. She became sorry and, holding the hands of Sarasvatî, remained silent. Then Gangâ became very angry ; Her lips began to quiver frequently Seeing the mad fiery nature of the red-eyed Sarasvatî, she told Lakṣmî :—" O Padme ! Leave that wicked foul-mouthed woman. What will she do to me ? She presides over speech and therefore likes always to remain with quarrels. Let Her shew Her force how far can she quarrel with me. She wants to test the strength of us. So leave Her. Let all know to-day our strength and prowess.

39-44. Thus saying, Gangâ became ready to curse Sarasvatî and addressing Lakṣmî, said :—" O Dear Padme ! As that woman has cursed you to become a river, " so I too curse her, " that she, too, be turned into a river and she would go to the abode of men, the sinners, to the world and take their heaps of sins. Hearing this curse of Gangâ, Sarasvatî gave her curse, " You, too,' will have to descend into the Bhurloka (the world) as a river, taking all the sins of the sinners. " O Nârada ! While there was going on this quarrel, the four-armed omniscient Bhagavân Hari came up there accompanied by four attendants of His, all four-armed, and took Sarasvatî in His breast and began to speak all the previous mysteries. Then they came to know the cause of their quarrels and why they cursed one another and all became very sorry. At that time Bhagavân Hari told them one by one :—

45-67. O Lakṣmî ! Let you be born in parts, without being born in any womb, in the world as the daughter in the house of the King Dharma-dhvaja. You will have to take the form of a tree there, out of this evil turn of fate. There Śankhachûḍa, the Indra of the Asuras, born of my parts will marry you. After that you will come back here and be my wife as now. There is no doubt in this. You will be named Tulasî, the purifier of the three worlds, in Bhârata. O Beautiful One ! Now go there quickly and be a river in your parts under the name Padmâvatî. O Gange ! You will also have to take incarnation in Bhârata as a river, purifying all the worlds, to destroy the sins of the inhabitants of Bhârata. Bhagiratha will take you there after much entreating and worshipping you; and you will be famous by the name Bhâgirathî, the most sanctifying river in the world. There, the Ocean born of my parts, and the King Śântanu also born of my parts will be your husbands. O Bhâratî! Let you go also and incarnate in part in Bhârata under the curse of Gangâ. O Good-natured One! Now go in full Amsas to Brahmâ and become His wife. Let Gangâ go also in Her fullness to Śiva Let Padmâ remain with Me. Padmâ is of a peaceful nature, void of anger, devoted to Me and of a Sâttvika nature. Chaste, good-natured, fortunate and religious woman like Padmâ are very rare. Those women that are born of the parts of Padmâ are all very religious and devoted to their husbands. They are peaceful and good-natured and worshipped in every universe. It is forbidden, nay, opposed to the Vedas, to keep three wives, three servants, three friends of different natures, at one place. They never conduce to any welfare. They are the fruitful sources of all jealousies and quarrels. Where, in any family females are powerful like men and males are submissive to females, the birth of the male is useless. At his every step, he meets with difficulties and bitter experiences. He ought to retire to the forest whose wife is foul-mouthed, of bad birth and fond of quarrels. The great forest is better for him than his house. That man does not get in his house any water for washing his feet, or any seat to sit on, or any fruit to eat, nothing whatsoever; but in the forest, all these are not unavailable. Rather to dwell amidst rapacious animals or to enter into fire than remain with a bad wife. O Fair One! Rather the pains of the disease or venom are bearable, but the words of a bad wife are hard to bear. Death is far better than that. Those that are under the control of their wives, know that they never get their peace of mind until they are laid on their funeral pyres. They never see the fruits of what they daily do. They have no fame anywhere, neither in this world nor in the next. Ultimately the fruit is this:—that they have to go to hell and remain there. His life is verily a heavy burden who is without any name or fame. Never it is for the least good that many co-wives remain at one place. When, by taking one wife only, a man does not become happy, then imagine, how painful it becomes to have many wives. O Gange! Go to Śiva. O Sarasvatî! Go to Brahmâ. Let the good-natured Kamalâ, residing on the lotus remain with Me. He gets in this world happiness and Dharma and in the next Mukti whose wife is chaste and obedient. In fact he is Mukta, pure and happy whose wife is chaste; and he whose wife is foul-natured, is rendered impure, unhappy and dead whilst he is living.

Here ends the Sixth Chapter of the Ninth Book on the coming in this world of Lakṣmî, Gangâ and Sarasvatî in the Mahâpurâṇam Śrîmad Devî Bhâgavatam of 18,000 verses by Mahaṛsi Veda Vyâsa.

CHAPTER VII.

1-2. Nârâyaṇa said :— "O Nârada ! Thus saying, the Lord of the World stopped. And Lakṣmî, Gangâ and Sarasvatî wept bitterly, embracing one another. All of them then looked to Śrî Kriṣṇa, and gave vent to their feelings one by one with tears in their eyes, and with their hearts throbbing with fears and sorrows.

3-4. Sarasvatî said :— "O Lord ! What is, now, the way out of this curse, so severe and paining since our births ? How long can helpless women live, separated from their husbands ? O Lord ! I certainly say that I will sacrifice my body when I go to Bhârata, by taking recourse to yoga. The Mahâtmâs always protect all the persons without fail.

5-6. Gangâ said :—"O Lord of the Universe ! Why have I been abandoned by You. What fault have I committed ? I will quit my body. And You will have to partake of the sin due to the killing of an innocent woman. He is surely to go to hell, even if he be the Lord of all, who forsakes in this world an innocent wife. "

7-15. Padmâ said :—" O Lord ! Thou art of the nature of Sattva Guṇa in fullness ; what wonder, then, how Thou hast become angry ! " However let Thou be pleased now with Sarasvatî and Gangâ. Forgiveness is the best quality of a good husband. I am ready just now to go to Bhârata when Sarasvatî has cursed me. But tell me, how long I will have to stay there ? After how many days I shall be able to see again Thy lotus-feet ? The sinners will wash away their dirts of sins in my waters by their constant baths and ablutions ? By what means shall I be freed again and get back to Thy lotus-feet. How long shall I have to remain in my part, the daughter of Dharma Dhvaja, at the expiry of which I will be able to see Thee again ? How long shall I have to assume the form of Tulasî tree, the abode of Thine. O Thou, the Ocean of mercy ! Say, when wilt Thou deliver me ? And if Gangâ have to go to Bhârata, by the curse of Bhâratî, when shall She be freed of the curse and sin and when shall She see back Thy feet ? Again if Sarasvatî have to go to Bhârata out of Gangâ's curse, when will that period of curse expire ? How many days after shall She be able to come back to Thy feet ? Now, be pleased to cancel Thy order for them to go to Brahmâ and Śiva respectively. O Nârada ! Thus speaking to Jagannâtha, the Devî Kamalâ bowed down at His feet and embracing them by Her own hairs of the head, cried frequently.

16-37. Now the lotus-navelled Hari, always eager to shew favour to the devotees, smiled and with a gracious heart took up Padmâ on His breast and said :—" O Sures'vari ! I will keep my own word, also I will act according as you like. O Lotus-eyed ! Hear. How the two ends can be made to meet. Let Sarasvatî go in her one part to have the form of a river and in her one-half part to Brahmâ and remain with me in Vaikuṇṭha in Her full parts. Gangâ will have to go in one part to Bhârata —to purify the three worlds, as she will be urged eagerly to do so by Bhagîratha. And She will remain in her one part in the matted hair of Chandra Śekhara (the Mahâdeva with Moon on his forehead), obtained with a great difficulty, and so will remain there purer than her natural pure state. And let her remain with me in full parts. O Padme! O Lovely-eyed One ! You are most innocent ; so part of your part will go to Bhârata and be the Padmâvatî river and you will be the Tulasî tree. After the expiry of five thousand years of Kali Yuga, your curse will expire. Again you all will come to My abode. O Padme ! Calamities are the causes of the happiness of the embodied beings. Without dangers no one can understand the true nature of happiness. The saint worshippers of My mantra who will perform their ablutions in your waters, will free you all of your curse by touch and sight. O Fair One ! By the sight and touch (Darṣan, Spars'an) of My bhaktas (devotees), all the sacred places of pilgrimage in the world will be purified. For uplifting and sanctifying the holy earth, My mantropâsakas, *i. e*, Śaivas, Śâktas, Gâṇapatyas, etc., that are devoted to Brahma all are residing in Bhârata. Where My Bhaktas reside and wash their feet, that place is undoubtedly reckoned as the holy places of pilgrimages. So much so that by the sight and touch of My devotees, the murderer of a woman, of a cow, of a Brâhmin, the treacherous and even the stealer of the wife of one's Guru will be sanctified and liberated while living. Those who do not perform the vow of Ekâdas'î, who do not perform Sandhyâs, who are Nâstikas (atheists), the murderers, all are freed of their sins by the sight and touch of My devotees. By the sight and touch of My devotees, those who live on their swords, pens, and the royal officials, the beggars in a village and the Brâhmaṇas who carry (deal in) bullocks are also freed of their sins. The traitors, the mischief makers of their friends, those who give false evidence, those that steal other's trust properties, are also freed of their sins by the sight and touch of My devotees. Those who are foul-mouthed, bastards, the husbands and sons of unchaste women are all purified by the sight and touch of My Bhaktas. The Brâhmin cooks of Śûdras, Brâhmiṇs of an inferior order (who subsist upon the offerings made to the images which he attends), the village mendicants, those who are not initiated by their Gurus, these all are purified by the sight and touch of My devotees. O Fair One ! The sins of those persons who do not maintain their fathers, mothers, brothers, wives, sons, daughters, sisters, the blind, friends, the families of the Gurus, the fathers-in-law, the mothers in-law are also removed by the sight and touch of My devotees. Those that cut the As'vattha trees, that slander My devotees, and the Brâhmins that eat the food of Śûdras, are also freed of their sins. Those who steal the Deva's articles, the Brâhmaṇa's articles, those that sell lac, iron, and daughters, those who commit Mahâ Pâtakas (Brahmahatyâ, Surâpânam, Steyam, Gurbanganâganah, Mahânti pâtakânyâhuh, tatsamsargahscha Pañchamam) and those that burn the Śûdrâ's dead bodies, these also are freed of their respective sins by the sight and touch of My devotees.

38-42. Mahâ Lakṣmî said :— "O Thou gracious to faithful attendants! What are the characteristics, the marks of those Bhaktas of Thine that Thou hast spoken of just now whose sight and touch destroy instantly the Mahâpâtakas (five great sins), that are destroyed after a long time by the water of the Tirthas and the earthen and stone images of the Gods. The sins of the vilest of men, devoid of Hari bhakti, vain and egoistic. cheats, hypocrites, slanderers of saints, vicious souls are destroyed by your Bhaktas, whose touch and ablutions sanctify the sacred places of pilgrimages : by the touch of the dust and water of whose feet, the earth is purified ; whom the Bhaktas of Bhârata always pray to see; and there is nothing higher than the meeting of those Bhaktas." Sûta said :— "O Great Riṣi ! Thus hearing the words of Mahâ Lakṣmî, the Lord smiled and began to speak about the secret things or the marks of the Bhaktas."

44 54. O Lakṣmî ! The marks of the Bhaktas are all mentioned very hiddenly in Śrutis and Purâṇas. These are very sanctifying, destructive of sins, giving happiness, devotion, and liberation. These are never to be described to deceitful persons ; these are the essences and to be kept hidden. But you are very simple and like my life. I therefore speak to you. Hear, O Fair One ! All the Vedas declare him to be holy and the best of men, in whose ears are pronounced from the mouth of a Guru, the Viṣṇu mantra. At the very moment of his being born into this world, one hundred generations back of that person, whether they be at that time in heaven or hell, get instantaneous liberation and if any of them happen to be born then as Jîvas, they become liberated at once while living and finally get Viṣṇupadam (the place of Viṣṇu). That mortal is My Bhakta (devotee) who is full of devotion to Me, who always repeats My glories and acts according to My directions, who hears with all his heart My topics, and hearing which, whose mind dances with joy, whose voice gets choked and

tears incessantly flow out from whose eyes, who loses his outward consciousness. Such a man is indeed, My Bhakta. My Bhaktas do not long for happiness, or Mukti, or the four states Sâlokya, Sâyujya, Sâmîpya and Sârṣṭi, nor the Brahmahood, nor the Devahood (the state of immortality); they want only to do Sevâ (service) to Me and they are solely intent on doing this. Even in dreams they do not desire the Indraship, Manuship, the state of Brahmâ, so very difficult to be had; nor do they want the enjoyment of kingdoms and heavens. My Bhaktas roam in Bhârata, eager to hear My glories, and always very glad to recite My sweet glorious deeds. The birth of such Bhaktas in Bhârata is very rare. They purify the world and go ultimately to My abode, the best of all Tîrthas (sacred places). Thus I have spoken O Padme! all that you wanted to hear. Now do as you like. Then Gangâ and others all went to obey the order of Śrî Hari, Who went to His own abode.

Here ends the Seventh Chapter of the Ninth Book on the curses of Gangâ, Sarasvatî, and Lakṣmî and the way to freedom thereof in the Mahâpurâṇam Śrîmad Devî Bhâgavatam of 18,000 verses by Maharṣi Veda Vyâsa.

CHAPTER VIII.

1-110. Nârâyana said:—A part of Sarasvatî descended in this Bhârata Puṇya Bhûmi (land of merits), owing to the curse of Gangâ; and She remained in full in Viṣṇu's region, the abode of Vaikuṇṭha. She is named Bhâratî, on account of Her coming to Bhârata; she is called Brâhmî because she is dear to Brahmâ; and She is called Vâṇî as She presides over Speech. Hari is seen everywhere, in tanks, in wells, in running streams (i.e., in Saras). Because He resides in Saras, therefore He is called Sarasvân. Vâṇî is the Śakti of that Sarasvân; therefore She is denominated Sarasvatî. The river Sarasvatî is a very sacred Tîrtha. She is the burning fire to the fuel of sins, of sinners. O Nârada! Through the curse of Sarasvatî, the Devî Gangâ also assumed the form of a river in part. She was brought down to this earth at the request of Bhagîratha. Hence she is called Bhâgîrathî. While Gangâ was rushing down to the earth Śiva capable to bear the great rush of Her, held Her on His head at the request of the Mother Earth. Lakṣmî also, through the curse of Sarasvatî came in part of parts to Bhârata as the river Padmâvatî. But She remained in full with Hari. Lakṣmî appeared also in Her other part as the well-known daughter Tulasî of the king Dharmadhvaja in India. Last of all, through Bhâratî's curse and by the command of Śrî Hari, she turned into the Tulasî tree, purifying the whole world. Remaining for five thousand years of Kali, all of them will quit their river appearances and go back to Hari. By the command of Śrî Hari, all the Tîrthas save Kâs'î and Bindrâban will go along with them to Vaikuṇṭha. Next at the expiry of the ten thousand years of Kali, Śâlagrâma Śilâ (the stone piece worshipped as Nârâyaṇa) Śiva, and Śiva Śakti and Puruṣottama Jagannâtha will leave the soil of Bhârata and go to their respective places, (*i.e.* the Mâhâtmyas of these will be extinct from Bhârata). There will then cease to be the saints (of Śiva Śâkta, Gâṇapatya and Vaiṣṇava sects, (eighteen) Purâṇas, the blowing of conch shells (auspicious signs), Śrâddhas, Tarpaṇas, and all the rites and ceremonies dictated by the Vedas. The worship and glorification of the Gods, the recitation of their praises, their names will be extinct. The Vedas with their Amgas will no longer be heard of. All these will disappear with them. The assembly of the Sâdhus, the true Dharma, the four Vedas, the village Devas and Devîs, the Vratas (vows) the practising of the austerities, fasting, all will disappear. All will be addicted to the Vâmâchâra ritual (the left-hand ritual Tântrik form of worship; sarcastically used in the sense of drinking wine and eating flesh, etc.) They will speak falsehood and be deceitful. If any body worships, his worship will be void of Tulasî leaves. Almost all will be deceitful, cruel, vain, egoistic, thievish and mischievous. Men will be at variance with one another; women will be at variance with one another; no fear will exist in marriage ties. Properties will be only of those that will make them (*i. e.* there will cease to be any inheritance from father to son and so forth). Husbands will be obedient to their wives; unchaste women will be in every house. Wives will rebuke their husbands by incessant noisings and chidings. Wives will be the sole mistresses of houses and husbands will stand before them as servants with folded palms. Fathers-in-law and mothers-in-law will be their servants. The brothers of wives, and their friends will be the managers of the household affairs. But there will be no friendship with one's own class fellows. The brothers and friends of the house owners (masters of the house) will appear quite strangers as if they are new-comers. Without the command of the housewives, the masters of the houses will be unable to do anything. The divisions of caste (Brâhmaṇa, Kṣattriya, Vaiṣya, and Śûdra) will entirely disappear. Far from practising Sandhyâ Bandanam and other daily practices, the Brâhmaṇas will cease to hold the holy threads even on their bodies. The four colour-classes will practise the doings of the Mlechchas, read the Śâstras of the Mlechchas and forsake their own Śâstras. The Brâhmins, Kṣattriyas, and Vais'yas will become the slaves of Śûdras, will become their cooks, runners and carriers of buffaloes. Every one will be devoid of truth. Earth will not yield any grains;

trees will not yield any fruits and women will be issueless. The cows will not yield milk; even if there be a little, milk, ghee will not come out of it. The affection between husband and wife will die out and the families will be devoid of truth. The King will not wield any power; the subjects will be over burdened with taxes. The ever flowing big rivers, the petty streams, the caves of mountains all will gradually have very little water in them. The Four Varṇas will be devoid of Dharma and Puṇya (merit, virtue). One in a lakh may be virtuous. Afterwards that too will cease. Men, women, boys, all will be ugly and deformed. They will utter bad words and vile sounds. Some villages and towns will be completely deserted by men and will look terrible; at some others few cottages with few inhabitants will be seen. Villages and towns will be jungles and jungles will become filled with men. The inhabitants of the forests will become heavily taxed and disconsolate. The beds of rivers and lakes will become dry owing to want of rains and will be cultivated. The Kulînas of high families will become very low. The whole earth will be filled with liars, untruthful cheats and hypocrites. The lands, though cultivated well, will yield grains in name. Those who are well known as the millionaires, they will become poor and those who are devoted to the Devas will be atheists. The towns folk will have no trace of mercy; rather they will hate and envy their neighbours and turn out murderers of men. In the Kali age, males and females will be, everywhere, of a dwarfish stature, diseased, shortlived, and of very little youthful virility. The hairs will turn out grey no sooner the people reach their sixteenth year. And they will be very old when they become twenty years old. The girls of eight years will have menstruation and will become pregnant. They will deliver every year. Old age will attack them when they become sixteen years old. Some women will have their husbands and children living. Otherwise almost all will be barren, childless. The four Varṇas will sell their daughters. The paramours of the mothers, wives, son's wives, daughters, and sisters will be the source of support to them all. No one will be able, without money, to collect the merits by repeating the name of Hari. Persons will make gifts for name and fame and ultimately will take back what they had made as gifts. If there be any gifts made by one's own self or by one's forefathers for a Deva purpose or for Brâhmiṇs or for the families of the Gurus, there will not be found wanting attempts to take back those gifts. Some will go to daughters, some to mothers-in-law, some to the wives of sons, some to sisters, some to mothers of co-wives, some will go to the brother's wives. In every house, those who are unfit to be mixed will be mixed with, excepting one's mother. In Kali Yuga who is whose wife? And who is whose husband? There will be no certainty; who is whose subject and what village is to whom? There will be no surety that such a property belongs to such and such a man. All will turn out to be liars, licentious, thieves, envious of other's wives, and murderers of men. In the houses of the Brâhmiṇs, Kṣattriyas, and Vais'yas, the three higher castes, the current of sin will flow. They will live by selling lac, iron, and salts prohibited by the Śâstras. The Brâhmiṇs will drive buffaloes, burn the dead bodies of the Śûdras, eat the food of the Śûdras and go to unchaste women. There will be no more faith existing in the five Riṣi Yajñas. Almost every Brâhmiṇ will not observe the vows of Amâvasyâ Nis'ipâlana. The holy threads will be cast away and the Sandhyâ Bandanam and cleanliness and good practices will cease altogether. The unchaste women who deal in giving loans, etc., and live on interests and the procuresses during menstruation will cook in Brâhmiṇ families. There will be no distinction of food, no distinction of wombs, no distinction of Âs'ramas, and no distinction of persons. All will turn out Mlechchas. O Nârada! Thus, when the Kali will have its full play, the whole world will be filled with Mlechchas, the trees will be one hand high and the men will be of the size, of a thumb. Then the most powerful Bhagavân Nârâyaṇa will incarnate in His part in the house of a Brâhmiṇ named Viṣṇujas'â as his son. Mounted on a long horse, holding a long sword He will make the world free of the Mlechchas in three nights. Then he will disappear from the face of the Earth and She will be without any sovereign and be filled with robbers. There will be incessant rain, for six nights and it will rain and rain and the whole earth will be deluged; no traces of men, houses, and trees. After this the Twelve Suns will rise simultaneously and by their rays the whole water will be dried up and the earth will become level. Thus the dreadful Kali will pass away when the Satya Yuga will come back, Tapasyâ and the true religion and Sattva Guṇa will prevail again. The Brâhmiṇs will practise Tapasyâ, they will be devoted to Dharma and the Vedas. The women will be chaste and religious in every house. Again the wise and intelligent Kṣattriyas devoted to the Brâhmaṇas will occupy the royal thrones and their might, devotion to Dharma and love for good deeds will increase. The Vais'yas will again go on with their trades and their devotion to their trade and the Brâhmiṇs will be reestablished. The Śûdras, too, will be again virtuous, and serve the Brâhmiṇs. Again the Brâhmiṇs, Ks'attriyas, and Vais'yas and their families will have Bhakti towards the Devî, be initiated in Devî Mantras and all will meditate on the Devî. Again there will be spread the knowledge of the Vedas, the Smritis, and the Purâṇas, all will go to their wives in menstruation periods. No Adharma (unrighteousness) will exist and the Dharma will reign in full, with all the parts (Kalâs) complete. When the Tretâ Yuga comes, the Dharma will be three footed; when the Dvâpara Yuga will come, the Dharma will be two-footed and when Kali will begin, the Dharma will be one-footed, and when Kali will reign supreme, no Dharma will exist, even in name. (O Nârada,! Now I will speak of time.) The seven days of the week, Sunday, &c., the sixteen tithis, Pratipada &c., the twelve months Vais'âkha &c., the six seasons Summer, &c., the two fortnights (dark and bright) and the two Ayaṇas (Northern and Southern) are rendered in vogue. One day consists of four Praharas, one night consists of four Praharas; a day and a night constitute one so-called day. Thirty such days make one month. In the computation of time, five kinds of years (Varṣas) were already mentioned (in the 8th Skandha). As the Satya, Tretâ, Dvâpara and Kali roll on turn by turn, so the days, months and years also roll on in turn. One day, according to the Devas, is equal to one year, according to men; three hundred and sixty human Yugas equal to one Deva Yuga. Sventy-one Deva Yugas make one Manvantara. The life period of Indra, the Lord of Śachî, is one Manvantara. Twenty-eight Indras' lives equal to one day of Hiraṇyagarbha (the golden wombed) Brahmâ. One hundred and eight such years equal to the life of one Brahmâ. When this Brahmâ dies, there is the Prâkrita Pralaya. The earth is not visible then. (The dissolution of Prakriti takes place.) The whole Brahmâṇḍa is deluged by water; Brahmâ, Viṣṇu, Mahes'vara and the other wise Riṣis get diluted in Para Brahma whose substance is all truth and consciousness. That time, the Prakriti Devî, too, gets merged in Para Brahma. The fall of Brahmâ and the dissolution of Prakriti are called the Prâkrita Pralaya. The duration of this Pralaya is one Nimeṣa of the Para Brahma Mûla Prakriti united with Mâyâ. All the Brahmâṇdas (universes) are destroyed at this time. When this Nimeṣa expires, the creation begins again in due order. So one cannot count the endless numbers of times when this creation and dissolution works are going on. So who can tell how many kalpas had past away, or how many Kalpas will come, how many Brahmâṇḍas were created or how many Brahmâṇḍas will be created. Who will be able to count how many Brahmâs, how many Viṣṇus or how many Mahes'varas there have been. But One and Only One Para Brahma Parames'vara (the Great God) is The Supreme Lord of these countless Brahmâṇḍas. This Parames'vara of the nature of Existence, Consciousness and Bliss is the Highest Spirit of all. All others, Brahmâ, Viṣṇu, Mahes'vara the

Great Virâț, the Smaller Virâț, all are His parts. This Brahma is Mûla Prakriti and from That has appeared Śrî Krişņa, the Lord of his left half which is woman (Ardha Nâris'vara). It is She that divided Herself into two forms; in Her one form, She resides as the two armed Krişņa in the region of Goloka; and as the four-armed Nârâyaņa in Vaikuņțha. All the things from Brahmâ, the Highest, to the mere grass the lowest, all are originated from Prakriti. And all the Prakriti-born things are transient. Thus the True, Eternal Para Brahma, beyond the three guņas, the Source of all creation, Whose substance is All-Will is the Only Substance beyond the region of Prakriti. He is without Upâdhis (conditions, as time, space, causation and attributes); He is without any form; and the forms that He assumes, they are for shewing His Grace to the devotees only. The Lotus-born Brahmâ is able by His Power of Knowledge to create the Brahmâņḍa. It is by His Grace that Śiva, the Lord of the yogis is named Mrityumjaya (the Conqueror of Death), the Destoyer of all, and the Knower of all Tattvas. By His Tapas, Śiva has realised Para Brahma and therefore has become the Lord of all, All-knowing, endowed with great Vibhûtis (lordly powers), the seer of all, omnipresent, the protector of all, the bestower of all prosperities. The devotion and service towards Para Brahma have alone made Śrî Vişņu - the Lord of all; and it is through the power of Para Brahma, that Mahâmâyâ Prakriti Devî has become omnipotent and the Goddess of all. Bhagavatî Durgâ has got His Grace by Her devotion and service to Him and has become Mûla Prakriti of the nature of Being, Consciousness and Bliss. And so has the Devî Sâvitrî, the Mother of the Vedas, become the presiding Deity of the Vedas and She is worshipped by the Brâhmaņas and the Knowers of the Vedas. That She presides over all the branches of knowledge, is worshipped by all the learned assemblies and by the whole Universe is the result only of worshipping the Prakriti Devî. That Lakşmî has become the bestower of all wealth and the presiding Deity of all the villages and the mistress of all, worshipped by all and the bestower of sons to all is also the result of worshipping Her. Thus it is through the worship of Prakriti that Durgâ, the Destroyer of all calamities and troubles has appeared from the left side of Śrî Krişņa; and Râdhâ has become the presiding Deity of His Prâņa (vital airs), and She is worshipped by all and possessed of all knowledge. It is by the worship of Śakti that Râdhikâ has so much excelled in love, has become the presiding Deity of the prâņa of Krişņa, has got His love and respect, has been placed on His breast and is exceedingly beautiful. With the object of getting Krişņa for her husband, She practised severe austerities for one thousand Deva years on the mountain Śatas'ringa in Bhârata to get the Mûla Prakriti's Grace. And when the Śakti Mûla Prakriti became graciously pleased towards Her, Śrî Kriṣṇa seeing Rādhikā increasing in beauty like the Crescent Moon took Her to His breast and out of tenderness wept and granted Her highest boons so very rare to others and said :—O Beautiful One! You better remain always in My breast and devoted to Me amongst all my wives; let you be superior to them all in good fortune, respect, love and glory. From to-day you are my greatest best wife. I will love you as the best amongst them all. O Dear! Always I will be submissive to you and fulfil what you say. Thus saying, Śrî Kriṣṇa selected her as his wife without any co-wives and made Her dear to His Heart. The other Devîs besides the five Prakritis, already mentioned, also derived superiorities by serving Mûla Prakriti. O Muni! What shall I say, everyone reaps the fruits as he practises Tapasyâ. Bhagavatî Durgâ practised on the Himâlyâs tapasyâ for one thousand Deva years and meditated on the lotus-feet of Mûla Prakriti and so has come to be worshipped by all. The Devî Sarasvatî practised tapasyâ for one lâkh Deva years and is come to be respected by all. The Devî Lakṣmî practised tapasyâ at Puṣkara for one hundred Divine Yugas and, by the Grace of Mûla Prakriti, has become the bestower of wealth to all. The Devî Sâvitrî worshipped Śakti for sixty thousand divine years in the Malaya mountain and is respected and worshipped by all. O Bibhu! Brahmâ, Viṣṇu, and Mahes'vara worshipped Śakti for one hundred Manvantaras and so have become the Preservers, etc., of this world. Śrî Kriṣṇa practised for ten Manvantaras terrible austerities and therefore obtained his position in the region of Goloka and is remaining there to-day in greatest bliss. Dharma Deva worshipped Śakti with devotion for ten Manvantars and has become the lives of all, worshipped by all, and the receptacle of all. O Muni! Thus all, whether the Devîs, Devas, Munis, Kings, Brâhmaṇas, all have got their respect in this world by the worship of Śakti. O Devarṣi! I have thus described to you all that I heard from the mouth of my Guru, in accordance with the rules of the Vedas. What more do you want to hear?

Here ends the Eighth Chapter of the Ninth Book on the Greatness of Kali in the Mahâ Purâṇam Srîmad Devî Bhâgavatam of 18,000 verses by Maharṣi Veda Vyâsa.

CHAPTER IX.

1-4. Śrî Nârada said:—In the twinkling of an eye of the Devi, the Pralaya takes place; and in that very time also the Brahmâṇḍa (cosmos) is dissolved, which is called the Pralaya of Prakriti. During this Pralaya, the Devî Vasundharâ (Earth) disappears; the whole world is deluged with water and all this appearance of five elements called Prapañcha vanishes in the body of Prakriti. Now where does Vasundharâ (Earth), thus vanished, reside? And how does She again appear at the beginning of the creation! What is the cause of her being so much blessed, honoured and capable to hold all and victorious. So tell about Her birth, the source of all welfare.

5-23. Śrî Nârâyaṇa said:—"O Nârada! So it is heard that the Earth appears at the very outset of the creation. Her appearance and disappearance so occur in all the Pralayas. (This earth) the manifestation of the great Śakti, sometimes becomes manifest in Her and sometimes remains latent in Her (the Śakti). It is all the will of that Great Śakti. Now hear the anecdote of appearance (birth) of the earth, the cause of all good, the source of destruction of all calamities, the destroyer of sin and the cause of furtherance of one's religious merits. Some say that this earth has come out of the marrow of the Daityas, Madhu and Kaiṭabha; but that is not the fact. Hear now the real fact. Those two Daityas were greatly pleased with Viṣṇu's valour and prowess in the fight between them and Viṣṇu; and they said:—"Kill us on that part of the earth which is not under water." From their words it is evident that the earth was existent during their life-time but she was not visible. After their death, the marrow came out after their bones. Now hear how the name "Medinî" came to be applied to the earth. She was taken out of the water, and the marrow came to be mixed with the earth. It is on account of this mixing that she is called Medini. Now I will tell you what I heard before in Puṣkara, the sacred place of pilgrimage, from the mouth of Dharma Deva, about the origin of earth, approved by the Śrutis, consistent, and good. Hear. When the mind of Mahâ Virâṭ, merged in water, expanded all over his body, it entered into every pore of his body. Next the Mahâprithvî or the Great Earth appeared at the time of Pañchî Karaṇa (mixing of one-half of each of the elements with one-eighth of each of the other four elements). This Mahâprithvî was broken into pieces and placed in every pore. It is this differentiated earth that appears during creation and disappears during Pralaya. From this mind, concentrated in every pore of the body of Mahâ Virât, is born this earth, after a long interval. In every pore in the skin of this Virâṭ Puruṣa there is one earth. She gets manifested and she disappears. This occurs again and again. When she appears, she floats on the water ; and when she disappears, she gets merged in the water. There is this earth (world) in every universe ; and along with her, there are mountains, forests, seven oceans, seven islands, Sumeru mountain, the Moon, the Sun and other planets, Brahmaloka, Viṣṇuloka (the abode of Vîṣṇu) Śivaloka and the regions of the other Devas, sacred places of pilgrimage, the holy land of Bhâratâvarṣa, the Kânchanî Bhûmi, seven heavens, seven Pâtâlas or nether regions, on the above Brahmaloka, and Dhruvaloka. This law holds good in every world in every universe. So every universe is the work of Mâyâ and thus it is transient. At the dissolution of Prakriti, Brahmâ falls. Again when creation takes place, the Maha Virât appears from Śrî Kriṣṇa, the Supreme Spirit. Eternal is this flow of creation, preservation and destruction ; eternal is this flow of time, Kâṣṭhâ ; eternal is this flow of Brahmâ, Viṣṇu and Mahes'a, etc. And eternal is this flow of Vasundharâ who is worshipped in the Vârâha Kalpa by the Suras, Munis, Vipras, Gandarbhas, etc. The Śruti says that the Presiding Deity of this eternal earth is the wife of Viṣṇu in His boar-form. Mangala (Mars) is the son of that earth and Mangala's son is Ghaṭes'n.

24-26. Nârada said :—" In what form was the Earth worshipped by the Devas in Vârâha Kalpa. The Vârâhi, the receptacle of all things, moving and non-moving, how did she appear, by what method of Pañchî Karaṇa, from the Mûlaprakriti ? What is the method of her worship in this Bhûrloka and in the Heavens (Svarloka). Also tell me, O Lord ! in detail, the auspicious birth of Mangala (Mars).

27-34. Nârâyaṇa spoke:—In ancient days, in the Vârâha Kalpa, Varâha Deva (the boar incarnation) when entreated and praised by Brahmâ, killed the Daitya Hiraṇyâkṣa and rescued the earth from the nether regions Rasâtala. He then placed the earth on the waters where she floated as the lotus leaf floats on water. In the meantime Brahmâ began to fashion the wonderful creation on the surface of the earth. Bhagavân Hari, in His boar form and brilliant like ten million suns saw the beautiful and lovely appearance of the presiding deity of the earth, possessed of amorous sentiments. He then assumed a very beautiful form, fit for amorous embraces. They then held their sexual intercourse and it lasted day and night for one Deva year. The beautiful Earth, in the pleasant amorous plays, fainted away ; for the intercourse of the lover with the beloved is exceedingly pleasant. And Viṣṇu, too, at the same time was very much exhausted by the pleasant touch of the body of the Earth. He did not become conscious even how days and nights passed away. When full one year passed away, they got back their senses and the amorous man then left his hold of the loved. He assumed easily his former Boar form and worshipped Her as the incarnate of the Devî, with incense, lights, offerings of food, with vermilion (Sindur, red-powder), sandal-paste, garments, flowers and various other offerings of food, etc. He then said :—

35-37. O Auspicious One ! Let Thou beest the receptacle of all things. All the Munis, Manus, Devas, Siddhas, and Dânavas, etc., will worship Thee with pleasure and willingness. On the day the Ambuvâchî ceremony closes, on the day when the house construction, *i. e.*, the foundation is laid, on the day when the first entry is made into the newly built houses, when the digging of the well or tank commences, and on the day when tilling the ground commences, all will worship Thee. Those stupid fools that will not observe this, will certainly go to hell.

38-41 The Earth spoke :—" O Lord ! By Thy command I will assume the form of Vârâhî (female boar) and support easily on my back this whole world of moving and non-moving things, but the following things, pearl, small shells, Śâlagrâm, (a black stone, usually round, found in the river Gandakî, and worshipped as a type of Viṣṇu), the phallus or emblem of Śiva, the images of the goddesses, conch-shells, lamps (lights), the Yantras, gems, diamonds, the sacred upanayana threads, flowers, books, the Tulasî leaves, the bead (Japa mâlâ), the garland of flowers, gold, camphor, Gorochanâ (bright yellow pigment prepared from the urine or bile of a cow). Sandal, and the water after washing the Śâlagrâma stone, I will not be able to bear. I will be very much pained in case I were to bear these on Me.

42-45. Śrî Bhagavân said :—" O Fair One ! The fools that will place the above articles on Thy back will go to the Kâlasutra hell for one hundred divine years. O Nârada ! Thus saying, the Bhagavân Nârâyaṇa remained silent. Now the Earth became pregnant and the powerful planet Mars was born. By the command of Śrî Hari, all began to meditate on Earth according to what is mentioned in Kâṇvas'âkhâ and began to praise Her. Offerings of food were given, uttering the root Mantra. Thus became extant all over the three worlds Her worship and praise.

46. Nârada said :—O Bhagavân ! Very sacred is the meditation, hymn and the root Mantra of the Earth. I am very anxious to hear them Kindly describe it in detail.

47-48. Nârâyaṇa said :—The Earth was first worshipped by Varâha Deva ; next She was worshipped by Brahmâ. Next She was worshipped by all the Munis, Devas, Manus and men. O Nârada ! Now hear the Dhyân, praise and Mantra of the Devî Earth.

49-51. The Earth was first worshipped by Bhagavân Viṣṇu with this root Mantra (mûl mantra). " Om Hrîm Śrîm Klîm Vasundharâyai Svâhâ. Next He said :—O Devî Earth ! O Thou Smiling One ! I worship Thee, who art worshipped by the three worlds, whose colour is white like white lotus, whose face is beautiful like the autumnal moon, who art the Store-house of all gems and jewels, and in whose womb all the precious stones and pearls are inbedded, and who has put on a raiment purified by fire. All then began to worship Her with this Mantra.

52-63. Śrî Nârâyaṇa said :—" Now hear the hymn sung before Her according to Kâṇva Śâkhâ :—O Thou, the Giver of Victory! Holder of water! Endowed with water, full of victory; Consort of the Boar Incarnation, Carrier of victory ! Bestow victory on me. O Thou Auspicious One ! The Store-house of all good, O Thou incarnate of all auspiciousness ! Bestower of good, Thou, the Source of all good to bestow all sorts of welfare ! Bestow all things that are good and auspicious to me in this world.

O Thou ! The Receptacle of all, the Knower of all, all powerful, the Bestower of all desires, O Devî Earth ! Give me the fruits that I desire.

O Thou ! Who art all merits Thou, the Seed of all religious merits, O Thou, the Eternal, the receptacle of all religious merits, the home of all religious persons, Thou bestowest merits to all.

O Thou ! The Store-house of all grains, enriched with all sorts of corns, Thou bestowest harvests to all ; Thou takest away all the grains in this world and again Thou producest all corns of various kinds here. O Earth ! Thou art all-in-all to the landlords, the Best Source of refuge and happiness. O Bestower of lands ! Give me lands. The above hymn yields great religious merits. He becomes the sovereign of the whole earth for millions and millions of births who rising early in the morning reads this stotra. Men who read this acquire merits due to giving away lands as gifts. People become certainly freed of their sins, if they read this stotra, who take back the lands after making them as gifts, who dig earth on the day of Ambuvâchî, who dig wells without permission on another's well, who steal other's lands, who throw their semen on earth, who place lamps on the earth. Religious merits, equivalent to one hundred horse sacrifices accrue from reading this stotra There is no doubt in this. This stotra of the great Devî is the source of all sorts of welfare and auspiciousness.

Here ends the Ninth Chapter of the Ninth Book on the origin of the Śakti of the earth in Śrî Mad Devî Bhâgavatam of 18,000 verses by Maharṣi Veda Vyâsa.

CHAPTER X.

1-3. Nârada said :—I am now desirous to hear about the merits acquired by making gifts of land, the demerits in stealing away lands, digging wells in other's wells, in digging earth on the day of Ambuvâchî, in casting semen on earth, and in placing lamps and lights on the surface of the earth as well the sins when one acts wrongly in various other ways on the surface of the earth and the remedies thereof.

4-30. Śrî-Nârâyaṇa said:—If one makes a gift of land in this Bhârata of the measure of a Vitasti (a long span measured by the extended thumb and little-finger) to a Brâhmaṇa who performs Sandhyâ three times a day and is thus purified, one goes and remains in Śiva Loka (the abode of Śiva). If one gives away in charity a land full of corn to a Brâhmin, the giver goes and lives in Viṣṇu Loka in the end for a period measured by the number of dust particles in the land. If one presents a village, a plot of land, or grains to a Brâhmiṇ, both the giver and the receiver, become freed of their sins and go to the Devî Loka (the abode of the Devî). Even if one be present when a proposal for a gift of land is being made and says "This act is good," one goes to Vaikuṇṭha with one's friends and relatives. He remains in the Kâlasutra hell as long as the Sun and Moon exist, who takes back or steals away the gift to a Brâhmiṇ, offered by himself or by any other body. Even his sons, grandsons, etc., become destitute of lands, prosperity, sons, and wealth and remain in a dreadful hell named Raurava. If one cultivates the grazing land for the cows and reaps therefrom a harvest of grains, one remains for one hundred divine years in the Kumbhîpâka hell. If one cultivates any enclosure for cows or tanks and grows grains on them, one remains in the Asipatra hell for a period equivalent to fourteen Indra's falls. One who bathes in another's tank without taking off five handfuls of earth from it, goes to hell and one's bath is quite ineffectual If anybody, out of his amorous passion casts his semen privately on the suface of the ground, he will have to suffer the torments of hell for as many years as are the numbers of dust particles on that area. If anyone digs ground on the day of Ambuvâchî, one remains in hell for four Yugas. If, without the permission of the owner of a well or tank, a stupid man clears the old well or tank and digs the slushy earth from the bottom, his labour goes in vain. The merit goes to the real owner. And the man who laboured so much goes to Tapta Kuṇḍa Naraka for fourteen Indra's life-periods. If any one takes out five handfuls of earth from another's tank, when he goes to bathe in it, he dwells in Brahma-Loka for a period of years amounting to the number of particles in those handfuls of earth. During one's father's or grandfather's Śrâdha ceremony, if one offers piṇḍa without offering any food (piṇḍa) to the owner of the soil, the Śrâdha performer goes certainly to hell. If one places a light (Pradîpa) directly on the earth without any holding piece at the bottom, one becomes blind for seven births; and so if one places a conch-shell on the ground (Śankha), one becomes attacked with leprosy in one's next birth. If any body places pearls, gems, diamonds, gold and jewels, the five precious things on the ground he becomes blind. If one places the phallic emblem of Śiva, the image of Śivânî, the Śâlagrâma stone on the ground, he remains for one hundred Manvantaras to be eaten by worms. Conchshells, Yantras (diagrams for Śakti worshippers), the water after washing Śilas (stones) *i. e.* Charaṇâmrita, flowers, Tulasî leaves, if placed on the ground, lead him who places these, verily to hells. The beads, garlands of flowers, Gorochana, (a bright yellow pigment prepared from the urine or bile of a cow), and camphor, when placed on the ground, lead him who places so to suffer the torments of hell. The sandal wood, Rudrâkṣa mâlâ, and the roots of Kus'a grass also, if placed on the ground, lead the doer to stay for one manvantara in the hell. Books, the sacred Upanayana threads, when placed on the ground make the doers unfit for Brâhmiṇ birth; rather he is involved in a sin equivalent to the murder of a Brâhmiṇ. The sacred Upanayana thread when knotted and rendered fit for holding, is worth being worshipped by all the castes. One ought to sprinkle the earth with curd, milk, etc., after one has completed one's sacrifices. If one fails to do this, one will have to remain for seven births in a hot ground with great torment. If one digs the earth when there is an earthquake or when there is an eclipse, that sinner becomes also devoid of some of his limbs in his next birth. O Muni! This earth is named Bhûmi since She is the abode of all; she is named Kâs'yapî since she is the daughter of Kas'yapa; is named Vis'vambharâ, since she supports the Universe; She is named Ananta, since she is endlessly wide; and She is named Prithivî since she is the daughter of the King Prithu, or she is extensively wide.

Here ends the Tenth Chapter of the Ninth Book on the offences caused towards the surface of the earth and punishments there of in hells—in the Mahâpurâṇam Śrî Mad Devî Bhâgavatam of 18,000 verses by Maharṣi Veda Vyâsa.

CHAPTER XI.

1-3. The Devarṣi Nârada said:—" O Thou, the foremost of the knowers of the Vedas ! I have heard the excellent narration of Earth. Now I want to hear the anecdote of Gangâ. I heard, ere long, that Gangâ, of the nature of Viṣṇu and appearing from the feet of Viṣṇu, the Is'varî of the Devas, appeared, due to the curse of Bhâratî, on Bhârata ; why has she come to Bharata ; in which Yuga and asked by whom did she come to Bhârata ? O Lord ! Now describe to me this auspicious anecdote capable to destroy sins and yield religious merits.

4-33. Nârâyaṇa said:—" O Child ! In ancient days there was born a prosperous Emperor King of Kings, in the Solar dynasty. He had two beautiful wives ; one was named Vaidarbhî, and the other was named Śaivyâ. Śaivyâ delivered a very lovely son ; his name was Asamanjâ. On the other hand, the queen Vaidarbhî desirous of getting a son, worshipped Śankara, the Lord of Bhûtas who became pleased and granted her request ; and Vaidarbhî became pregnant. After one hundred years of pregnancy she gave birth to one mass of flesh. Seeing this, the queen became very afflicted and taking refuge of Mahâdeva, began to cry loudly and very often. Bhagavân Śaṇkara, then, appeared there in a Brâhmiṇ form and cut that mass of flesh into thousand pieces. Those thousand pieces turned out into thousand very powerful sons. Their bodies looked more brillant than the mid-day sun. But they were all burnt to ashes by the curse of Kapila Muni. And the King began to lament bitterly and he entered into the forest. Asamajâ practised tapasyâ to bring the Gangâ for one lakh years when he quitted his body in course of time. His son Ams'umân practised tapasyâ for one lakh years to bring Gangâ unto Bhârata and he, too, died. Then the son of Amsumân, the intelligent Bhagiratha, a great devotee of Viṣṇu, free of old age and death and the store of many qualifications, practised tapasyâ for one lakh years to bring Gangâ on earth. At last he saw Śrî Kriṣṇa brillant like ten millions of summer suns. He had two hands ; there was a flute in his hand; he was full of youth in the dress of a cow-herd. A sight of His Gopâla Sundarî form, wearing a Sakhi's dress, makes one think that He is ever ready to show grace on His devotees. He is Para Brahma, whose Substance is Will ; he has no deficiencies. Brahmâ, Viṣṇu and Mahes'vara and the other Devas and Munis, etc.. all praise Him, who pervades everywhere. He is not concerned with anything ; yet He is the Witness of all. He is beyond the three guṇas, higher than Prakriti. A sweet smile is always in his face, which makes it the more lovely. There is none equal to him in showing Grace to the Bhaktas. His raiment is purified (uninflammable) by fire and he is decorated with gems, jewels and ornaments. The King Bhagîratha saw that unforeseen appearance, bowed down and began to praise over and over again. His whole body was filled with ecstacy. Then he clearly told what he wanted for the deliverance of his family. Bhagavân Śrî Kriṣṇa then, addressed Gangâ and said:—" O Sures'varî ! Go quickly and appear in Bhârata, under the curse of Bhâratî. By My command go quickly and purify the sons of Sagara. They will all be purified by the touch of the air in contact with the Ganges and rise up in divine aerial cars, assuming forms like Mine and they will come to My abode. They will there remain always as My attendants and they will not be involved in the sins that they committed in their previous births. O Nârada ! It is stated thus in the Vedas, that if the human souls, taking their births in Bhârata, commit sins for millions and millions of births, the sins will be completely destroyed if they touch once the air in contact with and carrying the particles of the Ganges. The sight of the Ganges and the touch of the Ganges water give religious merits ten times more than the touch with the air in contact with the Ganges water. People become freed of their sins then and there especially if they bathe in the Ganges. It is heard in the Śrutis that the bathing in the Ganges, if done according to rules, destroys all the sins *e.g.* the murder of a Brâhmin, etc., acquired in one thousand millions of births done consciously or unconsciously. The merits that are acquired by the bathing in the Ganges on a day of religious merit, cannot be described even by the Vedas. Whatever is mentioned in the Âgamas is but a mere trifle. Even Brahmâ, Viṣṇu and Mahes'a cannot describe fully the merits of the bathing in the Ganges. O Brâhmin ! Such is the glori of ordinary bathing. Now I will describe the effect of the Ganges bath done with a Sankalap (resolve) ; hear. Ten times more the result is obtained when the Ganges bathing is done with a resolve (Sankalap) than ordinary bath aud if one bathes on the day when the sun passes from one sign to another (in the Zodiac), thirty times more religious merits accrue. On the new Moon (Amâvyas) day, the Ganges bath gives the merits as above mentioned ; but when the Sun is in his Southern course (Dakṣ iṇâyaṇa) double the merits are obtained and when the sun is in his Northern course, ten times more religious merits are obtained. The Ganges bathing in the time of Châturmâsya, full Moon day, Akṣayâ Navamî or Akṣaya tritîyâ yields merits that cannot be measured. And if on the above Parva (particular periods of the year on which certain ceremonies are commanded) days both bathing, and making over gifts are done, there is no limit to the religious merits acquired; hundred times more than ordinary bath, religious merits are obtained. Great religious merits accrue from the Ganges bath on Manvantarâ tithi, Yugâdyâ, S'uklâ seventh day of the month of Mâgha, Bhîṣmâṣṭamî day, As'okâṣṭamî day, and Śrî Râma Navamî day. Again double the merits than those of the above arise from bathing in the Ganges during the Nandâ ceremony. The Ganges bath in the Das'aharâ tenth tithi gives merits equivalent to Yugâdyâ Snânam (bath). And if the bathing be done on Mahânandâ or in Mahâvâruṇî day, four times more religious merits accrue. Ten million times more religious merits accrue from the Ganges bathing on Mahâ Mahâ Vâruṇî day than ordinary bath. The Ganges bath in the Solar eclipse yields ten times more religious merits than in the Lunar eclipse. Again the Snânam in Ardhodaya Yoga yields hundred times more religious merits than that of the (solar) eclipse. Thus saying to Gangâ before Bhagîratha, the Lord of the Devas remained silent. The Devi Gangâ with her head bowed down with devotion, said :—

39—42. Gangâ said :—If I am after all, to go to Bhârata as Thou commandest and under the curse given previously by Bhâratî, then tell me how I would be freed of the sins that the sinners will cast on me. How long will I have to remain there? When, O Lord! Shall I be able to return to the Highest place of Viṣṇu? O Thou, the Inner Self of all! O All Knwoing! O Lord! Whatever else I desire, Thou knowest them all. So be pleased to instruct me on all these points.

43—69. Bhagavân Śrî Hari said :—" O Sures'varî! I know all that you desire; when you will assume the liquid form, the Salt Ocean will be your husband. He is My part and you are of the nature of Lakṣmî; so the union of the lover with the love stricken in the world will turn out a happy and qualified one. Of all the rivers Sarasvatî and others in Bhârata, that go to mix with the ocean, you will be the best and highly fortunate of them all. From today you will have to remain in Bhârata for a period of five thousand years, under the curse of Bhâratî. You will be able to enjoy daily and always the pleasures with the Ocean. O Devî! As you are a clever lady, so He is also apt and expert. The inhabitants of Bhârata will praise Thee and worship Thee with great devotion by the stotra which Bhagîratha has composed. He will derive the fruit of one horse-sacrifice who will meditate on Thee as per Kâṇvas'âkhâ and worship, praise and bow down to Thee daily. Even if one utter "Gangâ," "Gangâ," though one is one hundred Yojanas away from the Ganges, one will be freed of all sins and go to Viṣṇu-loka. Whatever sins will be cast in Thee by thousand sinners bathing in Thee will be destroyed by the touch of the devotees of Prakriti Devî. Even if thousands and thousands of sinners touch the dead bodies and bathe in Thee, all those will be destroyed when the Devî Bhaktas,the worshippers of Bhuvanes'varî and Mâyâ Vîja, will come and touch Thee. O Auspicious One! Thou wilt wash away the sins of the sinners, by Thy stay in Bhârata with other best rivers Sarasvatî and others. That will be at once a sacred place of pilgrimage where Thy glories will be chanted. By the touch of the dust of Thine, the sinner will be at once purified and he will dwell in the Devî-loka (Maṇi Dvîpa) for as many years as will be the dust there. All Hail to the Devî Bhuvenes'varî! He who will leave his body on Thy lap with full consciousness and remembering My name, will certainly go to My abode and will remain, as My chief attendant for an infinite period. He will see countless Prâkritik Layas (dissolutions of the Universe). Unless a man has collected hordes of religious merits, he cannot die in the Ganges; and if he dies on the Ganges he goes to Vaikunṭha as long as the Sun rises in this world. I get many bodies for him where he can enjoy the fruits of his Karma and I then give him My Svârûpya (Form resembling Mine) and make him My attendant. If any ignorant man, void of any Jñânam, quits his body by touching merely Thy water, I give him Sâlokya (place in My region) and make him My attendant. Even if one quits one's body in a far off place, uttering Thy Name, I give him place in My region for one life time of Brahmâ. And if he remembers Thee with devotion, and quits his mortal coil at another place, I give him Sârûpya (Form resembling Mine) for a period of endless Prâkritik Layas. He instantly gets on an aerial car made of jewels and goes with My attendants to the region of Goloka and gets form like Me. Those that worship daily My Mantra, that pass their days, eating the remnant of the food offered to Me, they need not have any distinction whether they die in Tîrath or not. They themselves can easily purify the three worlds. Getting on the excellent and best aerial car built of jewels, they go to the region of Go-loka. O Chaste One! Even if the friends of My devotees, be born in animal births, they also will be purified by the devotion shewn towards Me and getting on a jewelled aerial car will be able to go to Goloka, so difficult of access. Wherever the Bhaktas may be, if they simply remember Me with devotion, they will become liberated while living by the power of My Bhakti. Thus saying to Gangâ, Bhagavân Śrî Hari addressed Bhagîratha:—O Child! Now worship Gangâ Devî with devotion and chant hymns to Her. The pure Bhagîratha meditated with devotion as per Kanthuma Śâkhâ and worshipped the Devî and praised Her repeatedly. Then Gangâ and Bhagîratha bowed down to Śrî Krisṇa and He disappeared at once from their sight.

70. The Devarṣi Nârada said:—"O Thou the foremost of the Knowers of the Vedas! How, by what Kuthuma Sâkhâ, the noble King Bhagî-

ratha meditated on the Devî Gangâ; what stotra did he recite and what was the method with which he worshipped the Ganges.

71-75. Nârâyaṇa said:—"O Nârada! One should first take one's bath, and putting on a clean washed clothing should perform one's daily duties. Then one should control oneself and with devotion worship the six Devatâs Gaṇeṣa, Sun, Fire, Viṣṇu, Śiva and Śivâ, Thus one becomes entitled to worship. First worship is to be given to Gaṇes'a for the destruction of obstacles.; the Sun is to be next worshipped for health; Fire, for purification; Viṣṇu is then worshipped for getting wealth and power; Śiva is worshipped for knowlege and Śivânî is worshipped for Mukti. When these Devatâs are worshipped, one is entitled to worship the Deity. Otherwise contrary become the effects. Now I am saying what Dhyâṇam (meditation) did Bhagîratha practise towards the Devî Gangâ.

Here ends the Eleventh Chapter of the Ninth Book on the origin of the Ganges in the Mahâpurâṇam Śrî Mad Devî Bhâgavatam of 18,000 verses by Maharṣi Veda Vyâsa.

CHAPTER XII.

1-5. Nârâyaṇa said:—"O Nârada! Now about the meditation (Dhyân) of the Devî Gangâ as per Kâṇva Śâkhâ, which destroys all the sins. "O Gange! Of white colour like white lotuses! Thou destroyest all the sins of men. Thou hast appeared from the body of Śrî Kriṣṇa. Thou art powerful like Him. Thou art very chaste and pure. Thou hast worn the raiment, uninflammable and decorated all over with ornaments made of jewels. Thou art more brilliant than one hundred autumnal Moons. Thou art also well pleased with a smile on Thy lips. And Thou art always of steady youthful beauty (that never wanes). Thou art dear to Nârâyaṇa, calm and of peaceful temper, and proud of being His with His fortune. Thou bearest the braid of hair, decked with garlands of Mâlatî flowers; Thy cheeks are anointed with sandal dots, with Sindûra bindu (dots of red powder, vermilion) and well adorned with various artistic lines made of musk. Thy garment and Thy beautiful lips are more red than the ripe Bimba fruit (the red fruit of a cucurbitaceous plant); Thy teeth vie as it were, with the rows of pearls. How lovely are Thy eyes! How delightsome is Thy side-long glance! How close are Thy breasts like Bel fruits! Thy loins are thicker and more solid then the plantain trees, How do Thy feet look beautiful, defying the beauty of the Sthalapadma (ground Lotus)!

How do the red sandals look lovely with Kunkuma and alaktak (red powder)! What a red tinge Thy feet have shewn with the honey of

Pârijâta flower that is seen on the head of Indra). The Devas, the Siddhas, the Munis, offer always Arghyas (offerings of rice with Durba grass) at Thy feet; the ascetics bow down at Thy feet, and it seems as though so many lines of bees are on Thy lotus feet. O Mother! Thy lotus feet give liberation to those that want Mukti and enjoyment to those that want Bhukti (enjoyments). O Mother! Thou art the boon; Thou art the chief excellent; Thou grantest boons and Thou showest Thy favour to Thy devotees; Thou bestowest the Viṣṇupadam (the place of Viṣṇu); but Thou hast come from the feet of Viṣṇu. Thus meditating on the Devî Gangâ flowing by three routes (in Heaven, earth and infernal regions), the bestower of good things one should offer to the Devî sixteen things:—Â-sana, Pâdya, Arghya, water for bathing, ointment (anûlepana), Dhûpa (scents), Dîpa (lights), Naivedya (offerings of food), betel, cool water, clothings, ornaments, garlands, sandal-paste, Âchamanîya (water for sipping), and beautiful beddings and worship Her with these. Then, with folded hands, one should perform stotra to Her and bow down to Her with devotion. Thus the worshipper gets the fruits of A'svamedha sacrifice.

16. Nârada said:—"O Lord of the Devas! At present I am desirous to hear the sin-destroying and virtue—bestowing stotra (hymn) of Gangâ Devî, the Purifier of all those that are fallen from virtue, originated from the feet of Viṣṇu, the Lord of world and the husband of Lakṣmî. Kindly narrate all these in detail.

17-41. Nârâyaṇa said:—"O Nârada! Now I am narrating the stotra of Gangâ Devî, that destroys all sins and bestows all religious merits. Hear. I bow down to the Ganges who appeared from the body of Śrî Kriṣṇa, enchanted by the music of Śiva, and, who was bathed with the prespiration (water coming out of the body) of Śrî Râdhâ. I bow down to Gangâ Devî who first appeared in the circular dance (Râsa Maṇḍalam) in the region of Goloka and who always remains with Śankara. My obiesance to the Devî Gangâ who remains in the auspicious grand utsab of Râdhâ (Râsa Mâṇḍlam), crowded with Gopas and Gopîs, in the Full Moon night of the month of Kârtik. She is one koṭi yojanas wide and one lakh times one koṭi yojanas long in the region of Goloka. My Obeisance to Her! In Vaikuṇṭha, Gangâ is sixty lakh yojanas in width and four times that in lenght. My Obeisance to Her! In Brahma-loka, Gangâ is thirty lakh yojanas wide and five times as long. I bow down to Her. In Śiva-loka, She is thirty lakh yojanas wide and four times that in length. I bow down to Her. In Dhruva-loka, She is one lakh yojanas wide and seven times as long. I bow down to Her. In Chandraloka She is one lakh yojanas wide and five times as long. My obeisance to Śrî Gangâ Devi. I bow down to the Ganges who is sixty thousand yojanas wide in the Sûrya loka and ten times that in length. I bow down to Gangâ in Tapo-loka who is one lakh yojanas wide and five times that in length. My obeisance to Gangâ Devî in Janar-loka, who is one thousand yojanas wide and ten times that as long. I bow down to Gangâ in Mahar-loka who is ten lakh yojanas wide and five times that in length. My obeisance to Gangâ Devi in Kailâs'a who is one thousand yojanas wide and one hundred times as long. I bow down to Gangâ Devî who is known as Mandâkinî in Indra-loka, and who is one hundred yojanas wide and ten times than that in length. My obeisance to Gangâ Devî, known as Bhogavatî in Pâtâla who is ten yojanas wide and five times as long. I bow down to Gangâ Devî, known as Alakanandâ in this earth, who is two miles wide, in some places more wide and in some places less wide. I bow down to Gangâ Devî who was of the colour of milk in Satya yuga, of the colour of Moon in Tretâ Yuga of the colour of white sandal-paste in Dvâpara yuga. I bow down to Śrî Gangâ Devî who is as water in Kali yuga in this earth and as milk in Kali yuga in Heaven. O Child! By the touch of one molecule of the water of the Ganges, all the horrible sins incurred in ten million births, the murder of a Brâhmin and so forth, are burnt to ashes. Thus I have described in twenty-one verses the great stotra (human) of the sin-destroying and the virtue-increasing merits of Gangâ. He reaps the fruit of the A'svamedha sacrifice (Horse sacrifice), who daily sings this praise of Gangâ after worshipping Her with devotion. There is no doubt in this. The persons that are without any sons get sons hereby and those who have no wives get wives. The diseased get themselves free from their diseases, and the man who is under bondage, is liberated from that bondage. He who getting up early in the morning reads this stotra of Gangâ, becomes widely known even if he be not known at all and he becomes illumined with wisdom even if he be quite ignorant. Even if he sees a bad dream, he acquires the merit of bathing in the Ganges and of seeing good dreams.

42-44. Śrî Nârâyaṇa spoke :—" O Nârada ! With this stotra (hymn) did Bhagîratha praise the Gangâ Devî. Who then went with him to the spot where the Sagara's sons were burnt to ashes by the curse of Kapila. By the contact of the wind in touch with the particles of water of the Ganges, those sons of Sagara were instantly freed of their curses and they all repaired to Vaikuṇṭha. She is named Bhâgirathî, because Bhâgiratha brought Her to this earth. Thus I have discribed to you the story of the Ganges.

42-44. This anecdote is highly meritorious and the great step to liberation. What more do you now want to hear ? Say.

45-46. Nârada said :— " O Lord ! How did Gangâ come to flow through the three worlds by three routes, and thus purify them ? How was she carried and to which places ? How did the people of those localities accord respect to Her ? Kindly describe all these in detail.

47-79. Nârâyaṇa said :— " O Nârada ! On the Full Moon night of the month of Kârtik in the Râsa maṇḍalam, at the great festivity in honour of Râdhâ, Śrî Krisṇa worshipped Râdhâ and remained there. Next Râdhâ, worshipped by S'rî Krisṇa, was worshipped by Brahmâ and the other Devas, by Saunaka and the other Risis, who also stopped there with much gladness. At this moment the Devî Sarasvatî, the Presiding Deity of the Science of Music began to sing lovely songs regarding Krisṇa, in tune with vocal and instrumental music. Brahmâ became glad and presented to Sarasvatî a necklace of jewels ; Mahâ Deva gave her gems and jewels rare in this universe ; Krisṇa presented the best Kaustubha jewel ; Râdhikâ offered excellent invaluable necklace of jewels ; Nârâyâṇa presented to her the best and most excellent garland of jewels ; Laksmî gave her invaluable golden earrings decked with gems ; Visṇu-Mâyâ Mûla Prakriti, Bhagvatî Durgâ, who is Nârayaṇî, Îs'varî, Îs'ânî, presented Her devotion to Brahma, so very rare ; Dharma gave her devotion to Dharma and high fame ; Agni (fire) gave her excellent raiments purified by fire and Vâyu gave Her Nûpura (toe ornaments) made of gems and jewels. At this time, Mahes'vara, the Lord of Bhûtas (elements) began to sing, at the suggestion of Brahmâ, songs relating to Śri Krisṇa's grand Râsa festival. Hearing this, the Devas became very much enchanted and remained motionles like statues. With great difficulty, they regained their consciousness. Then they saw that there was no Râdhâ nor Krisṇa in the Râsa maṇḍala ; everything was deluged with water. The Gopas, Gopis, Devas and Brâhmaṇas began to cry loudly. Brahmâ in his meditation then came to know that Râdhâ and Krisṇa both have assumed this liquid appearance for the deliverance of the people of the world. Brahmâ and others, all began to praise Śrî Krisṇa and said:—" O All prevading One ! Now be pleased to show us Thy form and grant us our desired boons. At that instant a sweet incorporeal voice was clearly heard by all, as coming from air above, that, " I am the Self of all, pervading all ; and this my Śakti, Râdhâ, is also the Self of all, prevades all ; so there is no separation of us from you all even for a moment. It is only to show our favour to the devotees that we assume special forms. For this reason only there is separation of us from you as regards this body ! There is nothing else. Besides you have no necessity with our bodies. O Devas ! Now if my Manus, men, Munis, Vaisṇavas and you all, purified by Mantras, desire very much to see My Form clearly, then I tell you to request Mahes'vara to carry out My word. O Brahmâ ! O Creator ! Better ask

Mahâdeva, the World-Teacher, that He would better compose the beautiful Tantra S'âstra, in accordance with the limbs of the Vedas. And that the above S'âstra be full of Mantras, capable to yield desired fruits, Stotras (hymns) and Kavachas (protection mantras) and rules of due worship in proper order. And that also My Mantra, My Stotra, and My Kavacha be also given there in a hidden form. So that those people that are sinners might not understand their real meanings and thus turn out against Me. It may be that one in a thousand or in a hundred may worship My Mantra. And My Mantra worshippers, the saints, become purified and come to My Abode. If My Śâstra be not well made (*i. e.*, if every one be able to understand its meaning) and if every one be able to go from Bhûrloka to Goloka, then Thy labour in this creation of the world will all be in vain. Therefore dost Thou better create different worlds according to the differences of Sâttvik, Râjasik, and Tamo Guṇas ; then some will be the inhabitants of this Bhûrloka, some will be the inhabitants of Dyuloka according to their Karmas. O Brahman ! If Mahâ Deva promises earnestly in this assembly of the Devas, I will then exhibit My True Form. O Nârada ! Thus speaking, the Eternal Puruṣa Śrî Kriṣṇa remained silent. (*i. e.*, the aerial incorporeal voice stopped). Hearing this, Brahmâ, the Creator of the world, gladly informed Śiva of this. When the Lord of Knowledge, the Foremost of the Jñânins, Bhûtanâtha heard the words of the Creator, He took the Ganges water in His hands and swore that " I will complete the Tantra S'âstra, full of Râdhâ mantras and not opposed to the Vedas. " If one touches the Ganges water and speaks lies, one remains in the terrible Kâlasutra hell for a period of one Brahmâ's life time. O Dvija ! When Bhagavân Śankara said this before the assembly of the Devas in the region of Goloka, S'rî Kriṣṇa appeared there with Râdhâ. The Devas became exceedingly glad to see Him. They praised Him, the Best Puruṣa and they were all filled with rapture and again engaged themselves in the grand Râsa Festival. Some time after, Mâhâ Deva lighted the Torch of Mukti *i. e.* the Tantra S'âstra was published by Him, as promised. O Child ! Thus I have disclosed to you this anecdote, so very secret, and hard to be attained. Thus Śrî Kriṣṇa Himself, is verily the liquid Gangâ sprung in the region of Goloka. This holy Gangâ, born of the bodies of Kriṣṇa and Râdhâ inseparable from each other, grants enjoyment, lordship and liberation. Śrî Kriṣṇa, the Highest Self, has placed Her in various places ; so Gangâ is of the nature of Śrî Kriṣṇa and is everywhere, equally honoured everywhere in the Brahmâṇḍa (universe).

Here ends the Twelfth Chapter in the Ninth Book on the origin of Gangâ in the Mahâpurâṇam Srîmad Devî Bhâgavatam of 18,000 verses by Maharṣi Veda Vyâsa.

CHAPTER XIII.

1. Nârada said:—" O Lord of the Devas! Kindly say in what Loka did Gangâ go after 5000 (five thousand) years of the Kali Yuga?

2-4. Nârâyaṇa said:—The Bhâgîrathî Gangâ came down to Bhârata under the curse of Bhâratî; and when, the term expired, She went back, by the Will of God, to the region of Vaikuṇṭha. Also at the end of the period of their curses, Bhâratî and, Lakṣmî, too, left Bhârata and repaired to Nârâyaṇa. Gangâ, Lakṣmî, and Sarasvatî, these three and Tulasî all these four are so very dear to S'rî Hari.

5-6. Nârada said:—How did Gangâ appear from the lotus feet of Viṣṇu? Why did Brahmâ put Her in His Kamaṇḍalu? I have heard that Gangâ is the wife of S'iva; how then, came S'he to be the wife of Nârâyaṇa? Kindly describe all these in detail to me.

7-8. Nârâyaṇa said:—"O Muni! In ancient times, in the region of Goloka, Gangâ assumed the liquid appearance. She was born of the bodies of Râdhâ and Kriṣṇa. So She is of the nature of both of them and their parts. Gangâ is the presiding deity of water. S'he is unequalled in Her beauty in this world. She is full of youth and adorned with all ornaments.

9-43. Her face was like the autumnal mid-day lotus and sweet smile was always reigning on Her lips; Her form was very beautiful; Her colour was as bright as melted gold and She looked brilliant like the Autumnal Moon. Eyes and mind get cool and become pleasant at Her beauty and radiance; She was of purely Suddha Sattva; Her loins were bulky and hard and She was covered with excellent clothings all over Her body. Her breasts were plump and prominent; they were raised, hard, and nicely round. Her eyes very fascinating, always casting side-long glances. Her braids of hair situated a little oblique and the garland of Mâlatî flowers over it made Her look extremely handsome. The sandal-paste dot and the vermillion dot were seen on Her fore-head. On Her cheeks the leaves of musk were drawn and Her lips were red like Bandhûka flowers and they looked enchanting. Her rows of teeth looked like rows of ripe promegranates; the ends of Her cloth not inflammable by fire, worn in front in a knot round the waist. She sat by the side of Kriṣṇa, full of amorous desires, and abashed. She covered Her face with the end of Her cloth and was seeing, with a steadfast gaze the face of the Lord and She was drinking the nectar of His face with great gladness. Her lotus face bloomed and became gladdened at the expecation of a first amorous embrace. She fainted on seeing the Form of Her Lord and a thrill of joy passed all over Her body. In the meanwhile Râdhikâ came up there. Râdhâ was attended by thirty koṭis of Gopîs. She looked brilliant like tens of millions of Moons. Seeing Gangâ by the side of Śrî Kriṣṇa, Her face and eyes became reddened with anger like a red lotus. Her colour was yellow like champaka and Her gait was like a maddened elephant. She was adorned with various invaluable ornaments made of jewels. Her pair of clothings were tied round Her waist. They were decked with invaluable jewels and not inflammable by fire. (fire-proof). The Arghya offered by Śrî Kriṣṇa was on Her lotus-feet of the colour of a flowering shrub—Hibiscus mutabilis and She was going slowly step by step. The Riṣis began to fan Her with white Châmaras no sooner She, descending from the excellent aeroplane decked with jewels, began to walk. Below the point where the parting of the hairs on the head is done, there was the dot of Sindura on Her fore-head. It looked brilliant like a bright lamp flame. On both sides of this Sindurabindu, the dot of musk and the dot of Sandal-paste were seen. When She began to quiver with anger, Her braid, with Pârijâta garland round it began to tremble also. Her lips adorned with beautiful colours, began to quiver also. She took Her seat angrily on a jewel throne by the side of Śrî Kriṣṇa. Her attendants took their seats in their allotted positions. Seeing Râdhâ, Śrî Kriṣṇa got up at once from His seat with reverence and addressed Her, smiling and began to converse with Her in sweet words. The Gopîs, very much afraid and with their heads bent low, began to chant hymns to Her with devotion. Śrî Kriṣṇa also began to praise Her with stotras. At this moment Gangâ Devî got up and praised Her with various hymns and asked Her welfare with fear and with humble words. Out of fear, Her throat, lips and palate were parched up. She took refuge humbly at Śrî Kriṣṇa's feet. Śrî Kriṣṇa then took Gangâ Devî on His breast when She became calm and quiet. At this interval Sureśvarî Gangâ looked at Râdhâ, seated on a throne, lovely and sweet, as if She was burning with Brahma Fire. Since the beginning of creation, She is the Sole Lady of innumerable Brahmâs and She is Eternal. At the first sight, She looked young as if of twelve years old. Nowhere in any Universe can be seen a lady so beautiful and so qualified. She was peaceful, calm and quiet, lovely, infinite and having no beginning nor end. She was auspicious, well endowed with all auspicious signs, prosperous, and having, the good fortune of having a best husband. She was the foremost jewel amongst the ladies and appeared as if all the beauties were concentrated in Her. Râdhâ is the (left) half of Śrî Krisṇa's body; whether in age or in strength or in beauty she was in every way perfectly equal to Śrî Krisṇa. Laksmî and the Lord of Laksmî both worship Râdhâ. The excellent brilliance of Śrî Krisṇa was overpowered by the beauty of Râdhâ. Taking Her seat on the throne She began to chew betels offered by Her attendants (Sakhîs). She is the Mother of all the worlds; but no one is Her mother. She is fortunate, respected and proud. She is the Ruling Lady of Śrî Krisṇa's Life and Soul and ever dearer to Him than His Prâṇa (vital breath). O Devarsi! Gangâ, the Governess of the Devas, looked at Her over and over again with a steadfast gaze; but Her eyes and mind were not at all satiated. At this moment, Râdhâ addressed smilingly to Śrî Krisṇa, the Lord of the world, humbly and in sweet words. O My Lord! Who is that Lady sitting by Thy side, looking askance, eager and with a smiling countenance. She is enchanted with Thy beauteous form and fainting away. Her whole body is excited with rapturous joy. Hiding Her face with cloth She is frequently looking at Thee. Thou also dost look on Her smilingly and with desires. What are all these? Even during My presence in this Goloka, all these bad practices are being rampant.

44-51. It is Thou that art doing all these bad things often and often! We are female sex; what shall we do? We are naturally, of a very pleasing temper, simple. I bore and forgave all these out of our love. O Licentious One! Take Thy Beloved and go away quickly from this Goloka. Otherwise these things will not bid fair to Thee. Firstly, One day I saw Thee, united with Virajâ Gopî, in Chandana (Sandal wood) forest. What to do? At the request of the Śakhîs, I did forgive Thee. Then, hearing My footsteps, Thou didst fly away. Virajâ, out of shame, quitted Her body and assumed the form of a river. That is million Yojanas wide and four times as long. Even to this day that Virajâ is existing, testifying to Thy Glory (near Puri, Jagannâtha)! When I went back to My home Thou didst go to Virajâ again and cried aloud "O Viraje! O Viraje!" Hearing Your cry, Virajâ, the Siddha Yoginî arose from the waters, out of Her Yogic power, and when She showed Thee Her divine appearance, decked with ornaments, Thou didst draw Her to Thy side and cast Thy seed in Her. It is owing to the casting of that seed in the womb of Virajâ that the seven oceans have come into existence!

52-107. Secondly—One day I saw Thee in actual intercourse with the Gopî named Śobhâ! Hearing My footsteps, Thou fled'st away that day also.

Out of shame Śobhâ quitted Her body and departed to the sphere of Moon (Chandra Maṇḍal). The cooling effect of the Moon is due to this Śobhâ. When Śobhâ was thus distressed, Thou didst divide Her and put some parts to gems and jewels, part to gold, partly to excellent pearls and gems, partly on the face of women, partly to the bodies of Kings, partly to the leaves of trees, partly to flowers, partly to ripe fruits, partly to corns, partly to palaces and temples, partly to purified materials, partly to young and tender shoots and foliage, and partly to milk. Thirdly—I saw Thee united with Prabhâ Gopî in Bindrâban. Thou fled'st away, hearing My footsteps. Out of shame, Prabhâ quitted Her body and departed to the Solar atmosphere. This Prabhâ (lustre) is fierce luminosity of the Solar atmosphere. Out of the pangs of separation Thou criedest and didst divide Prabhâ and didst put some parts in Fire, partly amidst the Yakṣas, partly into lions, among men, partly amongst the Devas, partly in Vaiṣṇavas, partly in serpents, partly in Brâhmaṇas, partly in Munis, partly in ascetics, and partly in fortunate and prosperous ladies. Thou hadst to weep then after Thou hadst thus divided Prabhâ, for Her separation and and fourthly I saw Thee in love union with the Gopi Śânti in Râsa Maṇḍalam. On the coming of the spring season, one day Thou with garlands of flowers on Thy neck and with Thy body besmeared with sandal paste and decked with ornaments, wast sleeping on a bed of flowers with Śanti Gopî, decked with gems, in a temple made of gems and pearls and illumined by a lamp of jewels and Thou wast chewing the betel, given by Thy beloved. Hearing My sound Thou fled'st away. Śânti Gopi, too, out of fear and shame quitted Her body and disappeared in Thee. Therefore Śânti is reckoned as one of the noblest qualities. Out of the pain of separation. Thou didst divide the body of Śânti and distributed partly to forests, partly to Brahmâ, partly to Me, partly to Śuddha Sattvâ Lakṣmî, partly to Thy Mantra worshippers, partly to My Mantra worshippers, partly to the ascetics, partly to Dharma, and partly to the religious persons. Fifthly-Dost Thou remember that one day anointing all over Thy body fully with the sandal paste and good scent and with garlands on Thy neck, well dressed, decked with jewels, Thou wast sleeping with Kṣamâ (forgiveness) Gopî in ease and happiness, on a nice bedding intespersed with flowers and well scented. Thou wert so much overpowered by sleep after fresh intercourse that when I went and disturbed, then Thou two didst get up from the sweet sleep. I took away Thy yellow robes, the beautiful Muralî (flute), garlands made of forest flowers, Kaustubha gems, and invaluable earrings of pearls and gems. I gave it back to Thee at the earnest request of the Śakhis. Thy body turned black with sin and dire shame. Kṣamâ then quitted Her body out of shame and went down to the earth. Therefore Kṣamâ turned out to be the repository of best qualities. Out of affection to Her, Thou didst divide Her body and distributed them partly to Viṣṇu, partly to the Vaiṣṇavas, partly to Dharma, partly to the religious persons, partly to weak persons, partly to ascetics, partly to the Devas, and partly to the Pundits (literary persons). O Lord! Thus I have described Thy qualities as far as I know. What more dost Thou want to hear? Thou hast many more qualities! But I am not aware of them. Having thus spoken, the red-lotus eyed Râdhâ began to rebuke Gangâ sitting by the side of Śrî Kriṣṇa with Her head bent low out of shame. At this time Gangâ, who was a Siddha Yoginî came to know all the mysteries, and instantly disappeared from the assembly in Her own water form.

The Siddha Yoignî Râdhâ came to know also, by Her Yogic power, the secrets of Gangâ and became ready to drink the whole water in one sip. Gangâ, knowing this intention of Râdhâ, by Her Yogic power, took refuge of Kriṣṇa and entered into His feet. Then Râdhâ began to look out for Gangâ everywhere :—First She searched in Goloka, then Vaikuṇṭha, then Brahma-loka; then She searched all the Lokas one by one but nowhere did She find Gangâ. All the places in Goloka became void of of water; all turned out dried mud and all the aquatic animals died and fell to the ground. And Brahmâ, Viṣṇu, Śiva, Ananta, Dharma, Indra, Moon, Sun, Manus, Munis, Siddhas, ascetics all became very thirsty and their throats became parched. They then went to Goloka, and bowed down with devotion to Śrî Kriṣṇa, Who was the Lord of all, beyond Prakriti, the Supreme, worthy to be worshipped, the Bestower of boons, the Best, and the Cause of boons; Who is the Lord of Gopas and Gopîs; Who is formless, without any desire, unattached, without refuge, attributeless, without any enthusiasm, changeless, and unstained; Who is All Will and who assumes forms to show favour to His devotees; Who is Sattva, the Lord of truth, the Witness and eternal Puruṣa, and Who is the Highest, the Supreme Lord, the Best and Excellent, the Highest Self and the Supreme God. They began to hymn Him. All were filled with intense feelings with devotion; tears of love were flowing from their eyes and the bodies of all were filled with ecstacy, the hairs standing in ends. He was Para Brahma; His Substance was made of Transcendental Light, Who is the Cause of all Causes, who was seated in a wonderful throne, built of invaluable gems and jewels, who was being fanned by the Gopas with white chowries, who was seeing and hearing with great delight, and smiling countenance, the dancing and singing of the Gopîs, who was chewing the scented betel offered by Râdhâ and who was residing in the heart of His dearest Śrî Râdhâ, who was the Perfect, all pervading, and the Lord of the Râsa Circle. The Manus, Munis, and the ascetics all bowed down to Śrî Krisna, no sooner they beheld Him. Joy and wonder at once caught hold of their hearts. They then looked at one another and gave over to Brahmâ the task of communicating their feelings. The four faced Brahmâ, with Visnu on His right and Vâma Deva on His left, gradually came in front of Śrî Krisna. Wherever He cast His glance in the Râsa Mandalam, He saw Śrî Krisna, full of the Highest Bliss, of the nature of the Highest Bliss, sitting. All have turned out Krisnas; their seats were all uniform; all were two armed and with flutes in their hands; on every one's neck is the forest garland; peacock's tail was on the top of everyone's crest and Kaustubha jewels were on all their breasts. The Forms of all of them were very beautiful; very lovely and very peaceful. No difference at all between them whether in form, or in qualities, or in ornaments, or in radiance, in age, in lustre, in no respect no one was inferior to another. No one was imperfect; no one was deficient in lordliness. It was indeed very difficult to make out who was the master and who was the servant. Sometimes He is seen in His Teja form as the Great Light, and there is nothing else; sometimes there is that Clear Divine Form; sometimes He comes Formless; sometimes with form; and again sometimes both with and without form. Sometimes there is no Râdhâ; there is only Krisna; And sometimes again in every seat there is the Yugal Murti Râdhâ and Krisna combined. Sometimes Râdhâ assumes the form of Krisna. So the Creator Brahmâ could not make out whether Śrî Krisna was a female or a male. At last He meditated on Śrî Krisna in his heart-lotus and began to chant hymns to Him with devotion and prayed for forgiveness for his misdoings. When S'rî Krisna got pleased, the Creator, opening His eyes, saw S'rî Krisna on the breast of S'rî Râdhâ. There were His attendants on all the sides and the Gopîs all around. Seeing this, Brahmâ, Visnu, and Mahes'vara bowed down to Him and sang His praises.

108-113. Śrî Krisna, the Lord of Lakshmi, the Omnipresent, Cause of all, the Lord of all, and the Internal Ruler of all, knew their intentions and, addressing them, separately said:—"O Brahman! Is it all well with you? O Lord of Kamala! Come here. O Mahâdeva! Come here; let all be well to you. "You all have come to me for Gangâ. Gangâ has taken refuge under My feet out of fear for Râdhâ." Seeing Gangâ by My side, Râdhâ wanted to drink Her up. However I will give over Gangâ to the hands of you all; but you will have to pray to Râdhâ, so that Gangâ becomes fearless of Her." The lotus born Brahmâ smiled at S'rî Krisṇa's words and began to sing hymns to Râdhâ, Who is fit to be worshipped by all. The Creator Brahmâ, the Compiler of the Four Vedas, the Four-faced One praised Râdhâ with His Four heads, bent low and addressed Her thus :—

114-125. Brahmâ said:—"O Râdhe! Gangâ, appeared from Thee and the Lord S'rî Krisṇa. Both of you were transformed before into the liquid forms in the Râsâ Manḍalam, on hearing the music of S'ankara. And That Lquid Form is Gangâ. So She is born of Thee and S'rî Krisṇa. Hence She is like Thy daughter and to be loved as such. She will be initiated in Thy Mantra and She will worship Thee. The four armed Lord of Vaikunṭha will be Her husband. And when She will appear in parts on earth, the Salt Ocean will be Her husband. O Mother! The Gangâ that dwells in Goloka, is dwelling everywhere. O Governess of the Devas! Thou art Her mother; and She is always Thy Self born daughter. Hearing, thus, the words of Brahmâ, Râdhâ gave Her assent towards the protection of Gangâ. And then Gangâ appeared from the toe-tip of Śrî Krisṇa. The liquid Gangâ, then, assumed Her own form and, getting up from water, was received with great honour by the Devas. Bhagavân Brahmâ took a little of that Ganges water in His Kamanḍalu and Bhagavân Mahâdeva kept some of it in His own head.

The lotus born Brahmâ, then, initiated Gangâ into the Râdhâ Mantra and gave Her instructions, Râdhâ Stotra (hymn of Râdhâ) according to the Sâma Veda, Râdhâ Kavacha (protection mantras), Râdhâ Dhyân (meditation on Râdhâ), method of worship of Râdhâ, and Râdhâ's puraścharaṇa. Gangâ worshipped Râdhâ according to these instructions and went to Vaikunṭha. O Muni! Laksmî, Sarasvatî, Gangâ, and the world purifying Tulasî, these four became the wives of Nârâyaṇa. Krisṇa, then, smiled and explained to Brahmâ the history of Time, hardly to be comprehended by others. He then spoke :—"O Brahmâ! O Visṇu! O Mahes'vara! Now you better take Gangâ and I will now tell you what a change has been effected by this time. Hear.

126-130. You, the three Devas, the other Devas, Munis, Manus, Siddhas, and other Mahâtmâs that are present here, are living now. For this region of Goloka is not affected by Kâla (Time). Now the Kalpa is going to expire. So in the other regions than Goloka and Vaikunṭha, the Brahmâs, etc, that were existing in all other Universes, have all now dissolved in My Body. O Lotus-born! Save Goloka and Vaikunṭha, all are now under water, the pre-state of earth. Better go and create your own

Brahmâṇḍas and Gangâ will go to that newly created Brahmâṇḍa. I will also create other worlds and the Brahmâs thereof. Now you all better go with the Devas and do your own works respectively. You have waited here for a long interval. As many Brahmâs that have fallen all appear again. Thus saying Srî Kriṣṇa, the Lord of Râdhâ went to His Inner Chamber. The Devas also instantly retired from that spot and engaged themselves earnestly in the creation work. Gangâ remained as before till then in the region of Goloka, Vaikuṇṭha, Śivaloka, Brahma-loka, and in other places, by the command of S'rî Kriṣṇa. She is named Viṣṇupadî, because She appeared from the feet of Viṣṇu. Thus I have described to you this pleasant, essential story of Gangâ, leading to liberation. What more do you now want to hear? Say.

Here ends the Thirteenth Chapter the anecdote of Gangâ in the Ninth Book in the Mahapurâṇam Srî Mad Devî Bhâgavatam of 18,000 verses by Maharṣi Veda Vyâsa.

CHAPTER XIV.

1. Nârada said :—" O Lord! Gangâ, Lakṣmî, Sarasvatî, and the world purifying Tulasî, these four, are dearest to Nârâyaṇa. Out of these, Gangâ went did the region of Goloka to Vaikuṇṭha. So I have heard. But how did She come to be the wife of Nârâyaṇa, I have not heard. Kindly describe this.

3. Nârâyaṇa said :—Brahmâ came from Goloka to the region of Vaikuṇṭha accompanied by Gangâ.

4-23. Brahmâ said to Nârâyaṇa :—" O Lord! Gangâ, born of the bodies of Râdhâ and Kriṣṇa, full of youth, modest, extraordinarily beautiful, of pure Suddha Sattva, and void of anger and egoism, does not like to marry anyone save Thee as She is born of Thee. But Râdhâ is of a very proud nature and very wrathful. She was even ready to drink up Gangâ. But Gangâ at once and intelligently took refuge into the feet of Śrî Kriṣṇa. So the whole Goloka became void of water. Seing this, I have come here to know in particular the whole history of the ease. Then Śrî Kriṣṇa, the Knower and the Ruler of the hearts of all, came to know my heart and instantly caused Gangâ to issue from His toe and handed Her over to me. I bowed down to Śrî Kriṣṇa and now I have come with Gangâ to Thee. Now Thou dost marry the Sures'varî Gangâ according to the Gândharva rule of marriage. As Thou art a Deva of taste and humorous in the assembly of the Devas, so Gangâ is. As Thou art a gem amongst the males, so She is the gem amongst the females. And the union of a humorous man with a humorous woman is exceedingly pleasant. Now marry this Lady who has come of Her own accord to Thee. Śrî Mahâ Lakṣmî becomes annoyed with one who does not marry a woman who has come spontaneously. There is no doubt in this. The wise men do never insult the Prakriti. All the Puruṣas (males) are born of Prakṛiti and all the females are parts of Prakṛiti. So Prakṛiti and Puruṣa are both inseparable and verily one and the same. So these two should never insult each other. (If Thou sayest that Gangâ is attached to Kriṣṇa; how canst Thou marry Her. The reply is) As Śrî Krisṇa is beyond the attributes and beyond Prakṛiti, so Thou art also above Prakriti. The one-halfof Srî Kriṣṇa is two-armed; the other half of Śrî Kriṣṇa is four-armed. Râdhâ has appeared from the left side of S'rî Kriṣṇa. He Himself is the right half and Padmâ is His left-half. (As there is no difference between Râdhâ and Kamalâ so there is no difference between Śrî Kriṣṇa and Thee. Therefore as Gangâ is born of Thy body, she wants to marry Thee. As Prikṛiti and Puruṣa are really one and the same without any difference, so the males and females are one. Thus speaking to Nârâyaṇa, Brahmâ handed Gangâ over to Nârâyaṇa and went away. Nârâyaṇa, then, married Gangâ smeared with sandal paste and flowers, according to the rules of the Gandarbha marriage. The Lord of Lakṣmî then spent his time happily in enjoyment with Gangâ. Gangâ had to go to the earth (under the Bhârati's curse) and afterwards returned to Vaikuṇṭha As Gangâ appeared from the feet of Viṣṇu, She is denominated Viṣṇupadî. Gangâ Devî was very much overpowered with enjoyment in Her first intercourse with Nârâyaṇa; so much so that She remained, motionless. Thus Gangâ spent the days happily with Nârâyaṇa. Sarasvatîs jealousy towards Gangâ did not disappear, though She was advised by Lakṣmî Devî not to do so. Sarasvatî cherished incessantly the feeling of jealousy towards Gangâ. But Gangâ had not the least feeling of jealousy towards Sarasvatî.

At last, one day, when vexed too much, Gangâ became angry and cursed Sarasvatî to take Her birth in Bhârata. So Lakṣmî, Sarasvatî and Gangâ were the wives of Nârâyaṇa. Lastly Tulasî became the wife of Nârâyaṇa. So the number of wives of Nârâyaṇa amounted to four.

Here ends the Fourteenth Chapter in the Ninth Book on the story of Gangâ becoming the wife of Nârâyaṇa in the Mahâpuraṇam Śrî Mad Devî Bhâgavatam of 18,000 verses by Maharṣi Veda Vyâsa.

CHAPTER XV.

1-6. Nârada said:—"O Bhagavan! How came the pure chaste Tulasî to be the wife of Nârâyaṇa? Where was Her birth place? And what was She in Her previous birth? What family did She belong to? Whose daughter was She? And what austerities did She practise, that She got

Nârâyaṇa for Her husband, Who is above Prakriti, not liable to change whithout any effort, the Universal Self, Para Brahma andthe Highest God; Who is the Lord of all, omniscient, the Cause of all, the Receptacle of all, Omnipresent, and the Preserver of all. And how did Tulasî, the chief Devî of Nârâyaṇa, turn out into a tree? Herself quite innocent, how She was attacked by the fierce Asura? "O Remover of all doubts! My mind, plain and simple, has become restless. I am eager to hear all this. So kindly cut asunder all my doubts.

7-40. Nârâyaṇa said :—"O Nârada! The Manu Dakṣa Sâvarṇi was very religious, devoted to Viṣṇu, of wide renown, of a great name, and born with Viṣṇu's parts. Dakṣa Sâvarṇi's son Brahma Sâvarṇi was also very religious, devoted to Viṣṇu and of a pure Śuddha Sattva Guṇa. Brahma Sâvarṇi's son, Dharma Sâvarṇi was devoted to Viṣṇu and He was the master of his senses. Dharma Sâvarṇi's sons Rudra Sâvarṇi was also a man of restraint and very devoted. Rudra Sâvarṇi's son was Deva Sâvarṇi, devoted to Viṣṇu. Deva Sâvarṇi's son was Indra Sâvarṇi. He was a great Bhakta of Viṣṇu. His son was Vriṣadhvaja. But He was a fanatic Śaiva (devoted to S'iva). At his house S'iva Himself remained for three Yugas according to the Deva measure. So much so that Bhagavân Bhûtanâtha loved him more than His own son. Vriṣadhvaja did not recognise Nârâyaṇa, nor Lakṣmî nor Sarasvatî nor another body. He discarded the worship of all the Devas. He worshipped Śankara only. The greatly exciting Lakṣmî Pûjâ (worship of Mahâ Lakṣmî in the month of Bhâdra and Śrî Pañchamî Pûjâ in the month of Mâgha, which are approved of by the Vedas, Vriṣadhvaja put an entire stop to these and the Sarasvatî Pûjâ. At this the Sun became angry with the King Vriṣadhvaja, the discarder of the holy thread, the hater of Viṣṇu, and cursed Him thus :— "O King! As you are purely devoted to Śiva and Śiva alone, and as you do not recognise any other Devas, I say within no time, you will be deprived of all your wealth and prosperity." S'ankara, hearing this curse, became very angry and taking His trident, ran after the Sun. The Sun, becoming afraid, accompanied His father Kas'yapa and took refuge of Brahmâ. Bhagavân Śankara went to the Brahma Loka, with trident in His hands. Brahmâ became afraid of Mahâdeva and took Sun to the region of Vaikuṇṭha. Out of terror, the throats of Brahmâ, Kas'yapa, and Sun became parched and dry and they all went afraid for refuge to Nârâyaṇa, the Lord of all. They all bowed down to Him and praised Him frequently and finally informed Him of the cause of their coming and why they were so much afraid. Nârâyaṇa showed them mercy and granted them "Abhaya" (no fear). O You! Who are afraid, take rest. What cause of fear there can be to you, when I am here!"

Whoever remembers Me, wherever he may be, involved in danger or fear, I go there with the Sudars'an disc in My hand and save him. O Devas! I am always the Creator, Preserver and Destroyer of this universe In the form of Viṣṇu, I am the Preserver; in the form of Brahmâ, I am the Creator; and in the form of Mahes'a, I am the Destroyer. I am Śiva; I am you; and I am the Sûrya, composed of the three qualities. It is I who assumes many forms and preserves the universe. Better go to your respective places. What fear can ye suspect? I say, all your fears due to S'ankara, are verily removed from this day. Bhagavân S'ankara, the Lord of all, is the Lord of the Sâdhus. He always hears the words of His Bhaktas; and He is kind to them. He is their Self. Both the Sun and Śiva are dearer to Me than My life. No one is more energetic than S'ankara and the Sun. Mahâdeva can easily create ten million Suns and ten million Brahmâs. There is nothing impossible with Śûlapâṇi. Having no consciousness of any outer thing, immersed, day and night, in meditating on Me. with His whole heart concentrated, He is repeating with devotion My Mantra from His five faces and He always sings My glories. I am also thinking, day and night, of His welfare. Whoever worships Me in whichever way, I also favour him similarly. Bhagavân Mahâ Deva is of the nature of Śiva, all auspiciousness; He is the presiding deity of S'iva, that is, liberation. It is because liberation is obtained from Him, He is called Śiva. O dear Nârada! While Nârâyaṇa was thus speaking, the trident holder Mahâdeva, with his eyes red like reddened lotuses, mounting on His bull, came up there and getting down from His Bull, humbly bowed down with devotion to the Lord of Lakṣmî, peaceful and higher than the highest. Nârâyaṇa was then seated on His throne, decked with jewel ornaments. There was a crown on His crest; two earrings were hanging from His ears; the disc was in His hand, forest flower's garlands on His neck; of the colour of fresh blue rain cloud; His form exceedingly beautiful. The four-armed attendants were fanning Him with their four hands; His body smeared all over with sandal-paste and He is wearing the yellow garment. That Bhagavân, distressed with the thought of welfare for His Bhaktas, the Highest Self was sitting on a jewel throne and chewing the betel offered by Padmâ and with smiling countenance, seeing and hearing the dancing and singing of the Vidyâdharîs. When Mahâdeva bowed down to Nârâyaṇa, Brahmâ also bowed down to Mahâdeva. The Sun, too, surprised, bowed down to Mahâdeva with devotion. Kas'-yapa, too, bowed and with great bhakti, began to praise Mahâdeva. On the other hand, Śankara praised Nârâyaṇa and took His seat on the throne. The attendants of Nârâyaṇa began to fan Mahâdeva with white chowries. Then Viṣṇu addressed Him with sweet nectar like voice and said :—" O Mahes'vara! What brings Thee here? Hast Thou been angry?"

41-45. Mahâdeva said :—" O Viṣṇu! The King Vriṣadhavaja is My great devotee; he is dearer to Me than My life. The Sun has cursed him and so I am angry." Out of the affection for a son I am ready to kill Sûrya. Sûrya took Brahmâ's refuge and now he and Brahmâ have taken Thy refuge. And Those who being distressed take Thy refuge, either in mind or in word, become entirely safe and free from danger. They conquer death and old age. What to speak of them, then, of those who come personally to Thee and take Thy refuge. The remembrance of Hari takes away all dangers. All good comes to them. O Lord of the world! Now tell me what becomes of My stupid Bhakta who has become devoid of fortune and prosperity by the curse of Sûrya.

46-51. Viṣṇu said :—" O Śankara! Twenty-one yugas elapsed within this one-half Ghaṭikâ, by the coincidence of Fate (Daiva). Now go quickly to Thy abode. Through the unavoidable coincidence of the cruel Fate, Vriṣadhvaja died. His son Rathadhvaja, too, died. Rathadhvaja had two noble sons Dharmadhvaja and Kus'adhvaja. Both of them are great Vaiṣṇavas; but, through Sûrya's curse, they have become luckless. Their kingdoms are lost; they have become destitute of all property, prosperity and they are now engaged in worshipping Mahâ Lakṣmî. Mahâ Lakṣmî will be born in parts of their two wives. Then again, by the grace of Lakṣmî, Dharmadhvaja and Kus'adhvaja will be prosperous and become great Kings. O Śambhu! Your worshipper Vris'adhvaja is dead. Therefore Thou dost go back to Thy place. O Brahmâ, O Sun! O Kas'yapa! You all also better go to your places respectively. O Nârada! Thus saying, Bhagavân Viṣṇu went with His wife to the inner rooms. The Devas also went gladly to their own places respectively. And Mahâdeva, too, Who is always quite full within Himself, departed quickly to perform His Tapas.

Here ends the Fifteenth Chapter on the question of anecdote of Tulasî in the Ninth Book in the Mahâpurâṇam Śrî Mad Devi Bhâgavatam of 18,000 verses by Maharṣi Veda Vyâsa.

CHAPTER XVI.

1-30. Śrî Nârâyaṇa said :—O Muni! Dharmadhvaja and Kus'adhvaja practised severe tapasyâs and worshipped Lakṣmî. They then got separately their desired boons. By the boon of Mahâ Lakṣmî, they became again the rulers of the earth. They acquired great religious merits and they also had their children. The wife of Kus'adhvaja was named Mâlâvatî. After a long time, the chaste wife delivered one daughter, born of the parts of Kamalâ. The daughter, on being born, became full of wisdom. On being born, the baby began to sing clearly the Vedic mantrams from the lying-in-chamber. Therefore She was named Vedavatî by the Pundits. She bathed after her birth and became ready to go to the forest to practise severe tapas. Everyone, then, tried earnestly to dissuade her, devoted to Nârâyaṇa, from this enterprise. But she did not listen to anybody. She went to Puṣkara and practised hard tapasyâ for one Manvantara. Yet her body did not get lean a bit; rather she grew more plumpy and fatter. By degrees her youth began to shew signs in her body; one day she heard an incorporeal voice from the air above, "O Fair One! In your next birth Śrî Hari, adored by Brahmâ and other gods, will be your husband." Hearing this, her joy knew no bounds. She went to the solitary caves in the Gandhamâdan mountain to practise tapas again. When a long time passed away in this tapasyâ, one day the irresistible Râvaṇa came there as guest. No sooner Vedavatî saw the guest, than she gave him, out of devotion to the guest, water to wash his feet, delicious fruits, and cool water for his drink. The villain accepted the hospitality and sitting there, began to ask:—"O Auspicious One! Who are you? Seeing the fair smiling lady, with beautiful teeth, her face blooming like the autumnal lotus, of heavy loins, and of full breast, that villain became passionate. He lost entirely all consciousness and became ready to make violence on Her. Seeing this, the chaste Vedavatî, became angry and out of her tapas influence, astounded him and made him insensible to move. He remained motionless like an inanimate body. He could not move his hands nor feet nor could he speak. That wicked fellow, then mentally recited praises to her. And the praise of the Higher Śakti can never go futile. She became pleased and granted him religious merits in the next world. But she also pronounced this curse:—"That when you have touched my body out of passion, then you will be ruined with your whole family for my sake." Now see my power, O Nârada! Thus saying to Râvaṇa, Vedavatî left her body by her yogic power. Then Râvaṇa took her body and delivered it to the Ganges and he then returned to his own home. But Râvaṇa thought over the matter repeatedly and exclaimed. "What wonder have I seen! Oh! What a miracle this lady has wrought! Râvaṇa thus lamented. This Vedavatî, of pure character, took her birth afterwards as Sîtâ, the daughter of

Janaka. For the sake of this Sîtâ, Râvaṇa was ruined with his whole family. By the religious merits of her previous birth, the ascetic lady got Bhagavân Hari Srî Râma Chandra, the Fullest of the Full, for her husband and remained for a long time in great enjoyment with the Lord of the world; a thing very difficult to be attained! Though she was a Jâtismarâ (one who knows all about her past lives), she did not feel any pain due to her practising severe austerities in her previous birth; for when the pains end in success, the pains are not then felt at all. Sîtâ, in Her fresh youth enjoyed various pleasures in the company of her husband, handsome, peaceful, humorous and witty, the chief of the Devas, loved by the female sex, well-qualified, and just what she desired. But the all-powerful Time is irresistible; the truthful Râmachandra, the scion of the Raghu's family, had to keep up the promise made by his father and so he had to go to the forest, ordained by Time. He remained with Sîtâ and Lakṣmaṇa near the sea. Once the God Fire appeared to Him in the form of a Brâhmaṇa. Fire, in a Brâhmin-form, saw Râma Chandra morose and became himself mortified. Then the Truthful Fire addressed the truthful Râmachandra:— "O Bhagavân Râmachandra! I now speak to you how time is now coming to you. Now has come the time when your Sîtâ will be stolen."

31-48. The course of Destiny is irrestible; none else is more powerful than Time, Fate. So give over your Sîtâ, the World Mother to me and keep with you this Chhâyâ Sîtâ (the shadow Sîtâ; the false Sîtâ). When the time of Sîtâ's ordeal by fire will take place I will give Her back to you. The Devas united have sent me to you. I am not really a Brâhmin; but I am Agin Deva (eater of oblations). Râmachandra heard Fire and gave his assent. But his heart shattered. He did not speak of this to Lakṣmaṇa. By the yogic power Agni (Fire) created a Mâyâ Sîtâ. This Mâyâ Sîtâ, O Nârada, was perfectly equal to the real Sîtâ. Fire, then, handed this Mâyâ Sîtâ to the hands of Râmachandra. Hûtâsana (fire) took the real Sîtâ and said "Never divulge this to any other body" and went away. What to speak of divulging the secret to any other body, Lakṣmaṇa even could not know it. By this time Râma saw one deer, made of all gold. To bring that deer carefully to her, Sîtâ sent Râmachandra with great eagerness. Putting Sîtâ under Lakṣmaṇa's care, in that forest, Râma went himself immediately and pierced the deer by one arrow. That Mâyâ mrîga (the deer created by magic powers) on being pierced, cried out "Hâ Lakṣmaṇa! and seeing Hari before him and remembering the name of Hari, quitted his life. The deer body then vanished; and a divine body made its appearance in its stead. This new body mounting on an aerial car made of jewels, ascended to Vaikuṇṭha. That Mâyik (majic) deer was in its previous birth, a servant of the two gate-keepers of Vaikuṇṭha; but, for the sake of some emergency, he had to take up this Râkhṣasa birth. He again became the servant of two door-keepers of Vaikuṇṭha. On the other hand Sîtâ Devî, hearing the cry "Ha Lakṣmaṇa!" became very distressed and sent Lakṣmaṇa in search of Râma. No sooner did Lakṣmaṇa get out of the hermitage, the irresistible Râvaṇa took away Sîtâ gladly to the city of Lankâ (Ceylon). Now Râmachandra, seeing Lakṣmaṇa on the way in the forest, became merged in the ocean of sorrows and without losing any time came hurriedly to the hermitage where he could not find Sîtâ. Instantly he fell unconscious on the ground; and, after a long time, when he regained his consciousness, he lamented and wandered here and there in search of Her. After some days on the banks of the river Godâvarî, getting the information of Sîtâ, he built a bridge across the ocean with the help of His monkey armies. Then he entered with his army into Lankâ and slew Râvaṇa with arrows with all his friends. When Sîtâ's ordeal by fire came, Agni (Fire) handed over the real Sîtâ to Râmachandra. The Shadow Sîtâ then humbly addressed Agni and Râma Chandra "O Lord! What am I to do now? Settle my case.

49-53. Agni and Râmachandra both of them then said to Chhâyâ Sîtâ:— "O Devî! Go to Puṣkara and practise tapasyâ there; that place is the giver of religious merits and then you will be the Svarga Lakṣmî (Lakṣmî of Heaven). Hearing this, the Chhâyâ Sîtâ went and practised tapasyâ for the three divine lâkh years and became Mahâ Lakṣmî. This Svarga Lakṣmî appeared at one time from the sacrificial Kuṇḍa (pit). She was known as the daughter of Drupada and became the wife of the five Pâṇḍavas. She was Veda Vatî, the daughter of Kus'adhvaja in the Satya Yûgâ; Sîtâ, the wife of Râma and the daughter of Janaka in Tretâ Yuga; and Draupadî, the daughter of Drupada, in the Dvâpara Yuga. As she existed in the Satya, Tretâ, and Dvâpara Yugas, the Three Yugas, hence She is Trihâyaṇî.

54. Nârada said:— "O Chief of Munis! O Remover of doubts! Why had Draupadî five husbands? A great doubt has arisen in my mind on this point. Remove my doubt.

55-63. Nârâyaṇa said:— "O Devarṣi! When, in the city of Lankâ, the real Sîtâ came before Râma, then Chhâyâ Sîtâ, full of youth and beauty, became very anxious. Agni Deva and Râmachandra both told

Her to go to Puṣkara and worship Śamkara. While this Chhâyâ Sîtâ was practising austerities in Puṣkara, She became very anxious to get a good husband and asked from Mahâ Deva the boon "Grant me a husband" and repeated it five times. Śiva, the chief among the humorous, witty persons, hearing this, said "O Dear! You will get five husbands." and thus granted her the boon. Therefore She became the dearest wife of the five Pâṇḍavas. Now hear other facts. When the war at Lankâ was over, Śrî Râmachandra got his own dear wife Sîtâ, and installing Vibhîṣaṇa on the throne of Lankâ, returned to Ayodhyâ. He ruled for eleven thousand years in Bhârata and finally went to Vaikuṇṭha with his all his subjects. Vedavatî, the incarnation in part of Lakṣmî dissolved in the body of Kamalâ. Thus I have described to you the pure anecdote of Vedavatî. Hearing this destroys sins and increases virtue. The four Vedas reigned incarnate, in their true forms, on the lips of Vedavatî; hence She was named Vedavatî. Thus I have told you the anecdote of the daughter of Kus'adhvaja. Now hear the story of Tulasî, the daughter of Dharmadhvaja.

Here ends the Sixteenth Chapter in the Ninth Book on the incarnation of Mahâ Lakṣmî in the house of Kus'adhvaja in Śrî Mad Devî Bhâgvatam of 18,000 verses by Maharṣi Veda Vyâsa.

CHAPTER XVII.

1-19. Śrî Nârâyaṇa said:— "O Nârada! The wife of Dharmadhvaja was Mâdhavî. Going to the Gandhamâdan mountain, She began to enjoy, with great gladness, the pleasures with the king Dharmadhvaja. The bed was prepared, strewn with flowers and scented with sandal-paste. She smeared all over her body with sandal-paste. The flowers and cool breeze in contact with the sweet scent of sandal-paste began to cool the bodies. Mâdhavî was the jewel amongst women. Her whole body was very elegant. Besides it was adorned all-over with jewel ornaments. As she was humorous, so the king was very expert in that respect. It seemed as if the Creator created especially for Dharmadhvaja, the humorous lady Mâdhavî expert in amorous affairs. Both of them were skilled in amorous sports. So no one did like to desist from amorous enjoyments. One hundred divine years passed in this way, day and night passed unnoticed. The king then got back his consciousness and desisted from his amorous embraces. But the lustful woman did not find herself satisfied. However, by the Deva's influence, she became pregnant and conceived for one hundred years. In the womb there was the incarnation of Lakṣmî; and the body's lustre increased day by day. Then, on an auspicious day, on an auspicious moment, auspicious Yoga, auspicious Lagna, auspicious Amsa, and on an auspicious combination of planetary

-ulers and their houses, she delivered on the full moon night of the month of Kârtik one beautiful daughter, the incarnation in part of Lakṣmî. The face of the baby looked like the autumnal moon; Her two eyes resembled autumnal lotuses and her upper and lower lips looked beautiful like ripe Bimba fruits. The daughter began, no sooner it was born, to look on all sides of the lying-in-room. The palm and lower part of feet were red. The navel was deep and below that there were three wrinkles. Her loins were circular. Her body was hot in the winter and cold in the summer and pleasant to touch. Her hairs on the head were hanging like the roots of the fig tree. Her colour was bright like Champaka; She was a jewel amongst women. Men and women cannot compare her beauty. The holy wise men named Her Tulasî. As soon as she was born, she looked of the female sex, full in every way. Though prevented repeatedly by all, She went to the forest of Badarî for practising Tapasyâ. There she practised hard Tapasyâ for one lâkh divine years. Her main object was to get Nârâyaṇa for her husband. In summer she practised Panchatapâ (surrounded by fire on four sides and on the top); in the winter she remained in water and in the rainy season she remained in the open air and endured the showers of the rain, twenty thousand years. She passed away thus in eating fruits and water. For thirty thousand years she subsisted only on the leaves of trees. When the forty thousandth year came, she subsisted only on air and her body became thinner and thinner day by day. Then for ten thousand years afterwards she left eating anything whatsoever and without any aim, stood on only one leg. At this time the lotus-born Brahmâ, seeing this, appeared there to grant her boons. On seeing Him, Tulasî immediately bowed down to Brahmâ, the Four-faced One riding on His vehicle, the Swan. (*Note.*— The vehicle theory of the Devas came from Egypt. The Devas were without vehicles at first and were faced half-beasts. Then they were rendered men and their vehicles were fancied as beasts. The face of the Dûrgâ Devî was thought of as that of a tiger.]

20. He then addressed her and said :— "O Tulasî! Ask any boon that you like. Whether it be devotion to Hari, servantship to Hari, freedom from old age or freedom from death, I will grant that to you.

21-27. Tulasî said :— "Father! I now say you my mind. Hear. What is the use of hiding away my views out of fear or shame to One who knows everything reigning in One's Heart.

I am Tulasî Gopî (cowherdess); I used to dwell before in the Goloka. I was a dear she-servant of Radhikâ, the beloved of Kriṣṇa. I was also born of Her in part. Her Sakhis (female attendants) used to love me. Once in Râsa Maṇḍalam I was enjoyed by Govinda; but I was not satiated and while

I was lying down in an unconscious state, Râdhâ, the Governess-in-chief of the Râsa circle, came there and saw me in that state. She rebuked Gobinda and, out of anger, cursed me :—" Go at once and be born as a human being." At this Govinda spoke to me :—" If you go and practise Tapas in Bhârata, Brahmâ will get pleased and He will grant you boon. When you will get Nârâyaṇa, the Four-armed, born of Me in part as your husband. " O Father ! Thus speaking, Śrî Kriṣṇ ı disappeared out of sight. Out of Râdhâ's fear, I quitted my body and am now born in this world. Now grant me this boon that I get the peaceful, lovely, beautiful Nârâyaṇa for my husband."

28-37. Brahmâ said :—" O Child Tulasî ! The Gopa (cowherd) Sudâmâ was born of Śrî Kriṣṇa's body. At the present time he is very energetic, He too, under the curse of Râdhâ, has come and taken his birth amongst the Dânavas. He is named S'ankha Chûḍa. No one is equal to him in strength." In Goloka, when he saw you before, he was overpowered with passion for you. Only out of Râdhâ's influence, he could not embrace you. That Sudâmâ is Jâtismara (knows all about his previous births) ; and you, too, are Jâti Smarâ. There is nothing unknown to you. O Beautiful One ! You will now be his wife. Afterwards you will get Nârâyaṇa, the Beautiful and Lovely for your husband. Thus under the curse of Nârâyaṇa, you will be transformed into the world purifying Tulasî tree. You will be the foremost amongst the flowers and will be dearer to Nârâyaṇa than His life. No one's worship will be complete without Thee as leaf. You will remain as a tree in Bindrâban and you will be widely known as Vrindâbanî. The Gopas and Gopîs will worship Mâdhava with Your leaves. Being the Presiding Deity of the Tulasî tree, you will always enjoy the company of Kriṣṇa, the best of the Gopas. O Nârada ! Thus hearing Brahmâ's words, the Devî Tulasî became very glad. Smile appeared in her face. She then bowed down to the Creator and said :—

38-40. " O Father ! I speak now truly to Thee that I am not as devoted to the four-armed Nârâyaṇa as I am devoted to Śyâma Sundara, the two-armed. For my intercourse with Govinda Śrî Kriṣṇa was suddenly interrupted and my desire was not gratified. It is because of Śrî Govinda's words that I prayed for the four-armed. Now it appears certain that by Thy grace I will get again my Govinda, very hard to be attained. But, O Father ! Do this that I be not afraid of Râdhâ.

41-48. Brahmâ said :—"O Child ! I now give you the sixteen lettered Râdhâ mantra to you. By Her Grace you will be dear to Râdhâ as Her life. Râdhikâ will not be able to know anything of your secret dealings. O Fortunate! You will be dear to Govinda like Râdhâ. Thus saying, Brahmâ, the Creator of the world, gave her the sixteen lettered Râdhâ mantra, stotra, Kavacha and mode of worship and puras'charaṇa and He blessed her. Tulasî, then, engaged herself in worshipping Râdhâ, as directed. By the boon of Brahmâ, Tulasî attained Siddhi (success) like Lakṣmî. Out of the power of the Siddha mantra, She got her desired boon. She became fortunate in getting various pleasures, hard to be attained in this world. Her mind became quiet. All the toils of Tapasyâ disappeared. When one gets the fruit of one's labour, all the troubles then transform to happiness. She then finished her food and drink and slept on a beautiful bed strewn with flowers and scented with sandal paste.

Here ends the Seventeenth Chapter of the Ninth Book on the anecdote of Tulasî in Śrî Mad Devî Bhâgavatam of 18,000 verses by Maharṣi Veda Vyâsa.

CHAPTER XVIII.

1-26. Nârâyaṇa said:—"Thus highly pleased, Tulasî went to sleep with a gladdened-heart. She, the daughter of Vriṣadhvaja, was then in her blooming youth and while asleep. the Cupid, the God of five arrows, shot at her five arrows (by which one gets enchanted and swooned). Though the Devî was smeared with sandal paste and She slept on a bed strewn with flowers, her body was felt as if being burnt. Out of joy, the hairs stood on their ends all over her body; her eyes were reddened and her body began to quiver. Sometimes She felt uneasiness, sometimes dryness; sometimes She got faint; sometimes drowsiness and sometimes again pleasantness; sometimes she became conscious, sometimes sorrowful. Sometimes she got up from her bed; sometimes she sat; and sometimes she fell again to sleep. The flower-bed, strewn with sandal-paste, appeared to her full of thorns; nice delicious fruits and cold water appeared to her like poison. Her house appeared to her like a hole in a ground and her fine garments seamed to her like fire. The mark of Sindûra on her forehead appeared, as it were, a boil, a sore. She began to see in her dreams that one beautiful, well clothed, humorous, young man with smile in his lips, appeared to her. His body was besmeared with sandal-paste and decked with excellent jewels; garlands of forest flowers were suspending from his neck. Coming there, he was drinking the honey of her lotus face. He was speaking on love themes and on various other sweet topics. As if he was embracing amorously and enjoying the pleasures of intercourse. After the intercourse he was going away; again he was coming near.

The lady was addressing him " O Darling ! O Lord of my heart ! Where do you go. Come close. " Again when she became conscious, she began to lament bitterly. Thus on entering in her youth, the Devî Tulasi began to live in the hermitage of Badari (Plum fruit, It may signify womb. Those who visit Badari are not to enter again in any womb). On the other hand the great Yogi Śankhachûḍa obtained the Krişņa Mantra from Maharşi Jaigîşavya and got siddhi (success) in Puşkara Tîrtha (sacred place of pilgrimage where one crosses the world). Holding on his neck the Kavacha named Sarvamangalamaya and obtaining the boon from Brahmâ as he desired, he arrived at Badari, by Brahmâ's command. The signs of the blooming youth had just begun to be visible in the body of Śankhachûḍa as if the God of Love incarnated in his body ; his colour resembled that of white Champakas and all his body was decked with jewelled ornaments. His face resembled the autumnal full moon ; his eyes were extended like the lotus leaves. The beautiful form was seen to sit in an excellent aerial car, made of pearls and jewels. Two jewel earrings, nice and elegant, suspended upto his cheek ; his neck was adorned with Pârijâta flower garlands ; and his body was smeared with Kunkum and scented sandal-paste.. O Nârada ! Seeing Śankhachûḍa coming near to her, Tulasî covered her face by her clothings and she, with a smiling countenance, cast repeatedly sidelong glances on him and bent her head low abashed in the expectation of a fresh intercourse. How beautiful was that clear face of her ! It put down the autumnal moon in the background. The invaluable jewelled ornaments were on her toes. Her braid of hair was surrounded by sweet scented Mâlatî garlands. The invaluable jewelled wonderful earrings like the shape of a shark were hanging up to her cheek. Extraordinarily beautiful necklaces were seen being suspended to the middle of her breasts and added to the beauty thereof ; on her arms and hands were jewelled bangles and conch ornaments ; jewelled armlets and on fingers excellent jewelled rings were seen. O Muni ! Seeing that lovely beautiful chaste woman of good nature, Śankhachûḍa came to her and taking his seat addressed her as follows :—

27. " O Proud One ! O Auspicious One ! Who are you ? Whose daughter are you ? You look fortunate and blessed among women. I am your silent slave. Talk with me.

28-30. That beautiful eyed Tulasî, full of love, replied to Śankhachûḍa with smiling countenance and face bent low :—" I am the daughter of the great king Vrişadhvaja I have come to this forest for tapasyâ and am engaged in this. Who are you ? What business have you to talk with me ? Yau can go away wherever you like. I have heard in the Śâstras that persons born of a noble family never speak with ladies of a respectable family in privacy.

31-703. Only those that are lewd, void of any knowledge in the Dharma Śâstras, void of the Vedic knowledge and who are not Kulînas, like to speak with women in privacy. And those women, too, that look externally beautiful but very passionate and the Death of males, who are sweet tongued but filled with venom in their hearts, those who are sweet externally but like a sword internally, those that are always bent in achieving their own selfish ends and those that become obedient to their husbands for their own selfish ends otherwise behaving as they like, those that are filled inside with dirty things and outside looking pleasant in their faces and eyes, whose characters are pronounced as defiled, what intelligent, learned and noble-minded man can trust them? Those women do not discriminate who are their friends or who are their enemies; they want always new persons. Whenever they see a man well dressed, they want to satisfy their own passions. And they pretend with great care that they are very chaste. They are the vessels of passion; they always attract the minds of others and they are very enthusiastic in satisfying their own lust. They verbally shew that they want other men to go away but at hearts, feelings for intercourse remain preponderant; whenever they see their paramours in private, they laugh and become very glad but externally their shame knows no bounds. When they do not have their intercourses with their paramours, they become self-conceited; their bodies burn with anger and they begin to quarrel. When their passions are satisfied fully, they become glad and when there is a deficiency in that, they become sorrowful. For the sake of good and sweet food and cold drinks, they want beautiful young persons, qualified and humorous. They consider witty young persons clever in holding intercourses, more dearly than their sons. And if that beloved one becomes incapable or aged, then he is considered as an enemy. Quarrels and anger then ensue. They devour these men as serpents eat rats. They are boldness personified and they are the source of all evils and vices. Even Brahmâ, Viṣṇu and Mahes'a remain deluded before them. They cannot find out any clue of their minds. They are the greatest obstacle in the path of tapasyâ and the closed doors for liberation. Devotion to Hari cannot reach those women. They are the repositories of Mâyâ and they hold men fast by iron chains in this world. They are like magicians and false like dreams. They enchant others by external beauty; their lower parts are very ugly and filled with excrements, faeces, of foul scent and very unholy and smeared with blood. The Creator Bhagavân has created them as such, the Mâyâ to the Mâyâvis and the venom to those who want liberation, and as invisible to those that want to have them. Thus saying Tulasî stopped. O Nârada! Śankhachuda, then smilingly addressed her as follows:—"O Devî! What you have spoken is not wholly false; partly it is true and partly it is false. Now hear." The Creator has created this all-enchanting female form into two parts. One is praiseworthy and the other is not. He has created Lakṣmî, Sarasvatî, Durgâ, Sâvitrî, and Râdhâ and others as the primary causes of creation; so there are the prime creations. Those women that are born of their parts, are auspicious, glorious, and much praiseworthy. Śatarûpâ, Devahûti, Svadhâ, Svâhâ, Dakṣiṇâ Chhâyâvatî, Rohiṇî, Varunânî, Śachî, the wife of Kuvera. Diti, Aditi, Lopâmudrâ, Anasûyâ, Kauṭabhî (Koṭarî), Tulasî, Ahalyâ, Arundhatî, Menâ, Târâ, Mandodarî, Damayantî, Vedavatî, Gangâ, Manasâ, Puṣṭi, Tuṣṭi, Smriti, Medhâ, Kâlikâ, Vasundharâ, Saṣṭhî, Mangalachaṇḍî, Mûrti, wife of Dharma. Svasti, Śraddhâ; Śânti, Kânti, Kṣânti, Nidrâ, Tandrâ, Kṣudhâ, Pipâsâ, Sandhyâ, Râtri, Divâ, Sampatti, Dhriti, Kîrti, Krîyâ, Śobhâ, Prabhâ, Śivâ, and other women born of the Prime Prakritis, all are excellent in every Yuga. The prostitutes of the heavens are also born of the above women in their parts and parts of parts. They are not praiseworthy in the universe; they are all regarded as unchaste women. Those women that are of Sattva Guṇas are all excellent and endowed with influence. In the universe they are good, chaste and praiseworthy. This is not false. The Pandits declare them excellent. Those that are of Rajo Guṇas, and Tamo Guṇas are not so praiseworthy. Those women that are of Rajo Guṇas are known as middling. They are always fond of enjoyments, yield to them, and always ready to achieve their own ends. These women are generally insincere, delusive, and outside the pale of religious duties. Therefore they are generally unchaste. The Pandits consider them as middling. Those women that are of Tamo Guṇas are considered as worst. Those born of noble families can never speak with other wives in a private place or when they are alone. By Brahmâ's command I have come to you. O Fair One! I will marry you now according to the Gandharba method. My name is Sankhachûda. The Devas fly away from me out of terror. Before I was the intimate Śakhâ (friend) of Srî Hari, by the name of Sudâmâ. Now, by Râdhikâ's curse I am born in the family of the Dânavas. I was a Pâriṣad (attendant) of Śrî Kriṣṇa and the chief of the eight Gopas. Now, by Râdhikâ's curse I am born as Śankhachûḍa, the Indra of the Dânavas. By Śrî Kriṣṇa's grace and by His mantra, I am Jâtismarâ (know of my past births). You, too, are Jâtismarâ Tulsî. Śrî Kriṣṇa enjoyed you before. By

Râdhikâ's anger, you are now born in Bhârata. I was very eager to enjoy you then ; out of Râdhikâ's fear I could not.

72-87. Thus saying, Śankhachûḍa stopped. Then Tulasî gladly and smilingly replied :—" Such persons (like you) are famous in this world ; good women desire such husbands. Really, I am now defeated by you in argument. The man who is conquered by woman is very impure and blamed by the community. The Pitri Lokas, the Deva Lokas, and the Gandharbba Loka, too, look upon men, overpowered by women, as mean, despicable. Even father, mother, brother, etc., hate them mentally It is said in the Vedas that the impurities during birth and death are expiated by a ten days observances for the Brâhmaṇas, by twelve days observances for the Kṣattriyas, by fifteen days observances for the Vais'yas and by one month's observances for the Śûdras and other low castes. But the impurity of the man who is conquered by women cannot be expiated by any other means except (his dead body) being burned in the funeral pyre. The Pitris never accept willingly the piṇḍas and offerings of water (Tarpaṇas) offered by the women—conquered-men. So much so that the Devas even hesitate to accept flowers, water, etc., offered by them on their names. Those whose hearts are entirely subdued by men, do not acquire any fruits from their knowledge, Tapasyâ, Japam, five sacrifices, worship, learning and fame. I tested you to ascertain your strength in learning. It is highly advisable to choose one's husband by examining his merits and defects. Sin equivalent to the murder of a Brâhmin is committed if one gives in marriage one's daughter to one void of all qualifications, to an old man, to one who is ignorant, to a poor, illiterate, diseased, ugly, very angry, very harsh, lame, devoid of limbs, deaf, dumb, inanimate like, and who is impotent. If one gives in marriage a daughter to a young man of good character, learned, well qualified and of a peaceful temper, one acquires the fruits of performing ten horse sacrifices. If one nourishes a daughter and sells her out of greed for money, one falls to the Kumbhîpâka hell. That sinner drinks the urine and eats the excrements of that daughter, remaining in that hell. For a period equal to the fourteen Indra's life-periods they are bitten by worms and crows. At the expiry of this period, they will have to be born in this world of men as diseased persons. In their human births they will have to earn their livelihood by selling flesh and carrying flesh.

88-100. Thus saying, when Tulasî stopped, Brahmâ appeared on the scene and addressed Śankachûḍa :—" O Śankhachûḍa ! Why are you spending uselessly your time in vain talks with Tulasî ? Marry her soon by the Gândharba method. As you are a gem amongst males, so She is a gem amongst females. It is a very happy union between a humorus lover and a humorous beloved. O King! Who despises the great happiness when it is at one's hand! He who forsakes the pleasure is worse than a beast in this world. O Tulasî! And what for are you testing the nobly qualified person who is the tormentor of the Devas, Asuras and Dânavas. O Child! As Lakṣmî Devî is of Nârâyaṇa, as Râdhikâ is of Kriṣṇa; as is My Sâvitrî, as Bhava's is Bhavânî, as Boar's is Earth, as Yajna's is Dakṣîṇâ, Atri's Anasûyâ, Gautama's Ahalyâ, Moon's Rohiṇî, Brihaspati's Târâ, Manu's Śatarûpâ, Kandarpa's Rati, Kas'yapa's Aditi, Vas'iṣṭha's Arundhatî, Karddama's Devahûti, Fire's Svâhâ, Indra's Śachî, Gaṇes'a's Puṣṭi, Skanda's Devasenâ, and Dharma's Mûrti, so let you be the dear wife of Śaṅkhachûḍa. Let you remain with Śankhachûḍa, beautiful as he is, for a long time, and enjoy with him in various places as you like. When Śaṅkhachûḍa will quit his mortal frame, you would go to Goloka and enjoy easily with the two-armed Śrî Kriṣṇa, and in Vaikuṇṭha with the four-armed Kriṣṇa and with great gladness.

Here ends the Eighteenth Chapter of the Ninth Book on the union of Śankhachûḍa with Tulasî in the Mahâpurâṇam Śrî Mad Devî Bhâgavatam of 18,000 verses by Maharṣi Veda Vyâsa.

CHAPTER XIX.

1. Nârada said:—"O Bhagavan! Wonderful is the story that has been now recited by you. My ears are not satisfied. So tell me what happened afterwards."

2-94 Nârâyaṇa said:—"O Nârada! The Creator Brahmâ, blessing them, departed to His own abode. The Dânava married Tulaṣî under the Gandharba method. The celestial drums sounded and the flowers were showered. In the beautiful lovely house the Dânavendra, remained in perfect enjoyment. Tulaṣî, too, being busy with fresh intercourses, became almost mad after them. The chaste Tulasî and Śankhachûḍa both became deeply immersed in the ocean of bliss in their sexual union and began to enjoy sixty-four sorts of amorous sports. In the Śâstras on love affairs, all the connections of limbs with limbs that are described, as the lover and the loved desire, they both enjoyed these with perfect freedom and pleasure. The place was solitary; to add to it, the scenery was grand and lovely; so nothing remained untasted of the several tastes of amorous pleasures. On the banks of the river, in flower-gardens, they slept on the flower-beds smeared with sandal-paste, and enjoyed the amorous pleasures. Both were adorned with jewel ornaments; both were skilled in amorous practices; so no one desisted. The chaste Tulasî out of her nimbleness due to young age, easily stole into the heart of her husband. Śaṅkhachûḍa, too, a great expert in knowing other's amorous sentiments, attracted the heart of Tulasî. Tulasî obliterated the sandal marks from the breast of the King and the sign of tilak from his nose. The King also wiped away the dot of Sindur and Alakâ (vermillion) marks from Tulasî's forehead and put marks of nails on her round plump breasts. Tulasî also hurt the King's left side by her bracelets. Then the King bit the lips of Tulasî. Thus each one embraced the other, kissed each other and each one began to champoo the thighs, legs, etc. When both of them thus spent their time in amorous sports, they got up and began to dress themselves as they desired. Tulasî smeared Śaṅkhachûḍa's nose with red sandal-paste mixed with kunkum (saffron), smeared his body with sweet-scented sandal-paste, offered sweet-scented betels in his mouth, made him put on celestial garments (fireproof; brought from Fire) put unto his neck the wonderful garland of Pârijâta flowers, destructive of disease and old age, invaluable jewel rings on his hand. and offering him excellent gems, rare in the three worlds, said:—"O Lord! I am your maidservant" and uttering this repeatedly bowed down to the feet of her husband with devotion. She then got up and with smiling countenance began to look on his face with a steadfast gaze. The king Śaṅkhachûḍa then attracted his dear Tulasî to his breast and took off the veil fully from her face and began to look on that, next moment he kissed on her cheek and lips and gave her a pair of garments brought from the Varuṇa's house, a necklace of jewels, hard to get in the three worlds, the tinklets of Svâhâ, the wife of Agni, the Keyura (armlets) of the Sun's wife Chhâyâ, the two earrings of Rohiṇî, the wife of the Moon, the finger rings of Rati, the wife of Kâmadeva, and the wonderfully beautiful conch, given by Vis'va Karmâ, excellent bedding studded with pearls and jewels and various ornaments; and when he gave her all these things, he smiled. The king then put garlands on Tulasî's braid of hair, nicely variegated Alakâs on her cheek, three crescent lines of sweet-scented sandal paste within the Alakâr, dots of saffron all around that, the brillant Sindura mark looking like a flame, and red Altâ on the feet and toes; he then placed those feet on his breast and utterred repeatedly:—" I am your servant " and then held her on his breast. They then left the hermitage, in that state and began to travel in various places. In the Malaya mountain, in mountains after mountains, in solitary flower gardens, in the mountain caves, in beautiful sea-beaches, on the banks of the Puṣpabhadrâ river, cool with watery breeze, in various rivers and riversides, in Viṣpandana forest [illegible] with sweet songs of the birds of the vernal season. They then went from Viṣpandana forest to the Surasana forest, from the Surasana, forest to the Nandana forest. from the Nandana forest to the nice Chandana forests, from Chandana forest to Champaka, Ketakî ; Mâdhavî Kunda, Mâlatî, and Kumuda and lotus forests ; thence they went to the forest of desire gratifying trees (Kalpavrikṣa forest,) and Pârijâta trees. They then went to the solitary place Kânchan, thence to the Kânchî (forest) they then went to the Kiñjalaka forest, thence to the Kânchanâkar (the gold mine), thence to Kanchuka and various other forests echoed with the sweet sounds of cuckoos. There, on beds strewn with flowers and scented with sandal-paste they both enjoyed each other to their hearts' content and with great pleasure. But none of them, whether Śankhachûḍa or Tulasî, got quenched with their thirst. Rather their passions were inflamed like the fire on which clarified butter is poured (in sacrifices). The King of the Dânavas, then, brought Tulasî to his own kingdom and, there, in his own beautiful garden house, he incessantly enjoyed her. Thus the powerful king of the Dânavas passed away one Manvantara in the enjoyment of his kingdom. He spread his sway over the Devatâs, Asuras, Dânavas, Gandharbas, Kinnaras, and Râkṣasas. The Devas, dispossessed of their realms, wandered everywhere like beggars. At last they united in a body and went to the Brahmâ's assembly and there they began to cry and then related the whole history how the Dânava Śankhachûḍa oppressed them. Hearing all this, Brahmâ took them to Śankara and informed Him of the whole history of the case When Mahâdeva heard all this, He took them all to the highest place, Vaikuṇṭha devoid of old age and death. Going towards the first entrance of Nârâyana's, abode, they saw the gate-keepers watching the gate, taking their seats on jewel thrones. They all looked brilliant, clothed with the yellow garments, adorned with jewel ornaments, garlanded with forest flowers, all of Śyâma Sundara (dark blue, very beautiful) bodies. They were four-armed, holding on their hands conch, mace, discus and lotus ; sweet smile was on their faces and eyes beautiful like lotus leaves. On Brahmâ asking them for entrance to the assembly, they nodded their assent. He, then, accompanied by the Devas, passed one by one, sixteen gates and at last came before Nârâyaṇa. On reaching there, He saw that the assembly was completely filled with Devarṣis, and four-armed Nârâyaṇlike Pâriṣadas (attendants), decked with Kaustubha jewels. The sight of the Sabhâ (assembly) makes one think that the Moon has just arisen, shedding effulgent rays all round. By the will of S'rî Hari, excellent diamonds, invaluable gems and necklaces of gems and jewels were placed at various places. At other places rows of pearls were shedding their splendour and brilliance like the garlands of gems and jewels. At others, the mirrors were placed in a circle; and at various other places, the endless wonderful artistic picture lines were drawn. Again at other places, the jewels called *Padmarâgas* were artistically arranged as if the lotuses were there spreading their lustrous beauty all around. At many other places rows of steps were made of wonderful Syamantak jewels. All around the assembly, there were the excellent pillars, built of Indranîlam jewels. Over those pillars, sandal leaves strung on strings from pillar to pillar, were suspended. Golden jars, all brimful with water were located at various places. All around, the garlands of Pârijâta flowers were seen. The hall was decorated with sweet scented sandal trees, red like saffron and musk. Sweet scents were being emitted all round. The Vidyadhâris were dancing at places. The assembly hall measured one thousand Yojanas. Countless servants were engaged all over on various works. Brahmâ, Śankara, and the other Gods saw there Śrî Hari seated in the centre on an invaluable jewel throne, as a Moon looks surrounded by stars. There were the crown on His head, the ear-rings on His ears; garlands made of wild flowers were on his neck and His body was smeared all over with sandal paste and He was holding Kelipadma (a sort of lotus) in His hand. He was seeing, with a smiling countenance, the dancing and music before Him. He was full of peace, the Lord of Sarasvatî. Lakṣmî was holding gently His lotus feet and He was chewing the sweet scented betel offered by Her. Gangâ also was fanning Him devotedly with a white Châmara and the others were singing hymns to Him with their heads bent low with devotion. Brahmâ and the other Gods all bowed down to Him; their bodies were all filled with Pulaka (excessive joy causing hair stand on end); tears flowed from their eyes and their voices were choked out of emotion. The creator Brahmâ, then, with clasped hands informed Him, with head bowed down, of the whole history of Śankhachûḍa. Hearing this, the omniscient Hari, knowing the minds of all, smiled and spoke to Brahmâ all the interesting secrets:— "O Lotus born! I know all about S'ankhachûḍa. He was in his previous brith My great devotee, an energetic Gopa. Now I speak to you the ancient history of Goloka; hear. This story about Goloka is sin-destroying and highly meritorious. S'ankhachûḍa, in his previous birth was the Gopa Sudâmâ, My chief Pârisad (attendant). He has now become a Dânava on account of the dire curse pronounced by S'rî Râdhâ. One day when I went from My abode, accompanied by Virajâ Gopî, to the Râsa Mandala, My beloved Râdhâ, hearing this news from a maid servant, came up at once with Her whole host of Sakhis wrathful, to the Râsa Maṇḍalam (ball dance in Goloka) and, not being able to see Me, saw Virajâ turned into a river, She thought that I had disappeared. So She went back to Her own abode with Her Sakhis. But when I returned to the house with Sudâmâ, Râdhâ rebuked Me very much. I remained silent. But Sudâmâ could not bear and he rebuked Râdhâ in My presence, a thing quite intolerable to Her dignity! On hearing this rebuke, Râdhâ's eyes became red with anger and She immediately ordered Her Sakhis to drive him away. Sudâmâ began to tremble with fear. Immediately on Her command lakhs and lakhs of Sakhis got up immediately and drove that hot irresistible Sudâmâ away. Sudâmâ repeated his chafings and roarings. On hearing these, She cursed him ;—" You better be born in the womb of a Dânavi." Hearing the terrible curse, Sudâmâ bowed down to Me and went away crying ; then Râdhâ, who was all-mercy, became melted with mercy. And She prevented him repeatedly, not to go away. Râdhâ wept and told him, " O Child ! Wait. Where are you going ? No more you will have to go ; return." Thus saying She became very distressed. The Gopas and Gopis also began to weep. I then explaind to them. " In about half a moment Sudâmâ will come back, fufilling the conditions of the curse. O Sudâmâ ! Come here when the curse expires. " Then he appeased Râdhâ also. " Know that one moment (Kṣaṇ) in Goloka is equal to one Manvantara on earth. The Yogi Śaṅkhachûḍa, expert in Mâyâ and very powerful will soon return from the earth. Take this My weapon Śûla and go early to Bhârata. Śiva will slay the Dânava by this Śûlâstra. The Dânava holds always on his neck My auspicious Kavacha and will therefore become the conqueror of the universe. No one will be able to kill him as long as he holds the above Kavacha. So, first of all, I will go to him in the form of a Brâhmaṇa and ask from him the Kavacha. O Creator ! Thou also didst give him the boon that his death would occur when the chastity of of his wife would be destroyed. I will go and hold intercourse with his wife. Then his death will occur without fail. His wife after her death will come and become My dearest wife. Thus saying, Nârâyaṇa gave over to Mahâdeva the Śûlâstra. Then He went gladly to His inner compartments. On the other hand, Brahmâ and Rudra and the other Devas incarnated themselves in Bhârata.

Here ends the Nineteenth Chapter on the going of the Devas to Vaikuṇṭha after Tulasî's marriage with S'aṅkhachûḍa in the Mahâpurâṇam Śrî Mad Devî Bhâgavatam of 18,000 verses by Mahârṣi Veda Vyâsa.

CHAPTER XX.

1-21. Nârâyaṇa said :— Brahmâ, then putting S'iva to the task of killing S'aṅkhachûḍa went to His own abode. The other Devas returned to their homes. Here under the beautiful Baṭa tree, on the banks of the river Chandrabhâgâ, Mahâdeva pitched His big tent and encamped. Himself, to get the victory of the Devas. He, then, sent Chitraratha, the Lord of the Gandharbbas, as a messenger to S'aṅkhachûḍa, the Lord of the Dânavas. By the command of Mahâdeva, Chitraratha went to the city of the king of Daityas, more beautiful than Indra's place and more wealthy than the mansion of Kuvera. The city was five yojanas wide and twice as much in length. It was built of crystals of pearls and jewels. There were roadways on all sides. There were seven trenches, hard to be crossed, one after another, encircling the city. The city was built of countless rubies and gems, brilliant like flames. There were hundreds of roadways and markets and stalls, in the wonderful Vedis (raised platforms) built of jewels. All around were splendid palacial buildings of traders and merchantmen, filled with various articles There were hundreds and koṭis of beautiful buildings, adorned with various ornaments and built of variegated red stones looking like Sindûras. Thus he went on and saw, in the middle, the building of Sankhachûḍa, circular like the lunar sphere. Four ditches all filled with fiery flames, encircled one after another, his house. So the enemies could not in any way cross them ; but the friend could easily go there. On the top were seen turrets, built of jewels, rising high to the heavens. The gate-keepers were watching the twelve gates. In the centre were situated lakhs and lakhs of excellent jewel built houses. In every room there were jewelled steps and staircases and the pillars were all built of gems, and jewels, and pearls. Puṣpadanta (Chitraratha) saw all this and then went to the first gate and saw one terrible person, copper coloured, with tawny eyes, sitting with a trident in his hand and with a smiling countenance. He told he had come as a messenger and got his entrance. Thus Chitraratha went one after another to all the entries, not being prohibited at all though he told that he had come as a messenger on war service. The Gândharba reached one after another, the last door and said :— " O Door keeper !—Go quickly and inform the Lord of the Dânavas all about the impending war. When the messenger had spoken thus, the gate-keeper allowed him to go inside. Going inside, the Gandharba saw S'aṅkhachûḍa, of an excellent form, seated in the middle of the royal assembly, on a golden throne. One servant was holding on the king's head an umbrella, decked with divine excellent gems, the inner rod of the umbrella being made up of jewels, and decorated with expanded artificial flowers made of gems. The attendants were fanning him with beautiful white châmaras; he was nicely dressed, beautiful and lovely and adorned with jewel ornaments. He was nicely garlanded, and wore fine celestial garments. Three Koṭi Dânavas were surrounding him; and seven Koṭi Dânavas, all armed, were walking to and fro.

22-49. Puṣpadanta was thunderstruck when he saw thus, the Dânava, and he addressed him thus :— O King! I am a servant of Śiva; My name is Puṣpadanta; hear what Śiva has commanded me to tell you. "You better now give back, to the Devas, the rights that they had before" The Devas went to Śrî Hari and had taken His refuge. Śrî Hari gave over to Śiva one S'ûla weapon and asked the Devas to depart." "At present, the three eyed Deva is residing under the shade of a Baṭa tree on the banks of the Puṣpabhadrâ river. He told me to speak this to you, "Either give over to the Devas their rights, or fight with me." Please reply and I will speak to Him accordingly." Śakhachûḍa, hearing the messenger's words laughed and said "Tomorrow morning I will start, ready for war. Better go away to-day." The messenger went back to Śiva and replied to Him accordingly. In the meantime the following personages joined Śiva and remained seated on excellent aerial cars, built of jewels and gems. The following were the persons :—Skanda, Vîrabhadra, Nandî, Mahâkâla, Subhadraka, Vis'âlâkṣa, Bâṇa, Pingalâkṣa, Vikampana, Virûpa, Vikriti, Maṇibhadra, Vâskâla, Kapilâkṣa, Dîrgha Daṇgṣṭra, Vikaṭa, Tâmralochana, Kâlâkaṇṭha, Balîbhadra, Kâlajîhba, Kuṭîchara, Balonmatta, Raṇas'lâghî, Durjaya, Durgama, (these eight Bhairavas), eleven Rudras, eight Vasus, Indra, the twelve Âdityas, fire, moon, Vis'vakarmâ, the two As'vins, Kuvera, Yama, Jayanta, Nala, Kûbara. Vâyu, Varuṇa, Budha, Mangala, Dharma, Śanî, Is'âna, the powerful Kâmadeva. Ugradamṣṭrâ, Ugrachaṇḍâ, Koṭarâ, Kaiṭabhî, and the eight armed terrible Devî Bhadrakâlî. Kâlî wore the bloody red clothings and She smeared red sandal paste all over Her body.

Dancing, laughing; singing songs in tune, very jolly, She bids Her devotees discard all fear, and terrifies the enemies. Her lip is terrible, lolling, and extends to one Yojana. On Her eight arms She holds conch, disc, mace, lotus, axe, skin, bow and arrows. She was holding in Her hands, the bowl shaped human skull; that was very deep and one Yojana wide. Her trident reached up to the Heavens; Her weapon called S'akti (dart) extended to one Yojana. Besides there were Mudgara (mace), Musala (club), Vajra (thunderbolt), Kheṭa, (club), brilliant Phalaka (shield), the Vaiṣṇava weapon, the Varuṇa weapon, the Âgneyâstra (the fire weapon), Nâgapâs'a (the noose of serpents), the Nârâyaṇâstra, the Gandharva's weapons, the Brahmâ's weapons, the Gaḍuḍâstram, the Pârjanayâstram, the Pâs'upatâstram, the Jrimbhaṇâstram the Pârvatâstram, the Mahes'varâstram, the Vâyavyâstram, and the Sanmohanam rod and various other infallible divine weapons. Besides hundreds of other divine weapons were with Her. Three Koṭis of Yoginis and three Koṭis and a half of terrible Dâkinîs were attending Bhadrakâlî. Bhûtas, (demons) Pretas, Pis'âchas, Kusmâṇḍas, Brahma Râkṣasas, Râkhsasas, Vetâlas, Yakṣas and Kinnaras also were there in countless numbers. At this time Kârtikeya came there and bowed down to his father Mahâdeva. He asked him to take his seat on His left side and asked him to help. Then the army remained there in military array. On the other hand, when Śiva's messenger departed, Śankhachûḍa went to the zenana and informed Tulasî of the news of an impending war. No sooner She heard than her throat and lips and palate became dried. She then with a sorrowful heart spoke in sweet words:—"O my Lord! O my Friend! O the Ruler of My life! Wait for a moment and take your seat on My heart. Instil life in Me for a moment. Satisfy My desire of human birth. Let me behold you fully so that my eyes be satisfied. My breath is now very agitated. I saw by the end of the night one bad dream. Therefore I feel an internal burning. Thus at the words of Tulasî, the king S'ankhachûḍa finished his meals and began to address her, in good and true words, beneficent to her:—" O My Lady! It is Kâla (the time) that brings out these various combinations by which the Karmic fruit is enjoyed; it is Kâla that awards auspicious and inauspicious things; this Kâla is the Sole Master to impart pain, fear, and good and bad things.

54-84. Trees grow up in time; their branches, etc., come out in time; flowers appear in time and fruits come out in time. Fruits are ripened in time and after giving the fruits, they die out also in time. O Fair One! The universe comes into existence in time and dies away in time. The Creator, Preserver, and Destroyer of the universe, are creating, preserving and destroying the worlds with the help of time. Time guides them in every way. But the Highest Prakriti is the God of Brahmâ, Viṣṇu, and Mahes'a (i. e., the Creatrix of Time). This Highest Prakriti, the Highest God is creating, preserving and destroying this universe. She makes the Time dance. By Her mere Will, She has converted Her inseparable Prakriti into Mâyâ and is thus creating all things, moving and unmoving. She is the Ruler of all; the Form of all, and She is the Highest God. By Her is being done this creation of persons by persons, this preservation of persons by persons, and this destruction of persons by persons. So you better now take refuge of the Highest Lord. Know it is by Her command the wind is blowing, by Her command the Sun is giving heat in due time, by Her command Indra is showering rains; by Her command, Death is striding over the beings; by Her command fire is burning all things and by Her command the cooling Moon is revolving. She is the Death of death, the Time of time, Yama of yama (the God of death), the Fire of fire and the Destroyer of the destroyer. So take Her refuge. You cannot find and fix who is whose friend in the world; so pray to Her, the Highest God, Who is the Friend of All. Oh! Who am I? And who are you either? The Creator is the combiner of us two and so He will dissociate us two by our Karma. When difficulty arises, the ignorant fools become overwhelmed with sorrow; but the intelligent Pundits do not get at all deluded or become distressed. By the Wheel of Time, the beings are led sometimes into happiness; sometimes into pain. You will certainly get Nârâyaṇa for your husband; for which you practised Tapas before, in the hermitage of Vadari (the source of the Ganges, the feet of Viṣṇu). I pleased Brahmâ by my Tapasyâ and have, by his boon, got you as my wife. But the object for which you did your Tapasyâ, that you may get Hari as your husband, will certainly be fulfilled. You will get Gobinda in Vrindâbana and in the region of Goloka. I will also go there when I forsake this, my Demon body. Now I am talking with you here; afterwards we will meet again in the region of Goloka. By the curse of Râdhikâ, I have come to this Bhârata, hard to be attained. You, too, will quit this body and, assuming the divine form will go to S'rî Hari. So, O Beloved! You need not be sorry." O Muni! Thus these conversations took them the whole day and led them to the evening time. The king of the demons, S'ankhachûḍa then slept with Tulasî on a nicely decorated bed, strewn with flowers, and smeared with sandal paste, in the Ratna Mandir (temple built of jewels.) This jewel temple was adorned with various wealth and riches. The jewel lamps were lighted. Śankhachûḍa passed the night with his wife in various sports. The thin bellied Tulasî was weeping with a very sorrowful heart, without having taken any food. The king, who knew the reality of existence, took her to his breast and appeased her in various ways. What religious instructions he had received in Bhândîra forest from S'rî Kriṣṇa, those Tattvas, capable to destroy all sorrows and delusions, he now spoke carefully to Tulasî. Then Tulasî's joy knew no bounds. She then began to consider everything as transient and began to play with a gladdened heart. Both became drowned in the ocean of bliss; and the bodies of both of them were filled with joy and the hairs stood on their ends. Both of them, then, desirous to have amorous sports, joined themselves and became like Ardhanâris'vars and so one body. As Tulasî considered S'ankhachûḍa, to be her lord, so the Dânava King considered Tulasî the darling of his life. They became senseless with pleasureable feelings arising out of their amorous intercourses. Next moment they regained their consciousness and both began to converse on amorous matters. Thus both spent their time sometimes in sweet conversations, sometimes laughing and joking, sometimes maddened with amorous sentiments. As S'ankhachûḍa was clever in amorous affairs, so Tulasî was very expert. So none felt satiated with love affairs and no one was defeated by the other.

Here ends the Twentieth Chapter of the Ninth Book on the war preparations of S'ankhachûḍa with the Devas in the Mâhapurâṇam Srî Mad Devî Bhâgavatam of 18,000 verses by Mahârṣi Veda Vyâsa.

CHAPTER XXI.

1-33. S'rî Nârâyaṇa spoke:—Then the Dânava, the devotee of S'rî Krisṇa, got up from his flower strewn bed, meditating on S'rî Krisṇa, early in the morning time, at the Brahma Muhûrta. Quitting his night dress, he took his bath in pure water and put on a fresh washed clothing. He then put the bright Tilak mark on his forehead and, performing the daily necessary worship, he worshipped his Iṣṭa Devatâ (The Deity doing good to him). He then saw the auspicious things such as curd, ghee, honey, fried rice, etc., and distributed as usual, to the Brâhmaṇás the best jewels, pearls, clothing and gold. Then for his marching to turn out auspicious, he gave at the feet of his Guru Deva priceless gems, jewels, pearls, diamonds, etc., and finally he gave to the poor Brâhmiṇs with great gladness, elephants, horses, wealth, thousands of stores, two lâkhs of cities and one hundred koṭis of villages. He then gave over to his son, the charge of his kingdom and of his wife, and all the dominions, wealth, property, all the servants and maid servants, all the stores and conveyances. He dressed himself for the war and took up bows and arrows and arrow cases. By the command of the King, the armies began to gather. Three lakhs of horses, one lakh elephants, one ayuta chariots, three Koṭis of bowmen, three Koṭis armoured soldiers and three Koṭis of trident holders got themselves ready. Then the King counted his forces and appointed one Commander-in-Chief, (Mahâratha), skilled in arts of warfare, over the whole army. Thus the generals were appointed over the three lakh Akṣauhiṇî forces and their provisions were collected by three hundred Akṣauhiṇî men. He, then, thinking of Śrî Hari, started for war, accompanied by his vast army. *Note*:—One Akṣauhiṇî consists of a large army consisting of 21870 chariots, as many elephants, 65,610 horses, and 109,350 foot). He then mounted on a chariot built of excellent jewels and, headed by his Guru and all his other elders, went to S'ankara. O Nârada! Bhagavân Mahâdeva was at that time, staying on the banks of Puṣpabhadrâ. That place was Siddhâs'rama (the hermitage where the yogic successes had been obtained and can easily be acquired in future for the Siddhas as well a Siddha Kṣettra.) It was the place where the Muni Kapila practised Tapasyâ, in the holy land of Bhârata. It was bounded on the east by the western ocean, on the west by the Malaya mountain, on the south, by the S'ri Śaila mountain and on the north by the Gandha Mâdana Mountain. It was five yojanas wide and one hundred times as long. This auspicious river in Bhârata yields great religious merits and is always full of clear, sparkling running water. She is the favourite wife of the Salt Ocean and She is very blessed. Issuing from S'arâvatî Himâlayâs, She drops into the ocean. Keeping the river Gomatî (Goomti) by her left; She falls into the west ocean. Śankhachûḍa, arriving there, saw Mahâdeva under a Peepul tree near its root with a smiling countenance, like one Koṭi Suns seated in a yogic posture. His colour was white like a pure crystal; as if the Fire of Brahma was emitting from every pore of His body (burning with Brahma-Teja); He was wearing the tiger skin and holding the trident and axe. He dispels the fear of death of His Bhaktas; His face is quite calm. He, the Lord of Gauri, is the Giver of the fruits of Tapasyâ and of all sorts of wealth and prosperity. The smiling face of Âs'utoṣa (one who is pleased quickly) is always thinking of the welfare of the Bhaktas; He is the Lord of the Universe, the Seed of the universe, the All-form (all-pervading), and the Progenitor of the universe. He is omnipresent, All pervading, the Best in this universe, the Destroyer of this universe, the Cause of all causes, and the Saviour from the hells. He is the Awakener and Bestower of Knowledge, the Seed of all knowledges, and He Himself is of the nature of Knowledge and Bliss. Seeing that Eternal Puruṣa, the King of the Dânavas at once descended from his chariot and bowed down with devotion to Him and to Bhadra Kâlî on His left and and to Kârtikeya on his front. The other attendants did the same.—S'ankara, Bhadra Kali and Skanda all blessed him. Nandîs'vara and others got up from their seats on seeing the Dânava King and began to talk with each other on that subject. The King addressed S'iva and sat by Him. Bhagavân Mahâdeva, the Tranquil Self, then, spoke to him, thus:—"O King! Brahmâ, the knower of Dharma and the Creator of the world, is the Father of Dharma, The religious Marîchi, a devotee of Viṣṇu, is the son of Brahmâ. The religious Prajâpati Kas'yapa is also the Brahmâ's son. Dakṣa gladly gave over to Kas'yapa in marriage, his thirteen daughters. Danu, fortunate and chaste, is also one of them.

34-64. Danu had forty sons, all spirited and known as Dânavas. The powerful Viprachitti was the prominent amongst them. Viprachitti's son was Dambha, self controlled and very much devoted to Viṣṇu. So much so that for one lakh years he recited the Viṣṇu mantra at Puṣkara. His Guru (spiritual teacher) was S'ukrâchârya; and, by his advice, he recited the mantra of Śrî Kriṣṇa, the Highest Self. He got you as his son, devoted to Kriṣṇa. In your former birth, you were the chief attendant Gopa (cow-herd) of Kriṣṇa. You were very religious. Now, by Râdhikâ's curse, you are born in Bhârata, as the Lord of the Dânavas powerful, heroic, valorous, and chivalrous. All the things from Brahmâ down to a blade of grass, the Vaiṣṇavas regard as very trifling; even if they get Sâlokya, Sârṣṭi, Sâyujya and Sâmîpya of Hari, they do not care a straw for that. Without serving Hari, they do not accept those things, even if those are thrust on them. Even Brahmahood and immortality, the Vaiṣṇavas count for nothing. They want to serve Hari (Sevâ-bhâva). Indrahood, Manuhood, they do not care. You, too, are a real Kriṣṇa Bhakta. So what do you care for those things that belong to the Devas, that are something like false to you. Give back to the Devas their kingdoms thus and please Me. Let the Devas remain in their own places and let you enjoy your kingdom happily. No need now for further quarrels. Think that you all belong to the same Kas'yapa's family. The sins that are incurred, for example, the murder of a Brâhmin, etc., are not even one-sixteenth of the sins incurred by hostilities amongst the relatives. If, O King! You think that by giving away to the Devas their possessions, your property will be diminished, then think that no one's days pass ever in one and the same condition. Whenever Prakriti is dissolved, Brahmâ also vanishes. Again He appears by the Will of God. This occurs always. True, that knowledge is increased by true Tapasyâ; but memory fails then. This is certain. He who is the creator of this world, does his work of creation gradually by the help of his Knowledge-power (Jñâna-S'akti). In the Satya Yuga, Dharma reigns in full; in the Tretâ Yuga, one quarter is diminished; again in the Dvâpara only one-half remains. And in the Kali Yuga, only one quarter remains. Thus Dharma gets increase and decrease. At the end of the

Kali, the Dharma will be seen very feeble as the phase of the Moon is seen very thin on the Dark Moon night. See, again, the Sun is very powerful in summer ; not so in winter. At midday the Sun is very hot ; it does not remain so in the morning and evening ? The Sun rises at one time ; then he is considered as young ; at another time he becomes very powerful and at another time he goes down. Again in times of distress (i. e., during the cloudy days) the Sun gets entirely obscured. When the Moon is devoured by Râhû (in the Lunar Eclipse), the Moon quivers. Again when the Moon becomes liberated (i.e., when the eclipse passes away) She becomes bright again. In the Full-Moon night She becomes full but She does not remain so always. In the Dark fortnight She wanes every day. In the bright fortnight She waxes every day. In the bright fortnight, the Moon becomes healthy and prosperous and in the dark fortnight, the Moon becomes thinner and thinner as if attacked with consumption. In the time of eclipse She becomes pale and in the cloudy weather, She is obscured. Thus the Moon also becomes powerful at one time and weak and pale at another time. Vali now resides in Pâtâla, having lost all his fortunes ; but, at some other time, he will become Devendra (the Lord of the Devas). This earth becomes at one time covered with grains and the resting-place of all beings ; and, at another time, She becomes immersed under water. This universe appears at one time and disappears at another. Every thing, moving or non-moving, sometimes appears and again, at another time, disappears. Only Brahma, the Highest Self, remains the same. By His grace, I have got the name Mrityunjaya (the Conqueror of Death). I, too, am witnessing many Prâkritik dissolutions, I witnessed repeatedly many dissolutions and will in future, witness many dissolutions. The Paramâtman becomes of the nature of Prakriti. Again it is He that is the Puruṣa (male principle). He is the Self ; He is the individual soul (Jîva). He thus assumes various forms. And, again, Lo ! He is beyond all forms ! He who always repeats His Name and sings His Glory, can conquer, at some occasion, death. He is not to come under the sway of this brith, death, disease, old age and fear. He has made Brahmâ the Creator, Viṣṇu the Preserver and Me the Destroyer. By His Will, we are possessed of these influences and powers. O King ! Having deputed Kâla, Agni and Rudra, to do the destruction work, I Myself repeat only His name and sing His glory, day and night, incessantly. My name is, on that account, Mrityunjaya. By His Knowlege Power, I am fearless. Death flies away fast from Me as serpents fly away at the sight of Garûḍa, the Vinatâ's son. O Nârada ! Thus saying, Śambhu, the Lord of all, the Progenitor of all, remained silent. Hearing the above words of Śambhu, the King thanked Mahâdeva again and again and spoke in sweet humble words.

65-74. Śaukhachûḍa said:—"The words spoken by Thee are quite true. Still I am speaking a few words. Kindly hear." Thou hast spoken just now that very great sins are incurred by kindred hostilities. How is it, then, that He robbed Vali of his whole possessions and sent him down into Pâtâla.? Gadâdhara Viṣṇu could not recover Vali's glory. But I have done that. Why did the Devas kill Hiraṇyâkṣa and Hiranyâkas'ipu, S'ûmbha and the other Dânavas? In by gone days, we laboured hard when the nectar was obtained out of the churning of the ocean; but the best fruit was reaped by the Devas only. However, all these point that this universe is but the mere sporting ground of Paramâtman. Who has become of the nature of Prakriti (the polarities of the one and the same current to produce electric effects). Whomsoever He grants glory and fortune, he only gets that. The quarrel of the Devas and the Dânavas is eternal, Victory and defeat come to both the parties alternately. So it is not proper for Thee to come here in this hostility. For Thou art the God, of the nature of the Highest Self. Before Thee, we both are equal So it is a matter of shame, no doubt, for Thee to stand up against us in favour of the gods. The glory and fame that will result to Thee, if Thou art victorious, will not be so much as it will be if we get the victory. On the contrary the inglory and infamy that will result to Thee if Thou dost get dire defeat will be inconceivably much more than what would come to us if we are defeated. (For we are low and Thou art Great.)

75-79. Mahâdeva laughed very much when he heard the Dânava's words and replied:—"O King! You are descended from the Brâhmin family. So what shame shall I incur if I get defeat in this fighting against you. In former days, the fight took place between Madhu and Kaiṭabha; again between Hiranya Kas'ipu and Hiraṇyâkṣa and S'rî Hari. I also fought with the Asura Tripurâ. Again the serious fight took place also between S'umbha and the other Daityas and the Highest Prakriti Devî, the Ruler of all, and the Progenitrix of all and the Destructrix of all. And, then, you were the Pâriṣada attendant of Śrî Kriṣṇa, the Highest Self.

Note:—Śrî Kriṣṇa is the Eternal Puruṣa beyond the Guṇas. He creates Prakriti. All the creation is effected by Him. He is the Master of all the Śaktis. These Śaktis come from Him and go unto Him. Śrî Kriṣṇa plays with these Saktis, *these lines of Forces*, very powerful and terrible, indeed, that go to create, preserve and destroy the whole universe. These Lines of Forces have their three properties:—(1) Origin; (2) direction and (3) magnitude. And finally they come back to their origin. This makes one Kalpa, one Life, one Moment, one in the Full One. The Guṇas come out of these Śaktis, these Lines of Forces. Śrî Kriṣṇa is the Great Reservoir, the Great Centre of Forces, Powerful, Lovely and Terrible. All these events as described here, appear in the intermediate stages when the Fourth Dimension passes into the Third Dimension, etc. The Fourth Dimension does not at once turn out into the Third Dimension but it takes place by degrees. This explains our dreams, visions, etc. which, if seen when the mind is pure, turn out to be true.

80-82. So the Daityas, that were killed before, cannot be compared with you. Then why shall I feel shame in fighting against you? I am sent here by Srî Hari for saving the Devas. So either give back to the Devas their possessions, or fight with Me. No need in speaking thus quite useless talks O Nârada! Thus speaking, Bhagavân Śankara remained silent. Śankhachûḍa got up at once with his ministers.

Here ends the Twenty-first Chapter in the Ninth Book on the meeting of Mahâdeva and Śankhachûḍa for an encounter in conflict in the Mahâpurâṇam Srî Mad Devî Bhâgavatam of 18,000 verses by Maharṣi Veda Vyâsa.

CHAPTER XXII.

1-75 Śrî Nârâyaṇa spoke:—" Then the King of the Dânavas, very powerful, bowed down to Mahâdeva and ascended on the chariot with his ministers. Mahâdeva gave orders to His army to be ready at once. So Śankhachûḍa did. Terrible fight then ensued between Mahendra and Vriṣaparvâ, Bhâskara and Viprachitti, Nis'âkara and Dambha, between Kâla and Kâles'vara, between Fire and Gokarṇa, Kuvera and Kâlakeya between Vis'vakarmâ and Mâyâ, between Mrityu and Bhayamkar between Yama and Samhâra, between Varuṇa and Vikamka, between Budha and Dhritapriṣṭha, between Śani and Raktâkṣa, Jayanta and Ratnasâra, between the Vasus and Varchasas, between the two As'vin Kumâras and Dîptimân, between Nalakûbara and Dhûmra, between Dharma and Dhurandhara, between Maṅgala and Uṣâkṣa, Bhânu and Śovâkara, between Kandarpa and Piṭhara, between the eleven Âdityas and Godhâmukha, Chûrṇa and Khaḍgadhvaja, Kañchîmukha and Piṇḍa Dhûmra and Nandî, between Vis'va and Palâs'a, between the eleven Rudras and the eleven Bhayamkaras, between Ugrachaṇḍâ and the other Mahâmâris and Nandîs'vara and the other Dânavas. The battlefield, then, assumed a grim aspect, as if the time of Dissolution had come. Bhagavân Mahâdeva sat under the Vaṭa (peepul) tree with Kârtikeya and Bhadrakâlî. Śankhachûḍa, decked with his jewel ornaments, sat on th jewel throne, surrounded by koṭis and koṭis of Dânavas. The Śankara's army got defeated at the hands of the Dânavas. The Devas, with cuts and wounds on their bodies, fled from the battlefield, terrified. Kârtikeya gave words "Do'nt fear" to the Devas and excited them. Only Skanda resisted the Dânava forces In one moment he slew one hundred Akṣauhiṇî Dânava forces. The lotus eyed Kâlî also engaged in killing the Asuras. She became very angry and no sooner did She slay the Asura forces, than She began to drink their blood. She easily slew with Her one hand and at every time put into Her mouth ten lakhs, and hundred lakhs and Koṭis and Koṭis of elephants. Thousands and thousands of headless bodies (Kavandhas) came to be witnessed in the field. The bodies of the Dânavas were all cut and wounded by the arrows of Kârtikeya. They were all terrified and fled away. Only Vriṣaparvâ, Viprachitti, Dambha, and Vikamkaṇah remained fighting with Skanda with an heroic valour. Mahâmârî, too, did not shew his back and he fought out vigorously. By and by they all became very much confused and distressed; but they did not turn their backs. Seeing this terrible fight of Skanda, the Devas began to shower flowers. The killing of the Dânavas looked like a Prâkritik Dissolution. Śankhachûḍa, then, began to shoot arrows from his chariot.

The shooting of arrows by the king seemed as if rains were being poured in by the clouds Everything became pitch dark. Fires only were seen emitting their golden tongues The Devas, Nandîs'vara and others, fled away, terrified Only Kârtikeya remained in the battlefield. Then Śankhachûḍa began to throw terribly showers and showers of mountains, snakes, stones, and trees. So much so, that Kârtikeya was covered by them as the Sun becomes obscured by fog. The Demon King cut off the weighty quiver and the pedestal of Skanda and broke His chariot. By the divine weapons of the Dânava, the peacock (the vehicle) of Kârtikeya became exhausted. Kârtikeya threw one Śakti (weapon) on the breast of the Dânava; but before it fell, the Dânava cut off that, lustrous like the Sun and, in return, darted his Śakti. By that stroke, Kârtikeya became stunned for a moment; but he immediately regained his consciousness. He then took up the quiver that Bhagavân Viṣṇu gave him before and many other weapons; and ascending on another chariot, built of jewels, began to fight out violently and valiantly. Getting angry, he resisted all those showers of snakes, mountains and trees by his divine weapons. He resisted fire by his watery (Pâryannya) weapon. Then He cut off easily Śankhachûḍa's chariot, bow, armour, charioteer, and his bright crown and he threw on his breast one blazing Śakti of white colour. The Dânavendra fell unconscious; but, at the next moment, he regained his consciousness quickly, mounted on another chariot and took a fresh quiver. The Dânava was the foremost in his magic powers. He, by his power of Mâyâ, made a shower of arrows so much so that

Kârtikeya became completely covered by that multitude of arrows. Then the Dânava took one invincible Śakti, lustrous like one hundred Suns. It seemed that flames of fire were licking high as if the Disolution Time had come aright. Inflamed by anger, the Dânava threw that Śakti on Kârtikeya. It seemed, then, that a burning mass of fire fell on him. The powerful Kârtikeya became senseless. Bhadrakâlî immediately took Him on Her lap and carried him before S'iva. S'iva easily restored him to his life by his knowledge-power and gave him the indomitable strength. He then got up in full vigour. Bhadrakâlî went to the field to see the Kârtikeya's forces. Nandîs'vara and other heroes, the Devas, Gandharbas, Yakṣas, Râkṣasas and Kinnaras followed Her. Hundreds of war drums were sounded and hundreds of persons carried Madhu (wine). Going to the battle-ground, She gave a war-cry. The Dânava forces got fainted by that cry. Bhadrakâlî shouted aloud in auspicious peals after peals of laughter, Then She drank Madhu and danced in the battlefield. Ugra Damṣṭrâ, Ugrachaṇḍâ, Koṭavî, the Yoginîs, Dâkinîs, and the Devas all drank Madhu (wine). Seeing Kâlî in the battlefield, S'ankhachûḍa came up again and imparted the spirit of Fearlessnes to the Daityas, trembling with fear. Bhadrâkâlî projected, then, the Fire weapon, flaming like the Great Disolution Fire; but the king quickly put out that by the Watery weapon. Kâlî then projected the very violent and wondertul Varuṇâstra The Dânava cut off that easily with Gandharbâstra. Kâlî then threw the flame-like Mâhes'varâstra. The king made it futile by the Vaiṣṇavâstra. Then the Devî purifying the Nârâyaṇâstra with the mantra, threw it on the king. At this the king instantly alighted from his chariot and bowed down to it. The Nârâyaṇâstra rose high up like the Dissolution Fire. S'ankhachûḍa fell prostrate on the ground with devotion. The Devî threw, then, the Brahmâstra, purifying it with Mantra. But it was rendered futile by the Dânava's Brahmâstra. The Devî again shot the divine weapons purifying them with mantras; but they also were nullified by the divine weapons of the Dânava. Then Bhadrakâlî threw one Śakti extending to one Yojana. The Daitya cut it to pieces by his divine weapon. The Devî, then, being very much enraged, became ready to throw Pâs'upata Astra, when the Incorpereal Voice was heard from the Heavens, prohibiting Her, and saying "O Devî! The high-souled Dânava would not be killed by the Pâs'upata weapon. For Brahmâ granted him this boon that until the Viṣṇu's Kavacha will remain on his neck and until his wife's chastity be not violated, old age and death will not be able to touch him." Hearing this Celestial Voice, the Devî at once desisted. But She out of hunger, devoured hundreds and lakhs of Dânavas. The terrible Devî Kâlî, then, went with great speed to devour Śankhachûḍa but the Dânava resisted Her by his sharp divine weapons. The Devî then threw on him a powerful axe, lustrous like a summer Sun; but the Dânava cut it to pieces by his divine weapon. The Devî seeing this, became very angry and proceeded to devour him; but the Dânava King, the Lord of all Siddhis, expanded his body. At this, Kâli became violently angry and assuming a terrific appearance, went quickly and with the blow of one fist, broke his chariot and dropped down the charioteer. Then she hurled on the Asura one Śûla weapon, blazing like a Pralaya Fire. Śankhachûḍa easily held that by his left hand. The Devî became angry and struck the Dânava with Her fist; the Daitya's head reeled, and, rolling, he fell unconscious for a moment. Next moment regaining his consciousness he got up. But he did not fight hand to hand with the Devî. Rather he bowed down to Her. The weapons that the Devî threw afterwards were partly cut down by the Dânava and partly taken up by him and absorbed in him and thus rendered futile. Then Bhadrakâli caught hold of the Dânava and whirling him round and round threw him aloft. Then the powerful Śankha chûḍa fell down on the ground from high with great force; he immediately got up and bowed down to Her. He then gladly ascended on his beautiful chariot, built of excellent jewels. He did not feel any fatigue with the war and went on fighting. Then the Devî Bhadrakâli, feeling hungry began to drink the blood of the Dânavas and ate the fat and flesh. She came before Mahâdeva and described to Him the whole history of the warfare from beginning to end. Hearing the killing of the Dânavas, Mahâdeva began to laugh. She went on saying "The Dânavas that got out of my mouth while I was chewing them, are the only ones that are living. This number will be about one lâkh. And when I took up the Pâs'upata weapon to kill the Dânava, the Incorporeal Celestial Voice spoke: —" He is invulnerable by you." But the very powerful Dânava did no more fling any weapon on Me. He simply cut to pieces those that I threw on him.

Here ends the Twenty-Second Chapter in the Ninth Book on the fight between the Devas and Śankhachûḍa in the Mahâpurâṇam Śrî Mad Devî Bhâgavatam of 18,000 verses by Maharṣi Veda Vyâsa.

CHAPTER XXIII.

1-6. Nârâyaṇa said: --Śiva, versed in the knowledge of the Highest Reality, hearing all this, went himself with His whole host to the battle. Seeing Him, Sânkhachûḍa alighted from his chariot and fell prostrate before him. With great force he got up and, quickly putting on his armour, he took up his huge and heavy bow case. Then a great fight ensued between

Śiva and S'ankhachûḍa for full one hundred years but there was no defeat nor victory on either side. The result was stalemate. Both of them, Bhagavân and the Dânava quitted their weapons. Sankhachûḍa, remained on his chariot and Mahâdeva rode on His Bull. Hundreds and hundreds of Dânavas were slain. But extraordinarily endowed with divine power, S'ambhu restored to life all those of His party that were slain.

7-30. In the meanwhile, an aged Brâhmaṇa, very distressed in his appearence, came to the battlefield and asked S'ankhachûḍa, the King of Dânavas :—" O King ! Grant me what I beg of you ; you give away in charity all sorts of wealth and riches ; give me also what I desire ; give me, a Brâhmiṇ, something also. I am a quiet peaceable aged Brâhmiṇ, very very thirsty. Make your Promise first and then I will speak to you what I desire. (*Note.*—The Brâhmiṇs only are fit for receiving frauds and cheatings). The King S'ankachûḍa, with a gracious countenance and pleasing eyes swore before him that He would give him what he would desire. Then the Brâhmiṇ spoke to the King with great affection and Mâyâ :—" I am desirous of your Kavacha (amulet)." The King, then, gave him the Kavacha (the amulet, mantra written on a Bhurja bark and located in a golden cup). Bhagavân Hari (in the form of that Brâhmiṇ) took that Kavacha and, assuming the form of Śankhchûḍa came to Tulasî. Coming there, He made His Mâyâ (magic) mainfest and held sexual intercourse with her. At this time Mahâdeva took up the Hari's trident-aiming at the king of the Dânavas. The trident looked like the Mid-day Sun of summer, flaming like a Pralaya fire. It looked irresistible and invincible as if quite powerful to kill the enemies. In brilliance it equalled the Sudars'an Chakra (disc) and it was the chief of all the weapons. No other body than Śiva and Kes'ava could weild such a weapon. And everybody feared that but Śiva and Kes'ava. In length it was one thousand Dhanus and in width it was one hundred hands. It seemed lively, of the nature of Brahma, eternal and not capable to be noticed, whence and how it proceeded. The weapon could destroy, by its own free Lîlâ (Will) all the worlds. When Śiva held it aloft and amining at Śankhachûḍa, He hurled it on him, the King of the Demons quitted his bows and arrows and with mind collected in a yoga posture, began to meditate on the lotus-feet of Śrî Krisṇa with great devotion. At that moment, the trident, whirling round fell on Śankhachûḍa and easily burnt him and his chariot to ashes. He, then, assuming the form of a two-armed Gopa, full of youth, divine, ornamented with jewels, holding flute, mounted on a Divine Chariot, surrounded by koṭis and koṭis of Gopas who came there from the region of Goloka, whose bodies were built up of excellent jewels, and Śankhachûḍa then went up to the Heavens (Goloka, where Śrî Brindâbana is located in the middle). He went to Vrindâban, full of Rasas (sentiments) and bowed down at the lotus feet of Râdhâ Kriṣṇa with devotion. Both of them were filled with love when they saw Sudâmâ, and, with a gracious countenance and joyful eyes, they took him on their laps. On the other hand the Śûla weapon came with force and gladness back again to Kriṣṇa The bones of Śankhachûḍa, O Narada ! were transformed into conch-shells. These conch-shells are always considered very sacred and auspicious in the worship of the Devas. The water in the conch-shell is also very holy and pleasing to the Devas. What more than this, that the water in the conch-shell is as holy as the water of any Tîrtha. This water can be offered to all the Gods but not to Śiva. Wherever the conch-shell is blown, there Lakṣmî abides with great pleasure. If bathing be done with conch-shell water, it is equivalent to taking bath in all the Tîrthas. Bhagavân Harî resides direct in the conch-shell. Where Śankha is placed, there Hari resides. Lakṣmî also resides there and all inauspicious things fly away from there. Where the females and Śûdras blow the Śankhas, Lakṣmî then gets vexed and, out of terror, She goes away to other places. O Nârada ! Mahâdeva, after killing the Dânava, went to His own abode. When He gladly went away on His Vehicle, on the Bull's back, with His whole host, all the other Devas went to their respective places with great gladness. Celestial drums were sounded in the Heavens. The Gandharbas and the Kinnaras began to sing songs. And showers of flowers were strewn on Śiva's head. All the Munis and Devas and their chiefs began to chant hymns to Him.

Here ends the Twenty-Third Chapter of the Ninth Book on the killing of Śankhachûḍa in Śrî Mad Devî Bhâgavtam of 18,000 verses by Maharṣi Veda Vyâsa.

CHAPTER XXIV.

1. Nârada said:—How did Nârâyaṇa impregnate Tulasî ? Kindly describe all that in detail.

2-11. Nârâyaṇa said :—For accomplishing the ends of the Devas, Bhagavân Hari assumed the Vaiṣṇavî Mâyâ, took the Kavacha from Śankhchûḍa and assuming his form, went to the house of Tulasî. Dundubhis (celestial drums) were sounded at Her door, shouts of victory were proclaimed and Tulasî was informed. The chaste Tulasî, hearing that sound very gladly looked out on the royal road from the window. Then for auspicious observances, She offered riches to the Brâhmiṇs ; then She gave wealth to the panegyrists (or bards attached to the courts of princes), to the beggars, and the other chanters of hymns. That time Bhagavân Nârâyaṇa alighted from His chariot and went to the house of the Devî Tulasî, built of invaluable gems, looking excedingly artistic and beautiful. Seeing her dear husband before her, She became very glad and washed his feet and shed tears of joy and bowed down to Him. Then She, impelled by love, made him take his seat on the beautiful jewel throne and giving him sweet scented betels with camphor, began to say:—" To-day my life has been crowned with success. For I am seeing again my lord returned from the battle. Then she cast smiling glances askance at him and with her body filled with rapturous joy lovingly asked him the news of the war in sweet words :—

12-13. O Thou, the Ocean of mercy ! Now tell me of your heroic valour, how you have come out victorious in war with Mahâdeva who destroys countless universes. Hearing Tulasî's word, the Lord of Lakṣmî, in the guise of Śankhachûḍa, spoke these nectar-like words with a smiling countenance.

14-17. O Dear ! Full one Samvatsara the war lasted betwixt us. All the Daityas were killed. Then Brahmâ Himself came and mediated Peace, then, was brought about and by the command of Brahmâ. I gave over to the Devas their rights. When I returned to my home, S'iva went back to His S'ivaloka. Thus saying ! Hari, the Lord of the world, slept and then engaged in sexual intercourse with her. But the chaste Tulasî, finding this time her experience quite different from what She used to enjoy before, argued all the time within herself and at last questioned him :—

18-22. Who are you ? O Magician ! By spreading your magic, you have enjoyed me. As you have taken my chastity, I will curse you. Bhagavân Nârâyaṇa, hearing Tulasî's words and being afraid of the curse, assumed His real beautiful figure. The Devî then saw the Eternal Lord of the Devas before her. He was of a deep blue colour like fresh rain-clouds and with eyes like autumnal lotuses and with playful Lîlâs equivalent to tens and tens of millions of Love personified and adorned with jewels and ornaments. His face was smiling and gracious ; and he wore his yellow-coloured robe. The love-stricken Tulasî, seeing That Lovely Form of Vâsudeva, immediately fell senseless ; and at the next moment, regaining consciousness, she began to speak.

23-27. O Lord ! Thou art like a stone. Thou hast no mercy. By hypocricy Thou hast destroyed my chastity, my virtue and for that reason didst kill my husband. O Lord ! Thou hast no mercy ; Thy heart is like a stone. So Let Thee be turned into a stone. Those who declare Thee as a saint, are no doubt mistaken. Why didst Thou for the sake of others, kill without any fault, another Bhakta of Thine. Thus speaking, Tulasî overpowered with grief and sorrow, cried aloud and repeatedly gave vent to lamentations. Seeing her thus very distressed, Nârâyaṇa, the Ocean of Mercy, spoke to her to cheer her up according to the rules of Dharma.

28-102. O Honoured One ! For a long time you performed tapasyâ in this Bhârata, to get Me. S'ankhachûḍa, too, performed tapasyâ for a long time to get you. By that tapas, Śankhachûḍa got you as wife. Now it is highly incumbent to award you also with the fruit that you asked for. Therefore I have done this. Now quit your this terrestrial body and assume a Divine Body and marry Me. O Râme ! Be like Lakṣmî. This body of yours will be known by the name of Gaṇḍakî, a very virtuous, pure and pellucid stream in this holy land of Bhârata. Your hairs will be turned into sacred trees and as they will be born of you, you will be known by the name of Tulasî. All the three worlds will perform their Pûjâs with the leaves and flowers of this Tulasî. Therefore, O Fair-faced One ! This Tulasî will be reckoned as the chief amongst all flowers and leaves, In Heavens, earth, and the nether regions, and before Me, O Fair One, you will reign as the chief amongst trees and flowers. In the region of Goloka, on the banks of the river Virajâ, in the Râsa circle (the celestial ball dance,) where all amorous sentiments are played in Vrindâvana forest, in Bhâṇdîra forest, in Champaka forest, in the beautiful Chandana (Sandal) Forests and in the groves of Mâdhavî, Ketakî, Kunda, Mallikâ, and Mâlatî, in the sacred places you will live and bestow the highest religious merits. All the Tîrthas will reside at the bottom of the Tulasî tree and so religious merits will accrue to all. O Fair-faced One ! There I and all the Devas will wait in expectation of the falling of a Tulasî leaf. Any-body who will be initiated and installed with the Tulasî leaves water, will get all the fruits of being initiated in all the sacrifices. Whatever pleasure Hari gets when thousands and thousands of jars filled with water are offered to him, the same pleasure He will get when one Tulasî leaf will be offered to Him. Whatever fruits are acquired by giving Ayuta cows as presents, those will be also acquired by giving Tulasî leaves. Especially if one gives Tulasî leaves in the month of Kârtik, one gets the fruits same as above mentioned. If one drinks or gets the Tulasî leaf water at the momentous Time of Death, one becomes freed of all sins and is worshipped in the Viṣṇu Loka. He who drinks daily the Tulasî leaf water certainly gets the fruit of one lakh horse sacrifices. He who plucks or culls the Tulasî leaf by his own hand and holding it on his body, quits his life in a Tîrath, goes to Viṣṇu Loka. Whoever holds in his neck the garland made up of Tulasî wood, gets certainly the fruit of horse sacrifices at every step. He who does not keep his word, holding the Tulasî leaf in his hand, goes to the Kâlasûtra Hell as long as the Sun and Moon last. He who gives false evidence in the presence of the Tulasî leat, goes to the Kumbhîpâka Hell for the life-periods of fourteen Indras. He who drinks or gets a bit of the Tulasî leaf water at the time of death, certainly goes to Vaikuṇṭha, ascending on a car made up of jewels. Those who pluck or cull the Tulasî leaves in the Full Moon night, on the twelfth lunar day, on the passing of the sun from one sign to another, the mid-day, or on the twilights, on the night, while applying oil on their bodies, on the impurity periods, and while putting on night dresses, verily cut off the Nârâyaṇa's head. O Chaste One! The Tulasî leaf kept in the night, is considered sacred. It is considered good in Śrâddha, vow, ceremony, in the making over of any gift, in the installation of any image or in worshipping any Deva. Again, the Tulasî leaf fallen on the ground or fallen in water or offered to Viṣṇu, if washed out can be used in holy and other purposes. Thus, O Good One! You will remain as tree in this earth and will remain in Goloka as the Presiding Deity thereof and will enjoy daily the sport with Kriṣṇa. And also you will be the Presiding Deity of the river Gaṇḍakî and thus bestow religious merits in Bhârata; you will be the wife of the Salt Ocean, which is My part You are very chaste; in Vaikuṇṭha you will enjoy me as Ramâ lives with Me. And as for Me, I will be turned into stone by your curse; I will remain in India close to the bank of the river Gaṇḍakî. Millions and millions of insects with their sharp teeth will make rings, (the convolutions in the Sâlagrâma or sacred stones), on the cavities of the mountains there, representing Me. Of these stones, those that have one door (entrance hole), four convolutions, adorned by the garland of wild flowers (having a mark like this) and which look like fresh rain-cloud, are called Lakṣmî Nârâyaṇa Mûrtis (forms). And those that have one door, four convolutions and look like fresh rain-clouds but no garlands are called Lakṣmî Jânardana Chakras (discus). Those that have two doors, four convolutions, and decked with mark like cow's hoof and void of the garland mark are called Raghunâtha chakras. Those that are very small in size, with two Chakras and look like fresh rain-clouds and void of the garland marks are named Vâmana Chakras. Those that that are very small in size, with two Chakras and the garland mark added, know them to be the S'rîdhara Chakras. These always bring in prosperity to the household. Those that are big, circular, void of garland mark, with two circular Chakras, are known as Dâmodara forms. Those that are mediocre in size, with two Chakras and marked as if struck by an arrow, having marks of arrows and bow-cases are known as Raṇa-Râmas. Those that are middling, with seven Chakras, having marks of an umbrella and ornaments, are called Râjarâjes'varas. They bestow the royal Lakṣmî to persons. Those that have twice seven chakras, and are big, looking like fresh rain-clouds are named Anantaṣ. They bestow four fold fruits (Dharma, wealth, desire and liberation). Those that are in their forms like a ring, with two chakras, beautiful, looking like rain-clouds, having cow-hoof marks and of mediocre size, are named Madhusûdanaṣ. Those that have one Chakra are called Sudars'anas. Those that have their Chakras hidden are called Gadâdharas. Those that have two Chakras, looking horse-faced, are known as Haya. grîvas. O Chaste One! Those that have their mouths very wide and extended, with two Chakras, and very terrible, are known as Narasimhas. They excite Vairâgyas to all who serve them. Those that have two Chakras, mouths extended and with garland marks (ellipitical marks) are called Lakṣmî Nrisinghas. They always bless the householders who worship them. Those that have two Chakras near their doors (faces), that look even and beautiful, and with marks manifested are known as Vâsudevas. They yield all sorts of fruits. Those that have their Chakras fine and their forms like fresh rain-clouds and have many fine hole marks within their wide gaping facets are called Pradyumnas. They yield happiness to every householder. Those that have their faces of two Chakras stuck together and their backs capacious, are known as Sankarṣaṇas. They always bring in happiness to the householders. Those that look yellow, round and very beautiful are Aniruddhas. The sages say, they give happiness to the householders. Where there is the S'âlagrâma stone there exists Śrî Hari Himself; and where there is Hari, Lakṣmî and all the Tîrthas dwell there. Worshipping S'âlagram Śilâ, destroys the Brahmahatyâ (killing a Brâhmin) and any other sin whatsoever. In worshipping the Sâlagrâma stone looking like an umbrella, kingdoms are obtained; in worshipping circular Śilâs, great prosperity is obtained; in worshipping cart-shaped stones, miseries arise; and in worshipping stones, whose ends look like spears (Śûlas), death inevitably follows. Those whose facets are distorted, bring in poverty; and yellow stones bring in various evils and afflictions. Those whose Chakras look broken, bring in diseases; and those whose Chakras are rent asunder bring in death certainly. Observing vows, making gifts, installing images, doing Srâddhas, worshipping the Devas, all these become highly exalted, if done before the Śâligrâma Silâ. One acquires the merits of bathing in all the Tîrthas and in being initiated in all the sacrifices, if one worships the Sâligrâma Silâ. What more than this, that the merits acquired by all the sacrifices, all the Tîrthas, all vows, all austerities and reading all the Vedas are all acquired by duly worshipping by the holy Śâlagrâma Śilâ. He who performs his Abhiṣ'eka ceremony always with Śâlagrâma water (being sprinkled with Śâlagrâma water at the initiation and installation ceremonies), acquires the religious merits of performing all sorts of gifts and circumambulating the whole earth. All the Devas are, no doubt, pleased with him who thus worships daily the Śâlagrâma. What more than this, that all the Tîrthas want to have his touch. He becomes a Jivanmukta (liberated while living) and becomes very holy; ultimately he goes to the region of Śrî Hari and remains in Hari's service there and dwells with him for countless Prâkritic dissolutions. Every sin, like Brahma Hatyâ, flies away from him as serpents do at the sight of Gaḍuḍa. The Devî Vasundharâ (the Earth) becomes purified by the touch of the dust of his feet. At his birth, all his predecessors (a lakh in number) are saved. He who gets the Śâlagrâma Śilâ water during the time of his death, he is freed of all his sins and goes to the Viṣṇu Loka and gets Nirvâṇa; he becomes freed entirely from the effects of Karma and he gets, no doubt, dissolved and diluted for ever in (the feet of) Viṣṇu. He who tells lies, holding Śâlagrâma in his hands, goes to the Kumbhîpâka Hell for the life-period of Brahmâ. If one does not keep his word, uttered with the Śâlagrâma stone in his hand, one goes to the Asipatra Hell for one lakh manvantaras. He who worships the Śâlagrâma stone without offering Tulasî leaves on it or separates the Tulasî leaves from the stone, will have to suffer separation from his wife in his next birth. So if one does not offer the Tulasî leaves in the conchshell, for seven births he remains without his wife and he becomes diseased. He who preserves the Śâlagrâma stone, the Tulasî and the conchshell, in one place, becomes very learned and becomes dear to Nârâyaṇa. Look! He who casts his semen once in his wife, suffers intense pain, no doubt, at each other's separation So you become dear to Śankhachûḍa for one Manvantara. Now, what wonder! That you will suffer pain, at his bereavement. O Nârada! Thus saying, Śrî Hari desisted. Tulasî quitted her mortal coil and assumed a divine form, began to remain in the breast of Śrî Hari like Śrî Lakṣmî, Devî. Hari also went with her to Vaikuṇṭha Thus Lakṣmî, Sarasvatî, Gangâ, and Tulasî, all the four came so very dear to Hari and are recognised as Îs'varîs. On the other hand, the mortal coil of Tulasî, no sooner quitted by Tulasî, became transformed into the river Gaṇḍakî. Bhagavân Hari, too, became also converted into a holy mountain, on the banks thereof, yielding religious merits to the people. The insects cut and fashion many pieces out of that mountain. Of them, those that fall into the river, yield fruits undoubtedly. And those pieces that fall on the ground become yellow coloured; they are not at all fit for worship. O Nârada! Thus I have spoken to you everything. What more do you want to hear now? Say.

Here ends the Twenty-fourth Chapter of the Ninth Book on the glory of Tulasî in the Mahâpurâṇam Śrî Mad Devî Bhâgavatam of 18,000 verses by Maharṣi Veda Vyâsa.

CHAPTER XXV.

1-2 Nârada said:—When the Devî Tulasî has been made so dear to Nârâyaṇa and thus an object for worship, then describe Her worship and Stotra (the hymn of Tulasî) now. O Muni! By whom was She first worshipped? By whom were Her glories first sung? And how did She become therefore an object of worship? Speak out all these to me.

3. Sûta said:—Hearing these words of Nârada, Nârâyaṇa, laughing, began to describe this very holy and sin-destroying account of Tulasî.

4-15. Nârâyaṇa said:—Bhagavân Harî duly worshipped Tulasî, and began to enjoy her wtth Lakṣmî; He raised Tulasî to the rank of Lakṣmî and thus made her fortunate and glorious. Lakṣmî and Gangâ allowed and bore this new union of Nârâyaṇa and Tulasî. But Sarasvatî could not endure this high position of Tulasî owing to Her anger. She became self-conceited and beat Tulasî on some quarrel before Hari. Tulasî became abashed and insulted and vanished off. Being the Îs'varî of all the Siddis, the Devî, the Self-manifest and the Giver of the Siddhiyoga to the Jñânins, Tulasî, Oh! what a wonder, became angry and turned out as invisible to Śrî Hari even.

Not seeing Tulasî, Hari appeased Sarasvatî and getting Her permission went to the Tulasî forest. Going there and taking a bath in due accord, and with due rites, worshipped with His whole heart the chaste Tulasî and then began to meditate on Her with devotion. O Nârada! He gets certainly all siddhis who worships Tulasî duly with the ten lettered mantra:—" Śrîm Hrîm Klîm Aim Vrindâvanyai Svâhâ, " the King of mantras, yielding fruits and all gratifications like the Kalpa Tree. O Nârada! At the time of worship, the lamp of ghee, was lighted and dhûp, sindûra, sandal, offerings of food, flowers, etc., were offered to Her. Thus hymned by Hari, Tulasî came out of the tree, pleased. And She gladly took refuge at His lotus feet. Viṣṇu, then, granted her boon that "You will be worshipped by all; I will keep you in My breast and in My head and the Devas also will hold you on their heads." And He then took her to His own abode.

16. Nârada said :—"O Highly Fortunate One! What is Tulasî's dhyân, stotra and method of worship? Kindly describe all these.

17. Nârâyaṇa said:—When Tulasî vanished, Hari became very much agitated at her bereavement and went to Vrindâvana and began to praise her.

18-44. The Bhagavân said :—The Tulasî trees collect in multitudinous groups; hence the Pandits call it Vrindâ. I praise that dear Tulasî. Of old, She appeared in the Vrindâvana forest and therefore known as Vrindâvanî. I worship that fortunate and glorious One. She is worshipped always in innumerable universes and is, therefore, known as Vis'vapûjitâ (worshipped by all). I worship that Vis'vapûjitâ. By whose contact, those countless universes are always rendered pure and holy; and therefore She is called Vis'vapâvanî (purifying the whole universe). I am suffering from her bereavement, I remember the Devî. Without Tulasî, the Devas do not get pleased, though other flowers be heaped on them; therefore She is considered as the essence of all the flowers. Now I am in sorrow and trouble and I am very eager to see her, who is of the nature of purity incarnate. The whole universe gets delighted when the Bhaktas receive her; hence She is called Nandinî; so may She be pleased with me. There is nothing in the universe that can be compared to Her; hence She is called Tulasî, I take refuge of that dear Tulasî. That chaste dear one is the life of Kriṣṇa, hence She is known as Kriṣṇajîvanî. Now may She save my life. O Nârada! Thus praising, Ramâpatî remained there. The chaste Tulasî then came to His sight and bowed down to His lotus feet; when She becoming sensitive out of the insult, began to weep. Bhagavân Viṣṇu, seeing that sensitive dear one, immediately took her to His breast. Taking, then, Sarasvatî's permission, He took her to His own home and brought about, first of all, the agreement between her and Sarasvatî. Then He granted her the boon, "You will be worshipped by all, respected by all, and honoured by all; and all will carry you on their heads." I will also worship, respect and honour you and keep you on My head. Receiving this boon from Viṣṇu, the Devî Tulasî became very glad.

Sarasvatî then attracted her to her side, made her sit close to her. Lakṣmî and Gangâ both with smiling faces attracted her and made her enter into the house. O Nârada ! Whosoever worships her with her eight names Vrindâ, Vrindâvanî, Vis'vapûjitâ, Vis'vapâvanî, Tulasî, Puṣpasârâ, Nandanî and Kriṣṇa Jîvanî and their meanings and sings this hymn of eight verses duly, acquires the merit of performing As'vamedha Yajña (horse sacrifice). Specially, on the Full Moon night of the month of Kârtik, the auspicious birth ceremony of Tulasî is performed. Of old Viṣṇu worshipped her at that time. Whoever worships with devotion on that Full Moon combination, the universe purifying Tulasî, becomes freed of all sins and goes up to the Viṣṇu Loka. Offerings of Tulasî leaves to Viṣṇu in the month of Kârtik bring merits equal to those in giving away Ayuta Cows. Hearing this stotra at that period gives sons to the sonless persons, wives to the wife less persons and friends to friendless persons. On hearing this stotra, the diseased become free of their diseases, the persons in bondage become free, the terrified become fearless, and the sinners are freed of their sins. O Nârada ! Thus it has been mentioned how to chant stotra to her. Now hear her dhyân and method of worship. In the Vedas, in the Kâṇva Śâkhâ branch, the method of worship is given. You know that one is to meditate on the Tulasî plant, without any invocation (âvâhana) and then worship her with devotion, presenting all sorts of offerings as required to her. Now hear Her Dhyânam. Of all the flowers, Tulasî (the holy basil) is the best, very holy, and captivating the mind. It is a flame burning away all the fuel of sins committed by man. In the Vedas it is stated that this plant is called Tulasî, because there can be made no comparison with Her amongst all the flowers. She is the holiest of them all She is placed on the heads of all and desired by all and gives holiness to the universe. She gives Jîvanmukti, mukti and devotion to Śrî Hari. I worship Her. Thus meditating on Her and worshipping Her according to due rites, one is to bow down to Her. O Nârada ! I have described to you the full history of Śrî Tulasî Devî. What more do yo want to hear now, say.

Here ends the Twenty-fifth Chapter of the Ninth Book on the method of worship of Tulasî Devî in the Mahâpurâṇam Śrî Mad Devî Bhâgavatam of 18,000 verses by Maharṣi Veda Vyâsa.

CHAPTER XXVI.

1. Nârada said :—I have heard the anecdote of Tulasî. Now describe in detail the history of Sâvitrî. Sâvitrî is considered as the Mother of the Vedas. Why was She born, in days gone by ? By whom was She first worshipped and subsequently also ?

3. Nârâyaṇa said :—" O Muni ! She was first worshipped by Brahmâ. Next the Vedas worshipped her. Subsequently the learned men worshipped her. Next the King As'vapati worshipped Her in India. Next the four Varṇas (castes) worshipped Her.

5. Nârada said :—" O Brahman ! Who is that As'vapati ? What for did he worship? When the Devî Sâvitrî became adorable by all, by which persons was She first worshipped and by which persons subsequently.

6-14. Nârâyana said :—" O Muni ! The King As'vapati reigned in Bhadrades'a, rendering his enemies powerless and making his friends painless. He had a queen very religious ; her name was Mâlatî ; She was like a second Lakṣmî. She was barren ; and desirous of an issue, She under the instruction of Vasis'ṭha, duly worshipped Sâvitrî with devotion. But She did not receive any vision nor any command ; therefore She returned home with a grievous heart. Seeing her sorry, the king consoled her with good words and himself accompanied her to Puṣkara-with a view to perform Tapas to Sâvitrî with devotion and, being self-controlled, practised tapasyâ for one hundred years. Still he could not see Sâvitrî, but voice came to him. An incorpareal, celestial voice reached his ears :—" Perform Japam (repeat) ten lakhs of Gâyattri Mantram." At this moment Parâsara came up there. The king bowed down to him. The Muni said:—" O King ! One japa of Gâyatrî, destroys the days sins. Ten Japams of Gâyatrî destroy day and night's sins.

15-40. One hundred Gâyatrî Japams destroy one month's sins. One thousand Japams destroy one year's sins. One lakh Gâyattrî Japams destroy the sins of the present birth and ten lakh Gâyattrî Japams destroy the sins of other births. One hundred lakhs of Jâpams destroy the sins of all the births. If ten times that (*e. i.* 1,000 lakhs) be done, then liberation is obtained. (Now the method, how to make Jâpam). Make the palm of the (right) hand like a snake's hood ; see that the fingers are all close, no holes are seen ; and make the ends of the fingers bend downwards ; then being calm and quiet and with one's face eastward, practise Jâpam. Then count from the middle of the ring (nameless) finger and go on counting right-handed (with the hands of the watch) till you come to the bottom of the index finger. This is the rule of counting by the hand. O King ! The rosary is to be of the seed of white lotus or of the crystals ; it should be consecrated and purified. Jâpam is to be done then in a sacred Tîrtha or in a temple. Becoming self-controlled one should place the rosary on a banyan leaf or on a lotus leaf and smear it with cowdung ; wash it, uttering Gâyattrî Mantra and over it perform one hundred times Gâyattrî Jâpam intently in accordance with the rules. Or wash it with Pañchagavya, milk, curds, clarified butter, cow urine and cowdung), and then consecrate it well. Then wash it with the Ganges water and perform best the consecrations. O Râjarṣi ! Then perform ten lakhs of Japam in due order. Thus the sins of your three births will be destroyed and then you will see the Devî Sâvitrî. O King ! Do this Jâpam, being pure, everyday in the morning, mid-day, and in the evening. If one be impure and devoid of Sandhyâ, one has no right to do any action; and even if one performs an action, one does not get any fruit thereby. He who does not do the morning Sandhyâ and the evening Sandhyâ, is driven away from all the Brâhminic Karmas and he becomes like Sûdras. He who does Sandhyâ three times throughout his life, becomes like the Sun by his lustre and brilliance of tapas. What more than this, the earth is always purified by the dust of his feet. The Dvija who does his Sandhyâ Bandanam and remains pure, becomes energetic and liberated while living. By his contact all the tîrthas become purified. All sins vanish away from him as snakes fly away at the sight of Garuḍa. The Dvija who becomes void of Sandhyâ three times a day, the Devas do not accept his worship nor the Pitris accept his Piṇḍas. He who has no Bhakti towards the Mûla Prakriti, who does not worship the specific seed Mantra of Mâyâ and who does not hold festivities in honour of Mûla Prakriti, know him verily to be an Ajagara snake without poison. Devoid of the Viṣṇu mantra, devoid of the three Sandhyâs and devoid of the fasting on the Ekâdas'î Tithi (the eleventh day of the fortnight), the Brâhmiṇ becomes a snake devoid of poison. The vile Brâhmiṇ who does not like to take the offerings dedicated to Hari and who does the washerman's work and eats the food of Śûdra and drives the bufalloes, becomes a snake devoid of poison. The Brâhmin who burns the dead bodies of the Śûdras, becomes like the man who is the husband of an unmarried girl. The Brâhmiṇ also who becomes a cook of a Śûdra, becomes a snake void of poison. The Brâhmiṇ who accepts the gifts of a Śûdra, who performs the sacrifice of a Śûdra, who lives as clerks and warriors becomes like a snake void of poison. The Brâhmiṇ who sells his daughter, who sells the name of Hari or eats the food of a woman who is without husband and son, as well as of one who has just bathed after her menstruation period, becomes like a serpent void of poison. The Brâhmiṇ who takes the profession of pimps and pampers and lives on the interest, is also like a serpent void of poison. The Brâhmiṇ who sleeps even when the Sun has risen, eats fish, and does not worship the Devî is also like a poisonless serpent. Thus stating all the rules of worship in order, the best of the Muṇis told him the Dhyânam, etc., of the Devî

Sâvitrî, what he wanted. Then he informed the King of all the mantras and went to his own Âs'rama. The king, then worshipped accordingly and saw the Devî Sâvitrî and got boons.

41-43. Nârada said :—What is the Sâvitrîs Dhyân, what are the modes of her worship, what is stotra, mantra, that Parâs'ara gave to the King before he went away? And how did the King worship and what boon did he get? This great mystery, grand and well renowned in the Srutis, about Sâvitrî, I am desirous to hear in brief on all the points.

44-78. Nârâyaṇa said :—On the thirteenth day (the trayodas'î, tithi) of the black fortnight in the month Jyaiṣṭha or on any other holy period, the fourteenth day (the chaturdas'î tithi) this vow is to be observed with great care and devotion. Fourteen fruits and fourteen plates with offerings of food on them, flowers and incense are to be offered and this vow is to be observed for fourteen years consecutively. Garments, holy threads and other articles are also offered and after the Vrata is over, the Brâhmins are to be fed. The lucky pot (mangal ghaṭ) is to be located duly according to the rules of worship with branches and fruits. Gaṇes'a, Agni, Viṣṇu, Śiva and Śivâ are to be worshipped duly.

In that ghaṭ Sâvitrî is to be next invoked and worshipped. Now hear the Dhyânan of Sâvitrî, as stated in the Mâdhyan Dina Śâkhâ, as well the stotra, the modes of worship, and the Mantra, the giver of all desires. I meditate and adore that Sâvitrî, the Mother of the Vedas, of the nature of Praṇava (Om), whose colour is like the burnished gold, who is burning with Brâhma teja (the fire of Brahma), effulgent with thousands and thousands of rays of the midday summer Sun, who is of a smiling countenance adorned with jewels and ornaments, wearing celestial garment (purified and uninflammable by fire), and ready to grant blessings to Her Bhaktas; who is the bestower of happiness and liberation, who is peaceful and the consort of the Creator of the world, who is all wealth and the giver of all riches and prosperity, who is the Presiding Deity of the Vedas andwho is the Vedas incarnate, I meditate on Thee. Thus reciting the Dhyânam, mantra and meditating on Her, one is to offer Naivedyas (offerings of food) to Her and then place one's fingers on one's head; one is to meditate again, and then invoke the Devî within the pot. One should next present fourteen things, uttering proper mantras according to the Vedas. Then one must per-form special poojâ and chant hymns to the Devî and worship Her. The fourteen articles of worship are as under :—

(1) Seat (Âsan); (2) water for washing feet (Pâdya), (3) offering of rice and Durba grass (Arghya), (4) water for bath (Snânîya), (6) anointment with sandalpaste and other scents (Anulepana), (7) incense (Dhûpa), (8) Lights (Dipa), (9) offerings of food (Naivedya), (10) Betels (Tambûl), (11) Cool water, (12) garments, (13) ornaments, (14) garlands, scents, offering of water to sip, and beautiful bedding. While offering these articles, one is to utter the mantras, this beautiful wooden or golden seat, giving spiritual merits is being offered by me to Thee. This water from the Tîrthas, this holy water for washing Thy feet, pleasant, highly meritorious pure, and as an embodiment of Poojâ is being offered by me to Thee. This holy Arghya with Durba grass and flowers and the pure water in the conch-shell is being offered by me to Thee. (as a work of initial worship). This sweet scented oil and water being offered by me to Thee with devotion for Thy bathing purposes. Kindly accept these. O Mother! This sweet-scented water Divine-like, highly pure and prepared of Kunkuma and other scented things I offer to Thee. O Parames'varî! This all-auspicious, all good and highly meritorious, this beautiful Dhûpa, kindly take, O World Mother! This is very pleasant and sweet scented; therefore I offer this to Thee. O Mother! This light, manifesting all this Universe and the seed, as it were, to destroy the Darkness is being offered by me to Thee. Devî! Kindly accept this delicious offering of food, highly meritorious, appeasing hunger, pleasant, nourishing and pleasure giving. This betel is scented with camphor, etc., nice, nourishing, and pleasure—giving; this is being offered by me to Thee. This water is nice and cool, appeasing the thirst and the Life of the World. So kindly accept this. O Devî! Kindly accept this silken garment as well the garment made of Kârpâsa Cotton, beautifying the body and enhancing the beauty. Kindly accept these golden ornaments decked with jewels, highly meritorious, joyous, beauteous and prosperous. Kindly accept these fruits yielding fruits of desires, obtained from various trees and of various kinds. Please have this garland, all auspicious and all good, made of various flowers, beauteous and generating happiness. O Devî! Kindly accept this sweet scent, highly pleasing and meritorious. Please take this *Sindura*, the best of the ornaments, beautifying the forehead, highly excellent and beautiful. Kindly accept this holy and meritorious threads and purefied by the Vedic mantrams and made of highly holy threads and knitted with highly pure knots. Uttering thus, offer the above articles that are to be offered to the Devî, every time the specific seed mantra being uttered. Then the intelligent devotee should recite the stotras and subsequently offer the Dakṣiṇâs (presents) with devotion to the Brâhmaṇas. The Radical or the Specific Seed Mantra mantra is the eight lettered mantra Srîm Hrim Klim Svâitrai Svâhâ; So the sages know. The Stotra, as stated in the Mâdhyandîna

Śâkhâ, gives fruits of all desires. I am now speaking to you of that mantra, the Life of the Brâhmaṇas. Listen attentively. O Nârada! Sâvitrî was given to Brahmâ, in the ancient times of old in the region of Goloka by Kriṣṇa; but Sâvitrî did not come Brahma loka with Brahmâ. Then by the command of Kriṣṇa, Brahmâ praised the mother of the Vedas. And when She got pleased, She accepted Brahmâ as Her husband.

79-87. Brahmâ said:—"Thou art the everlasting existence intelligence and bliss; Thou art Mûlaprakriti; thou art Hiraṇya Garbha; Thou didst get pleased, O Fair one! Thou art of the nature of fire and Energy; Thou art the Highest; Thou art the Highest Bliss, and the caste of, the twice-born. Dost thou get appeassed, O Fair One! Thou art eternal, dear to the Eternal; thou art of the nature of the Everlasting Bliss. O Devî, O Thou, the all auspicious One! O Fair One! Beest thou satisfied. Thou art the form of all (omnipresent)! Thou art the essence of all mantras of the Brâhmanas, higher than the highest! Thou art the bestower of happines and the liberator O Devî, O Fair One! Beest thou appeased. Thou art like the burning flame to the fuel of sins of the Brâhmanas! O Thou, the Bestower of Brahma teja (the light of Brahma) O Devî! O Fair One! Best appeased. By Thy mere remembrance, all the sins to me by body, mind and speech are burnt to ashes. Thus saying, the Creator of the world reached the assembly there. Then Sâvitrî came to the Brahmaloka with Brahmâ. The King As'vapati chanted this stotra to Sâvitrî and saw Her and got from Her the desired boons. Whosoever recites this highly sacred king of Stotras after Sandhyâ Bandanam, quickly acquires the fruits of studying the Vedas.

Here ends the Twenty Sixth Chapter of the Ninth Book on the narration of Sâvitrî in Śrîmad Devî Bhâgavatam of 18,000 verses by Maharṣi Veda Vyâsa.

CHAPTER XXVII.

1-2. Nârâyaṇa said:—"O Nârada! After having chanted the above hymn to the Goddess Sâvitrî and worshipped Her in accordance with due rites and ceremonies, the king As'vapati saw the Devî, effulgent like the lustre of thousand suns. She then smilingly told the king, as a mother to her son, whilst all the quarters were illumined with the lustre of Her body:—

3-14. Sâvitrî said:—"O King! I know your desire. Certainly I will give what you and your wife long for. Your chaste wife is anxious for a daughter, while you want a son. So, one after another, the desires of both of you will be fulfilled. Thus saying, the Devî went to the Brahma Loka. The King also returned to his house. First a daughter was born to him. As the daughter was born, as if a second Lakşmî was born after worshipping Sâvitrî, the King kept her name as Sâvitrî. As time rolled on, the daughter grew, day by day, like the phases of bright fortnight moon, into youth and beauty. There was a son of Dyumat Sena, named Satyavâna, always truthful, good natured and endowed with various other qualifications. The daughter chose him for her bridegroom. The King betrothed her with jewels and ornaments, to Satyavâna, who gladly took her home. After one year expired, the truthful vigorous Satyavâna gladly went out, by his father's command, to collect fruits and fuel. The chaste Sâvitrî, too, followed him. Unfortunately Satyavâna fell down from a tree and died. Yama, the God of Death, saw his soul as a Puruşa of the size of one's thumb and took it and went away. The chaste Sâvitrî began to follow Him. The high souled Yama, the Foremost of the Sadhus, seeing Sâvitrî following Him, addressed her sweetly:— "O Sâvitrî! Whither are you going in your this mortal coil? If you like to follow after all, then quit your this body.

15-25. The mortal man, with his transient coil of these five elements, is not able to go to My Abode. O Chaste One! The death time of your husband arrived; therefore Satyavâna is going to My Abode to reap the fruits of his Karma. Every living animal is born by his Karma. He dies again through his life long Karma. It is his Karma alone that ordains pleasure, pain, fear, sorrows, etc. By Karma, this embodied soul here becomes Indra; by Karma he can become a Brahmâ's son. What more than this that Jiva, by his Karma, can be in Hari's service and be free from birth and death! By one's own Karma all sorts of Siddhis and immortality can be obtained; the four blessed regions as Vişnu's Sâlokya, etc., also can be obtained by Karma. What more than this that by Karma, a being becomes divine, human, or a King, or Śiva or Gaņes'a! The state of Munîndra, asceticism, Kşattriyahood, Vais'yahood, Mlechhahood, moving things, stones, Râkşasahood, Kinnaras, Kingship, becoming trees, beasts, forest animals, inferior animals, worms, Daityas, Dânavas, Asuras, all are fashioned and wrought by Karma and Karma alone. O Narada! Thus speaking, Yama remained silent.

Here ends the Twenty-seventh Chapter of the Ninth Book on the birth etc. of Sâvitrî in Śrî Mad Devî Bhâgavatam of 18,000 verses by Maharşî Veda Vyâsa.

CHAPTER XXVIII.

1-4. Nârâyaṇa said :—" O Nârada! Hearing the words of Yama, the chaste intelligent Sâvitrî, replied with great devotion:—" O Dharmarâjan! What is Karma? Why and how is its origin? What is the cause of Karma? Who is the embodied soul (bound by Karma)? What is this body? And who is it that does Karma? What is Jnâna? What is Buddhi? What is this Prâṇa of this embodied Jîva? What are the Indriyas? And what are their characteristics? And what are the Devatâs thereof? Who is it that enjoys and who is it that makes one enjoy? What is this enjoyment (Bhoga)? And what is the means of escape from it? And what is the nature of that State when one escapes from enjoyment? What is the nature of Jîvâtmâ? And what of Paramâtmâ? O Deva! Speak all these in detail to me.

5-21. Dharma said:—Karma is of two kinds—good and bad. The Karma that is stated in the Vedas as leading to Dharma is good; all other actions are bad. The God's service, without any selfish ends (Sankalap) and without the hope of any fruits thereof (ahaitukî), is of such a nature as to root out all the Karmas and gives rise to the highest devotion to God. A man who is such a Bhakta of Brahma becomes liberated, so the Śrutis say. Who then does the Karma and who is it that enjoys? (*i. e.* no such body). To such a Bhakta to Brahma, there is no birth, death, old age, disease, sorrow nor any fear. O Chaste One! Bhakti is two-fold. This is stated by all in the Śrutis. The one leads to Nirvâṇa and the other leads to the nature of Hari. The Vaiṣṇavas want the Bhakti to Hari *i. e.* the Saguṇa Bhakti. The other Yogis and the best knowers of Brahma want the Nirguṇa Bhakti. He who is the Seed of Karma, and the Bestower for ever the fruits of Karma, Who is the Karma Incarnate and the Mûla Prakriti, is the Bhagavân; He is the Highest Self. He is the Material Cause of Karma. Know this body to be by nature liable to dissolve and die. Earth, air, âkâs'a, water, and fire these are the threads, as it were, of the work of creation of Brahma Who is of the nature of Being. " Dehî " or the Embodied Soul is the Doer of Karma, the Kartâ; he is the enjoyer; and Âtmâ (self) is the prompter, the stimulator within to do the Karma and enjoy the fruits thereof. The experiencing of pleasures and pains and the varieties thereof is known as Bhoga (enjoyment). Liberation, Mukti is the escape there from.

The knowledge by which Âtmâ (sat) and Mâyâ (Asat) are discriminated is called Jñânam (Brahma Jñânam). The knowledge is considered as the root discriminator of various objects of enjoyments. (i. e. by which the various objects are at once recognised as different from Âtman). By Buddhi is meant the right seeing of things, (as certain) and is considered as the seed of Jñânam. By Prâṇa is known as the different Vâyus in the body. And this Prâṇa is the strength of the embodied. Mind is the chief, the best, of the senses, it is a part of Îs'vara: its characteristic is its doubtful uncertain state. It impels to all actions, irresistible. It is inascertainable, invisible; it obstructs the Jnâna. The senses are seeing, hearing, smelling, touching and tasting. These are the several limbs, as it were, of the embodied and the impellors to all actions. They are both enemies and friends as they give pain (when attached to wordly objects) and happiness (when attached to virtuous objects) both. The Sun, Vâyu, Earth, Brahmâ and others are their Devatâs. The Jîva is the holder, the sustainer of Prâṇa, body, etc. The Paramâtmâ, the Highest Self, is the Best of all, Omnipresent, transcending the the Guṇas, and beyond Prakriti. He is the Cause of all causes and He is the Brahma Itself. O Chaste One! I have replied, according to the Śâstras to all your questions. These are Jnânas of the Jnânins. O Child! Now go back to your house at pleasure.

22-30. Sâvitrî said:—Whither shall I go, leaving my Husband and Thee, the Ocean of Knowledge? Please oughtest to answer the queries that I now put to Thee. What wombs do the Jîvas get in response to which Karmas? What Karmas lead to the Heavens? And what Karmas lead to various hells? Which Karmas lead to Mukti? And which Karmas give Bhakti? What Karmas make one Yogî and what Karmas inflict diseases? Which Karmas make one's life long? or short? Which Karmas again make one happy? And what Karmas make one miserable? Which Karmas make one deformed in one's limbs, one-eyed, blind, deaf, lame or idiotic? Which Karmas again make one mad? Make one very much avaricious or of a stealing habit? What Karmas make one possess Siddhis? Or make one earn the four Lokas Sâlokya, etc.? What Karmas make one a Brâhmiṇ or an ascetic? Or make one go to Heaven or Vaikuṇṭha? What Karmas enable one to go to Goloka, the par excellence and free from all diseases? How many are the hells? What are their names and how do they appear? How long will one have to remain in each hell? and what Karmas lead to what diseases? O Deva, Now tell me about these that I have asked to you and oblige.

Here ends the Twenty-Eighth Chapter of the Ninth Book on the story of Sâvitrî in Śrî Mad Devî Bhâgavatam of 18,000 verses by Maharṣi Veda Vyâṣa.

CHAPTER XXIX.

1. Nârâyaṇa said:—Yama got thunderstruck at these queries of Sâvitrî. He then began to describe, with a smiling countenance, the fruition of the several works of the Jîvas.

2-8. He said:—" O Child ! You are now a daughter only twelve years old. But you speak of wisdom like the Highest Jnânins and Yogîs, Sanaka and others. O Child ! By virtue of the boon granted by Sâvitrî, you have become incarnate of Her in part. The King As'vapati got you before by performing severe penances. As Lakṣmî is dear and fortunate with regard to Viṣṇu, as Mahâdevî is to Mahâdeva, Aditi to Kas'yapa, Ahalyâ to Gautama, so you are to Satyavâna in respect of affection and good-luck and other best qualities. As Śachî is to Mahendra, as Rohiṇî is to Moon, as Rati is to Kâma, as Svâhâ is to Fire, as Svadhâ is to the Pitris, as Sanjñâ is to the Sun, as Varuṇânî is to Varuna, as Dakṣiṇâ is to Yajna, as Earth is to Varâha, as Devasenâ is to Kârtika, so you are fortunate and blessed with respect to Satyavâna. O Sâvitrî ! I myself grant you this boon of my own accord. Now ask other boons. O highly fortunate One ! I will fulfil all your desires.

9-12. Sâvitrî said :—" O Noble One ! Let there be one hundred sons of mine by Satyavâna. This is the boon that I want. Let there be one hundred sons of my Father as well ; let my Father-in-law get back his (lost) eyesight and may he get back his lost kingdom. This is another boon that I want. Thou art the Lord of the world. So grant me this boon, too, that I may have this my very body for a lâkh years when I may go to Vaikuṇṭha with Satyavâna. Now I am eager to hear the various fruitions of Karmas of several Jîvas. Kindly narrate them and oblige.

13-70. Dharma said:—You are very chaste. So what you have thought will verily come to pass. Now I describe the fruition of Karmas of the Jîvas. Listen. Excepting this holy land of Bhârata, nowhere do the people enjoy wholly the fruition of their two-fold Karmas, good and bad. It is only the Suras, Daityas, Dânavas, Gandharvas, Râkṣasas, and men that do Karmas. The beasts and the other Jîvas do not do Karmas. The special Jîvas e. g. men, etc., experience the fruition of their Karmas in Heavens, hells and in all the other Yonis (wombs). Specially, as the Jîvas roam in all the different Yonis, they enjoy their Karmas, good or bad, as the case may be, carved in their previous births. The good works get fructified in Heavens; and the bad works lead the Jîvas to hells. This Karma can be got rid of by Bhakti. This Bhakti is of two kinds :—(1) Nirguṇâ of the nature of Nirvâṇa ; and (2) towards Prakriti, of the nature of Brahma, and with Mâyâ inherent. Diseases come as the result of bad and ignorant actions ; and healthiness comes from good and certain scientific Karmas. Similar are the remarks for short and long lives for happiness and pain. By bad works, one becomes blind or deformed in body. So by doing excellent Karmas, one acquires Siddhis, etc.. These are spoken generally. I will now speak in detail ; listen. This is very secret even in Purâṇas and Smritis. In this Bhâratavarṣa, men are the best of all the various classes of beings. The Brâhmans are the best of men and are best in all Kinds of Karmas. They are responsible, too, for their actions. O Chaste One ! Of the Brâhmiṇs, again, those that are attached to the Brâhmaṇas are the best. The Brâhmaṇas are of two kinds as they are Sakâma (with desires) or Niṣkâma (without desires). The Niṣkâmî Brâhmaṇas are superior to the Sakâmî Brâhmaṇas. For the Sakâmîs are to enjoy the fruits of their Karmas, while the Niṣkamî Brahmânas are perfectly free from any such disturbances (they have not to come back to this field of Karma). The Niṣkâma Bhaktas, after they quit their bodies, go to a place free from sickness or disease, pure and perfect. From there they do not come back. The Niṣkâma Bhaktas assuming the divine forms go to the Goloka and worship the Highest God, the Highest Self, the two-armed Kriṣṇa The Sakâmî Vaiṣṇavas go to Vaikuṇṭha ; but they come back in Bhârata and get into the wombs of the twice-born. By degrees they also become Niṣkâma when they certainly acquire pure undefiled Bhakti. The Brâhmaṇas and Vaiṣṇavas that are Sakâmîs in all their births, never get that pure undefiled intellect and never get the devotion to Viṣṇu. The Brâhmaṇas, living in the Tîrthas (sacred places of pilgrimages) and attached to Tapas go to Brahmaloka (the region of Brahmâ) ; they again come down to Bhârata. Those that are devotedly attached to their own Dharma (religion) and reside in places other than Tîrthas, go to Satyaloka and again come to Bhârata. The Brâhmaṇas, following their own Dharma and devoted to the Sun go to the world of the Sun and again come to Bhârata. And those who are devoted to Mûla Prakriti and devoted to Niṣkâma Dharma go to Maṇi Dvîpa and have *not* to come back from thither. The Bhaktas of Śiva, Śakti, and Gaṇe'sa, and attached to their own Dharmas respectively go to the Śiva Loka and return from thence. Those Brâhmaṇas that worship the other Devas and attached to their own Dharmas go to those regions of theirs respectively and again come to Bhârata. Attached to their own Dharmas, the Niṣkâmî, Bhaktas of Hari go by their Bhakti step by step to the region of Śrî Hari. Those that are not attached to their own Dharmas and do not worship the Devas and always bent on doing things as they like without any regard to their Âchâras go certainly to hells. No doubt in this. The Brâhmaṇas and the other three Varṇas, attached to their own Dharmas all enjoy the fruits of their good works. But those who do not do their Svadharma, go verily down into hells. They do not come to Bhârata for their rebirth, they enjoy their fruits of Karmas in hells! Therefore the four Varṇas ought to follow their own Dharmas of the Brâhmaṇas, they are to remain attached to their own Dharmas and give their daughters in marriage to the similarly qualified Brâhmaṇas. They then go to the Chandraloka (the region of the Moon). There they remain for the life periods of the fourteen Indras. And if the girl be given, with ornaments, the results obtained would be twice. If the girl be given with a desire in view, then that world is obtained; but if the girl be given without any desire but to fulfil the God's will and God's satisfaction only, then one would not have to go to that world. They go to Viṣṇu Loka, bereft of the fruits of all Karmas. Those that give to the Brâhmaṇas pasture ground and cattle, silver, gold, garment, fruits and water, go to the Chandraloka and live there for one Manvantara They live long in those regions by virtue of that merit. Again those that give gold, cows, copper, etc., to the holy Brâhmaṇas, go to the Sûrya Loka (the region of the Sun) and live there for one Ayuta years (10,000 years), free from diseases, etc, for a long time. Those that give lands and lots of wealth to the Brâhmiṇs, go to the Viṣṇu Loka and to the beautiful Śveta Dvîpa (one of the eighteen minor divisions of the known continents). And there they live as long as the Sun and Moon exist. O Muni! The meritorious persons live long in that wide region. Note:—Śveta Dvîpa may mean Vaikuṇṭha, where Viṣṇu resides. Those who give with devotion dwelling places to the Brâhmaṇas, go to the happy Viṣṇu Loka. And there, in that great Viṣṇu Loka, they live for years equal to the number of molecules in that house. He who offers a dwelling house in honour of any Deva, goes to the region of that Deva and remains there for a number of years equivalent to the number of particles in that house. The lotus-born Brahmâ said that if one offers a royal palace, one obtains a result four times and if one offers a country, one gets the result one hundred times that; again if one offers an excellent country, twice as much merit one acquires. One who dedicates a tank for the expiation of all one's sins, one lives in Janar Loka (one of the pious regions) for a period equivalent to the number of particles therein). If any man offers a Vâpî (a well) in preference to other gifts, one gets ten fold fruits thereby. If one offers seven Vâpîs, one acquires the fruits of offering one tank. A Vâpî is one which is four thousand Dhanus long and which is as much wide or less (*Note* :—Dhanu equals a measure of four hastas). If offered to a good bridegeroom, then the giving of a daughter in marriage is equivalent to a dedication of ten Vâpîs. And if the girl be offered with ornaments, twice the merits accrue. The same merit accrues in clearing the bed of the mud of a pond as in digging it. So for the Vâpî (well). O Chaste One! He who plants an As'vattha tree and dedicates it to a godly purpose, lives for one Ayuta years in Tapar Loka. O Sâvitrî! He who dedicates a flower garden for the acquirement of all sorts of good, lives for one Ayuta years in Dhruva Loka.

O Chaste One! He who gives a Vîmâṇa (any sort of excellent carriage) in honour of Viṣṇu, in this Hindoos thân, lives for one Manvantara in Viṣṇuloka. And if one gives a Vimâṇa of variegated colours and workmanship, four times the result accrues. And one who gives a palanquin, acquires half the fruits. Again if anybody gives, out of devotion, a swinging temple (the Dol Mandir) to Bhagavân Śrî Hari, lives for one hundred Manvantras, in the region of Viṣṇu. O Chaste One! He who makes a gift of a royal road, decorated with palacial buildings on either side, lives with great honour and love in that Indraloka for one Ayuta years. Equal results follow whether the above things are offered to the Gods or to the Brâhmaṇas. He enjoys that which he gives. No giving, No enjoying. After enjoying the heavenly pleasures, etc., the virtuous person takes birth in Bhârata as a Brâhmin or in other good families, in due order, and ultimately in the Brâhmaṇa families. The virtuous Brâhmaṇa, after he has enjoyed the heavenly pleasures, takes his birth again in Bhârata in Brâhmaṇa, Kṣattriya or in Vais'ya families. A Ksattriya or a Vais'ya can never obtain Brahmanahood, even if he performs asceticism for one Koṭi Kalpas. This is stated in the Śrutis. Without enjoying the fruits, no Karma can be exhausted even in one hundred Koṭi Kalpas. So the fruits of the Karmas must be enjoyed, whether they be auspicious or inauspicious. By the help of seeing the Devas and seeing the Tîrthas again and again, purity is acquired. O Sâvitrî! So now I have told you something. What more do you want to hear? Say.

Here ends the Twenty-Ninth Chapter of the Ninth Book on the anecdote of Sâvitrî on the fruits of making gifts and on the effects of Karmas in Śrî Mad Devi Bhâgvatam of 18,000 verses by Maharṣi Veda Vyâsa.

CHAPTER XXX.

1. Sâvitrî said :—" O Dharmarâjan ! Kindly tell me in detail about those works that lead the meritorious persons to the Heavens and various other spheres.

2-20. Dhûrmaraj said :—" O Child ! He who gives rice and food to the Brâhmaṇas in India, goes to the Sivaloka where he dwells with great respect for years equivalent to the measure of that food. This " Anna-dâna " (the giving of boiled rice and other eatables) is a great dân (charity) and this can be done not only to the Brâhmaṇas but to the other castes also, where similar results also follow. There is, or will be, no other charity superior to this charity of anna (rice, boiled it may be and other eatables.) For here no distinction is made as to what caste will get it or not, nor the discrimination of time, when to give such a charity. O Child ! Seats (Âsanas) given to the Devas and the Brâhmaṇas, carry the donor to the Viṣṇu Loka, where he dwells for Ayuta years with great respect and love. Giving excellent cows yielding milk to Brâhmanas take the donor to Viṣṇuloka, where he is glorified and remains for years equivalent to the number of pores in that cow or those cows. And if cows be given on a meritorious day, four times the merits accrue, and if given in a sacred place of pilgrimage, hundred times the result occurs; and if given in a tîrath, where Nârâyaṇa is worshipped, koṭi times the results accrue. He who gives with devotion, cows to the Brâhmaṇas in Bhârata, remains in the Chandraloka for one Ayuta years and is glorified. He who gives a two-mouthed cow to a Brâhmaṇa, goes to Viṣṇuloka and remains there for as many years as there exist the numbers of hairs on the body of that cow and is glorified. A gift of a beautiful white umbrella to a Brâhmaṇa makes one go to Varuṇaloka for Ayuta years where he remains with great pleasure. Giving garments to the diseased Brâhmaṇas makes one fit to remain with glory in Vâyuloka for one ayuta years. Giving to a Brâhmaṇa the Sâlagrâma with garments makes one remain with glory in Vaikuṇṭha as long as there exist the Sun and Moon. Giving a beautiful bedding to a Brâhmaṇa, glorifies a man in the Chandraloka as long as there exist the Sun and Moon. To give lights to the Devas and Brâhmaṇa glorifies a man in Agniloka (the region of Fire) for one Manvantara. To give elephants to the Brâhmaṇas in Bhârata, makes one sit in the same throne with Indra for his life period

Giving horses to the Brâhmaṇas makes one remain in Varuṇaloka for fourteen Indras' life periods. Giving a good palanquin to a Brâhmaṇa makes one remain in the Varuṇaloka for fourteen Indras' life-periods. Giving a good site or a good orchard to a Brâhmaṇa leads one to the Vâyuloka where he remains with glory for one Manvantara. Giving a white châmara and fan to a Brâhmaṇa, leads the donor to the Vâyuloka where he remains for one ayuta years. Giving grains and jewels make one long-lived and both the donors and receivers go certainly to Vaikuṇṭha.

21-40. He who always recites the name of Śrî Hari, lives for ever and Death goes far far away from him. The intelligent man that celebrates the Swinging Festival (Dol Jâtrâ) in the last quarter of the Full Moon night in this land of Bharata, becomes liberated while living, enjoying pleasures in this world, goes in the end to Viṣṇuloka, where he remains for one hundred Manvantaras; there is no doubt in this. If the Swinging Festival be performed under the influence of the asterism Uttara Phâlgunî then the fruits become doubled; this is the saying of Brahmâ Himself. The performer lives to the end of a Kalpa. To give til (Sesamum) to a Brâhmaṇ, leads one to Śiva Loka, where one enjoys for a number of years equal to the number of til. Then one is born in a good yoni and becomes longlived and happy. To give a copper plate yields double the effect. To give in India a chaste wife with garments and ornaments to a Brâhman (and then to purchase her with an equivalent in gold) leads one to Chandra Loka where one remains for fourteen Indra's life periods and enjoys day and night the celestial Apsarâs. Thence the donor goes to the Gandharba Loka for one ayuta years and day and night enjoys Urvas'î. Then he gets for thousand births chaste, fortunate, wealthy, gentle and sweet-speaking, beautiful wives. He who gives nice and delicious friuts to the Brâhmaṇas, remains with glory in the Indra Loka for a number of years equivalent to the fruits. He gets again a good Yoni (birth) and gets excellent sons. To give thousand trees while there are fruits on them, or nice friuts only to the Brâhmaṇas, makes one enjoy the Heavens for a long, long time and he then comes back to Bhârata. To give various things and good edifices with grains, etc., to the Brâhmaṇas leads one to the regions of the Devas where he remains for one hundred Manvantaras. Then he gets a very good birth and becomes the master of abundant wealth. He who gives with devotion to the Brâhmaṇas lands certainly goes for one hundred Manvantaras and remains there in glory for one hundred Manvantras; and, coming again to be born in good wombs, they become Kings. The earth does not leave him for hundred births. He becomes prosperous, wealthy and possesses many sons and becomes the lord of his subjects. He who gives a good village with pasture land and cows, dwells with glory in Vaikuṇṭha for one lakh manvantaras. Then he gets a good brith (becomes born in a high caste family) and obtains a lakh villages. The earth quits him not even if he be born a lakh times. (This is very bad then, to one who does not like to be born again).

41-60. He who gives a village inhabited by good and obedient subjects with ripe excellent grains, various tanks, trees and adorned with fruits and leaves dwells in Kailâṣa with great glory for ten lakh Indra's life periods. Getting again born in a high family, he becomes Râjâ Dhirâja in Bhârata and obtains Niyuta towns. There is no doubt in this. The earth quits him not, even if he be born âyuta times. Really he gets the highest prosperity in this earth. He who gives to a Brâhmaṇa one hundred towns and countries, inhabited by good or mediocre subjects, with wells, tanks, and various trees, remains with glory in Vaikuṇṭha for one koṭi manvantaras. Then he becomes born in this earth in a high caste family, becomes the Lord of Jambudvîpa and attains in this earth great prosperity like Indra. The earth quits him not even if he comes here Koṭi times; in reality he is a Mahâtmâ (a great-sould man), Râjrâjes'vara (the Lord of Kings) and lives upto the end of a Kalpa. He who gives his whole property to a Brahmiṇ, gets in the end four times that; there is no doubt in this. He who gives Jambu Dvîpa to an ascetic Brâhmaṇa, gets undoubtedly in the end one hundred times the fruit. If you give away Jambu Dvîpa, the whole earth; if you travel all the Tîrthas, if you perform all sorts of asceticisms, if you give shelter to all, if you make gifts of all sorts, know that you will have to come again to be reborn in this earth; but if you become a devotee of Mûla Prakriti, then be sure that you w'ont have to come here and be reborn. The devotees of Mûla Prakriti go to Maṇi Dvîpa, the Highest place of Śrî Bhuvanes'arî Devî and remain there and they see the fall of innumerable Brahmâs. The worshippers of the Devî Mantra when they quit their mortal coils, assume divine appearances endowed with Bibhûtis (manifestations of powers) and free from birth, death and old age, assume the Sârûpya (the same form) of the Devî and remain in Her Service. They reside in Maṇidvîpa and see the part Pralayas. The Devas die, the Siddhas die, the whole universe vanishes; but the Devî Bhaktas never die and they remain free form birth, death, and old age. He who offers Tulasî leaf to Bhagavân Hari in the month of Kârtik resides for three yugas in the temple of Hari. Getting again a good birth, he acquires the devotion to Śrî Hari and becomes the Foremost of those who restrain their senses. He who bathes in the Ganges early before the rising of the Sun remains in enjoyment in the temple of Hari for sixty thousand yugas. Getting again a good birth, he gets the Viṣṇu Mantra, and, quitting his mortal coil, becomes united with the Feet of Sri Hari.

61-77. He has not to come back from Vaikuṇṭha to this earth. He remains in Hari's Service and gets the same form of Hari. He who bathes daily in the Ganges, becomes purified like the Sun and gets the result of performing the Horse-sacrifice at every step. The earth becomes purified by the dust of his feet and he enjoys in Vaikuṇṭha as long as the Sun and Moon exist. Then again he becomes born in a good and beautiful womb, and is liberated by acquiring the devotion to Hari. He becomes very energetic and the foremost of the ascetics, pure, religious, learned, and self-restrained. When the Sun comes midway between Pisces and Cancer and heats intensely the earth, the man who in Bhârata gives cool water to drink to the people, resides in happiness in Kailâs'a for fourteen Indras' life periods. Getting again a good birth here, he becomes beautiful, happy, devoted to Śiva, energetic and expert in the Vedas, and the Vedâṅgas. He who gives to a Brâhmaṇa the Śaktu (sattu) in the month of Vais'âkhe enjoys in the Śiva temple for as many years as there are number of particles in that quantity of sattu (powders in parched oat). He who performs the Kriṣṇa Janmâṣṭamî vow in this Bhârata, is freed from the sins incurred in his hundred births; there is no doubt in this. The observer of the vow remains in great enjoyment in Vaikuṇṭha for fourteen Indras' life periods, gets again a good birth here and acquires Hari-Bhakti. He who performs the Śivarâtri vow in this Bhârata Varṣa, resides with great joy in Śiva Loka for seven manvantaras. He who offers the Bel leaves to Śiva in Śivarâtri time, resides with great joy in Śiva's Abode for as many yugas as there are number of leaves. Getting again a good birth here, he acquires the devotion to Śiva and becomes learned, prosperous and possesses sons, subjects and lands. He who performs vow and worships Śankara in the month of Chaitra or Mâgha and who, with a branch of a tree in hand, dances day and night for one month, or half a month, for ten days or for seven days, dwells in Śiva Loka for as many yugas as the number of days he dances. He who performs the vow of Śrî Râma Navamî, lives in the abode of Viṣṇu for seven Manvantaras in great joy. Getting again a good birth, he becomes devoted to Śrî Râma, the foremost of those who have self restraint and he becomes very wealthy.

78-87. He who performs the Sâradîyâ Pûja" (the great Durgâ Pûjâ in the month of autumn) of the Mûla Prakriti with incense, lights, offerings of food, and animal sacrifices of buffaloes, goats, sheep, rhinoceros, frogs or other animals, together with dancing, music, and various other auspicious things, resides in the Śiva Loka for seven Manvantaras. Getting an excellent birth, and a pure understanding, he gets unbounded prosperity, sons and, no doubt, grandsons and he becomes a very powerful sovereign possessing many horses and elephants. There is no doubt in this. Again he who worships daily with devotion for a fortnight beginning from the eighth day of the bright fortnight the Mahâ Devî Lakṣmî, remains in the region of Goloka for fourteen Indras' life periods. Then, obtaining an excellent birth, he becomes a sovereign. He who in the full moon night in the month of Kârtik prepares a Râsa maṇḍal with one hundred Gopas and Gopîs and worships Śrî Kriṣṇa and Râdhâ in Śalagrâma or in images with sixteen varieties of offerings remains in Goloka for Brahmâ's life-time and coming again to Bhârata acquires an unflinching devotion to Śrî Kriṣṇa.

88-99. And when this Bhakti becomes greatly intensified, he gets initiated into Śrî Hari mantra and after quitting his mortal coil, he goes to the Goloka. Then he gets the Sârûpya (the same form) of Kriṣṇa and becomes the chief Pârisad (attendant of Kriṣṇa) and, becoming free from old age, he has no fear to fall again down to this earth. He who observes the Ekâdas'î day, remains fasting and performing penances in the bright or dark eleventh day, remains in Vaikuṇṭha in great enjoyment and comfort. Then, again coming into this Bhârata he becomes a devotee of Hari. And when that Bhakti is intensified he becomes solely devoted to Hari and quitting his mortal coil, goes again to the Goloka and gets the Sârûpya of Kriṣṇa and becomes His Pâriṣada (attendant). Then, freed of old age and death, he does not fall. He who worships Indra in the month of Bhâdra in the twelfth day of the white fortnight is worshipped in the regions of Indra for sixty thousand years. He who performs in Bhârata the worship of the Sun on Sunday Sankrânti (when the Sun goes from one sign to another) and the bright seventh Tithi, according to due rules and ceremonies and eats the food called Haviṣyânna (rice boiled in ghee), dwells in the Sûryaloka for fourteen Indra's life periods. Then coming to Bhârata, he becomes free from all diseases and becomes prosperous. He who worships Sâvitrî on the fourteenth day of the black fortnight dwells in the region of Brahmâ for seven Manvantaras with great eclât and glory. Coming again to Bhârata he enjoys beauty, unequalled valour, long life, knowledge and prosperity. He who worships on the fifth day of the bright fortnight in the month of Mâgha, with his senses controlled and full of devotion, the Devî Sarasvatî with sixteen articles of food, resides in Maṇi Dvîpa for one day and one night of Brahmâ.

100-140. On getting re-birth, he becomes a poet and a learned man. He who daily gives with devotion for his whole life, cow and gold to a Brâhmaṇa dwells in Viṣṇu Loka for twice as many years as there are the numbers of hairs on the bodies of these cows and plays and jests with Viṣṇu and doing auspicious things he finds pleasure. In the end he comes again to this Bhârata and becomes the King of Kings. He becomes fortunate, prosperous, possesses many sons, becomes learned, full of knowledge and happy in every way. He who feeds a Brâhmaṇa here with sweetmeats goes to Viṣṇu Loka and enjoys there for as many years as there are hairs on the body of the Brâhmin. In the end he comes again to Bhârata and becomes happy, wealthy, learned, long lived, fortunate and very powerful. He who utters the name of Hari or gives the name (*i.e.* the mantra) of Hari to others, is worshipped in Viṣṇu loka for as many yugas as the number of times, the name or mantra was uttered. Coming again to Bhârata, he becomes happy and wealthy. And if such things be done in Nârâyaṇa Kṣettra, koṭi times the above results ensue. He who repeats the name of Hari koṭi times in Nârâyaṇa Kṣettra, becomes, no doubt, freed of all sins and liberated while living and he will not get rebirth. He lives always in Vaikuṇṭha. He gets the Sâlokya (the same region of Viṣṇu, is not liable to fall, becomes a Bhakta of Viṣṇu. He who daily worships the earthen phallic symbol (after making it daily) for his whole life, goes to the Śiva Loka and dwells there for as many years as there are the number of particles of earth. Getting rebirth he becomes the King of Kings. He who worships daily the Sâlagrâma stone and eats the water (after bathing it) is glorified in Vaikuṇṭha for one hundred Brahmâ's lives and becomes born again. When he acquires the rare Hari Bhakti and quiting his mortal coil goes to Viṣṇu Loka, whence he is not to return. He who performs all the Tapasyâs (asceticims) and observes all the vratas (vows), dwells in Vaikuṇṭha for fourteen Indras' life peroids. Getting rebirth in Bhârata he becomes the King of Kings and then he becomes liberated. He is not to return any more. He who bathes in all the Tîrthas and makes a journey round the whole world, gets Nirvâṇa. He is not reborn. He who performs the Horse-Sacrifice in this holy land Bhârata enjoys half the Indraship for as many years as there are hairs on the body of the horse. He who performs a Râjasûya Sacrifice, gets four times the above result. Of all the sacrifices, the Devî Yajña, or the Sacrifice before the Devî is the Best. O Fair One! Of old, Viṣṇu, Brahmâ, Indra and when Tripurâsura was killed, Mahâ Deva did such a sacrifice. O Beautiful One! This sacrifice before the Śakti is the highest and best of all the sacrifices. There is nothing like this in the three worlds. This Great Sacrifice was done of yore by Dakṣa when he collected abundant sacrificial materials of all sorts. And a quarrel ensued on this account between Dakṣa and Śankara. The Brâhmins conducting the sacrifice cursed the Nandî and others. And Nandî cursed the Brâhmaṇas. Mahâdeva, therefore, disallowed the going on of sacrifice and brought it to a dead stop. Of yore the Prajâpati Dakṣa did this Devî Yajña; it was done also by Dharma, Kas'yapa; Ananta, Kardama, Svâyambhuva Manu, his son Priyavrata, Śiva, Sanat Kumâra, Kapila and Dhruva. The performance of this sacrifice brings fruits equal to performing thousands and thousands of Râjasûya sacrifices. Therefore there is no other sacrifice greater than this Devî Yajña. One becomes surely endowed with a long life of one hundred years and is liberated while living. He becomes equal to Viṣṇu in knowledge, energy, strength, and asceticism. This is as true as anything. O Child! This Devî Yajña is the best and highest of all the sacrifices as Viṣṇu is the highest amongst the Devas; Nârada, amongst the Vaiṣṇavas; the Vedas, amongst all the Śâstras; the Brâhmaṇas amongst all the castes; the Ganges amongst the sacred places of pilgrimages, Śiva amongst the Holy of Holies, the Ekâdas'î vow amongst all the Vratas; Tulasî, amongst all the flowers; the Moon, amongst the asterisms; Garuḍa, amongst the birds; Prakriti, Râdhâ, Sarasvati and Earth amongst the females; the mind, amongst the quick-going and restless senses; Brahmâ, amongst the Prajâpatis; Brahmâ, amongst all the subjects; Vrindrâban, amongst all the forests; Bhârat Varṣa, amongst all the Varṣas; Lakṣmî, amongst the prosperous; Sarasvatî, amongst the learned; Durgâ, amongst the chaste; Radhikâ, amongst the fortunate. If one hundred horse sacrifices are performed, Indrahood is sure to be obtained. It is by the influence of bathing in all the Tîrthas, performing all the sacrifices, observing all the Vratas, practising all the austerities, studying all the Vedas and circumambulating the whole earth, that this Highest Śakti's service is obtained and this service of Śakti is the direct cause of Mukti (liberation). To worship the lotus-feet of the Devî is the best and highest, is stated in all the Purâṇas, in all the Vedas, and in all the Itihâsas. To sing the glories of Mûla Prakriti, to meditate on Her, to chant Her Name and attributes, to remember Her stotras, bow down before Her,, to repeat Her Name, and to drink daily Her Pâdodoka (water after washing Her feet) and the offerings already offered to Her, these are approved of by all; and everyone desires this. So worship, worship this Mûla Prakriti, Who is of the nature of Brahma, and, lo! Who is again endowed with Mâyâ. O Child! Take your husband and live happily with him in your home. O Child! Thus I have described to you the fruition of the Karmas. This is auspicious to every human being, desired by all and approved of by all. The Real Knowledge springs from this. There is no doubt in this.

Here ends the Thirtieth Chapter of the Ninth Book on the conversation between Śâvitrî and Yama and on the fruition of Karmas in the Great Purâṇam Śrî Mad Devî Bhâgavatam of 18,000 verses by Maharṣi Veda Vyâsa.

CHAPTER XXXI.

1-2. Nârâyaṇa said :—" O Nârada ! Hearing thus the supreme nature of Mûla Prakriti from Dharmarâja Yama, the two eyes of Sâvitrî were filled with tears of joy and her whole body was filled with a thrill of rapture, joy and ecstacy. She again addressed Yama:—" O Dharmarâja ! To sing the glories of Mûla Prakriti is the only means of saving all. This takes away the old age and death of both the speaker and the hearer.

3-12. This is the Supreme Place of the Dânavas, the Siddhas, the ascetics. This is the Yoga of the Yogins and this is studying the Vedas of the Vaidiks. Nothing can compare even to one-sixteenth of the sixteenth parts of the (full) merits of those who are in Śakti's Service ; call it Mukti, immortality, or attaining endless Siddhis, nothing can come to it. O Thou, the Foremost of the Knowers of the Vedas ! I have heard by and by everything from Thee. Now describe to me how to worship Mûla Prakriti and what are the ends of Karmas, auspicious and inauspicious. Thus saying, the chaste Sâvitrî bowed down her head and began to praise Yama in stotras according to the Vedas. She said:—" O Dhamarâjan ! The Sun practised of yore very hard austerities at Puṣkara and worshipped Dharma. On this, Dharma Himself became born of Sûrya as his son. And Thou art that son of Sûrya, the incarnation of Dharma. So I bow down to Thee. Thou art the Witness of all the Jîvas ; Thou seest them equally ; hence Thy name is Samana. I bow down to Thee. Sometimes Thou by Thy own will takest away the lives of beings. Hence Thy name is Kritânta. Obeisance to Thee ! Thou holdest the rod to distribute justice and pronounce sentence on them and to destroy the sins of the Jîvas ; hence Thy name is Daṇḍadhara ; so I bown down to Thee.) Note:—Any Jîva, in course of his travelling towards Mukti, can expect to pass through the stage Yamaship ; and if he pleases, he can become a Yama.) At all times Thou destroyest the universe. None can resist Thee. Hence Thou art named Kâla ; so obeisance to Thee ! Thou art an ascetic, devoted to Brahma, self-controlled, and the distributor of the fruits of Karmas to the Jîvas; Thou restrainest Thy senses. Hence Thou art called Yama. Therefore I bow down to Thee.

13-17. Thou art delighted with Thy Own Self; Thou art omniscient; Thou art the Tormentor of the sinners and the Friend of the Virtuous. Hence Thy name is Puṇya Mitra; so I bow down to Thee. Thou art born as a part of Brahmâ; the fire of Brahma is shining through Thy body. Thou dost meditate on Para Brahma. Thou art the Lord. Obeisance to Thee! O Muni! Thus praising Yama. She bowed down at the feet of Him. Yama gave her the mantra of Mûla Prakriti. How to worship Her and He began to recite the fruition of good Karmas. O Nârada! He who recites these eight hymns to Yama early in the morning, getting up from his bed, is freed of the fear of death. Rather he becomes freed of all his sins. So much so, that even if he be a veritable awful sinner and if he recites daily with devotion this Yamâṣṭakam. Yama purifies him thoroughly.

Here ends the Thirty-first Chapter of the Ninth Book on the Yama's giving Śakti Mantra to Sâvitri in the Mahâpurâṇam Śri Mad Devî Bhâgavatam of 18,000 verses by Maharṣi Veda Vyâsa.

CHAPTER XXXII.

1-28. Nârâyaṇa said:— Then, initiating her with the Great Seed, the Âdi Radical Mantra of the Mahâ Śakti, Śrî Bhûvaneas'varî *in accordance with due rules*, the son of Sûrya began to recite the various effects of various Karmas, auspicious and inauspicious. Never do the persons go to hell when they perform good Karmas; it is only the bad works that lead men to hells. The different Purâṇas narrate various heavens. The Jîvas go to those places as the effects of their various good Karmas. The good Karmas do not lead men to hells; but the bad Karmas do lead them veritably to various hideous hells. In different Śâstras, different hell-pits are ascertained. Different works lead men to different hells. O Child! Those hell-pits are very wide, deep, painful and tormenting, very horrible and ugly. Of these! Eighty six pits or Kuṇḍas are prominent. Many other Kuṇḍas exist. Now listen to the names of the Kuṇḍas mentioned in the Vedas. Their names are:—Vahni Kuṇḍa, Tapta Kuṇḍa, Kṣâra Kuṇḍa, Bhayânaka Kuṇḍa, Viṭ Kuṇḍa, Mûtra Kuṇḍa, Śleṣma Kuṇḍa, Gara Kuṇḍa, Dûṣikâ Kuṇḍa, Vasâ Kuṇḍa, Śukra-Kuṇḍa, Śoṇita Kuṇḍa, As'rû Kuṇḍa, Gâtramala Kuṇḍa, Karṇamala Kuṇḍa, Majjâ Kuṇḍa, Mâmsa Kuṇḍa, impassable Nakra Kuṇḍa, Loma Kuṇḍa, Kes'a Kuṇḍa, impassable Asthi Kuṇḍa, Tâmra Kuṇḍa, the exceedingly hot and painful Lauha Kuṇḍa (the pit of molten iron). Charma Kuṇḍa, the hot Surâ Kuṇḍa, sharp Thorny Kuṇḍa, Viṣa Kuṇḍa, the hot Taila Kuṇḍa, very heavy Astra Kuṇḍa, Krimi Kuṇḍa, Pûya Kuṇḍa, terriable Sarpa

Kuṇḍa, Mas'aka Kuṇḍa, Dams'a Kuṇḍa, dreadful Garala Kuṇḍa, Vajra Damṣṭra Vris'chika Kuṇḍa, Śara Kuṇḍa, Sûla Kuṇḍa, awful Khadga Kuṇḍa, Gola Kuṇḍa, Nakra Kuṇḍa, sorrowful Kâka Kuṇḍa, Manthâna Kuṇḍa, Vîja Kuṇḍa, painful Vajra Kuṇḍa, hot Pâs'âṇa Kuṇḍa, sharp Pâṣâṇa Kuṇḍa. Lâlâ Kuṇḍa, Masî Kuṇḍa Chakra Kuṇḍa Vakra Kuṇḍa very terrible Kurma Kuṇḍa, Jvâlâ Kuṇḍa, Bhasma Kuṇḍa, Dagdha Kuṇḍa, and others. Besides these, there are the Taptasûchî, Asipatra, Kṣuradhâra, Sûchîmukha, Gokhâmûkha, Kûmbhîpâka, Kâlasûtra, Matsyoda, Krimi Kantuka, Pâms'ubhojya, Pâs'aveṣṭa, Sûlaprota, Prakampana Ulkâmakha, Andhakûpa, Vedhana, Tâḍana, Jâlarandhra, Dehachûrṇa, Dalana, Śoṣaṇa, Kaṣa, Śûrpa, Jvâlâmûkha, Dhûmândha, Nâgaveṣṭana and various others. O Sâvitri! These Kuṇḍas give much pain and torment greatly the sinners; they are under the constant watch of innumerable servants. They hold rods in their hands; some of them have nooses; others hold clubs, Śaktis, awful scimitars; they are fierce fanatics, maddened with vanity. All are filled with Tamoguṇas, merciless, irresistible, energetic, fearless and tawny-eyed (like copper). Some of them are Yogîs; some are Siddhas, they assume various forms. When the sinners are about to die, they see these servants of Yama. But those who do their own duties, who are Śâktas, Sauras, or Gâṇapatyas or those who are virtuous Siddha Yogis, they never see the servants of Yama. Those who are engaged in their own Dharmas, who are possessed of wisdom, who are endowed with knowledge, who are mentally strong, who are untouched by fear, who are endowed with the feelings of the Devas, and those who are real Vaiṣṇavas, they never see these servants of Yama. O Chaste One! Thus I have enumerated to you the Kuṇḍas. Now hear who live in the Kuṇḍas.

Here ends the Thirty-second Chapter of the Ninth Book on the enumeration of various hells for sinners in the Mâhâpurâṇam Śrî Mad Devî Bhâgavatam of 18,000 verses by Maharṣi Veda Vyâsa.

CHAPTER XXXIII.

1-19. Dharmarâjan siad: "Those that are in Hari's service, pure, the Siddhas in Yoga (those that have attained success in Yoga), the performers of Vratas (vows), the chaste, the ascetics, the Brahmachâris never go to hells. There is no doubt in this. Those persons that are proud of their strong positions and who use very harsh burning words to thier friends, they go to Vahni Kuṇḍa and live there for as many years as there are hairs on his body; next they attain animal births for three births and get themselves scorched under the strong heat of the Sun. He goes to the Tapta Kuṇḍa hell who does not entertain any Brâhmaṇ guest with any eatables who comes to his house hungry and thirsty. He lives there for as many years as there are hairs on his body and he has to sleep on a bed of fire, very tormenting. Then he will have to be born for seven births as birds. If anybody washes any clothing with any salt on Sunday, or on the day of Samkrânti (when the Sun enters another sign), or an any new-moon day or on any Śrâddha day (when funeral ceremonies are performed), he will have to go to the Kṣâra Kuṇḍa hell where he remains for as many years as there are threads in that clothing and finally he becomes born for seven births as a veritable washerman. The wretch that abuses Mûla Prakriti, the Vedas, the Śâstras, Purâṇas, Brahmâ, Viṣṇu, Śiva and the other Devas, Gaurî, Lakṣmi, Sarasvatî and the other Devîs, goes to the hell named Bhayânaka Narakakuṇḍa. There is no other hell more tormenting than this. The sinners live here for many Kalpas and ultimately become serpents. There is no sin greater than the abuse of the Devî. There is no expiation for it. So one ought never to abuse the Devî. If one discontinues the allowances given by oneself or other persons to the Devas or Brâhmaṇas, one goes to Viṣṭhâ Kuṇḍa and has to eat the fæces there for sixty thousand years and finally to be born in Bhârata as worms in faeces the same number of years. If any person without the owner's permission digs another's tank dried of water, or makes water in the water of any tank, he goes to Mûtra Kuṇḍa and drinks urine for as many years as there are the particles in that tank. Then he becomes born in this Bhârata as an ox for one hundred years. If any person eats good things himself without giving any portion thereof to the member of his family, he goes to Śleṣma Kuṇḍa where he eats phlegm, for full one hundred years. Then he becomes born as Preta (disembodied spirits) in this Bhârata for hundred years and drinks phlegm, urine and puss; then he becomes pure. He who does not support his father, mother, spiritual teacher, wife, sons, daughters and the helpless persons, goes to Gara Kuṇḍa where he eats poison for full one hundred years. Finally he becomes born and wanders as Bhûtas (disembodied spirits). Then he becomes pure.

20-41. He who becomes angry and shrinks his eyes at the sight of a guest who has come to his house offends the Devas or Pitris, who do not accept the water offered to them by that villain. On the contrary, he earns all the sins of Brahmahatyâ (murder of a Brâhmin and so forth) and finally goes to Dûṣikâkuṇḍa where he remains for one hundred years and eats polluted things. Then wandering as Bhûtas for one hundred years he becomes purified. If anybody makes a gift of any article to a Brâhmin and then again gives that article to a different man, he goes to Vasâ Kuṇḍa where he eats marrows for one hundred years. Then he has to roam about in India for seven births as a Krikalâsa (lizard) and finally he becomes born as a very poor man with a very short life. If any woman or any man makes another of a different sex eat semen, out of passion, he goes to Śukra Kuṇḍa where he drinks semen for one hundred years. Then he crawls about as worms for one hundred years. And then he gets purified. If anybody beats a Brâhmaṇa who is a family preceptor and causes his blood to come out, he will have to go to Rakta Kuṇḍa where he has to drink blood for one hundred years, Finally he has to roam about for seven births in India as tigers; then he becomes pure by degrees. If any body mocks and laughts at any devotee of Kriṣṇa who sings with rapt consciousness and sheds tears of joy, he will have to go to As'ru Kuṇḍa where he drinks tears for one hundred years. Then he has to roam as a Chaṇḍâla for three births and then he becomes pure. He who always cheats his friends, lives for one hundred years in Gâtramala Kuṇḍa. Then roaming about for three births as an ass and for three briths as a fox concurrently, he becomes purified. Out of vanity, if anybody jests at a deaf person, he goes to Karṇamalakuṇḍa where he eats for one hundred years the wax of the ear. Next he comes to the earth as a deaf and a very poor man for seven births, when at last he gets purified. If anybody commits murder out of greed to support his family, he goes to the hell Majjâkuṇḍa where he eats marrow for one lakh years. Next he becomes a fish for seven births, for seven births he becomes a mosquitto, for three births he becomes a boar, for seven births he becomes a cock, deer and other animals concurrently ; at last he gets purified. If any stupid person sells the daughter whom he has supported, out of greed for money, he goes to Mâṇsakuṇḍa and lives there for as many years as there are hairs on her body. The Yama's servants beat him with their clubs. His head becomes overloaded with the burden of the flesh; and, out of hunger, he licks the blood coming out of his head. Next that sinner comes to Bhârata and for sixty years becomes a worm in any daughter's faesces, for seven births he becomes a hunter; for three births, a boar; for seven births, cock; for seven births, frog ; for seven births, leech; and for seven births, crow; when he gets purified. One who shaves on the day of observing vows, fasting and funeral ceremony day, becomes impure and unfit to do any action, and, in the end, he goes to the Nakha Kuṇḍa where he receives blows of clubs and eats nails for one hundred Deva years. If anybody worships, out of carelessness, the earthen Śiva phallic symbol with any hairs on it, he goes to the hell Kes'a Kuṇḍa where he remains for as many years as there are particles in that hair; then he gets to the yoni (womb) of a Yâvanânî (a Mlechcha woman) out of Hara's wrath. After one hundred years he becomes freed from that and then he becomes a Râkṣasa; there is no doubt in this. He who does not offer Piṇḍas to the Viṣṇupâda in honour of his Pitris at Gayâ goes to the hell Asthikuṇḍa where he remains for as many years as there are dirts on his body. Then he becomes a man; but for seven births he becomes lame and poor. Then he gets purified. The stupid man who commits outrage and violence on his pregnant wife, resides for one hundred years in the hot Tâmra Kuṇḍa (where coppers are in a molten condition). He who takes the food of a childless widow and the same of any woman that has just bathed after menstruation goes for one hundred years to the hot Lauha Kuṇḍa (where iron is in a molten condition). For seven births he becomes then a crow and for seven births he becomes born of a washerwoman, full of sores and boils, and poor. Then he gets purified.

51-61. If one touches the things of the Devas after touching skins or impure hydes, one remains in the Charma Kuṇḍa for full one hundred years. If any Brâhmiṇ eats a Śûdra's food, requested by him, he lives for one hundred years in the hot Surâ Kuṇḍa. Then for seven births he performs, the funeral rites for a S'ûdra ; at last he becomes pure. If any foul-mouthed person uses always harsh and filthy language to his master, he will have to go to Tîkṣṇa Kanṭaka Kuṇḍa where he eats thorns. Besides, the Yama's servants give severe beatings to him with their clubs. For seven births he will have to become horses when he gets purified. If any man ministers poison to another and so takes away his life, he will have to remain for endless years in Viṣakuṇḍa, where he will have to eat poison. Then he will have to pass for one hundred years as a murderer Bhilla, full of sores and boils, and for seven births he will have to be a leper when at last he gets purified. Being born in this holy land Bhûratavarṣa, if any man strikes a cow with a rod or any driver does so whether by himself or by his servant, he will have to dwell certainly in the hot Lauha Kuṇḍa for four yugas. He will have to pass as many years as a cow as there are hairs on that cow when ultimately he gets purified. If anybody strikes any other body with a red-hot iron dart (Kunta weapon), he will have to dwell in the Kunta Kuṇḍa for ayuta years. Then he will have to remain for one birth in a good womb, with a diseased constitution, when ultimately he will be purified.

62-85. If any Brâhmiṇ villain eats, out of greed, any flesh (not sacrificed before the goddess) or anything not offered to Hari, he will have to remain in the Krimi Kuṇḍa where he eats those things for as many years as there are hairs on his body. Then he will have to pass for three births as Mlechchas when ultimately he becomes born in a Brâhmin family. If any Brâhmin performs the S'radh of a Śûdra, eats the food pertaining to a Śrâdh of a Śûdra or burns the dead body of a Śûdra, he will have to dwell certainly in Pûya Kuṇḍa, where, being beaten by the rod of Yama, he eats the puss, etc., for as many years as there are hairs on his body. Then he becomes reborn in this Bhârata as one greatly diseased, poor, deaf and dumb and ultimately he will have to roam for seven births as a Śûdra. He who kills a black serpent on whose hood there is the lotus mark, lives in Sarpa Kuṇḍa for as many years as there are hairs on his body and he is bitten by serpents there and beaten by the servants of Yama and eats the excresceences of snakes and finally becomes born as a serpent. Then he becomes a man shortlived and having the cuticaneous disease and ringworm. And his death also comes out of snake-bite. He who kills mosquittoes and other small fanged-animals, that earn their substance rightly and pass so their lives, goes to Dams'a mas'a Kuṇḍa where he is eaten by mosquittoes and other fanged-creatures and lives there without food and crying, weeping, for as many years as the number of lives destroyed. Besides the Yama's servants tie his hands and feet and beat him. Then he becomes born as flies when ultimately he becomes purified. He who beats and chastises any man not fit to be chastised and beaten and as well as a Brâhmaṇa, goes to Vajra Damṣṭra Kuṇḍa, full of worms, and lives there day and night for as many years as there are the number of hairs on the chastised person. When he is bitten by the worms and beaten by Yama's servants, he cries sometimes, weeps sometimes, and becomes very miserable. Next he is reborn as a crow for seven births when ultimately he gets purified. If any foolish king punishes and gives trouble to his subjects out of greed of money, he goes to Vriṣchika Kuṇḍa where he lives for as many years as there are hairs on the bodies of his subjects. There is no doubt in this. Finally he becomes born in this Bhârata as a scorpion ; then a man diseased and defective in limbs, when ultimately he becomes freed of his sins. If any Brâhmiṇ carries or raises weapons, washes the clothes of others who do not perform Sandhyâs and abandons his devotion to Hari, he lives in Sarâdi Kuṇḍa for as many years as there are hairs on his body ; he is, then, pierced by arrows. Finally he becomes purified. If any king maddened by his own folly and fault, shuts his subjects in a dark cell and kills them, then he will have to go to a dreadful dark hell filled with worms having fanged teeth and covered with dirt. This hell is named Gola Kuṇḍa. He lives there bitten by insects for as many years as there are hairs on the bodies of his subjects. Finally he becomes a slave of those subjects, when he gets purified.

86-103. If anybody kills the sharks and crocodiles, etc., that rise out of the water spontaneously, he will have to remain, then, in Nakra

Kuṇḍa for as many years as there are thorns or edged points on those animals. Then he will have to be born as crocodiles, etc., for some time, when he will be purified. If any man, overpowered with lust, sees another's wife's uncovered breast, loins, and face, he will have to remain in Kâka Kuṇḍa for as many years as there are hairs in his own body. Here the crows take out his eyes. Finally for three births he gets himself burned by Fire when he becomes pure. He who steals in India the gold of the Devas and the Brâhmaṇas, dwells certainly in Manthâna Kuṇḍa for as many years as there are hairs on his body. My servants give him good beatings, and cudgellings; his eyes are covered by Manthâna Daṇḍa insects (or animals) and he eats their dirty faeces. Then he is reborn as a man but for three births he becomes blind and for seven births he becomes very poor, cruel, and a sinful goldsmith and then he is born a Svarṇavaṇik (Sonâr bene). O Fair One! He who steals in India copper or iron, silver or gold, dwells in Vîja Kuṇḍa for as many years as there are hairs on his body. There the Vîjas (a kind of insect) cover his eyes and he eats the ex-crescences of those insects. My messengers torment him. Finally he gets purified. If any body steals in India any Devatâ or the articles of a Devatâ, he dwells in Vajra Kuṇḍa for as many years as there are hairs on his body. There his body gets burnt up. My messengers torment him and he cries and weeps and remains without any food. Then he gets purified. If any body steals the metal gold or silver, cows, or garments of any Deva or a Brâhmaṇa, certainly he dwells in hot Pâṣâṇa Kuṇḍa for as many years as there are hairs on his body. Next for three births he becomes a tortoise and all sorts of white birds. Finally for three births he becomes a leper and for one birth he becomes a man with white marks on his body. Next for seven births he becomes diseased with a severe colic pain and bad blood and lives short. When he gets purified. If any body steals brass or Kâmsya properties of any Deva or a Brâhmaṇa, he will have to remain in the sharp Pâṣâṇa Kuṇḍa for as many years as there are hairs on his body. Next he becomes born in Bhârata for seven births as horses; and ultimately his both the testacles get enlarged and he gets diseases in his legs when he gets purified. If any body verily eats the food of an adulterate woman or lives on her alms, he will have to go to the Lâlâ Kuṇḍa for as many years as there are hairs on his body. My messengers torment him there and he eats the saliva and thus lives miserably. Than he gets eye diseases and colic; when ultimately he gets purified.

104-126. If any Brâhmaṇa lives on writing only or on the service of Mlechchas, he lives in Masi Kuṇḍa very painfully, eating ink, tormented by My messengers for as many years as there are hairs on his body. Then he becomes a black animal for three births and for another three births he becomes a black goat. Then he becomes a Tâl tree when he gets purified. If any body steals a Deva's or a Brâhmaṇa's grains, or any other good materials, betel, Âsan (seat) or bedding, he lives in Chûrṇa Kuṇḍa for one hundred years, tormented by My Dûtas (messengers). Next for three births he gets himself born as a goat, cock, and monkey. Finally he becomes born as a man with the heart disease, without any issue, poor, and short lived. When, at last, he gets purified. If any body steals any Brâhmiṇ's property and thereby does chakra pûjâ (the famous chakra circle worship in Tantra), or prepares a potter's wheel or any other wheels, he will have to go to Chakra Kuṇḍa and remain there for one hundred years, tormented by My messengers. Then he will be born for three births as an oilman suffering from very severe diseases when he will ultimately be poor, without any issue and diseased. Finally he gets purified. If any body casts a sinful eye on any Brâhmaṇa or on cows, he will have to remain in Vakra Kuṇda for one hundred Yugas. Next for three births he becomes a cat, for three births he becomes a vulture; for three births he becomes a boar; for three births he becomes a peacock; for seven births he becomes a man deformed and defective in limbs, his wife being dead, without any issue. Finally he becomes purified. If any person born in a Brâhmin family eats the flesh of a tortoise that is prohibited, he lives in Kûrma Kuṇḍa, for one hundred years, eaten by tortoises. Then he becomes for three births a tortoise; for three births, a boar; for three births a cat; for three births, a peacock; till at last he gets purified. If anybody steals clarified butter or oil of any Devas or a Brâhmaṇa he will have to go to Jvâlâ Kuṇḍa or Bhasma Kuṇḍa. That sinner remains in oil for one hundred years and gets soked through and through. Then for seven births he becomes a fish and a mouse when he gets purified. If anybody, born here in this holy land Bhârata, steals-sweet scented oil of a Deva or of a Brâhmaṇa, the powdered myrobalan or any other scent, he goes to Dagdha Kuṇḍa where he lives, burnt day and night for as many years as there are hairs on his body. For seven births he becomes born emitting a nasty smell, for three births he becomes musk (mriga-nâbhi;) for seven births, as a Manthâna insect. Then he becomes born as a man. If, out of envy, a powerful man appropriates to his purpose another's ancestral property by cheating, by using force, he goes to the hot Sûchî Kunda, being tormented there like a Jîva dropped in the midst of a very hot oil tank, full of boiling oil. His body is, then, being burnt up severely as the result of his own Karma; the wonder being that his body never gets completely destroyed nor reduced to ashes. For seven manvantaras he lives there without any food. My messengers give him good beatings and cudgellings and chastise him; he cries aloud. Next he gets himself born as worms of faeces for sixty thousand years. When he becomes born as a pauper without owning any land. Thus that villain, getting a fresh lease of human birth, begins again to do fresh good acts.

Here ends the Thirty-third Chapter of the Ninth Book on the description of the destinies of different sinners in different hells in Srî Mad Devî Bhâgavatam of 18,000 verses by Maharṣi Veda Vyâsa.

CHAPTER XXXIV.

1-28. Dharma Râja Yama said :—"O Fair One! If, in this Bhârata, any murderer, merciless and fierce, kills any man, out of greed for money, he goes and miserably dwells in the Asipattra hell for fourteen Indra's life periods. And if that murderer kills a Brâhmaṇa, he lives in that hell for one hundred manvantaras. While in hell, his body becomes fiercely cut and wounded by the swords. There My messengers chastise him and beat him and he cries aloud and passes his time without any food. Then he becomes born for one hundred years as a Manthâna insect, for hundred births as a boar, for seven births as a cock; for seven births as a fox, for seven births as a tiger; for three births, as an wolf; for seven births, as a frog; then as a buffaloe when he becomes freed of his sins of murders. If any body sets fire to a city or a village, he will have to live in Kṣuradhâra Kuṇḍa for three yugas with his body severed. Then he becomes a Preta (disembodied spirit) and travels over the whole earth, being burnt up with fire. For seven births he eats unclean and unholy food and spends his time as a pigeon. Then for seven births he becomes diseased with a severe colic pain, for seven births as a leper; when ultimately he gets a pure human body. If any-body whispers in one's ear another's calumny and thus glorifies himself and abuses and vilifies the Devas and Brâhmaṇas, he goes and remains in Sûchî Kuṇḍa for three Yugas, and he is pierced there by needles. Then he becomes a scorpion for seven births, a serpent for seven births, and an insect (Bhaṣma Kîṭa) for seven births; then he gets a diseased human body when, at last, he becomes purified. If any-body breaks into another's house and steals away all the household articles, cows, goats or buffaloes, he goes to Gokâ Mukha Kuṇda where faeces are like cow's hoofs, there, beaten by My servants, for three Yugas. (Gokâ is Gokṣura, hoof of a cow). Then, for seven births, he becomes a diseased cow; for three births, a sheep; for three births, a goat; and finally he becomes a man. But in this man-birth he is born first as diseased, poor, deprived of wife and friends, and a repenting person; when ultimately he is freed of his sin. If any-body steals any ordinary thing, he goes to Nakra Mukha Kunda and lives there for three years, greatly tormented by My messengers. Next for seven births, he becomes a diseased ox. Then he attains a very diseased man-birth, and ultimately he is freed of his sins. Such are the horrible results. If anybody kills a cow, elephant, horse, or cuts a tree, he goes to Gaja Dams'a Kuṇḍa for three yugas. There he is punished by My messengers freely by the teeth of elephants. Then he attains three elephants' births, three horse-births; then he becomes born as a cow and ultimately he is born a Mlechcha when he becomes pure. If anybody obstructs any thirsty cow from drinking water, he goes to Krimi Kuṇḍa and Gomukha Kuṇḍa filled with hot water and lives there for one manvantara. Next when he attains a human birth he owns not any cattle nor any wealth; rather he is born as a man, very much diseased, in low castes, for seven births when he becomes freed. If anybody, being born in Bhârata, kills cows, Brâhmiṇs, women, beggars, causes abortions or goes to those not fit to be gone into, he lives in the Kumbhîpâka hell for fourteen Indra's life periods. There he is pulverised always by My messengers. He is made to fall sometimes in fire, sometimes over thorns, sometimes in hot oil, sometimes in hot water, sometimes in molten iron or copper. That great sinner gets thousand vulture births, hundred boar births, seven crow births and seven serpent births. He then becomes worms of fæces for sixty thousand years. Thus travelling frequently in ox births he at last becomes born as a very poor leper.

29-31. Sâvitrî said:—"O Bhagavan! What is, according to the Sâstras, Brahmahatyâ (murdering a Brâhmin) and Gohatyâ (killing a cow)? Who are called Agamyâs (women unfit to be approached)? Who are designated as void of Sandhyâ (daily worship of the twice born castes)? Who can be called uninitiated? Who are said to take Pratigrahas (gifts) in a Tîrath? What are the characteristics of a real Grâmayâjî (village priests), Devala, (Brâhmaṇa of an inferior order who subsists upon the offerings made to the images which he attends), the cook of a Sûdra, of one who is infatuated (Pramatta) and the Vriṣalîpati (one who has married an unmarried girl twelve years old in whom menstruation has commenced; a barren woman). Kindly describe all these to me.

32-91. Dharmarâjan said:—"O Fair Sâvitrî! If anybody makes a distinction between Krisṇa and His Image or between any Deva and his image, between Śiva and His phallic emblem, between the Sun and the stone Sûrya Kânta (a precious stone of a bright and glittering colour) between Gaṇes'a and Durgâ, he is said to be guilty of the sin Brahmahattyâ. If anybody makes any difference (superiority or inferiority) between his own Iṣta Deva (his Deity), his Spiritual Teacher, his natural father, and mother, is certainly involved in the sin of Brahmahattyâ. He who shews any difference (superiority or inferiority) between the devotees of Viṣṇu and those of other Devas, is said to commit Brahmahattyâ. He who makes any difference in matters of respect between the waters of the feet of any Brâhmaṇa and those of Sâlagrâma stone, is said to commit Brahmahattyâ. The difference between the offerings to Hari and Hara leads to Brahmahattyâ. He who shews any difference between Krisṇa, Who is verily the God of gods, the Cause of all causes, the Origin of all, Who is worshipped by all the Devas, Who is the Self of all, Who is attributeless and without a second yet Who by His Magic powers assumes many forms and who is Is'âna, is said to commit, indeed, the Brâhmhattyâ. If any Vaiṣṇava (a devotee of Viṣṇu) abuses and envies a Śâkta (a devotee of Śâkti), he commits Brahmahattyâ. He who does not worship, according to the Vedas, the Pitris and the Devas or prohibits others in doing so, commits Brahmahattyâ. He who abuses Hriṣikes'a, Who is the Highest of the Holy things, Who is Knowledge and Bliss and Who is Eternal, Who is the only God to be served by the Devas and Vaiṣṇavas, and those Who are worshippers of His Mantra, and those who do not worship themselves are said to commit Brahmabattyâ. He who abuses and vilifies Mûlâprakriti Mahâ Devî, Who is of the nature of Causal Brahma (Kâraṇa Brahma), Who is All Power and the Mother of all, Who is worshipped by all and Who is of the nature of all the Devas and the Cause of all causes, Who is Âdyâ Śakti Bhagavatî, is said to commit Brahmahattyâ. He who does not observe the Holy Śrî Krisṇa Janmâṣṭamî, Śrî Râma Navamî, Śivarâtri, the Ekâdas'i happening on Sunday, and five other holy Pârvaṇas (festivals), commits Brahmahattyâ; is considered more sinful than a Chânḍâla. He who in this land of Bharata, digs earth on the day of Ambuvâchî or makes water etc. in the waters of the tanks, is involved in the sin of Brahmahattyâ. He who does not support his spiritual teacher, mother, father, chaste wife, son and daughter, though they are faultless, commits Brahmahattyâ. He whose marriage does not take place during his whole life-time, who does not see the face of his son, who does not cherish devotion to Hari, who eats things unoffered to Śrî Hari, who never worshipped throughout his life Viṣṇu or an earthen symbol of Śiva, verily commits Brahmahattyâ. O Fair One! Now I will recite the characteristics, according to the S'âstras, of Gohattyâ, (Killing a cow). Listen. If anybody does not prohibit one, seeing one to beat a cow,or if he goes between a cow and a Brâhmiṇ, he is involved in the sin of Gohathyâ. If any illiterate Brâhman, carrying an ox, daily beats with a stick, the cows, certainly he commits the Gohattyâ. If anybody gives the remains of another's meal to a cow to eat, or feeds a Brâhmin who carries, rather moves or drives, cows and oxen ; or eats himself the food of such a Brâhmin driver, he commits Gohattyâ Those who do sacrifices of the husband of a barren woman (Vriṣali) or eat his food, commit sin equal to one hundred Gohattyâs ; there is no doubt in this. Those who touch fire with their feet, beat the cows or enter the temple bathing but not washing their feet, commit Gohattyâ. Those who eat without washing their feet or those who sleep with their feet wetted with water and those who eat just after the Sun has risen, commit Gohattyâ. Those who eat the food of women without husbands or sons or the food of pimps and pampers or those who do not perform their Sandhyâs thrice, commit Gohattyâ. If any woman makes any difference between her husband and the Devatâ, or chastises and uses harsh words to her husband, she commits Gohattyâ. If any body destroys cow's pasture land, tanks, or land for forts and cultivates there grains, he commits Go-hattyâ. He who does not do Prâyas'chitta (expiation, atonement) for the expiation of the sin of Gohattyâ done by his son (for fear of his son's life), commits the sin himself. If any trouble arises in the state or from the Devas, and if any master does not protect then his own cows, rather torments them, he is said to commit Gohattyâ. If any Jiva oversteps the image of a Deva, fire, water, offerings to a god, flowers, or food, he commits the great sin Brahma hattyâ. When a guest comes, if the master of the house always says "there is nothing, nothing with me; no, no" and if he be a liar, cheat and an abuser of the Devas, he commits the above sin. O fair One! Whoever seeing his spiritual teacher, and a Brâhman, does not bow down and make respectful obeisance to them, commits Gohattyâ. If any Brâhmin, out of sheer anger, does not utter blessings to a man who bows down or does not impart knowledge to a student, he commits Gohattyâ. O Fair One! Thus I have described to you the characteristics, approved by Ŝâstras, of cow-killing (Gohattyâ). and murdering a Brâhmin (Brahmahattyâ). Now hear which women are (Agamyâs) not fit to be approached and those which are fit to be approached (Gamyâs). One's own wife is fit to be approached (Gamyâ) and all other women are Agamyâs, so the Pundits, versed in the Vedas, declare. This is a general remark; now hear everything in particular. O Chaste One! The Brâhmin wives of Ŝûdras or the Ŝûdra wives of Brâhmaṇas are Atyâgamyâs (very unfit to be approached) and blameable both in the Vedas and in the society. A Śûdra going to a Brâhmaṇî woman commits one hundred Brahmahatyâs; so a Brâhmana woman going to a Śûdra goes to the Kumbhîpâka hell. As a Sudra should avoid a Brâhmaṇi, so a Brâhmana should avoid a Śûdra woman. A Brâhmana going to a Śûdra woman is recognised a Briṣalipati (one who has married an unmarried girl twelve years old in whom menstruation has commenced. So much so that that Brâhmaṇa is considered an outcast and the vilest of the Chândâlas. The offerings of Piṇdas by him are considered as fæces and water offered by him is considered as urine. No where whether in the Devaloka or in the Pitriloka, his offered Piṇdas and water are accepted. Whatever religious merits he has acquired by worshipping the Devas, and practising austerities for Koṭi births, he loses all at once by the greed of enjoying the Śûdra woman. There is no doubt in this A Brâhmin, if he drinks wine, is considered as the husband of a Vriṣalî, eating faeces. And if he be a Vaiṣnava, a devotee of Viṣnu, his body must be branded with the marks of a Taptamudrâ (hot seal); and if he be a Śaiva, his body is to be branded with the Tapta Śûla (hot trident). The wife of a spiritual teacher, the wife of a king, step-mother, daughter, son's wife, mother-in-law, sister of the same father and mother, the wife of one's brother (of the same father and mother), the wife of a maternal uncle, the father's mother, mother's mother, the mother's sister, sisters, the brother's daughter, the female disciple, the disciple's wife, the wife of the sister's son, the wife of the brother's son, th ese all are mentioned by Brahmâ as Atyâgamyâs (very unfit to be approached). The people are hereby warned. If anybody, overpowered by passion, goes to these Atyâgamyâ women, he becomes the vilest of men. The Vedas consider him as if going to his mother and he commits one hundred Brahmâhat'yâ sins. These have no right to do any actions. They are not to be touched by any. They are blamed in the Vedas, in the society everywhere. Ultimately they go to the dreadful Kumbhîpâka hells. O Fair One! He who performs Sandhyâs wrongly or reads it wrongly or does not perform at all the three Sandhyâs daily, is called as void of Sandhyâ. He is said to remain uninitiated who does not, out of sheer vanity, receive any Mantra, whether he be a Vaiṣṇavite, Śaivite, or a Sun worshipper or the Ganes'a worshipper. Where there is the running stream of the Ganges, lands on either side, four hands in width, are said to be the womb of the Ganges (Gangâ Garbha) Bhagavân Nârâyana incessantly dwells there. This is called the Nârâyaṇa (Kṣetra). One goes to Viṣnupada who dies in such a place. Vârâṇas'î (Benares), Vadarî, the Confluence of the Ganges with the ocean (Gangâ-Sâgara), Puṣkara, Hari Hara Kṣettra (in Behar near Châprâ), Prabhâsa,

Kâmarûpa, Hardwar, Kedâra, Mâtripura, the banks of the river Sarasvatî, the holy land Bindrâban, Godâvarî, Kaus'ikî, Triveṇî (Allahabad), and the Himâlayâs are all famous places of pilgrimages. Those who willingly accept gifts in these sacred places are said to be Tîrthapratigrâhîs (the acceptors of the gifts in the Tîrthas). These Tîrthaprathigrâhîs go in the end to Kumbhîpâka hell. The Brâhmaṇa who acts as priests to the Śûdras is called Śûdrayâjî; the village priests are called Grâmayâjîs. Those who subsist on the offerings made to the gods are called Devalas. The cooks of the Śûdras are called Sûpakâras. Those who are void of Sandhyâ Bandanams are called Pramattas (mad). O Bhadre! These are the marks of the Vrisalîpatis that I have (now) enumerated. These are the Great Sinners (Mahâ Pâtakas). They go ultimately to the Kumbhîpâka hell. O Fair One! I now state by and by the other Kuṇḍas (hells) where other people go. Listen.

Here ends the Thirty fourth Chapter of the Ninth Book on the description of the various hells in the Mahâ Purâṇam Śrimad Devî Bhâgavatam of 18,000 verses by Maharṣi Veda Vyâsa.

CHAPTER XXXV.

1-59. Dharmarâja said:—"O Chaste One! Without serving the Gods, the Karma ties can never be severed. The pure acts are the seeds of purities and the impure acts lead to impure seeds. If any Brâhmaṇa goes to any unchaste woman and eats her food, he will have to go ultimately to the Kâlasûtra hell. There he lives for one hundred years when ultimately he gets a human birth when he passes his times as a diseased man and ultimately he gets purified. Those women who are addicted to their (one) husbands only are called Pativratâs. Those addicted to two persons are named Kulaṭâs; to three, are called Dharṣiṇîs; to four, called Pums'-chalîs; to five, six persons, called Veṣyâs; to seven, eight, nine persons are called Pungîs; and to more than these, are called Mahâves'yâs. The Mahâves'yâs are unfit to be touched by all the classes. If any Brâhṇmaa goes to Kulaṭâ, Dharṣiṇî, Pumschalî, Pungî, Ves'yâ and Mahâves'yâs, he will have to go to the Matsyoda Kuṇḍa. Those who go to Kulaṭâs remain there for one hundred years; those who go to Dharṣiṇîs, remain for four hundred years, those who go to Pums'chalîs for six hundred years; those who go to Ves'yâs, for eight hundred years; those who go to Pungîs, remain for one thousand years and those who go to Mahâves'yâs remain in the Matsyoda Kuṇḍa for ten thousand years. My messengers chastise and beat and torment them very severely. And when their terms expire, the Kulaṭâ-goers become Tittiris (a bird), the Dharṣiṇî-goers become crows, the Pums'chalî-mongers become cuckoos, the Ves'yâ haunters become wolves; the Pungî-goers become for seven births boars. If any ignorant person eats food during the lunar and solar eclipses, he goes to Aruntuda Kuṇḍa for as many years as there are particles in that food. He then becomes born diseased with Gulma (a chronic enlargement of spleen) having no ears nor teeth, and after passing his time so, he becomes freed of his previous sin. If anybody makes a promise to give his daughter to one but he gives actually to a different person, he goes to Pâms'u Kuṇḍa where he eats ashes for one hundred years. Again if anybody sells his daughter, he sleeps on a bed of arrows in Pams'uveṣṭa Kunda for one hundred years, chastised and beaten by My messengers. If any Brâhmaṇa does not worship with devotion the phallic emblem of Śiva, he goes to the dreadful Śûlaprota Kunda for that heinous sin. He remains there for one hundred years; then he becomes a quadruped animal for seven births and again he becomes born a Devala Brâhmin for seven births when he becomes freed. If any Brâhmana defeats another Brâhmana in a bad useless argument and trifles him and makes him tremble, he goes to the Prakampana Kunda for as many years as there are hairs on his body. If any woman, being very furious with anger, chastises and uses harsh words to her husband, she goes to Ulkâmukha Kuṇḍa for as many years as there are hairs on his body. My servants put fiery meteors or torches in her mouth and beat on her head. At the end of the term, she becomes a human being but she has to bear the torments of widow hood for seven births. Then she is again born as diseased; when at last she gets herself freed. The Brâhmana woman, enjoyed by a Śûdra, goes to the terrible dark Andhakûpa hell, where she remains, day and night, immersed in the impure water and eats that for fourteen Indra's life periods. Her pains are unbounded and My messengers beat her severely and incessantly.

At the expiry of the term in that hell, She becomes a female crow for thousand births, a female boar for one hundred births, a female fox for one hundred births, a hen for one hundred years, a female pigeon for seven births, and a female monkey for seven births. Then she becomes a Chândâlî in this Bhârata, enjoyed by all. Then she becomes an unchaste woman with the pthisis disease, a washerwoman, and then an oilwoman with leprosy when she becomes freed. O Fair One! The Ves'yâs live in the Vedhana, and Jalarandhra hells; the Pungîs live in the Dandatâdana hell; the Kulaṭâs live in the Dehachûrna hells; the Svairinîs live in the Dalana hells; the Dharṣiṇîs live in Śoṣana hells. Their pains know no bounds at all those places. My messengers always beat and chastise them and they eat always the urine and faeces for one Manvantara. Then, at the expiry of their hell period, they become worms of faeces for one lakh years when they become freed. If a Brâhmana goes to another Brâhmana's wife, if a Kṣattriba, Vais'ya and Śûdra do so, they go to the Kaṣâya hell. There they drink the hot Kaṣâya water for twelve years when they become purified. The lotus-born Brahmâ has said that the wives of Brâhmins, Kṣattriyas, etc., live in hells like Brâhmins, Kṣattriyas, etc., and they then get freed. If a Kṣattriya or a Vais'ya goes to a Brâhmin's wife, he is involved in the sin of his going to his mother and goes and lives in the Śûrpa hell. There the worms of the size of a Śûrpa bit that Kṣattriya, that Vais'ya and that Brâhmaṇa's wife. My messengers chastise them and they have to eat the hot urine. Thus they suffer pains for fourteen Indra's life periods. When they become boars for seven births and goats for seven births, when at last they are freed. Now if any body makes a false promise or swears falsely, taking the Tûlasî leaf in his hands, if anybody makes a false promise, taking the Ganges water, Śâlagrâma stone, or any other images of God in his hand; if any body swears falsely, placing his right palm on the palm of another; if anybody swears falsely, being in a temple or touching a Brâhmaṇa or a cow; if any body acts against his friends or others, if he be treacherous or if he gives a false evidence; then all these persons go to Jvâlâ Mukha hell, and remain there for fourteen Indra's life periods, chastised and beaten by My messengers and feeling pain as if one's body is being burnt by red hot coal. One who gives a false evidence, with the Tûasî (holy basil) in his hand becomes a Chânḍâla for seven births; one who makes a false promise with the Ganges water in his hand, becomes a Mlechcha for five births; one who swears falsely while touching the Śâlagrâma stone, becomes a worm of the foeces for seven births; one who swears falsely, touching the image of the God, becomes a worm in a Brâhmin's house for seven births; one who gives a false evidence touching with the right hand, becomes a serpent for seven births; then he becomes born as a Brâhmin, void of the knowledge of the Vedas, when he becomes freed. One who speaks falsely, while in a temple, is born as a Devala for seven births.

45-47. If one swears falsely, touching a Brâhmaṇa, one becomes a tiger. Then he becomes dumb for three births, then for three births he becomes deaf, without wife, without friends, and his family becomes extinct. Then he becomes pure. Those that rebel against their friends, become mongoose; the treacherous persons become rhinoceroses; the hypocrite and treacherous persons become tigers and those who give false evidences become frogs. So much so, that their seven generations above and seven generations below go to hell. If any Brâhmaṇa does not perform his daily duties (Nitya Karma), he is reckoned as Jaḍa (an inert matter). He has no faith in the Vedas. Rather he laughs at the Vedic customs. He does not observe vows and fastings; he blames others who give good advices. Such persons live in Dhûmrândhakâra hell where they eat dark smoke only. Then he roams about as an aquatic animal for one hundred births successively. Then he becomes born as various fishes when he is freed. If anybody jests at the wealth of a Deva or a Brâhmaṇa, then he with his ten generations above and below becomes fallen and he himself goes to the Dhûmrândhakâra hell, terribly dark and filled with smoke. There his pains know no bounds and he lives there for four hundred years, eating smoke only. Then he becomes a mouse for seven births, and he becomes various birds and worms, various trees and various animals when ultimately he gets a human birth. If a Brâhmin earns his livelihood by being an astrologer or if he be a physician and lives thereby or if he sells lac, iron, or oil, etc., he goes to the Nâgav ṣṭana Kuṇḍa hell where he lives for as many years as there are hairs on his body, tied up by snakes. Then he becomes born as various birds; ultimately he gets a human birth and becomes an astrologer for seven births and a physician for seven births. Then for sometime he becomes a cowherd (milkman), for sometimes a blacksmith; for sometimes a painter, when he becomes freed of his sin. O Chaste One! Thus I have described to you all the famous Kuṇḍas or hells. Besides there are innumerable small Kuṇḍas. The sinners go there and suffer the fruits of their own Karmas and travel through various wombs. O Fair One! What more do you now want to hear? Say.

Here ends the Thirty-Fifth Chapter of the Ninth Book on the description of the various hells for the various sinners in the Mahâ Purâṇam Śrî Mad Devî Bhâgavatam of 18,000 verses by Maharṣi Veda Vyâsa.

CHAPTER XXXVI.

1-7. Sâvitri said:—"O Dharmarâjan! O Highly Fortunate One! O Thou! Expert in the Vedas and the Amgas thereof! Now kindly describe that which is the essence of the various Purâṇas and Itihâsas, which is the quintessence, which is dear to all, approved of by all, which is the seed by which the Karmic ties are cut asunder, which is high, noble and happy is this life. Kindly describe the above by which man can acquire all his desires, and what is the only source of all the good and auspicious things. And by knowing which man has not to face any dangers or troubles, nor has he to go to the dreadful hells that thou hast severally just now described and that by which men can be freed of those various wombs. Kindly now describe all these. O Bhagavan ! What is the size of the several kuṇḍas or hells that Thou hast just now enumerated ? How do the sinners dwell there ? When a man departs, his body is reduced to ashes. Then of what sort is that other body by which the sinners enjoy the effects of their Karmas ? and why do not those bodies get destroyed when they suffer so much pains for so long a time ? What sort of body is that ? Kindly describe all these to me.

8-33. Nârâyaṇa spoke :—Hearing the questions put forward by Sâvitrî, Dharmarâja remembered Srî Hari and began to speak on subjects that sever the bonds of Karma :—" O Child ! O One of good vows ! In the four Vedas, in all the books on Dharma, (Smritis) in all the Samhitâs, all the Itihâsas, all the Purâṇas, in the Nârada Pañcharâtram, in the other Dharma Śâstras and in the Vedângas, it is definitely stated that the worship of the Pañcha Devatâs (the five Devatâs) Śiva, Śakti, Viṣṇu, Ganes'a, and Sûrya is the best, the highest, the destroyer of the old age, disease, death, evils and sorrows, the most auspicious and leading to the highest bliss. In fact, the worship of these Pañcha Devatâs is the source of acquiring all the Siddhis (the success) and saves one from going to the hells. From their worship springs the Bhaktic Tree and then and then only the Root of the Tree of all Karmic bonds is severed for ever and ever. This is the step to Mukti (final liberation) and is the indestructible state. By this one can get Sâlokya, Sârṣṭi, Sârûpya, and Sâmîpya, the different state of beatitudes in which the soul (1) resides in the same world with the Deity, (2) possesses the same station, condition, or rank, or equality with the Supreme Being in power and all the Divine attributes (the last of the four grades of Mukti, (3) possesses the sameness of form or gets assimilated to the Deity or (4) gets intimately united, identified or absorbed into the Deity, O Auspicious One ! The worshipper of these five Devatâs has never to see any of the hells, watched by My messengers. Those who are devoid of the devotion to the Devî see My abode ; but those who go to the Tîrthas of Hari, who hold Harivâsaras (festivities on the days of Hari) who bow down at the feet of Harî and worship Hari, never come to My abode named Samyamana. Those Brâhmaṇas that are purified by their performing the three Sandhyâs and by their following the pure Âchâras (customs and observances), those that find no pleasure until they worship the Devi, those that are attached to their own Dharmas and their own Âchâras, never come to My abode.

My terrible messengers, seeing the devotees of Śiva, run away out of terror as snakes ran away terrified by Gaḍuḍa I also order My messengers with nooses in their hands never to go to them. My messengers go mostly to other persons than the servants of Harî. No sooner do My Messengers see the worshippers of the Kriṣṇa Mantra, than they run away as snakes get terrified at the sight of Gaḍuḍa. Chitragupta, too, one of the beings in Yama's world, recording the vices and virtues of mankind), strike off the names of the Devî worshippers, out of fear and prepare Madhuparka, etc, for them (a mixture of honey; respectful offering made to a guest or to the bridegroom on his arrival at the door of the father of the bride). They rise higher than the Brahma Lokas and go to the Devî's abode, i.e., to Maṇidvîpa. Those that are the worshippers of the Śakti Mantra and are highly fortunate, whose contact removes the sins of others, they deliver the thousand generations (from the downward course). As bundles and bundles of dry grasses become burnt to ashes, no sooner they are thrown into fire, so the delusion at once becomes itself deluded at the sight of the forms of those devotees. At their sight, lust, anger, greed, disease, sorrow, old age, death, fear, Kâla (time that takes away the life of persons), the good and bad karmas, pleasures and enjoyments drop off to a great distance. O Fair One! Now I have described to you the states of those persons that are not under the control of Kâla, good and bad karmas, pleasures and enjoyments etc., and those that do not suffer those pains. Now I am speaking of this visible body. Listen. Earth, water, fire, air, and ether are the five Mahâ Bhûtas (the great elements); these are the seeds of this visible body of the person and are the chief factors in the work of creation. The body that is made up of earth and other elements is transient and artificial, i.e., that body becomes burnt to ashes. Within this visible body, bound, is there a Puruṣa of the size of a thumb; that is called the Jîva Puruṣa; the subtle Jîva assumes those subtle bodies for enjoying the effects of karmas. In My world, that subtle body is not burnt by the burning fire. If that subtle body be immersed in water, if that be beaten incessantly or if it be struck by a weapon or pierced by a sharp thorn, that body is not destroyed. That body is not burnt nor broken by the burning hot and molten material, by the red hot iron, by hot stones by embracing a hot image or by falling into a burning cauldron. That body has to suffer incessant pains. O Fair One! Thus I have dwelt on the subject of the several bodies and the causes thereof according to the Śâstras. Now I will describe to you the characters of all the other Kuṇḍas. Listen.

Here ends the Thirty-sixth Chapter of the Ninth Book on the destruction of the fear of the Yama of those who are the worshippers of the Five Devatâs, in the Mahâ Purâṇam Śrî Mad Devî Bhâgavatam of 18,000 verses by Maharṣi Veda Vyâsa.

CHAPTER XXXVII.

1-60. Dharmarâja said :—All the Kuṇḍas (hells) are circular in form like the Full Moon. Of these, the Vahṇikuṇḍa has the fire lit at its bottom, by the help of various kinds of stones. This Kuṇḍa will not be destroyed till Mahâpralaya comes. Here the sinners are tormented severely. It looks like a blazing coke. The flames are rising from it one hundred hands high. In circumference those flames are two miles. This is named Vahṇikuṇḍa. It is full of sinners crying loudly. It is constantly watched by My messengers who are chastising and punishing the sinners. Next comes the Tapta Kuṇḍa. It is filled with hot water and full of rapacious animals. The sinners there are severely beaten by My messengers and they are always crying out very loudly, which is being echoed and re-echoed all around terribly. It extends for one mile. This Kuṇḍa is filled with hot salt water and the abode of many crows. Then there is the Bhayânaka Kuṇḍa. It extends for two miles and it is filled with sinners. They are being punished by My messengers and they are incessantly crying " Save us, Save us. "

Next comes the Viṣṭhâ Kuṇḍa. It is filled with fœces and excrements, where the sinners are moving without any food and with their palates and throats dry. Its size is two miles and it is very bad and ugly, with foetid and nasty smell. It is always filled with sinners, who are being chastised by My Dûtas (messengers) and eat those foeces and excrements. The worms therein are constantly biting and stinging them and they are crying " deliver us, deliver us." Then comes the hot Mûttra Kuṇḍa. It is filled with the hot urine and the worms thereof. The great sinners always dwell here. It measures four miles ; and it is quite dark. My Dûtas always beat them and their throats, lips, palates are all dry. Then comes the Śleṣma Kuṇḍa. It is filled with phlegm and the insects thereof. The sinners dwell in phlegm and eat that phlegm. Then comes the Gara Kuṇḍa. It is filled with (factitious) poison. It measures one mile. The sinners eat this poison and dwell here. The worms thereof bite them. They tremble at the chastisement of My Dûtas and cry aloud. My messengers look like serpents, with teeth like thunderbolt and they are very furious and fierce, with their throats dry and their words very harsh. Then comes Dusikâ Kuṇḍa. It is filled with the rheum and dirt of the eyes and it measures one mile. Innumerable worms are born therein. Numberless sinners live there, and as they move, the insects immediately bite and sting them. Next comes the Vasâ Kuṇḍa It is filled with the serum or marrow of the flesh and it measures one-half mile. The sinners dwell there, chastised and punished by My messengers. Then comes the Śukra Kuṇḍa. It measures two miles in diameter. The insects, born in the semen, bite the sinners, and they move on and on. Then comes the Rakta Kuṇḍa, with very offensive, fœted smell. It is deep like a well and filled with blood. The sinners dwell here, drinking blood. The insects therein are always biting them. Then follows the As'ru Kuṇḍa. It measures in size one fourth the measure of the well (above-mentioned). It is always filled with hot tears of the eyes ; and many sinners are seen there living weeping and crying and being bitten by the snakes. Then there is the Gâtra Mala Kuṇḍa. The sinners are chastised and punished there by My messengers and being bitten by the insects thereof, they eat the dirts of the body and dwell there. Then comes the Karṇa Mala Kuṇḍa. The sinners eat the wax of the ear and fill the place. The insects always bite them and they are crying aloud. It measures one fourth the measure of a Vâpî. Then comes the Majjâ Kuṇḍa. It is filled with fat and marrow, emitting foeted offensive odour. It measures one fourth the measure of a Vâpî. The great sinners always dwell there. Then comes the Mâmsa Kuṇḍa. This is filled with the greasy flesh. It measures (one-fourth) that of a Vâpi. Those who sell their daughters dwell here. My messangers always chastise and punish them and horrible insects bite and sting them a d they cry, out of fear and agony, "Save us, Save us," and eat at times that flesh. Then come in succession the four Kuṇḍas Nakha, Loma and others. They also measure each one-fourth that of a Vâpi. The sinners dwell there, always chastised by My messengers. Next comes the very hot Tâmra Kuṇḍa. Burning cokes exist on the top of very hot coppers. There are lakhs and lakhs of very hot copper figures in that Kuṇḍa The sinners, being compelled by My messengers, are made to embrace each of these hot copper figures and they cry loudly and live there. It measures four miles. Then come the burning Angâra Kuṇḍa and the hot Lauha Dhâra Kuṇḍa. Here the sinners are made to embrace the hot iron figures and, feeling themselves burnt, cry out of fear and agony. Whenever My messengers punish them, they immediately cry out "Save us, Save us." It measures eight miles ; and it is pitch dark and very awful. This is named the hot Lauha Kuṇḍa. Then come the Charma Kuṇḍa and Surâ Kuṇḍa. The sinners, beaten by My men, eat the skin and drink the hot urine and dwell there. Then comes the Śâlmalî Kuṇḍa; it is overspread with thorns and thorny trees, causing intense pain. It measures two miles. Millions and millions of great sinners are made by My men to fall from the tops of those trees down below where their bodies get pierced by very sharp thorns, six feet long; and thus they dwell there, beaten by My men. Out of thirst, their palates get dried up; and they cry out repeatedly "Water, Water." Out of fear, they get very anxious and then their heads get broken by the clubs brought down on them by My men. So they move there like the beings burnt in very hot oil. Then comes the Viṣoda Kuṇḍa. It measures two miles in diameter and is filled with the poison of the serpent called Takṣakas. My men punish the sinners and they drink the poison thereof and dwell there. Then comes the hot Taila Kuṇḍa. There are no insects here. Only the great sinners dwell. All around burning coals are flaring and when My men beat the sinners, they run hither and thither. It is filled with horrible intense darkness and it is exceedingly painful. It looks dreadful and measures two miles. Then comes the Kunta Kuṇḍa. Sharp pointed iron weapons like tridents are placed in order all round. The sinners, pierced by those weapons, are seen encircling the Kuṇḍa. It measures one-half mile. Beaten by My men, their throats and lips get dried up. Then comes the Krimi Kuṇḍa. It is filled with terrible worms and insects, snake, like-with sharp teeth, of the size of a Śanku (a Sâl tree) deformed and hideous looking; and it is filled with pitch darkness, terrible to look at. Beaten by My men, the great sinners dwell there. Then comes the Pûya Kuṇḍa. It measures eight miles in diameter (or in circumference ?). The sinners dwell and eat the puss; thereof and, are beaten by My men. Then comes the Sarpa Kuṇḍa. Millions and millions of snakes of the length of a Tâl tree are existing there. These serpents encircle the sinners and as they bite them, My men also beat them at the same time. So there arises a general hue and cry. "Save us, Save us; we are done for." Then come in order the Dams'a Kuṇḍa, Mas'aka Kuṇḍa, and the Garala Kuṇḍa. These are filled with gad-flies, mosquittoes, and poison respectively. Each of them measures one mile. The sinners' hands and feet are tied up. So when the gad-flies and mosquittoes fiercely sting them, and My men violently beat them simultaneously, they raise a loud uproar and are made to move on, in their tied states by My persons. Their bodies get thoroughly reddened and covered with blood by the stinging of the flies, etc. Then come the Vajra Kuṇḍa and the Vris'chika Kuṇḍa filled respectively with Vajra insects and the scorpions. Each of them measures one-half that of the Vâpî. The sinners that dwell there, are incessantly bitten by insects (Vajras and scorpions. Then come in order the Śara Kuṇḍa, Śûla Kuṇḍa, and the Khaḍga Kuṇḍas. They are filled respectively with arrows, spikes, and scimitars. Each of them measures one half that of the Vâpî. The sinners are pierced by arrows, etc., and become covered over with blood and dwell there. Then comes the Gola Kuṇḍa. It is filled with boiling hot water and it is pitch dark. The sinners live there, bitten by the insects. This Kuṇḍa measures half that of the Vâpî. The insects bite them and My men beat them; so their fear knows no bounds; everyone of them is weeping and crying loudly. This Kuṇḍa is filled with hideously offensive smells. So the pains of the sinners are infinite. The Nakra Kuṇḍa comes next. It measures half the Vâpî, is filled with millions and millions of crocodiles living in water. The horrible looking deformed sinners live there. The Kâka Kuṇḍa then follows. The sinners here are being bitten by hundreds of deformed crows eating foeces, urines and phlegm. Then come the Manthâna Kuṇḍa and Vîja Kuṇḍa. These are filled respectively with insects called Manthâna and Vîja. Each of them measures one hundred Dhanus. (One Dhanu-four hastas.) Those insects are stinging the sinners and they cry out very loudly. Then follows the Vajra Kuṇḍa. It measures one hundred Dhanus. Many insects with their teeth as hard as thunderbolt live there and bite the sinners who cry out loudly. It is pitch dark. Then comes the hot Pâṣâṇa Kuṇḍa. It measures twice that of the Vâpî. It is so built of hot stones as it resembles a burning mass of coal. The sinners become restless with the heat and turn round and round in the middle. Then comes the Pâsâṇa Kuṇḍa and the Lâlâ Kuṇḍa. The Pâsâṇa Kuṇḍa is made up of the sharp pointed stones, having sharp edges. Innumerable sinners dwell there. Many red beings live in the Lâlâ Kuṇḍa. Then comes the Ma-î Kuṇḍa. Its size is one hundred Dhanus and its depth is two miles. It is made up of hot stones, each measuring the Anjana mountain. The sinners, beaten and driven by My persons, move on and on in the middle. Then comes the Chûrṇa Kuṇḍa. It measures two miles (in circumference) and is filled with (seven) chûrṇas (powders). The sinners, driven and beaten My men, go on, restless hither and thither and eat the powders and get themselves burnt. Then comes the Chakra Kuṇḍa. Here a potter's wheel with sixteen sharp-edged spokes is constantly whirling round and round; the sinners are being crushed by this wheel.

61-80. Then comes the Vakra Kuṇḍa. Its depth is eight miles. It is fashioned very much curved; and with and sharp slope it has gone down. It is built on the plan of a mountain cave, filled with hot water and it is enveloped with deep dense darkness. The aquatic animals there are biting the sinners, who get very much restless and are crying out very loudly. Then comes the Kûrma Kuṇḍa. Here millions and millions of tortoises in the water awfully distorted, are biting the sinners. Then comes the Jvâlâ Kuṇḍa. It is built of fierce fiery flames. It measures two miles in circumference. The sinners here are always in great difficulty, with intense pain and crying out loudly. Next follows the Bhasma Kuṇḍa. It measures two miles The sinners get themselves well burnt in hot ashes and live there; eating the ashes. It is filled with hot stones and hot irons. The sinners here are always being burnt in hot irons and hot stones and their throats and palates are being parched up. Then comes the Dagdha Kuṇḍa. It is deep and horrible. It measures two miles in circumference. My messengers threaten always the sinners there. Then comes the Sûchî Kuṇḍa. It is filled with salt water. Waves are always rising there. It is filled with various aquatic animals making all sorts of noises. It measures eight miles in circumference and it is deep and dark. The sinners here cannot see each other and are bitten by the animals. Pained very much, they cry out loudly. Then comes the Asipattra Kuṇḍa. On the top surface of the Kuṇḍa there is a very big Tâl tree very high. The edges of the leaves of this tree are sharp like the edge of a sword. One mile below this Tâl tree is situated the Kuṇḍa. The sharpedged Tâl leaves, then, fall on the bodies of the sinners from the height of a mile and they get cut and wounded; blood comes out of them and the sinners, in great pain, cry out "save, save." It is very deep, very dark and filled with Rakta Kîṭa a kind of blood like insects. This is the horrible Asipatra Kuṇḍa. Next comes the Kṣura Dhâra Kuṇḍa, measuring one hundred Dhanus (one Dhanu-four hastas). It is filled with keenedged weapons, as sharp as nice razors. The blood of the sinners is flowing here profusely. Then comes the Sûchî Mukha Kuṇḍa, filledwith sharp weapons of the form of long needles. It measures fifty Dhanus. The sinners get pierced by them and are constantly emitting blood. Their intense pain knows no bounds. Then comes the Gokâmukha Kuṇḍa; inhabited by a sort of insect, called Gokâ. They look like mouths; hence they are named Gokâmukha. It is deep like a well and it measures twenty Dhanus. The great sinners suffer an intense amount of pain there. They have got to keep their mouths always downwards as the Gokâ insects always bite and sting them. Then comes the Nakra Kuṇḍa. It resembles like the mouth of a crocodile and measures sixteen Dhanus. It is deep like a well and numbers of sinners dwell there. Then comes the Gaja Dams'a Kuṇḍa. It measures one hundred Dhanus. Next comes the Gomukha Kuṇḍa. It measures thirty Dhanus and resembles the mouth of a cow. It gives incessant pains and troubles to the sinners.

81-101. Then comes the Kumbhipâka Kuṇḍa. It is like a wheel resembling that of the Kâlachakra, very horrible; and it is rotating incessantly It looks like a water-jar, measuring eight miles, and it is quite dark. Its depth is one lakh Puruṣas of the height of 100,000 persons. There are many other Kuṇḍas, Tapta Taila Kuṇḍa and Tapta Taila Tâmra Kuṇḍa, etc., within it. This Kuṇḍa is filled with almost unconscious great sinners and insects. They beat each other and cry out loudly. My messengers also threaten them with clubs and Muṣalas. So at times they fall dizzy-headed, at times they get unconscious, and sometimes they get up and cry. O Fair One! The numbers of sinners here equal to four times that of all the other sinners in all the other Kuṇḍas. They know no death, however much you beat them. Their lives persist. For the body is built up for sufferance, it is indestructible. This Kumbhipâka Kuṇḍa is the chief of all the Kuṇḍas. This Kuṇḍa where the sinners are tied to a thread built by Kâla, where My men lift the sinners on high at one time, and sink them down below at another time, where the sinners becoming suffocated for a long time, get unconscious, where their sufferings know no bounds, where it is filled with boiling oil, is named the Kâlasutra Kuṇḍa. Then comes the Matsyoda Kuṇḍa, hollow like a well. It is filled with boiling water and it measures twenty-four Dhanus. Next comes the Abaṭoda Kuṇḍa. It measures one hundred Dhanus. The sinners get their bodies burned and chastised by My persons, live there. No sooner they drop into the water of this Kuṇḍa, than they are attacked with all sorts of diseases. Then comes the Krimikantaka Kuṇḍa. The sinners are bitten by the Krimi Kantaka insects and cry out loudly, creating a general consternation and live there. Its another names is Aruntuda Kuṇḍa. Next comes the Pâmśu Kuṇḍa. It measures one hundred Dhanus. It is overspered with burning rice husks. The sinners eat those hot husks and live there. Then comes the Pas'aveṣtana Kuṇḍa. It measures two miles. No sooner the sinners fall in this Kuṇḍa than they are twined round by this rope or Pâs'a. Hence its name. Then comes the Sûlaprota Kuṇḍa. It measures twenty Dhanus. No sooner the sinners fall here than they are encircled with the Sûlâstra (darts). Then comes the Prakampana Kuṇḍa. It measures one mile. It is filled with ice-cold water. The sinners, going there, shiver at once. Next follows the Ulkâ Kuṇḍa. It measures twenty Dhanus. It is filled with burning torches and meteors. My messengers thrust the torches and meteors into the mouths of the sinners living there Next comes the Andha-Kûpa Kuṇḍa. It is pitch-dark, shaped like a well, circular and very horrible. The sinners beat each other and eat the insects thereof. Their bodies are burnt with hot water; they cannot see anything on account of dire darkness.

102-118. The Kuṇḍa where the sinners are pierced by various weapons is known as the Vedhana Kuṇḍa. It measures twenty Dhanus. Then comes the Daṇḍatāḍana Kuṇḍa. It measures sixteen Dhanus. The sinners dwell here, threatened by My messengers. Then comes the Jâlarandhra Kuṇḍa. Here the sinners live encompassed by a great net as fishes, etc., are tied in a net. Next comes the Deha-chúrṇa Kuṇḍa. It is quite dark and its depth is that of the height of one koṭi persons; its circumference is twenty Dhanus. The sinners, here, encompassed by iron chains are made to fall below where their bodies are reduced to powders and they are inert and almost unconscious. The Kuṇḍa where the sinners are crushed and threatened by My messengers is known as the Dalana Kuṇḍa; it measures sixteen Dhanus in circumference. Next comes the Śoṣana Kuṇḍa. It is deep up to the height of one hundred persons and it is very dark. It measures thirty Dhanus. On falling on the hot sand, the throats and palates of sinners get dried up. Their pain knows no bounds. Hence it is called the Śoṣana Kuṇḍa. Then comes the Kaṣa Kuṇḍa. It measures one hundred Dhanus. It is filled with the juices of skins and its smell is very offensive. The sinners eat those astringent waters and live there. Then comes the Śūrpa Kuṇḍa. It measures twelve Dhanus and is extended like a winnowing basket. It is filled with hot iron dust and many sinners live there, eating those foetid iron dusts. Next comes the Jvâlâmukha Kuṇḍa. It is filled with red hot sand. From the (bottom) centre rises a flame, overspreading the mouth of the Kuṇḍa. It measures twenty Dhanus. The sinners are burnt here by the flame and live awfully; they get fainted no sooner they are dropped in this Kuṇḍa. Then comes the Dhumrândha Kuṇḍa. It is dark, quite filled with smoke. Within that the hot bricks are placed. The sinners get suffocated with smoke; and their eyesight becomes also obstructed. It measures one hundred Dhanus. Then comes the Nâgabeṣṭana Kuṇḍa. It is encircled and filled with the serpents. No sooner the sinners are let fall there, than they are surrounded by the snakes. O Sâvitrî! Thus I have spoken to you about the eighty-six Kuṇḍas and their characteristics. Now what more do you want to hear? Say.

Here ends the Thirty-seventh Chapter of the Ninth Book on the eighty-six Kuṇḍas and their characteristics in the Mahâ Purâṇam Śrî Mad Devî Bhâgavatam of 18,000 verses by Maharṣi Veda Vyâsa.

CHAPTER XXXVIII.

1-6. Sâvitri said :—"O Lord ! Give me the devotion to the Devî to that Âdyâ Śakti Bhagavatî Mahâ Mâye, Parames'varî Mâyî that is the Essence of all essences, the Door of final liberation to the human beings, and the Cause of delivering them from hells, that is the Root of all the Dharmas that lead to Mukti, that destroys all the inauspiciousness, that takes away the fear of all the Karmas, and that takes away always all the sins committed before. O Thou, the Foremost amongst the knowers of the Vedas ! How many kinds of Muktis are there in this world ? What is the True Bhakti ? What are its characteristics ? What is to be done by which the enjoyment of the karmas done can be desisted and nullified ? O Bhagavan ! The woman kind has been created by the Creator as devoid of any Tattvajnâna or true knowledge ; now tell me something about this True Knowledge. All the charities, sacrifices, bathing in the sacred places of pilgrimages, observing vows and austerities cannot be compared with one-sixteenth of imparting knowledge to those who are ignorant (of true knowledge). Mother is hundred times superior to father; this is certain; but the Spiritual Teacher, the Giver of True Knowledge, is hundred times more to be reverenced and worshipped than the mother. O Lord !

7-79. Dharmarâja said :—" O Child ! What boons you desired of Me before, I granted them all to you. Now I grant this boon to you that "Let the devotion towards the Śakti now arise in your mind" O Auspicious One ! You want to hear the reciting of the Glories of Śrî Devî; by this, both he who puts forward the question and he who hears the answer, all their families are delivered. When the Śeṣa Nâga Ananta Deva with His thousand mouths is unable to recite the glories of the Devî, when Mahâdeva cannot describe with His five mouths, when the Creator Brahmâ is incapable to recite Her glories with His four mouths, when Viṣṇu, the Omniscient, falls back, when Kârtikeya with His six mouths cannot sufficiently describe, when Gaṇes'a, the Guru of the Gurus of the great yogis is incapable, when the Pundits, the knowers of the four Vedas, the Essence of all the Śâstras, cannot know even a bit of Her, when Sarasvatî becomes inert in going to describe Her glories ; when Sanatkumâra, Dharma, Sanâtana, Sananda, Sanaka, Kapila, Sûrya and other sons of the Creator have fallen back, when the other Siddhas, Yogîndras, Munîndras are quite incapable to glorify the deeds of Prakriti Devî, then how can I recite fully the Glories of Her ? Whose lotus-feet Brahmâ,

Viṣṇu, Śiva and others meditate ; and lo ! when it becomes difficult for Her devotees even to think of Her, then what wonder is there that She will be so very rare to others ! Brahmâ, skilled in the knowledge of the Vedas knows more of Her than what other ordinary persons know so little of Her auspicious Glories. More than Brahmâ, Gaṇes'a, the Guru of the Jnânins, knows; again Śambhu, the Omniscient, knows the best of all. For, in ancient times, the knowledge of the Prakriti Devî was given to Him by Kriṣṇa, the Highest Spirit in a solitary place in the Râsa Maṇḍalam in the region of Goloka. Mahâdeva, again, gave it to Dharma in the Śivaloka ; Dharma again gave the Prakriti Mantra to My father. My father became successful (Siddha) in the worship of Prakriti Devî when he practised austerities. Of old, the Devas wanted to offer to me the Government of the Yama Loka; but as I was very much dispassionate towards the world, I became unwilling and became ready to perform austerities. Then my Father told the Glories of Prakriti Devî. Now I describe to you what I heard from my Father and what is stated in the Vedas, though very difficult to comprehend. Listen carefully. O Fair Faced One ! As the eternal space does not know its own extent, so Prakriti Devî Herself knows not Her own Glories ; then what can be said of any other person on this ! She is the Self of all, endowed with all powers and lordship, the Cause of all causes, the Lord of all, the Origin of all and the Preserver of all; She is Eternal, always with Her Cosmic Body, full of everlasting bliss, without any special form, unrestrained, having no fear, without any disease and decay, unattached, the Witness of all, the Refuge of all, and Higher than the Highest ; She is with Mâyâ and She is Mûla Prakriti ; the objects created by Her being known as the Prâkrit creation ; Who remains as Prakriti and Puruṣa inseparable from each other as Agni and Her burning force ; the Mahâ Mâyâ, of the nature of everlasting existence, intelligence and bliss. Though formless, She assumes forms for the gratification of the desires of Her Bhaktas. She created first the beautiful form of Gopâla Sundarî i. e, the form of Śri Kriṣṇa very lovely and beautiful, captivating the mind. His body is blue like the fresh rain cloud ; He is young and dressed like that of a cow-herd. Millions of Kandarpas (the Love deity) are, as it were, playing in His body. His eyes vie with the midday lotus of the autumn. The beauty of His face throws under shade the millions and millions of the Full Moon. His body is decorated with invaluable ornaments decked with jewels. Sweet smile reigns over in His lips ; it is adorned moreover with His yellow coloured invaluable robe. He is Parama Brahma. His whole body is burning with the Brahma Teja, the Fire of Brahma.

His Body is Fiery. He is lovely, sweet to look at, of a peaceful temper, the Lord of Râdhâ and He is Infinite. (*Note*: —The Universe, as we see, is unreal like what we see in the Kaleidoscope; various apparent pictures of an endless variety of beautiful colours and forms.) He is sitting on a jewel throne in the Rása Mandalam, and is incessantly looked upon by the smiling lovely Gopis at one and the same time. He is two-armed. A garland made of wild flowers is hanging from His neck. He is playing on His flute. His breast is resplendent with Kaustubha gem that He always wears. His body is anointed with Kunkuma (saffron), aguru (the fragrant and cooling paste of the Aguru wood), musk, and sandal-paste. The garland of beautiful Champaka and Mâlatî flowers is hanging from His neck. On His head, the beautiful crest is being seen, a little obliquely situated in the form of the beautiful Moon. Thus the Bhaktas, filled with Bhaktis, meditate on Him. O Child! It is through His fear that the Creator is doing His work of creation of this Universe; and is recording the Prârabdha fruits of their Karmas. It is through His fear that Visnu is awarding the fruits of Tapas and preserving the Universe. By His command the Kâlagni Rudra Deva is destroying all. By Whose favour Śiva has become Mrityumjaya, the Conqueror of Death and the Foremost of the Jnânis; knowing whom Śiva has become Himself endowed with knowledge and the Lord of the knowers of knowledge, full of the Highest Bliss, devotion and dispassion. Through Whose fear the wind becomes the foremost of runners and carries things, the Sun gives heat, Indra gives rain, Yama destroys, Agni burns, and Water cools all the things. By Whose command the Regents of the (ten) quarters of the sky are watching and preserving nice orders; through Whose fear the planets are describing their several orbits. Through Whose fear, trees flower and yield fruits; By Whose command the Kâla destroys all. By Whose command all the beings whether on land on in water are quitting their lives in time; until the proper time comes no man dies not die even if he be pierced whether in battle or in danger. By Whose command the wind supports the water; the water supports the tortoise; the tortoise supports the Ananta and the Ananta supports the earth; the earth supports the oceans, mountains and all the jewels. The earth is of the nature of forgiveness, *i. e.* endures all. For this reason all things, moving and non-moving, rest on Her and again melt away in Her. Seventy-one Divine Yugas constitute one Indra's life period. Twenty-eight Indra's life periods constitute Brahmâ's one day and one night. Thus thirty days constitute Brahmâ's one month; so two months constitute one Ritu (season); six Ritus make one year. Thus one hundred years constitute Brahmâ's-

life. When Brahmâ dies, Śrî Hari's eye closes. That is the Prâkritik
Pralaya. At this time, everything, moving and non-moving, from
the Deva loka to Bhûr loka (earth) dies. The Creator Brahmâ gets
dissolved in the navel of Śrî Krishṇa. The four-armed Viṣṇu, of
Vaikuṇṭha, sleeps on Kṣîra Samudra, the ocean of milk, i. e., He dissolves
on the left side of Śrî Krishṇa, the Highest Spirit. All the other
Śaktis (forces) dissolve in Mûla Prakriti, the Mâyâ of Viṣṇu. The
Mûla Prakriti Durgâ, the Presiding Deity of Buddhi (reason) dissolves
in the Beddhi of Krishṇa. Skanda, the part of Nârâyaṇa, dissolves
in His breast. Gaṇeśa, the foremost of the Devas, born in part of
Krishṇa, dissolves in the arm of Śrî Krishṇa. And those who are born
in parts of Padmâ, dissolve in Her body and Padmâ dissolves in the
body of Râdhâ. All the cow-herdesses and all the bodies of the Devas
dissolve in Râdhâ's body. But Râdhâ, the Presiding Deity of the
Prâṇa of S'rî Krishṇa, dissolves in the Prâṇa of Śrî Krishṇa. Sâvitrî,
the four Vedas and all the Śâstras dissolve in Sarasvatî ; and Sarasvatî gets dissolved in the tongue of Śrî Krishṇa, the Highest Self.
The Gopas in the region of Goloka dissolve in the pores of His skin ;
the Prâṇa Vâyu of all dissolve in His Prâṇa Vâyu ; the fire dissolves in
the fire in His belly ; water dissolves in the tip of His tongue, and
the Vaiṣṇavas, (devotees of Viṣṇu), drinking the nectar of Bhakti, the
Essence of all essences, dissolve in His lotus-feet. All smaller Virâṭs
dissolve in the Great Virâṭ and the Great Virâṭ dissolves in the Body
of S'rî Krishṇa. O Child! He is Krishṇa, on the pores of Whose
skin are situated endless Universes ; at the closing of Whose eyes,
the Prâkritic Pralaya comes and on the opening of Whose eyes, the creation
takes place. The closing and opening of the eyes takes the same
time. Brahmâ's creation lasts one hundred years and the Pralaya
lasts one hundred years. O One of good vows! There is no counting
how many Brahmâs or how many creations and dissolutions have taken
place. As one cannot count the number of dusts, so one cannot count
the creations and dissolutions. This is the Great Unspeakable Wonder!
Again on Whose closing of the eyes the Pralaya takes place and on whose
opening of the eyes the creation takes place, out of the will of God,
That Krishṇa dissolves at the time of Pralaya in Prakriti. This Highest Śakti, the Mûla Prakriti is the Only One without a second ; it is
the only one Nirguṇa and the Highest Puruṣa. It is considered as
"Sat" existing, by the Seers of the Vedas. Such a thing as Mûla
Prakriti is the unchanged state (Muktî). During the Pralaya, this only
One Mûla Prakriti appears as Jnâna Śakti or the Knowledge Force.
Who can in this universe recite Her glories? Mukti is of four kinds.

(1) Sâlokya, (2) Sârûpya, (3) Sâmîpya and (4) Nirvâṇa. So it is stated in the Vedas. Out of them Bhakti towards the Deva is the highest; so much so that the Deva Bhakti is superior to Mukti. Mukti gives Sâlokya, Sârûpya, Sâmîpya, and Nirvâṇa. But the Bhaktas do not want anything. They want service of the Lord. They do not want anything else. The state of becoming Śiva, of becoming an Amara or an immortal, becoming a Brahmâ, the birth, death, disease, old age, fear, sorrow, or wealth, or assuming a divine form, or Nirvâṇa or Mokṣa all are looked on alike by the Bhaktas with disregard and contempt. Because Mukti is without any service while Bhakti increases this service. Thus I have told you the difference between Bhakti and Mukti. Now hear about the cutting off of the fruits of the past Karmas. O Chaste one! This service of the Highest Lord severs the ties of Karmas (past acts). This service is really the True Knowledge. So, O Child! I have now told you the Real Truth, leading to auspicious results. Now you can go freely as you desire. Thus saying to Sâvitrî, Yama, the son of Sûrya, gave life back to her husband and blessing her, became ready to go to His own abode. Seeing Dharmarâja ready to go away, Sâvitrî became sorry to have the bereavement of a good company, bowed down at His feet and began to cry. Yama, the Ocean of Mercy, hearing the crying of Sâvitri began to weep and told the following words:—

80-96. Dharma said:—" O Child! You enjoy in this holy Bhârata happiness for one lakh years and you will in the end go to the Devîloka or Maṇi Dvîpa. Now go back to your house and observe for fourteen years the vow called Sâvitrî-vrata for the mukti of women. This Vrata is to be observed on the fourteenth day of the white fortnight in the month of Jyaiṣṭha. Then observe the Mahâ-Lakṣmî Vrata. Its proper time is the eighth day of the bright fortnight of the month of Bhâdra. For sixteen years consecutively without any break this vow is to be observed. The woman who practises with devotion this vow, goes to the abode of Mûla Prakriti. You would worship on every Tuesday in every month the Devî Mangala Chaṇḍikâ, the giver of all good; on the eighth day in the bright fortnight you should worship Devî Ṣaṣṭhî (i.e. Devasenâ); you should worship Manasâ Devî, the giver of all siddhis, on the Saṁkrânti day (when the Sun enters another sign) in every year; you should worship Râdhâ, the Central Figure of Râsa, more than the Prâṇa of Kriṣṇa on every Full Moon night in the month of Kârtik and you should observe fasting on the eighth day in the bright fortnight and worship the Viṣṇu Mâyâ Bhagavatî Devî, the Destructrix of all difficulties and dangers.

(*Note.*—The Râsa is the playing out of the Vedântic saying of Brahma as "Raso vai Sah;" He is of the nature of Rasa, the most sweet and lovely Divine Principle which unites the Rasika and the Rasikâ). The chaste woman having husband and sons who worships the World Mother Mûla Prakriti, whether in Yantra, or in Mantra or in image, enjoys all pleasures in this world; and, in the end, goes to the Devîloka or Maṇi Dvîpa. O Child! The worshipper Sâdhaka (one who is in one's way to success) must worship all the manifestations of the Devî, day and night. At all times one must worship the omnipresent Durgâ, the Highest Îśvarî. There is no other way to attain blessedness than this. Thus saying, Dharmarâja went to His own abode. Sâvitrî, too, with her husband Satyavân went to her home. Both Sâvitrî and Satyavân, when they reached home, narrated all their stories to their friends and acquaintances. In time, by the blessing of Yama, Sâvitrî's father got sons and father in-law recovered his eyesight and kingdom and Sâvitrî Herself got sons. For one lakh years, Sâvitrî enjoyed pleasures in this holy land of Bhârata, and ultimately went with her husband to the Devîloka Sâvitrî is the Presiding Deity of the Sûryamaṇḍalam, the solar orb. The Sun is the central Para Brahma. The Gâyatrî Mantra, the Presiding Devî, proves the existence of the Highest Brahma in the centre of the Sun. Therefore She is called Sâvitrî. Or Her name is Sâvitrî because all the Vedas have come out of Her. Thus I have narrated the excellent anecdote of Sâvitrî, and the fruitions of the Karmas of the several Jîvas. Now what more do you want to hear? Say.

Here ends the Thirty-eighth Chapter in the Ninth Book on the glories of the Devî and on the nature of Bhakti in the Mahâ Purâṇam Śrî Mad Devî Bhâgavatam of 18,000 verses by Maharṣi Veda Vyâsa.

CHAPTER XXXIX.

1-3 Nârada said:—"O Lord! I have heard in the discourse on Sâvitrî and Yama about the Formless Devî Mûla Prakriti and the glories of Sâvitrî, all true and leading to the endless good. Now I want to hear the story of the Devî Lakṣmî. O Thou, the Chief of the knowers of the Vedas! What is the nature of Lakṣmî? By whom was She first worshipped? and by what Mantra? Kindly describe Her glories to me.

4-33. Nârâyaṇa said:—Of old, in the beginning of the Prâkritik Creation, from the left side of Kriṣṇa, the Supreme Spirit, appeared in the Râsamaṇḍalam (the Figure Dance) a Devî. She looked exceedingly handsome, of a dark blue colour, of spacious hips, of thin waist, and with high breast, looking twelve years old, of steady youth, of a colour of white Champaka flower and very lovely. The beauty of Her face throws under shade millions and millions of autumnal full moons. Before Her wide expanded eyes, the midday lotus of the autumnal season becomes highly ashamed. By the Will of God, this Devî suddenly divided Herself into two parts. The two looked equal in every respect; whether in beauty, qualities, age, lovelines, colour, body, spirit, dress, ornaments, smile, glance, love, or humanity, they were perfectly equal.

Now she who appeared from the right side is named Râdhâ and she who came from the left side is named Mahâ Lakṣmî. Râdhâ wanted first the two armed Śrî Kriṣna, Who was Higher than the highest; then Mahâ Lakṣmî wanted Him. Râdhâ came out of the right side and wanted first Kriṣna; so Kriṣna, too, divided himself at once into two parts. From His right side came out the two-armed and from his left side came out the four-armed The two-armed person first made over to Mahâ Lakṣmi the four-armed One; then the two-armed Person Himself took Râdhâ. Lakṣmî looks on the whole universe with a cooling eye; hence She is named Lakṣmî and as She is great, She is called Mahâ Lakṣmî. And for that reason the Lord of Râdhâ is two-armed and the Lord of Lakṣmî is four-armed. Râdhâ is pure Aprâ kritic Śuddha Sattva (of the nature of pure Sattva Guṇa, the illuminating attribute) and surrounded by the Gopas and Gopîs. The four-armed Puruṣa, on the other hand, took Lakṣmî (Padmâ) to Vaikuṇṭha. The two-armed person is Kriṣna; and the four-armed is Nârâyaṇa. They are equal in all respects. Mahâ Lakṣmî became many by Her Yogic powers. (*i. e.* She remained in full in Vaikuṇṭha and assumed many forms in parts). Mahâ Lakṣmî of Vaikuṇṭha is full, of pure Sattva Guṇa, and endowed with all sorts of wealth and prosperity. She is the crest of woman-kind as far as loving one's husbands is concerned. She is the Svarga Lakṣmî in the Heavens; the Nâga Lakṣmî of the serpents, the Nâgas, in the nether regions; the Râja Lakṣmî of the kings and the Household Lakṣmî of the householders. She resides in the houses of householders as prosperity and the most auspicious of all good things. She is the progenetrix, She is the Surabhi of cows and She is the Dakṣiṇâ (the sacrificial fee) in sacrifices. She is the daughter of the milk ocean and she is Padminî, the beauty of the spheres of the Moon and the Sun. She is the lustre and beauty of the ornaments, gems, fruits, water, kings, queens, heavenly women, of all the houses, grains, clothings, cleansed places, images, auspicious jars, pearls, jewels, crest of jewels, garlands, diamonds, milk, sandal, beautiful twigs, fresh rain cloud, or of all other colours. She was first worhipped in Vaikuṇṭha by Nârâyaṇa. Next She was worshipped by Brahmâ and then by Sankara with devotion. She was worshipped by Viṣṇu in the Kṣhirode Samudra. Then she was worshipped by Svâyambhuva Manu, then by Indras amongst men, then by Munis, Riṣis, good householders, by the Gandharbas, in the Gandharbaloka; by the Nâgas in the Nâgaloka. She was worshipped with devotion by Brahmâ for one fortnight commencing from the bright eighth day in the month of Bhâdra and ending on the eighth day of the dark fortnight in the three-worlds. She was worshipped by Viṣṇu, with devotion in the three worlds on the meritorious Tuesday in the months of Pauṣa, Chaitra, and Bhâdra. Manu, also, worshipped Her on the Pauṣa Sankrânti (the last day of the month of Pauṣa when the Sun enters another sign) and on the auspicious Tuesday in the month of Mâgha. Thus the worship of Mahâ Lakṣmî is made prevalent in the three worlds. She was worshipped by Indra, the Lord of the Devas and by Mangala (Mars) on Tuesday. She was then worshipped by Kedâra, Nîla, Subala, Dhruva, Uttânapada, Śakra, Bali, Kas'yapa, Dakṣa, Kardama, Sûrya, Priyavrata, Chandra, Vâyu, Kuvera, Varuṇa, Yama, Hutâsana and others. Thus Her worship extended by and by to all the places. She is the Presiding Deity of all wealth; so She is the wealth of all.

Here ends the Thirty-ninth Chapter of the Ninth Book on the story of Mahâ Lakṣmî in the Mahâ Purâṇam Śrî Mad Devî Bhâgavatam of 18,000 verses by Maharṣi Veda Vyâsa.

CHAPTER XL.

1-2. Nârada said:—"O Lord! How did the eternal Devî Mahâ Lakṣmî, the dweller in Vaikuṇṭha, the beloved of Nârâyaṇa, the Presiding Deity of Vaikuṇṭha, come down to the earth and how She, became the daughter of the ocean? By whom was She first praised? Kindly describe all these in details to me and oblige.

3-10. Nârâyaṇa said:—O Nârada! In ancient days when on Durvâsâs curse, Indra was dispossessed of his kingdom, all the Devas came down to earth. Lakṣmî, too, getting angry, quitted the Heavens, out of pain and sorrow and went to Vaikuṇṭha and took the shelter of Nârâyaṇa. The Devas, then, went to Brahmâ with their hearts full of sorrow and, taking Him from there, they all went to Nârâyaṇa in Vaikuṇṭha. Going there they all took refuge of the Lord of Vaikuntha. They were very much distressed and their throats, palates and lips were quite dry. At that time Lakṣmî, the wealth and prosperity of all, came down on earth by the command of Nârâyaṇa and became born in part as the daughter of the ocean. The Devas, then, with the Daityas churned the Kṣîroda Ocean and, out of that, Mahâ

Lakṣmî appeared. Viṣṇu looked on Her. Her joy knew no bounds. She smiling, granted boons to the Devas and then offered a garland of flowers on the neck of Nârâyaṇa (as a symbol of marriage celebrated) O Nârada! the Devas, on the other hand, got back their kingdoms from the Asuras. They then worshipped and chanted hymns to Mahâ Lakṣmî and since then they became free from further dangers and troubles.

11-12. Nârada said :—"O Bhagavan! Durvâsâ was the best of the Munis; he was attached to Brahma and had spiritual knowledge. Why did he curse Indra? What offence had he committed? How did the Devas and Daityas churn the ocean? How, and by what hymns Lakṣmî became pleased and appeared before Indra? What passed on between them. Say all this, O Lord.

13-25. Nârâyaṇa said :—In ancient days, Indra the Lord of the three worlds, intoxicated with wine and becoming lustful and shameless, began to enjoy Rambhâ in a lonely grove. After having enjoyed her, he became attracted to her; his mind being wholly drawn to her, he remained there in that forest, his mind becoming very passionate. Indra then saw the Muni Durvâsâ on his way from Vaikuṇṭha to Kails'a burning with the fire of Brahma. From the body of the Riṣi, emitted, as it were, the rays of the thousand mid-day Suns. On his head was the golden matted hair. On his breast there was the hoary holy thread; he wore torn clothes; on his hands there was the Daṇḍa and Kamaṇḍalu; on his forehead there was the bright Tilaka in the form of the Crescent Moon.

(Tilaka— a sectarian mark on the forehead made with coloured earth or sandalpaste.) One hundred thousand disciples, thoroughly-versed in the Vedas and the Vedângas, were attending him. The intoxicated Purandara, seeing him, bowed down to him and he began to chant with devotion hymns to his disciples also. They were very glad. The Riṣi with his disciples then blessed Indra and gave him one Pârijâta flower.

When the Muni was returning from the region of Vaikuṇṭha, Viṣṇu, gave him that beautiful Pârijâta flower. Old age, death, disease, sorrows, etc., all are removed by the influence of the flower; and the final liberation is also attaind. The Devendra was intoxicated with his wealth; so taking the flower given by the Riṣî, he threw it on the head of the elephant Airâvata. No sooner the elephant touched the flower, than he became suddenly like Viṣṇu, as it were, in beauty, form, qualities, fire and age. The elephant, then, forsook Indra and entered into a dense forest. The Lord of the Devas could, in no way, get him under his control. On the other hand, the Muni Durvâsâ seeing that Mahendra had thus dishonoured the flower, became inflamed with rage and cursed him saying "O Indra! You are so mad with wealth that you have dishonoured me. The flower that I gave you so lovingly, you have thrown that, out of vanity, on the elephant's head !

26-45. No sooner one gets the food, water, fruits that had been offered to Viṣṇu, one should eat that at once. Otherwise one incurs the sin of Brahmahattyâ. If anybody forsakes the things offered to Viṣṇu, that he has got perchance, he becomes destitute of wealth, prosperity, intelligence, and his kingdom. And if he eats the food already offered to Viṣṇu with devotion, he then elevates his hundred families passed before him and he himself becomes liberated while living. If anybody daily eats Viṣṇu's Naivedyam (food offered to Viṣṇu) and bows down before Him or worships Hari with devotion and chants hymns to Him, he becomes like Viṣṇu in energy and wealth. By mere touch with the air round about his body, the places of pilgrimage become all purified. O You Stupid ! The earth becomes purified by the contact of the dust of the feet of such a one devoted to Viṣṇu. If anybody eats the food unoffered to Hari and flesh that is not offered to any Deity ; if he eats the food of any unchaste woman, any woman without husband and sons, the food offered at any Śûdra's Śrâdh (funeral) ceremony, the food offered by a Brâhmaṇa, who is a priest to the Śûdras in honour of a Śiva Lingam, the food of a Brâhmaṇ priest who subsists on the presents of a temple, the food of one who sells his daughter, the food of one who subsists on dealings with womb concerns, the leavings of others, the stale food left after all others had eaten, the food of the husband of an unmarried girl (twelve years old in whom menstruation has commenced), the driver of oxen, the food of one uninitiated in one's Iṣṭamantram, of one who burns a corpse, of a Brâhmin who goes to one not fit for going, the food of a rebel against friends, of one who is faithless, treacherous who gives false evidence, the food of a Brâhmin who accepts offerings in a sacred place of pilgrimage, all his sins (incurred in the ways above-mentioned) will be removed if he eats the prasâdam of Viṣṇu, i.e. the food offered to Viṣṇu. Even if a Châṇḍâla be attached to the service of Viṣṇu, he sanctifies his millions of persons born in his family before him. And the man who is devoid of the devotion to Hari is not able even to save himself. If anybody takes unknowingly the remains of an offering (such as flowers) made to Viṣṇu he will certainly be freed from all the sins incurred in his seven births. And if he does this knowingly and with intense devotion, he will certainly be freed of all sorts of sins incurred in his Koṭi births. So, O Indra! I am a devotee of Śrî Hari. And when you have cast away the Pârijâta flower offered by me on the elephant's head, then I say unto you that the Mahâ Lakṣî will leave you and She will go back to Nârâyaṇa. I am highly devoted to Nârâyaṇa; so I do not fear anybody, I fear neither the Creator, nor Kâla, the Destroyer, nor old age, nor death; what to speak of other petty persons! I do not fear your father Prajâpati Kas'yapa nor do I fear your family priest Brihaspati. Now he, on whose head there lies the flower Pârijâta offered by me, verily he should be worshipped by all means. Hearing these word of Durvâsâ, Indra became bewildered with fear, and being greatly distressed and holding the feet of Muni, cried out loudly. He said :—" The curse is now well inflicted on me; and it has caused my delusion vanish. Now I do not want back my Râja Lakṣmî from you; instruct me on knowlege. This wealth is the source of all coils; it is the cause of the veil to all knowledge, it hides the final liberation and it is a great obstacle on the way to get the highest devotion.

47-67. The Muni said :—" This birth, death, old age, disease, and afflictions, all come from wealth and the manipulation of great power. Being blind by the darkness of wealth, he does not see the road to Mukti. The stupid man that is intoxicated with wealth is like the one that is intoxicated with wine. Surrounded by many friends, he is surrounded by the unbreakable bondage. The man that is intoxicated with wealth, blind with property and overwhelmed with these things has no thought for the real knowledge. He who is Râjasik, is very much addicted to passions and desires; he never sees the path to Sattvaguṇa. The man that is blind with sense-objects is of two kinds, firstly, Râjasik and secondly Tâmasik. He who has no knowledge of the Sâstras is Tamasik and he who has the knowledge of the Śâstras is Râjasik. O Child of the Devas! Two paths are mentioned in the Śâstras; one is Pravritti, going towards the sense objects and the other is Nivritti, going away from them. The Jivas first follow the path of Pravritti, the path that is painful, gladly and of their own accord like a mad man. As bees, blind with the desire of getting honey, go to the lotus bud and get themselves entangled there, so the Jîvas, the embodied souls, desirous first of getting enjoyments come to this very painful circle of births and deaths, this wordly life, which in the end is realised as vapid and the only cause of old age, death, and sorrow and get themselves enchained there.

For many births he travels gladly in various wombs, ordained by his own Karmas, till at last by the favour of gods, he comes in contact with the saints. Thus one out of a thousand or out of an hundred finds means to cross this terrible ocean of world. When the saintly persons kindle the lamp of knowledge and shew the way to Mukti, then the Jîva makes an attempt to sever this bondage to the world. After many births, many austerities and many fastings, he then finds safely the way to Mukti, leading to the highest happiness. O Indra! What you asked me, I thus heard from my Guru. O Nârada! Hearing the words of the Muni Durvâsâ Indra became dispassionate towards the Sam-Ara. Day by day his feeling of dispassion increased. One day, when he returned to his own home from the hermitage of the Muni, he saw the Heavens overspread by the Daityas and it had become terrible. At some places outrage and oppression knew no bounds; some places were devoid of friends; at some places, some persons had lost their fathers, mothers, wives, relations; so no rest and repose could be found. Thus, seeing the Heavens in the hands of the enemies, Indra went out in quest of Brihaspati, the family preceptor of the Devas. Seeking to and fro Indra ultimately went to the banks of the Mandâkinî and saw that the Guru Deva had bathed in the waters of the Mandâkinî and sitting with his face turned towards the East towards the Sun, was meditating on Para Brahma, Who has His faces turned everywhere. Tears were flowing from his eyes and the hairs of the body stood erect with delight. He was elderly in knowledge; the spritual Teacher of all, religous, served by all great men; he was held as most dear to all the frends. Those who are Jñânins regard him as their Gurus. He was the eldest of all his brothers; he was considered as very unpopular to the enemies of the Devas. Seeing the family priest Brihaspati merged in that state of meditation, Indra waited there. When after one Prahara (three hours), the Guru Deva got up, Indra bowed down to his feet and began to weep and cry out repeatedly. Then he informed his Guru about his curse from a Brâhmin, his acquiring the true knowledge as so very rare, and the wretched state of Amarâvatî, wrought by the enemies.

68-92. O Best of Brâhmaṇas! Hearing thus the words of the disciple, the intelligent speaker Brihaspati spoke with his eyes reddened out of anger. "O Lord of the Devas! I have heard everything that you said; do not cry; have patience; hear attentively what I say. The wise politicians of good behaviour, with moral precepts, never lose their heads and get themselves distressed in times of danger. Nothing is everlasting; whether property or adversity; all are transient;

they only give troubles. All are under one's own Karma; one is master of one's own Karma. What had been done in previous births, so one will have to reap the fruits afterwards. (Therefore property or adversity, all are due to one's own Karma.) This happens to all persons eternally, births after births. Pain and happiness are like the ring of a rolling wheel. So what pain is there? It is already stated that one's own Karma must be enjoyed in this Holy Bhârata. The man enjoys the effects of his own Karmas, auspicious or inauspicious. Never the Karma gets exhausted in one hundred Koṭi Kalpas, without their effects being enjoyed. The Karma, whether auspicious or inauspicious must be enjoyed. Thus it is stated in the Vedas and as well by Śrî Kriṣṇa, the Supreme Spirit. Bhagavan Śrî Kriṣṇa addressed Brahmâ, the lotus-born, in the Sâma Veda Sâkhâ that all persons acquire their births, whether, in Bhârata or in any other country, according to the Karma that he had done. The course of a Brâhmaṇa comes though this Karma; and the blessings of a Brâhmaṇa come again by this Karma. By Karma one gets great wealth and prosperity and by Karma again one gets poverty. You may take one hundred Koṭi births; the fruit of Karma must follow you. O Indra! The fruit of Karma follows one like one's shadow. Without enjoyment, that can never die. The effects of Karma become increased or dicreased according to time, place, and the person concerned. As you will give away anything to persons, of different natures, in different times and in different places, your merit acquired will also vary accordingly. Gifts made on certain special days bring in Koṭi times the fruits (merits, puṇyam) or infinite times or even more than that. Again gifts, similar in nature, made in similar paces yield puṇyam the same, in character also. Gifts made in different countries yield puṇyams, Koṭi times, infinite times, or even more than that. But similar things given to similar persons yield similar puṇyams. As the grains vary in their natures as the fields differ, so gifts made to different persons yield different grades of puṇyas infinitely superior or infinitely inferior as the case may be.

Giving things to a Brâhmaṇa on any ordinary days yields simple puṇya only. But if the gift be made to a Brâhmaṇ on an Amavasyâ day (new moon day) or on a Sankrânti day (the day when the Sun enters another's sign) then hundred times more puṇyam is acquired. Again charities made on the Châturmâsya period (the vow that lasts for four months in the rainy season) or on the full moon day, yield infinite puṇyams. So charities made on the occasion of the lunar eclipses yield Koṭi times the result and if made on the occasion of the solar eclipse yield ten times more puṇyams. Charities made on Akṣayaya Tritîyâ or the Navamî day yield infinite and endless results. So charities on other holy days yield religious merits higher than those made on ordinary days. As charities made on holy days yields religious merits, so bathing, reciting mantrams, and other holy acts yield meritorious results. As superior results are obtained by pious acts; so inferior results are obtained by impious acts. As an earthen potter makes pots, jars, etc., out of the earth with the help of rod, wheel, earthen cups or plates and motion, so the Creator awards respective fruits to different persons, by the help of this thread (continuity) of Karma. Therefore if you want to have cessation of this fruition of Karma, then worship, Nârâyaṇa, by whose command all these things of Nature are created. He is the Creator of even Brahmâ, the Creator, the Preserver of Viṣṇu, the Preserver, the Destroyer of Śiva, the Destroyer and the Kâla (the great Time) of Kâla (the Time). Śankara has said :—He who remembers Madhusûdana (a name of Viṣṇu) in great troubles, his dangers cease and happiness begins. O Nârada! The wise Brihaspati thus advised Indra and then embraced him and gave him his hearty blessings and good wishes.

Here ends the Fortieth Chapter of the Ninth Book on the birth of Lakṣmî in the discourse of Nârada and Nârâyaṇa in the Mahâ Purâṇam Śrî Mad Devî Bhâgavatam of 18,000 verses by Maharṣi Veda Vyâsa.

CHAPTER XLI.

1-2. Nârâyṇa said :—" O Twice-born! Indra then remembered Hari and took Brihaspati, the Guru of the Devas, to the assembly of Brahmâ, accompanied by the other Devas. They soon reached the region of Brahmâ and no sooner they saw Him, than Indra and the other Devas and Bihaspati all bowed down to Him.

3-25. Brihaspati, the Âchârya of the Devas, then communicated all to Brahmâ. Hearing this, He smiled and spoke, addressing Indra :—" O Indra! You have been born in My race; nay, you are My grandson; the Ârya Brihaspati is your Guru; you yourself are the ruler of the Devas and you are very wise and sagacious; the mother of your father is the powerful Dakṣa. a great Viṣṇu Bhakta. How is it, then that when the three sides of the family are pure, one would turn out so haughty and arrogant! Whose mother is so much devoted to her husband, whose father, mother's father and mother's, brother are self-controlled and of pure Sattva Guṇa, he is not expected to be so very haughty! Every man may be guilty to Hari for the three faults :—For some fault due to that of his father, or of his mother's father, or of Guru, the Spiritual Teacher. Bhagavân Nârâyaṇa, resides in this great holy temple of our this physical body controlling the hearts of all. At whatever moment, Śrî Nârâyaṇa quits this temple-body, at that momant this body becomes dead. I myself am the mind; Śankara is the Knowledge, Viṣṇu is the vital breaths, Bhagvatî Durgâ is the intelligence (Buddhi), sleep, etc., the powers of Prakriti; when these are being reflected on by the Âtman, Jiva is formed with a body for enjoyment called Bhoga Śarîrabhrit. When a king departs, his attendants also follow him; so when this Âtmân departs from this temple of body, his attendants mind, buddhi, etc., instantly depart from this body and follow the Âtman. O Indra! We all, are verily, the parts of Śrî Krişņa. I myself, Śiva, Ananta Deva, Vişņu, Dharma, Mahâ Virât, you all are His parts and entirely devoted to Him. And you have shown contempt for His flowers. Bhagavân Śankara, the Lord of the Bhutas, worshipped the lotus-feet of Śri Krişņa with that flower. The Rişi Durvâsâ gave you that flower. But you showed disrespect to it. The flower, Pârijâta, after being offered at the lotus-feet of Krişņa, should be placed on the head of an Immortal; His worship is to be done first; and it is the foremost amongst the Devas. So you are now being afflicted by the inevitable course of Fate; Fate is the most powerful of all. Who can save that unlucky man against whom Fate has turned? Seeing that you have rejected the flower offered to Śrî Krişņa, Śrî Lakşmî Devî has left you out of anger. Now come with Me and with your family priest Brihaspati to Vaikuņtha and worship the Lord of Lakşmî; then by His grace you may get back your Heavens. Thus saying, Brahmâ with Indra and all the other Devas, went to the Eternal Puruşa, Bhagavân Nârâyaņa and saw that He was full of Fire and Energy like one hundred koți summer mid-day Suns, yet perfectly cool and calm. He has no beginning, and no end, nor any middle. He is Infinite. The four-armed Pârişadas, Sarasvatî, the four Vedas, and the Ganges, all were surrounding Him. Seeing Him, Brahmâ and the other Devas bowed down with devotion and began to chant hymns to Him with tears in their eyes. Brahmâ, then, informed Him of everything when all the Devas, dispossessed of their places, began to weep before Him. Nârâyaņa saw that the Devas were very afraid and much distressed. They had no jewel ornaments as before, no vehicles (Vâhanas), nor the Daivic splendour as before, not that brilliance; always fearful. Then Nârâyaņa, the Destroyer of fear, seeing the Devas in that state, addressed Brahmâ and the other Devas:—"O Brahman! O Devas! Discard all fears. What fear can overcome you? I am here. I will give you again the immoveable prosperous Râjya Lakşmî (the Lakşmî of the kings).

26-47. But for the present, I give you some advice proper for this moment. Listen. There are endless universes where exist innumerable persons. All of them are under Me. So know verily, that

I am under them also. My devotees regard Me as the Highest They know no other than Me ; they are fearless ; so I do not remain in that house where My devotees are dissatisfied. I instantly quit that house with Lakṣmî. Durbâsâ Riṣi is born in part of Śankara. He is highly devoted to Me. He is a pakkâ Vaiṣṇava. He cursed you and, as a matter of fact, I and Lakṣmî instantly left your house.

Lakṣmî does not reside in that house where conchshells are not blown, where there are no Tulasî trees, where there is no worship of Śiva and Śivâ, where the Brâhmaṇas are not fed. O Brâhmaṇ ! O Devas ! Where I and My Bhaktas are blamed, Mahâ Lakṣmî becomes greatly displeased. She instantly goes away out of that house. Lakṣmî does not stay even for a moment in that house where the stupid person, without any devotion for me, takes his food on the Harivâsara Ekâdas'î day (the eleventh day of the moon's wane or increase) or on My anniversay birthday. If anybody sells My name or his own daughter, where the guests are not served, Lakṣmî quits that house instantly and goes away.

(Note :—That Guru is the Real Guru, who, being capable, imparts the name of God to worthy persons without taking any fee at all.) If the son of an unchaste woman be a Brahmaṇa, he and the husband of an unchaste woman are great sinners. If anybody goes to such a person's house or eats the food of a Śûdra during a Srâddha ceremony, Lakṣmî becomes very angry and vacates that house. Being a Brâhmiṇ, if one burns a Sudra's corpse, one becomes very wretched and the vilest of the Brâhmiṇs. Lakṣmî never stays for a moment more in that house. Being a Brâhmiṇ, if he be a Śûdra's cook and drives oxen, Lakṣmî fears to drink water there and quits his house. Being a Brâhmi ṇ, if his heart be unholy, if he be cruel, envies others and blames per sons, if he officiates as a priest for the Śûdra, Lakṣmî Devî never stays in h is house. The World-Mother never stays even for a moment in his house who eats at the house of one who marries an unmarried girl twelve years old in whom menstruation has commenced. He who cuts grass by his nails, or writes on the ground with his nails, or from whose house a Brâhmaṇa guest goes back disappointed, Lakṣmî ne ver stays in his house. If any Brâhmaṇa eats food at the ea rly sunrise, sleeps during the day or engages in a sexual intercourse during the day, Lakṣmî never stays in his house. Lakṣmî slips away from that Brâhmaṇa who is devoid of Âchâra (rules of conduct), who accepts gifts from Śûdras, from him who remains uninitiated in his Mantram. The ignorant man who sleeps naked and with his feet wet, who laughs always, and always talks at random on disconnected subjects like a mad man, is forsaken at once by Lakṣmî. Lakṣmî becomes angry and goes away from the house of that man who applies oil all over his body first and then touches the bodies of others and always makes some sounding noise on several parts of his body. If any Brâhmaṇa forsakes observing vows, fastings, the Sandhyâ ceremony, purity and devotion to Viṣṇu, Kamalâ (Lakṣmî) does not remain in his house any longer. If anybody blames always the Brâhmaṇas and shews his hatred always towards the Brâhmaṇas, if he does injury to the animals, and if he does not indulge in his heart anything of pity, kindness, Lakṣmî, the Mother of the Worlds, quits him. O Lotus-born! But where Hari is worshipped and Hari's Name is chanted, Lakṣmî, the Mother of all auspiciousness, remains there. Lakṣmî remains where the glories of Śrî Kriṣṇa and His Bhaktas are sung.

48-59. Lakṣmî always remains there with the greatest gladness where conch-shells are blown, where there are conchsells,the Sâlagrâma stone, the Tulasi leaves and the service and meditation of Lakṣmî are daily done.

Where the phallic emblem of Śiva is worshipped, and His glories sung, where Sri Durgâ is worshipped and Her glories are sung, Lakṣmî, the Dweller in the Lotus, remains there. Where the Brâhmaṇas are honoured and they are gladly feasted, where all the Devas are worshiped; the chaste Lakṣmî, the Lotus-faced, remains there. Thus saying to the Devas, the Lord of Lakṣmî said':—O Devî! Go without any any delay to the Kṣiroda Ocean and incarnate there in part. He then addressed Brahmâ and said:—"O Lotus-born! You also better go there and churn the Kṣiroda Ocean; when Lakṣmî will arise, give Her to the Devas." O Devarsi! Thus saying, the Lord Kamalâ went to His inner compartment. On the other hand the Devas, after a long time, reached the shores of the Kṣiroda Ocean. The Devas and the Daityas then made the Golden Mountain (the Sumeru) the churning rod, the Deva Kurma (the tortoise), the churning pot and Ananta Deva (the thousand headed serpent) the churning cord and began to churn the ocean. While churning was going on, by and by arose Dhanvantarî, Amrita (the nectar), the horse Uchchaihs'ravâ, various other invaluable jewels that were desired, the elephant Airâvata and the beautiful eyed Lakṣmî. Viṣṇupriyâ, Srî Lakṣmî Devî, no sooner She got up from the ocean, she, the chaste woman, presented on the neck of Nârâyaṇa, of beautiful appearance, the Lord of all, Who slept on the Kṣiroda ocean the garland (indicative of accepting Him for her bridegroom). Then Brahmâ and Mahes'vara and the other Devas gladly worshipped Her and chanted hymns. At this time Lakṣmî Devî being pleased, cast a favourable glance towards the homes of the Devas, in order to free them from their curse. Then, by the grace of Mahâ Lakṣmî and by the granting of the boon by Brahmâ, the Devas got back their own possessions from the hands of the Daityas. O Nârada! Thus I have described to you the story of Lakṣmî Devî, the Essence of all Essences, and very pleasant to hear. Now what more do you want to hear? Say.

Here ends the Forty-first Chapter of the Ninth Book on the churning of the ocean and on the appearing of Lakṣmî in the Mahâ Purâṇam Śrî Mad Devî Bhâgavatam of 18,000 verses by Maharṣi Veda Vyâsa.

CHAPTER XLII.

1-50. Nârada said:—O Bhagavan! I have heard about the glories of Hari, about the Tattvajñânam (the True Knowledge) and the story of Lakṣmî. Now tell me Her Dhyânam (meditation) and Stotram (recitation of hymns) of Her. Nârâyana said:—"O Nârada! Indra then, bathed first in the Tîrath (holy place) and, wearing a cleansed cloth, installed, first of all, an earthen jar (ghaṭa) on the beach of the Kṣiroda Ocean. Then he worshipped with devotion Gaṇes'a, Sûrya, Fire, Viṣṇu, Śiva, and Śivâ, the six deities with scents and flowers. Next Indra invoked Mahâ Lakṣmî, of the nature of the highest powers and greatest prosperity, and began to worship Her as Brahmâ, who was acting as an officiating priest in the presence of the Munis, Brâhmaṇas, Brihaspati, Hari and the other Devas, had dictated him. He first smeared one Pârijata flower with sandal paste and reciting the meditation mantra of Mahâ Lakṣmî offered it to Her feet. The meditation mantra that was recited by Devendra, was what Bhagavân Hari first gave to Brahmâ. I am now telling you that. Listen.

"O Mother! Thou residest on the thousand-petalled lotus. The beauty of Thy face excels the beauty of koṭi autumnal Full Moons. Thou art shining with Thy own splendour. Thou art very beautiful and lovely Thy colour is like the burnished gold; Thou art with form, chaste, ornamented all over with jewel ornaments; Thou art wearing the yellow cloth and look! What beauty is coming out of it! Always a sweet smile reigns on Thy lips. Thy beauty is constant; Thou art the bestower of prosperity to all. O Mahâ Lakṣmî! I meditate on Thee." Thus meditating on Her endowed with various attributes with this mantra, Indra worshipped devotedly with sixteen upachâras (articles offered). Every upachâra (article) was offered with the repetition of mantra. All the things were very excellent, right and commendable. "O Mahâ Lakṣmî!

Vis'vakarmâ has made this invaluable Âsan (a carpet seat) wonderfully decked with jewels; I am offering this Âsan to Thee. Accept." O Thou residing in the Lotus! This holy Ganges water is considered with great regard and desired by all. This is like the fire to burn the fuel in the shape of the sins of the sinners. O Thou! The Dweller in the Lotus! This Dûrbba grass, flowers, this Arghya (offering) of the Ganges water perfumed with sandalpaste, I am offering to Thee. Accept. O Beloved of Hari! This sweet scented flower oil and this sweet scented Âmalaki fruit lead to the beauty of the body; therefore I present this to Thee. Accept. O Devî! I am presenting this cloth made of silk to Thee; âccept. O Devî! This excellent ornament made of gold and jewels, which increases the beauty, I am presenting to Thee. Accept. O Beloved of Kriṣna! I am presenting this sweet scented holy Dhûpa prepared from various herbs and plants, exquisitely nice and the root of all beauty, to Thee. Accept. This sweet scented pleasant sandalpaste I offer to Thee, O Devî! Accept. O Ruler of the Devas! I present this pleasing holy Dîpa (lights) which is the eye of this world and by which all the darkness is vanished; accept. O Devî! I present to Thee these very delicious offerings of fruits, etc., very juicy and of various kinds. Accept. O Deves'î! This Anna (food) is Brahma and the chief means to preserve the life of living beings. By this the nourishment of the body and the mental satisfaction are effected. Therefore I am presenting this food to Thee. Accept. O Mahâ Lakṣmî! I am presenting this most delicious Paramânna, which is prepared out of rice, milk and sugar, to Thee. Accept. O Devî! I am presenting this most delicious and pleasant svastika prepared of sugar and clarified butter to Thee; accept. O Beloved of Achyuta! I am presenting to Thee various beautiful Pakkâunas, ripe delicious fruits and clarified butter out of cow's milk; accept. O Devî! The sugarcane juice, when heated, yields a syrup which again heated yields very delicious and nice thing called *Gur*. I am presenting this Gur to Thee; accept. O Devî! I am presenting to Thee the sweetmeats prepared out of the flour of Yava and and wheat and Gur and clarified butter; accept. I am presenting with devotion the offering made of Svastika and the flour of other grains; accept. O Kamale! I am presenting to Thee this fan and white châmara, which blows cool air and is very pleasant when this body gets hot; accept. O Devî! I am presenting this betel scented with camphor by which the inertness of the tongue is removed; accept. O Devî! I am presenting this scented cool water, which will allay the thirst and which is known as the life of this world; accept. O Devî! I am presenting this cloth made of cotton and silk that increases the beauty and splendour of the body. Accept. O Devî! I am presenting to Thee, the ornaments made of gold and jewels which are the source of beauty and love-liness. Accept. O Devî ! I am presenting to Thee these pure garlands of flowers which blossom in different seasons, which look very beautiful and which give satisfaction to the Devas and to the kings. Accept. O Devî ! I am presenting to Thee this nice scent, this very holy thing to Thee by which both the body and mind become pure, which is most auspicious and which is prepared of many fragrant herbs and plants ; accept. O Beloved of the God Krïṣṇa ! I am presenting this Âchamanîya water to Thee for rinsing the mouth, pure and holy, and brought from holy places of pilgrimages ; accept. O Devî ! I am presenting to Thee, this bed made of excellent gems and jewels and flowers, sandalpaste, clothings and ornaments; accept. O Devî ! I am presenting to Thee all those things that are extraordinary, very rare in this earth and fit to be enjoyed by the Devas and worthy of their ornaments ; accept. O Devarṣi ! Uttering those mantras, the Devendra offered those articles, with intense devotion according to the rules. He, then, made Japam of the Mûla Mantra (the Radical Seed Mantra) ten lakhs of times. Thus his Mantra revealed the Deity thereof and thus came to a successful issue. The lotus-born Brahmâ gave this Mantra "Śrîm, Hrîm Klîm Aim Kamalavâsinyai Svâhâ", to the Devendra. This is like a Kalpavrikṣa (the tree in Indra's garden yielding whatever may be desired). This Vaidik mantra is the chief of the mantras. The word "Svâhâ" is at the end of the mantra. By virtue of this Mantra, Kuvera got his highest prosperity. By the power of this Mantra, the King-Emperor Dakṣa Sâvarṇi Manu and Mangala became the lords of the earth with seven islands. Priyavrata, Uttânapâda, and Kedârarâja all these became Siddhas (were fructified with success) and became King-Emperors. O Nârada ! When Indra attained success in this Mantra, there appeared before him Mahâ Lakṣmî, seated in the celestial car, decked with excellent gems and jewels. The Great Halo, coming out of Her body made manifest the earth with seven islands. Her colour was white like the white champaka flower and Her whole body was decked with ornaments. Her face was always gracious and cheerful with sweet smiles. She was ever ready to shew Her kindness to the Bhaktas. On Her neck there was a garland of jewels and gems, bright as ten million Moons. O Devarṣi ! No sooner did Indra saw that World Mother Mahâ Lakṣmî, of a peaceful appearance, than his body was filled with joy and the hairs of the body stool on ends. His eyes were filled with tears ; and, with folded palms, he began to recite stotras to Her, the Vaidik stotras, yielding all desires, that was communicated to him by Brahmâ.

51-75. Indra said:—" O Thou, the Dweller in the lotus ! O Nârâyaṇi! O Dear to Kriṣṇa ! O Padmâsane ! O Mahâ Lakṣmî !

Obeisance to Thee! O Padmadalekṣaṇe! O Padmanibhânane! O Padmâsane! O Padme! O Vaiṣṇavî! Obeisance to Thee! Thou art the wealth of all; Thou art worshipped by all; Thou bestowest to all the bliss and devotion to Śrî Harî. I bow down to Thee. O Devî! Thou always dwellest on the breast of Krisṇa and exercisest Thy powers over Him. Thou art the beauty ot the Moon; Thou takest Thy seat on the beautiful Jewel Lotus. Obeisance to Thee! O Devî! Thou art the Presiding Deity of the riches; Thou art the Great Devî; Thou increasest always Thy gifts and Thou art the bestower of increments. So I bow down to Thee. O Devî! Thou art the Mahâ Lakṣmî of Vaikuṇṭha, the Lakṣmî of the Kṣiroda Ocean; Thou art Indra's Heavenly Lakṣmî; Thou art the Râja Lakṣmî of the Kings; Thou art the Griha Lakṣmî of the householders; Thou art the household Deity of them; Thou art the Surabhî, born of the Ocean; Thou art the Dakṣ'iṇâ, the wife of the Sacrifices; Thou art Aditi, the Mother of the Devas; Thou art the Kamalâ, always dwelling in the Lotus; Thou art the Svâhâ, in the offerings with clarified butter in the sacrificial ceremonies; Thou art the Svadhâ Mantra in the Kâvyas (an offering of food to deceased ancestors). So obeisance to Thee! O Mother! Thou art of the nature of Viṣṇu; Thou art the Earth that supports all; Thou art of pure Śuddha Sattva and Thou art devoted to Nârâyaṇa. Thou art void of anger, jealousy. Rather Thou grantest boons to all. Thou art the auspicious Sâradâ; Thou grantest the Highest Reality and the devotional service to Harî. Without Thee all the worlds are quite stale, to no purpose like ashes, always dead while existing. Thou art the Chief Mother, the Chief Friend of all; Thou art the source of Dharma, Artha, Kâma and Mokṣa! As a mother nourishes her infants with the milk of her breasts, so Thou nourishest all as their mother! A child that sucks the milk might be saved by the Daiva (Fate), when deprived of its mother; but men can never be saved, if they be bereft of Thee! O Mother! Thou art always gracious. Please be gracious unto me. O Eternal One! My possessions are now in the hands of the enemies. Be kind enough to restore my kingdoms to me from my enemies' hands. O Beloved of Hari! Since Thou hast forsaken me, I am wandering abroad, friendles, like a beggar, deprived of all prosperities. O Devî! Give me Jnânam, Dharma, my desired fortune, power, influence and my possessions. O Nârada! Indra and all the other Devas bowed down frequently to Mahâ Lakṣmî with their eyes filled with tears. Brahmâ, Śankara, Ananta Deva, Dharma and Kes'ava all asked pardon again and again from Mahâ Lakṣmî. Lakṣmî then granted boons to the Devas and before the assembly gladly gave the garland of flowers on the neck of Ke'sava. The Devas, satisfied, went back to their own places. The Devi, Lakṣmi, too, becoming very glad went to Śrî Hari sleeping in the Kṣiroda Ocean. Brahmâ and Mahes'vara, both became very glad and, blessing the Devas, went respectively to their own abodes. Whoever recites this holy Stotra three times a day, becomes the King Emperor and gets prosperity and wealth like the God Kuvera. Siddhi (success) comes to him who recities this stotra five lakhs of times. If anybody reads regularly and always this Siddha Stotra for one month, he becomes very happy and he turns out a Râjarâjendra.

Here ends the Forty-second Chapter of the Ninth Book on the Dhyânam and Stotra of Mahâ Lakṣmî in the Mahâ Purâṇam Śrî Mad Devî Bhâgavatam of 18,000 verses by Maharṣî Veda Vyâsa.

CHAPTER XLIII.

1-4.—Nârada said:—" O Riṣi Nârâyaṇa ! O Highly Fortunate One ! O Lord ! Thou art equal to Nârayâṇa whether in beauty or in qualities, or in fame or in energy or in everything Thou art equal to Nârâyaṇa. Thou art the foremost of the Jñânins; there cannot be found a second like Thee as a Siddha Yogî, the ascetics and the Munis. And Thou art the crest of the knowers of the Vedas. I have heard the wonderful anecdote of Mahâ Lakṣmî that Thou hast told me. Now tell me any other thing that is unknown, very good in everyway, in accordance with Dharma, in the Vedas, and that which is not as yet written in the Purâṇas.

5-6. Nârâyaṇa said:—"There are many wonderful hidden anecdotes that are not published as yet in the Purâṇas. What you have heard is very small in fact. Please mention me what you like to hear, what you think as best amongst them and I will describe that to you.

7-8. Nârada said :—"When clarified butter is poured as libations in all the sacrificial ceremonies to the gods, Svâhâ is to be uttered everywhere as excellent, and commendable ; so Svadhâ is to be repeated in the offerings when the oblations are offered to the Pitris, the deceased ancestors. Then, again, Dakṣinâ (the sacrificial fee)is always to be paid as right and excellent. So, O Knower of the Vedas ! I like to hear the accounts of Svadhâ, and Dakṣinâ and their merits. Please now tell me about them.

9. Sûta said:—"Hearing the words of Nârada, Nârâyaṇa Riṣi smiled and began to speak the very ancient words of the Purâṇas.

10-11. Nârâyaṇa said:—Before the creation, the Devas assembled in the beautiful Brahmâ's Council to decide on their food question."

They all brought to the notice of Brahmâ the scarcity about their food. Brahmâ promised to remove their food difficulties and began to chant hymns to Hari.

12. Nârada said:—"O Lord! Bhagavân Nârâyaṇa Himself incarnated in part as Sacrifice. Are not the Devas satisfied when the Brâhmaṇas pour oblations of ghee to the Devas in those sacrifices?

13-17. Nârâyana said:—"O Muni! The Devas, in fact, did not get the offerings of the clarified butters that were poured in with devotion in sacrificial acts by the Brâhmaṇas and Kṣattriyas. So they were very much depressed and went again to the council of Brahmâ and informed Him that they could not get any food for themselves. On hearing this, Brahmâ at once meditated and took refuge of Srî Kriṣṇa; Krisṇa advised them to worship Mûla Prakriti. Brahmâ then, by the command of Srî Krisṇa, began to meditate on Prakriti, worship Her and chant hymns to Her. Then from the part of Prakriti, an all-powerful Devî appeared. She was very beautiful, Shyâmâ (of a blue colour) and very lovely. This Devî was Svâhâ. She looked always gracious with smile in Her face; it seemed that She was always ready to show favour towards the Bhaktas. She appeared before Brahmâ and said:—"O Lotus born! Want any boon you desire."

18-22. Hearing Her words, the Creator spoke reverentially:—"O Devî! Let Thou be the burning power of Fire; without Thee Fire would not be able to burn anything. At the conclusion, of any Mantra, whoever taking Thy name, will pour obtations in the Fire to the Gods, will cause those oblations to go to the Gods and reach them. And then they will be very glad. O Mother! Let Thou be the wealth of Fire. the beauty and housewife of Fire; let Thou be incessantly worshipped in the regions of the Gods and amongst men and other beings. Hearing these words of Brahmâ, Svâhâ Devî became very sad and expressed Her own intentions:—"I will get Kriṣṇa as my husband; let me perform Tapasyâ as long as it takes. This is my object. All other things are false as dreams.

23-28. I always meditate with devotion on the lotus-feet of Śrî Kriṣṇa, serving Which You have become the Creator of this world, Śambhu has become the Conqueror of death, Ananta Deva is supporting this universe, Dharma is the Witness of the virtuous, Gaṇeśâ is getting first of all, the first worship. Prakriti Devi has become the adorable of all and the Munis and the Riṣis respected by all. O Child! Having spoken thus to the Lotus-born, Padmâ, with Her lotus-face, meditating incessantly on the Lotus-Feet of Śrî Kriṣṇa, free from any disease, started to perform tapasyâ for attaining Him. She, first of all, stood on one leg and practised austerities for one lakh years. Then She saw the Highest Puruṣa Śrî Kriṣṇa, Who is beyond Prâkriti and Her attributes. The beautiful amorous Svâhâ, seeing the Lovely Form of the Lord of Love, fainted.

29-43. The omniscient Bhagavân Kriṣṇa knowing Her intentions, took Her to His lap, reduced very much in body by long continued Tapasyâ, and He said :—"O Devî ! Thou shalt be My wife in the next Varâha Kalpa. Then Thou wilt be the daughter of Nagnajit and wilt be known by the name of Nâgnajitî." O Beloved ! At present let Thou be the Energy of Fire and be His wife. By My boon Thou wilt be worshipped by all. Fire will make Thee the Lady of His house and take the utmost care of Thee. Thou wilt be able to enjoy easily with Him. O Nârada ! Thus saying to Svâhâ, Bhagavân disappeared. On the other hand, Fire came in there by the command of Brahmâ, with a doubtful mind and began to meditate on Her, the World Mother as per Sâma Veda and worshipped Her. He then pleased and married Her with mantrams, etc. For one hundred divine years they enjoyed each other. In a very solitary place while they were enjoying each other, Svâhâ Devî felt pregnant. For full twelve divine years She retained Her pregnancy. Then She delivered gradually three sons Dakṣiṇâgni, Gârhyapatyâgni, and Âhavanîyâgni. The Riṣis, Munis, Brâhmaṇas, Kṣattriyas poured oblations of clarified butter pronouncing the terminal mantra "Svâhâ." He who pronounces this excellent terminal Mantra "Svâhâ" gets immediate success in his actions. Then all the mantras without "Svâhâ in the end became impotent as snakes become when void of poison, the Brâhmaṇas when they are devoid of the knowlege of the Vedas, the wife when she does not serve her husband, the men whenthey turn illiterate and the trees, when void of fruits and branches. O Child ! The Brâhmaṇas then became satisfied. The Devas began to receive the oblations. With the "Svâhâ" mantra everything turned out fruitful. Thus I have described to you the ancedote of "Svâhâ." One who hears this essential ancedote gets his happiness enhanced and the Mokṣa in his hands. What more do you want to hear ? Say.

44. Nârada said :—I like to hear how Fire worshipped Svâhâ and recited stotras (hymns of praise) to Her. Kindly tell me the method of worship, the Dhyânam and Stotra.

45-49. Nârâyana said :—"O Best of Brâhmaṇas ! I now tell you the meditation (Dhyânam) as per Sâma Veda, the method of worship and stotra. Listen attentively. At the commencement of any sacrificial ceremony, one should first of all worship whether on the Sâlagrâma stone or in an earthen jar (ghaṭa), the Devî Svâhâ and then commence the ceremony with the expectation of getting the desired fruit. The following is the Dhyânam (meditation) of Svâhâ Devî :—"O Devî Svâhâ! Thou art embodied of the Mantras; Thou art the success of the Mantras; Thou art Thyself a Siddhâ: Thou givest success and the the fruits of actions to men. Thou dost good to all. Thus meditating, one should offer Pâdya (water for washing the feet), etc., uttering the basic Mantra; success then comes to him. Now hear about the Radical Seed Mantra. The said mantra (mûla mantra) is this:—"Om Hrîm Śrîm Vahnijâyâyai Devyai Svâhâ." If the Devî be worshipped with this Mantra, all the desires come to a successful issue.

50-54. Fire recited the following stotra:—"Thou art Svâhâ, Thou art the Beloved of Fire, Thou art the wife of Fire; Thou pleasest all; Thou art the Śakti, Thou art the action, Thou art the bestower of Kâla (time); Thou dost digest the food; Thou art the Dhruvâ; Thou art the resort of men; Thou art the burning power; Thou canst burnt everything, Thou art the essence of this world; Thou art the deliverer from the terrible world; Thou art the life of the gods and Thou nourishest the Gods." O Nârada! He who reads with devotion these sixteen names, gets success both in this world as well as in the next. None of his works become deficient in any way; rather all the works are performed successfuly and with a successful issue. Reading this stotra, one who has no wife, gets wife. So much so that the man who recites the stotra gets for his wife equal to Rambhâ, the heavenly nymph, and passes his time in greatest bliss.

Here ends the Forty-third Chapter of the Ninth Book on the history of Svâhâ in Śri Mad Devî Bhâgavatam, the Mahâ Purâṇam, of 18,000 verses by Maharṣi Veda Vyâsa.

CHAPTER XLIV.

1-18. Nârâyaṇa said:—"O Nârada! I will tell you now the excellent anecdote of Svadhâ, pleasing to the Pitris and enhancing the fruits of the Śrâdh ceremony when foods are offered to the Pitris. Listen. Before the creation, the Creator created seven Pitris. Four out of them are with forms and the other three are of the nature of Teja (light).

Note:—Kavyavâhoanalah Somo Yamaschaivâryamâ tathâ, Agniśvâttâh Barhiṣadah Somapâ Pitri devatah. These seven Pitris are according to the other Purâṇas. Seeing the beautiful and lovely forms of the Pitris, He made arrangements for their food in the form of Śrâddhas and

Tarpaṇas, etc. (funeral ceremony and peace-offerings), etc. (Śrâdh, solemn obsequies performed in honour of the manes of deceased ancestors.) Taking bath, performing Srâdh ceremony upto Tarpaṇam (peace-offerings), worshipping the Devas and doing Sanddhyâ thrice a day these are the daily duties of the Brâhmaṇas. If any Brâhmaṇa does not perform daily the Trisandhyâs, Srâddha, Tarpaṇam, worship and the reciting of the Vedas, he becomes devoid of fire like a snake without any poison. He who does not perform the devotional service of the Devî, who eats food not offered to Śrî Hari, who remains impure till death, is not entitled to do any karma whatsoever. Thus, introducing the Śrâddhas, etc., for the Pitris, Brahmâ went to His own abode. The Brâhmaṇas went on doing the Śrâddhas for the Pitris, but the Pitris could not enjoy them and so they remained without food and were not satisfied. They all, being hungry and sad, went to the Council of Brahmâ and informed Him everything from beginning to end. Brahmâ then created out of His mind one daughter very beautiful, full of youth and having a face lovely, as if equal to one hundred moons. That woman was best in all respects whether in form, beauty, qualities or in learning. Her colour was white like the white Champaka flower and her body was adorned all over with jewel ornaments. This form was very pure, ready to grant boons, auspicious and the part of Prakriti. Her face was beaming with smiles; her teeth were very beautiful and her body shewed signs of Lakṣmî (*i.e.*, of wealth and prosperity) Her name was Svadhâ. Her lotus-feet were situated on one hundred lotuses. She was the wife of the Pitris. Her face resembled that of a lotus and Her eyes looked like water lilies. She was born of the lotus born Brahmâ. The Grand-father Brahmâ made over that daughter of the nature of Tuṣṭi (Contentment) to the hands of the Pitris and they were satisfied. Brahmâ advised the Brâhmaṇas privately that whenever they would offer any thing to the Pitris, they should offer duly with the mantra Svadhâ pronounced at the end. Since then the Brâhmaṇas are offering everything to the Pitris, with the Mantra Svadhâ uttered in the end. Svâhâ is laudable. when offerings are presented to the Gods and Svadhâ is commendable when offerings are made to the Pitris. But in both the cases, Dakṣiṇâ is essential. Without Dakṣiṇâ (sacrificial fee), all sacrifices are useless and worthless. The Pitris, Devatâs, Brâhmaṇas, the Munis, the Manus worshipped the peaceful Svadhâ and chanted hymns to Her with great love. The Devas, Pitris, Brâhmaṇas, all were pleased and felt their ends achieved when they got the boon from Svadhâ Devî. Thus I have told you everything about Svadhâ. It is pleasing to all. What more do you want to hear? Say. I will answer all your questions.

19. Nârada said :—"O Thou, the Best of the Knowers of the Vedas! O Muni Sattama! I want now to hear the method of worship, the meditation and the hymns of Svadhâ Devî. Kindly tell me all about this.

20-27. Nârâyaṇa said :—"You know everything about the all-auspicious Dhyân, Stotra, as stated in the Vedas; then why do you ask me again? However I will speak out this for the enhancement of knowledge." On the thirteenth day of the Dark Fortnight in autumn when the Maghâ asterism is with the Moon and on the Śrâddha day. One should worship with care Svadhâ Devî; then one should perform Śrâddha. If, out of vanity, a Brâhmin performs Śrâdh without first worshipping Svadtâ Devî then he will never get the fruits of Tarpaṇam or Śrâdh. "O Devî Svadhe! Thou art the mind-born daughter of Brahmâ, always young and worshipped by the Pitris. Thou bestowest the fruits of Śraddh. So I meditate on Thee. Thus meditating, the Brâhmin is to pronounce the motto (mûla mantra) and offer the Pâdyam, etc., on the Sâlagrâm stone or on the auspicious earthen jar. This is the ruling of the Vedas. The motto is "Om Hrîm, Śrîm, Klîm, Svadhâ Devyai Svâhâ. She should be worshipped with this Mantra. After reciting hymns to the Devî, one is to bow down to the Svadhâ Devî. O Son of Brahmâ! O Best of Munis! O Skilled in hearing! I now describe the stotra which Brahmâ composed at the beginning for the bestowal of the desired fruits to mankind. Listen. Nârâyaṇa said :—"The instant the Mantra Svadhâ is pronounced, men get at once the fruits of bathing in the holy places of pilgrimages. No trace of sin exists in him at that time; rather the religious merits of performing the Vâjapeya sacrifice accrue to him.

28-36. "Svadhâ," "Svadhâ," "Svadhâ," thrice this word if one calls to mind, one gets the fruits of Śrâdh, Tarpaṇam, and Bali (offering sacrifices). So much so, if one hears with devotion during the Śrâdh time the recitation of the hymn to Svadhâ, one gets, no doubt, thefruit of Śrâdh. If one recites the Svadhâ mantra thrice every time in the morning, midday and evening) every day, one gets an obedient, chaste wife begetting sons. The following is the hymn (Stotra) to Svadhâ :— "O Devî Svadhe! Thou art dear to the Pitris as their vital breaths and thou art the lives of the Brâhmaṇas. Thou art the Presiding Deity the of Śrâdh ceremonies and bestowest the fruits thereof. "O Thou of good vows! Thou art eternal, true, and of the nature of religious merits. Thou appearest in creation and disappearest in dissolution. And this appearing and disappearing go on for ever. Thou art Om, thou art Svasti, Thou art Namas Kâra (salutation); Thou art Svadhâ, Thou art Dakṣiṇâ, Thou art the various woks as designated in the Vedas. These the Lord of the world has created for the success of actions." No sooner Brahmâ, seated in His assembly in the Brahma Loka, reciting this stotra remained silent, than Ṣavdhâ Devî appeared there all at once. When Brahmâ handed over the lotus-faced Svadhâ Devî over to the hands of the Pitris, and they gladly took Her to their own aboles. He who hears with devotion and attention this stotra of Svadhâ, gets all sorts of rich fruits that are desired and the fruits of bathing in all the Tîrthas,

Here ends the Forty-fourth Chapter of the Ninth Book on the story of Svadhâ Devî in the discourse between Nârada and Nârâyaṇa in the Mahâ Purâṇam Śrî Mad Devî Bhâgavatam of 18,000 verses by Maharṣi Veda Vyâsâ

CHAPTER XLV.

1-63. Nârâyaṇa said:—The excellent, most sweet stories of Svâhâ and Svadhâ are told; now I will tell you the story of Dakṣiṇâ; hear attentively. In early days, in the region of Goloka, there was a good-natured Gopî named Sus'îlâ, beautiful, Râdhâ's companion and very dear to Srî Hari. She was fortunate, respected, beautiful, lovely, prosperous, with good teeth, learned, well qualified and of exquisitely handsome form. Her whole body was tender and lovely like Kalâvatî (one versed in 64 arts; moon) She was beautiful and her eyes were like water lilies. Her hips were good and spacious; Her breasts were full; she was Shyâmâ (a kind of women having colour like melted gold; body being hot in cold and cool in summer; of youthful beauty); as well She was of the Nyagrodha class of women (an excellent woman, Stanau Sukaṭhinau Yasyâ Nitambe cha Vis'âlatâ, Madhye Ksîṇâ bhavedyâ Sânyagrodha parimaṇḍalâ). Always a smile sweetened Her face; and that looked always gracious. Her whole body was covered with jewel ornaments. Her colour was white like the white champakas. Her lips were red like the Bimba fruits; Her eyes were like those of a deer.

Sus'ilâ was very clever in amorous sciences. Her gait was like a swan. She was specially versed in what is called Premâ Bhakti (love towards God) So She was the dearest lady of Śrî Kriṣṇa. And She was of intense emotional feelings. She knows all the sentiments of love; she was witty humorous, and ardent for the love of Śrî Kriṣṇa, the Lord of the Râsa circle. She sat by the left side of Srî Kriṣṇâ in the presence of Râdhâ. Śrî Kriṣṇa, then cast His glance on Râdhâ, the Chief of the Gopis and hung down His head through fear. Râdhâ's face turned red; the two eyes looked like red lilies; all Her bodies began to quiver out of anger and Her lips began to shake. Seing that state of Radhâ, Bhagvân Śrî Kriṣṇa dissappeared, fearing that a quarrel might ensue. Sus'îlâ and other Gopîs seeing that the peaceful Kriṣṇa of Sattvâ Guna and of lovely form had dis appeared, began to tremble with fear. Then one lakh Koṭi

Gopîs seeing Krişņa absent and Râdhâ angry, became very much afraid and bowing their heads down with devotion and with folded palms began to say frequently. "Râdhe! Protect us, protect us, and they took shelter at Her feet. O Nârada! Three lâkh Gopas also including Sudâmâ and others took shelter at the lotus feet of Śrî Râdhâ out of fear. Seeing, then, Krîşņa absent and Her companion Sus'ilâ running away, Râdhâ cursed her thus:—"If Susila" comes again to this Goloka, she will be reduced to ashes." Thus cursing Her companion Sus'ilâ out of anger, Râdhâ, the Darling of the Deva of the Devas, and the Lady of the Râsa circle went to the Râsâ circle and called on Krişņa, the Lord of the same. Not being able to find out Śrî Krîşņa, a minute appeared a yuga to Her and she began to say:—"O Lord of Prâņas! O Dearer than My life! O Presiding Deity of my life! O Krişņa! My life seems to depart from Thy absence! Come quickly and shew Thyself to me. O Lord! It is through the favour of one's husband that the pride of women gets increased day by day. Women's safeguards of happiness are their husbands. Therefore women, who are helpless creatures, ought always to serve their husbands according to Dharma. The husband is the wife's friend, presiding deity and the sole refuge and the chief wealth. It is through husbands that women derive their pleasures, enjoyments. Dharma, happiness, peace and contentment. If husbands are respected, wives are respected and if husbands are dishonoured, women are dishonoured too. The husband is the highest thing to a woman. He is the highest friend. There is no better friend than him. The husband is called Bhartâ because he supports his wife; he is called Pati, because he preserves her; he is called Svâmî, because he is the master of her body; he is called Kântâ because he bestows the desired things to her; he is called Bandhu, because he increases her happiness; he is called Priya, because he gives pleasure to her; he is called Is'a, because he bestows prosperity on her; he is called Prâņes'vara, because he is the lord of her Prâņa; and he is called Ramaņa, because he gives enjoyment to her. There is no other thing dearer than husband. The son is born of the husband; hence the son is so dear. The husband is dearer to a family woman than one hundred sons. Those who are born in impure families, cannot know what substance a husband is made up of. Taking Baths in all the Tîrthas, giving Dakşiņâs in all the Yajñas (sacrifice). circumambulating round the whole earth, performing all austerities, observing all vows, making all great gifts, holy fastings, all that are dictated in the Śâstras, serving the Guru, the Brâhmaņas and the Devas all cannot compare to even one sixteenth part with serving faithfully the feet of the husband. The husband is the highest; higher than the Spiritual Teacher (Guur), higher than the Brâhmaṇas, higher than all the Devas. As to man, the Spiritual Teacher who imparts the Spiritual Knowledge is the Best and Supreme, so to the women their husbands are the best of all. Oh! I am not able to realise the glory of my Dearest, by Whose favour I am the Sole Ruler of one lakh Koṭî Gopîs, one lakh Koṭî Gopas, innumerable Brahmâṇḍas, and all the things thereof, and all the lokas (regions) from Bhu (earth) to Goloka. Oh! The womanly nature is insurmountable. Thus saying, Râdhikâ began to meditate with devotion on Śrî Krisṇa, Tears began to flow incessantly from Her eyes. She exclaimed "O Lord! O Lord! O Ramaṇa! Shew Thyself to me." I am very much weak and distressed from Thy bereavement." Now the Dakṣiṇâ Devî, driven out from Goloka, practised Tapasyâ for a long time when She entered into the body of Kamalâ. The Devas, on the other hand, performed a very difficult Yajña; but they could not derive any fruit therefrom. So they went to Brahmâ, becoming very sad. Hearing them, Brahmâ meditated on Viṣṇu for a long time with devotion. At last Viṣṇu gave Him a reply. Viṣṇu got out of the body of Mahâ Lakṣmî a Martya Lakṣmî (Lakṣmî of the earth) and gave Her Dakṣiṇâ to Brahmâ. Then with a view to yield to the Devas the as a fruits of their Karmas, Brahmâ made over to the Yajña Deva (the Deva presiding the sacrifice) the Devî Dakṣiṇâ, offered by Nârâyaṇa. Yajña Deva, then, worshipped Her duly and recited hymns to Her with great joy. Her colour was like melted gold; her lustre equalled koṭi Moons; very lovely, beautiful, fascinating; face resembling water lilies, of a gentle body; with eyes like Padma Palâśa, born of the body of Lakṣmî, worshipped by Brahmâ, wearing celestial silken garments, her lips resembling like Bimba fruits, chaste, handsome; her braid of hair surrounded by Mâlatî garlands; with a sweet smiling face, ornamented with jewel ornaments, well dressed, bathed, enchanting the minds of the Munis, below the hair of her forehead the dot of musk and Sindûra scented with sandalpaste, of spacious hips, with full breasts, smitten by the arrows of Kâma Deva (the God of Love.) Such was the Dakṣiṇâ Devî. Seeing Her, the Yajña Deva fainted. At last he married her according to due rites and ceremonies. Taking her to a solitary place, he enjoyed her for full divine one hundred years with great joy like Lakṣmî Nârâyaṇa. Gradually then Dakṣiṇâ became pregnant. She remained so for twelve divine years. Then she duly delivered a nice son as the fruit of Karma. When any Karma becomes complete, this son delivers the fruits of that Karma. Yajña Deva with His wife Dakṣiṇâ and the above named Karmaphala, the bestower of the fruits of actions, gives the desired fruits to all their sacrificial acts and Karmas. So the Pundits, the knowers of the Vedas, say. Really he, henceforth, began to give fruits to all the persons of their acts, with his wife Dakṣiṇâ and son, the bestower of the fruits of the actions. The Devas were all satisfied at this and went away respectively to their own abodes. Therefore, the man who performs Karmas, generally known as Karma Kartâs, should pay the Dakṣiṇâ (the Sacrificial fee) and so he completes at once his actions. It is stated in the Vedas, that no sooner the Karma Kartâ pays the Dakṣiṇâ, than he obtains the fruits of his Karmas at once. In case the Karma Kartâ, after he has completed his acts, does not pay either through bad luck or through ignorance, any Dakṣiṇâ to the Brâhmaṇas, its amount is doubled if a Muhûrta, passes away and if one night elapses, its amount is increased, to one hundred times. If three nights pass away, and the Dakṣiṇâ not paid, the amount last brought forward, is increased again to hundred times ; if a week passes, the last amount is doubled, and if one month passes away, the Dakṣiṇâ is multiplied to one lakh times. If one year passes away, that is increased to ten millions of times and the Karma, also, bears no fruit. Such a Karma Kartâ is known as taking away unfairly a Brâhmaṇa's property and is regarded as impure. He has no right to any further actions. For that sin, he becomes a pauper and diseased. Lakṣmî Devî goes away from his house, leaves him, cursing him severely. So much so that the Pitris do not accept the Śrâdh, Tarpaṇam offered by that wretched fellow. So the Devas do not accept his worship, nor the Fire accepts the oblations poured by him. If the person that performs sacrifices does not pay the sacrificial fee that he resolves to pay and he who accepts the offer does not demand the sum, both of them go to hell. But if the performer of the sacrifices does not pay when the priests demand the fee, then the Yajamâna (the performer of the sacrifices) only falls down to hell as the jar, severed from the rope, falls down. The Yajamâna (pupil) is denominated as a Brahmasvâpahârî (one who robs a Brâhmaṇa's property) ; he goes ultimately to the Kumbhipâka hell. There he remains for one lakh years punished and threatened by Yama's messengers. He is then reborn as a Chânḍâla, poor and diseased. So much so that his seven generations above and his seven generations below go to hell.

64-65. O Nârada ! Thus I have narrated to you the story of Dakṣiṇâ. What more do you want to hear ? Say. Nârada said :—" O Best of Munis ! Who bears the fruits of that Karma where no Dakṣiṇâ is paid. Describe the method of worship that was offered to Dakṣiṇâ by Yajna Deva." Nârâyaṇa said :—Where do you find the fruit of any sacrifice without Dakṣiṇâ ? (*i.e.* nowhere.) That Karma only gets fruits where Dakṣiṇâs are paid. And the fruits of the acts void of any Dakṣinâ, Bali who lives in the Pâtâla only enjoys; and no one else.

67-71. For, in olden times, it was ordained by Vâmana Deva that those fruits would go to the king Vali. All those that pertain to Śrâdh not sanctioned by the Vedas, the charities made without any regard or faith, the worship offered by a Brâhmiṇ who is the husband of a Vriṣala (an unmarried girl twelve years in whom menstruation has commenced), the fruits of sacrifices done by an impure Brâhmaṇa (a Brahman who fails in his duties), the worship offered by impure persons, and the acts of a man devoid of any devotion to his Guru, all these are reserved for the king Bali. He enjoys the fruits of all these. O Child! I am now telling you the Dhyân, Stotra, and the method of worship as per Kaṇva Śâkhâ of Dakṣiṇâ Devî. Hear. When Yajña Deva, in ancient times got Dakṣiṇâ, skilful in action, he was very much fascinated by her appearance and being love-stricken, began to praise her:—"O Beautiful One! You were before the chief of the Gopîs in Goloka. You were like Râdhâ; you were Her companion; and you were loved by Śrî Râdhâ, the beloved of Śrî Kriṣṇa.

72-97. In the Râsa circle, on the Full Moon night in the month of Kârtik, in the great festival of Râdhâ, you appeared from the right shoulder of Lakṣmî; hence you were named Dakṣiṇâ. O Beautiful One! You were of good nature before; hence your name was Sus'ilâ. Next you turned due to Râdhâ's curse, into Dakṣiṇâ. It is to my great good luck that you were dislodged from Goloka and have come here. O highly fortunate One! Now have mercy on me and accept me as your husband. O Devî! You give to all the doers of actions, the fruits of their works. Without you, their Karmas bear no fruit. So much so, if you be not present in their actions the works never shine forth in brilliant glory. Without Thee, neither, Brahmâ, nor Viṣṇu nor Mahes'a nor the Regents of the quarters, the ten Dikpâlas, can award the fruits of actions. Brahmâ is the incarnate of Karma. Mahes'vara is the incarnate of the fruits of Karmas; and I Viṣṇu myself is the incarnate of Yajñas. But Thou art the Essence of all. Thou art the Parâ Prakriti, without any attributes, the Para Brahma incarnate, the bestower of the fruits of actions. Bhagavân Śri Kriṣṇa cannot award the fruits of actions without Thee. O Beloved! In every birth let Thou be my Śakti. O Thou with excellent face! Without Thee, I am unable to finish well any Karma. O Nârada! Thus praising Dakṣinâ Devî, Yajña Deva stood before Her. She, born from the shoulder of Lakṣmî, became pleased with His Stotra and accepted Him for Her bridegroom. If anybody recites this Dakṣinâ stotra during sacrifice, he gets all the results thereof.

If anybody recites this stotra in the Râjasûya sacrifice, Vâjapaya, Gomedha (cow sacrifice) Naramedha (man sacrifice), As'vamedha (horse sacrifice), Lângala Sacrifice, Viṣṇu Yajña tending to increase one's fame, in the act of giving over wealth or pieces of lands, digging tanks or wells, or giving fruits, in Gaja medha (elephant sacrifice), in Loha Yajña (iron sacrifice), Svarna Yajña (gold sacrifice), Ratna Yajña (making over jewels in sacrifices), Tâmra Yajña (copper), Śiva Yajña, Rudra Yajña, Śakra Yajña, Bandhuka Yajna, Varuṇa Yajña (for rains), Kaṇḍaka Yajna, for crushing the enemies, Sachi Yajna, Dharma Yajña, Pâpa mochana Yajña, Brahmâṇî Karma Yajña, the auspicious Prakriti Yâga, sacrifices, his work is achieved then without any hitch or obstacle. There is no doubt in this. The stotra, thus, is mentioned now; hear about the Dhyânam and the method of worship. First of all, one should worship in the Śâlagrâma stone, or in an earthen jar (Ghaṭa) Dakṣiṇâ Devî. The Dhyânam runs thus :—" O Dakṣiṇâ ! Thou art sprung from the right shoulder of Lakṣmî ; Thou art a part of Kamalâ ; Thou art clever (Dakṣa) in all the actions and Thou bestowest the fruits of all the actions." Thou art the Śakti of Visṇu, Thou art revered, worshipped. Thou bestowest all that is auspicious; Thou art purity ; Thou bestowest purity, Thou art good natured. So I meditate on Thee. Thus meditating, the intelligent one should worship Dakṣiṇâ with the principal mantra. Then with the Vedic Mantras, pâdyas, etc. (offerings of various sorts) are to be offered. Now the mantra as stated in the Vedas, runs thus :—" Om Śrîm, Klîm, Hrîm, Dâkṣiṇâyai Svâhâ." With this mantra, all the offerings, such as pâdyas, arghyas, etc., are to be given, and one should worship, as per rules, Dakṣiṇâ Devî with devotion. O Nârada ! Thus I have stated to you the anecdote of Dakṣiṇâ. Happiness, pleasure, and the fruits of all karmas are obtained by this. Being engaged in sacrificial acts, in this Bhâratavarṣa, if one hears attentively this Dhyânam of Dakṣiṇâ, his sacrifice becomes defectless. So much so that the man who has got no sons gets undoubtedly good and qualified sons ; if he has no wife, he gets a best wife, good natured, beautiful, of slender waist, capable to give many sons, sweet speaking, humble, chaste, pure, and Kulîna; if he be void of learning, he gets learing ; if he be poor he gets wealth ; if he be without any land, he gets land and if he has no attendants, he gets attendants. If a man hears for one mouth this stotra of Dakṣiṇâ Devî, he gets over all difficultis and dangers, bereavements from friends, troubles, inprisonments, and all other calamities.

Here ends the Forty-fifth Chapter of the Ninth Book on the anecdote of Dakṣiṇâ in the Mahâ Purâṇam Śrî Mad Devî Bhâgavatam of 18,000 verses by Maharṣi Veda Vyâsa.

CHAPTER XLVI.

1. Nârada said:—" O Thou, the foremost of the Knowers of the Vedas! I have heard from you the anecdotes of many Devis. Now I want to hear the lives of other Devîs also. Kindly describe.

2. Nârâyaṇa said:—" O Best of the Brâhmaṇas! The lives and glorious deeds of all the Devîs are described separately. Now say, which lives you want to hear.

3. Nârada said:—" O Lord! Ṣaṣṭhî, Mangala Chaṇḍî, and Manasâ, are the parts of Prakriti. Now I want to hear the lives of them.

4-22. Nârâyaṇa said:—" O Child! The sixth part of Prakriti is named as Ṣaṣṭhî. The Devî Ṣaṣṭhî is the Presiding Deity of infants and children; She is the Mâyâ of Viṣṇu and She bestows sons to all. She is one of the sixteen Mâtrikâs. She is known by the name of Devasenâ. She performs Vratas (vows); She is the chaste and dearest wife of Skanda. She decides on the longevity of children and is always engaged in their preservation. So much so, that this Siddha Yoginî always keeps the children on her side.

O Best of Brâhmaṇas! I will now talk about the method of worshipping this Devî and the history about Her bestowing children that I heard from Dharma Deva. Hear. Sváyambhuva Manu had one son Priyavrata. He was a great Yogîndra and remained in practising austerities. So he was not inclined to have any wife. At last by the effort and request of Brahmâ, he got himself married. But many days passed, and he could not see the face of a son. Then Maharṣi Kas'yapa became his priest in the Putreṣṭi Sacrifice (to get a son); and when the sacrifice was over, he gave the sacrificial offering called charu to his wife Mâlinî. On eating the charu, the queen Mâlinî become pregnant. For twelve Deva years she held the womb. After twelve years she delivered a full developed son, of a golden colour; but the son was lifeless and his two eyeballs were upset. At this, the friends' wives became very sorry and began to weep. The mother of the child became so very sorrowful that she became senseless. O Muni! The King himself took the son on his breast and went to the burning ground. There with his child on his breast he began to cry aloud. Rather he got himself ready to quit his own life than leave the son from away his breast. At this time he saw in the space overhead an aerial car, white as crystal, made of excellent jewels, coming towards him. The car was shining with its own lustre, encircled with woven silken cloth, which added to its beauty. Innumerable garlands of variegated colours gave it a very nice and charming appearance. On that car was seated a Siddha Yoginî, very beautiful, of a lovely appearance of a colour like that of white champakas, always youthful, smiling, adorned with jewel ornaments, ever gracious to show favour to the devotees. On seeing Her, the King Priyavrata placed the child from his breast on the ground and began to worship Her and chant hymns to Her with great love and devotion. And he then asked that peaceful lady, the wife of Skanda, Who was shinning like a summer sun :—" O Beautiful ! Who art Thou ? Whose wife art Thou and whose daughter art Thou ? From Thy appearance it seems that Thou art fortunate and respected amongst the female sex.

23-24. O Nârada ! In ancient times, when the Daityas dispossessed the Devas of their positions, this Lady was elected as a general and got victory for the Devas; hence She was named Devasenâ. Hearing the words of the King Priyavrata, Devasenâ, who fought for the Devas and was all good to the whole world, said:—

25-35. O King ! I am the mind-born daughter of Brahmâ. My name is Devasenâ. The Creator before created Me out of His mind and made Me over to the hands of Skanda. Amongst the Mâtrikâs, I am known as Ṣaṣṭhî, the wife of Skanda. I am the sixth part of Prakriti ; hence I am named Ṣaṣṭhî. I give sons to those who have no sons, wives to those who have no wives, wealth to the poor, and I give works to those who are workers (karmîs.)

Happiness, pain, fear, sorrow, joy, good, and wealth and adversity all are the fruits of Karmas. As the result of one's Karmas, people get lots of sons and it is due to the result of one's Karma again that people are denuded of all the issues of their family. As the result of Karma, the people get dead sons; and as the result of Karma the people get long lives. All enjoy the fruits of their Karmas, whether they be well qualified, or deformed or whether they have many wives, or whether they have no wife, whether they be beautiful, religious, diseased, it is all through Karmas, Karmas. Disease comes out of their Karmas. Again they get cured by their Karmas. So, O King ! It is stated in the Vedas that Karma is the most powerful of all. Thus saying, Devasenâ took the dead child on her lap ; and, by the wisdom, early made the child alive. The King saw, the child, of a golden colour got back his life and began to smile. Thus bidding goodbye to the King, Devasenâ took the child and became ready to depart. At this the King's palate and throat got dry and he began again to chant hymns to Her. The Devî Saṣṭhi became pleased at the stotra made by the King. The Devî then addressed the King and said :—"O King ! All that is stated in the Vedas, is made up of Karmas. You are the son of Svâyambhuva Manu, and the Lord of the three worlds. You better promulgate My worship in the three worlds and you yourself worship Me. Then I will give you your beautiful son, the lotus of your family. Your son, born in part of Nârâyaṇa, will be famous by the name of Suvrata. He will be well-qualified, a great literary man, able to remember his conditions in his former lives, the best of Yogis, performer of one hundred Yajñas, the best of all, bowed down by the Kṣattriyas, strong as one lakh powerful elephants, wealthy, fortunate, pure, favourite of literary persons, learned and bestower of the fruits of the ascetics, renowned and bestower of wealth and prosperity to the three worlds. Thus saying Devasenâ gave the the child to the king. When the king promised that he would promulgate Her worship, the Devî granted him boons and went up to the Heavens.

43. The king, too, becoming very glad and surrounded by his ministers, returned to his own abode and informed all about the son. The ladies of the house, become highly delighted when they heard everything. On the occasion of the son's getting back his life, the king performed everywhere auspicious ceremonies. The worship of Ṣasṭhî Devî commenced. Wealth was bestowed to the Brâhmiṇs. Since, then, on every sixth day of the bright fortnight in every month, great festivals in honour of Ṣaṣṭhî Devî began to be celebrated. Since then, throughout the kingdom, on every sixth day after the birth of a child in the lying-in-chamber, Ṣasṭhî Devî began to be worshipped. On the twenty-first day, the auspicious moment, at the ceremoney of giving rice to a child for the first time, when sixth months old, and on all other auspicious ceremonies of the children, Ṣasṭhî Devî's worship was made extant and the king himself performed those worships with great care and according to due rules. Now I will tell you about the Dhyânam and method of worship and stotra as I heard from Dharma Deva, and as stated in Kauthuma Śâkhâ. Hear. He has said :—In a Śâlagrâma stone, in a jar, on the root of a Baṭa tree, or drawing the figure on the floor of the rooms, or making an image of Ṣasṭhî Devî, the sixth part of Prakriti and installing it, one should worship the Devî. The Dhyânam is this :—"O Devasenâ ! Thou art the bestower of good sons, the giver of good luck ; Thou art mercy and kindness and the progenitor of the world ; Thy colour is

bright like that of the white Champaka flowers. Thou art decked with jewel ornaments. Thou art pure, and the highest and best Devî. Obeisance to The I mediate on Thee." Thus meditating, the worshipper should place flower on his own head. Then again meditating and uttering the principal mantra one is to offer the Pâdya (water for washing feet), Arghya, Âchamanîya, scents, flowers, dhûp, lights, offerings of food and best roots and fruits and one should worship thus with various things Saṣṭhî Devî "Om Hrîm Ṣaṣṭhî Devyai Svâhâ is the principal Mantra of Ṣaṣṭhî Devî. This great Mantra of eight letters a man should repeat as his strength allows. After the Japam, the worshipper should chant hymns with devotion and undivided attention and then bow down. The Stotra (hymn) of Ṣaṣṭhî Devî as per Sâma Veda is very beautiful and son-bestowing. The lotus-born Brahmâ has said :—If one repeats (makes Japam) this eight lettered mantra one lakh of times, one gets certainly a good son. O Best of Munis! Now I am going to say the auspicious stotra of Ṣaṣṭhî Devî as composed by Priyavrata. Hear.

58-73. One's desires are fulfilled when one reads this very secret stotra. Thus the King Priyavrata said :—" O Devî, Devasenâ! I bow down to Thee. O Great Devî! Obeisance to Thee! Thou art the bestower of Siddhis; Thou art peaceful; obeisance to Thee! Thou art the bestower of good; Thou art Devasenâ; Thou art Ṣaṣṭhî Devî, I bow down to Thee! Thou grantest boons to persons; Thou bestowest sons and wealth to men. So obeisance to Thee! Thou givest happiness and mokṣa; Thou art Ṣaṣṭhî Devî; I bow down to Thee. Thou thyself art Siddha; so I bow down to Thee. O Ṣaṣṭhî Devî! Thou art the sixth part of this creation; Thou art Siddha Yoginî, so I bow down to Thee. Thou art the essence, Thou art Sâradâ; Thou art the Highest Devî. So I bow down again and again to Thee. Thou art the Presiding Deity Ṣasthî Devî of the children; I bow down to Thee. Thou grantest good; Thou Thyself art good and Thou bestowest the fruits of all Karmas. O Thou O Ṣasthî Devi! Thou shewest thy form to thy devotees; I bow down to Thee! Thou art Śuddha Sattva and respected by all the persons in all their actions. Thou art the wife of Skanda. All worship Thee. O Ṣasthî Devî! Thou hadst saved the Devas. So obeisance to Thee O Ṣaṣṭhî Devi! Thou hast no envy, no anger; so obeisance to Thee. O Sures'varî! Give me wealth, give me dear things, give me sons. Give me respect from all persons; give me victory; slay my enemies. O Maheṣvarî! Give me Dharma; give me name and fame; I bow down again again to Ṣasthi Devî. O Ṣaṣṭhî Devî! worshpiped reverentially by all! Give me lands, give me subjects, give me learning; have welfare for me; I bow down again and again to Ṣaṣṭhî Devî, O Nârada! Thus praising the Devî, Priyavrata got a son, renowned and ruling over a great kingdom through the favour of Ṣaṣṭhî Devî. If any man that has no son, hears this stotra of Ṣiṣṭhî Devî for one year with undivided attention, he gets easily an excellent son, having a long life. If one worships for one year with devotion this Devasenâ and hears this stotra, even the most barren woman becomes freed from all her sins and gets a son. Through the grace of Ṣaṣthî Devî, that son becomes a hero, well qualified, literate, renowned and long-lived. If any woman who bears only a single child or delivers dead children hears with devotion for one year this stotra, she gets easily, through the Devî's grace, a good son. If the father and mother both hear with devotion, this story during the period of their child's illness, then the child becomes cured by the Grace of the Devî.

Here ends the Forty-sixth chapter of the Ninth Book on the anecdote of Ṣiṣṭhî Devi in the Mahâ Purâṇam Srî Mad Devî Bhagvatam of 18,000 verses by Maharṣi Veda Vyâsa.

CHAPTER XLVII.

1-25. Nârâyaṇa said:—"O Nârada! I have now narrated the anecdote of Ṣiṣṭhî as stated in the Vedas. Now hear the anecdote of Mangala Chaṇḍî, approved of by the Vedas and respected by the literary persons. The Chaṇḍî, that is very skilled in all auspicious works and who is the most auspicious of all good things, is Mangal Chaṇḍîkâ. Or the Chaṇḍî who is an object of worship of Mangala (Mars), the son of earth and the bestower of desires is Mangala Chaṇḍîkâ. Or the Chaṇḍî who is an object of worship of Mangala of the family of Manu who was the ruler of the whole world composed of seven islands and the bestower of all desires is Mangala Chaṇḍî. Or it may be that the Mûla Prakriti, the Governess, the Ever Gracious Durgâ assumed the form of Mângla Chaṇḍî and has become the Iṣṭa Devatâ of women. When there was the fight with Tripurâsura, this Mangala Chaṇḍî, higher than the highest was first worshipped by Mahâdeva, stimulated by Viṣṇu, on a critical moment. O Brâhmin! While the fighting was going on, a Daitya threw out of anger one car on Mahâdeva and as that car was about to fall on Him, Brahmâ and Viṣṇu gave a good advice when Mahâdeva began to praise Durgâ Devî at once. Durgâ Devî that time assuming the form of Mangala Chaṇḍî appeared and said "no fear no fear" Bhagavân Viṣṇu will be Thy Carrier buffalo. I will be also Thy Śakti in the action and Hari, full of Mâyâ, will also help Thee. Thou better slayest the enemy that dispossessed the Devas. O Child! Thus saying, the Devî Mangala

Chaṇḍî disappeared and She became the Śakti of Mahâ Deva. Then with the help of the weapon given by Viṣṇu, the Lord of Umâ killed the Asura. When the Daitya fell, the Devas and Riṣis began to chant hymns to Mahâdeva with devotion and with their heads bent low. From the sky, a shower of flowers fell instantaneously on Mahâ Deva's head. Brahmâ and Viṣṇu became glad and gave their best wishes to Him. Then ordered by Brahmâ and Viṣṇu, Śankara bathed joyously. Then He began to worship with devotion the Devî Mangala Chaṇḍî with pâdya, Arghya, Âchamanîya and various clothings. Flowers, sandal paste, various goats, sheep, buffaloes, bisons, birds, garments, ornaments, garlands, Pâyasa (a preparation of rice, ghee, milk and sugar), Piṣtaka, honey, wine, and various fruits were offered in the worship. Dancing, music, with instruments and the chanting of Her name and other festivals commenced. Reciting the Dhyân as in Mâdhyandina, Mahâdeva offered everything, pronouncing the principal Radical Mantra. "Om Hrim Śrim Klîm Sarva-pujye Devî Mangala Chaṇḍike Hum Phat Svâhâ" is the twenty-one lettered Mantra of Mangala Chaṇḍî. During worship, the Kalpa Vrikṣa, the tree yielding all desires, must be worshipped. O Nârada! By repeating the Mantra ten lakhs of times, the Mantra Siddhi (success in realising the Deity inherent in the Mantra) comes. Now I am saying about the Dhyânam of Mangala Chaṇḍi as stated in the Vedas and as approved by all. Listen. "O Devî Mangala Chaṇḍike! Thou art sixteen years old; Thou art ever youthful; Thy lips are like Bimba fruits, Thou art of good teeth and pure. Thy face looks like autumnal lotus; Thy colour is like white champakas; Thy eyes resemble blue lilies; Thou art the Preserver of the world and thou bestowest all sorts of prosperity. Thou art the Light in this dark ocean of the world. So I meditate on Thee." This is the Dhyânam. Now hear the stotra, which Mahâdeva recited before Her.

26-37. Mahâdeva said:—Protect me, Protect me. "O Mother! O Devî Mangal Chaṇḍike! Thou, the Destroyer of difficulties! Thou givest joy and good. Thou art clever in giving delight and fortune. Thou the bestower of all bliss and prosperity! Thou, the auspicious, Thou art Mangala Chaṇḍikâ. Thou art Mangalâ, worthy of all good, Thou art the auspicious of all auspicious; Thou bestowest good to the good persons. Thou art worthy to be worshipped on Tuesday (the Mangala day); Thou art the Deity, desired by all. The King Mangala, born of Manu family always worships Thee. Thou, the presiding Devî of Mangala; Thou art the repository of all the good that are in this world. Thou, the Bestower of the auspicious Mokṣa. Thou, the best of all; Thou, the respository of all good; Thou makest one cross all the Karmas; the people worship Thee on every Tuesday; Thou bestowest abundance of Bliss to all." Thus praising Mangala Chaṇḍikâ with this stotra, and worshipping on every

Tuesday, Śambhu departed. The Devî Sarva Mangalâ was first worshipped by Mahâdeva. Next she was worshipped by the planet Mars; then by the King Mangala; then on every Tuesday by the ladies of every household. Fifthly she was worshipped by all men, desirous of their welfare. So in every universe Mangal Chaṇḍikâ, first worshipped by Mahâdeva, came to be worshipped by all. Next she came to be worshipped everywhere, by the Devas, Munis, Mânavas, Manus. O Muni! He who hears with undivided attention this stotra of the Devî Mangala Chaṇḍikâ, finds no evils anywhere. Rather all good comes to him. Day after day he gets sons and grandsons and so his prosperity gets increased, yea, verily increased!

38-58. Nârâyaṇa said:—O Nârada! Thus I narrated to you the stories of Ṣaṣṭhi and Mangla Chaṇḍikâ, according to the Vedas. Now hear the story of Manasâ that I heard from the mouth of Dharama Deva.

Manasâ is the mind-born daughter of Maharṣi Kas'yapa; hence she is named Manasâ; or it may be She who plays with the mind is Manasâ. Or it may be She who meditates on God with her mind and gets rapture in Her meditation of God is named Manasâ. She finds pleasure in Her Own Self, the great devotee of Viṣṇu, a Siddha Yoginî. For three Yugas She worshipped Śrî Kriṣṇa and then She became a Siddha Yoginî. Śrî Kriṣṇa, the Lord of the Gopîs, seeing the body of Manasâ lean and thin due to austerities, or seeing her worn out like the Muni Jarat Kâru called her by the name of Jarat Kâru. Hence Her name has come also to be Jarat Kâru. Kriṣṇa, the Ocean of Mercy, gave her out of kindness, Her desired boon; She worshipped Him and Śrî Kriṣṇa also worshipped Her. Devî Manasâ is known in the Heavens, in the abode of the Nâgas (serpents), in earth, in Brahmaloka, in all the worlds as of very fair colour, beautiful and charming. She is named Jagad Gaurî as she is of a very fair colour in the world. Her other name is Śaivî and she is the disciple of Śiva. She is named Vaiṣṇavî as she is greatly devoted to Viṣṇu. She saved the Nâgas in the Snake Sacrifice performed by Parikṣit, she is named Nages'varî and Naga Bhaginî and She is capable to destroy the effects of poison. She is called Viṣahari. She got the Siddha yoga from Mahâdeva; hence She is named Siddha Yoginî; She got from Him the great knowledege, so she is called Mahâ Jñanayutâ, and as she got Mritasamjîvanî (making alive the dead) she is known by the name of Mritasanjivanî. As the great ascetic is the mother of the great Muni Âstîk, she is known in the world as Âstîka mâtâ. As She is the dear wife of the great high-souled Yogî Muni Jarat Kâru, worshipped by all, she is called as Jarat Kârupriya. Jaratkâru, Jagadgaurî, Manasâ, Siddha Yoginî, Vaiṣṇavî,

Nâga Bhagini, Śaivi, Nâges'varî, Jaratkârupriyâ, Âstikamâtâ, Viṣahari, and Mahâ Jñanayutâ these are the twelve names of Manasâ, worshipped everywhere in the Universe. He who recites these twelve names while worshipping Manasâ Devî, he or any of his family has no fear of snakes. If there be any fear of snakes in one's bed, if the house be infested with snakes, or if one goes to a place difficult for fear of snakes or if one's body be encircled with snakes, all the fears are dispelled, if one reads this stotra of Manasâ. There is no doubt in this. The snakes run away out of fear from the sight of him who daily recites the Manasâ stotra. Ten lakhs of times repeating the Manasâ mantra give one man success in the stotra. He can easily drink poison who attains success in this stotra. The snakes become his ornaments; they carry him even on their backs. He who is a great Siddha can sit on a seat of snakes and can sleep on a bed of snakes. In the end he sports day and night with Viṣṇu.

Here ends the Forty-seventh Chapter of the Ninth Book on Manasâ's story in the Mahâ Purâṇam Śri Mad Devî Bhâgavatam of 18,000 verses by Maharṣi Veda Vâysa.

CHAPTER XLVIII.

1-30. Nârâyaṇa said:—"O Nârada! I will now speak of the Dhyânam and the method of worship of Śri Devî Manasâ, as stated in the Sâma Veda. Hear. "I meditate on the Devî Manasâ, Whose colour is fair like that of the white champaka flower, whose body is decked all over with jewel ornaments, whose clothing is purified by fire, whose sacred thread is the Nâgas (serpent), who is full of wisdom, who is the foremost of great Jñanins, who is the Presiding deity of the Siddhas, Who Herself is a Siddha and who bestows Siddis to all." O Muni! Thus meditating on Her, one should present Her flowers, scents, ornaments, offerings of food and various other articles, pronouncing the principal Seed Mantra. O Nârada! The twelve lettered Siddha Mantra, to be mentioned below, yields to the Bhaktas their desires like the Kalpa Tree. Now the Radical mantra as stated in the Vedas is "Om Hrîm Śrîm Klim Aim Manasa Devyai Svâhâ" Repetition of this, five lakhs of times, yields success to one who repeats. He who attains success in this mantra gets unbounded name and fame in this world. Poison becomes nectar to him and he himself becomes famous like Dhanvantari. O Nârada! If anybody bathes on any Samkrânti day (when the sun enters from one sign to another) and going to a private room (hidden room), invokes the Devî

Manasâ Is'ânâ and worships Her with devotion, or makes sacrifices of animals before the Devî on the fifth day of the fortnight, he becomes certainly wealthy, endowed with sons and name and fame. Thus I have described to you the method of worship of Manasâ Devî. Now hear the anecdote of the Devî as I heard from Dharma. In olden days, men became greatly terrified on earth from snakes and took refuge of Kas'yapa, the supreme amongst the Munis. The Maharsi Kas'yapa became very afraid. He then with Brahmâ, and by His command composed a mantra following the principal motto of the Vedas. While composing this mantra, he intensely thought of the Devî, the Presiding Deity of that Mantra, through the power of his Tapasyâ and through the mental power, the Devî Manasâ appeared and was named so, as She was produced from the sheer influence of mind. On being born, the girl went to the abode of Ŝankara in Kailâsa and began to worship Him and chant hymns to Him with devotion. For one thousand Divine years, the daughter of Kas'yapa served Mahâdeva when He became pleased. He gave her the Great Knowledge, made Her recite the Sâma Veda and bestowed to her the eight-lettered Krişņa mantra which is like the Kalpa Tree. Ŝrîm, Hrîm Klîm Krişņâya Namah was the eight lettered Mantra. She got from Him the Kavacha (amulet) auspicious to the three worlds, the method of worship and all the rules of Puraşcharaņa (repetition of the name of a deity attended with burnt offerings, oblations, etc.) and went by His command to perform in Puşkara very hard austerities. There she worshipped Krişņa for the three Yugas. Ŝrî Krişņa then appeared before Her." On seeing Krişņa, immediately the girl, worn out by austerities, worshipped Him, and she was also worshipped by Ŝrî Krişņa. Krişņa granted her the boon "Let you be worshipped throughout the world" and departed. O Nârada! She was thus first worshipped by the Supreme Spirit, the Deva Krişņa; secondly by Ŝankara; thirdly by the Maharşi Kas'yapa and the Devas. Then she was worshipped by the Munis, Manus, Nâgas, and men; and She became widely renowned in the three worlds. Kas'yapa gave Her over to the hands of Jaratkâru Muni. At the request of the Brâhmiņ Kas'yapa, the Muni Jarat Kâru married Her. After the marriage, one day, being tired with his long work of Tapasyâ, Jarat Kâru laid his head on the hip and loins of his married wife and fell fast asleep. Gradually the evening came in. The sun set. Then Manasâ thought "If my husband fails to perform the Sandhyâ, the daily duty of the Brâhmaņas, he would be involved in the sin of Brahmahatyâ." It is definitely stated in the Ŝâstras, that if any Brâhmaņa does not perform his Sandhyâ in the morning and in the evening, he becomes wholly impure and the sins

Brahmahattyâ and other crimes come down on his head." Arguing thus, these thoughts in her mind, as commanded by the Vedas, at last she awakened her husband, who then got up from his sleep.

31-39. The Muni Jarat Kâru said:—" O Chaste One! I was sleeping happily. Why have you thus interrupted my sleep? All his vows turn out useless who injures her husband." Her tapas, fastings, gifts, and other meritorious works all come to vain who do things unpleasant to her husband. If she worships her husband, she is said to have worshipped Śrî Krişņa. For the sake of fulfilling the vows of the chaste women, Hari himself becomes their husbands. All sorts of charities, gifts, all sacrifices, fastings, practising all the virtues, keeping to truth, worshipping all the Devas, nothing can turn out equal to even one-sixteenth part of serving one's husband. She ultimately goes with her husband to the region of Vaikuņţha, who serves her husband in this holy land Bhârata. She comes certainly of a bad family who does unpleasant acts to her husband or who uses unpleasant words to her husband. She goes to the Kumbhîpâka hell as long as the Sun and Moon last and then she becomes born as a Chaņdâlî, without husband and son. Speaking thus, Jarat Kâru, the best of the Munis, became angry and his lips began to tremble. Seeing this, the best Manasâ, shivering with fear, addressed her husband:—

I have broken your sleep and awakened you, fearing you might miss your time of Sandhyâ. I have committed an offence. Punish me as you think. I know that a man goes to the Kâlasûtra hell as long as the Sun and Moon last in this world, who throws an obstacle when any man eats, sleeps or enjoys with the opposite sex. O Nârada! Thus saying, the Devî Manasâ fell down at the feet of her husband and cried again and again. On the other hand, knowing the Muni angry, and ready to curse her, the Sun came there with Sandhyâ Devî. And He humbly spoke to him with fear:— " O Bhagavan! Seeing Me going to set, and fearing that you may miss Dharma, your chaste wife has awakened you. O Brâhmin! Now I am also under your refuge; forgive me. O Bhagavan! You should not curse Me. The more so, a Brâhmaņa's heart is as tender as the fresh butter. The anger of a Brâhman lasts only half the twinkling of an eye (Kşaņ). When a Brâhmaņa becomes angry, he can burn all this world and can make a new creation. So who can possess an influence like a Brâhmaņa. A Brâhmiņ is a part of Brahmâ; he is shining day and night with the Tejas of Brahma. A Brâhmaņa meditates always on the Eternal Light of Brahma. O Nârada! " Hearing the words of the Sun, the Brâhmiņ became satisfied and blessed Him. The Sun also went to His own place, thus blessed duly. To keep his promise, the Brâhmiņ Jaratkâru quitted

Manasâ. She became very sorry and began to cry aloud with pain and anguish. Being very much distressed by the then danger, she remem bered Her Iṣṭa Deva, Mahâdeva, Brahmâ, Hari and Her father Maharṣi Kas'yapa. On the very instant when Manasâ remembered, Śrî Kriṣṇa, the Lord of the Gopis, Mahâdeva, Brahmâ and Maharṣi Kas'yapa appeared there. Then seeing his own desired Deity Śrî Kriṣṇa, superior to Prakriti, beyond the attributes, Jaratkâru began to praise Him and bowed down to Him repeatedly. Then bowing down to Mahâdeva, Brahmâ and Kas'yapa, he enquired why they had come there. Brahmâ, then, instantly bowed down at the lotus-feet of Hriṣîkes'a and spoke in befitting words at that time if the Brâhmiṇ Jaratkâru leaves at all his legal wife, devoted to her own Dharma, he should first of all have a son born of her to fulfil his Dharma. O Muni! Any man can quit his wife, after he has impregnated her and got a son. But if without having a son, he leaves his wife, then all his merits are lost as all water leaks out of a sieve or a strainer. O Nârada! Hearing thus the words of Brahmâ, the Muni Jaratkâru by his Yogic power recited a Mantra and touching the navel of Manasâ spoke to her:—"O Manasâ! A son will be born in your womb self-controlled, religious, and best of the Brâhmaṇas.

61-77. That son will be fiery, energetic, renowned, well-qualified, the foremost of the Knowers of the Vedas, a great Jnânin and the best of the Yogîs. That son is a true son, indeed, who uplifts his family who is religious and devoted to Hari. At his birth all the Pitris dance with great joy. And the wife is a true wife who is devoted to her husband, good-natured and sweet-speaking and she is religious, she is the mother of sons, she is the woman of the family and she is the preserver of the family. He is the true friend, indeed, the giver of one's desired fruits, who imparts devotion to Hari. That father is a true father who shows the way to devotion to Hari. And She is the True Mother, through whom this entering into wombs ceases for ever, yea, for ever! That sister is the true kind sister from whom the fear of Death vanishes. That Guru is the Guru who gives the Viṣṇu Mantra and the true devotion to Viṣṇu. That Guru is the real bestower of knowledge who gives the Jñânam by which Śrî Kriṣṇa is meditated in whom this whole universe, moving and non-moving from the Brahmâ down to a blade of grass, is appearing and disappearing. There is no doubt in this. What knowledge can be superior to that of Śrî Kriṣṇa. The knowledge derived from the Vedas, or from the sacrifices, or from any other source is not superior to the service to Śrî Kriṣṇa. The devotion and knowledge of Śrî Hari is the Essence of all knowledge; all else is vain and mockery. It is through this Real Knowledge; that this bondage from this world is severed. But the Guru who does not impart this devotion and knowledge of Śrî Hari is not the real Guru ; rather he is an enemy that leads one to bondage. Verily he kills his disciple when he does not free him. He can never be called a Guru, father or friend who does not free his disciple from the pains in the various wombs and from the pains of death. Verily he can never be called a friend who does not show the way to the Undecaying Śrî Krişņa, the Source of the Highest Bliss. So, O Chaste One! You better worship that Undecaying Para Brahma Śrî Krişņa, Who is beyond the attributes. O Beloved! I have left you out of a pretence; please excuse me for this. The chaste women are always forgiving ; never they become angry because they are born of Sattvaguņas. Now I go to Puşkara for Tapasyâ ; you better go wherever you like. Those who have no desire have their minds always attached to the lotus feet of Śrî Krişņa. O Nârada ! Hearing the words of Jaratkâru, the Devî Manasâ became very much distressed and bewildered with great sorrow. Tears began to flow from her eyes. She then humbly spoke to her dearest husband :—" O Lord ! I have not committed any such offence, as you leave me altogether when I have thus broken your sleep.

73-115. However kindly show Thyself to me when I will recollect you. The bereavement of one's friend is painful ; more than that is the breavement of a son. Again one's husband is dearer than one hundred sons ; so the breavement of one's husband is the heaviest of all. To women, the husband is the most beloved of all earthly things ; hence he is called Priya, *i. e.*, dear. As the heart of one who has only one son is attached to that son, as the heart of a Vaişņava is attached to Śrî Hari ; as the mind of one-eyed man to his one eye, as the mind of the thirsty is attached to water, as the mind of the hungry is attached to food, as the mind of the passionate is attached to lust, as the mind of a thief is attached to the properties of others, as the mind of alewd man to his prostitute, as the mind of the learned is attached to the Śâs'tras, as the mind of a trader is attached to his trade, so the minds of chaste women are attached to their husbands. Thus saying, Manasâ fell down at the feet of her husband. Jaratkâru, the ocean of mercy, then, took her for a moment on his lap and drenched her body with tears from his eyes. The Devî Manasâ, too, distressed at the breavement of her husband also drenched the lap of the Muni with tears from her eyes. Some time after, the true knowledge arose in them and they both became free from fear. Jaratkâru then enlightened his wife and asked her to meditate on the lotus feet of Śrî Krişņa the Supreme Spirit repeatedly ; thus saying he went away for his Tapasyâ. Manasâ, distressed with sorrow, went to his Işța Deva Mahâdeva on Kailâs'a. The auspicious Śiva and Pârvatî both consoled her with knowledge and advice. Some days after, on an auspicious day and on an auspicious moment she gave birth to a son born in part of Nârâyaṇa, and as the Guru of the Yogis and as the Preceptor of the Jñânins. When the child was in mother's womb, he heard the highest knowledge from the mouth of Mahâdeva; therefore he was born as a Yogîndra and the Spiritual Teacher of the Jñanins. On his birth, Bhagavân Śankara performed his natal ceremonies and performed various auspicious ceremonies. The Brâhmaṇas chanted the Vedas for the welfare of the child; various wealth and jewels and Kirîṭas and invaluable gems were distributed by Śankara to the Brâhmaṇas; and Pârvatî gave one lakh cows and various jewels to others. After some days, Mahâdeva taught him the four Vedas with their Angas (six limbs) and gave him, at last, the Mrityumjaya Mantra. As in Manasâ's mind there reigned the devotion to her husband, the devotion to her Iṣṭa Deva and Guru, the child's name was kept Âstika.

Âstika then got the Mahâ Mantra from Śankara and by his command went to Puṣkara to worship Viṣṇu, the Supreme Spirit. There he practised tapasyâ for three lakh divine years. And then he returned to Kailâsa, to bow down to the great Yogî and the Lord Śankara. Then, bowing down to Śankara, he remained there for some time when Manasâ with her son Âstika went to the hermitage of Kâs'yapa, his father. Seeing Manasâ with son, the Maharṣi's gladness knew no bounds. He fed innumerable Brâhmaṇas for the welfare of the child, and distributed lakhs and lakhs of jewels. The joy of Aditi and Diti (the wives of Kas'yapa) knew no bounds; Manasâ remained there for a long, long time with his son. O Child! Hear now an anecdote on this. One day due to a bad Karma, a Brâhmaṇa cursed the king Parikṣit, the son of Abhimanyu; one Riṣi's son named Śringî, sipping the water of the river Kaus'ikî cursed thus:—"When a week expires, the snake Takṣaka will bite you, and you will be burnt with the poison of that snake Takṣaka." Hearing this, the King Parikṣit, to preserve his life, went to a place, solitary where wind even can have no access and he lived there. When the week was over, Dhanvantari saw, while he was going on the road, the snake Takṣaka who was also going to bite the king. A conversation and a great friendship arose between them; Takṣaka gave him voluntarily a gem; and Dhanvantari, getting it, became pleased and went back gladly to his house. The king Parikṣit was lying on his bed-stead when Takṣaka bit the king. The king died soon and went to the next world. The king Janamejaya then performed the funeral obsequies of his father and commenced afterwards the Sarpa Yajña (a sacrifice where the snakes are the victims). In that sacrifice, innumerable snakes gave up their lives by the Brahma Teja (the fire of the Brâhmins). At this, Takṣaka became terrified and took refuge of Indra. The Brâhmiṇs, then, in a body, became ready to burn Takṣaka along with Indra, when, Indra and the other Devas went to Manasâ. Mahendra, bewildered with fear, began to chant hymns to Manasâ. Manasâ called his own son Âstika who then went to the sacrificial assembly of the king Janamejaya and begged that the lives of Indra and Takṣaka be spared. The king, then, at the command of the Brâhmaṇas, granted their lives. The king, then, completed his sacrifice and gladly gave the Dakṣiṇâs to the Brâhmiṇs. The Brâhmaṇas, Munis, and Devas collected and went to Manasâ and worshipped Her separately and chanted hymns to Her. Indra went there with the various articles and He worshipped Manasâ with devotion and with great love and care ; and He chanted hymns to Her. Then bowing down before Her, and under the instructions of Brahmâ, Viṣṇu and Mahes'a, offered her sixteen articles, sacrifices and various other good and pleasant things. O Nârada ! Thus worshipping Her, they all went to their respective places. Thus I have told you the anecdote of Manasâ. What more do you want to hear. Say.

Nârada said :—" O Lord ! How did Indra praise Her and what was the method of His worshipping Her ; I want to hear all this.

117-124. Nârâyaṇa said :—Indra first took his bath; and, performing Âchamana and becoming pure, He put on a fresh and clean clothing and placed Manasâ Devî on a jewel throne. Then reciting the Vedic mantras he made Her perform Her bath by the water of the Mandâkinî the celestial river Ganges, poured from a jewel jar and then He made Her put on the beautiful clothing, uninflammable by fire. Then He caused sandalpaste to be applied to Her body all over with devotion and offered water for washing Her feet and Arghya, an offering of grass and flowers and rice, etc., as a token of preliminary worship. First of all the six Devatâs Gaṇes'a, Sun, Fire, Viṣṇu, Śiva, and Śivâ were worshipped. Then with the ten lettered mantra "Om Hrîm Śrîm Manasâ Devyai Svâhâ" offered all the offerings to Her. Stimulated by the God Viṣṇu, Indra worshipped with great joy the Devî with sixteen articles so very rare to any other person. Drums and instruments were sounded. From the celestial heavens, a shower of flowers was thrown on the head of Manasâ. Then, at the advice of Brahmâ, Viṣṇu and Mahes'a, the Devas and the Brâhmaṇas, Indra, with tears in his eyes, began to chant hymns to Manasâ, when his whole body was thrilled with joy and hairs stood on their ends.

125-145. Indra said :—" O Devî Manase ! Thou standest the highest amongst the chaste women. Therefore I want to chant hymns to

Thee. Thou art higher than the highest. Thus art most supreme. What I now praise Thee? Chanting hymns is characterised by the descan cription of one's nature; so it is said in the Vedas. But, O Prakriti! I am unable to ascertain and describe Thy qualities. Thou art of the nature of Śuddha Sattva (higher than the pure sattva unmixed with any other Guṇas); Thou art free from anger and malice. The Muni Jaratkâru could not forsake Thee; therefore it was that he prayed for Thy separation before. O Chaste One! I have now worshipped Thee. Thou art an object of worship as my mother Aditi is. Thou art my sister full of mercy; Thou art the mother full of forgiveness. O Sures'varî! It is through Thee that my wife, sons and my life are saved. I am worshipping Thee. Let Thy love be increased. O World-Mother! Thou art eternal; though Thy worship is extant everywhere in the universe, yet I worship Thee to have it extended further and further. O Mother! Those who worship Thee with devotion on the Sankrânti day of the month of Âṣâḍha, or on the Nâga Pañchamî day, or on the Sankrânti day of every month or on every day, they get their sons and grandsons, wealth and grains increased and become themselves famous, well gratified, learned and renowned. If anybody do not worship Thee out of ignorance, rather if he censures Thee, he will be bereft of Lakṣmî and he will be always afraid of snakes. Thou art the Griha Lakṣmî of all the householders and the Râja Lakṣmî of Vaikuṇṭha. Bhagavân Jarat Kâru, the great Muni, born in part of Nârâyaṇa, is Thy husband. Father Kâ'syapa has created Thee mentally by his power of Tapas and fire to preserve us; Thou art his mental creation; hence thy name is Manasâ. Thou Thyself hast become Siddhâ Yoginî in this world by thy mental power hence thou art widely known as Manasâ Devî in this world and worshipped by all. The Devas always worship Thee mentally with devotion; hence the Pundits call Thee by the name of Manasâ. O Devî! Thou always servest Truth, hence Thou art of the nature of Truth. He certainly gets Thee who always thinks of Thee verily as of the nature of truth. O Nârada! Thus praising his sister Manasâ and receiving from her the desired boon, Indra went back, dressed in his own proper dress, to his own abode. The Devî Manasâ, then, honored and worshipped everywhere, and thus worshipped by her brother, long lived in Her father's house, with Her son.

One day Surabhi (the heavenly cow) came from the Goloka and bathed Manasâ with milk and worshipped Her with great devotion and revealed to Her all the Tattva Jñânas, to be kept very secret. (This is now made the current story wherever any Lingam suddenly becomes visible.) O Nârada! Thus worshipped by the Devas and Surabhi, the Devî Manasâ went to the Heavenly regions. O Muni! One gets no fear from snakes who recites this holy Stotra composed by Indra and worships Manasâ;his family descendants are freed from the fear due to snakes. If anybody becomes Siddha in this Stotra, poison becomes nectar to him. Reciting the stotra five lakhs of times makes a man Siddha in this Stotra. So much so that he can sleep on a bed of snakes and he can ride on snakes.

Here ends the Forty-eighth Chapter of the Ninth Book on the anecdote of Manasâ in the Mahâ Purâṇam Śrî Mad Devî Bhâgavatam of 18,000 verses by Maharṣi Veda Vyâsa.

CHAPTER XLIX

1. Nârada said :—" O Bhagavan ! Who was that Surabhi, who came down from the region of Goloka. I want to hear Her life. Kindly describe.

2-23. Nârâyaṇa spoke :—" O Devarṣi ! The Devî Surabhi sprang in the Goloka. She was the first in the creation of cows ; and, from Her, all the other cows have come. She is the Presiding Deity of the cows. I will now speak Her history from the very beginning. Hear. Before, She appeared in the holy Brindâban. One day the Lord of Râdhâ, surrounded by the Gopîs, was going gladly with Râdhâ to the Holy Vrindâvan. There he began to enjoy in a solitary place with great pleasure. He is All Will and suddenly a desire arose in His mind that He would drink milk. Then He created easily the Devî Surabhi, full of milk, with Her calf, from His own left side. The calf of Surabhi is nothing else but Her wish personified. Seeing Surabhi, Śrîdâma milked Her in a new earthen jar. The milk is more sweet than even the nectar and it prevents birth and death ! The Lord of the Gopîs drank the milk. What milk dropped out of the jar, created a big tank ! The tank measured one hundred Yojanas in length and in breadth and is known in Goloka by the name of Kṣîrasâgara. The Gopikâs and Râdhâ play therein. At the will of Śrî Kriṣṇa, Whose Nature is All Will, that tank become full of excellent gems end jewels. Then, from every pore of Surabhi, there appeared suddenly one lakh koṭi Kâmadhenus (cows who yield according to one's desires). So much so that every Gopa who used to live there in Goloka had one Kâmadhenu and each house had one such. Their calves again became so many that no limit can be put to them. Thus, by degrees, the whole universe was filled with cows. This is the origin of the Cow Creation. O Nârada ! Surabhi was first worshipped by Bhagavân Śrî Kriṣṇa. Therefore She is so much honoured everywhere. On the day next the Dewâli night (new moon in the month of October), Surabhi was worshipped by the command of Śrî Kriṣṇa. This is heard from the mouth of Dharma Deva. O Child ! Now hear the Dhyânam, Stotra, and the method of worship of Surabhi as mentioned in the Vedas. I will now speak on this." "Om Surabhyai namah," is the principal six-lettered mantra of Surabhi. If anybody repeats this mantra one lakh times, he becomes Siddha in this mantra. This is like Kalpa Vrikṣa (a tree yielding all desires) to the devotees. The Dhyânam of Surabhi is mentioned in the Yajur Vedas. Success, prosperity, increase and freedom come as the result of worshipping Surabhi. The Dhyânam runs as follows :—" O Devî Surabhi ! Thou art Lakṣmî, Thou art best, Thou art Râdhâ ; Thou art the chief companion of Śrî Râdhâ, Thou art the first and the source of the cow-creation Thou art holy and Thou sanctifiest the persons ; Thou fufillest the desires of the devotees and Thou purifiest the whole universe. Therefore I meditate on Thee." Reciting this Dhyânam, the Brâhmaṇas worship the Devî Surabhi in jars, on the heads of cows, or on the pegs where cows are fastened or on Sâlagrâma stone or in water or in fire. O Muni ! He who worships with devotion on the next day morning after Divâlî night, becomes also worshipped in this world. Once a day in the Vârâhakalpa Surabhi did not yield milk, by the influence of Viṣṇu Mâyâ. The Devas became very anxious. Then they went to the Brahmaloka and began to praise Brahmâ. At His advice, Indra began to chant hymns (Stotra) to Surabhi :—

24-33. The Devendra said :—" O World-Mother ! O Devî ! O Mahâ Devî ! O Surabhi ! Thou art the source of the cow creation. Obeisance to Thee ! Thou art the dear companion of Râdhâ ; Thou art the part of Kamalâ ; Thou art dear to Śrî Kriṣṇa ; Thou art the mother of cows, I bow down to Thee. Thou art like the Kalpa Vrikṣa (a tree yielding all desires), Thou art the Chief of all ; Thou yieldest milk, wealth and prosperity and increase thereof. So I dow down to Thee. Thou art auspicious, Thou art good, Thou bestowest cows. Obeisance to Thee ! Thou givest fame, name and Dharma. So I bow down to Thee." O Nârada ! Thus hearing the praise sung by Indra, the eternal Surabhi, the originator of the world, became very glad and appeared in the Brahmaloka. Granting boon to Mahendra, so very rare to others and desired by him, Subrabhi went to the Goloka. The Devas, also, went back to their own abodes. The whole world was now full of milk ; clarified butter came out of the milk ; and from clarified butter sacrifices began to be performed and the Devas were fed and they became pleased. O Child ! He who recites this holy Stotra of Surabhi with devotion, gets cows, other wealth, name, fame and sons. The reciting of this Stotra qualifies one as if he had bathed in all the sacred places of pilgrimages and he had acquired the fruits of all the sacrifices. Enjoying happiness in this world, he goes in the end to the Temple of Śri Krişņa There living long in the service of Krişņa, he becomes able to be a son of Brahmâ.

Here ends the Forty-ninth Chapter of the Ninth Book on the anecdote of Surabhi in the Mahâ Purâņam Śrî Mad Devî Bhâgavatam of 18,000 verses by Maharşi Veda Vyâsa.

CHAPTER L.

1-4. Nârada said:—" O Bhagavan! I have heard all the anecdotes of Prakriti, as according to the Śâstras, that lead to the freedom from birth and death in this world. Now I want to hear the very secret history of Śrî Râdhâ and Durgâ as described in the Vedas. Though you have told me about their glories, yet I am not satisfied. Verily, where is he whose heart does not melt away on hearing the glories of both of them! This world is originated from their parts and is being controlleds by them. The devotion towards them frees one easily from the bonds of Samsâra (rounds of birth and death). O Muni! Kindly describe now about them.

5-44. Nârâyaņa said:—" O Nârada! I am now describing the characters of Râdhâ and Durgâ, as described in the Vedas: listen. I did not describe to anybody this Secret which is the Essence of all essences and Higher than the highest. This is to be kept very secret. Hearing this, one ought not to divulge it to any other body. Râdhâ presides over the Prâņa and Durgâ presides over the Buddhi. From these two, the Mûlâprakriti has originated this world. These two Śaktis guide the whole world. From the Mahâvirâț to the small insect, all, moving or non-moving, are under the Mûlaprakriti. One must satisfy them. Unles these two be satisfied, Mukti cannot be obtained.

Therefore one ought to serve Mûlâ Prakriti for Her satisfaction. Now of the two in Mûlâ Prakriti, I will describe fully the Râdhâ Mantra. Listen. Brahmâ, Vişņu, and others always worship this mantra. The principal mantra is " Śri Râdhâyai Svâhâ." By this six lettered mantra Dharma and other fruits all are obtained with ease. If to this six lettered Mûla mantra Hrîm be added, it yields gems and jewels as desired. So much so, if thousand koți mouths and one hundred koți tongues are obtained, the glory of this mantra cannot be described. When the incorporeal voice of Mûla Prakriti was heard in the Heavens, this mantra was obtained, first by Krişņa in the Râsa Maņdalam in the region of Goloka where all love sentiments are played: (The Vedas declare him as Raso vai Sah). From Krişņa, Vişņu got the Mantra; from Vişņu, Brahmâ got; from Brahmâ

Virâṭ got, from Virât, Dharma, and from Dharma I have got this Mantra. Repeating that Mantra, I am known by the name of Riṣi. Brahmâ and the other Devas meditate always on the Mûlâ Prakriti with greatest joy and ecstacy. Without the worship of of Râdhâ, never can the worship of Śrî Kriṣṇa be done. So men, devoted to Viṣṇu, should first of all worship Râdhâ by all means. Râdhâ is the Presiding Deity of the Prâṇa of Śrî Kriṣṇa. Hence Śrî Kriṣṇa is so much subject to Râdhâ. The Lady of the Râsa Maṇḍalam remains always close to Him. Without Her Śrî Kriṣṇa could not live even for a moment. The name Râdhâ is derived from "Râdhnoti" or fulfills all desires. Hence Mûlâ Prakriti is termed Râdhâ. I am the Riṣi of all the mantras but the Durgâ Mantra mentioned in this Ninth Skandha. Gâyatrî is the chhanda (mantra) of those mantras and Râdhikâ is the Devatâ of them. Really, Nârâyaṇa is the Riṣi of all the mantras; Gâyatrî is the chhanda; Praṇava (om) is the Vîja (seed) and Bhuvanes'varî (the Directrix of the world) is the Śakti. First of all the principal mantra is to be repeated six times; then meditation of the great Devî Râdhikâ, the Śakti of the Râsa is to be done, as mentioned in the Sâma Veda. The meditation of Râdhâ is as follows:—O Devî Radhike! Thy colour is like white Champaka flower; Thy face is like the autumnal Full Moon; Thy body shines with the splendour of ten million moons, Thy eyes look beautiful like autumnal lotus; Thy lips are red like Bimba fruits, Thy loins are very heavy and decked with the girdle (Kânchî) ornament; Thy face is always gracious with sweet smiles; Thy breasts defy the frontal globe of an elephant. Thou art ever youthful as if twelve years old; Thy body is adorned all over with ornaments! Thou art the waves of the ocean of Śringâra (love sentiments.) Thou art ever ready to shew Thy grace to the devotees; on Thy braid of hair garlands of Mallikâ and Mâlatî are shining; Thy body is like a creeping plant, very gentle and tender; Thou art seated in the middle of Râsa Maṇḍalam as the Chief Directrix; Thy one hand is ready to grant boons and another hand expresses "Have no fear." Thou art of a peaceful appearance; Thou art ever youthful; Thou art seated on a jewel throne; Thou art the foremost guide of the Gopîkâs; Thou art dearer to Kriṣṇa than even His life; O Parame'svarî! The Vedas reveal Thy nature. Meditating thus, one is to bathe the Devî on a Śâlagrâma stone, jar, yantra or the eight petalled lotus and then worship Her duly. First the Devî is to be invoked; then Pâdya and Âsana, etc., are to be offered, the principal Mantra being pronounced at every time an offering is given. After giving water for washing both the feet, Arghya is to be placed on the head and Âchamanîyam water to be offered three times on the face. Madhuparka (an oblation of honey, milk etc.) and a cow giving a good quantity of milk are next to be offered. Then the yantra is to be thought of as the bathing place where the Devî is to be bathed. Then Her body is to be wiped and a fresh cloth given for putting on. Sandalpaste and various other ornaments are next to be given. Various garlands of flowers with Tulasi Manjari (flower stalks) Pârijâta flower and Satapatra etc., then, are to be offered. Then within the eight petals, the family members of the Devî are to be thought of; worship is next to be offered in the right hand direction (with the hands of the watch). First of all, Mâlâvatî on the petal in front of (on the east) the Devî, then Mâdhavî on the southeast corner, then Ratnamâlâ on the south, Sus'ilâ on the south-west Sas'ikalâ on the west, Pârijâtâ on the north-west, Parâvatî on the north and the benefactious Sundarî on the north-east corner are to be worshipped in order. Outside this, Brâhmî and the other Mâtrikâs are to be worshipped and on the Bhûpûras (the entrances of the yantra,) the Regents of the quarters, the Dikpâlas and the weapons of the Devî, thunderbolt, etc., are to be worshipped. Then all the attendant Deities of the Devî are to be worshipped with scents and various other articles. Thus finishing the worship, one should chant the Ṣtotra (hymns) named Sahasra-nâma (thousand names) Ṣtotra with care and devotion. O Nârada! The intelligent man who worships thus the Râses'varî Devî Râdhâ, becomes like Viṣṇu and goes to the Go-loka.

He who performs the brith—day anniversary of Śrî Râdhâ on the Full-Moon day of the month of Kârtik, gets the blessings of Śrî Râdhâ who remains near to him. For some reason Râdhâ, the dweller in Goloka was born in Brindâban as the daughter of Vriṣavânu. However, according to the number of letters of the mantras that are mentioned in this chapter, Puraṣcharaṇa is to be made and Homa, one-tenth of Puraṣcharana, is to be then performed. The Homa is to be done with ghee, honey, and milk the three sweet things mixed with Til and with devotion.

45. Nârada said:—"O Bhagavan; Now describe the Stotra (hymn) Mantra by which the Devî is pleased.

46-100. Nârâyaṇa said:—"O Nârada!" Now I am saying the Râdhâ Stotra. Listen. "O Thou, the Highest Deity! the Dweller in Râsa Maṇḍalam! I bow down to Thee; O Thou, the Chief Directrix of the Râsa Maṇḍalam; O Thou dearer to Kriṣṇa than His life even, I bow down to Thee. O Thou, the Mother of the three Lokas! O Thou the Ocean of mercy! Be pleased. Brahmâ, Viṣṇu and the other Devas bow down before Thy lotus feet. Thou art Sarasvatî ; Thou art Sâvitrî ; Thou art Śankarî I bow down to Thee ; Thou art Gangâ ; Thou art Padmâvatî ; Thou art Ṣaṣṭhî ; Thou art Mangala Chaṇḍikâ; Thou art Manasâ ; Thou art Tulasî; Thou art Durgâ; Thou art Bhagavatî ; Thou art Lakṣmî ; Thou art all, I bow down to Thee. Thou art the Mûlâ Prakriti ; Thou art the Ocean of mercy. Obesiance to Thee! Be merciful to us and save us from this ocean of Samsâra (round of brith and death). O Nârada ! Any body who remembers Râdhâ and reads this Stotra three times a day does not feel the want of any thing in this world. He will ultimately go to Goloka and remain in the Râsa Maṇḍalam. O Child ! This great secret aught never to be given out to any. Now I am telling you the method of worship of the Durgâ Devî. Hear. When any one remembers Durgâ in this world, all his difficulties and troubles are removed. It is not seen that anybody does not remember Durgâ. She is the object of worship of all. She is the Mother of all and the Wonderful Śâkti of Mahâdeva. She is the Presiding Deity of the intellect (Buddhi) of all and She controls the hearts of all and She removes the great difficulties and dangers of all. Therefore She is named Durgâ in the world. She is worshipped by all, whether a Śaiva or a Vaiṣṇava. She is the Mûlâ Prakriti and from Her the creation, preservation and destruction of the universe proceed. O Nârada ! Now I am saying the principal nine lettered Durgâ Mantra, the best of all the Mantras. "Aim Hrîm Klîm Châmuṇḍâyai Vichche" is the nine lettered Vîja mantra of Śrî Durgâ ; it is like a Kalpa Vrikṣa yielding all desires. One should worship this mantra by all means. Brahmâ Viṣṇu, and Mahes'a are the Riṣis of this mantra ; Gâyatrî, Uṣṇik and Anuṣṭhubha are the chhandas; Mahâkâlî, Mahâ Lakṣmî and Sarasvatî are the Devatâs ; Rakta Dantikâ, Durgâ, and Bhrâmarî are the Vîjas. Nandâ, Sâkambharî, and Bhîmâ are the Śaktis and Dharma (Virtue), Artha (wealth) and Kâma (desires), are the places of application (Viniyoga). Assign the head to the Riṣi of the mantra (Nyâsa); assign the chhandas to the mouth and assign the Devatâ to the heart. Then assign the Śakti to the right breast for the success and assign the Vîja to the left breast.

Than perform the Ṣaḍaṃga Nyâsa as follows :—Aim Hridayâya namah, Hrîm Śi'rase Svâhâ, Klîm Śikhâyâm Vaṣaṭ, Châmuṇḍâyai Kavachâya Hum, Vichche Netrâbhyâm Vauṣaṭ, "Aim Hrîm Klîm Châmuṇḍâyai Vichche" Karatalapriṣṭhâbhyâm Phaṭ. Next say touching the corresponding parts of the body :—" Aim namah Śikhâyâm, Hrîm Namah " on the right eye ; " Klîm Namah " on the left eye, Châm Namah " on the right ear, ' Mum namah " on the left ear, ṇḍâm Namah " on the nostrils ; Vim Namah on the face ; " Chchem Namah " on the anus and finally " Aim Hrîm Klîm Châmuṇḍâyai Vichche " on the whole body. Then do the meditation (dhyân) thus :—" O Châmuṇḍe ! Thou art holding in Thy ten hands ten weapons viz, Khadga (axe) Chakra (disc) Gadâ (club), Vâṇa (arrows), Châpa (bow), Parigha, Sûla (spear), Bhûs'uṇḍî Kapâla, and Khadga. Thou art Mahâ Kâlî ; Thou art three-eyed ; Thou art decked with various ornaments. Thou shinest like Lilânjan (a kind of black pigment). Thou hast ten faces and ten feet. The Lotus born Brahmâ chanted hymns to Thee for the destruction of Madhu Kaiṭabha I bow down to Thee." Thus one should meditate on Mahâ Kâlî, of the nature of Kâmavîja (the source whence will comes). Then the Dhyânam of Mahâ Lakṣmî runs as follows :—" O Mahâ Lakṣmî, the destroyer of Mahiṣâsura ! Thou holdest the garland of Akṣa (a kind of seed), Paras'u (a kind of axe), Gadâ (club), Iṣu (arrows), Kulis'a (the thunderbolt) Padma (Lotus), Dhanu (bow), Kuṇḍikâ (a student's waterpot, Kamaṇdalu), Daṇḍa (rod for punishment), Śakti (a kind of weapon), Asi (sword), Charma (shield) Padma (a kind of waterlily), Ghaṇṭâ (bell,) Śurâpâtra) (a pot to hold liquor), Śûla (pickaxe) Pâs'a (noose) and Sudarṣana (a kind of weapon. Thy colour is of the Rising Sun. Thou art seated on the red Lotus. Thou art of the nature Mâyâvîja (the source whence female energy comes). So Obeisance to Thee ! (The Vija and the Devî are one and identical). Next comes the Dhyânam of Mahâ Sarasvatî as follows :— O Mahâ Sarasvatî ! Thou holdest bell, pickaxe, plough (Hala), Conch shell, Muṣala (a kind of club), Sudars'ana, bow and arrows. Thy colour is like Kunda flower ; Thou art the destroyer of Śumbha and the other Daityas ; Thou art of the nature of Vâṇîvîja (the source whence knowledge, speech comes). Thy body is filled with everlasting existence, intelligence and bliss. Obeisance to Thee ! O Nârada ! Now I am going to say on the Yantra of Mahâ Sarasvatî. Listen. First draw a triangle. Draw inside the triangle eight petalled lotus having twenty-four leaves. Within this draw the house. Then on the Yantra thus drawn, or in the Śalagrâma stone, or in the jar, or in image, or in the Vâṇalingam, or on the Sun, one should worship the Devî with oneness of heart. Then worship the Pîṭha, the deities seated also on the dais, *i. e.*, Jayâ, Vijayâ, Ajitâ, Aghorâ, Mangalâ and other Pîṭha Śaktis. Then worship the attendant deities called Âvaraṇa Pûjâ :—Brahmâ with Sarasvatî on the east, Nârâyaṇa with Lakṣmî on the Nairirit corner, Śankara with Pârvatî on the Vâyu corner, the Lion on the north of the Devî, and Mahâsura on the left side of the Devî ; finally worship Mahiṣa (buffalo). Next worship

Nandajâ, Raktadantâ, Śâkambharî, Śivâ, Durgâ, Bhîmâ, and Bhrâmarî. Then on the eight petals worship Brâhmî, Mâhes'varî, Kaumârî, Vaiṣṇavî, Vârâhî, Nâra Simhî, Aindrî, and Châmuṇḍâ. Next commencing from the leaf in front of the Devî, worship on the twenty-four leaves Viṣṇu Mâyâ, Chetanâ, Buddhi, Nidrâ (sleep), hunger, shadow, Śakti, thirst, peace, species (Jâti), modesty, faith, fame, Lakṣmî (wealth), fortitude, Vriti, Śruti memory, mercy, Tuṣṭi, Puṣṭi (nourishment), Bhrânti (error) and other Mat-rikâs. Next on the corners of the Bhûpura (gates of the Yantra), Ganes'a Kṣettrapâlas, Vaṭuka and Yoginîs are to be worshipped. Then on the outside of that Indra and the other Devas furnished with weapons are to be worshipped as per the aforesaid rules. For the satisfaction of the World-Mother various nice offerings and articles like those given by the royal personages are to be presented to the Mother; then the mantra is to be repeated, understanding its exoteric and esoteric meanings. Then Saptas'atî stitra (Chaṇḍî pâṭha) is to be repeated before the Devî. There is no other stotra like this in the three worlds. Thus Durgâ, the Deity of the Devas, is to be appeased every day. He who does this gets within his easy reach Dharma, Artha, Kâma, and Mokṣa, the four main objects of human pursuits (virtue, wealth, enjoyment and final beatitude). O Nârada! Thus I have described to you the method of worship of the Devî Durgâ. People get by this what they want. Hari, Brahmâ, and all the Devas, Manus, Munis, the Yogîs full of knowledge, the Âs'ramîs, and Lakṣmî and the other Devas all meditate on Śivâni. One's birth is attained with success at the remembrance of Durgâ. The fourteen Manus have got their Manuship and the Devas their own rights by meditating on the lotus feet of Durgâ. O Nârada! Thus I have described to you the very hidden histories of the Five Prakritis and their parts. Then, verily, the four objects of human pursuits Dharma, Artha, Kâma and Mokṣa are obtained by hearing this. He who has no sons gets sons, who has no learning gets learning and whoever wants any thing gets that if he hears this. The Devî Jagad-dhâtrî becomes certainly pleased with him who reads with his mind concentrated on this for nine nights before the Devî. The Devî becomes obedient to him who daily reads one chapter of this Ninth Skandha and the reader also does what is acceptable to the Devî. To ascertain beforehand what effects, merits or demerits, would accrue from reading this Bhâgavata, it is necessary by examining through the hands of a virgin girl or a Brâhmin child, the auspicious or inauspicious signs. First make a Sankalap (resolve) and worship the book. Then bow down again and again to the Devî Durgâ. Then bring there a virgin girl, bathed well and worship her duly and have a golden pencil fixed duly in her hand and placed in the middle on the body. Then calculate the auspicious or inauspicious effects, as the case may be, from the curves made by that pencil. So the effects of reading this Bhâgavata would be. If the virgin girl be indifferent in fixing the pencil within the area drawn, know the result of reading the Bhâgavata would be similar. There is no doubt in this.

Here ends the Fiftieth Chapter of the Ninth Book on the Glory of Śakti in the Mahâpurâṇam Śrîmat Devî Bhâgavatam of 18,000 verses by Maharṣi Veda Vyâsa.

Here ends the Ninth Book.

The Ninth Book Completed.

Extracts from the Calcutta Review-No. XLVII, March 1855.

The Śâktas.--Their characteristics and Practical influence in society.

In the Mârkaṇḍeya Purâṇam, Nature (Prakriti) is said "to have assumed three transcendent forms, according to her three Guṇas or qualities, and in each of them to have produced a pair of divinities, Brahmâ and Sarasvatî, Mahes'a and Kâlî, Viṣṇu and Lakṣmî, after whose intermarriage, Brahmâ and Sarasvatî formed the mundane egg, which Mahes'a and Kâli divided into halves; and Viṣṇu, together with Lakṣmî, preserved from destruction.

The Tantras, which are full of mysteries and mystical symbols, while they admit the three first forms of the female principle to be severally the representatives of the three primary Guṇas, derive their origin from the conjunction of Bindu, or the sound called Anusvâra, and marked (·) with the Bîja or roots of mantras or incantations. Every specific mantra, or a mantra, peculiar or exclusively belonging to any divinity, consists of Bîja or root, and the Anusvâra, which together from what is called a Nâda; and it is from the Nâda, or the combination of the two symbols, that the Three forms of Śakti are said to have had their origin. But this symbolical representation, the Tantras, which exalt Śiva and his bride, above all other divinities, mean, that Bindu and Bîja severally represent Śiva and Śakti, the parents of all other gods and goddesses. Thus:—"The *Bindu*, which is the soul of *Śiva*, and the *Bîja* which is the soul of Śakti, together form the Nâda, from which the three Śaktis are born (Kriyâ Sâra Tantra). Here is another attempt of the worshippers of Śiva and his Śakti to identify their guardian divinities with the Supreme Brahma.

In the Gorakṣa Samhitâ, we read as follows, "*Will, action, and intelligence* are in order the sources of Gaurî, the wife of Śiva, Brâhmî, the wife of Brahmâ and Vaiṣṇavî, the wife of Viṣṇu. The theory dismisses altogether the notion of the three Guṇas, and substitutes will, action, and intelligence in their place.

Again the Śâstras, it appears, have increased the number of the female divinities, according as they have increased the number of the male deities or their incarnations. The Kurma Purânam gives five forms of the original Śakti: "And she (Mûlâ Prakriti) became in the act of creation fivefold by the will of the supreme." And the forms which, according to this authority the original Prakriti is said to have assumed, are:—1st, Durgâ, the bride, Śakti, or Mâyâ of Śiva; 2nd, Lakṣmî, the bride, Śakti, or Mâyâ of Viṣṇu; 3rd Sarasvatî, the same of Brahmâ, or in the Brahma Vaivartta Purâṇam of Hari, whilst the fourth, Sâvitrî is the bride of Brahmâ. The fifth division, Râdhâ, is unquestionably, as Dr. Wilson very justly remarks, "a modern intruder into the Hindu pantheon."

In every successive creation of the universe, the Mûlâ Prakriti is said "to assume the different gradations of 'Amsa-rûpiṇî, Kalâ-rûpiṇî, and Kalâmsa-rûpiṇî, or manifests herself in portions, parts and portions of parts and further subdivisions. Thus the writers of the Purâṇas state:— "In every creation of the world, the Devî, through Divine Yoga assumes divine forms and becomes Amsa-rûpâ, Kalâ-rûpâ, and Kalâmsa-rûpa, or Ams'âmsa-rûpî. The Amsas form the class in which all the more important manifestations of the Śakti are comprehended, the Kalâs include all the secondary Goddesses, and the Kalâmsas and Ams'âms'as are subdivisions of the latter, and embrace all womankind, who are distinguished as good, middling or bad, according as they derive their being from the parts of their great original, in which the Sattva, Rajo and Tamo Guṇa predominates. At the same time, being regarded as manifestations of the one Supreme Spirit, they are all entitled not only to respect but to veneration. "Whoever," says the Brahma Vaivartta Purâṇam, offends or insults a female' incurs the wrath of Prakriti, whilst he who propitiates a female, particularly the youthful daughter of a Brâhmin, with clothes, ornaments and perfumes, offers worship to Prakriti Herself."

We shall next determine the questions,—What is a Śâkta, and what is the complexion of his faith? By Śâktas are understood the worshippers of Śakti. This is true only when we take the term Śakti in its restricted sense. This term, which had originally but one primary signification, has in the course of time come to be used in two different senses, a general and a limited one. When taken in its widest sense, it means the allegorical representation of the active energy of God and is synonymous with

Mûlâ Prakriti, the primitive source of Gods and men. In its limited sense, it is confined to Śiva Śakti, the Tâmasî, the offspring of darkness, and the last of the first three forms of the original Prakriti. It is Śakti in this latter sense, the bride of Śiva, whom, in her manifold forms, the Śâktas worship. The followers of the Śiva Śakti then are alone called S'aktas.

Every Hindu may pay his adoration to all the thirty-three Koțis of Gods and Goddesses composing the Hindu pantheon, but one and one only of the five divinities, Vişņu. S'iva, Sûrya, Gaņapati and S'akti must be his Işța Devatâ or tutelar divinity. Here is the marked distinction between general worshippers and special followers. To render this distinction more clear, we observe, that there are certain *general* formulâs and prayers forming the ritual of worship of every particular divinity. These may be learnt by any Hindu from the Sâstras, or from the mouth of a Brâhman and used in the adoration of any God or Goddess, according to choice or necessity. But besides these general mantras, which may be made use of by any Hindu, without any distinction of sect, there are the Bîja or specific formulâs, which are received only from the hallowed lips of the Guru or spiritual guide. These are kept in great secrecy and repeated mentally every day, as a matter of highest religious duty. The God or Goddess, whose Bîja or Mûla mantra is received in the prescribed manner, by any devotee, becomes his guardian divinity; and the person, thus initiated, becomes the special follower of that divinity. The S'âktas, then, are the special followers of the Śakti of Śiva. They may in general worship any other God or Goddess, but the bride of Śiva, in one or other of her horrid manifestations, must be their guardian deity. The following passage, quoted from the works of Mr. Colebrooke, will much elucidate the subject.

That the Hindus belong to various sects, is universally known. Five great sects, exclusively worship a single deity. One recognises the five divinities, which are adored by the other sects respectively; but the followers of this most comprehensive scheme mostly select one object of daily devotion and pay adoration to other deities on particular occasions only. The Hindu theologists have entered into vain disputes on the question, which, among the attributes of God, shall be deemed characteristic and pre-eminent Śankarâchârya, the celebrated commentator on the Vedas, contended for the attributes of S'iva; and founded or confirmed the sect of S'aivas, who worship Mahâdeva as the supreme being, and deny the independent existence of Vişņu and other Deities. Mâdhava Âchârya and Vallava Âchârya have, in like manner, established the sect of Vaişņavas who adore Vişņu as God. The Sauras (less numerous than the two sects above mentioned) worship the Sun, and acknowledge no other divinity. The Gâṇapatyâs adore Gaṇes'a, as uniting in his person all the attributes of the Deity. Before I notice the fifth sect, I must remind the reader, that the Hindu Mythology has personified the abstract and active powers of the divinity; and has ascribed sexes to these mythological personages. The S'akti, or energy of an attribute of God, is female and is fabled as the consort of that personified attribute, * * * The exclusive adorers of the Śakti of Śiva, are the Sâktas. (Asiatic Researches, Vol. VII, pp. 279).

The Śâktas, who adopt the female principle in the last of her three principle modifications, as their special divinity,—instead of deriving her origin from the supreme Brahm, use to her the language which is invariably applied to the preferential object of worship in every sect, and contemplate her as the only source of life and existence. She is declared to be equally in all things, and that all things are in her, and that besides her there is nothing. In short, she is identified with the Supreme Being. Thus it is written in the Kâs'î Khaṇda:—"Thou art predicated in every prayer—Brahmâ and the rest are all born from Thee. Thou art one with the four objects of life, and from Thee they come to fruit. From Thee this whole universe proceeds, and in Thee, asylum of the world, all is, whether visible or invisible, gross or subtle in its nature: what is, Thou art in the Śakti form and except Thee nothing has ever been. "The Sakti of Siva being indentified with Śaktimân, the Deity, is declared to be not only superior to Her Lord, but the Cause of Him. Of the two objects (Śiva and Śakti) which are eternal, the greater is the Śakti." Again Śakti gives strength to Śiva; without Her he could not stir a straw. She is, therefore the Cause of Śiva. (Sankara Vijaya)

Although the Purâṇas do, to a certain extent, authorize the adoration of Śakti, yet the principal rites and incantations are derived from a different source. Of the Purâṇas, those which in particular inculcate the worship of the female principle, are the Brahma Vaivartta, the Skanda, and the Kâlikâ. But neither in them, nor in any other Purâṇam, do we find the Bîja or radical mantras which the Śaktas receive from their spiritual guides. These, as well as the greater portion of the formulas intended for general worshippers, are received from an independent series of works, known by the collective name of Tantras. The fabulous origin of the Tantras is derived from revelations of Śiva to Pârvatî, and confirmed by Viṣṇu. It is therefore called Âgama, from the initials of the three words in a verse of the Sadala Tantra. Comming from the mouth of Śiva, heard by the mountain born Goddess, admitted by the son of Vasudeva, it is thence called Âgama.

In the Śiva Tantra, Śiva is made to say:—"The five scriptures (the four Vedas and the Purâṇas) issued from my five mouths, are the East, West, South, North, and Upper. The five are known as the paths to final liberation. There are many scriptures, but none are equal to the upper scripture (meaning the Tantras)."

Accordingly, the observances and ceremonies they prescribe, have indeed, in Bengal, superseded the original or the Vaidik ritual. They appear also, says Dr. Wilson, to have been written chiefly in Bengal and the eastern districts, many of them being unknown in the West and South-India and the rites they teach having there failed to set aside the ceremonies of the Vedas, although they are not without an important influence upon the belief and the practices of the people."

The Śakti of Śiva, whom the Śaktas make the particular object of their devotion, in preference to and exclusion of all other gods and goddesses, is said to have first assumed sixty (60) different forms, each of which is believed to have a great many modifications. Each of these secondary manifestations of the Śakti is again said to have taken a variety of forms, and so on almost without end. Even the cow and the jackals are declared to be parts of Bhagavati and venerated by the benighted natives of the country. Of the sixty primary forms of the Śiva Śakti, ten are held to be the chief being distinguished by the name of Das'a Mahâ Vidyâ or ten great Vidyâs. Their names are as follows:—(1) Kâlî, (2) Târâ, (3) Śoḍaṣî, (4) Bhuvanes'varî, (5) Bagalâ, (6) Chhinnamastâ, (7) Dhûmâvatî, (8) Bhairavî, (9) Mâtangî and (10) Kamalâtmikâ. These are the forms in which the Śâktas generally adore the bride of Śiva as their guardian divinity. The Śaktas are divided into two leading branches, the Dakṣiṇâchâris and the Vâmâchâris; or the followers of the right hand and left hand ritual. With the former, the chief authorities, among the Tantras, which are too numerous to be enumerated in this place are the Mantra Mahodadhi, Śâradâ Tilaka, Kâlikâ Tantra, etc., While the impure ritual adopted by the latter is contained chiefly in the Kulachûḍâmaṇi, Rudra Yâmala, Śyâmâ Rahasya, Yoni Tantra, and similar works.

The Vâmîs or the left-hand worshippers, adopt a form of worship contrary, to that which is usual, and they not only worship the Śakti of Śiva in all her terrific forms, but pay adoration to her numerous fiend-like attendants, the Yoginis, Dâkinis, and the Śâkinîs,

In common with the other branch of the S'âktas, S'iva is also admitted to a share of their worshipful homage, especially in the form of Bhairava, as it is with this modification of the deity, that the Vâmâ worshipper is required to conceive himself to be identified, just before he engages himself in the orgies peculiar to his sect. Thus, " I am Bhairava, I am the omniscient, endowed with qualities. The object presented to the followers of the left-hand ritual, is nothing less than an identification with Śiva and his Śakti after death, and the possession of supernatural powers in this life. It has no precedent either in the Purâṇas or in the Vedas. It is quite peculiar in itself, and perfectly distinct from every other form of worship. The Kulârnava Tantra declares:—" The Vedas are preeminent over all works, the Vaiṣṇava sect excels the Vedas, the Śaiva sect is preferable to that of Viṣṇu and the right-hand Śâkta to that of Śiva—the left hand is better than the right-hand division, and the Siddhânta is better still, the Kaula is better than the Siddhânta, and there is none better than it. The Vâmâchâris in general, and the Kaulas, in particular, make a great secret of their faith, not because they are in any way ashamed to avow the impure rites they perform, but because, by being made public, the rites are said to lose their efficacy, and become abortive. " Inwardly Śâktas, outwardly Śaivas, and in society nominally Vaiṣṇavas, the Kaulas assuming various forms traverse the earth.

The form of worship varies according to the end proposed by the worshippers: but in all the forms, the five Makâras are indispensably necessary. These are Mâmsya, Matsya, Madya, Maithuna, and Mudrâ (flesh, fish, spirituous liquor, women and certain mystical gesticulations). They are called Makâra, because they all begin with the letters m (म). Thus we read in Śyâmâ Rahasya:—" Wine, flesh, fish, Mudrâ, and Maithuna, are the five-fold Makâra, which takes away all sin." Appropriate mantras are also indispensable, according to the immediate object of the adorer. These incantations are no more intelligible to us than Egyptian hieroglyphics, and consist of meaningless monosyllabic combinations of letters. They are very great in number and are all declared to be highly efficacious, if properly used according to the dictates of the Tantras. Take the Prasâda mantra. It is composed of two letters, H and S, and is one of the very few to which any meaning is attempted to be attached. The Kulârnava says:—The letter H is the expirated and S the inspirated letter, and as these two acts constitute life, the mantra they express is the same with life, the animated world would not have been formed without it, and exists but as long as it exists, and it is an integral part of the universe, without being distinct from it, as the fragrance of flowers, and sweetness of sugar, oil of sesamum seed, and Śakti of Śiva.

He who knows it, needs no other knowledge, he who repeats it, needs practice no other act of adoration. The authority here cited is very elaborate upon the subject.

The rites practised by the Vâmâchâris are so grossly obscene, as to cast into shade the worst inventions which the most impure imagination can conceive (unbridled debauchery with wine and women).

Solitude and secrecy being strictly enjoined to the Vâmîs they invariably celebrate their rites at midnight and in most unfrequented and private places. Those, whose immediate object is the attainment of super-human powers, or whose end is specific, aiming at some particular boon or gift, are more strict on the point, lest they reap no fruits of their devotion. They never admit a companion, not even of their own fraternity, into the place of their worship. Even when they are believed by the credulous Hindus to have become Siddhas, that is, possessed of supernatural powers; or, in other words, when they have acquired sufficient art to impose upon their ignorant and superstitious countrymen, and have established their reputation as men capable of working miracles, they take every care not to disclose the means through which they have attained the object of their wish, unless revealed by some accidental occurrence or unlooked for circumstance. Those whose object is of a general character, hold a sort of convivial party, eating and drinking together in large numbers, without any great fear of detection. But yet they always take care to choose such secluded spots for the scenes of their devotion as lie quite concealed from the public view. They generally pass unnoticed and are traced out only when we make it our aim to detect them by watching over their movements like a spy. At present, as their chief desire appears to be only the gratification of sensual appetites, they are at all times found to be more attentive to points which have direct reference to the indulgence of their favourite passions, than those minor injunctions which require of them secrecy and solitude.

We shall now enumerate some of the leading rites observed by the Vâmâchâris of this country. The drinking of spirituous liquors, more or less, is with them no less a habit than a religious practice. Here it should be observed that the orthodox Vâmîs will never touch any foreign liquor or wine, but use only the country doasta, which they drink out of a cup formed either of the nut of a cocoa, or of a human skull. They hold the bowl on the three ends of the three fingers of the left hand, *viz*., the thumb, the little finger, and the one next to the thumb, closing the two other fingers. The liquor is first offered to their especial divinity in quart bottles or pints but more frequently in chaupalas and earthen jars, and then distributed round the company, each member having a cup exclusively his own. If there be no company, the worshipper pours the liquor into his own cup, and after holding it in the manner just described, repeats his Bîja Mantra, while covering it with his right hand. The Vâmâchâri, then, whether he be a sole worshipper or a member of a party, brings the cup filled with the heart-stirring liquid in contact with his forehead, as a mark of homage paid, and then empties it at a single sip. No symptom of nausea must be shewn, and no spittle must be thrown, indicating dis-relish of the celestial nectar to which the liquor is said to be converted by the repetition of the holy text. Three times the cup must go round over and over, before any food can be put to the mouth. There are certain technicalities in vogue among these, which they use in their parties. For instance, when boiled rice is to be served, they say distribute the flowers; the drinking cup is called pâttra; onions, nutmegs; the bottles, jantras, etc. They call themselves and all other men that drink wine, bîrs or heroes, and those that abstain from drinking, pas'us, *i.e.*, beasts. At the time of the principal initiation, or mantra grahaṇa, that is, when the specific of Bîja mantra is received from the Guru, he and his new disciple drink together, the former at intervals giving instructions to the latter as to the proper mode of drinking.

Many ludicrous anecdotes are told of Kaula gurus and disciples, when heated with the intoxicating drug; when their brains are excited by drinking copiously, their conduct towards each other does little agree with the relation which subsists between them. Some times the relation is quite inverted and the disciple acts the part of the Guru, and puts his feet on his head which the latter quietly submits to this height of profanation on the part of the former.

There is still another variety of the Vâmîs who substitute certain mixtures in the place of wine. These mixtures are declared in the Tantras to be equivalent to wine, and to possess all its intrinsic virtues without the power of intoxication; such as the juice of the cocoanut received in a vessel made of Kânsâ, the juice of the water lemon mixed with sugar, and exposed to the Sun; molasses dissolved in water, and contained in a copper vessel; the juice of the plant called Somalatâ, etc. etc.

In all the ceremonies, which not only comprehend the worship of the Śakti, but are performed for the attainment of some proposed object, the presence of a female, as the living representative, and the type of the goddess, is indispensably necessary. Such ceremonies are specific in their nature, and are called Sâdhanâs. Some who are more decent than the rest of the sect, join with their wives in the celebration of the gloomy rites of Kâli. Others make their beloved mistresses partners in the joint devotion. Here the rite assumes a blacker aspect. The favourite concubine is disrobed, and placed by the side or on the thigh of her naked paramour. In this situation, the usual calmness of the mind must be preserved and no evil lodged in it. Such is the the requisition of the Śâstras, say the Vâmîs, when reproached for their brutal practices. But here we first remind them of the fivefold Makâra, and then ask them the plain question, how many among them can really boast of ever attaining to such a state of perfection, and such thorough control over the passions, as to keep them unruffled, or from being inflamed in the midst of such exciting causes.

In this way is performed the rite called the Mantra Sâdhanâ. It is, as must be expected, carried on in great secrecy, and is said to lead to the possession of supernatural powers. The religious part of it is very simple, consisting merely of the repetition of the Mûla Mantra which may or may not be preceded by the usual mode of Śakta worship. Hence it is called the Mantra Sâdhanâ, to distinguish it from other sorts of Sâdhanâs, which we shall presently notice. After ten p. m. the devotee under pretence of going to bed, retires into a private chamber, where, calling in his wife or mistress, and procuring all the necessary articles of worship, such as wine, grains, water, a string of beads, etc., he shuts the doors and the windows of the room, and sitting before a lighted lamp, joins with his fair partner in drinking upto one, two, or three o'clock in the morning.

One of our neighbours, a rich and respectable man in the native community, was in the habit of holding private meetings with his mistress every night, for the purpose of making the Sâdhanâ. He had a string of beads made of chânḍâl's teeth, which is yet preserved in his family, as a precious relic. The beads are believed to be endowed with a sort of animation, to drink or absorb milk, and to shew the appearance of grim laughter when wine is sprinkled over it. We have ourselves seen the rosary and tried its alleged virtues, but found nothing in it verifying the above statements.

There is another sort of devotion, called the "Śava Sâdhanâ," the object of which is to acquire an interview with and command over the impure spirits, such as the Dânâs, Tâlas, Betâlas, Bhûtas, Pretas, Śâkinîs, Dâkinîs, and other male and female goblins, so that they may be ready at command to do whatever task the worshipper shall be pleased to commit to their charge. In this horrible ceremony, a dead body is necessary. The corpse of a chândâla is preferable to any other. But that which is declared to be the most meritorious, forming the shortest path to the acquisition of dominion, is the body of a chândâla, having died a violent death, on Tuesday or Saturday, days sacred to Kâlî and on the day of the total waue of the moon. Such a conjunction of circumstances can rarely take place, and consequently any dead body serves the purpose. The rite assumes different forms. According to some authorities, the adept is to be alone at midnight in a s'masâna, or a place where dead bodies are either buried or burned, and there to perform the prescribed rights, seated on the corpse. According to others, he must procure in the dead of night, four lifeless bodies, cut off their heads, and then bring them home. Placing these at the four corners of a square board, he should take his seat upon it, which with the worshipper upon it, must be supported by the four heads. In this latter method, the Guru is sometimes seated in the front, for giving necessary directions, as well as for the purpose of encouraging the novice and to prevent his sinking down under fear. But whatever be this preliminary step, the leading features in either case are the same. The worshipper must be furnished with spirituous liquors, and fried rice, and grain. Thus supplied, he, after worshipping the Śakti in the usual manner' must continue repeating his Mûla Mantra without interruption. This sort of prayer is called Japam. Ere long, he is said to be troubled with a hundred fears and assailed by a thousand hideous appearances. Infernal beings, some skeleton-like, and others pale as death, some one-legged and others with feet turned backwords, some with flaming brands taken from funeral piles in their hands, and others tall as palm trees, emaciated, with hideous faces, and worms hanging from every part of their bodies, now dance round him, now terrify him with frowning countenances, and now threaten him with destruction. The corpse itself, upon which he has taken his seat, seems suddenly to revive, its pale eyes begin to sparkle and wear a furious look, now it laughs and then opens wide its mouth, as if to devour him, who is thus oppressing it with his burden, and, Oh! dreadful to mention, now it attempts to rise and mount in the air. The heads also are said to show the same fearful appearances. In the midst of these terrors, the devotee is required to persevere, to keep steadily in view the object of his devotion, to fix his mind, firmly on his tutelar goddess and to pay no regard to the fiend-like phantoms. To the reviving corpse and heads, he is directed to present wine and food, with the view of pacifying them. If by giving way to fear, he tries to escape by flight, he instantly falls down insensible on the ground, and either dies on the spot or turns mad for life. But if, in spite of such apalling dangers, he can continually maintain his ground, the evil spirits gradually cease to frighten him, and are at last enslaved to his absolute will, like the genii represented in the story of Aladdin's Wonderful Lamp.

We now come to the blackest part of the Vâmâ worship. The ceremony is entitled Śrî Chakra, Pûrṇâbhiṣeka, the ring or full initiation. This worship is mostly celebrated in mixed societies composed of motely groups of persons of various castes, though not of creeds. This is quite extraordinary, since, according to the established laws of the caste system, no Hindu is permitted to eat with an inferior. But here the law is at once done away with, and persons of high caste, low caste, and no caste, sit, eat, and drink together. This is authorised by the Śâstras in the following text:—"Whilst the Bhairavi Tantra (the ceremony of the Chakra) is proceeding, all castes are Brâhmaṇas—when it is concluded they are again distinct. (Śyâmâ Rahasya). Thus, while the votaries of Śakti observe all the distinctions of caste in public, they neglect them altogether in the performance of her orgies.

The principal part of the rite called the Chakra is the Śakti Sâdhanâ, or the purification of the female representing the Śakti. In the ceremony termed the Mantra Sâdhanâ, we have already noticed the introduction of a female, the devotee always making his wife or mistress partner in the devotion. This cannot be done in a mixed society. For although the Vâmîs are so far degenerated as to perform rites such as human nature, corrupt as it is, revolts from with detestation, yet they have not sunk to that depth of depravity as to give up their wives to the licentiousness of men of beastly conduct. Neither is it the ordination of the Śâstras. For this purpose, they prescribe females of various descriptions, particularly, "a dancing girl, a female devotee, a harlot, a washerwoman, or barber's wife, a female of the Brahmanical or Śudra tribe, a flower girl or a milk-maid (Devi Rahasya). Some of the Tantras add a few more to the list, such as, "a princess, the wife of a Kâpâlî or of a châṇḍâla, of a Kulâla or of a conch-seller" (Rebati Tantra). Others increase the number to twenty-six, and a few even to sixty-four. These females are distinguished by the name of Kula Śakti. Selecting and procuring females from the preceding classes, the Vâmâchâris are to assemble at midnight in some sequestered spot in eight, nine or eleven couples, the men representing Bhairavas or Vîras, and the woman Bhairavîs or Nâyikâs. In some cases a single female representing the S'akti is to be procured. For this purpose a woman of a black complexion is always preferred. In all cases, the Kula Śakti is placed disrobed, but richly adorned with ornaments on the left of a circle (chakra) described for the purpose, whence the ceremony derives its name. Sometimes she is made to stand, stark naked, with protuberant tongue and dishevelled hair. She is then purified by the recitation of many mantras and texts, and by the performance of the mudrâ or gesticulations. Finally she is sprinkled over with wine, and if not previously initiated, the Bîja mantra is thrice repeated in her ear. To this succeeds the worship of the guardian divinity; and after this, that of the female to whom are now offered broiled fish, flesh, fried peas, rice, spirituous liquors, sweetmeats, flowers and other offerings, which are all purified by the repeating of incantations and the sprinkling of wine. It is now left to her choice to partake of the offerings, or to rest contended simply with verbal worship. Most frequently she eats and drinks till she is perfectly satisfied, and the refuse is shared by the persons present. If, in any case, she refuses to touch or try either meat or wine, her worshippers pour wine on her tongue while standing, and receive it as it runs down her body in a vessel held below. This wine is sprinkled over all the dishes which are now served among the votaries.

Such is the preliminary called the purification of S'akti. To this succeeds the devotional part of the ceremony. The devotees are now to repeat their radical mantra, but in a manner unutterably obscene. Then follow things too abominable to enter the ears of men, or to be borne by the feelings of an enlightend community ; things of which a Tiberius would be ashamed, and from which the rudest savage would turn away his face with disgust. And these very things are contained in the directions of the S'âstrâs, "Dharmâ dharma Havirdîpte Svâtmâgnau manasâs'ruchâ, Suṣumnâ Vartmanâ Nityâ Mokṣavrittim juhomyaham. Svâhântam mantra muchhârya Mûlam smaram param. * * * *. Târa dvayântaragatam Paramânanda Kâraṇam. Om Prakâs'âkâs'a Hastâbhyâm avalambya Unmanî Śruchâ, Dharmâ dharma Kalâsteha Pûrṇa Vahnau juhomyaham. * * * *. Sampûjya Kântâm santarpya statvâ nattvâ paraṣparam, Samhâra Mudrayâ Mantrî Śakti Vîrâṇ visarjjayet." Those who abide by the rules of the Śastras are comparatively few; the generality confine themselves chiefly to those parts that belong to gluttony, drunkenness and whoredom, without acquainting themselves with all the minute rules and incantations of the Śastras. The chakra is nothing more than a convivial party, consisting of the members of a single family, or at which men are assembled and the company are glad to eat flesh and drink spirits under the pretence of a religious observance.

The Sâktas delineate on their foreheads three horizontal and semicircular lines, with ashes, obtained, if possible, from the hearth on which a consecrated fire is perpetually maintained. But as such ashes are not always procurable, they generally draw lines of red sandal or vermillion. They sometimes add a red streak up the middle of the forehead, with a red circlet at the root of the nose. The circular spot, they mark, when they avow themselves, either with saffron or with turmeric and borax, but most frequently with red sandal, which, however, properly belongs to the Śaiva sect.

The beads are made either of coral, or of a certain species of stone called sphatic, or of human bone, or the teeth of a Châṇḍâla. This last sort is said to be replete with miracles, and is much valued by the Vâmâchâris. The seeds of the Rudrâkṣa and more specially what they call the Sunkhya Guṭikâ are highly prized by the Dakṣiṇâs

There is another set of impostors who pretend to have obtained dominion over the impure spirits. These go about doing miracles among the ignorant Hindus, by whom they are called in for various purposes, generally for curing diseases, barrenness, etc. They invariably come at night, in a body of two, three or four persons, one of whom is always a ventriloquist. They require to be brought Jyavâ flowers, which are sacred to Kâlî, sweetmeats, curds, etc., which being placed on the floor of a room, they and the visitors enter the room. The worship of the Śakti is now performed and then the lights are extinguished. The chief actor then begins to call his vassal goblin by name, saying, "Arambaraye, Arambaraye," and a hollow voice answers from a distance. "Here I am coming." Soon after a variety of sounds are heard as if some one knocking at the door, windows, roof, etc., or if it be a cot, the thatches shake, the bamboos crack, etc., in short, the room is filled with the presence of the spirit. Now the head inpostor asks him a number of questions as to the nature of the disease to be cured, and then begs some medicine to be given, on which a sound is heard, as if something were thrown on the floor. The lights being then brought in, roots of plants or some such things are discovered. In this way, the commanders of ghosts impose upon the credulous Hindus. The process is called Chaṇḍujâgâna, or awakening the ghost. The impostors always fail before men of sense in their attempt to call in the ghost.

The tenets of the Śaktas open the way for the gratification of all the sensual appetites, they hold out encouragement to drunkards, thieves and dacoits; they present the means of satisfying every lustful desire; they blunt the feelings by authorising the most cruel practices, and bad man to commit abominations which place them on a level worse than the beasts. The Śaktya worship is impure in itself, obscene in its practices, and highly injurious to the life and character of men."

Extracts from the Calcutta Review No XLVII, March 1855.

Pages 31-67.

By H. H. Wilson, L. L. D., and F. R. S. Calcutta, 1846.

THE TENTH BOOK.

CHAPTER I.

1-6. Nârada said:—" O Nârâyaṇa ! O Thou, the Supporter of this whole world ! The Preserver of all ! Thou hast described the glorious characters of the Devî, that take away all the sins. Kindly describe now to me the several forms that the Devî assumed in every Manvantara in this world as well as Her Divine Greatness. O Thou, full of mercy ! Describe also how and by whom She was worshipped and praised ; how She, so kind to the devotees, having been thus pleased, fulfilled their desires. I am very eager to hear these, the very best and blissful characters of the Devî. Śrî Nârâyaṇa said:—" Hear, O Maharṣi ! The glories and greatness of the Devî Bhagavatî leading to the devotion of the devotees, capable of giving all sorts of wealth and destroying all sins." From the navel lotus of Viṣṇu, the holder of the Chakra (discus), was born Brahmâ, the Creator of this universe, the great Energetic One, and the Grand Sire of all the worlds.

7-14. The four faced Brahmâ, on being born, produced from His mind Svâyambhuva Manu and his wife Śatarûpâ, the embodiment of all virtues. For this very reason, Svâyambhuva Manu has been known as the mind-born son of Brahmâ. Svâyambhuva Manu got from Brahmâ the task to create and multiply ; he made an earthen image of the Devî Bhagavatî, the Bestower of all fortunes, on the beach of the sanctifying Kṣîra Samudra (ocean of milk) and he engaged himself in worshipping Her and began to repeat the principal mystic mantra of Vâgbhava (the Deity of Speech). Thus engaged in worship, Svâyambhuva Manu conquered by and by his breath and food and observed Yama, Niyama and other vows and became lean and thin. For one hundred years he remained standing always on one leg and became successful in controlling his six passions lust, anger etc. He meditated on the feet of that Âdyâ Śakti (the Primordial Śakti) so much that he became inert like a vegetable or mineral matter. By his Tapas the Devî, the World Mother appeared before him and said :—" O King ! Ask divine boons from Me." Hearing these joyous words, the King wanted his long cherished and heart-felt boon, so very rare to the Devas.

15-22. Manu said:—" O Large eyed Devî ! Victory to Thee, residing in the hearts of all ! O Thou honoured, worshipped ! O Thou ! the Upholdress of the world ! O Thou, the Auspicious of all auspicious !

By Thy Gracious Look, it is that the Lotus born has been able to create the worlds ; Viṣṇu is perserving and Rudra Deva is destroying in a minute. By Thy command it is that Indra, the Lord of Śachî, has got the charge of controlling the three Lokas ; and Yama, the Lord of the departed, is awarding fruits and punishing according, to their merits or demerits, the deceased ones. O Mother ! By Thy Grace, Varuṇa, the holder of the noose, has become the lord of all aquatic creatures and is preserving them ; and Kuvera, the lord of the Yakṣas, has become the lord of wealth. Agni (fire), Nairṛit, Vâyu (wind), Îs'âna and Ananta Deva are Thy parts and have grown by Thy power. Then, O Devî ! If Thou desirest to grant me my desired boon, then, O Thou ! the Auspicious One ! Let all the great obstacles to my work of procreating in this universe and increasing my dominions die away. And if any body worships this great Vâgbhava Mantra or any body hears with devotion this history or makes others hear this, they all shall be crowned with success and enjoyment and Mukti be easy to them.

23-24. Specially they would get the power to remember their past lives, acquire eloquence in speaking, all round beauty, success in obtaining know ledge, success in their deeds and especially in the increase of their posterity and children. O Bhagavatî ! This is what I want most.

Here ends the First Chapter of the Tenth Book on the story of Svâyambhuva Manu in the Mahâpurâṇam Śrî Mad Devî Bhâgavatam of 18,000 verses by Maharṣi Veda Vyâsa.

CHAPTER II.

1-6. The Devî said:—" O King ! O Mighty-armed One ! All these I grant unto you. Whatever you have asked for, I give them to you. I am very much pleased with your hard Tapasyâ and with your Japam of the Vâgbhava Mantra. Know Me that My power is infallible in killing the Lords of the Daityas. O Child ! Let your kingdom be free from enemies and let your prosperity be increased. Let your devotion be fixed on Me and in the end you will verily get Nirvâṇa Mukti. O Nârada ! Thus granting the boon to the highsouled Manu, the Great Devî disappeared before him and went to the Bindhya Range. O Devarṣi ! This Bindhya mountain increased in height so much so that it was well nigh on the way to prevent the course of the Sun when it was arrested by Maharṣi Agastya, born of a kumbha (water jar). The younger sister of Viṣṇu, Varades'varî, is staying here as Bindhyavâsinî. O Best of the Munis ! This Devî is an object of worship of all.

7-8. Saunaka and the other Riṣis said :—O Sûta ! Who is that Bindhya Mountain ? And why did He intend to soar high up to the Heavens to resist the Sun's course ? And why was it that Agastya, the son of Mitrâvaruṇa quieteued that rising mountain ? Kindly describe all these in detail.

9-15. O Saint ! We are not as yet satisfied with hearing the Glories of the Devî, the ambrosial nectar, that have come out of your mouth. Rather our thirst has been increased. Sûta said :—" O Riṣis ! There was the Bindhya Mountain, highly honoured and reckoned as the chief of the mountains on the earth. It was covered with big forests and big trees. Creeping plants and shrubs flowered these and it looked very beautiful. On it were roaming deer, wild boars, buffaloes, monkeys hares, foxes, tigers and bears, stout and cheerful, with full vigour and all very merrily. The Devas, Gandharbbas, Apsarâs, and Kinnaras come here and bathe in its rivers ; all sorts of fruit trees can be seen here. On such a beautiful Bindhya Mountain, came there one day the ever joyful Devarṣi Nârada on his voluntary tour round the world. Seeing the Maharṣi Nârada, the Bindhya Mountain got up and worshipped him with pâdya and arghya and gave him a very good Âsana to sit. When the Muni took his seat and found himself happy, the Mountain began to speak.

16-17. Bindhya said :—" O Devarṣi ! Now be pleased to say whence you are coming ; your coming here is so very auspicious! My house is sanctified today by your coming. O Deva ! Your wandering is, like the Sun, the cause of inspiring the beings with freedom from fear. So, O Nârada ! Kindly give out your intention as to your coming here which seems rather wonderful.

18-28. Nârada said ! " O Bindhya ! O Enemy of Indra ! (Once the mountains had a very great influence. Indra cut off their wings and so destroyed their influence. Hence the mountains are enemies of Indra). I am coming from the Sumeru Mountain. There I saw the nice abodes of Indra, Agni, Yama, and Varuṇa. There I saw the houses of these Dikpâlas (the Regents of the several quarters), which abound in objects of all sorts of enjoyments. Thus saying, Nârada gave out a heavy sigh. Bindhya, the king of mountains, seeing the Muni heaving a long sigh, asked him again with great eagerness. " O Devarṣi ! Why have you heaved such a long sigh ? Kindly say." Hearing this, Nârada said :—" O Child ! Hear the cause why I sighed. See ! The Himâlayâ Mountain is the father of Gaurî and the father-in-law of Mahâdeva ; therefore he is the most worshipped of all the mountains. The Kailâs'a Mountain again, is the residence of Mahâdeva ; hence that is also worshipped and chanted as capable of destroying all the sins. So the Niṣadha, Nîla, and Gandhamâdana and other mountains are worshipped at their own places. What more than this, that the Sumeru Mountain, round whom the thousandrayed Sun, the Soul of the universe, circumambulates along with the planets and stars, thinks himself the supreme and greatest amongst the mountains "I am the supreme; there is none like me in the three worlds." Remembering this self-conceit of Sumeru, I sighed so heavily. O Bindhya! We are ascetics and though we have no need to discuss those things, yet by way of conversation I have told this to you. Now I go to my own abode."

Here ends the Second Chapter of the Tenth Book on the conversation between Nârada and the Bindhya Mountain in the Mahâ Purâṇam Śrî Mad Devî Bhâgavatam of 18,000 verses by Maharṣi Veda Vyâsa.

CHAPTER III.

1-16. Sûta said:—"O Riṣis! Thus advising, the Devarṣi, the great Jñânî and Muni going wherever he likes, went to the Brahmaloka. After the Muni had gone, the Bindhya became immersed in great anxiety and, becoming always very sorrowful, could not get peace. "What shall I do now so as to overthrow Meru? Until I do that, I won't be able to get the peace of my mind or my health. The highsouled persons always praised me for my enthusiasm and energy. Fie to my energy, honour, fame and family! Fie to my strength and heroism! O Riṣis! With all these cogitations in his mind, Bindhya came finally to this crooked conclusion:—"Daily the Sun, stars and planets circumambulate round the Sumeru; hence Sumeru is always so arrogant; now if I can resist the Sun's course in the heavens by my peaks, He will not be able to circumambulate round the Sumeru. If I can do this, certainly I will be able to curb the Sumeru in his pride. Thus coming to a conclusion, Bindhya raised his arms that were the peaks high up to the heavens and blocking the passage in the Heavens remained so and passed that night with great uneasiness and difficulty, thinking when the Sun would rise and he would obstruct His passage. At last, when the morning broke out, all the quarters were clear. The Sun, destroying the darkness, rose in Udaya Giri. The sky looked clear with His rays; the lotus, seeing Him, blew out with joy; while the excellent white water-lilies, at the bereavement of the Moon, contracted their leaves and closed as if at the separation of one's lover, gone to a distant place. The people began to do their own works on the appearance of the day; the worship of the gods, the offerings to the Gods, the Homas and the offerings to the Pitris were set a going on (in the morning, afternoon and evening respectively). The Sun marched on in His course. He divided the day into three parts, morning, mid-day, and after-noon. First of all he consoled the eastern quarter which seemed like a woman suffering from the bereavement of her lover; then he consoled the south eartern corner; then as He wanted to go quickly towards the south, His horses could not go further. The charioteer Aruṇa, seeing this, infomed the Sun what had happened.

17. Aruṇa spoke :—"O Sun! The Bindhya has become very jealous of the Sumeru as You circumambulate round the Sumeru Mountain daily. He has risen very high and obstructed your course in the Heavens, hoping that you would circumambulate round him. He is thus vying with the Sumeru Mountain.

18-26. Sûta said :—"O Riṣis! Hearing the words of Aruṇa, the charioteer, the Sun began to think thus :—"Oh! The Bindhya is going to obstruct My course! What can a great hero not do, when he is in the wrong path? Oh! My horses' motions are stopped to-day! The fate is the strongest of all (Because Bindhya is strong to-day by Daiva, therefore he is doing this). Even when eclipsed by Râhu (the ascending node) I do not stop for a moment even; and now obstructed in My passage, I am waiting here for a long time. The Daiva is powerful; what can I do? The Sun's course having been thus obstructed, all from the Gods to the lowest became helpless and could not make out what to do. Chitragupta and others ascertain their time through the Sun's course; and that Sun is now rendered motionless by the Bindhya mountain! What a great adverse fate is this! When the Sun was thus obstructed by the Bindhya out of his arrogance, the sacrifices to the Devas, the offerings to the Pitris all were stopped; the world was going to rack and ruin. The people that lived on the west and south had their nights prolonged and they remained asleep. The people of the east and the north were scorched by the strong rays of the Sun and some of them died; some of them lost their health and so forth. The whole earth became devoid of Śrâddhas and worships and a cry of universal distress arose on all sides. Indra and the other Devas became very anxious and began to think what they should do at that moment.

Here ends the Third Chapter of the Tenth Book on the obstruction of the Sun's course by the Bindhya Mountain in the Mahâ Purâṇam Śrî Mad Devî Bhâgavatam of 18000 verses by Maharṣi Veda Vyâsa.

CHAPTER IV.

1-2. Sûta said:—O Riṣis! Then Indra and all the other Devas, taking Brahmâ along with them and placing Him at the front, went to Mahâdeva and took His refuge. They bowed down to Him and chanted sweet and great hymns to Him, Who holds Moon on His forehead, the Deva of the Devas, thus:—

3-1. O Thou, the Leader of the host of Gods! Victory to Thee! O Thou, Whose lotus feet are served by Umâ, Victory to Thee! O Thou, the Giver of the eight Siddhis and Vibhûtis (extraordinary powers) to Thy devotees, Victory to Thee! O Thou, the Background of this Great Theatrical Dance of this Insurmountable Mâyâ! Thou art the Supreme Spirit in Thy True Nature! Thou ridest on Thy vehicle, the Bull, and residest in Kâilâs'a; yet Thou art the Lord of all the Devas. O Thou, Whose ornament is snakes, Who art the Honoured and the Giver of honours to persons! O Thou! the Unborn, yet comprising all forms, O Thou Śambhu! That findest pleasure in this Thy Own Self! Victory to Thee!

6-9. O Thou, the Lord of Thy attendants! O Thou, Giris'a! The Giver of the great powers, praised by Mahâ Viṣṇu! O Thou, That livest in the heart lotus of Viṣṇu, and deeply absorbed in Mahâ Yoga! Obeisance to Thee! O Thou that can'st be known through Yoga, and nothing but the Yoga itself; Thou, the Lord of the Yoga! We bow down to Thee. Thou awardest the fruits of yoga to the Yogins. O Thou, the Lord of the helpless! The Incarnate of the ocean of mercy! The Relief of the diseased and the most powerful! O Thou, whose forms are the three guṇas, Sattva, Rajo, Tamas! O Thou! Whose Emblem (carrier) is the Bull (Dharma); Thou art verily the Great Kâla; yet Thou art the Lord of Kâla! Obeisance to Thee! (The Bull represents the Dharma or Speech).

10. Thus praised by the Devas, who take the offerings in sacrifices the Lord of the Devas, whose emblem is Bull, smilingly told the Devas in a deep voice:—

11. O Thou, the excellent Devas! The residents of the Heavens! I am pleased with the praises that you have sung of Me. I will fulfil the desires of you, all the Devas.

12-15. The Devas said:—"O Lord of all the Devas! O Giris'a! O Thou whose forehead is adorned with Moon! O Thou, the Doer of good to the distressed. O Thou, the Powerful! Dost Thou do good to us. O Thou, the Sinless One! The Bindhya Mountain has become jealous of the Sumeru Mountain, and has risen very high up in the Heavens and he has obstructed the Sun's course, thereby causing great troubles to all. O

Thou, the Doer of good to all! O Is'âna! Dost Thou check the mountain's abnormal rise. How can we fix time if the Sun's course be obstructed! And when there is no knowledge, what is now the time, the sacrifices to the Devas and the offerings to the Pitris are now almost dead and gone O Deva! Who will now protect us? We see Thee as the Destroyer of the fear of us and of those who are terrified. O Deva! O Lord of Giris'â! Be pleased with us.

16-18. Śrî Bhagavân said:—"O Devas! I have no power to curb the Bindhya Mountain. Let us go to the Lord of Ramâ and pay our respects to Him. He is our Lord, fit to be worshipped. He is Gobinda, Bhagavân Viṣṇu, the Cause of all causes. We will go to Him and tell Him all our sorrows. He will remove them.

19. Hearing thus the words of Girîs'a, Indra and the other Devas with Brahmâ placed Mahâdeva at their front and went to the region of Vaikuṇṭha, trembling with fear.

Here ends the Fourth Chapter of the Tenth Book on the going of the Devas to Mahâdeva in the MahâPurâṇam Srîmad Devî Bhâgavatam of 18,000 verses by Maharṣi Veda Vyâsa.

CHAPTER V.

1-5. Sûta said:—Then the Devas, on arriving at Vaikuṇṭha, saw the Lord of Lakṣmî, the Deva of the Devas, the World-Teacher, with his eyes beautiful like Padma Palâsa (lotus-leaves), shining with brilliance and began to praise Him in a voice choked with intense feelings of devotion, thus:—"Victory to Viṣṇu! O Lord of Ramâ! Thou art prior to the Virâṭ Puruṣa." O Enemy of the Daityas! O Thou, the Generator of desires in all and the Bestower of the fruits of those desires to all! O Gobinda! Thou art the Great Boar and Thou art of the nature of Great Sacrifices! O Mahâ Viṣṇu! O Lord of Dharma! Thou art the Cause of the origin of this world! Thou didst support the earth in Thy Fish Incarnation for the deliverance of the Vedas! O Thou Satyavrata of the form of a Fish! We bow down to Thee. O Thou! The Enemy of the Daityas! The Ocean of mercy! Thou dost do the actions of the Devas out of mercy. O Thou! the Tortoise Incarnation! That grantest Mukti to others! Obeisance to Thee!

6-18. O Thou! That didst assume the form of a Boar for the destruction of the Daityas Jaya and others and for raising the earth from the waters! Obeisance to Thee! Thou didst assume that form—Half man and half Lion—of the Nrisimha Mûrti and tore asunder

Hiraṇya Kas'ipu, proud of his boons, by Thy nails. We bow down
to Thee! Obeisance to Thee! That in Thy Dwarf Incarnation,
didst deceive Bali, whose head got crazed by the acquisition of the
kingdom over the three Lokas. We bow down to Thee, that in Thy
Paras'u Rāma Incarnation, didst slay Kārta Viryûryuna, the thousand
handed, and the other wicked Kṣattr iyas! Obeisance to Thee! That
wert born of the womb of Reṇukâ as the son of Jamadagni.
Obeisance to Thee, of great prowess and valour, that in Thy Rāma
Incarnation as the son of Das'aratha, didst cut off the heads of
the wicked Rākṣasa, the son of Pulastya! We bow down again and
again to Thee, the Great Lord, that in Thy Kriṣṇa incarnation, didst
deliver this earth from the clutches of the wicked King Duryodhana,
Kamsa and others and didst establish the religion by removing the then
prevailing vicious ideas and doctrines. We bow down to Thy Buddha
Incarnation, that Great Deva who didst come down here to put a
stop to the slaughtering of the innocent animals and to the performance of the wicked sacrificial ceremonies! Obeisance to the Deva!
When almost all the persons in this world will turn out in future
as Mlechchas and when the wicked Kings will oppress them, right and
left, Thou wilt then incarnate Thyself again as Kalki and redress all the
grievances! We bow down to Thy Kalki Form! O Deva! These are Thy
Ten Incarnations, for the preservation of Thy devotees, for the killing of
the wicked Daityas. Therefore Thou art called as the Great Reliever
of all our troubles. O Thou! Victory to Thee! The Deva Who
assumess the forms of women and water for destroying the ailings of
the devotees! Who else can be so kind! O Thou, the Ocean of mercy!
O Riṣis! Thus praising the yellow robed Viṣṇu, the Lord of all the
Devas, the whole host of the Devas bowed down to Him and made
Shâṣṭâmgas. Then Viṣṇu Gadâdhara, hearing their hymns, gladdened
them and spoke : —

19-27. Śrî Bhagavânn said: —" O Devas! I am pleased with your
stotra. You need not be sorrowful. I will remove all your troubles
that have become unbearable to you. O Devas! I am very
glad to hear the praises that you have offered on Me. Better ask
boons from Me. I will grant them though very rare even and obtained
with difficulty. Any person who rises early in the morning and recites
with devotion this stotra sung by you, will never experience any
sorrow. O Devas! No poverty, no bad symptoms, no Vetâlas nor
planets nor Brahma Râkṣaṣas nor any misfortunes will overtake him.
No disease, due to Vâta (windy temperament), Pitta (bile) and Kapha
(phlegm) nor untimely death will visit him. His family will not

be extinct and happiness will always reign there. O Devas! This stotra can give every thing. Both the enjoyment and freedom will come within any one's easy access. There is no doubt in this. Now what is your difficulty? Give out. I will remove it at once There is not a bit of doubt in this. Hearing these words of Śrî Bhagavân, the Devas became glad and spoke to Viṣṇu.

Here ends the Fifth Chapter of the Tenth Book on the Devas' going to Viṣṇu, in the Mahâ Purâṇam Śrî Mad Devî Bhâgavatam of 18,000 verses by Maharṣi Veda Vyâsa.

CHAPTER VI.

1-6. Sûta said:—"O Riṣis! Hearing the words of the Lord of Lakṣmî, all the Devas became pleased and they spoke:—The Devas said:—"O Deva of the Devas! O Mahâ Viṣṇu! O Thou, the Creator, Preserver and the Destroyer of the Universe! O Viṣṇu! The Bindhya mountain has risen very high and it has stopped the Sun's course. Therefore all the works on earth are suspended. We are not receiving our share of Yajñas. Now where we will go, what we will do, we do not know. Śrî Bhagavân said:—"O Devas! There is now in Benares the Muni Agastya of indomitable power, in devoted service of that Primordial Śakti Bhagavatî, the Creatrix of this Universe. This Muni alone can put a stop to this abnormal Bindhya Range. Therefore it behoves you all to go to that fiery Dvijā Agastya at Benares where the people get Nirvâṇa; the Highest Place and pray to him (to kindly fulfil your object).

7-19. Sûta said:—"O Riṣis! Thus ordered by Viṣṇu, the gods felt themselves comforted and, saluting Him, went to the city of Benares.

In a moment they went to the Holy City of Benares, and bathing there at the Maṇikarṇikâ ghâṭ, worshipped the Devas with devotion and offered Tarpaṇas to the Pitris and duly made their charities. Then they went to the excellent Âs'rama of the Muni Agastya. The hermitage was full of quiet quadruped animals; adorned with various trees, peacocks, herons, geese and Chakravâkas and various other birds tigers, wolves, deer, the wild boars, rhinoceros, young elephants, Ruru deer and others. Though there were the ferocious animals, yet the place was free from fear and it looked exceedingly beautiful. On arriving before the Muni, the gods fell prostrate before him and bowed down again and again to him. They then chanted hymns to him and said:—O Lord of Dvijas! O Thou honoured and most worshipful! Victory to Thee. Thou art sprung from a water jar. Thou art the destroyer of

Vâtâpi, the Asura. Obeisance to Thee! O Thou, full of Śrî, the son of Mitrâvaruṇa! Thou art the husband of Lopâmudrâ. Thou art the store house of all knowledge. Thou art the source of all the Śâstras. Obeisance to Thee! At Thy rise, the waters of the ocean become bright and clear; so obeisance to Thee! At Thy rise (Canopus) the Kâs'a flower blossoms. Thou art adorned with clots of matted hair on Thy head and Thou always livest with Thy disciples. Śri Râma Chandra is one of Thy chief disciples. O great Muni! Thou art entitled to praise from all the Devas! O Best! The Store-house of all qualities! O great Muni! We now bow down to Thee and Thy wife Lopâmudrâ! O Lord! O very Energetic! We all are very much tormented by an unbearable pain inflicted on us by the Bindhya Range and we therefore take refuge of Thee. Be gracious unto us. Thus praised by the gods, the highly religious Muni Agastya, the twice born, smiled and graciously said :—

20-27. O Devas! You are the lords of the three worlds, superior to all, highsouled, and the preserver of the Lokas. If you wish, you can favour, disfavour, do anything. Especially He who is the Lord of heavens, whose weapon is the thunderbolt, and the eight Siddhis are ever at his service is your Indra, the Lord of the Devas. What is there that he cannot do? Then there is Agni, Who burns everything and always carries oblations to the gods and the Pitris, Who is the mouth piece of the Devas. Is there anything impracticable with him! O Devas! Then again Yama is there amongst you, the Lord of the Râkṣasas, the Witness of all actions, and always quick in giving punishment to the offenders, that terrible looking Yama Râja. What is there that he can not accomplish?

20-27. Still, O Devas! if there be anything required by you that awaits my co-operation, give out at once and I will do it undoubtedly. Hearing these words of the Muni, the Devas became very glad and joyfully began to say what they wanted. O Maharṣi! The Bindhya mountain has risen very high and thwarted the Sun's course in the Heavens. A cry of universal distress and consternation has arisen and the three worlds are now verging to the ruins. O Muni! Now what we want is this that Thou, by Thy power of Tapas, curbest the rise of this Bindhya Mountain. O Agastya! Certainly, by Thy fire and austerities, that mountain will be brought down and humiliated. This is what we want.

Here ends the Sixth Chapter of the Tenth Book on the Devas' praying to the Muni Agastya for checking the abnormal rise of the Bindhya Range in the Mahâ Purâṇam Śrî Mad Devî Bhâgavatam of 18,000 verses by Maharṣi Veda Vyâsa.

CHAPTER VII.

1-21. Sûta said:—Hearing the words of the Devas, Agastya, the Best of the Brâhmiṇs promised that he would carry out their works. "O Riṣis! All the Devas then became very glad when the Muni, born of the water jar, promised thus. They then bade good-bye to him and went back gladly to their own abodes. The Muni then spoke to his wife thus:—"O daughter of the King! The Bindhya Mountain has baffled the progress of the Sun's course and has thus caused a great mischief. What the Munis, the Seers of truths said before referring to Kâsî, all are now coming to my mind when I am thinking why this disturbance has overtaken me. They said that various hindrances would come to him at every step, who is a Sâdhu intending to settle at Kâs'i. Let him who wants Mukti, never quit Kâs'i, the Avimukta place, in any case. But, O Dear! To-day I have got one hindrance during my stay at Kâs'î. Thus talking with much regret on various subjects with his wife, the Muni bathed in the Maṇikarṇikâ ghâṭ, saw the Lord Vis'ves'vara worshipped Daṇḍapâṇî and went to the Kâla Bhairava. He said in the following terms:—"O Mighty armed Kâlabhai'rava! Thou destroyest the fear of the Bhaktas; Thou art the God of this Kâs'î City. Then why art Thou driving me away from this Kâs'idhâm. O Lord! Thou removest all the obstacles of the devotees and Thou preservest them. Then why, O Destroyer of the sorrows of the Bhaktas! Art Thou removing me from here? Never I blamed others; nor did I practise any hypocrisy with any person nor did I lie; then under what sin, Thou art driving me away from Kâs'î. O Riṣis! Thus praying to Kâla Bhairava, the Muni Agastya, born of water jar and the husband of Lopâmudrâ, went to Sâkṣi Gaṇes'a, the Destroyer of all evils and seeing and worshipping Him, went out of Kâs'î and proceeded to the south. The Muni, the ocean of great fortune, left Kâs'î; but he became very much distressed to leave it and he remembered it always. He began to march on with his wife. As if riding on his car of asceticism he arrived at the Bindhya mountain in the twinkling of an eye and saw that the Mountain had risen very high and obstructed the passage of the Sun in the Heavens. The Bindhya Mountain, seeing the Muni Agastya in front, began to tremble and as if desirous to speak something to the earth in a whisper became low and dwarfish and bowed down to the Muni and fell down with devotion in sâṣṭâṅgas with devotion just like a stick dropped flat on the ground before the Muni.

Seeing the Bindhya thus low, the Muni Agastya became pleased and spoke with a gracious look :—"O Child! Better remain in this state until I come back. For, O Child! I am quite unable to ascend to your lofty heights. Thus saying, the Muni became eager to go to the south ; and, crossing the peaks of the Bindhya, alighted gradually again to the plains. He went on further to the south and saw the Śrî Śaila Mountain and at last went to the Malayâchala and there, building his Âs'rama (hermitage), settled himself. O Saunka ! The Devî Bhagavatî, worshipped by the Muni went to the Bindhya Mountain and settled there and became known, in the three worlds, by the name of Bindhyavâsinî.

22-26. Sûta said :—Any body who hears this highly pure narrative of the Muni Agastya and Bindhya, becomes freed of all his sins. All his enemies are destroyed in no time. This hearing gives knowledge to the Brâhmaṇas, victory to the Kṣattriyas, wealth and corn to the Vais'yas and happiness to the Sûdras.

If any body once hears this narrative, he gets Dharma if he wants Dharma, gets unbounded wealth if he wants wealth and gets all desires if he wants his desires fulfilled. In ancient times Svâyam bhuva Manu worshipped this Devî with devotion and got his kingdom for his own Manvantara period. O Saunaka ! Thus I have described to you the holy character of the Devî in this Manvantara. What more shall I say ? Mention please.

Here ends the Seventh Chapter of the Tenth Book on the checking of the rise of the Bindhya Range in the Mahâ Purâṇam Śrî Mad Devî Bhâgavatam of 18,000 verses by Maharṣi Veda Vyâsa.

CHAPTER VIII.

1. Saunaka said:—"O Sûta ! You have described the beautiful narrative of the first Manu Svâyambhuba. Now kindly describe to us the narratives of other highly energetic Deva-like Manus.

2-3. Sûta said:—"O Riṣis ! The very wise Nârada, well versed in the knowledge of Śrî Devî, hearing the glorious character of the first Svâyam bhuba Manu, became desirous to hear of the other Manus and asked the Eternal Nârâyaṇa:—"O Deva ! Now favour me by reciting the origins and narratives of the other Manus.

4. Nârâyaṇa said:—"O Devarṣi ! I have already spoken to you everything regarding the first Manu. He had worshipped the Devî Bhagavatî, and thus he got his foeless kingdom. You know that then.

5-24 Manu had two sons of great prowess, Priyavrata and Uttânapâda. They governed their kingdoms with fame. The son of this Priyavrata, of indomitable valour, is known by the wise as the second Svârochişa Manu. Dear to all the beings, this Svârochişa Manu built his hermitage near the banks of the Kâlindî (the Jumnâ) and there making an earthen image of the Devî Bhagavatî, worshipped the Devî with devotion, subsisting on dry leaves and thus practaised severe austerities. Thus he passed his twelve years in that forest; when, at last, the Devî Bhagavatî, resplendent with brilliance of the thousand Suns, became visible to him. She got very much pleased with his devotional stotrams. The Devî, the Saviour of the Devas, and Who was of good vows, granted to him the sovereignty for one Manvantara. Thus the Devî became famous by the name Târiņî Jagaddhâtrî. O Nârada ! Thus, by worshipping the Devî Târiņî, Svârochişa obtained safely the foeless kingdom. Then establishing the Dharma duly, he enjoyed his kingdom with his sons; and, when the period of his manvantara expired, he went to the Heavens. Priyavrata's son named Uttama became the third Manu, On the banks of the Ganges, he practised tapasyâ and repeated the Vîja Mantra of Vâgbhaba, in a solitary place for three years and became blessed with the favour of the Devî. With rapt devotion he sang hymns wholly to the Devî with his mind full; and, by Her boon, got the foeless kingdom and a continual succession of sons and grandsons. Thus, enjoying the pleasures of his kingdom and the gifts of the Yuga Dharma, got in the end, the excellent place, obtained by the best Râjarşis. A very happy result. Priyavarata's another son named Tâmasa became the fourth Manu. He practised austerities and repeated the Kâma Vîja Mantra, the Spiritual Password of Kâma on the southern banks of the Narmadâ river and worshipped the World Mother. In the spring and in the autumn he observed the nine nights' vow (the Navarâtri) and worshipped the excellent lotus eyed Daves'î and pleased Her. On obtaining the Devî's favour, he chanted excellent hymns to Her and made praņâms. There he enjoyed the extensive kingdom without any fear from any foe or from any other source of danger. He generated, in the womb of his wife, ten sons, all very powerful and mighty, and then he departed to the excellent region in the Heavens.

The young brother of Tâmasa, Raivata became the Fifth Manu and practised austerities on the banks of the Kâlindî (the Jumnâ) and repeated the Kâma Vija Mantra, the spiritual password of Kâma, the resort of the Sâdhakas, capable to give the highest power of speech and to yield all the Siddhis, and thus he worshipped the Devî. He obtained excellent heavens, in-domitable power, unhampered and capable of all success and a continual line of sons, grandsons, etc. Then the unrivalled excellent hero Raivata Manu established the several divisions of Dharma and enjoying all the worldly pleasures, went to the excellent region of Indra.

Here ends the Eighth Chapter of the Tenth Book on the origin of Manu in the Mahâpurâṇam S'rî Mad Devî Bhâgvatam of 18,000 verses by Maharsi Veda Vyâsa.

CHAPTAR IX.

1-7. Nârâyaṇa said:—"O Nârada! I will now narrate the supreme glories of the Devî and the anecdote how Manu, the son of Anga, obtained excellent kingdom by worshipping the Devî Bhagavatî. The son of the king Anga, named Châkṣuṣa became the Sixth Manu. One day he went to the Brahmarṣi Pulaha Riṣi and taking his refuge said:—"O Brahmarṣi! Thou removest all the sorrows and afflictions of those that come under Thy refuge; I now take Thy refuge. Kindly advise Thy servant how he may become the Lord of an endless amount of wealth. O Muni! What can I do so that I may get the sole undisputed sway over the world? How my arms can weild the weapons and manipulate them so that they may not be baffled? How my race and line be constant and my youth remain ever the same, undecayed? And how can I, in the end, attain Mukti? O Muni! Kindly dost Thou give instructions to me on these points and oblige. Hearing thus, the Muni wanted him to worship the Devî and said:—" O King! Listen attentively to what I say you to-day. Worship to-day the all auspicious Śakti; by Her grace, all your desires will be fulfilled.

8. Châkṣuṣa said:—"O Muni! What is that very holy worship of Śrî Bhagavatî? How to do it? Kindly describe all these in detail.

9-20. The Muni said:—"O King! I will now disclose all about the excellent Pûja of the Devî Bhagavatî. Hear. You recite (mentally) always the seed mantra of Vakbhava (Speech) (The Deity being Mahâ Sarasvatî). If any one makes japam (recites slowly) of the Vâkbhava Vîja thrice a day, one gets both the highest enjoyment here and, in the end, release (Mukti) O Son of a Kṣattriya! There is no other Vîja Mantra (word) better than this of Vâk (the Word). Through the Japam of this Vîja Mantra comes the increase of strength and prowess and all successes. By the Japam of this, Brahmâ is so powerful and has become the Creator; Viṣṇu preserves the Universe and Mahes'vara has become the Destroyer of the Universe. The other Dikpâlas (the Regents of the quarters) and the other Siddhas have become very powerful by the power of this Mantra, and are capable of favouring or disfavouring others. So, O King! You, too, worship the Devî of the Devas, the World Mother and ere long you will become the Lord of unbounded wealth. There is no doubt in this. O Narada! Thus advised by Pulaha Riṣi, the son of the King Anga went to the banks of the Virajâ river to practise austerities. There the king Châkṣuṣa remained absorbed in making Japam of the Vâgbhava Vîja Mantra and took for his food the leaves of the trees that dropped on the ground and thus practised severe austerities.

The first year he ate leaves; the second year he drunk water and in the third year he sustained his life by breathing air simply and thus remained steady like a pillar. Thus he remained without food for twelve years. He went on making Japam of the Vâgbhava Mantra and his heart and mind became purified. While he was sitting alone, absorbed in the meditation of the Devî Mantra, there appeared before him suddenly the Parames'varî, the World Mother, the Incarnate of Lakṣmî. The Highest Deity, full of dauntless fire and the Embodiment of all the Devas, spoke graciously in sweet words to Châkṣuṣa, the son of Anga.

21-29. O Regent of the earth! I am pleased with your Tapasyâ. Now ask any boon that you want. I will give that to you. Châkṣuṣa said:—"O Thou, worshipped by the Devas! O Sovereign of the Deva of the Devas! Thou art the Controller Inside; Thou art the Controller Outside. Thou knowest everything what I desire in my mind. Still, O Devî! When I am so fortunate as to see Thee, I say "Thou grantest me the kingdom for the Manvantara period." The Devî said:—"O Best of the Kṣattriyas! I grant unto you the kingdom of the whole world for one manvantara. You will have many sons, very powerful, indeed, and well qualified. Your kingdom will be free from any danger till at last you will certainly get Mukti. Thus granting the excellent boon to Manu, She disappeared then and there, after being praised by Manu, with deep devotion. The Sixth Manu, then favoured by the Devî, enjoyed the sovereignty of the earth and other pleasures and became the best of the Manus. His sons became the devotees of the Devî, very powerful and expert and became respected by all and enjoyed the pleasures of the kingdom. Thus getting the supremacy by the worship of the Devî, the Châkṣuṣa Manu became merged in the end in the Holy Feet of the Devî.

Here ends the Ninth Chapter of the Tenth Book on the narrative of Châkṣuṣa Manu in the Mahâpurâṇam Śrîmad Devî Bhâgavatam of 18,000 verses by Maharṣi Veda Vyâsa.

CHAPTER X,

1-4. Nârâyaṇa said:—Now the Seventh Manu is the Right Hon'ble His Excellency the Lord Vaivasvata Manu Śrâddha Deva, honoured by all the kings, and the Enjoyer of the Highest Bliss, Brahmânanda. I will now speak of this seventh Manu. He, too, practised austerities before the Highest Devî and by Her Grace, got the sovereignty of the earth for one Manvantara.

The Eighth Manu is the Sun's son, known as Sâvarṇi. This personage, a devotee of the Devî, honoured by the kings, gentle, patient, and powerful king Sâvarṇi worshipped the Devî in his previous births; and, by Her boon, became the Lord of the Manvantara.

5. Nârada said:—"O Bhagavan! How did this Sâvarṇi Manu worship in his previous birth the earthen image of the Devî. Kindly describe this to me.

6-13. Nârâyaṇa said: "O Nârada! This Eighth Manu had been, before, in the time of Svârochiṣa Manu (the second Manu), a famous king, known by the name of Suratha, born of the family of Chaitra, and very powerful. He could well appreciate merits, clever in the science of archery, amassed abundance of wealth, a generous donor, a very liberal man and he was a celebrated poet and honoured by all. He was skilled in all arts of warfare with weapons and indomitable in crushing his foes. Once on a time, some of his powerful enemies destroyed the city of Kolâ, belonging to the revered king and succeeded in beseiging his capital wherein he remained. Then the king Suratha, the conqueror of all his foes went out to fight with the enemies but he was defeated by them. Taking advantage of this opportunity, the king's ministers robbed him of all his wealth. The illustrious king then went out of the city and with a sorrowful heart rode alone on his horse on the plea of having a game and walked to and fro, as if, absent-minded.

14-25. The king, then, went to the hermitage of the Muni Sumedhâ, who could see far-reaching things (a Man of the Fourth Dimensions). It was a nice, quiet Âs'rama, surrounded by quiet and peaceful animals and filled with disciples. There in that very sacred Âs'rama, his heart became relieved and he went on living there.

One day, when the Muni finished his worship, etc., the king went to him and saluted him duly and humbly asked him the following:—"O Muni! I am suffering terribly from my mental pain. O Deva on the earth! Why I am suffering so much though I know everything, as if I am quite an ignorant man. After my defeat from my enemies, why does my mind become now compassionate towards those who stole away my kingdom. O Best of the knowers of the Vedas! What am I to do now? Where to go? How can I make me happy? Please speak on these. O Muni! Now I am in want of your good grace. The Muni said :—"O Lord of the earth! Hear the extremely wonderful glories of the Devî that have no equal and that can fructify all desires. She, the Mahâ Mâyâ, Who is all this world, is the Mother of Brahmâ, Viṣṇu and Mahes'a. O King! Know verily that it is She and She alone, that can forcibly attract the hearts of all the Jîvas and throw them in dire utter delusion. She is always the Creatrix, Preservrix and Destructrix of the Universe in the form of Hara. This MahâMâyâ fulfills the desires of all the Jîvas and She is known as the insurmountable Kâlarâtri. She is Kâlî, the Destructrix of all this universe and She is Kamalâ residing in the lotus. Know that this whole world rests on Her and it will become dissolved in Her. She is therefore, the Highest and Best. O King! Know, verily, that he alone can cross the delusion (Moha) on whom the Grace of the Devî falls and otherwise no one can escape from this Anâdi Moha.

Here ends the Tenth Chapter of the Tenth Book on the anecdote of the King Suratha in the Mahâ Purâṇam Śrî Mad Devî Bhâgavatam of 18,000 verses by Maharṣi Veda Vyâsa.

CHAPTER XI.

1-2. The king Suratha spoke :—"O Best of the twice born! Who is that Devî that you spoke just now? Why the Devî deludes all these beings? What for does She do so? Whence is the Devî born? What is Her Form? and what are Her qualities? O Brâhmin! Kindly describe all these to me.

3-9. The Muni spoke :—"O King! I will now describe the nature of the Devî Bhagavatî and why does She take Her Form in due time. Listen. In ancient days, when Bhagavân Nârâyaṇa, the king of the Yogis, was lying in deep sleep on the ocean on the bed of Ananta, after He had destroyed the Uuiverse, there came out of the wax of his ear the two, Dânavas, Madhu and Kaiṭabha, of monstrous appearances. They wanted to kill Brahmâ, who was lying on the lotus coming out of the navel of Bhagavân. Seeing the two Daityas Madhu and Kaiṭabha and seeing also Hari asleep the Lotus-born Brahmâ became very anxious and thought :— Now Bhagavân is asleep; and these two indomitable Daityas are ready to kill me. Now what am I to do? Where to go? How shall I get ease? "O Child! Thus thinking, the high souled Lotus born suddenly came to a practical conclusion. He said :—"Let me now take refuge to the Goddess Sleep, Nidrâ, the Mother of all and under Whose power Bhagavân Hari is now asleep.

10-24. Brahmâ then began to praise Her thus :—"O Devî of the Devas! O Upholdress of the world! Thou grantest desires of Thy devotees. O Thou auspicious! Thou art Para Brahma! By Thy Command all are doing respectively their works in their proper spheres! Thou art the Night of Destruction (Kâla Râtri); Thou art the Great Night (Mahâ Râtri). Thou art the greatly terrible Night of Delusion (Moha Râtri); Thou art omnipresent; omniscient; of the nature of the Supreme Bliss. Thou art regarded as the Great. Thou art highly worshipped; Thou art alone in this world as highly intoxicated; Thou art submissive to Bhakti only; Thou art the Best of all the things; Thou art sung as the Highest; Thou art modesty; Thou art Puṣṭi (nourishment); Thou art forgiveness (Kṣamâ); Thou art Beauty (Kânti); Thou art the embodiment of mercy; Thou art liked by all; Thou art adorned by the whole world; Thou art of the nature of wakefulness, dream and deep sleep; Thou art the Highest; Thou art alone Highest Deity; Thou art highly attached to the Supreme Bliss. There is no other thing than Thee. There is One only and that is Thee. Hence Thou art denominated as One; Thou becomest again the two by contact with Thy Mâyâ. Thou art the refuge of Dharma, Artha and Kâma; hence Thou Thou art Three; Thou art the Turîya (the fourth state of consciousness) hence Thou art Four. Thou art the God of the five elements; hence Thou art Panchamî (five); Thou presidest over the six passions Kâma, anger etc.; hence Thou art Ṣaṣṭhî; Thou presidest over the seven days of the week and Thou grantest boons seven by seven; hence Thou art Seven. Thou art the God of the eight Vasus; hence Thou art Aṣṭamî; Thou art full of the nine Râgas and nine parts and Thou art the Goddess of nine planets; hence Thou art Navamî. Thou pervadest the ten quarters and Thou art worshipped by the ten quarters; hence Thou art named Das'amî (the tenth day of the fortnight); Thou art served by the Eleven Rudras, the Goddeses of eleven Gaṇas and Thou art fond of Ekâdas'î Tithi; hence Thou art denominated Ekâdas'î; Thou art twelve armed and the Mother of the twelve Âdityas; hence Thou art Dvâdas'î; Thou art dear to the thirteen Gaṇas; Thou art the presiding Deity of Visve Devâs and Thou art the thirteen months including the Malas Mâsa (dirty month), hence Thou art Trayodas'î. Thou didst grant boons to the fourteen Indras and Thou gavest birth to the fourteen Manus; hence Thou art Chaturdas'î. Thou art knowable by the Pañchadas'î. Thou art sixteen armed and on Thy forehead the sixteen digits of the Moon are always shining; Thou art the sixteenth digit (ray) of the Moon named Amâ; hence Thou art Ṣoḍas'î. O Deves'î! Thou, though attributeless and formless, appearest in these forms and attributes. Thou hast now enveloped in Moha and Darkness the Lord of Ramâ, the Bhagavân, the Deva of the Devas. These Daityas, Madhu and Kaiṭabha are indomitable and very powerful. So to kill them, Thou better dost awake the Lord of the Devas.

25-34. The Muni said:—Thus praised by the Lotus-born, the Tâmasi Bhagavatî (the Goddess of sleep and ignorance), the Beloved of Bhagavân, left Viṣṇu and enchanted the two Daityas.

On being awakened, the Supreme Spirit Viṣṇu, the Lord of the world, the Bhagavân, the Deva of the Devas, saw the two Daityas. Those two monstrous Dânavas, beholding Madhu Sûdana, came up before Him, ready to fight. The hand-to-hand fight lasted amongst them for five thousand years. Then the two Dânavas, maddened by their great strength, were enchanted by the Mâyâ of Bhagavatî and told the Supreme Deity "Ask boon from us" Hearing this, the Bhagavân Âdi Puruṣa (the Prime Man) asked the boon that both of them would be killed that day by Him. Those two very powerful Dânavas spoke to Hari again "Very Well. Kill us on that part of the earth which is not under water." O King! Bhagavân Viṣṇu, the Holder of the conch and club, spoke:—"All right. Indeed! Let that be so.

Saying this He placed their heads on His thigh and severed them with His disc (chakra). O King! Thus Mahâ Kâlî, the Queen of all the Yogas arose on this occasion when the praise was offered Her by Brahmâ. O King! Now I will describe another account how this Mahâ Lakṣmî appeared on another occasion. Listen.

Here ends the Eleventh Chapter of the Tenth Book on the killing of Madhu Kaiṭabha in the Mahâ Purâṇam Srî Mad Devî Bhâgavatam of 18,000 verses by Maharṣi Veda Vîyâsa.

CHAPTER XII.

1-6. The Muni said:—"O King! The powerful Asura Mahiṣa, born of a She-buffalo, defeated all the Devas and became the Lord of the whole universe. That indomitable Dânava seized forcibly all the rights of the Devas and began to enjoy the pleasures of the kingdom over the three worlds. The Devas, thus defeated, were expelled from their abodes in Heavens. They took Brahmâ as their Leader and went to the excellent regions where Mahâ Deva and Viṣṇu resided and informed them of all that had been done by that vicious Asura Mahiṣa. They said:—"O Deva of the Devas! The insolent Mahiṣâsura has become unbearable and he has taken possessions of the rights and properties of the whole host of the Devas and he is now enjoying them. Both of you are quite capable to destroy the Asura. So why do you not devise means to annihilate him in no time!"

7-10. Hearing these pitiful words of the Devas, Bhagavân Viṣṇu became quite indignant. Śankara, Brahmâ and the other Devas all were inflamed with anger. O King! From the face of the angry Hari, then emanated an Unusual Fire, brilliant like thousand Suns. Then by and by emanated fires also from the bodies of all the Devas who were filled then with joy. From the mass of fire thus emanated there came out a beautiful Female Figure. The face of this figure was formed out of the fire that emanated from the body of Mahâ Deva. Her hairs were formed out of the fire of Yama and Her arms were formed out of the fire that emanated from Viṣṇu.

11-21. O King! From the fire of the Moon came out two breasts; from the fire of Indra came out Her middle portion; from the fire of Varuṇa, appeared Her loins and thighs; from the fire of Earth, Her hips were formed; from the fire of Brahmâ, Her feet were formed; from the fire of the Sun, Her toes were formed; from the fire of the Vasus, Her fingers were formed; from Kuvera's fire, Her nose came out; from the excellent tejas of Prajâpati, teeth; from the fire of Agni, Her three eyes; from the fire of the twilights, Her eye-brows and from the fire of Vâyu, Her ears appeared.

11-21. O Lord of men! Thus Bhagavatî Mahiṣamardinî was born of the Tejas (fiery substances) of the Devas. Next Śiva gave Her the Śûla (weapon spear); Viṣṇu gave Sudars'ana (Chakra;) Varuṇa gave the conchshell; Fire gave Śakti (weapon); Vâyu gave Her bows and arrows; Indra gave Her thunder bolt and the bell of the elephant Airâvata; Yama gave Her the Destruction Staff (Kâla Daṇḍa); Brâmâ gave Her the Rudrâkṣa, rosary and Kamaṇḍalu; the Sun gave Her, in every pore the wonderful rays; the Time (Kâla) gave Her sharp axe and shield; the oceans gave Her the beautiful necklace and new clothes two in number); Vis'vakarmâ gladly gave Her the crown, ear-rings, kaṭaka, Angada, Chandrârdha, tinklets; and the Himâlayâs gave Her the Lion as Her Vehicle and various gems and jewels.

22-30. Kuvera, the Lord of wealth gave Her the cup filled with the drink; Bhagavân Ananta Deva gave Her a necklace of snakes (Nâghâra). Thus the World Mother, the Devî, became honoured by all the Devas. The Devas, very much oppressed by Mahiṣâ sura, then, chanted various hymns of praise to the World Mother Mâhes'vari Mahâ Devî.

22-30. Hearing their Stotras, the Deves'î, worshipped by the Devas, shouted aloud the War-Cry. O King! Mahiṣâsura, startled at that War-Cry, came to Bhagavatî with all his army corps. Then that great Asura Mahiṣa hurled various weapons in the air and overcast the sky with them and began to fight with great skill. The several generals Chikṣura, Durdhara, Durmukha, Vâṣkala, Tâmraka, Viḍâlâkṣa and various other innumerable generals as if Death incarnate, accompanied Mahiṣa, the chief Dânava. A fierce fight then ensued. Then the Devî Who enchants all the beings, became redeyed with anger and began to kill the generals of the against party. When the generals were killed one by one Mahiṣâsura, skilled in the science of magic, came up quickly to the front of the Devî.

31-40. The Lord of the Dânavas, then, by his magic power, began to assume various forms. Bhagavatî, too, began to destroy his those forms. Then the Daitya, the crusher of the Devas, assumed the form of a buffalo and began to fight. The Devî then fastened the animal, the Asura, the Death of the Devas, tightly and cut off his head by Her axe. The remainder of his forces, then, fled away in terror and disorder with a loud cry. The Devas became very glad and began to chant hymns to the Devî. O King! Thus the Lakṣmî Devî appeared to kill Mahiṣâsura. Now I will describe how Sarasvatî appeared. Listen. Once on a time the two very powerful Daityas Śumbha and Nis'umbha were born. They attacked the Devas, oppressed them and siezed their houses and rights. The Devas became dispossessed of their kingdoms and went to the Himâlayâs and offered stotras to the Devî with the greatest devotion:—"O Deves'î! O Thou, skilled in removing the difficulties of the Bhaktas! Victory to Thee! O Thou, the Sinless One! Old age and death cannot touch Thee. O Thou! Death incarnate to the Dânavas! O Deves'î! O Thou, of mighty valour and prowess! O Thou, the embodiment of Brahmâ, Viṣṇu and Mahe'sa! Unbounded is Thy might; Thou canst be easily reached by the power of devotion. O Thou, the Creator, Preserver and Destroyer! O Mâdhavî! O Thou, the Giver of Bliss! Thou dancest with great joy at the time of the dissolution of all the things (Pralaya).

41-50. O Thou, full of mercy! O Deva Deve'sî! Be gracious unto us. O Thou, the Remover of the sufferings of the refugees! We now come unto Thy protection. The terror of Śumbha and Nis'umbha is like an endless ocean unto us. Save, save us from their fast clutches. O Devî! save us O King! verily. When the Devas praised thus, the daughter of the Himâlayâs, Bhagavatî became pleased and asked "What is the matter?" In the meanwhile, there emitted from the physical sheath of the Devî, another Devî Kaus'ikî who gladly spoke to the Devas:—"O Suras! I am pleased with Thy Stotra. Now ask the boon that you desire. The Devas then asked for the following boon:—" O Devî! The two famous Daityas Śumbha and Nis'umbha have attacked forcibly the three worlds. The wicked Lord of the Dânavas, Śumbha, has overcome us by the power of his arm and is now tormenting us without any break. Kindly devise some means to kill him." The Devî said:—"O Devas! Be patient. I will kill these two Daityas, Śumbha and Nis'umbha and thus remove the thorn on your way. At an early date I will do good to you" Thus saying to Indra and the other Devas, the merciful Devî disappeared at once before their eyes. The Devas with their hearts delighted went to the beautiful Sumeru Mountain and dwelt there in the caves thereof.

41-50. Here the servants of Śumbha and Nis'umbha Chaṇḍa and Muṇḍa, while they were making their circuits, saw the exquisitely beautiful Devî, the Enchantress of the world, and came back to Śumbha, their King and said:—

51-60. "O Destroyer of enemies! O Giver of honour! O Great King! You are the Lord of all the Daityas and are fit to enjoy all the gems and jewels. To-day we have seen an extraordinary beautiful woman jewel. She is fit to be enjoyed by you. So now you would better bring that perfectly beautiful woman and enjoy. No such enchanting women can be seen amongst the Asura women Nâga Kanyâs Gandharbba women, Dânavîs or men." Hearing thus the words of the servant, Śumbha, the tormentor of the foes, sent a Daitya named Sugrîva as a messenger to Her. The messenger went to the Devî as early as possible and spoke to Her all that Śumbha had told him. "O Devî! The Asura Śumbha is now the conqueror of the three worlds and respected by the Devas. O Devî!

He is now enjoying all that is best, the gems and jewels. O Devî! I am his messenger sent here to convey to you his message as follows:—"O Devî! I am the sole enjoyer of all the jewels. O Beautiful-eyed! You are a gem; so you would worship me. O Fair One! All the gems and jewels that are in the Deva loka, in the Daitya loka, or amongst the regions of men, are under my control. So you would lovingly worship me." The Devî said:—"O Messenger! True that you are speaking for your King; but I made a promise before. How can I act against it? O Messenger! Hear what I promised.

61-70. Whoever in the three worlds will conquer Me by sheer force and thus crush My vanity, whoever will be as stong as Myself, He can enjoy Me. So the King of Daityas can prove My promise true and by sheer force can marry Me. What is there with him that he cannot do? So, Messenger! Go back to your master and tell him all this so that the powerful Śumbha may fulfil My promise. Hearing thus the words of the Great Devî, the messenger went back to Śumbha and informed him everything regarding the Devî's sayings. The very powerful Lord of the Daityas, Śumbha became very angry at the unpleasant words of the messenger and commanded the Daitya named Dhumrâkṣa:—"O Dhumrâkṣa! Listen to my words with great attention. Go and catch hold of that wicked woman by her hairs and bring her to me. Go quickly; do not delay. Thus commanded, the very powerful and the best of the Daityas, Dhumrâkṣa, went at once to the Devî with sixty thousand Daityas and cried aloud to Her:—

"O Auspicious One! You would better worship quickly our Lord Śumbha, who is very powerful and mighty; you will then acquire all sorts of pleasures; else I will hold you by your hairs and take you to the Lord of the Daityas.

71-80. Thus addressd by Dhumrâkṣa Daitya, the enemy of the Devas, the Devî said:—"O Powerful One! O Daitya! What you have spoken is perfectly right, but tell me first what you or your king Śumbha can do to Me? When the Devî said thus, the Daitya Dhûmralochana rushed on Her at once with arms and weapons. With one loud noise, Mâhes'varî burnt him immediately to ashes. O King! The other forces were partly crushed by the Lion, the vehicle of the Devî and partly fled away in disorder to all the quarters; some became senseless out of fear. Śumbha, the Lord of the Daityas, became very angry to hear this. His face assumed a terrible form with eyebrows contracted. Then he became impatient with anger and sent in order Chaṇḍa, Muṇḍa and Raktabîja.

The three powerful Daityas went to the battle and tried their might to capture the Devî. The Devî Jagaddhâtrî, of violent prowess, seeing that these three Daityas were coming to Her, killed them by Her trident and laid them prostrate on the ground. Hearing their death with all their army, Śumbha and Nis'umbha came in their own persons arrogantly to the battlefield. Śumbha and Nis'umbha fought for a time with the Devî a terrible fight and became tired, when the Devî killed them outright. When the Bhagavatî, Who is all this world, killed Śumbha and Nis'umbha, the Devas began to praise Bhagavatî, the Supreme Deity of Vâk (Word) incarnate.

81-93. O King! Thus I have spoken to you in due order the manner in which the beautiful Kâlî, Mahâ Lakṣmî and Sarasvatî incarnated themselves on the earth. That Supreme Deity, the Devî Parames'varî thus creates, preserves, and destroys the Universe. You better take refuge of that highly adored Devî, that causes the distinction and the delusion of this Universe. Then only you will attain success. Nârâyaṇa said:—The king Suratha, hearing these beautiful words of the Muni, took refuge of the Devî, that yields all desired objects. He built an earthen image of the Devî and, with concentrated attention, thought wholly of the Devî and began to worship Her with devotion. When the worship was over, he offered sacrifices of the blood of his body to the Devî. Then the World-Mother, the Deity of the Devas, became pleased and appeared before him and asked him:—Accept the boon that you desire. When the Devî said thus, the king asked from the Mahes'varî that excellent knowledge whereby the ignorance is destroyed and as well the kingdom free from any dangers or difficulties. The Devî said:—"O King! By My boon, you will get your foeless kingdom in this very birth as well as the Jñânam that removes ignorance. O King! I will tell you also what you will be in the next birth. Hear. In your next birth, you will be the son of the Sun and be famous as Sâvarṇi Manu. By My boon you will be the Lord of the Manvantara, become very powerful and you will get good many sons. Thus granting him this boon, the Devî disappeared. By the Grace of the Devî, Suratha became the Lord of the Manvantara. O Sâdhu! Thus I have described to you the birth and deeds of Sâvarṇi. He who hears or reads this anecdote with devotion, will be a favourite of the Devî.

Here ends the Twelfth Chapter of the Tenth Book on the anecdote of Sâvarṇi Manu in the Mahâpurâṇam Srî Mad Devi Bhâgavatam of 18,000 verses by Maharṣi Veda Vyâsa.

CHAPTER XIII.

1-10. Śrî Nârâyaṇa spoke :—" O Child Nârada ! Hear now the wonderful anecdotes of the births of the remaining other Manus. The mere remembrance of these birth anecdotes causes Bhakti to grow and well up towards the Devî. Vaivasvata Manu had six sons :—viz., Karuṣa, Pṛiṣadhra, Nâbhâga, Diṣṭa, Saryâti, and Tris'aṇku. All of them were stout and strong. Once they all united went to the excellent banks of the Jumnâ and began to practise Prâṇâyama without taking any food and became engaged in worshipping the Devî. Each of them built separately an earthen image of the Devî and worshipped Her with devotion and with various offerings. In the beginning,they took the dry leaves of the trees that dropped of themselves for their food ; then they drank water only, then breathed air only; then the smoke from the fire of the Homa; then they depended on the Solar Rays. Thus they practised tapasyâ with great difficulties. The continual worship of the Devî with the greatest devotion made them conscious of their clear intellect, destructive of all sorts of vanities and delusions, and the Manu's sons thought only of the Hallowed Feet of the Devî ; their intellects were purified and they were greatly wondered to see within their Self the whole Universe. Thus they practised their Tapasyâ full twelve years when Bhagavatî, the Ruling Principle of this Univers resplendent with the brilliance of the thousand Suns, appeared before them. The princes with their intelligences thus purified saw Her, bowed downt and, with their lowly hearts, began to chant hymns to Her with greates devotion. " O Îs'âni ! O Merciful ! Thou art the Devî presiding over all. Thou art the Best. So Victory to Thee ! Thou art known by the Vâgbhava Mantra. Thou gettest pleased when the Vâgbhava Mantra is repeated. O Devî ! Thou art of the nature of Klîm Kâra (of the form of Klîm). Thou gettest pleased with the repetition of Klîm Mantra. O Thou, that gladdenest the Lord ! Thou bestowest joy and pleasure in the heart of the King of Kâma. O Mahâ Mâyâ ! When Thou art pleased, Thou givest that Unequalled Kingdom. O Thou that increasest the enjoyments ! Thou art Viṣṇu, Sûrya, Hara, Indra and the other Devas." When the highsouled princes praised Her thus, Bhagavatî became pleased and spoke to them the following sweet words :—" O Highsouled Princes ! You all have worshipped Me and practised, indeed, very hard tapasyâs and thus you have become sinless and your intellects and hearts have become thoroughly purged and thus purified. Now ask boons that you desire. I will grant them ere long to you. The Princes said: "O Devî! We want unrivalled Kingdoms, many sons of long longevity, continual enjoyment of pleasures, fame, energy, freedom in all actions, and as well the good and keen intelligence. These will be benificial to us. The Devî said:—Whatever you have desired, I grant them to you all. Besides I give you another boon. Listen attentively. By My Grace you all will be the Lords of the Manvantaras and acquire strength that will experience no defeat, and you will get prosperity, fame, energy, powers, and a continual line of descent and abundant full enjoyments.

22-32. Nârâyaṇa said:—After the World Mother Bhrâmarî Devî granted them these boons, the princes chanted hymns to Her and then She instantly vanished. The very energetic princes acquired in that birth excellent kingdoms and abundance of wealth. They all had sons and thus established their families, and became the Lords of Manvantara in their next births. By the Grace of the Devî, the first of the princes Karuṣa became the Ninth Manu, the exceedingly powerful Dakṣa Sâvarṇi; the second prince Priṣadhra became the Tenth Manu, named Meru Sâvarṇi; the third prince, the highly enthusiastic Nâbhâga became the Eleventh Manu, named Sûrya Sâvarṇi; the fourth prince Diṣṭa became the Twelfth Manu, named Chandra Sâvarṇi; the powerful fifth prince Śaryâti became the Thirteenth Manu named Rudra Sâvarṇi and the sixth prince Tris'anku became the Fourteenth Manu named Viṣṇu Sâvarṇi and became the celebrated Lord of the world.

33-41. Nârada questioned:—"O Wise One! Who is that Bhrâmari Devî? What is Her Nature? What for She takes birth? Kindly describe all this beautiful and pain destroying anecdotes to me. I am not satiated with the drinking of the nectar of the Glories of the Devî; my desire to hear further more is as strong as ever. As the drink of the nectar takes away death, so the drink of this anecdote of the Devî takes away the fear of death. Nârâyaṇa said:—"O Nârada! I will now narrate the wonderful glories of that unthinkable, unmanifested World-Mother, leading to Mukti. Hear, as a Mother behaves towards Her child kindly and without any hypocrisy, so the World-Mother in all Her lives manifests Her merciful sincere dealings for the welfare of the humanity. In days gone by, in the nether regions, in the city of the Daityas, there lived a powerful Daitya named Aruṇa. He was a furious Deva Hater and a pâkkâ hyprocrite. With a view to conquer the Devas, he went to the banks of the Ganges in the Himâlayâs, practised a very hard Tapasyâ, to Brahmâ, taking Him to be the Protector of the Daityas. First influenced by Tamo Guṇa, he withheld in his body the five Vâyus and partook only the dry leaves and repeated the Gâyattrî Mantra and practised austerities. Thus he practised for full ten thousand years. Then for another ten thousand years the Daitya lived drinking some drops of water only; then for another ten thousand years he remained by inhaling air only; and then for another ten thousand years he did not take any thing and thus practised he his wonderful Tapasyâ.

42-49. Thus practising his Tapasyâ, a sort of wanderful halo of light emitted from his body and began to burn the whole world. This thing then appeared a great wonder. All the Devas then exclaimed. "Oh! What is this! Oh! What is this! And they trembled. All were very much terrified and took refuge of Brahmâ. Hearing all the news from the Devas, the four faced Bhagavân rode on His vehicle, the Swan, and with the Gâyatrî went very gladly to where the Daitya was practising his austerities and saw that the Daitya was immersed in meditation with his eyes closed; and he looked, as it were, blazing with fire, as if a second Fire himself. His belly had become dried up, body withered and the nerves of the bodies, too, became almost visible; only the life breath was lingering there. Brahmâ then spoke to him:—"O Child! Auspices to you! Now ask the boon that you desire. Hearing these gladdening nectar-like words from the mouth of Brahmâ, Aruṇa, the chief of the Daityas opened his eyes and saw Brahmâ in his front. Seeing Brahmâ before him with a rosary of beads and Kamaṇḍalu in his hand and attended by Gâyatrî and the four Vedas, muttering the name of the Eternal Brahma, the Daitya rose up and bowed down to Him and sang to Him various Stotras.

50-59. Then the intelligent Daitya asked from Brahmâ the following boon that "I shall not die. Grant this." Brahmâ then gently explained to him:—"O Best of the Dânavas! See that Brahmâ, Viṣṇu, Mahes'vara and others are not free from this limitation of death! What to speak then for others! I cannot grant you a boon that is an impossibility. Ask what is possible and just. The intelligent persons never show an eagerness to an impossibility." Hearing the above words of Brahmâ, Aruṇa again said with devotion:—"O Deva! If Thou art unwilling to grant me the above boon, then, O Lord! Grant me such a boon, as is practicable, that my death shall not be caused by any war, nor by any arms or weapons, nor by any man or any woman, by any biped or quadruped or any combinations of two and grant me such a boon, such a large army as I can conquer the Devas." Hearing the words of the Daitya, Brahmâ said "Let that be" so and went back instantly to His own abode. Then, puffed up with that boon, the Daitya Aruṇa called on all the other Daityas that lived in the nether regions. The Daityas, that were under his shelter, came and saluted him, as their king and, by his command, they sent messengers to the Heavens to fight with the Devas. Hearing from the messenger that the Daityas were willing to fight with the Devas, Indra trembled with fear and went instantly with the Devas to the abode of Brahmâ. Taking Brahmâ, too, along with them from there, they went to the Viṣṇu Loka and took Viṣṇu with them and all went to the Śiva Loka.

60-70. There they all held a coference how to kill the Daitya, the enemy of the Gods. While, on the other hand, Aruṇa, the king of the Daityas surrounded by his army, went ere long to the Heavens.

O Muni! The Daitya, then, through the power of his Tapas, assumed various forms and seized the rights and possessions of the Moon, the Sun Yama, Agni and all the others. All the Devas, then, dislodged from their stations went to the region of Kailâs'a and represented to Sankara about their own troubles and dangers respectively. Then, what was to be done on this subject, on this, great discussions cropped up. When Brahmâ said, that the death of the Daitya would not ensue from any fight, with any arms or weapons, from any man or woman, biped, quadruped or from any combination of the above two. Then the Devas became all anxious and could not find out any solution at that instant, when the Incorporeal Voice was clearly heard in the Heavens :—Let you all worship the Queen of the Universe. She will carry out your work to succees. If the king of the Daityas, always engaged in mutering the Gâyattrî, forsakes the Gâyattrî any how, then his death will occur. Hearing this gladdening Celestial Voice, the Devas held the council with great caution. When it was settled what ought to be done, Indra asked Brihaspati and said :—"O Guru Deva! You would better go to the Daitya for the carrying out of the Devas' ends and do so that he forsakes the Devî Gâyattrî Parames'varî. We will all now go and meditate on Her. When She will be pleased, She will help us.

71-77. Thus commanding Brihaspati and thinking that the beautiful Protectress of Jâmbû Nada would protect them the Devas all started to worship Her and, going there, began the Devî Yajna and with great devotion muttered the Mâyâ Vîja and practised asceticism. On the other hand, Brihaspati went ere long in the garb of a Muni to the Daitya Aruṇa. The king of the Daityas then asked him :—"O Best of Munis! Whence and why have you come here. Say, O Muni! Where have you come? I am not one of your party. Rather I am your enemy. Hearing the above words, Brihaspatî said :—When you are worshipping incessantly the Devî whom we too worship, then say how you are not a one on our side! "O Saint! The vicious Daitya, hearing the above words and deluded by the Mâyâ of the Devas, forsook the Gâyattrî Mantra out of vanity and therefore he became weak, bereft of the Holy Fire.

78-85. Then Brihaspati, having succeeded in his work there, went to the Heavens and saw Indra and told him everything in detail. The Devas became satisfied and worshipped the Highest Deity. O Muni! Thus a long interval passed, when one day the World Mother, the Auspicious Devi appeared before them. She was resplended with the brilliance of ten million suns and looked beautiful like ten millions of Kandarpas (Gods of love). Her body was anointed with variegated colours, etc.; She wore a pair of clothings; a wonderful garland suspended from Her neck; Her body was decked with various ornaments and in the fists of Her hands there were worderful rows of hornets (large black bees). Her one hand was ready to grant boons and Her other hand was ready to hold out "no fear." On the neck of Bhagavatî, the Ocean of Mercy, and peaceful, were seen the variegated garlands with large black bees all round. Those male and female bees singing incessantly all round Her the Hrîmkâra Mantra (the First Vibration of Force), koṭis of black bees surrounded Her. The All-auspicious Bhagavatî, praised by all the Vedas, Who is all in all, composed of all, Who is all good, the Mother of all, Omniscient, the Protectress of all, was adorned fully with dress.

86-96. Seeing suddenly the Devî, in their front Brahmâ and the other Devas became surprised and by and by they got relieved and gladly began to chant hymns of praise to Bhagavatî, Whose Glories have been written in the Vedas.

The Devas said:—"O Devî! Obeisance to Thee! Thou art the Highest Knowledge and the Creatrix, Preservrix and the Destructrix of the Universe. O Thou, the Lotus-eyed! Thou art the Refuge of all! So we bow down to Thee. O Devî! Thou art collectively and individually Vis'va, Taijasa, Prâjña, Virâṭ and Sûtrâtmâ. O Bhagavatî. Thou art differentiated and undifferentiated; Thou art the Kûṭastha Chaitanya (the Unmoveable, Unchangeable Consciousness). So we bow down to Thee. O Durge! Thou art unconcerned with the creation, preservation and destruction; yet Thou punishest the wicked and art easily available by the sincere devotion of Thy Bhaktas. O Devî! Thou scorchest and destroyest the ignorance and sin of the embodied souls. Hence Thou art named Bhargâ. So we bow down to Thee. O Mother! Thou art Kâlikâ, Nîla Sarasvatî, Ugra Târâ, Mahogrâ; Thou assumest many other forms. So we always bow down to Thee. O Devî! Thou art Tripura Sundrî, Bhaiarabî, Mâtangî, Dhûmâvatî, Chhinnamastâ, Sâkambhari and Rakta Dantikâ. Obeisance to Thee! O Bhagavati! It is Thou that didst appear as Lakṣmî out of the milk ocean (Kṣîra Samudra). Thou hadst destroyed Vritrâsura, Chaṇḍa, Muṇḍa, Dhûmralochana, Rakta Bîja, Sumbha, Nis'umbha and the Exterminator of the Dânavas and thus, Thou didst do great favours to the Devas. So, O Gracious Countenced! Thou art Vijayâ and Gangâ; O Sârade! We bow down to Thee. O Devî! Thou art the earth, fire, Prâṇa and other Vâyus and other substances. O Merciful! Thou art of the form of this Universe; the Deva form, and the Moon, Sun and other Luminons forms and of the Knowledge Form.

97-109. O Devî! Thou art Sâvitrî; Thou art Gâyatrî; Thou art Sarasvatî; Thou art Svadhâ, Svâhâ, and Dakṣiṇâ. So we bow down to Thee. Thou art, in the Vedas, the Âgamas, "Not this" "Not this" Thou art what is left after the negation of all this. This all the Vedas declare of Thy True Nature thus as the Absolute Consciousness in all. Thus Thou art the Highest Deity So we worship Thee. As Thou art surrounded by large black bees, Thou art named Bhrâmarî. We always make obeisance to Thee! Obeisance to Thee! Obeisance to Thy sides! Obeisance to Thy back! Obeisance to Thy front! O Mother! Obeisance to Thy above! Obeisance to Thy below! Obeisance to everywhere round of Thee! O Thou, the Dweller in Maṇî Dvîpa! O Mahâ Devî! Thou art the Guide of the innumerable Brahmâṇḍas! O World Mother! Let Thou be merciful to us. O Devî! Thou art higher than the highest. O World Mother! Victory be to Thee! All Hail! O Goddess of the universe! Thou art the Best in the whole universe; Victory to Thee! O Lady of the world! Thou art the mine of all the gems of qualities. O Parames'varî! O World Mother! Let Thou be pleased unto us." Nârâyaṇa said:—Hearing those sweet, ready and confident words of the Devas, the World Mother said in the sweet tone of a Mad Cuckoo:— "O Devas! As far as granting boons to others is concerned, I am ever ready. I am always pleased with you. So, O Devas! Say what you want." Hearing the words of the Devî, the Devas began to express the cause of their sorrows. They informed Her of the wicked nature of the vicious Daitya, the neglect of the Devas, the Brâhmaṇas and the Vedas and the ruins thereof, and the dispossession of the Devas of their abodes and the receiving by the Daitya of the boon from Brahmâ; in fact, everything what they had to say, duly and vigorously. Then the Bhagavatî Bhrâmarî Devî sent out all sorts of black bees, hornets, etc., from Her sides, front and forepart.

110-120. Innumerable lines of black bees then were generated and they joined themselves with those that got out of the Devî's hands and thus they covered the whole earth. Thus countless bees began to emit from all sides like locusts. The sky was overcast with the bees; and the earth was covered with darkness. The sky, mountain peaks, trees, forests all became filled with bees and the spectacle presented a grand dismal sight. Then the black bees began to tear asunder the breasts of the Daityas as the bees bite those who destroy their beehives. Thus the Daityas could not use their weapons nor could they fight nor exchange any words. Nothing they could do; they had no help but to die. The Daityas remained in the same state where they were and in that state they wondered and died. No one could talk with another. Thus the principal Daityas died within an instant. Thus completing their destruction, the bees came back to the Devî. All the people then spoke to one another "Oh! What a wonder!" "Oh! What a wonder! Or like this:—" Whose. Mâyâ is this! What a wonder that She will do like this!" Thus Brahmâ, Viṣṇu and Mahes'a became merged in the ocean of joy and worshipped the Devî Bhagavatî with various offerings and shoutings of chants "Victory to the Devî" and showered flowers all around. The Munis began to recite the Vedas. The Gandharbas began to sing.

121-127. The various musical instruments, Mridangas, Murajas, the Indian lutes, Dhakkâs, Damarus, Śankhas, bells, etc., all sounded and the three worlds were filled with their echoes. All with folded palms chanted various hymns of praise to the Devî and said "O Mother! Îsânî! Victory to Thee!" The Mahâ Devî became glad and gave to each separate boons and when they asked "for unshakeable devotion to Thy lotus feet," She granted them that also and disappeared before them. Thus I have described to you the glorious character of the Bhrâmârî Devî. If anybody hears this very wonderful anecdote, he crosses at once this ocean of the world. Along with the gloriess and greatness of the Devî, if one hears the accounts of Manus, then all auspiciousness comes to him. He who hears or recites daily this Greatness of the Devî, becomes freed from all his sins and he gets himself absorbed in the thoughts of the Devî (Sâjuya). *Note.*—The Mantra is here not merely the Seed, the Spiritual Password, but it connotes, besides the idea of the password, the Âdi First vibration and it exhibits the *First Spiritual Form*, endowed with the highest feelings of Faith, Wisdom, Bliss and Joy, displayed with the grandest colours, startling thrills, rapt enchanting signs, gestures, and postures, the shooting forth of all powers, the sources of Siddhis, that cannot be ordinarily conceived in the worldly concerns. Their faint echoes govern this mighty world. The Mantras are seated in the six chakras or plexuses or the six Laya centres in the spinal cord. Within these chakras, the transformations of the Tattvas take place. Some vanish. Some appear and so on. Remark :—In this chapter we find clearly the mention of the several names of the ten Das'a Mahâ Vidyâs.

Here ends the Thirteenth Chapter of the Tenth Book of the account of Brâhmarî Devî in the Mahâpurâṇam Śrî Mad Devî Bhâgavatam of 18,000 verses by Maharṣi Veda Vyâsa and here ends as well the Tenth Book.

[The Tenth Book completed.]

THE ELEVENTH BOOK.

CHAPTER I.

1-13. Nârada said:—"O Bhagavan! O Thou, the Eternal One! O Nârâyaṇa! O Lord of the past and the future! Thou art the Creator and the Lord of all the beings that lived in the past and that will come into existence in the future. Thou hast described to me the highly wonderful and excellent anecdote of the Exalted Devî. How She did assume the forms of Mahâkâlî, Mahâ Lâkṣmî, Mahâ Sarasvatî and Bhrâmarî, for the fulfilment of the Devas' purposes and how the Devas got back their possessions by the Grace of the Devî. All you have described. O Lord! Now I want to hear the rules of Sadâchâra (right way of living), the due observance of which by the devotees pleases the World-Mother. Kindly describe them. Nârâyaṇa said:—"O Knower of Truth! Now I am telling you those rules of the right way of living, which rightly observed, always please Bhagavtî. Listen first, I will talk of the Brâhmiṇs, how their welfare is secured, what the Brâhmaṇas ought to do on getting up early in the morning from their bed. From the sunrise to the sunset the Brâhmaṇas should do all the daily and occasional duties (Nitya and Naimittik Karmas) and they are to perform the optional works for some particular object such as Puttreṣṭi Yajña and other good works (not acts of black majic as killing, causing pain and inconveniences to others, etc. It is the Self alone and not the Father, Mother, etc., nor any other body that helps us on our way to that happiness in the next world. Father, Mother, wife, sons and others are helps merely to our happiness in this world. None of them are helpful to us in bettering our states in the next world.

1-13. Deliverance of one's Self depends verily on his own Self. Therefore one should always earn and store dharma (religion) and observe always there the right conduct to help one in the next world. If Dharma be on our side, this endless sea of troubles can be safely crossed. The rules of right living as ordained by Manu in Śrutis and Manu Smritis are the principal Dharmas. The Brâhmaṇas should always be observant to their Dharma as ordained in the Śastras, Śruti and Smriti. Follow the right conduct and then you will get life, posterity and increase of happiness easily here and hereafter. By right conduct, food is obtained and sins are easily destroyed; the right conduct is the auspicious principal

Dharma of men. Persons of right living enjoy happiness in this world as well as in the next. Those, who are veiled in darkness by Ignorance and thus wildly enchanted, can verily see their way to Mukti if they follow the Great Light revealed to them by Dharma and the right conduct. It is by Sadâchâra, that superiority is attained. Men of right conduct always do good deeds. From good deeds, knowledge comes. This is the advice of Manu.

14-24. Right way of living is the best of all the Dharmas and is a great Tapasyâ (asceticism). The knowledge comes from this Right Living. Everything is attained thereby. He who is devoid of Sadâchâra, is like a Sûdra, even if he comes of a Brâhmin family. There is no distinction whatsoever betwen him and a Sûdra: Right conduct is of two kinds :—(1) as dictated by the Śâstras, (2) as dictated by the popular custom, Laukika). Both these methods should be observed by him who wants welfare for his Self. He is not to forsake one of them. O Muni ! The village Dharma, the Dharma of one's own caste, the Dharma of one's own family, and the Dharma of one's own country all should be observed by men. Never, Never he is to do anything otherwise. With great loving devotion that is to be preserved. Men who practise wrong ways of living, are censured by the public ; they always suffer from diseases. Avoid wealth and desires that have no Dharma in them. Why ? If in the name of Dharma, painful acts (*e. g.* killing animals in sacrifices) are to be Committed, those are blamed by the people ; so never commit them. Avoid them by all means. Nârada said :—" O Muni ! The Śâstras are not one, they are many and they lay down different rules and contradictory opinions, How then Dharma is to be followed ? And according to what Dharma Śâstra ? Nârâyaṇa said :—Śruti and Smriti are the two eyes of God ; the Purâṇam is His Heart. Whatever is stated in the Śruti, the Smriti and the Purâṇams is Dharma ; whatever else is written in other Śâstras is not Dharma. Where you will find differences between Śruti, Smriti and Purâṇas, accept the words of the Śruits as final proofs. Wherever Smriti disagrees with the Purâṇas, know the Smritis more authoritative.

And where differences will crop up in the Śrutis themselves, know that Dharma, too, is of two kinds. And where the differences will crop up in the Smritis themselves, consider, then, that different things are aimed at. In some Purâṇas, the Dharma of the Tantras is duly described ; but of these, which go against the Vedas, they are not to be accepted by any means.

25-37. Tantra is accepted as the authoritative proof then and then only when it contradicts not the Vedas. Whatever goes clearly against the Vedas can in no way be accepted as a proof. In matters concerning Dharma, the Vedas is the Sole Proof. Therefore that which is not against the Vedas can be taken as proof; otherwise not. Whoever acts Dharma according to other proofs than what is ordained in the Vedas, goes to the hell in the abode of Yama to get his lesson. So the Dharma that is by all means to be accepted as such, is what is stated in the Vedas. The Smrits, the Purâṇas, or the Tantra Śâstras can be taken also as authoritative when they are not conflicting to Vedas. Any other Śâstras can be taken as authoritative when it is fundamentelly coincident with the Vedas. Else it can never be accepted.

25-37. Those who do injury to others even by the blade of a Kus'a grass used as a weapon, go to hell with their heads downwards and their feet upwards. Those that follow their own sweet free will, that take up any sort of dress (*e. g.* Bauddhas), those that follow the philosophical doctrines called Pâs'upatas, and the other hermits and saints and persons that take up other vows contrary to the religions of the Vedas, for example, the Vaikhânasa followers, those who brand their bodies by the hot Mudrâs, at the places of pilgrimages, *e. g.* Dvârkâ, etc., they go to hell with their bodies scorched by red hot brands (Tapta Mudrâs). So persons should act according to the excellent religions commanded by the Vedas. Everyday he should get up from his bed early in the morning and think thus: —" What good acts have I done, what have I given as charities ? Or what I advised others to do charities what greater sins (Mahâpâtakas) and what smaller sins have I committed?" At the last quarter of the night he should think of Para Brahma. He should place his right leg on his left thigh and his left on his right thigh crosswise keeping his head straight up and touching the breast with his chin, and closing his eyes, he should sit steadily so that the upper teeth should not touch the lower jaw.

He should join his tongue with his palate and he should sit quiet, restraining his senses. He should be Śuddha Sattva. His seat should not be very low. First of all he should practice Prâṇâyâma twice or thrice; and within his heart he should meditate the Self of the shape of the Holy Flame or the Holy Light. (Om Mani Padmi Hum.)

38-49. He should fix his heart for a certain time to that Luminous Self whose Eyes are everywhere. So the intelligent man should practise Dhâraṇâ. Prâṇâyâma is of six kinds:—(1) Sadhûma (when the breaths are not steady), (2) Nirdhûma (better than the Sadhûma),

(3) Sagarbhâ (when united with one's mantra), (4) Agarbha (when the practice is without the thought of any mantra), (5) Salakṣya (when the heart is fixed on one's Deity) and (6) Alakṣya (when the heart is not fixed on one's Deity). No yoga can be compared with Prâṇâyâma. This is equal to itself. Nothing can be its equal. This Prâṇâyâma is of three kinds, called Rechaka, Pûraka and Kumbhaka. The Prâṇâyâma consists of three letters, A, U, M, *i. e.* of the nature of "Om". Or, in other words the letter A, of the Praṇava Om indicates Pûraka, the letter "U" denotes Kumbhaka and the letter "M" denotes Rechaka. By the Iḍâ Nâḍi (by the left nostril) inhale as long as you count "A" (Viṣṇu) thirty-two times; then withold breath, *i. e.*, do Kumbhaka as long as you count "U" (Śiva) sixtyfour times and by the Pingalâ Nâḍi (the right nostril) do the Rechaka, *i. e.*, exhale the breath as long as you count "M" (Brahmâ) for sixteen times. O Muni! Thus I have spoken to you of the Sadhûma Prâṇâyâma. After doing the Prâṇâyâma as stated above, pierce the Six Chakras (*i. e.*, plexuses) (called Ṣaṭchakra bheda) and carry the Kula Kuṇḍalinî to the Brahma Randhra, the brain aperture, or to the thousand petalled lotus in the head and meditate in the heart the Self like a Steady Flame. (The Nâḍis are not those which are known to the Vaidya or the Medical Śâstras. The latter are the gross physical nerves. The Nâḍis here are the Yoga Nâḍis, the subtle channels (Vivaras) along which the Prâṇik currents flow. Now the process of piercing the six Chakras (or nerve centres or centres of moving Prâṇik forces) is being described. Within this body, the six nerve centres called Padmas (Lotuses) exist. They are respectively situated at the (1) Mûlâdhâra (half way between Anus and Linga Mûla), called the Sacral Plexus; (2) Linga Mûla (the root of the genital organs), ; called postatic plexus; (this is also called Svâdhiṣṭhâna) (3) Navel, the Solar Plexus (4) Heart, the cardiac Plexus, (5) Throat (6) Forehead, between the eye brows there-the lotus in the forehead, called the cavernous plexus (Âjnâ Chakra) has two petals; in these two petals, the two letters "Ham" "Kṣam" exist in the right hand direction (with the hands of the watch; going round from left to right keeping the right side towards one circumambulated as a mark of respect). I bow down to these which are the two-lettered Brahma. The lotus that exists in the throat laryngeal or pharyngeal plexus has sixteen petals (viśuddhâ chakra); in these are in due order in right hand direction the sixteen letters (vowels) a, â, i, î, u, û, ṛi, ṛî, lri, lrî, e, ai, o, au, am, aḥ; I bow down to these which are the sixteen lettered Brahma. The lotus that exists in the heart, the cardiac plexus (anâhata chakra), has twelve petals; wherein are the twelve letters k, kh, g, gh, ṅ, ch, chh, j, jh, ñ, ṭ, ṭh; I bow to to these twelve lettered Brahma. The Solar

plexus forms the Great Junction of the Right and Left sympathetic chains Îḍâ and Pingalâ with the Cerebro spinal Axis. The lotus that exists in the navel, called the Solar Plexus, or Epigastric plexus (Maṇipura Chakra) has ten petals wherein are the ten letters ḍ, ḍh, ṇ, t, th, d, dh, n, p, ph, counting in the right hand direction (that is clockwise) (and the action of this clock is vertical in the plane of the spinal cord ; also it may be horizontal). The lotus that exists at the root of the genital organ, the genital plexus or postatic plexus has six petals. The petals are the configurations made by the position of Nâdis at any particular centre. Svâdhiṣṭhâna chakra or Svayambhu Linga, wherein are situated the six letters, b, bh, m, y, r, l; I bow down to this six-lettered Brahma. (These are the Laya Centres). The lotus that exists in the Mûlâdhâra, called the sacral or sacrococcygeal plexus has four petals, wherein are the four letters v, s′, ṣ, s. I bow down to these four-lettered Brahma. In the above six nerve centres or Laya Centres, or lotuses, all the letters are situated in the right hand direction (clockwise). (*Note.*—All the nerves of the body combine themselves in these six nerve centres or Laya Centres. Each of these centres is spheroidal and is of the Fourth Dimension. At each centre many transitions take place, many visions take place, many forces are perceived and wonderful varieties of knowledge are experienced. These are called the Laya Centres. For many things vanish into non-existence and many new Tattvas are experienced.) Thus meditating on the Six Chakras or plexuses, meditate on the Kula Kuṇḍalinî, the Serpent Fire. She resides on the four petalled lotus (Centre of Sakti) called Mûlâdhâra Chakra (Coccygeal plexus) ; She is of Rajo Guṇa ; She is of a blood red colour, and She is expressed by the mantra "Hrîm," which is the Mâyâvîja ; she is subtle as the thread of the fibrous stock of the water lily. The Sun is Her face ; Fire is Her breasts; he attains Jîvan mukti (liberation while living) within whose heart such a Kula Kuṇḍalini arises and awakens even once. Thus meditating on Kula Kuṇḍalinî, one should pray to Her :—Her sitting, coming, going, remaining, the thought on Her, the realisation of Her and chanting hymns to Her, etc., all are Mine, Who is of the nature of all in all ; I am that Bhagavatî ; O Bhagavatî ! All my acts are Thy worship ; I am the Devî ; I am Brahma, I am free from sorrow. I am of the nature of Everlasting Existence, Intelligence and Bliss. Thus one should meditate of one's ownself. I take refuge of that Kula Kuṇḍalinî, who appears like lightning and who holds the current thereof, when going to Brahmarandhra, in the brain, who appears like nectar when coming back from the brain to the Mûlâdhâra and who travels in the Suṣumnâ Nâḍî in the spinal cord. Then one is to meditate on one's own Guru, who is thought of as one with God, as seated in one's brain and then worship Him mentally. Then the Sâdhaka, controlling himself is to recite the following Mantra "The Guru is Brahmâ, the Guru is Viṣṇu, it is the Guru again that is the Deva Mahes'vara ; it is Guru that is Para Brahma. I bow down to that Śrî Guru.

Here ends the First Chapter of the Eleventh Book on what is to be thought of in the morning in the Mahâ Purâṇam Śrî Mad Devî Bhâgavatam of 18,000 verses by Maharṣi Veda Vyâsa.

CHAPTER II.

1-42. Nârâyaṇa said :—Even if a man studies the Vedas with six Amgas (limbs of the Vedas), he cannot be pure if he be devoid of the principle of right living (Sadâchâra) and if he does not practise it. All that is in vain. As soon as the two wings of the young ones of birds appear, they leave their nests, so the chhandas (the Vedas) leave such a man devoid of Sadâchâra *at the time of his death.* The intelligent man should get up from his bed at the Brâhma muhûrta and should observe all the principles of Sadâchâra. In the last quarter of night, he should practise in reciting and studying the Vedas. Then for some time he should meditate on his Iṣṭa Deva (his Presiding Deity). The Yogî should meditate on Brahma according to the method stated before. O Nârada ! If meditation be done as above, the identity of Jîva and Brahma is at once realised and the man becomes liberated while living. After the fifty-fifth Daṇḍa (from the preceding sunrise *i. e,* 2 hours before the sunrise comes the Uṣâkâla ; after the fifty seventh daṇḍa comes the Aruṇodayakâla ; after fifty eighth Daṇḍa comes the morning time ; then the Sun rises. One should get up from one's bed in the morning time. He should go then to a distance where an arrow shot at one stretch goes. There in the south-west corner he is to void his urines and faeces. Then the man, if he be a Brahmachârî, should place his holy thread on his right ear and the householder should suspend it on his neck only. That is, the Brahmachârî, in the first stage of of his life should place the holy thread over his right ear ; the householder and the Vânaprasthîs should suspend the holy thread from the neck towards the back and then void their faeces, etc. He is to tie a piece of cloth round his head ; and spread earth or leaves on the place where he will evacuate himself. He is not to talk then nor spit nor inhale hard. One is not to evacuate oneself in cultivated lands, that have been tilled, in water, over the burning pyre, on the mountain, in the broken and ruined temples, on the ant-hills, on places covered with grass, on road side, or on holes where living beings exist. One ought not to do the same also while walking. One ought to keep silence during both the twilights, while one is passing urine or voiding one's faeces, or while one is holding sexual intercourse, or before the presence of one's Guru, during the time of sacrifice, or while making gifts, or while doing Brahma Yajña. One ought to pray before evacuating, thus :—"O Devas! O Riṣis! O Pis'âchas! O Uragas! O Râkṣasas! You all who might be existing here unseen by me, are requested to leave this place. I am going to ease myself here duly." Never one is to void oneself while one looks at Vâyu (wind), Agni (fire), a Brâhmaṇa, the Sun, water or cow. At the day time one is to turn one's face northward and at the night time southward, while easing oneself and then one is to cover the faeces, etc., with stones, pebbles, leaves or grass, etc. Then he is to hold his genital organ with his hand and go to a river or any other watery place ; he is to fill his vessel with water then and go to some other place.

The Brâhmaṇa is to use the white earth, the Kṣattriya is to take the red earth, the Vais'ya is to use the yellow earth and the Sûdra is to apply the black earth and with that he is to cleanse himself. The earth under water, the earth of any temple, the earth of an anthill, the earth of a mouse hole, and the remnant of the earth used by another body for washing are not to be used for cleansing purposes. The earth for cleansing faeces is twice as much as that used in case of urine clearance ; in the cleansing after sexual intercourse thrice as much. In urine cleansing the earth is to applied in the organ of generation once, thrice in the hand. And in dirt clearing, twice in the organ of generation. five times in anus, ten times in the left hand and seven times in both the hands. Then apply earth four times first in the left feet and then on the right feet. The house holder should clear thus : the Brahmachârî is to do twice and the Yatis four times. At every time the quantity of wet earth that is to be taken is to be of the size of an Âmalakî fruit ; never it is to be less than that. This is for the clearance in the day time. Half of these can be used in the night time. For the invalids, one-fourth the above measurements ; for the passers-by, one-eighth the above dimensions are to be observed. In case of women, Śûdras, and incapable children, clearings are to be done till then when the offensive smell vanishes. No numbers are to be observed. Bhagvân Manu says—for all the Varṇas the clearing is to be done till then when the offensive smell vanishes. The clearing is to be performed by the left hand. The right hand is never to be used. Below the navel, the left hand is to be used ; and above the navel the right hand is to be used for clearing. The wise man should never hold his water pot while evacuating himself. If by mistake he catches hold of his waterpot, he will have to perform the penance (prâyaśchitta).

If, out of vanity or sloth, clearing be not done, for three nights, one is to fast, drinking water only, and then to repeat the Gâyatrî Mantra and thus be purified. In every matter, in view of the place, time and materials, one's ability and power are to be considered and steps are to be taken accordingly. Knowing all this, one should clear oneself according to rule. Never be lazy here. After evacuating oneself of faeces, one is to rinse one's mouth twelve times; and after passing urine and clearing, one is to rinse four times. Never less than that is to be done. The water after rinsing is to be thrown away slowly downwards on one's left. Next performing Âchaman one is to wash one's teeth. He is to take a tiny piece, twelve Ângulas (fingers) long (about one foot) from a tree which is thorny and gummy. The cleansing twig (for teeth) is thick like one's little finger. He is to chew the one end of it to form a tooth brush. Karanja, Udumbara (figtree), Mango, Kadamba, Lodha, Champaka and Vadarî trees are used for cleansing teeth. While cleansing teeth, one is to recite the following mantra:—"O Tree! Wherein resides the Deity Moon for giving food to the beings and for killing the enemies! Let Him wash my mouth to increase my fame and honour! O Tree! Dost Thou please give me long life, power, fame, energy, beauty, sons, cattle, wealth, intellect, and the knowledge of Brahma." If the cleansing twig be not available and if there be any prohibition to brush one's teeth that day (say Pratipad day, Amâvas, Ṣaṣṭhi and Navamî), take mouthfuls of water, gargle twelve times and thus cleanse the teeth. If one brushes one's teeth with a twig on the new moon day, the first, sixth, ninth and eleventh day after the Full or New Moon or on Sunday, one eats the Sun (as it were, by making Him lose his fire), makes his family line extinct and brings his seven generations down into the hell. Next he should wash his feet and sip pure clean water thrice, touch his lips twice with his thumb, and then clear the nostrils by his thumb and fore finger. Then he is to touch his eyes and ears with his thumb and ring finger, touch his navel with his thumb and little finger, touch his breast with his palm and touch his head with all his fingers.

Here ends the Second Chapter of the Eleventh Book on cleansing the several parts of the body in the Mahâpurâṇam Śrî Mad Devî Bhâgvatam of 18,000 verses by Maharṣi Veda Vyâsa.

CHAPTER III.

1-21. Śrî Nârâyaṇa said:—"O Nârada! 'There are the six kinds of Âchamana:—(1) Śuddha, (2) Smârta, (3) Paurâṇik, (4) Vaidik, (5) Tântrik and (6) "Śrauta. The act of cleaning after evacuating oneself of urine and faeces is known as Śuddha Śaucha. After cleaning, the Âchaman, that is performed according to rules, is named as Smârta and Paurâṇik. In places where the Brahma Yajña is performed, the Vaidik and Śrauta Âchamanas are done. And where acts e. g. the knowledge of warfare are being executed, the Tântrik Âchaman is done. Then he is to remember the Gâyatrî Mantra with Praṇava (om) and fasten the lock of hair on the crown of his head, thus controlling all the hindrances (Bighna Bandhanam). Sipping again, he is to touch his heart, two arms, and his two shoulders. After sneezing, spitting, touching the lower lip with teeth, accidentally telling a lie, and talking with a very sinful man, he is to touch his right ear (Where the several Devas reside). On the right ear of the Brâhmaṇas reside Fire, Water, the Vedas, the Moon, the Sun, and the Vâyu (wind). Then one is to go to a river or any other reservoir of water, and there to perform one's morning ablutions and to cleanse his body thoroughly. For the body is always unclean and dirty and various dirts are being excreted out of the nine holes (doors) in the body. The morning bath removes all these impurities. Therefore the morning bath is essentially necessary. The sins that arise from going to those who are not fit for such purposes, from accepting gifts from impure persons or from the practice of any other secret vices all are removed by the morning ablutions. Without this bath, no acts bear any fruit. Therefore every day, this morning bath is very necessary. Taking the Kus'a grass in hand, one is to perform one's bath and Sandhyâ. If for seven days, the morning ablutions are not taken, and if for three days, the Sandhyâs are not performed, if for twelve days, the daily Homas be not performed, the Brâhmaṇas become Śûdras. The time for making the Homa in the morning is very little ; therefore lest ablutions be done fully which would take a long time and hence the time for the Homa might elapse, the morning bath should be performed quickly. After the bath the Prâṇâyâma is to be done. Then the full effects of bath are attained. There is nothing holier in this world or in the next than reciting the Gâyatrî. It saves the singer who sings the Gâyatrî ; hence it is called Gâyatrî. During the time of Prâṇâyâma, one must control one's Prâṇa and Apâṇa Vâyus i. e. make them equal. The Brâhmiṇ, knowing the Vedas and devoted to his Dharma, must practise Prâṇâyâma three times with the repetition of Gâyatrî and Praṇava and the three Vyârhitis (Om Bhu, Om Bhuvar, Om Svah).

While practising, the muttering of Gâyatri is to be done three times. In Prâṇâyâma, the Vaidik mantra is to be repeated, never a Laukika Mantra is to be uttered. At the time of Prâṇâyâma, if any body's mind be not fixed, even for a short while, like a mustard seed on the apex of a cow-horn, he cannot save even one hundred and one persons in his father's or in his mother's line. Prâṇâyâma is called Sagarbha when performed with the repetition of some mantra; it are called Agarbha when it is done simply with mere meditation, without repeating any mantra. After the bathing, the Tarpaṇam with its accompaniments, is to be done; *i. e.* the peace offerings are made with reference to the Devas, the Riṣis, and the Pitris (whereby we invoke the blessings from the subtle planes where the highsouled persons dwell.) After this, a clean pair of clothes is to be worn and then he should get up and come out of the water. The next things preparatory to practise Japam are to wear the Tilaka marks of ashes and to put on the Rudrâkṣa beads. He who holds thirty-two Rudrâkṣa beads on his neck, forty on his head, six on each ear (12 on two ears), twenty four beads on two hands (twelve on each hand) thirty-two beads on two arms (sixteen on each), one bead on each eye and one bead on the hair on the crown, and one hundred and eight beads on the breast, (251 in all) becomes himself Mahâ Deva. One is expected to use them as such. O Muni! You can use the Rudrâkṣas after tieing, stringing together with gold or silver always on your Śikhâ, the tuft of hair on the head or on your ears. On the holy thread, on the hands, on the neck, or on the belly (abdomen) one can keep the Rudrâkṣa after one has repeated sincerely and with devotion the five lettered mantra of Śiva, or one has repeated the Prâṇâva (Om). Holding the Rudrâkṣa implies that the man has realised the knowledge of Śiva-Tattva. O Brahman! The Rudrâkṣa bead that is placed on the tuft or on the crown hair represents the Târa tattva *i. e.*, Om Kâra; the Rudrâksa beads that are held on the two ears are to be thought of as Deva and Devî, (Śiva and Śivâ).

22-37. The one hundred and eight Rudrâkṣa beads on the sacrificial thread are considered as the one hundred and eight Vedas (signifying the Full Knowledge, as sixteen digits of the Moon completed; on the arms, are considered as the Dik (quarters); on the neck, are considered as the Devî Sarasvatî and Agni (fire). The Rudrâksa beads ought to be taken by men of all colours and castes. The Brâhmaṇas, Kṣattriyas and Vais'yas should hold them after purifying them with Mantras *i. e.* knowingly; whereas the Śûdras can take them without any such purification by the Mantras. *i. e.* unknowingly. By holding or putting on the Rudrâksa beads, persons become the Rudras incarnate in flesh and body. There is no doubt in this. By this all the sins arising from seeing, hearing, remembering, smelling, eating prohibited things, talking incoherently, doing prohibited things, etc., are entirely removed with the Rudrâksa beads on the body; whatever acts, eating, drinking, smelling, etc., are done, are, as it were, done by Rudra Deva Himself. O Great Muni! He who feels shame in holding and putting on the Rudrâkşa beads, can never be freed from this Samsâra even after the Koṭi births. He who blames another person holding Rudrâkşa beads has defects in his birth (is a bastard). There is no doubt in this. It is by holding on Rudrâkşa that Brahmâ has remained steady in His Brahmâhood untainted and the Munis have been true to their resolves. So there is no act better and higher than holding the Rudrâkşa beads. He who gives clothing and food to a person holding Rudrâkşa beads with devotion is freed of all sins and goes to the Śiva Loka. He who feasts gladly any holder of such beads at the time of Śrâdh, goes undoubtedly to the Pitri Loka. He who washes the feet of a holder of Rudrâkşa and drinks that water, is freed of all sins and resides with honour in the Śiva Loka. If a Brâhmaṇa holds with devotion the Rudrâkşa beads with a necklace and gold, he attains the Rudrahood. O Intelligent One! Wherever whoever holds with or without faith and devotion the Rudrâkşa beads with or without any mantra, is freed of all sins and is entitled to the Tattvajñâna. I am unable to describe fully the greatness of the Rudrâkşa beads. In fact, all should by all means hold the Rudrâkşa beads on their bodies.

Note.—The Number one hundred and eight (108) signifies the One Hundred and Eight Vedas, the Brahmaṇ, the Source of all Wisdom and Joy.

Here ends the Third Chapter of the Eleventh Book on the glories of the Rudrâkşa beads in the Mahâ Purâṇam Śrî Mad Devî Bhâgavatam of 18,000 verses by Maharşi Veda Vyâsa.

CHAPTER IV.

1-11. Nârada said :—"O Sinless one! The greatness of the Rudrâkşa seed that you have descibed is verily such. Now I ask why is this Rudrâkşam so much entitled to worship by the people. Please speak clearly on this point. Nârâyaṇa spoke :—"O Child! This is the very question that was asked once by Kârtika, the sixfaced One, to Bhagavân Rudra, dwelling in Kailâs'a. What He replied, I say now. Listen. Rudra Deva spoke :—"O Child Ṣaḍânana. I will dwell briefly on the secret cause of the greatness of the Rudrâkşa seed. Hear. In days of yore, there was a Daitya called Tripurâ who could not be conquered by any body. Brahmâ, Vişṇu and the other Devas were defeated by him. They then came to Me and requested Me to kill the Asura. At their request, I called in my mind the Divine Great weapon, named Aghora, beautiful and terrible and containing the strength of all the Devas, to kill him. It was inconceivable and it was blazing with fire.

For full divine one thousand years I remained awake with eyelids wide open in thinking of the Aghora weapon, the destroyer of all obstacles, whereby the killing of Tripurâsura might be effected and the troubles of the Devas be removed. Not for a moment my eyelids dropped. There by my eyes were affected and drops of water came out of any eyes.—Note here. How enemies are to be killed. It requires great thought, great concentration, great yoga and great powers.) O Mahâsena ! From those drops of water coming out of my eyes, the great tree of Rudrâkṣam did spring for the welfare of all. This Rudrâkṣa seed is of thirty-eight varieties. From My Sûrya Netra. *i. e.*, My right eye, symbolizing the Sun, twelve yellow coloured (Pingala colour) varieties have come ; and from my left eye representing the Moon, the Soma Netra, sixteen varieties of white colour and from my third eye on the top, representing Fire *i.e.* the Agni Netra, ten varieties of black colour have come out. Of these the white Rudrâkṣams are Brâhmins and they are used by the Brâhmaṇas ; the red coloured ones are the Kṣattriyas and should be used by the Kṣattriyas and the black ones are Śûdras and should be used by the Vaiṣyas and the Śûdras.

12-19. One faced Rudrâkṣa seed is the Śiva Himself, made manifest and rendered vivid; even the sin incurred in killing a Brâhmaṇa is destroyed thereby. Two faced or two headed Rudrâkṣam is like the Deva and the Devî. Two sorts of sins are destroyed thereby. The three faced Rudrâkṣam is like fire ; the sin incurred in killing a woman is destroyed in a moment. The four faced Rudrâkṣa seed is like Brahmâ and removes the sin of killing persons. The five faced Rudrâkṣam is verily an image of Rudra; all sorts of sins, e, g. eating prohibited food, going to the ungoables, etc., are destroyed thereby. The six faced Rudrâkṣam is Kârtikeya. It is to be worn on the right hand. One becomes freed of the Brahmahatyâ sin. There is no manner of doubt in this. The seven faced Rudrâkṣam is named Ananga. Holding this frees one from the sin of stealing gold, etc., O Mahâsena! The eight faced Rudrâkṣa is Vinâyaka. Holding this frees one from the sin of holding an illicit contact with a woman of a bad family and with the wife of one's Guru, etc., and other sins as well. It enables one to acquire heaps of food, cotton, and gold ; and in the end the Highest Place is attained.

20-35. The fruit of holding the eight faced Rudrâkṣa seed has been said. Now I will talk of the nine-faced Rudrâkṣam. It is verily the Bhairava made manifest. On the left hand it should be worn. By this, the people get both Bhoga (enjoyment) and Mokṣa (liberation) and they become powerful like Me and get themselves freed at once, without the least delay, of the sins incurred by committing thousands of abortions, hundreds of Brahmahattyâs (killing the Brâhmaṇas). Holding the ten-faced Rudrâkṣa is verily wearing Janârdana, the Deva of the Devas. The holding of which pacifies the evils caused by planets, Pis'âchas, Vetâlas Brahma Râkṣasas, and Pannagas. The eleven-faced Rudrâkṣam is like the Eleven Rudras. The fruits, the efficacy of which I now describe. Hear. The fruits obtained through the performance of one thousand horse sacrifices, one hundred Vâjapeya sacrifices, and making gifts of one hundred thousand cows are obtained thereby.

If one wears the twelve-headed Rudrâkṣasm on one's ear, the Âdityas get satisfied. The fruits of performing Gomedha and As'vamedha sacrifices are obtained thereby. No fear comes from horned buffaloes, armed enemies and wolves and tigers and other murderous animals. Also the several diseases of the body never come to him. The holder of the twelve-faced Rudrâkṣa seed feels always happy and he is the master of some kingdoms. He becomes freed of the sins incurred in killing elephants, horses, dear, cats, snakes, mice, frogs, asses, foxes and various other animals.

O Child ! The thirteen faced Rudrâkṣam is very rare ; if anybody gets it, he becomes like Kârti Keya and gets all desires fulfilled ; and the eight siddhis are under his grasp. He learns how to make gold, silver and other metals ; he attains all sorts of enjoyments. There is no manner of doubt in this. O Ṣaḍânana ! If anybody holds the thirteen faced Rudrâkṣam, he becomes freed from the sins incurred in killing mother, father and brothers.

O Son ! If one holds on one's head the fourteen-faced Rudrâkṣam always, one becomes like Śiva. O Muni ! What more shall I speak to you ! The Devas pay their respects to one holding the fourteen faced Rudrâkṣas and he in the end attains the Highest Goal, the state of Śiva. His body becomes verily the body of Śiva.

36-40. The Devas always worship the Rudrâkṣa seed; the highest goal is attained by wearing the Rudrâkṣam. The Br'ahmanas should hold on their heads at least one Rudrâkṣam with devotion. A rosary of twenty-six Rudrâkṣams is to be made and tied on the head. Similarly a rosary of fifty seeds is to be worn and suspended on the breast ; sixteen each on each of the two arms ; twenty-four Rudrâkṣams to be worn on the wrists, twelve on each. O Ṣaḍânana ! If a rosary be made of one hundred and eight, fifty or twenty-seven Rudrâkṣams and if japam be done with that, immeasurable merits are obtained. If anybody wears a rosary of one hundred and eight seeds, he gets at every moment the fruit of performing the As'vamedha sacrifices and uplifts his twenty-one generations and finally he resides in the Śiva Loka.

Here ends the Fourth Chapter of the Eleventh Book on the Greatness of the Rudrâkṣam in the Mahâpurâṇam Śrî Mad Devî Bhâgavatam of 18,000 verses by Maharṣi Veda Vyâsa.

CHAPTER V.

1-14. Îs'vara said:--"O Kârtikeya! Now I will speak how to count the Japam (repetition of the mantra) with the rosary. Hear. The face of Rudrâkṣam is Brahmâ; the upper summit point is Śiva and the tail end of Rudrâkṣam is Viṣṇu. The Rudrâkṣam has two-fold powers:— It can give Bhoga (Enjoyment) as well as Mokṣa (Liberation). Then string or tie together, like a cow's tail, and like the snake's coiling a body, twenty-five five faced Rudrâkṣa seeds, thorny and of red, white, mixed colours bored through and through. The rosary is to taper as a cow's tail tapers down. In stringing the beads into a rosary, it should be seen that the flat face of one Rudrâkṣam is in front of the flat face of another Rudrâkṣam; so the tail, the pointed end of one, must come in front of the tail or the narrower end of another. The Meru or the topmost bead of the string must have its face turned upwards and the knot should be given over that. The rosary, thus strung, yields success of the Mantra (mantra-siddhi) When the rosary is strung, it is to be bathed with clear and scented water and afterwards with the Pañchagavya (cow-dung, cow urine, curd, milk, and ghee); then wash it with clear water and sanctify it with the condensed electrical charge of the Mantra. Then recite the Mantra of Śiva (Six limbed, with "Hûm" added and collect the rosaries. Then repeat over them the Mantra "Sadyojâta, etc., and sprinkle water over it one hundred and eight times. Then utter the principal mantra and place them on a holy ground and perform Nyâsa over it, *i. e.*, think that the Great Cause Śiva and the World-Mother Bhagavatî have come on them. Thus make the Samskâra of the rosary (*i. e.*, purify it) and you will find then that your desired end will be attained successfully. Worship the rosary with the Mantra of that Devatâ for which it is intended. One is to wear the Rudrâkṣa rosary on one's head, neck or ear and controlling one self, one should make japam with the rosary On the neck, head, breast, or the ears or on the arms, the rosary should he held with the greatest devotion. What is the use in saying about it so often? It is highly meritorious and commendable to holds always the Rudrâkṣam. Especially on such occasions as taking baths making gifts, making japams, performing the Homas, or sacrifices to Viṣve Devâs, in performing the Poojâs of the Devas, in making Prâyaschittams (penances), in the time of Śrâdh and in the time of initiation, it is highly necessary to hold Rudrâkṣam. A Brâhmiṇ is sure to go to hell if he performs any Vaidik act without wearing any Rudrâkṣam. Note :—It would be offering an insult to Śiva !

15-29. It is advisable to use the true Rudrâkṣam with gold and jewel, on the head, neck or on one's hand. Never use the Rudrâkṣam worn by another. Use Rudrâkṣam always with devotion; never use it while you are impure. Even the grass that grows with the air in contact with the Rudrâkṣa tree, goes verily to a holy region for ever. Jâbâla Muni says in the Śruti:—If a man wearing Rudrâkṣam commits a sin, he gets deliverance from that sin. Even if animals hold Rudrâkṣam, they become Śiva; what of men! The devotees of Śrî Rudra should always use at least one Rudrâkṣa on the head. Those great devotees, who with Rudrâkṣam on take the name of the Highest Self Śambhu, get themselves freed of all sorts of sins and pains. Those who are ornamented with Rudrâkṣam are the best devotees. It is highly incumbent on those who want their welfare to wear Rudrâkṣam. Those who hold Rudrâkṣam on their ears, crown hair, neck, hands, and breast, get Brahmâ, Viṣṇu, and Mahes'vara under them as their Vibhûtis (manifestations, powers). The Devas and all those Riṣis that started the Gotra, the Âdipuruṣas (the first chief men in several families), held with reverence the Rudrâkṣams. All the other Munis, that descended from their families, the ardent followers of Śrauta Dharma, the pure souled, held the Rudrâkṣams. It may be, that many might not like at first to hold this Rudrâkṣam, the visibile giver of liberation and so well written in the Vedas; but after many births, out of the Grace of Mahâdeva, many become eager to take the Rudrâkṣams. The Munis' that are the Jâbâla Sâkhîs are famous in expounding the inestimable greatness of Rudrâkṣams.

The effect of holding Rudrâkṣams is well known in the three worlds. Puṇyam (great merit) arises from the mere sight of Rudrâkṣams; ten million times that merit arises by its touch; and by wearing it, one hundred Koṭi times the fruit arises and if one makes Japam every day, then one lakh koṭi times the puṇyam arises. There is no manner of questionings in this.

30-36. He who holds in his hand, breast, neck, ears, head, the Rudrâkṣams, becomes an image of Rudra. There is no manner of doubt in this. By holding Rudrâkṣams, men become invulnerable of all the beings, become respected, like Mahâ Deva, by the Devas and Asuras and they roam on the earth like Rudra. Even if a man be addicted to evil deeds and commits all sorts of sins, he becomes respected by all, on holding Rudrâkṣams. By this men are freed of the sin of taking Uchhiṣṭa and of all the other sins. Even if you suspend a Rudrâkṣam rosary on the neck of a dog and if that dog dies in that state, he gets liberation! Then what to speak of others! By holding Rudrâkṣams, men even if they be devoid of Japam and Dhyânam, become freed of all sins and attain the highest state. Even if one holds merely one Rudrâkṣa seed purified and surcharged with Mantra Sakti, he uplifts his twentyone generations, gets to Heaven and resides there with respect. I am speaking now further of the Greatness of Rudrâkṣam.

Here ends the Fifth Chapter of the Eleventh Book on the Rudrâkṣam rosaries in the Mahâ Purâṇam Śrî Mad Devî Bhâgavatam of 18,000 verses by Maharṣi Veda Vyâsa.

CHAPTER VI.

1-21. Îs'vara said:—"O Kârtikeya! Kus'agranthi, Jîvapattrî and other rosaries cannot compare to one-sixteenth part of the Rudrâkṣa rosary. As Viṣṇu is the best of all the Puruṣas, the Gangâ is the best of all the rivers, Kas'yapa, amongst the Munis, Uchchaihsravâ amongst the horses, Mahâ Deva amongst the Devas, Bhagavatî amongst the Devîs, so the Rudrâkṣam rosary is the Best of all the rosaries. All the fruits that occur by reading the stotras and holding all the Vratas, are obtained by wearing the Rudrâkṣam bead. At the time of making the Akṣaya gift, the Rudrâkṣam bead is capable of giving high merits. The merit that accrues by giving Rudrâkṣam to a peaceful devotee of Śiva, cannot be expressed in words. If anybody gives food to a man holding the Rudrâkṣam rosary, his twenty one generations are uplifted and he ultimately becomes able to live in the Rudrâ Loka. He who does not apply ashes on his forehead and who does not hold Rudrâkṣam and is averse to the worship of Śiva is inferior to a chândâla. If Rudrâkṣam be placed on the head then the flesh-eaters, drunkards, and the associates with the vicious become freed of their sins. Whatever fruits are obtained by performing various sacrifices, asceticism and the study of the Vedas are easily attained by simply holding the Rudrâkṣam rosary. Whatever merits are obtained by reading the four Vedas and all the Purâṇas and bathing in all the Tîrthas an the results that are obtained by immense practise in learning all are, obtained by wearing Rudrâkṣam. If at the time of death, one wears Rudrâkṣam and dies, one attains Rudrahood. One has not to take again one's birth. If anybody dies by holding Rudrakṣam on his neck or on his two arms, he uplifts his twenty-one generations and lives in the Rudra Loka. Be he a Brâhmaṇ or a Châṇḍâla, be he with qualities or without qualities, if he applies ashes to his body and holds Rudrâkṣam, he surely attains Śivahood. Be he pure or impure; whether he eats uneatables or be he a Mlechha or a Châṇḍâla or a Great Sinner, any body if he holds Rudrâkṣam is surely equal to Rudra. There is no doubt in this.

If any body holds Rudrâkṣam on his head he gets Koṭi times the fruit; on his ears, ten Koṭi times the fruit, on his neck, one hundred Koṭi times the fruit; on his holy thread, ayuta times the fruit; on his arm, one lâkh Koṭi times the fruit and if one wears Rudrâkṣam on one's wrist, one attains Mokṣa. Whatever acts, mentioned in the Vedas be performed with Rudrâkṣam on, the fruits obtained are unbounded. Even if a man be without any Bhakti and if he wears on his neck the Rudrâkṣa rosary though he does always vicious acts, he becomes freed of the bondage of this world. Even if a man does not hold Rudrâksa but if he be always full of devotion towards the Rudrâksam, he attains the fruit that is got by wearing the Rudrâkṣam and he attains the Śiva Loka and is honoured like Śiva. As in the country of Kikaṭa, an ass which used to carry Rudrâkṣam seed got Śivahood after his death, so any man, whether he be a Jñâni (wise) or Ajnâni (unwise), gets Śivahood if he holds Rudrâksam. There is no doubt in this.

2?-28. Skanda said :—" O God ! How is it that in the country of Kîkaṭa (Bihar), an ass had to carry Rudrâkṣa ; who gave him the Rudrâkṣams ! And what for did he hold that ?

Bhagavân Îs'vara said :—" O Son! Now hear the history of the case. In the Bindhya mountain one ass used to carry the load of Rudrâkṣam of a traveller. Once the ass felt tired and became unable to carry the load and fell down on the road and died. After his death the ass came to Me by My Grace, becoming Mahes'vara with trident in his hand and with three eyes. O Kârtikeya ! As many faces as there are in the Rudrâkṣam, for so many thousand Yugas the holder resides with honour in the Śiva Loka. One should declare the greatness of Rudrâkṣam to one's own disciple ; never to disclose its glories to one who is not a disciple nor a devotee of Rudrâkṣam nor to him who is an illiterate brute. Be he a Bhakta or not a

Bhakta, be he low or very low, if he holds Rudrâkṣam, then he is freed from all sins. No equal can be to the merit of him who holds the Rudrâkṣams.

29-39. The Munis, the Seers of truth, describe this holding on of Rudrâkṣam as a very great vow. He who makes a vow to hold one thousand Rudrâkṣams, becomes like Rudra; the Devas bow down before him. If thousand Rudrâkṣams be not obtained, one should hold at least sixteen Rudrâkṣams on each arm, one Rudrâkṣam on the crown hair; on the two hands, twelve on each; thirty-two on the neck; forty on the head; six on each ear and one hundred and eight Rudrâkṣams on the breast; and then he becomes entitled to worship like Rudra. If any body holds Rudrâkṣam together with pearls, Prabâla, crystal, silver, gold and gem (lapis lazuli), he becomes a manifestation of S'iva. If a body, through laziness even, holds Rudrâkṣam, the sin cannot touch him as darkness cannot come near light. If any body makes japam of a mantram with a Rudrâksa rosary, he gets unbounded results. Such a merit giving Rudrâkṣam, if one such Rudrâkṣam be not found in any one's body, his life becomes useless, like a man who is void of Tripuṇḍrak (three curved horizontal marks made on the forehead by the worshippers of S'iva). If any body simply washes his head all over with Rudrâkṣam on, he gets the fruit of bathing in the Ganges. There is no doubt in this. One faced Rudrâkṣam, the five faced, eleven faced and fourteen faced Rudrkṣams are highly meritorious and entitled to worship by all. The Rudrâkṣam is S'ankara made manifest; so it is always worshipped with devotion. The greatness of Rudrâksam is such as it can make a king out of a poor man. On this point, I will tell you an excellent Purânic anecdote.

40-49. There was a Brâhmin, named Girinâtha in the country of Kosala. He was proficient in the Vedas and Vedâmgas, religious and very rich. He used to perform sacrifices. He had a beautiful son named Guṇanidhi. The son gradually entered into his youth and looked beautiful like Kandarpa, the God of Love. While he was studying at his Guru Sudhiṣaṇa's house, he, by his beauty and youth captivated the mind of his Guru's wife named Muktâvalî. The Guru's wife became so much enchanted by his extraordinary beauty that she, being unable to control herself, mixed with him and for some time remained with him in secret enjoyment. Then feeling inconveniences, due to the fear of his Guru, to enjoy her freely, used poison to the Guru, killed him and then he began to live freely with her. Next when his father, mother came to know about this, he put to death instantly his father and mother, administering poison to them. He became addicted to various pleasures and his wealth was exhausted gradually. He began to steal in Brâhmaṇs' houses and became addicted very much to drinking. His relatives outcasted him from the society for his bad behaviour and banished him outside the town. He then went into a dense forest with Muktâvalî; and he began to kill the Brâhmiṇs for their wealth. Thus a long time passed away; when at last he fell into the jaws of death.

50-54. Then to take him to the region of Death, thousands of the Yama's messengers came; at the same time the Śiva's messengers came from Śiva-Loka. O Kârtikeya! A quarrel then ensued between both the parties of Yama and Śiva," The Yama's messengers, then, said:— "O Servers of Śambhu! What are the merits of this man that you have come to take him? First speak to us of his merits." Śiva's messengers spoke—"Fifteen feet below the ground where this man died, there exists the Rudrâkṣam. O Yama's messengers! By the influence of that Rudrâkṣam, all his sins are destroyed; and we have come to take him to Śiva." Then the Brahmin Guṇanidhi assumed a divine form and, getting on an aerial car went with S'iva's messengers before S'iva. "O One of good vows! Thus I have described briefly to you the greatness of Rudrâkṣam. This is capable to remove all sorts of sins and yield great merits.

Here ends the Sixth Chapter of the Eleventh Book on the Greatness of Rudrâkṣams in the Mahâpurâṇam S'rî Mad Devî Bhâgavatam of 18,000 verses by Maharsi Veda Vyâsa.

CHAPTER VII.

1-4. S'rî Nârâyaṇa said:—"O Nârada! When Girîs'a thus explained to Kârtikeya the greatness of Rudrâkṣam, he became satisfied. Now I have spoken to you of the glories of the Rudrâkṣams as far as I know. Now, as to our subject of right way of acting, I will now speak on other things that ought to be known. Listen. The seeing of Rudrâkṣam brings in a lakh times of Puṇyam and koṭi times the merit arises from touching that; holding it brings in koṭi times merit; again if one makes the japam of a Mantra with that Rudrâkṣam, one obtains merit one hundred lakh koṭi times and one thousand lakh koṭi times the merit. The merit in holding the Rudrâkṣam is far superior to that in holding Bhadrâkṣam. The Rudrâkseam seed that is of the size of an Âmalakî is the best; which is the of the size of a plum, is middling; and which is of the size of a gram is the worst.

this is my word and promise. The Rudrâkṣam tree is of four kinds :—Brâhmaṇa, Kṣattriya, Vais'ya, and S'ûdra. The white colour is Brâhmaṇa; the red colour is Kṣattriya; the yellow colour is Vais'ya and the black coloured Rudrâkṣam seed is Śûdra. The Brâhmaṇas are to use the white coloured Rudrâkṣams; the Kṣattriyas, the red coloured ones, the Vais'yas, the yellow coloured ones; and the Sûdras, the black ones. Those Rudrâkṣa seeds that are nicely circular, smooth, hard, and whose thorns or points are distinctly visible, are the best. Those that are pierced by insects, broken in parts, whose thorns are not clearly visible, with swells and holes and those that are coated over, these six varieties of Rudrâkṣams are faulty. Those Rudrâkṣams that have their holes by nature running through and through are best; and those that have their holes pierced by men are middling. The Rudrâkṣa seeds that are all of uniform shape, bright, hard, and beautifully circular should be strung together by a silken thread. How to test the Rudrâkṣa seed? As gold is tested by a touch stone; so the Rudrâkṣam is tested by drawing lines on it; those on which the lines are most uniform, bright and beautiful are the best and they should be worn by the Śaivas. One should hold one Rudrâkṣam on the crown hair, thirty on the head, thirty six on the neck; sixteen on each arm, twelve on each wrist, fifty on the shoulders, one hundred and eight Rudrâkṣams in the place of the sacrificial thread; and the devotee should have two or three rounds on the neck. On the earrings, on the crown of the head, the head, on bracelets, on armlets, on necklace, on the ornament worn on the loins one should hold Rudrakṣam always, whether one sleeps or eats. Holding three hundred Rudrâkṣams is the lowest; holding five hundred is middling; holding one thousand Rudrâkṣams is the best; so one ought to wear one thousand Rudrâksams. At the time of taking Rudrâksam, on one's head, one should utter the Mantra of Îsâna; the mantra of Tat Puruṣa while holding on one's ears; Aghora mantra on one's forehead and heart; and the vîja of Aghora mantra *i. e.* "hasau" while holding on one's hands. One should wear the rosary of fifty Rudrâkṣa seeds, suspended up to the belly, uttering the Vâmadeva mantra, *i. e.*, Sadyojâtâdi, etc., the five Brahma mantras, and the six-limbed Śiva mantra. One is to string every Rudrâkṣa seed, uttering the root mantra and then hold it. One-faced Rudrâkṣa reveals Paratattva (the highest Tattva); when worn, the knowledge of the highest Tattva arises; the Brahma is seen then. The two-faced Rudrâkṣam is Ardhanârîs'vara, the Lord of the other half which represents woman (in the same person); if worn, Ardhanârîsvara Śiva is always pleased with that man who holds it. The three-faced Rudrâkṣam is Fire made manifest; it destroys in a moment the sin of killing a woman.

The three-faced Rudrâkṣam is the three Agnis, Dakṣiṇâgni, Gârhapatya, and Âhavaniya ; Bhagavân Agni is always pleased with that man who wears the three-faced Rudrakṣam. The four-faced Rudrâkṣam in Brahmâ Himself. The wearer gets his prosperity enhanced, his diseases destroyed, the divine knowledge springs in him and his heart is always pleased. The five-faced Rudrâkṣam is the five faced Śiva Himself; Mahâdeva gets pleased with him who holds it. The Presiding Deity of the six faced Rudrâkṣam is Kârtikeya. Some Pandits take Gaṇapati to be the Presiding Deity of the six-faced Rudrâkṣam. The presiding Deity of the seven-faced Rudrâkṣam is the seven Mâtrikâs, the Sun and the seven Riṣis. By putting on this, the prosperity is increased, health and the pure knowledge are established. It should be put on when one becomes pure. The Presiding Deity of the eight-faced Rudrâkṣam is Brâhmî, the eight Mâtrikâs. By holding this, the eight Vasus are pleased and the river Ganges is also pleased. The putting on of this makes the Jîvas truthful and pleasant-minded. The Devatâ of the nine-faced Rudrâkṣam is Yama ; holding this puts off the fears of Death. The Devatâ of the eleven-faced Rudrâkṣam is ten quarters the ten quarters are pleased with him who wears the ten-faced Rudrâkṣam. The Devatâ of the eleven mouthed Rudrâkṣam is the eleven Rudras and Indra. Holding this enhances happiness The twelve-faced Rudrâkṣam is Visṇu made manifast ; its Devatâs are the twelve Âdityas ; the devotees of Śiva should hold this. The thirteen-faced Rudrâkṣam, if worn, enables one to secure one's desires; he does nowhere experience failures. The Kâma Deva becomes pleased with him who wears this. The fourteen-faced Rudrâkṣam destroys all diseases and gives eternal health. While holding this, one ought not to take wine, flesh, onion, garlic, Sajnâ fruit, Châltâ fruit and the flesh of the boar which eats excrements, etc., During the Lunar and Solar eclipses, during the Uttarâyaṇa Śamkrânti or the Dakṣiṇâyana Samkrânti, during the full Moon or the New Moon day, if Rudrâkṣam be worn, one becomes instantly freed of all one's sins.

Here ends, the Seventh Chapter of the Eleventh Book on the greatness of one faced etc., Rudrâkṣam in the Mahâ Purâṇam Śrî Mad Devî Bhâgavatam of 18,000 verses by Maharṣi Veda Vyâsa.

CHAPTER VIII

1-21. Nârâyaṇa said :—" O Great Muni ! Now I shall tell you the rules of Bhûta Śuddhi i. e. the purification of the elements of the body (by respiratory attraction and replacement, etc.) Firstly, think of the Highest Deity Kuṇḍalinî (the Serpent Fire) as rising up in the hollow canal Suṣumnâ in the Spinal Cord from the Mulâdhâra (the sacral plexus) to the Brahmarandhra (the aperture supposed to be at the crown of the head). Next, the devotee is to meditate on the Mantra "Hamsa" and consider his Jîvâtmâ (the embodied soul) united with Para Brahma. Then think from leg to the knees in the form of a square Yantra (diagram as furnished with Vajra thunderbolt) (represented by 63 lines at the four corners); consider this square as the earth, of a golden colour and represented by the letter "Lam," representing the Seed Mantra of earth. Next from the knee to the navel consider the semi-moon and at its two ends consider that the two lotuses are situated. Consider this as the circle of water, of white colour, represented by the letter "Vam" the Seed Mantra of water. Then again from the navel to the heart consider it as of a triangular form and the Svastik mark at its three angles and think it as of fire and represented by the letter "Ram" its root Mantra, of red colour. Next from the heart to the centre of the eyebrows, consider as marked with six dots, with the Seed Mantra "Yam" of a smoke-coloured colour (dark-red) and of a circular appearance and consider it as air. Then again from the centre of the eyebrows to the crown of the head consider as Âkâs'a Maṇḍalam (a region of ether) beautiful and clear and with "Ham" as its vîja letter. Thus thinking consider firstly the earthy principle originated from watery principle, dissolved in water. Then think water as dissolved in fire, its cause; fire dissolved in air, its cause; and air dissolved in Âkâsa, ether, its cause; then consider Akâsa dissolved in its cause Ahamkâra, egoism; then again Ahamkâra dissolved in the Great Principle (Mahattatva); and Mahattatva again in its cause Prakriti and consider Prakriti again diluted in its cause, the Supreme Self. Then consider your ownself as the Highest Knowledge and only that. Think, then, of the Pâpa Puruṣa, the Sinful Man in your body. The size of this Man is that of a thumb and it is situated in the left abdomen. The head of him is represented by Brahmahatyâ (murdering a Brâhmaṇ); his arm as stealing gold; his heart as drinking wine; his loins as going to the wife of his Guru, his legs as mixing with people who go to their Guru's wives, and his toes as representing other sins and venial offences. The Sinful Man holds axes and shield in his hands; he is always angry, with his head bent down and his appearance is very horrible. Inhale air through the left nostril thinking of "Vam" the Root Mantra of air and make Kumbhaka *i. e.*, fill the whole body with that air, and hold it inside, purifying the sinful man; then repeating "Ram," the seed Mantra of fire, think the sinful man with his own body burnt down to ashes. Then exhale outside through the right nostril those ashes of the Sinful Man. Next consider the ashes due to the burning of the Sinful Man, as rolled and turned into a round ball with the nectar seed of the Moon. Think steadily this ball as transformed into a golden egg by the Seed Mantra "Lam" of the earth. Repeat then, "Ham" the seed Mantra of Akâs'a and think yourself as an ideal being pure and clear, and shape thus your body and the several limbs.

Create, then, fresh in an inverse order from the Brahma the elements Akâs a, air, fire, water, earth and locate them in their respective positions. Then by the Mantra "Soham" separate the Jivâtmâ from the Paramâtmâ and locate the Jîvâtmâ in the heart. Think also that the Kuṇḍalinî has come to the Sacral Plexus, after locating the Jivâtmâ, turned into nectar by contact with the Highest Self, in the heart. Next meditate on the vital force, the Prâṇa Śakti, thus located as follows:—There is a red lotus on a wide boat in a vast ocean of a red colour; on this lotus is seated the Prâṇa S'akti. She has six hands holding, in due order, the trident, the arrows made of sugarcane, noose, goad, five arrows and a skull filled with blood. She is three-eyed. Her high breasts are decorated; the colour of Her body is like the Rising Sun. May She grant us happiness. Thus meditating on the Prâṇa Śakti, Who is of the nature of the Highest Self, one ought to apply ashes on his body in order to attain success in all actions. Great merit arises from the application of ashes (besmearing ashes) on the body. I will now dwell on this subject in detail. Listen. This point of holding ashes on to the body is particularly proved in the Vedas and Smritis.

Here ends the Eighth Chapter in the Eleventh Book on Bhûta S'uddhi (purification of elements in the body) in the Mahapurânam Sri Mad Devî Bhâgavatam of 18,000 verses by Maharsi Veda Vyâsa.

CHAPTER IX.

1-43. Śrî Nârâyaṇa said:—The Brâhmaṇas that will perform duly the Śirovrata, to be described in the following, are the only ones who will attain very easily the highest knowledge, destroying all Avidyâ or Ignorance. So much so that the rules of right living and right conduct as ordained in the Śrutis and Smritis are not necessary to be observed by those who duly and devotedly perform the Śirovrata (*i. e.* vow of the head; *i. e.* vow to apply ashes on the forehead). O Learned One! It is through this Śirovrata that Brahmâ and the other Devas have been able to get their Brahmâhood and the Devahood. The ancient sages glorified highly this Śirovrata. Brahmâ, Viṣṇu, Rudra and the other Devas all performed this Śirovrata. O Wise One! Those that performed duly this S'irovrata, all became sinless though they were sinful in every way. Its name is S'irovrata, inasmuch as it is mentioned in the first part of the Atharva Veda. Only this vrata (vow) is called S'irovrata; no other thing is denominated by this name. By no other merit can this be acquired. O Muni! Different names are assigned to this vrata in different Śâkhâs; in fact, they are all one and the same.

N. B.—Pâsupata vrata, S'ivavrata, etc., are the different names assigned to it. In all the S'âkhâs, the One Substance, Intelligence solidified named S'iva and the knowledge thereof is mentioned. This is "S'irovrata." He who does not perform this Śirovrata, is irreligious and he is banished from all religious acts, though he is well-qualified in all branches of learning. There is no manner of doubt in this. This S'irovrata is like the blazing fire in destroying wholly the forest of sins. All knowledge flashes before him who performs this Śirovrata. The Atharva Śruti expounds the subtle and particularly incomprehensible things; this Śruti declares the above S'irovrata as daily to be done; so it is one of the daily observances. "Fire is ashes," "water is ashes" "earth is ashes," "air is ashes," "ether or Akâs'a is ashes," "all this mainfest Universe is ashes." These six mantras stated in the Atharva Veda are to be recited; after this, ashes are to be besmeared all over the body. This is named the S'irovrata. The devotee is to put on these ashes named S'irovrata during his Sandhyopâsanâ (practising Sandhyâ thrice a day) so long as the Brahma Vidyâ (the knowledge of Brahma) does not arise in him. One is to make a ankalap (resolve) of twelve years before one starts with this Vrata. In cases of incapability, a period of one year or six months, or three months or at least twelve days are to be adopted. That Guru is considered very cruel and his knowledge will come to an end who hesitates and does not impart the knowledge of the Vedas and other things to him who is purified by observing this Śirovrata. Know him certainly as a very merciful Guru who illumines the heart by Brahma Vidyâ just as God is very merciful and compassionate to all the living beings. One who performs one's own Dharmas for many births, acquires particular faith in this Śirovrata; others can have no faith in this. Rather he gets animosity for this vrata, because of the abundance of ignorance in him. So one ought never to advise on spiritual knowledge to an enemy who has no faith, rather who has hatred for any such thing. Those only that are purified by the observance of S'irovrata are entitled to Brahma Vidyâ; and none others. So the Vedas command:—Those are to be advised on Brahma Vidyâ who have performed S'irovrata. Even the animal becomes freed of his animalism, as a result of this vrata; no sin occurs in killing that animal; this is the decision of the Vedânta. It has been repeatedly uttered by Jâvâla Riṣi that the Dharma of the Brâhmaṇas is to put on the Tripuṇḍra (three curved lines of ashes on the forehead). The householders are instructed to put on this Tripuṇḍra by repeating the mantra "triyamvaka" with Om prefixed. Those that are in the stage of the Bhikṣus (Sannyâsis, etc.,) are to put on this Tripuṇḍra uttering thrice the mantra "Om Hasaḥ" Such is regularly stated in Jâvâla Śruti. The house holders and the Vânapras this (foresters) are to put on this Tripuṇḍra, uttering Triyamvaka mantra purified with "Haum" the praṇava of Śiva prefixed.

Those that are the Brahmachâris are to use daily this Tripuṇḍra uttering the mantra "Medhâvî," etc. The Brâhmaṇas are to apply the ashes in three curved lines on the fore head. The God Śiva is always hidden under the cover of ashes; so the Śaivas, the devotees of Śiva are to use the Tripuṇḍra. The Brahmaṇas are to use daily this Tripuṇḍra. Brahmâ is the Prime Brâhmin. When He used Tripuṇḍra on His forehead, what need to tell, then, that every Brâhmaṇ ought always to use it! Never fail, out of error, to besmear your body with the ashes as prescribed in the Vedas and worship the S'iva Lingam. The Sannyâsins are to apply Tripuṇḍra on their forehead, arms, chest, uttering the Triyamvaka mantra with Om' prefixed and also the five lettered mantra of S'iva " Om Namah S'ivâya.' The Brahmachâris should use Tripuṇḍra of ashes, obtained from their own fire, uttering the mantra " Triyâyuṣam Jamadagneh, etc., or the mantra " Medhâvî, etc. The S'ûdras in the service of the Brâhmiṇs are to use the ashes with devotion, with the mantra "Namah Śivâya." The other ordinary persons can use the Tripuṇḍra without any mantra. To besmear the body all over with ashes and to put on the Tripuṇḍra is the essence of all Dharma; therefore this should be used always. The ashes from the Agnihotra Sacrifice or from Virajâgni (Virajâ fire) are to be carefully placed on a clean and pure basin. Cleansing hands and feet, one is to sip (perform Âchamana) twice, and then, taking the ashes in the hand, utter the five Brahma mantras " Sadyoyâtam prapadyâmi, etc., and perform short Prâṇâyâma thrice; he is, then, to utter the seven mantras " Fire is ashes" " water is ashes," " earth is ashes" " Teja is ashes," " wind is ashes,' " ether is ashes," " All this whatsoever is ashes" and purify and impregnate the ashes with the mantra by blowing out air through the mouth. Then one is to think of Mahâ Deva, repeating the mantra "Om Apojyoti, etc., and apply dry ashes of white colour all over the body and become sinless. After this he is to meditate on the Mahâ Viṣṇu, the Lord of the universe and on the Lord of the waters and repeat again the mantras "Fire is ashes " and mix water with the ashes. He is, then, to think of S'iva and apply ashes on his forehead. He is to think of the ashes as S'iva Himself and then, with mantras appropriate to his own Âs'rama (stages of life) use the Tripuṇḍra on his forehead, chest and shoulders.

By the middle finger and ringfinger he is to draw the two lines of the ashes from the left to the right and by his thumb draw a third line of ashes from the right to the left. These Tripuṇḍras are to be used in the morning, midday and in the evening.

Here ends the Ninth chapter of the Eleventh Book on the rules of S'irovrata, in the Mahâpurâṇam Srî Mad Devî Bhâgavatam of 18,000, verses by Maharṣi Veda Vyâṣa.

CHAPTER X.

1-33. Nârâyaṇa said :—"O Knower of Brahma! O Nârada! The ashes prepared from ordinary fire are secondary (Gauṇa). The greatness of this secondary ashes is to be considered by no means trifling; this also destroys the darkest ignorance and reveals the highest knowledge. It is of various kinds. Amongst the secondary ashes, that prepared from Virajâgni is the best; it is equivalent to that obtained from Agnihotra Yajña and it is as glorious. The ashes obtained from the marriage sacrificial fire, that obtained from the burning of the Samidh fuel, what is obtained from the conflagration of fire are known as the secondary ashes. The Brâhmaṇas, Kṣattriyas and Vais'yas should use the ashes from the Agnihotra and the Virajâ Fire. For the householders, the ashes from the marriage sacrificial fire are good. For the Brahmachâris, the ashe from the Samid fuel are good and for the Śûdras the fire of the cook ing place of the Veda knowing Brâhmaṇas is good. For the other persons, the ashes obtained from the conflagration of fire are good. Now I will talk of the origin of the ashes obtained from the Virajâ fire. The chief season of the Virajâ fire sacrifice is the Full-moon night with Chitrâ asterism with the Moon. If this does not take place, the sacrifice may be performed at other seasons; and it should be remembered that the fit place is where one adopts as one's dwelling place. The auspicious field, garden or forest is also commendable for the above sacrifice. On the Trayodas'î Tithi, the thirteenth night preceding the full-moon night, one is to complete one's bathing and Sandhyâ; then one is to worship one's Guru and bow down before Him Then, receiving his permission, the sacrificer is to put on pure clothing and perform the special Pûjâ. Then with his white sacrificial thread, white garlands, and white sandalpaste one is to sit on the Kus'a seat with sacrificial (Kus'a) grass in one's hands. With his face towards the east or north he is to perform Prâṇâyâma thrice.

Then he is to meditate on Śivà and Bhagavatî and get mentally their permissions. O Deva Bhagavan! O Mother Bhagavatî! "I will perform this vow for my life-time" Thus making the resolve, he should start with this sacrifice. But this is to be known that this Vrata can be performed for twelve years, for six years, for three years, for one year, for six months, for twelve days, for six days, for three days, even at least for one day. But in every case, he must take mentally the permission of the Deva and the Devî. Now, to perform the Virajâ Homa, one is to light the fire according to one's Grihya Sûtras and then perform Homa with ghee, Samidh (fuel) or with charu (an oblatoin of rice, milk, and sugar boiled together). Then on the fourteenth lunar day (Chaturdas'î) one is to pray "Let the tattvas (principles) in me be purified" and then perform the Homa ceremony with Samidh, etc., as above-mentioned. Now recollecting that "My principles in my body are purified," he is to offer oblations to the fire. In other words, uttering "Priththitattvas me sudhyatâm jyotiraham virajâ vipâpmâ bhûyâsam Svâhâ" one is to offer oblations to the Fire. Thus uttering the five element (Mahâbhutas), five tanmâtrâs, five Karmendriyas (organs of action), five Jnânendriyas (organs of perception), five Prâṇas, seven dhâtus Tvak, etc., mind, buddhi (intellect), Ahamkâra (egoism), Sattva, Raja, Tamah guṇas, Prakriti, Puruṣa, Râga, Vidyâ, Kalâ (arts etc.,) Daiva (Fate), Kâla (time), Mâyâ Śuddhavidyâ, Mahes'vara, Sadâ Śiva, Śakti Śivatattva, etc., respectively by its own name, one is to offer oblations to the fire by the five-lettered Virajâ Mantra; then the sacrificer will become pure. Then form a round ball of fresh cowdung and purifying it by Mantram place it on fire and carefully watch it. On that day, the devotee is to take Haviṣyânna (a sacred food of boiled rice with ghee). On the morning of the Chaturdas'î, he is to perform his daily duties as above and then to perform Homa on that fire, uttering the five lettered Mantra. He is not to take any food the rest of the time. On the next day, that is, on the full-moon day, after performing the morning duties, he is to do the Homa ceremony, uttering the Five lettered Mantra and then take leave of the Fire (invoked for worship). He is, then, to raise up the ashes. Then the devotee is to keep Jaṭâ (matted hair) or to shave clean his head or to keep only one lock of hair on the crown of the head. He is to take his bath, then; and if he can, then he should be naked or put on a red coloured cloth, hide, or one piece of rag or bark; he is to take a staff and a belt. Washing his hands and feet and sipping twice he by his two hands, is to pulverise the ashes" and, uttering the six Atharvan Mantras, "Fire is ashes and so forth" apply ashes from his head to foot. Then, as before, he is to apply ashes, gradually to his arms, etc., and all over the body uttering the Praṇava of Siva, "Vam, Vam." He is to put on the Triyâyusa Tripuṇḍra on his forehead." After he has done, this, the Jîva (the embodied self) becomes Śiva (the Free Self) and he should behave him self like Śiva. O Nârada ! Thus, at the three Sandhyâ-periods, he is to do like this. This Pâs'upata vrata is the source of enjoyment as well as liberation and as well as of the cessation of all brutal desires. By the performance of this vrata the devotee is to free himself gradually of his animal feelings and then to worship Bhagavân Sadâ Śiva in the form of a phallic symbol. The above bath ashes is highly meritorious and it is the source of all happiness. By holding the ashes, one's longevity is prolonged, one gets even great bodily strength, becomes healthy and his beauty increases and he gets nourishment. This using of ashes is for the preservation of one's own self ; it is the source of one's good and of all sorts of happiness and prosperity. Those who use ashes (Bhas'ma) are free from the danger of plague and other epidemic diseases ; this bhasma is of three sorts as it leads to the attainment of peace, nourishment, or to the fufilment of all desires.

Here ends the Tenth Chapter of the Eleventh Book on the subject Gauṇa Bhasma (secondary ashes) in the Mahâpurâṇam Srîmad Devî Bhâgavatam of 18,000 verses by Maharṣi Veda Vyâṣa.

CHAPTER XI.

Nârada asked :—" O Bhagavan ! How is the above Bhasma of three kinds ? I am eager to hear this. Kindly describe this to me." Nârâyaṇa said :—" O Nârada ! I am now talking of the three kinds of ashes ; hearing this even destroys one's sins and brings in good fame. When a cow evacuates her dung, just as the cow dung leaves her and is far from reaching the ground, one should catch it with one's hand and this cow-dung burnt with "Sadyojâtâdi *i. e.*, Brahma Mantra" becomes ashes which are called "Śântika Bhaṣma," *i. e.*, ashes producing peace. Before the cowdung is about to reach the ground, the devotee should take it with his hand and uttering the six lettered Mantra, he is to burn the cowdung. The ashes from this are called Pauṣṭik Bhaṣma, *i. e.*, ashes leading to nourishment.

If the cowdung be burned with the Mantra "Haum," the ashes of this are called "Kâmada Bhasma *i. e.*, ashes leading to the granting of desires. O Nârada ! On the full moon day, new moon day or on the eighth lunar day, a man is to get up from his bed early in the morning and be pure and go the cow enclosure. He is to salute the cows and take the cowdung, uttering the Mantra Haum. If he be a Brâhmiṇ, he is to collect the white cow dung ; if he be a Kṣattriya, he would take the red cow.

dung; a Vais'ya, yellow cowdung and if he be a Śûdra, he will take the black cowdung. Then by the mantra "Namah" he is to form that into a ball and cover it with the husk of rice or some other grain and dry it in a sacred place, repeating the mantra "Haum". Bring fire from a forest or from the house of a Veda-knowing Brâhmin and reduce the cowdung to ashes by this mantra, uttering the mantra Haum. Next take out the ashes carefully from the fire place (Agni Kuṇḍa) and place it in a new jar or pot, again remembering the mantra "Haum". Mix with the ashes the Ketakî dust, the Pâṭala flower dust, the root of the fragrant grass called khas khas, saffron and other sweet scented things with the mantra "Sadyojâtam prapadyâmi," etc. First perform the water bath, then the bath of the ashes. In case one cannot have the water bath, one is to have the ash bath. Washing the hands, feet and head with the mantra "Is'ânah Sarvavidyânâm," etc., and uttering "Tatpuruṣa" one is to besmear one's face with ashes and by the mantra "Aghora" apply ashes on one's chest; with the mantra Vâmadeva." he is to use ashes on his navel; and with the mantra "Sadyo Jâta, etc.," all over his body; he is to quit his former cloth and put on another fresh cloth. Wash your hands and feet and sip (do Âchaman). It will serve the purpose if one simply uses Tripuṇdrak and if one does not besmear the whole body with ashes. Before the midday one is to use Bhasma with water; but after the midday with dry ashes one is to draw the Tripuṇḍra lines of ashes with the forefinger, middlefinger and ringfinger. The head, forehead, ears, neck, heart, and the arms are the places whereon the Tripuṇḍras are used. On the head, the ashes are applied with five fingers and with the mantra "Haum"; on the forehead, the Tripuṇḍra is applied with mantra Svâhâ by the forefinger, mindlefinger and ringfinger; on the right ear, it is applied with "Sadyojâta" mantra; on the left ear, with "Vâmadeva" Mantra; on the neck with Aghora mantra by the middlefinger; on the chest with "Namaḥ" mantra by the forefinger, middlefinger and ringfinger; on the right arm with vaṣaṭ mantra by the three fingers; on the left arm with "Hum" mantra by the three fingers; and on the navel, the ashes are to be applied with the mantra Îs'ânaḥ sarva devânâm by the middlefinger. The first line in every Tripuṇḍra is Brahmâ; the second line is Viṣṇu; and the third, the topmost line is Mahâ Deva. The line of ashes that is marked by one finger is Îs'vara. The head is the place of Brahmâ; the forehead is the site of Îs'vara; the two ears are the seats of the two As'vins and the neck is where Gaṇes'a resides. The Kṣattriyas, Vais'yas, and Śûdras are to use Tripuṇḍras without any mantra; they are also not to use the ashes on the whole of the body. The lowest classes (e. g. the chândâlas, etc.,) and the uninitiated persons are to use the Tripuṇḍraks without any mantra.

Here ends the Eleventh Chapter of the Eleventh Book on the description of the greatness of the three kinds of Bhaṣmas in the Mahâpurâṇam Śrî Mad Devî Bhagavatam of 18,000 verses by Maharṣi Veda Vyâsa.

CHAPTER XII.

1-20. Śrî Nârâyaṇa said :—" O Devarṣi Nârada ! Hear now the great secret and the fruits of besmearing one's body with ashes, yielding all desires. The pure cowdung of the Kapila (brown) cow is to be taken up by the hand before it reaches the ground. It should not be like mire i. e., not like a liquid ; it should not be also very hard nor should it emit a bad stench. And in case if the cowdung that has already fallen on the earth, has to be taken, it should be scraped off from the top and bottom ; make it into a ball and then burn it in a pure fire, repeating the principal mantra. Take the ash and tie it in a piece of cloth and keep it in a pot. The pot in which the ashes are to be kept should be nice and good, hard, clean and sprinkled over for purification. Uttering the principal mantra, one is to keep the ashes in the pot. The pot may be of metal, wood, earth, or cloth ; or it can be kept in any other nice pot. The ashes can be kept in a silken bag where the mohurs are kept. In going to a distant land, the devotee can take the ashes himself or kept with his accompanying servant. When it is to be given to somebody, it is to be given with both the hands ; never with one hand. Never keep it in an unholy place. Never apply feet to the ashes, nor throw it in an ordinary place nor ever cross it by your legs. Use always the ashes after purifying it with mantra. These rules of holding the Bhasma are according to the Smritis. By holding Bhasma in this way, the devotee becomes, no doubt, like Śiva. The ashes, that the Vaidik devotees of S'iva prepare are to be taken with devotion. All can ask for that, But the ashes that the followers of the Tantra cult prepare, are taken by the Tântriks only ; it is pohibited to the Vaidiks. The Sûdras, Kâpâlikas, and other heretics (e. g., Jains, Buddhists) can use the Tripuṇḍras. Never do they conceive in their minds that they would not take the Tripuṇḍra. The holding on of Bhasma (ashes) is according to the Vedas. Therefore one who does not apply it falls down. The Brâhmaṇas must use the Tripuṇḍras, repeating the mantra; and they are to besmear their whole body with ashes; if they don't do so, they are surely fallen. He can never expect to get liberation even after koṭi births who does not besmear his body with ashes devotedly and who does not hold the Tripuṇḍras. O Nârada! The vile man who does not hold Bhasma duly, know the birth of that man as futile as is the birth of a hog. Consider that body as a burning ground which does not bear the Tripuṇḍra marks. The virtuous man should not cast a glance at him even. Fie on that forehead which does not carry the Tripuṇḍra! Fie on that village which has not a single temple of Śiva! Fie on that birth which is void of the worship of Śiva! Fie on that knowledge which is void of the knowledge of Śiva. Know them to be the slanderers of Śiva who mock at Tripuṇḍra. Those that put on the Tripuṇḍras, bear Śiva in their forehead. The Brâhmin who is Niragnik (without the holy fire) is not nice in every way. So if the worship of Śiva be not done with any Tripuṇḍra is not praiseworthy, even it be attended with abundance of other offerings. Those who do not besmear their bodies with ashes or who do not use the Tripuṇḍras, get their previous good deeds converted into bad ones.

21-42. Unless the Tripuṇḍra mark is taken up according to the Śâstras, the Vaidik Karmas (works) or those performed according to the Smritis prove injurious; the good works whatsoever done by any man count for nothing; the holy words heard seem as if unheard and the study of the Vedas counted as if not studied.

The study of the Vedas, Sacrifices, Charities, asceticisms, vows and fastings of that man, who does not use the Tripuṇḍra, all become fruitless. Without using Bhasma (ashes) if one wants liberation, then that desire is equivalent to live after taking poison. There is no doubt in this. The Creator has not made the forehead vertically high nor round; but he has made it slightly slanting and curved fit to have the Tripuṇḍra. Making thus the forehead, the Creator wants, as it were, to inform everyone that every one ought to use Tripuṇḍra marks; the curved lines also are made visible for this purpose. Still the igorant illiterate man does not put up the Tripuṇḍra. Unless the Brâhmaṇas use the curved Tripuṇḍras, their meditation won't be successful; they will not have liberation, knowledge, nor their asceticism would bear any fruit. As the Śûdras have no right in the study of the Vedas, so the Brâhmans have not any right to perform the worship of Śiva, etc., unless they use the Tripuṇḍras. First of all, facing eastward, and washing hands and feet, he ought to make a resolve and then to take a bath of the ashes mentally, controlling his breath. Then taking the ashes of the Agnihotra sacrifice he is to put some ashes on his own head, uttering "Îs'âna" mantra. Then he is to recite the Puruṣa Sûkta Mantra and apply ashes on his face; with the Aghora mantra on his chest; with the Vâmadeva mantra, on his anus; with Sadyojâta mantra on his legs; and with the mantra Om, he is to besmear his whole body with ashes. This is called the bath of fire by the Munis. So bring all the actions to a successful issue one is to take first of all this bath of fire. Washing his hands, then, he is to make Âchaman duly; and, according to the above-mentioned rules, he is to apply ashes on his fore head, heart, and all round the neck with the five mantras above mentioned; or with each mantra he is to apply the Tripuṇḍras. Thus all works are fructified and he gets the right to do all the Vaidik actions. The Sudras, even, are not to use the ashes touched by the lowest classes. All the actions ordained by the S'astras are to be done after being besmeared with ashes of the Agnihotra sacrifice; otherwise no action will bear any fruit. All his truth, purity, Japam, offering, oblations to the sacrifice, bathing in the holy places of pilgrimage, and worshipping the gods become useless, who does not hold Tripuṇḍra. No fear of disease, sins, famine, or robbers comes to the Brâhmins who use Tripuṇḍra and rosary of Rudrâkṣa and thus remain always pure. In the end, they get the Nirvâṇa liberation. During the time of Srâddhas (solemn obsequies performed in honour of the manes of deceased ancestors) the Brahmins purify the rows where persons are fed; so much so that the Devas glorify them. One must use the Tripuṇḍra marks before one performs any Srâddha, Japam sacrifice, offering oblations or worshipping the Visvedevâs; then one gets deliverance from the jaws of death. O Nârada! I am now speaking further of the greatness in holding the Bhasma; listen.

Here ends the Twelfth Chapter of the Eleventh Book on the greatness in holding the Tripuṇḍra and Bhasma in the Mahâpurâuan S'rî Mad Devî Bhagâvatam of 18,000 verses by Maharsi Veda Vyâsa.

CHAPTER XIII.

1-20. Nârâyaṇa said:—O Best of Munis! What shall I describe to you the effects of using the Bhasma! Only applying the ashes takes aways the Mahâpâtaks (great sins) as well as other minor sins of the devotee. I speak this truly, very truly unto you. Now hear the fruits of using simply the ashes. By using Bhasma, the knowledge of Brahma comes to the Yatis; the desires of enjoyments are eradicated; the improvement is felt in all the virtuous actions of the householders and the studies of the Vedas and other Śâstras of the Brahmachâris get their increase. The Śûdras get merits in using Bhasmas and the sins of others are destoyed. To besmear the body with ashes and to apply the curved Tripuṇḍras is the source of good to all beings. The Śruti says so. That this implies the performance of sacrifies by all, is also asserted in the Srutis. To apply ashes to the whole of the body and to use Tripuṇḍra is common to all the religions; it has nothing, in principle, contradictory to others. So the S'ruti says. This Tripuṇḍra and the besmearing with ashes is the special mark of the devotees of S'iva; this again is asserted in the S'ruti This Bhasma and the Tripuṇḍra are the special marks by which one is characterised; it is said so in the Vaidik Śruti. S'iva, Viṣṇu, Brahmâ, Indra, Hiraṇyagarbha, and their Avatâras, Varuṇa and the whole host of the Devas all gladly used this Tripuṇḍra and ashes. Durgâ, Lakṣmî, and Sarasvatî, etc., all the wives of the gods daily anoint their bodies with ashes and use the Tripuṇḍras. So even the Yakṣas, Râkṣasas, Gandharbhas Sidhas, Vidyâdharas, and the Munis have applied Bhasma and Tripuṇḍra This holding on of ashes is not prohibited to anybody; the Brahmaṇas, Ksattriyas, Vais'yas, S'ûdras, mixed castes, and the vile classes all can use this Bhasma and Tripuṇḍra. O Nârada! In my opiniom they only are the Sadhus (saints) who use this Tripuṇḍra and besmear their bodies with ashes. In seducing this Lady Mukti (liberation is persionfined here as a lady) one is to have this gem of S'iva Lingam, the five lettered Mantra Namah Sivâyâ as the loving principle, and holding on the ashes as the charning medicine, (as in seducing any ordinary woman, gems, jewels and ornaments, love and charming medicines are necessary). O Nârada! Know the place where the person, who has besmeared the body with ashes and who has used Tripuṇḍra takes his food as where S'ankara and Śankarî have taken their food together. Even if anybody himself not using the Bhasma, follows another who has used the Bhasma, he will be soon honoured in the society even if he a sinner. What more than this, if anybody himself not using the ashes, praises another who uses the Bhasma, he is freed from all his sins and gets soon honour and respect in the society. All the studies of the Vedas come to him though he has not studied the Vedas, all the fruits of hearing the Śrutis and the Purâṇas come to him, though he has not heard them, all the fruits of practised Dharma come to him though he has not practised any, if he always uses this Tripuṇḍra on his forehead and gives food to a beggar who uses Tripuṇḍra on his forehead. Even in countries as Bihar (Kîkaṭa, etc, that have got a bad name) if there be a single man in the whole country whose body is besmeared with ashes and who uses this Tripuṇḍra, that is considered then as Kâs'î (Benares city). Any body, of a bad or of a good character, be he a Yogî or a sinner, using Bhasma, is worshipped like my son, Brahmâ. O Nârada! Even if an hypocrite uses Bhasma, he will have a good future, which cannot be attained even by performing hundreds of sacrifices. If any body uses Bhasma daily either through good companion or through neglect, he will be entitled, like me, to the highest worship. O Nârada! Brahmâ, Viṣṇu, Mahes'vara, Pârvatî, Lakṣmî, Sarasvatî and all the other Devas become satisfied with simply holding on this Bhasma. The merits that are obtained by using only the Tripuṇḍra, cannot be obtained by gifts, sacrifices, severe austerities, and going to sacred places of pilgrimages. They cannot give one-sixteenth part of the result that accrues from holding the Tripuṇḍra. As a King recognises a person as his own, whom he has given some object of recognition, so Bhagavân Śankara knows the man who uses Tripuṇḍras as His own person. They that hold Tripuṇḍras with devotion can have Bholâ Nâtha under their control; no distinction is made here between the Brâhmaṇas and Chaṇḍâlas. Even if any body be fallen from the state of observing all the Âchâras or rules of conduct proper to his Âs'rama and if he be faulty in not attending to all his duties, he will be Mukta (freed) if he has used even once this Bhasma Tripuṇḍra. Never bother yourself with the caste or the family of the holder of the Tripuṇḍras. Only see whether the sign Tripuṇḍra exists in his forehead. If so, consider him entitled to respect. O Nârada! There is no mantra higher than this Śiva Mantra; there is no Deity higher than Śiva; there is no worship of greater merit-giving powers than the worship of Śiva; so there is no Tîrtha superior to this Bhasma. This Bhasma is not an ordinary thing; it is the excellent energy (semen virile) of fire of the nature of Rudra. All sorts of troubles vanish, all sorts of sins are destroyed by this Bhasma. The country where the lowest castes reside with their bodies besmeared with ashes, is inhabited always by Bhagavân Śankara, Bhagavatî Umâ, the Pramathas (the attendants of Śiva) and by all the Tîrthas. Bhagavân S'ankara, first of all, held this Bhasma as an ornament to his body by purifying it first with "Sadyo Jâta," etc., the five mantras. Therefore if any body uses the Bhasma Tripuṇḍra according to rules on his forehead, the writings written at the time of his birth by Vidhâtâ Brahmâ will all be cancelled, if they had been bad. There is no doubt in this.

Here ends the Thirteenth Chapter of the Eleventh Book on the greatness of Bhasma in the Mahâpurâṇam Śrî Mad Devî Bhâgavatam of 18,000 verses by Maharṣi Veda Vyâsa.

CHAPTER XIV.

1-17. Nârâyaṇa said:—"O Nârada! Whatever is given as charities to any man besmeared with the holy ashes, takes away instantly all the sins of the donor. The Śrutis, Smritis, and all the Purâṇas declare the greatness of this Bhasma. So the twice-born must accept this Whoever holds this Tripuṇḍra, of this holy ashes at the three Sandhyâ times, is freed from all his sins and goes to the region of Śiva. The Yogî who takes a bath of ashes throughout his body during the three Sandhyâs, gets his Yoga developed soon. By this bath of ashes, many generations are lifted up. O Nârada! This ash bath is many times superior to the water bath. To take once a bath of ashes secures to one all the merits acquired by bathing in all the sacred places of pilgrimages. There is no doubt in this. By this bath of ashes, all the Mahâpâtakas (great heinous sins) and other minor sins as well are instantly destroyed as heaps of wood are brought down to ashes in a moment by the fire. No bath is holier than this one. This is first mentioned by Śiva and He took Himself this bath. Since then this bath of ashes has been taken with great care by Brahmâ and the other Devas and the Munis for their own good in all the virtuous actions. This bath of ashes is termed the bath of fire. So he who applies ashes on his head, gets the state of Rudra while he is in this body of five elements. Those who are delighted to see persons with this ashes on their bodies are respected by the Devas, Asuras, and Munis. He who honours and gets up on seeing a man besmeared with ashes is respected even by Indra, the Lord of Heavens. Even if any body eats any uneatables, then the sin incurred thereby wo'nt touch him, if his body be then besmeared with ashes. He who first takes a water bath and then an ash-bath, be he a Brahmachârî or an house-holder or an anchorite (Vânaprasthî) is freed of all sins and gets in the end the highest state. Specially for the Yatis (ascetics), this ash bath is very necessary. This ash bath is superior to the water bath. For the bonds of Nature, this pleasure and pain, are cut asunder by this ash bath. The Munis know this Prakriti as moist and wet; and therefore Prakriti binds men. If any body desires to cut asunder this bondage of the body, he will find no other remedy for this in the three worlds than this Holy Bath of ashes.

18-54. In ancient days the ashes were first offered to the Devî gladly by the Devas for their protection, their good and purification, when they first saw the ashes. Therefore any body who takes this bath of fire, gets all his sins destroyed and he goes to S'iva Loka. He who daily uses this ashes has not to suffer from the oppression of the Râkṣasas, Pis'âchas, Pûtanâs and the other Bhûtas or from disease, leprosy, the chronic enlargement of spleen, all sorts of fistulae, from eighty sorts of rheumatism, sixty four kinds of bilious diseases, twenty two varieties of phlegmatic diseases and from tigers, thieves, and other vicious planetary influences. Rather he gets the power to suppress all these as a lion kills easily a mad elephant. Any body who first mixes the ashes with pure cold water and then besmears his body with that and puts on the Tripuṇḍras, attains soon the Highest Brahma. He who holds the Tripuṇḍra of ashes becomes sinless and goes to the Brahma loka. He can even wipe off the ordnances of the fate on his forehead to go to the jaws of Death, if he uses, according to the S'astras, the Tripuṇḍras on his forehead. If the ashes be used on the neck, then the sin, incurred through the neck, is completely destroyed. If the ashes be used on the neck, then the sin incurred by the neck, in eating uneatable things is entirely destroyed. If the ashes be held on the arms, then the sin incurred by the arms is destroyed. If it be held on the breast, the sin done mentally is destroyed. If it be held on the navel, the sin incurred by the generative organ is destroyed. If it be held on the anus, then the sin incurred by the anus is destroyed. And if it be held on the sides, then the sin incurred in embracing other's wives is destroyed. So, know fully, to use ashes is highly commendable. Everywhere three curved lines of ashes are to be used. Know these three lines as Brahmâ, Viṣṇu and Mahes'a; Dakṣiṇâgni, Gârhapatya fire and Âhavanîya fire; the Sattva, Rajas and Tamas qualities, Heaven, earth and Pâtâla (nether regions). If the wise Brahmin holds properly the ashes his Mahâpâtakas are destroyed. He is not involved in any sin. Rather he, without any questionings, gets his liberation. All the sins, in the body besmeared with ashes, are burnt down by the ashes, which is of the nature of fire, into ashes. He is called Bhasmaniṣṭha (a devotee of Bhasma *i. e.* ashes) who takes a bath of ashes, who besmears his body with ashes, who use the Tripuṇḍras of ashes, who sleeps in ashes, He is called also Âtmaniṣṭha (a devotee of Âtman (Self). At the approach of such a man, the Demons, Pis'âchas, and very serious diseases run away to a distance. There is no doubt in this. In as much as these ashes reveal the knowledge of Brahma, it is called Bhasita from Bhasma, to shine; because it eats up the sins, it is called Bhasma; because it increases the eight supernatural powers Animâ, etc., it is called

Bhûti; because it protects the man who uses it, it is called "Rakṣâ." As the sins are all destroyed by the mere remembrance of Bhagavân Rudra, so seeing the person using the Tripuṇḍra, the demons, bad spirits and other vicious hosts of spirits fly away quickly, trembling with fear. As a fire burns a great forest by its own strength, so this bath of ashes burns the sins of those who are incessantly addicted to sins. Even if at the time of death one takes a bath of ashes, though he has committed an inordinate amount of vices, all his sins are soon destroyed. By this bath ashes, the Self is purified, the anger is destroyed; the senses are calmed down. The man who uses even once this Bhasma comes to Me; he has not to take any more births in future. On Monday Amâvasyâ (also on the full moon day) if one sees the S'iva Lingam, with his body besmeared all over with ashes, one's sins will all be destroyed. (All the sins are not seen; hence the tithi is called Amâvas.) If people use Bhasma daily, all their desires will be fructified whether they want longevity, or prosperity or Mukti. The Tripuṇḍra that represents Brahmâ, Viṣṇu and S'iva is very sacred. Seeing the man with Tripuṇḍra on, the fierce Râkṣasas or mischievous creatures flee to a distance. There is no doubt in this. After doing the S'aucha (necessary cleanliness) and other necessary things, one bathes in pure cold water and besmears his body with ashes from head to foot. By taking the water bath only, the outward unclean things are destroyed. But the ash bath not only cleanse the outer external uncleanliness but cleanse also all the internal uncleanliness. So even if one does not take tâe water bath, one ought to take this ash bath. There is to be no manner of doubt in this.

44-47. All the religious actions performed without this ash bath seem as if no actions are done at all. This ash bath is stated in the Vedas. Its another name is the Fire Bath. By this ash bath both outside and inside are purified. So a man who uses ashes gets the entire fruit of worshipping S'iva. By the water Bath only the outside dirt is removed; but by this bath of ashes, outside dirts and inside dirts, both are fully removed. If this water bath be taken many times daily, still without an ash bath, one's heart is not purified. What more shall I speak of the greatness of ashes, the Vedas only appreciate its glories rightly! Yea, very rightly!

48-50. Or Mahâ Deva, the Gem of all the Devas, knows the greatness of this Bhasma. Those who perform rites and works prescribed by the Vedas, without taking this bath of ashes, do not get even a tithe of the fruits of their works done. Only that man will be entitled to the entire fruits of the Vedas who perform this bath of ashes duly. This is the opinion of the Vedas. This bath of ashes purifies more the things that are already pure ; thus the Śruti says. That wretch who does not take the bath of ashes as aforesaid is a Great Sinner. There is no doubt in this. By this bath greater interminable merits accrue than what is obtained by innumerable baths taken by the Brâhmaṇas on the Vâruṇî momentous occasion. So take this bath carefully in the morning, mid-day and evening. This bath of ashes is ordained in the Vedas. So know those who are against this bath mentioned in the Vedas, are verily fallen! After evacuating oneself of one's urine and faeces, one ought to take this bath of ashes. Otherwise men will not be purified. Even if one performs duly the water bath and if one does not take this bath of ashes, that man will not be purified. So he cannot get any right to do any religious actions. After evacuating one's abdomen of the outgoing air, after yawning, after holding sexual intercourses, after spitting and sneezing, and after easing oneself of phlegm, one ought to take this bath of ashes. O Nârada! Thus I have described to you here the greatness of Śrî Bhasma. I am again telling you more of it specially. Listen attentively.

Here ends the Fourteenth Chapter of the Eleventh Book on the greatness in holding the Bibhûti (ashes) in the Mahâpurâṇam Srî Mad Devî Bhâgavatam of 18,000 verses by Maharṣi Veda Vyâsa.

CHAPTER XV.

1-10. Nârâyana said :—Only the twice born are to take this Tripuṇḍra on the forehead and the other parts of the body after carefully purifying the ashes by the mantra Agniriti Bhasma, etc. The Brâhmaṇs, Kṣattriyas, and Vais'yas are known as the twiceborn, (the Dvijas). So the Dvijas ought to take daily this Tripuṇḍra with great care. O Brâhmaṇa! Those who are purified with the ceremony of the holy thread, are called the Dvijas. For these the taking of Tripuṇḍra as per Śruti is very necessary. Wthout taking this Vibhûti, any good work done is as it were not done. There is no doubt in this. Even the japam of Gâyatrî is not well performed if this Bhasma be not used. O Best of Munis! The Gâyatrî is the most important and the chief thing of the Brâhmanhood. But that is not advised if the Tripuṇḍra be not taken. O Munis! As long as the ashes born of Agni are not applied on the forehead, one is not entitled to be initiated in the Gâyatrî Mantra. O Brahman! Unless ashes be applied on the forehead, no one will recognise you as a Brâhmaṇa. For this reason I take this holding of the merit-giving Tripuṇḍra as the cause of the Brâhmanhood. I speak this verily unto you, that he is recognised as a Brâhmaṇa and literary on whose forehead there is seen the white ashes purified by the mantra. He is entitled to the state of a Brâhmaṇa who is naturally very eager to collect the ashes as he collects the invaluable gems and jewels.

11-20. Those who are not naturally eager to collect the Bhasma as they are naturally eager to collect gems and jewels, are to be known as Chândâlas in some of their previous births. Those who are not naturally joyous in holding Tripuṇḍra, were verily Chândâlas in their previous births.; This I tell you truly very truly.

Those who eat roots and fruits without holding ashes go to the terrible hells. "He who worships Śiva without having' Bibhûti" on his forehead, that wretch is a Siva hater and goes to hell after his death. He who does not hold Bibhûti is not entitled to any religious act."

Without taking Bibhûti, if you make a gift of Tulâ Puruṣa made of gold, you won't get any fruits. Rather you will have to go to hell!

As the Brâhmaṇas are not to perform their Sandhyâs without their holy threads, so without this Bibhûti, one ought not also to perform one's Sandhyâ.

If at times a man by chance has no holy thread, he can do his Sandhyâ by muttering the Gâyatrî or by fasting. But there is no such rule in holding Bhasma.

If one performs Sandhyâ, without having any Vibhûti, he is liable to incur a sin; as without holding this Bhasma, no right can come to him to perform his Sandhyâ.

As a man of a lowest caste acts contrary and incurs a sin if he hears the Veda mantra, so a twice-born incurs a sin if he performs Sandhyâ without having his Tripuṇḍra. The twiceborn must therefore collect his thoughts with his heart intent on this Tripuṇḍra whether it be according to Śrauta or Smârta method—or in absence thereof the Laukika Bhasma. Of whatsoever sort is the Bhasma, it is always pure. In the Sandhyâ and other actions of worship, the twiceborn ought to be very careful and punctilious in using this Bhasma.

21-31. No sin can enter into the body of one besmeared with ashes. For this reason, the Brâhmaṇas ought always to use ashes with great care. One is to hold the Tripuṇḍra, six Angulas high or greater by the fore, middle and ring fingers of the right hand. If any body uses Tripuṇḍra, shining and brilliant, and extending from eye to eye, he becomes, no doubt, a Rudra. The ring-finger is the letter "A," the middle finger is "U" and the fiorefinger is "M"; so the Tripuṇḍra marks drawn by the above three fingers is of the nature of the three guṇas. The Tripuṇḍra should be drawn by the middle, fore, and ring fingers in a reverse way (from the left of the forehead to its right). I will now tell you an anecdote, very ancient. Listen. Once Durvâsâ, the head of the ascetics, with his body besmeared with ashes and with Rudrâkṣam, all over, on his body went to the region of the Pitris, uttering loudly "O S'ankara, of the Form of All! O S'iva! O Mother Jagadambe, the Source of all auspiciousness! The Pitris Kavya-Vâlâs, etc., (Kavya Vâlanalaḥ Somaḥ Yamaḥ schaivâryamâ Tathâ, Agnisvâttvâ, Varhisadaḥ, Somapâḥ Pitri Devatâh) got up, received him heartily and gave him seats and shewed him great honours and respect and held many pure conversations with the Muni. During their talk, the sinners of the Kumbhipâka hell were crying "Oh! Alas! We are killed, we are being killed" Oh! We are being burnt!; some others cried "Oh! Oh! We are cut down." Thus various cries and lamentations reached their ears.

32-40. Hearing their piteous cries, Durvâsâ, the prince of the Riṣis, asked with a grievous heart the Pitris "Who are those crying?" The Pitris replied:—There is a city close to our place called "Samyamanî Purî" of the King Yama where the sinners are punished. Yama gives punishment to the sinners there. O Sinless One! In that city the King Yama lives with his terrible black-coloured messengers, the personifications of Kâla (the Destruction). For the punishment of the sinners, eighty-six hells exist there. The place is being guarded always by the horrible messengers of Yama. Out of those hells, the hell named Knmbhîpâka is very big and that is the chief of the hells. The ailings and torments of the sinners in the Kumbhîpâka hell cannot be described in hundred years. O Muni! The Śiva-haters, the Viṣṇu-haters, the Devî-haters are made to fall to this Kuṇḍa. Those who find fault with the Vedas, and blame the Sun, Gaṇes'a and tyrannise the Brâhmaṇas fall down to this hell. Those who blame their mothers, fathers, Gurus, elder brothers, the Smritis and Purâṇas and those as well who take the Tapta Mudrâs (hot marks on their bodies) and

Tapta Śûlas (*i. e.*, those who being Śaivas act as they like) those who blame the religion (Dharma) go down to that hell.

41-50. We hear constantly their loud piteous cries, very painful te hear; hearing which naturally gives rise to feelings of indifference (Vairâgyam)." Hearing the above words of the Pitris, Durvâsâ, the prince of the Munis, went to the hell to see the sinners. O Muni! Going there, the Muni bent his head downwards and saw the sinners when, instantly the sinners began to enjoy pleasures more than those who enjoy in the Heavens. The sinners became exceedingly glad. Some began to sing, some began to dance, some began to laugh some sinners began to play one with one another in great ecstacy. The musical instruments Mridaṇga, Muraja, lute, Dhakkâ, Dundubhis, etc., resounded with sweet sonorous tones (in accordance with five resonants). The sweet fragrant smell of the flowers of Vâsanti creepsers spread all round. Durvâsâ Muni became surprised to see all this. The messengers of Yama were startled and immediately went to their King Yama and said :—" O Lord! Our King! A wondrous event occurred lately. The sinners in the Kumbhîpâkâ hell are now enjoying pleasures more than those in the Heavens. O Bibhu! How can this take place! We cannot make out the cause of this. O Deva! We all have become terrified and have come to you. Hearing the words of the messengers, Dharmarâja, mounting on his great bufflao, came there instantly and seeing the state of the sinners sent news immediately to the Heavens.

51-60. Hearing the news Indra came there with all the Devas, Brahmâ came there from His Brahmaloka; and Nârâyaṇa came there from Vaikuṇṭha. Hearing this, the regents of the quarters, the Dikpâlas came there with all their attendants from their respective abodes. They all came there to the Kumbhîpâka hell and saw that all the beings there are enjoying greater pleasures than those in the Heavens. They all were astonished to see this; and they could not make out why this had happened. "What a wonder is this! This Kuṇḍa has been built for the punishment of the sinners. When such a pleasure is now being felt here, the people wo'nt fear anything henceforth to commit sins. Why is this order of the Vedas created by God reversed? Why has God undone His own doing? What a wonder is this! Now a great miracle is before our sight." Thus speaking, they remained at a fix. They could not make out the cause of this. In the meanwhile Bhagavân Nârâyaṇa after consulting with the other Devas went with some Devas to the abode of

Śankara in Kailâsa. They saw there that Śrî Bhagavân S'ankara (with crescent of the Moon on His forehead) was playing there attended always by the Pramathas and adorned with various ornaments like a youth, sixteen years old. His parts of the body were very beautiful as if the mine of loveliness. He was conversing on various delightful subjects with His consort Pârvatî and pleasing Her mind. The four Vedas were there personified. Seeing Him, Nârâyana bowed down and informed him clearly of all the wonderful events. He said :—

61-75. "O Deva! What is the cause of all this? We cannot make out anything! O Lord! Thou art omniscient. Thou knowest everything. So kindly mention how is this brought about!" Hearing Viṣṇu's words, Bhagavân S'ankara spoke graciously in sweet words, grave as the rumbling of a rain-cloud: "O Viṣnu! Hear the cause of this. What wonder is there? This is all due to the greatness of Bhasma (ashes)! What cannot be brought about by Bhasma! The great S'aiva Durvâsâ went to see the Kumbhîpâka hell, besmearing his whole body with Bhasma and looked downwards while he was looking at the sinners. At that time, accidentally a particle of Bhasma from his forehead was blown by air to the bodies of the sinners in the hell. Thereby they were freed of their sins and they got so much pleasure! Such is the greatness of Bhasma! Henceforth the Kumbhîpâka will no more be a hell. It will be a Tîrtha (holy place of pilgrimage) of the residents of the Pitrilokas. Whoever will bathe there will be very happy. There is no doubt in this. Its name will be henceforth the Pitri Tîrtha.

O Sattama! My Lingam and the form of Bhagavatî ought to be placed there. The inhabitants of the Pitri Loka would worship them. This will be the best of all the Tîrthas extant in the three Lokas. And if the Pitris'varî there be worshipped, know that the worship of the Trilokî is done. Nârâyaṇa said :—Hearing thus the words of Śankara, the Deva of the Devas, He thanked Him and, taking His permission came to the Devas and informed them of everything what Śankara had said. Hearing this, the Devas nodded their heads and said "Sâdhu (well, very well))" and began to glorify the greatness of Bhasma. O Tormenter of the enemies! Hari, Brahmâ and the other Devas began to eulogise the glories of ashes. The Pitris became very glad to get a new Tîrtha. The Devas planted a S'iva Lingam and the form of the Devî on the banks of the new Tîrtha, and began to worship them regularly day by day. The sinners that were there suffering, all ascended on the celestial chariot and got up to Kailâsa. Even to-day they are all dwelling in Kailâsa and are known by the name of the Bhadras. The hell Kumbhîpâka came to be built afterwards in another place.

76-84. Since that day the Devas did not allow any other devotee of Śiva to go to the newly created hell Kumbhîpâka. Thus I have described to you the excellent greatness of the Bhasma. O Muni ! What more can there be than the glories of the Bhasma ! O Best of Munis ! Now I am telling you of the usage of Ûrdhapuṇḍra (the vertical marks) according to the proper province of the devotees. Listen. I will now speak what I have ascertained from the study of the Vaiṣṇava Śâstras, the measure of Ûrdhapuṇḍra, according to the Anguli measurements, the colour, mantra, Devatâ and the fruits thereof. Hear. The earth required is to be secured from the crests of hills, the banks of the rivers, the place of Śiva (Śiva Kṣettram), the ocean beaches, the ant-hill, or from the roots of the Tulasî plants. The earth is not to be had from any other places. The black coloured earth brings in peace, the red-colour earth brings in powers to bring another to one's control ; the yellow-coloured earth increases prosperity ; and the white-coloured earth gives Dharma (religion). If the Ûrdhapuṇḍra be drawn by the thumb, nourishment is obtained ; if it be drawn by the middle finger, longevity is increased ; if it be drawn by nameless or ring finger, food is obtained and if it be drawn by the fore finger, liberation is attained. So the Ûrdhapuṇḍras ought to be drawn by these fingers, only be careful to see that the nails do not touch at the time of making the mark. The shape of the Ûrdhapuṇḍra (the vertical mark or sign on the fore-head) is like a flame or like the opening bud of a lotus, or like the leaf of a bamboo, or like a fish, or like a tortoise or like a conch-shell.

85-95. The Ûrdhapuṇḍra, ten Angulis high is the super best ; nine Angulis high, is best ; eight Angulis high, is good ; the middling Ûrdhapuṇḍra is of three kinds as it is of seven Angulas, six Angulas, or five Angulas. The lowest Ûrdhapuṇḍra is again of three kinds as it is four Angulas, three Angulas or two Angulas high. On the Ûrdhapuṇḍra of the forehead, you must meditate Kes'ava, on the belly you must think of Nârâyaṇa ; on the heart, you must meditate on Mâdhava ; and on the neck, you must meditate on Govinda. So on the right side of the belly, you must meditate on Madhûsûdana ; on the roots of the ears, on Trivikrama ; on the left belly, on Vâmana ; on the arms, on Śrîdhara ; on the ears, Hriṣîkes'a ; on the back, Padmanâbha ; on the shoulders Dâmodara ; and on the head Brahmarandhra you must meditate on Vâsudeva Thus the twelve names are to be meditated. In the morning or in the evening time when you are going to make the Pûjâ or Homa, you are to take duly, single-in-intent, the above names and make the marks of Ûrdhapuṇḍras. Any man, with Ûrdhapuṇḍra on his head, is always pure, whether he be impure, or of unrighteous conduct or whether he commits a sin mentally. Wherever he dies, he comes to My Abode even if he be of a Chândâla caste. My devotees (Vîra Vaiṣṇavas or Mahâvîra Vaiṣṇavas) who know My Nature must keep an empty space between the two lines of Ûrdhapuṇḍra of the form of the Viṣṇupada (the feet of Viṣṇu) and those who are my best devotees are to use nice Ûrdhapuṇḍras, made of turmeric powder, of the size of a spear (Śûla), of the form of the feet of Viṣṇu (Viṣṇu padah).

96. The ordinary Vaiṣṇavas are to use with Bhakti, the Ûrdhapuṇḍras without any empty space, but the form of it is to be like a flame, the blosson of a lily or like a bamboo leaf.

97-110. Those who are Vaiṣṇavas in name only can use Ûrdhapuṇḍra of both the kinds, with or without any empty space. They incur no sin if they use one without an empty space. But those who are My good devotees, incur sin it they do not keep an empty space between the two vertical lines (in the Ûrdhapuṇḍra three vertical lines are used). The Vaiṣṇavas who use excellent vertical rod like Ûrdhapuṇḍras keeping an empty space in the middle and uttering the mantra "Kesvâya Namaḥ" build My Temple there. In the beautiful middle space of Ûrdhapuṇḍra, the Undecaying Viṣṇu is playing with Lakṣmî. That wretch, the twice-born who uses Ûndhapuṇḍra without any empty space kills Viṣṇu and Lakṣmî, seated there. The stupid who uses Ûrdhapuṇḍra without a vacant space goes successively to twenty-one hells. The Ûrdhapuṇḍra should be of the size of a clear straight rod, lotus, flame, a fish with sharp straight edges and with vacant spaces between them. O Great Muni ! The Brâhmaṇa should always use the Tripuṇḍra like the lock of hair on the crown of his head and like his Sacrifical tharead ; otherwise all his actions will be fruitless. Therefore in all ceremonies and actions the Brâhmaṇas ought to use Ûrdhapuṇḍras of the form of a trident, a circle or of a square form. The Brâhmaṇa who knows the Vedas is never to use the semi-moonlike mark (Tilak) on his head. The man who is of the Brâhmin caste and follows the path of the Vedas should not even by mistake use any other mark than those above-mentioned. Other sorts of puṇḍras (marks) that are mentioned in other Vaiṣṇava Śâstras for the attainment of fame, beauty, etc., the Veda-knowing Brâhmaṇas should not use them. The Vaidik Brâhmaṇas should not use even in error any other Tilaks than the curved Tripuṇḍras.

If, out of delusion, the man, following the path of the Vedas, uses other sorts of Tripuṇḍras, he would certainly go down to hell.

111-118. The Veda-knowing Brâhmaṇas would certainly go down to hell if they use other sorts of Tripuṇḍras on their bodies. Only the Tilakas, prescribed in the Vedas ought to be used by those who are devoted to the Vedas. Those who do not observe the duties of the Vedas would use Tilaks approved of by other Śâstras. Those should use marks approved of by the Vedas whose Deity is that of the Vedas. Those who follow the Tantra Śâstras different from the Vedas, should use marks approved of by the Tantras.

Mahâ Deva is the Veda's Deity—and, ready to deliver from the bondages of the world, He has prescribed the Tilakas prescibed in the Vedas for the benefit of the devotees. The marks prescribed by Viṣṇu, also a Deity of the Vedas, are also those of the Vedas. His other Avatâras also use marks approved of by the Vedas. The Tripuṇḍras and the besmearing of the body with ashes are according to the Vedas. In the Tantra S'astra different from the Vedas, there is the usage of Tripuṇḍra and other marks. But they are not to be used by the Vaidiks. No never.

Those who follow the path of the Vedas should use the curved Tripuṇḍras and Bhasma on their foreheads according to the rules prescribed in the Vedas.

He who has obtained the highest state of Nârâyaṇa *i. e.*, who has realised My Nature, ought to use always on their foreheads Śûla marks scented with fragrant sandalpaste.

Here ends the Fifteenth Chapter of the Eleventh Book on the rules of using the Tripuṇḍra and Ürdhapuṇḍra marks in the Mahâpurâṇam Śrî Mad Devî Bhâgavatam of 18,000 verses by Maharṣi Veda Vyâsa.

CHAPTER XVI.

1-24. Nârâyaṇa said:—Now I am speaking of the very holy Sandhyopâsanâ (method of Sandhyâ worship of Gâyatrî, the Presiding Deity of the morning, mid-day and evening, and of the twice-born. Listen. The greatness of using Bhasma has been described in detail. No further need be stated on the subject. I shall talk, first of all, of the morning Sandhyâ. The morning Sandhyâ is to be done early in the morning while the stars are visible. When the Sun is in the meridian, the mid-day Sandhyâ is to be performed; and while the Sun is visibly going down, the evening Sandhyâ is to be recited over. Now again, the distinctions are made in the above three Sandhyâs:—The morning Sandhyâ with stars seen is the best; with stars disappeared, middling; and with the Sun risen above the horizon-inferior. So the evening Sandhyâ, again, is of three kinds:—best, middling, and inferior. When the Sun is visibly disappearing, the evening Sandhyâ is the best; when the Sun has gone down the horizon, it is middling and when the stars are visible, it is inferior. The Brâhmaṇas are the root of the Tree, the Sandhyâ Vandanam; the Vedas are the branches; the religious actions are the leaves. Therefore its root should be carefully preserved. If the root be cut, no branches or leaves of the tree will remain. That Brâhmaṇa who knows not his Sandhyâ or who does not perform the Sandhyâs is a living Śûdra. That Brâhmana after his death verily becomes a dog. Therefore the Sandhyâs must be observed every day. Otherwise no right comes at all to do any action. At the sunrise and the sunset the time for Sandhyâ is two Daṇḍas (48 minutes) and if Sandhyâ be not done or rather neglected in the interval, the Prâyas'chitta (penance) is to be paid duly (performed duly). If the proper time for Sandhyâ expires, one more offering of Arghya is to be made in addition to the three Arghayas daily made; or the Gâyatri is to be repeated one hundred and eight times before the Sandhyâ is commenced. In whichever time any action ought to be done, worship, first of all, the Sandhyâ Devî, the Presiding Deity of that time and do the actions proper to that time afterwards. The Sandhyâ performed in dwelling houses is ordinary; the Sandhyâ done in enclosures of cows is middling and on the banks of the rivers is good and the Sandhyâ performed before the Devî's temple or the Devî's seat is very excellent. The Sandhyopâsanâ ought to be done before the Devî, because that is the worship of the very Devî. The three Sandhyâs done before the Devî give infinitely excellent fruits. There is no other work of the Brâhmaṇas better than this Sandhyâ. One can rather avoid worshipping Śiva or Viṣṇu; because that is not daily done as obligatory; but the Sandhyopâsanâ ought to be done daily. The Gâyatrî of the Great Devî is the Essence of all the mantras in the Vedas. In the Veda Śâstras, the worship of Gâyatrî is most definitely pronounced. Brahmâ and the other Devas meditate in the Sandhyâ times on this Devî Gâyatrî and make a japam of that. The Vedas always make japams of Her. For this reason the Gâyatrî has been mentioned as the object of worship by the Vedas. The Brâhmaṇas are called Śâktas inasmuch as they worship the Primal Śakti (Force) Gâyatri, the Mother of the Vedas. They are not Śaivas nor Vaiṣṇavas.

Firstly make the ordinary Âchaman three times, and, while inhaling, drink a little of the water of Âchaman, repeating "Om Kes'avâya Svâhâ, Om Nârâyaṇâya Svâhâ, Om Mâdhavâya Svâhâ. Then wash your two hands, repeating "Om Gobindâya Namah, Om Viṣṇave Namaḥ." Then by the root of the thumb rub the lips repeating "Om Madhû sûdanâya Namah, Om Trivikramâya Namaḥ." So rub the mouth, repeating "Om Vâmamâya Namaḥ, Om Śrîdharâya Namaḥ." Then sprinkle water on the left hand, saying "Om Hrisîkes'âya Namaḥ." Sprinkle water on the legs, saying Om Padmanâbhâya Namaḥ." Sprinkle water on the head, saying "Om Dâmodarâya Namaḥ." Touch the mouth with the three fingers of the right hand, saying "Om Samkarṣaṇâya Namaḥ." Touch the nostrils with the thumb and forefinger saying "Om Vâsudevâya Namaḥ, Om Pradyumnâya Namaḥ." Touch the eyes with the thumb and ringfinger, saying "Om Aniruddhâya Namaḥ, Om Puruṣottamâya Namaḥ. Touch the ears with the thumb and ringfinger saying "Om Adhokṣajâya Namaḥ, Om Nârasimhâya Namaḥ." Touch the navel with the thumb and little finger saying "Om Achyutâya Namaḥ." Touch the breast with the palm, saying "Om Janârdanâya Namaḥ." Touch the head saying "Om Upendrâya Namaḥ." Touch the roots of the two arms saying "Om Haraye Namaḥ, Om Kriṣṇâya Namaḥ."

25-50. While sipping the Âchaman water on the right hand, touch the right hand with your left hand; otherwise the water does not become pure. While doing Âchaman, make the palm and the fingers all united and close, of the form of a Gokarṇa (the ear of a cow) and spreading the thumb and the little finger, drink the water of the measure of a pea. If a greater or less quantity be sipped, then that would amount to drinking liquor. Then thinking of the Praṇava, make the Prâṇâyâma, and repeat mentally the Gâyatrî with her head and the Turîya pâda *i. e.* Âpojyotiḥ rasomritam Brahma Bhurbhuvah svarom. Inhale the air by the left nostril (Pûrak), close both the nostrils (kumbhak) and exhale the air, by the right nostril (rechak). Thus Prâṇâyâma is effected. While doing Pûrak, Kumbhak and Rechak repeat the Gâyatrî every time; hold the right nostrial with the right thumb and hold the left nostril with the ringfinger and little finger (*i. e.*, do'nt use forefinger and middle finger).

The Yogis who have controlled their minds say that Prâṇâyâma is effected by the three processes Pûraka, Kûmbhaka and Rechaka. The external air is inhaled in Pûraka; air is not exhaled nor inhaled (it is retained inside) in Kumbhaka; and air is exhaled in rechaka. While doing Pûraka, meditate, on the navel, the four-armed high-souled Viṣṇu, of the blue colour (Syâma) like the blue lotus. While doing Kumbhaka, meditate in the heart lotus the four-faced grandsire Brahmâ Prajâpati, the Creator seated on the lotus and while doing Rechaka meditate, on the forehead, on the white sindestroying Śankara, pure as crystal. In Pûraka, the union with Viṣṇu is obtained; in Kumbhaka, the knowledge of Brahmâ is attained and in Rechaka, the highest position of Îs'vara (Śiva) is attained. This is the method of Âchaman according to the Purâṇas. Now I am speaking of the all sin-destroying Vaidik Âchaman. Listen. Reciting the Gâyatri mantra "Om Bhurbhuvaḥ." Sip a little water; this is the Vaidik Âchaman after repeating the seven great Vyâhritis Om Bhuḥ; Om Bhuvaḥ, Om Svaḥ Om Mahaḥ, Om Janaḥ, Om Tapaḥ, Om Satyam, repeat Gâyatrî and the head of the Gâyatrî Âpojyoti Rasomritam Brahma Bhurbhuvaḥ svarom) and practise Prâṇâyâma three times. Hereby all sins are destroyed and all virtues spring Now another sort of Prâṇâyâma Mudrâis described :—The Vânaprasthîs and Grihasthas would do Prâṇâyâma with five fingers, holding the tip of the nose; the Brahmachâris and Yatis would do Prâṇâyâma with the thumbs, little finger, and ring finger (avoiding middle and fore). Now I am speaking of the Aghamarṣaṇa Mârjana mantra. Listen. The Mantra of this Mârjana is "Âpohiṣṭhâ Mayobhuvah, etc. There are three mantras in this. There are three Pâdas in every mantra, prefix Om to every pâdas (thus ninetimes Om is to be prefixed); at the end of every pâda sprinkle water on the head with the sacrificial thread and the Kus'a grass. Or at the end of every mantra do so. By the above Mârjana (cleaning) the sins of one hundred years are instantly destroyed. Then making Âchaman (taking a sip of water to rinse the mouth before worship), repeat the three Mantras "Om Suryas'cha mâ manyus'cha, etc. By this act, the mental sins are destroyed. As mârjana is done with Praṇava, Vyârhitis, and Gâyatrî, so make Mârjana by the three mantras "Âpohiṣṭhâ, etc." Make your right palm of the shape of a cow's ear; take water in it and carry it before your nose and think thus :—"There is a terrible sinful person in my left abdomen, his colour is dark black and he is horrible looking. Recite, then, the mantras "Om ritamcha satyamchâbhîdhyât, etc." and "Drupâdâdiva Mumuchâna, etc." and bring that Sinful Person through your right nostril to the water in the palm. Do'nt look at that water; throw it away on a bit of stone to your left. And think that you are now sinless. Next, rising from the seat, keep your two feet horizontal and with the fingers save forefinger and thumb, take a palmful of water and with your face towards the Sun, recite the Gâyatrî three times and offer water to the Sun three times. Thus, O Muni! The method of offering the Arghyas has been mentioned to you.

51-80. Then circumambulate, repeating the Sûrya Mantra. The one thing to be noted in offering Arghyas is this:—Offer once in the midday, and three times in the morning and three times in the evening. While offering the Arghya in the morning, bend yourself a litte low; in offering the arghya in the midday, stand up; and while offering the arghya in the evening, it can be done while sitting. Now I will tell you why the Arghya is offered to the Sun. Hear. Thirty Koṭi Râkṣasas known as the Mandehas, always roam on the path of the Sun (the mental Sun also). They are great heroes, treacherous and ferocious. They always try to devour the Sun, while they assume terrible forms. For this reason the Devas and the Riṣis combined offer the water with their folded hands to the Sun, while they perform the great Sandhyâ Upâsanâ. The water thus offered, becomes transformed into the thunderbolt and burns the heads of the cruel demons (and throws them on the island Mandehâruṇa) Therefore the Brâhmanas daily do their Sandhyopâsana. Infinite merits accrue from this Sandhyâ Upâsanâ. O Nârada! Now I am speaking to you of the Mantras pertaining to the Arghya. No sooner they are pronounced the full effects of performing the Sandhyâs are obtained. I am That Sun; I am That Light; I am That Âtman (Self); I am Śiva; I am the Light of Âtman; I am clear: and transparently white; I am of the nature of all energy; and I am of the nature of Rasa (the sweetness, all the sweet sentiments.) O Devî! O Gâyatrî! O Thou! Who art of the nature of Brahma! Let Thee come and preside in my heart to grant me success in this Japa Karma. O Devî! O Gâyatrî! Entering into my heart, go out again with this water. But Thou wouldst have to come again." Sit thus on a pure seat and with a single intent repeat the Gâyatrî, the Mother of the Vedas. O Muni! In this Sahdhyopâsanâ, the Khhecharî Mudrâ ought to be done after practising the Prâṇyâmâ. Hear now the meaning of the Khecharî Mudrâ. When the soul of a being leaves the objects of senses, it roams in the Âkâs'a *i. e*, it becomes aimless when the tongue also goes to the Âkâs'a and roams there; and then the sight is fixed between the eyebrows; this is called the Khhecharî Mudrâ. There is no Âsana (seat) equal to Siddhâsana and there is no Vâyu (air) equal to the Khumbaka Vâya (suspension of air in the body).

O Nârada! There is no Mudrâ equal to the Khecharî Mudrâ. One is to pronounce Praṇava in Pluta (protracted) accents like the sound of a bell and, suspending his breath, sit quiet motionless in Sthirâsana without any Ahamkâra (egoisin). O Nârada! I am now talking of

Siddhâsana and its characteristic qualities. Hear. Keep one heel below the root of the genital and the other heel below the scrotum ; keep the whole body and breast straight and motionless ; withdraw the senses from their objects and look at the point, the pituitary body, between the eyebrows. This posture is called the Siddhâsan and is pleasant to the yogis. After taking this seat, invoke the Gâyatrî " O Mother of the Vedas ! O Gâyatrî ! Thou art the Devî granting boons to the Bhaktas. Thou art of the nature of Brahma. Be gracious unto Me. O Devî ! Whoever worships Thee in the day gets his day sins destoyed and in the night, night sins destroyed O Thou ! Who art all the letters of the alphabet ! O Devî ! O Sandhye ! O Thou who art of the nature of Vidyâ ! O Sarasvatî ! O Ajaye ! O Thou immortal ! Free from disease and decay. O Mother ! Who art all the Devas ! I bow down to Thee. In voke the Devî again by the mantra " Ojosi, etc ," and then pray:—" O Mother ! Let my japam and other acts in Thy worship be fulfilled with success by Thy Grace." Next for the freedom of the curse of Gâyatrî, do the things properly. Brahmâ gave a curse to Gâyatrî ; Vis'vâmitra gave a curse to Her and Vas'iṣṭha also cursed Her. These are the three curses ; they are removed in due oder by recollecting Brahmâ, Vis'vâmitra and Vas'iṣṭha. Before doing Nyâsa, oneought to collect oneself and remember the Highest Self ; think in the lotus of the heart that Puruṣ a (Person) who is Truth, who is all this Universe, who is the Hghest Self and who is All knowledge and who cannot be comprehended bywords. Now I am speaking of the Amganyâsa of Sandhyâ; Hear. First utter Om and then utter the mantra.

Touch the two legs, saying " Om Bhuḥpâdâbhyâm namaḥ "
Touch the Knees, saying " Om Bhuva Jânubhyâm namaḥ "
Touch the hip, saying " Om Svaḥ Kaṭibhyâm namaḥ "
Touch the navel, saying " Om Maharnâbhyai namaḥ "
Touch the heart, saying " Om Janaḥ Hridayâya namaḥ "
Touch the throat, saying " Om Tapaḥ Kaṇṭhâya namaḥ "
Touch the forehead, saying " Om Satyam Lalâṭâya namaḥ "
Thus perform the Vyârhiti nyâsa.

Next perform the Karâmganyâsa thus :—Om Tat savituḥ ramguṣṭhâbhyâm namaḥ (referring to the thumb) ; " Om Vareṇyam Tarjanîbhyâm namaḥ " referring to the forefinger) ; Om bhargo devasya madhyamâ bhyâm namaḥ (referring to the middle finger) ; " Om Dhîmahi anâmikâbhyâm namah (referring to the ringfinger) ; Om dhîyo yonaḥ, Kaniṣṭhâbyâm namaḥ (referring to the little finger) ; " Om prachodayât kara tala priṣṭhâbhyâm namaḥ " referring to the upper part and lower part of the palm and all over the dody).

81-106. Now I am speaking of the Amganyâsa. Hear. " Om tat savitur brahmâ tmane hridayâya namaḥ " (referring to the heart.)

"Om Varenyam Vişņvâtmane Śirase namaḥ" (referring to the head); "Om bhargo devasya Rudrâtmane Śikhâyai namaḥ." (referring to the crown of the head); "Om dhîmahi Śaktyâtmane Kavachâya namaḥ" referring to the Kavacha; "Om dhîyoyonaḥ Kâlâtmane netratrayâya namaḥ" referring to the three eyes; "Om prachodayât sarvâtmane astrâya namaḥ" (referring to the Astra or armour, protecting the body.) Now I am speaking of the Varṇanyâsa. O Great Muni! Hear. This Varṇanyâsa is performed by the letters in the Gâyatrî mantra. If anybody does this, he becomes freed of sins.

"Om Tat namaḥ" on the two toes; (touching them).
"Om Sa namaḥ" on the two heels; (touching them).
"Om Vi namaḥ" on the legs;
"Om Tu namah" on the two knees;
"Om Va namaḥ" on the two thighs;
"Om re namaḥ" on the anus.
"Om ṇi namaḥ" on the generative organ;
"Om ya namaḥ" on the hip;
"Om bha namaḥ" on the navel;
"Om Rgo namaḥ" on the heart;
"Om De namaḥ" on the breasts;
"Om va namaḥ" on the heart;
"Om sya namaḥ" on the throat;
"Om dhî namaḥ" on the mouth;
"Om ma namaḥ" on the palate;
"Om hi namaḥ" on the tip of the nose;
"Om dhi namaḥ" on the two eyes;
"Om yo namaḥ" on the space between the eye-brows;
"Om yo namaḥ" on the forehead;
"Om naḥ namaḥ" to the east;
"Om pra namaḥ" to the south
"Om cho namaḥ" on the west;
"Om da namaḥ" on the north;
"Om yâ namaḥ" on the head;
"Om ta namaḥ" on the whole body from head to foot.

Some Jâpakas (those who do the Japam) do not approve of the above nyâsa. Thus the Nyâsa is to be done. Then meditate on the Gâyatrî or the World-Mother. The beauty of the body of the Gâyatrî Devî is like that of the full blown Javâ flower. She is seated on the big red lotus on the back of the Haṇsa (Flamingo); She is holding the red coloured garland on Her neck and anointed with red coloured ungument. She has four faces;

every face has two eyes. On her four hands are a wreath of flowers, a sacrificial ladle, a bead, and a Kamaṇḍalu. Sha is blazing with all sorts of ornaments. From the Devî Gâyatrî has originated first the Rig. veda. Brahmâ worships the virgin Gâyatrî on the idea of Śrî Parames'varî Gâyatrî has four feet; The Rig Veda is one; the Yajurveda is the second, the Sâmaveda is the third and the Atharva veda is the fourth foot. The Gâyatrî has eight bellies; the east side is the one; the south is the second; the west is the third; the north is the fourth; the zenith is the fifth; the nadir is the sixth; the intermediate space is the seventh and all the corners are the eighth belly. Gâyatrî has seven Śiras (heads); Vyâkaraṇam (Grammar) is one; Śikṣâ is the second (that Amga of the Veda, the science which teaches the proper pronunciation of words and laws of euphony); Kalpa is the third (the Vedânga which lays down the ritual and prescribes rules for ceremonial and sacrificial acts); Nirukta is the fourth (the Vedânga that contains glossarial explanation of obscu e words, especially those occurring in the Vedas); Jyotish or astronomy is the fifth; Itahâsa (history) and Purâṇas is the sixth head; and Upaniṣadas is the seventh head. Agni (fire) is the month of Gâyatrî; Rudra is the Śikhâ (the chief part); Her gotra (lineage) is Sâmkhyâyaṇa; Viṣṇu is the heart of Gâyatrî and Brahmâ is the armour of Gâyatrî. Think of this Mahes'varî Gâyatrî in the middle of the Solar Orb. Meditating on the Gâyatrî Devî as above, the devotee should shew the following twenty-four Mudrâs (signs by the fingers, etc., in religious worship) for the satisfaction of the Devî :—(1) Sanmukh; (2) Sampûṭ; (3) Vitata (4) Vistrita; (5) Dvimukha; (6) Trimukha; (7) Chaturmukha; (8) Panchamukha; (9) Ṣaṇmukha; (10) Adhomukha; (11) Vyâpaka; (12) Anjali; (13) Śakaṭa (14) Yamapâs'a; (15) fingers intertwined end to end; (16) Vilamba (17) Muṣṭika; (18) Matsya; (19) Kûrma; (20) Varâha; (21) Simhâkrânta; (22) Mahâkrânta; (23) Mudgara; (24) Pallava. Next make japam once only of one hundred syllabled Gâyatrî. Thus twenty-four syllabled Sâvitrî, " Jâtavedase sunavâma, etc. forty-four syllabled mantra; and the thirty two syllabled mantra " Tryamvakam Jajâmahe etc., These three mantras united make up one hundred lettered Gâyatrî. (The full context of the last Mantra is this :—Om Haum Om yum saḥ—Trayamvakam yajâmahe Sugandhim Puṣṭi Vardhanam. Urbbârukamiva bandhanân mrityo mûksiya mâ mritât Bhur Bhhuvaḥ. Svarom Yum Svaḥ Bhurbhuvah Svarom Haum Next make japam of Bhurbhuvah Svah, twenty four lettered Gâyatrî with Om. O Nârada! The Brâhmanas are to perform daily the Sandhyo pâsânâ repeating Gâyatri, completely adopting the rules above prescribed and then he will be able to enjoy completely pleasures, happiness and bliss.

Here ends the Sixteenth Chapter of the Eleventh Book on the description of Sandhyâ Upâsânâ in the Mahâpuram Śrî Mad Devi Bhâgvatam of 18,000 verses by Maharsi Veda Vyâsa.

CHAPTER XVII.

1-5. Nârâyaṇa said :—If one divides or separates the pâdas while reciting or making Japam of the Gâyatrî, one is freed from the Brâhmin icide, the sin of Brahmahatyâ. But if one does so without breaking the pâdas, *i.e.*, repeats at one breath, then one incurs the sin of Brahmahatyâ. Those Brâhmaṇas who do the Japam of the Gâyatri without giving due pause to the pâdas, suffer pains in hells with their heads downwards for one hundred Kalpas. (O Gâyatrî ! Thou art of one foot, of two feet, of three feet and of four feet. Thou art without foot, because Thou art not obtained. Salutation to Thy Fourth Foot beautiful and which is above the Trilokî (Rajas). This cannot obtain that. Firstly, Gâyatrî is of three kinds :—" Samputâ" ; " Ekomkârâ", and " Ṣaḍomkârâ." There is also the Gâyatrî, with five Praṇavas, according to the Dharma Śâstras and Purâṇas. There is something to be noted while muttering or making the japam of the Gâyatrî :—Note how many lettered Gâyatrî you are going to repeat (make japam). When you have repeated one-eighth of that, repeat (make japam) the Turîya pâda of Gâyatrî (*i.e*, the fourth Pâda, the mantram parorajase Sâvadomâ prâpat) etc., (see the daily practises, page 107.) once and then complete repeating the Gâyatrî. If the Brâhmaṇa makes the Japam (the silent muttering) in the above way he gets himself uninted with Brahma. Other modes of making the Japam do not bear any fruit. Om Gâyatryasye kapadî dvipapî Tripadî chatus padasi nahi padyase namaste Tûryâya dars'atâyapadâya paro Rajase Sâbado mâ prâpat. Gâyatrî is one-footed in the form of Trilokî, two-footed, the Trayî Vidyâ from thy second foot ; tripadî (all Prâṇas are thy third foot, chatuṣpadi, as the Puruṣa apadi without any foot, Parorajase above the Rajas, the dust ; asau-that ; adah this not prâpat may obtain. The Yogis who are Ûrdharetâs (hold Brahma charyam, continence) are to make Japam of the Samputâ Gâyatri (*i. e.*, with Om) Gâyatrî with one pranava and as well the Gâyatrî with six pranavas. The householder Brahmachârî or those who want mokṣa are to make Japam of Gâyatrî with Om prefixed.

6. Those householders who affix Om to the Gâyatrî do not get the increase of their families.

7-8. The Turîya pâda (foot) of Gâyatrî is the mantra "Parorajase Sâvodomâ prâpat". (Brihad. up. v. 14. 7). Salutation to Thy beautiful Fourth Foot which is above the Trilokî (Rajas). This cannot obtain that. The presiding deity of this mantra is Brahma. I am now speaking of the full Dhyânam (meditation) of this Brahma so that the full fruit of the Japam (recitation) may be obtained. There is a full blown lotus in the heart; its form is like the Moon, Sun, and the Spark of Fire; *i. e.*, of the nature of praṇava and nothing else. This is the seat of the inconceivable Brahma. Think thus. Now on that seat is seated well the steady constant subtle Light, the essence of Âkâs'a, the everlasting existence, intelligence and bliss, the Brahma. May He increase my happiness. (see page 107 the daily practice of the Hindus by R. B. Sris Chandra Basu, on the Invocation of the Gâyatrî).

Note.—Aum! Gâyatryasyekapadî dvipadî, tripadî, chatuṣpadasi, nahi padyase namaste turyâya dars'atâya padâya parorajase, sâvado mâprâpat O Gâyatrî! Thou art of one foot (in the form of Triloki), of two feet (the Trayî vidyâ from Thy second foot) of three feet (all Prâṇa, etc., are Thy third foot and of four feet (as the Puruṣa). Thou art without foot because Thou art not obtained. Salutation to Thy beautiful fourth foot which is above the Triloki (Rajas). This can not obtain that.

9. Now I am speaking of the Mudrâ of the Turîyâ Gâyatrî:—(1) Tris'ûla, (2) Yoni, (3) Surabhi, (4) Akṣamâlâ, (5) Linga, (6) Padma and (7) Mahâmudrâ. These seven Mudrâs are to be shewn.

10-14. What is Sandhyâ, that is Gâyatrî; there is no difference whatsoever between the two. The two are one and the same. Both are of the nature of Existence, Intelligence and Bliss. The Brâhmaṇas would daily worship Her and bow down before Her with greatest devotion and reverence. After the Dhyânam, first worship Her with five upachâras or offerings. Thus:—

Om lam prithivyâtmane gandham, arpayâmi namo namaḥ." "Om Ham âkâs'âtmane puṣpam arpayâmi namo namaḥ." "Om ram Vahnyâtmane dîpam arpayâmi namo namaḥ." "Aum vam amritâtmane naivedyam arpayâmi namo namaḥ." Om yam ram lam vam ham puṣpânjalim arpayâmi namo namaḥ." Thus worshipping with five upachâras, you must shew Mudrâs to the Devî.

15-16. Then meditate on the Form of the Gâyatrî mentally and slowly repeat the Gâyatrî. Do not shake head, neck and while making japam, do not shew your teeth. According to due rules repeat the Gâyatrî one hundred and eight times, or twenty-eight times. When unable, repeat ten times; not less than that.

17-20. Then raise the Gâyatrî placed before on the heart (seat) by the mantra "Gâyatrasyai kapadî Dvipadî, etc., and then bid farewell to Her after bowing down to Her and repeating the mantra "Omuttame Śikhare Devî bhûmyâm parvata mûrdhani Brâhmaṇa ebhyobhya anujnâtâ Gachcha Devî yathâsukham" (on the highest top of the mountain summit in earth (i. e. on the Meru mountain) dwells the goddess Gâyatrî. Being pleased with Thy worshippers go back, O Devî! to Thy abode as it pleaseth Thee." (See page 110, The Daily Practices of the Hindus.)

The wise men never mutter nor recite the Gâyatrî mantra within the water. For the Maharṣis say that the Gâyatrî is fire-faced (agnimukhî). After the farewell shew again the following mudrâs:— Surabhi Jñân, Sûrpa, Kûrma, Yoni, Padma, Linga and Nirvâna Mudrâs.

Then address thus:—"O Devî!" "O Thou who speakest pleasant to Kas'yapa" O Gâyatrî! Whatever syllables I have missed to utter in making Japam, whatever vowels and consonants are incorrectly pronounced, I ask Thy pardon for all my above faults." O Nârada! Next one ought to give peace offerings to the Gâyatrî Devî.

21-33. The Chchhanda of Gâyatrî Tarpaṇam (peace offerings to Gâyatrî) is Gâyatrî; the Riṣi is Vis'vâmitra; Savitâ is the Devatâ; its application (Niyoga) is in the peace offerings.

"Om Bhûḥrigvedapuruṣam tarpayâmi."
"Om Bhuvaḥ Yajurvedapuruṣam tarpayâmi."
"Om Svah Sâmaveda puruṣam tarpayâmi."
"Om Mahaḥ Atharvaveda puruṣam tarpayâmi."
"Om Janaḥ Itihâsapurâṇa puruṣam tarpayâmi."
"Om Tapaḥ Sarvâgama puruṣam tarpayâmi."
"Om Satyam Satyaloka puruṣam tarpayâmi."
"Om Bhûḥ bhûrloka puruṣam tarpayâmi."
"Om Bhubaḥ bhuvoloka puruṣam tarpayâmi."
"Om Svaḥ svarloka puruṣam tarpayâmi."
"Om Bhûḥ rekapadâm Gâyatrîm tarpayâmi."
"Om Bhuvo dvitîyapadâm Gâyatrîm tarpayâmi."
"Om Svastripadâm Gâyatrîm tarpayâmi."
"Om Bhûrbhûvah Svas'chatuspadâm Gâyatrîm tarpayâmi."

Pronouncing these, offer the Tarpaṇams. Next add the word Tarpayâmi to each of the following words "Ûṣasîra, Gâyatrîm, Sâvitrîm, Sarasvatîm Vedamâtaram, Prithvîm, Ajâm, Kaus'îkîm, Sâmkritîm, Savajitîm, etc.," and offer Tarpaṇams. After the Tarpanam is over, offer the peace-chantings, (Sântivâri) repeating the following mantras.

"Om Jâta vedase sunavâma somam, etc."

"Om Mânastoka, etc."

"Om Tryamvakam Yajâmahe, etc."

"Om Tachchhamyoh, etc."

Then touch all the parts of your bodies, repeating the two mantras "Om atodeva, etc." And reciting the mantram "Svonâ Prithivi," bow down to the earth, after repeating one's name, Gotra, etc.

34-45. O Nârada! Thus the rules of the morning Sandhyâ are prescribed. Doing works so far, bid farewell to the above-mentioned Gâyatrî. Next finishing the Agnihotra Homa sacrifice, worship the five Devatâs, Śivâ, Śiva, Ganes'a, Sûrya and Viṣṇu. Worship by the Puruṣa Sûkta mantra, or by Hrîm mantra, or by Vyahriti mantra or by Śrîschate Lakṣmîs'cha, etc.," place Bhavani in the centre; Viṣṇu in the north-east corner, Śiva in the south-east corner; Gaṇesa in the south-west corner, and the Sun in the north-west corner; and then worship them. While offering worship with the sixteen offerings, worship by repeating sixteen mantras. As there is no other act more merit-giving than the worship of the Devî, so the Devî should first of all be worshipped. Then worship in due order the five Devatâs placed in five positions. As the worship of the Devî is the chief object, so in the three Sandhyâs, the worship of the Sandhya Devî is approved of by the Śrutis. Never worship Viṣṇu with rice; Ganes'a with Tulasî leaves; the Devî Durga with Durba grass and Śiva with Ketakî flower. The under-mentioned flowers are pleasing to the Devî:—Mallikâ, Jâti, Kuṭaja, Panasa, Palâsa, Vakula, Lodha, Karavîra, Śiṇs'apa, Aparâjitâ, Bandhûka, Vaka, Madanta, Sindhuvâra, Palâs'a, Durbbâ, Śallakî, Mâdhavî, Arka, Mandâra, Ketakî, Karṇikâra, Kadamba, Lotus, Champaka, Yûthikâ, Ṭagara, etc.

46-47. Offer incenses Guggul, Dhûpa and the light of the Til oil and finish the worship. Then repeat the principal (mûla) mantra (make Japam). Thus finishing the work, study the Vedas in the second quarter of the next day; and in the third quarter of that day feed father, mother and other dependent relatives, with money earned by one's own self according to the traditions of one's family.

Here ends the Seventeenth Chapter of the Eleventh Book on the description of Sandhyâ and other daily practices in the Mahâpurâṇam Śrî Mad Devî Bhâgvatam of 18,000 verses by Maharṣi Veda Vyâsa.

CHAPTER. XVIII.

1. Nârada spoke:— " O Bhagavan ! I am now very eager to hear the special Pûjâ of Śrî Devî. The people get their desires fulfilled if they worship Her.

2-23. Nârâyaṇa said:—" O Devarṣi ! I shall now specially speak to you how the World Mother Bhagvatî is worshipped ; by worhipping Whom one easily gets objects of enjoyments, liberation and the destruction of all evils. Controlling one's speech and making Âchaman, one must make one's sankalap and perform Bhûtas'uddhi, Mâtrikânyâsa, ṣaḍanganyâsa, placing conchshell and doing other necessary acts. Offering the ordinary Arghya, one should give special Arghya and with the mantra " Astrâya Phaṭ sprinkle over all the articles brought for worship: Taking the Guru's permission, he is to go on with his Pûjâ. First worship the pîṭha or seat whereon the Devî would be placed ; then perform dhyân (meditation of the Devî.) Then with great devotion, offer to the Deva, the seats (Âsana) and other articles of worship ; then perform the bath of the Devî by the water of the Panchâmrita (the five nectars). If anybody performs the bath cerenony of Śrî Devî with one hundred jars of sugarcane juice, he will not have to incur any future birth.

He who performs this bath, and recites the Veda Mantras, with mango juice or sugarcane juice gets for ever Lakṣmî ever and ever and Sarasvatî bound at his doors. He who gets this sacred bath of the Devî with grape juice, along with his relatives and acquaintances dwells in the Devî-loka for as many years as there are atoms in the juice. He who bathes the Devî with the Vedic mantras, and with water scented with camphor, the fragrant aloe wood (aguru), saffron, and musk, becomes freed at once of the sins acquired in his hundred births. He who bathes the Devî with jars of milk, lives in the ocean of milk (kṣîra samudra) for one Kalpa. So he who does this bathing ceremony with jars of curd, becomes the lord of Dadhikuṇḍa (the reservoir of curd). He who performs the Snânams of the Devî with honey, ghee and sugar becomes the lord of these things. He who bathes the Devî with one thousand jars, becomes happy in this world as in the next. *Note* :—Make the liquid current flow pure in your body is the esoteric meaning of the bath. If you give Her a pair of silken clothes, you will go to the Vâyu-Loka. If you give Her the jewel ornaments, you will become the Lord of gems and jewels. (Make your mind like the gem.) If anybody gives saffron, sandalpaste, musk, Sindûra and Âlaktak (red things), he will go to the Heavens and become there the Indra, the Lord of the Devas, in the next birth. Various flowers ought to be offered in Śrî Bhagavatî's worship; or the flowers of the season offered to the Devî will lead the devotee to Kailâs'a. The devotee that offers the beautiful Bel leaves to the Devî never experiences anywhere pains and difficulties. The devotee who writes the Vîja mantra of Mâyâ "Hrîm Bhuvanes'varyai Namaḥ" with red sandalpaste thrice on the tri-leaves of the Vilva tree leaf and offers this to the lotus feet of the Devî, becomes Manu by the merit of this virtuous act! The devotee becomes the Lord of the whole universe who worships the Devî Bhagavatî with ten millions of entire Vilva leaves, fresh, green and spotless.

24-40. If any devotee worships with ten millions of entire fresh green Kuṇḍa flowers, with eight scents, he gets surely the Prajâpatihood. The worship of the Devî with ten millions of Mallikâ and Mâlatî flowers besmeared with eight scents makes a man the four faced (Brahmâ); and one hundred millions of such flowers will make the devotee a Viṣṇu. In days of yore, Viṣṇu worshipped the Devî in the aforesaid way and so got His Viṣṇuhood. If any devotee worships the Devî with one hundred Koṭis of Mallikâ or Mâlatî flowers, the man becomes certainly Sutrâtmâ Hiraṇyagarbha. In ancient days Hiraṇyagarbha worshipped thus the Devî with great devotion and so he became Hiraṇyagarbha! (These Hiraṇyagarbha, Brahmâ, Viṣṇu and Mahes'a were mere ordinary men before. See the Brihadâraṇyaka Upaniṣada). *Note.*—The eight scents refer to Jaṭâ mamsî Kapiyutâ Śaktergandhâṣ ṭakam! So will be the results if Javâ, Vandhûka and Dâḍimî flowers be offered in the worship. Various other beautiful flowers can be offered duly to the Devî by the devotee. The merits accruing from such offers are not known even to the God Îs'vara. The flowers that spring in their proper seasons are to be offered every year to the Devî, repeating Her thousand names enumerated in the Twelfth Book or in the Kurma Purâṇa. If the above worship be offered to the Devî, then that man, whether he be a sinner or a great sinner, will be freed from all the sins and after leaving his mortal coil, he will get, no doubt, the lotus feet of the Śrî Devî Bhagavatî. Offer Dhûpa made of black Aguru, camphor, sandalpaste, red sandalpaste, Sihlaka and Guggula, saturated with ghee in such a way as the whole room of Śrî Bhagavatî scents with pure fragrant smell. The Devî Bhagavatî becomes pleased with this and offers the lordship of the three Lokas to the devotee. The devotee, who offers daily the light of camphor to the Devî, goes to the Sûrya Loka. There is no doubt in this. With one's whole heart, one should give one hundred or one thousand lights to the Devî. The devotee should offer heaps of food consisting of six Rasas, the plates and dishes for chewing, sucking, licking and drinking, that is, all kinds of food solid, and liquid, mountain-like high. Always give food on golden flat plates and cups and various delicious sweet juicy nice heavenly fruits, nicely arranged on trays, cups and saucers. When Śrî MahÂdevî Bhuvane'svarî gets pleased, the whole universe gets pleased. For the whole Universe is all Devî; as a rope is mistaken for a snake, so this MahÂdevî is mistaken for the universe.

41-59. Offer a jar of drinking Ganges water, cool and nice, scented with camphor to the Devî; then offer betels with camphor, cardamum, cloves, and various delicious scents. These all are to be offered with great devotion so that the Devî may be pleased. Next have music with lovely mridangas, flutes, murajas, Dhabkâs and dundubhis and so please Her. The Veda mantras are to be recited, the Purâṇas are to be read and the hymns to be chanted. With whole head and heart offer to the Devî the umbrella and châmara, the two kingly offerings. Then circumambulate round Her and prostrate before Her and ask Her kindness and pray to Her to forgive all faults and shortcomings. The Devî is pleased with anybody who remembers Her even once! What wonder then that She will be pleased with all these offerings! The Mother is naturally merciful to her child. When She is loved with devotion, then She becomes very merciful. There is nothing strange here! On this point I will recite to you the history of Vrihadratha Râjarṣi. Hearing which gives rise to Bhakti and Love.

Once in a certain region in the Himâlayâs there lived a bird called Chakravâk. It flew over many countries and went once to Kâs'idhâm. As a fruit of his Prârabdha Karma, that bird, desirous to find some rice beans, voluntarily went like an orphan round about the temple of Śrî Annapûrṇâ Devî. There circumambulating round the Devî Bhagavatî the bird left the city Kâs'î, that grants liberation and flew away to another country. In time the bird left his body and went to Heavens. There he assumed a heavenly form of a youth and began to enjoy various pleasures. Thus he enjoyed for two Kalpas. Then he got back to the earth and took his birth as the best in the Kṣattriya family. He became celebrated as the King Vrihadratha in this world. That King was truthful, controlled his senses, and practised Śamyama and deep concentration and knew everything of the past, the present and the future. He conquered all the enemies and performed various sacrifices and became the Emperor of the sea-girt earth and acquired the very rare faculty in the knowledge of everything of his previous births. The Munis came to know of this from various rumours and came to the King. The King Vrihadratha duly entertained those guests. The Munis took their seats and asked:—"O King! We hear that all the events of previous births are vividly reflected in your memory. On this point great doubts have come upon us. Kindly describe in detail—By what Puṇyam (merits,) you have come to know all about previous births and the knowledge of the past, the present and the future. We have come to you to know how you got this wonderful supersensual knowledge. Kindly say to us sincerely everything about this and oblige.

60-71. Nârâyaṇa said:—" O Brahman! The very religious King Vrihadratha heard them and began to speak out all the secret causes for his knowledge of the past, the present and the future, thus:—"O Munis! Hear how I acquired this knowledge. In my previous birth I was a very low bird chakravâk. Once, out of my ignorance, I circumambulated round the temple of the Devî Bhagavatî Annapurṇâ at Kas'î. And, as the result of that, I lived in the Heavens for a period of two Kalpas and I have got this birth and I have got the knowlege of the past, the present and the future. O You of good vows! Who can ascertain what amount of merits accrues from remembering the Feet of the World-Mother. Remembering Her glories, I always shed tears of joy. Those who do not worship the adorable Deity Jagadambâ are the Great Sinners and they are treacherous. Fie on their births! The worship of Śiva or Viṣṇu is not eternal. Only the Jagadambâ's worship is eternal. Thus it is stated in the Śrutis. What more shall I speak on this worship of the World-Mother, which is void of the least trace of any doubt. Everyone ought to serve devotedly the lotus feet of the Devî Bhagavatî. There is no other act more glorious in this world than serving the feet of Jagadambâ. It is highly necessary to serve the Highest Deity, whether in Her Saguṇa, or in Her Nirguṇa aspect. (Eat the sugarcandy, holding it in any way. It makes no difference). Nârâyaṇa said:—Hearing the aforesaid words of the virtuous Râjarṣi Vrihadratha, the Munis went back to their respective abodes. Such is the power of the Devî Jagadambikâ! So who can question about the certainty of the high merits arising from the Jagadamvikâ's worship and who will not reply, when so questioned? Their births are really fruitful who possess faith in the Devî worship;

but of those who have no such faith, there is some wrong mixture, no doubt, in their births.

Here ends the Eighteenth Chapter of the Eleventh Book on the Greatness of the Devî Pûjâ in the Mahapurâṇam Śrî Mad Devî Bhâgavatam of 18,000 verses by Maharṣi Veda Vyâsa.

CHAPTER XIX.

1-24. Nârâyana said:—"O Nârada ! Now I am speaking of the auspicious mid day Sandhyâ, the practice of which leads to the wonderfully excellent results. Listen. Here the Âchamana and other things are similar to those of the morning Sandhyâ. Only in meditation (Dhyânam) there is some difference. I will now speak of that. The name of the midday Gâyatrî is Sâvitrî. She is ever a youthful maiden, of white colour, three-eyed ; She holds in Her one hand a rosary, in Her other hand a trident and with Her two other hands She makes signs to Her Bhaktas to dispel fear and to grant boons. Riding on the bull, She recites the Yayur Vedas ; She is the Rudra Śakti with Tamo guṇas and She resides in Brahmaloka. She daily traverses in the path of the Sun. She is Mâyâ Devî, beginningless ; I bow down to Her. After meditating on the Âdyâ Devî Bhagavati perform âchamanas and other things as in the morning Sandhyâ. Now, about the offering of Arghya (an offer of green grass, rice, etc., made in worshipping a God or Brahman). Collect flowers for Arghya ; in the absence of flowers, the Bael leaves and water will serve the purpose. Facing the Sun, and looking upwards, offer the Arghya to the Sun upwards. Then perform other acts as in the morning Sandhyâ. In midday, some offer Arghya to the Sun, only with the recitation of the Gâyatrî mantra. But that is not approved of by the tradition and community ; there is the likelihood of the whole work being thwarted or rendered fruitless. For, in the morning and evening Sandhyâs, the Râkṣashas named the Mandehâs become ready to devour the Sun. This is stated in the Śrutis. Therefore the midday offering of the Arghya is not for the destruction of the Daityas but for the satisfaction of the Devî; so with the mantra "Âkriṣṇena, etc.," the offering of Arghya can be effected ; and the reciting of the infallible Gâyatrî mantra is only to create disturbance in the shape of thwarting the action. So in the morning and evening, the Brâhmaṇa is to offer the Sûryârghya, repeating the Gâyatrî and Praṇava; and in the midday to offer flowers and water with the mantra "Âkriṣṇene, rajasâ etc , else it will go against the Śruti. In the absence of flowers, the Durba grass, etc., can be offered carefully as the Arghya; and the full fruits of the Sandhyâ will be secured. O Best of Devarṣis! Now hear the important points in the Tarpaṇam (peace offerings). Thus :—

"Om Bhuvaḥ puruṣam tarpayâmi namo namaḥ."
"Om Yajurvedam tarpayâmi namo namaḥ."
"Om Maṇḍalam tarpayâmi namo namaḥ."
"Om Hiraṇyagarbham tarpayâmi namo namaḥ."
"Om antarâtmânam tarapayâmi namo namaḥ."
"Om Sâvitrîm tarapayâmi namo namaḥ."
"Om Devamâtaram tarpayâmi namo namaḥ."
"Om Sâmkritim tarpayâmi namo namaḥ."
"Om Yuvatîm sandhyâm tarpayâmi namo namah."
"Om Rudrâṇîm tarpayâmi namo namaḥ."
"Om Nîmrijâm tarpayâmi namo namaḥ."
"Om Bhurbhuvaḥ Svaḥ puruṣam tarpayâmi namo namaḥ."

Thus finish the midday Sandhyâ nga Tarpaṇam." Now, with your hands raised high up towards the Sun, worship Him by the two mantras :—praising thus :—"Om Udutyam Jâtavedasam, etc.," "Om Chitram Devâṇâm, etc." Next repeat the Gâyatrî. Hear its method. In the morning, repeat the Gâyatrî at the proper moment with hands raised; in the evening time with hands lowered and in the midday with hands over the breast. Begin with the middle phalanx (joint) of the nameless finger, then the phalanx at its root, then the phalanx at the root of the little finger, its middle phalanx and its top, then the tops of the nameless, fore and ring fingers, then the middle and finally the root of the ring finger (in the direction of the hands of the watch; avoiding the middle and root phalanx of the middle finger). Thus ten times it is repeated. In this way if the Gâyatrî be repeated one thousand times, the sins arising from killing a cow, father, mother, from causing abortions, going to the wife of one's Guru, stealing a Brâhmaṇa's property, a Brâhmaṇ's field, drinking wine, etc., all are destroyed. Also the sins acquired in three births by mind, word, or by the enjoyments of sensual objects are thereby then and there instantly destroyed. All the labours of him, who works hard in the study of the Vedas without knowing the Gâyatrî, are useless. Therefore if you compare on the one hand the study of the four Vedas with the reciting of the Gâyatrî, then the Gayatrî Japam stands higher. Thus I have spoken to you of the rules of the mid-day Sandhyâ. Now I am speaking of Brahma Yajña. Hear.

Here ends the Nineteenth Chapter of the Eleventh Book on the midday Sandhyâ in the Mahâpuraṇâm Śrî Mad Devî Bhâgavatam of 18,000 verses by Maharṣi Veda Vyâsa.

CHAPTER XX.

1-25. The twice born (Brâhmaṇa) is firstly to sip three times (make Âchamana); then to make the mârjana (sprinkle water) twice; he is to touch the water by the right hand and sprinkle water on his two feet. Next, he is to sprinkle with water his head, eyes, nose, ears, heart, and head thoroughly. Then speaking out the Des'a and Kâla (place and time) he should commence the Brahma Yajña. Next for the destruction of all the sins and for getting liberation, he should have the Darbha (sacrificial grass, and the Kuśa grasses,) two on his right hand, three on his left hand, one grass each on his seat, sacrificial thread, his tuft, and his heels. No sin can now remain in his body.

"I am performing this Brahma Yajña for the satisfaction of the Devatâ according to the Sûtra" thus thinking, he is to repeat the Gâyatrî thrice. Then he is to recite the following mantras :—" Agnimîle purohitam, etc.," "Yadamgeti" "Agnirvai," "Mahâvratanchaiva panthâ," "Athâtaḥ Śamhitâyâs'cha vidâmaghavat," "Mahâvratasya," Îṣetvorjetvâ," Agna âyâhi" Śanno Devî rabbîṣṭaye," Tasya "Samâmnâyo" Briddhirâdaich" "Śikṣâm pravakṣyâmi," "Pañcha Samvatsareti," "Mayarasataja-bhetyeva," "Gaurgmâ," also he is to recite the two following Sûtras :—"Athâto Dharma Jijñâsâ," "Athâto Brahma Jijñâsâ." Next he is to recite the mantra Tachhamyoḥ" and also the mantra "Namo Brahmaṇe namo stvagnaye namaḥ prithivyai nama Oṣadhibhyoḥ namah". (These mantras are the famous mantras of the Rig Veda). Next perform the Deva-tarpaṇam, thus:—"Om Prajâpati stripyatu", "Om Brahmâ tripyatu", "Om Vedâs tripyantu," "Om Riṣayastri pyantu", "Om Devâstrip, antu," "Om Sarvaṇi chhandâmsi tripyantu", "Om Om Kâra stripyatu", "Om Vaṣaṭ Kâra stripyatu", "Om Vyârhitayas tripyantu", Om Sâvitrî tripyatu", "Om Gâyatrî tripyatu", Om Yajnâ stripyantu, Om Dyâvâ prithivyau tripyatâm. Om antarîkṣam tripyatu, Om Ahorâtrâni tripyantu, Om Sâmkkyâ stripyantu, Om Siddhâ stripyantu, Om Samudrâ stripyantu, Om Nadyâs tripyantu, Om girayas tripyantu, Om Ksettrauṣ adhivana spati gandharvâ Psarasas tripyantu, Om nâgâ vayâmsi gâvascha sâdhyâ viprâsta thaira cha, yakṣâ rakṣâṇsi bhutanî tyeva mantâni tripyantu. Next, suspending the sacrificial thread from the neck perform the Riṣi tarpaṇam, thus:—Om Śatarchinas tripyantu, Om mâdhyamâs tripyantu,

Om Gritsamada stripyatu, Om Vis'vâmitra stripyatu, Om Vâmadeva stripyatu, Om Atri stripyatu

Om Bharadvâjastripyatu.

Om Vas'iṣṭhastripyatu.

Om Pragâthastripyatu,— Pâvamânyastripyantu. Next, holding the sacrificial thread over the right shoulder and under the left arm, perform the Tarpaṇam, thus:—

Om Kṣudrasûktâ stripyantu.

Om Mahâsûktâstripyantu, Om Sanaka stripyatu.

Om Sananda stripyatu.

Om Sanâtana stripyatu.

Om Sanat Kumâra stripyatu.

Om Kapila stripyatu.

Om Âsuristripyatu.

Om Vohalistripyatu.

Om Pañchas'ikha stripyatu.

Om Sumantu Jaimini Vais'ampâyana Paila Sûtra Bhâṣya bhârata Mahâ Bhârata Dharmâchâryâh stripyantu.

Om Jânantîvâha vigârgya Gautama Śâkalya vâbhravya Mâṇḍavya Mâṇḍûkeyâ stripyantu.

Om Gârgî Vâchakṇavî tripyatu.

Om Vaḍavâ prâtitheyî tripyatu.

Om Sulabhâ maitreyî tripyatu.

Om Kahola stripyatu.

Om Kauṣîtaka stripyatu.

Om Mahâ Kauṣitaka stripyatu.

Om Bhâradvâja stripyatu.

Om Paimga stripyatu.

Om Mahâpaimga stripyatu.

Om Sujajña stripyatu.

Om Sâmkhyâyana stripyatu.

Om Aitareya stripyatu.

Om Mahaitareya stripyatu.

Om Vâṣkala stripyatu.

Om Sâkala stripyatu.

Om Sujâta vaktra stripyatu.

Om Audavâhi stripyatu.

Om Saujâmi stripyatu.

Om Śaunaka stripyatu,

Om Âs'valâyana stripyatu.

26-54. Let all the other Âchâryas be satisfied. Om Ye Ke châsmat kule Jâtâ aputrâ gotriṇo mritâḥ. te grihṇantu mayâ dattam vastraniṣpîḍi to dakam." Saying thus offer water squeezed out of a cloth. O Nârada! Thus I have spoken to you of the rules of Brahma Yajña. Whoever performs thus the Brahma Yajña gets the fruits of studying all the Vedas. Then performing, in due order, the Vais'va deva, Homa, Śrâddha, serving the guests, and feeding the cows, the devotee is to take his meals during the fifth part of the day along with the other Brâhmaṇas. Then the sixth and the seventh parts of the day he is to spend in reading histories and the Purâṇas. Then the eighth part of the day he is to devote in seeing the relatives, talking with them and receiving visits from other persons; then he will be prepared to perform the evening Sandhyâ. O Nârada! I am now talking of the evening Sandhyâ. Listen. Śrî Bhagavatî is pleased very quickly with him who performs the evening Sandhyâ. First make the Âchaman and make the Vâyu (air) in the body steady. With heart tranquilled and with the seat Baddha Padmâsana, be calm and quiet while engaged in performing the Sandhyâ. At the commencement of all actions prescribed in the Śrutis and Smritis, first perform the Sagarbha Prâṇâyma. In other words recite the mantra mentally for the due number of moments and make the Prâṇâyama. Simply meditating is called Agarbha Prâṇâyama. Here no mantra is necessary to be recited. Then have the Bhutas'uddhi (have the purifications of the elements) and make the Sankalap. First of all, the purification of elements, etc., are to be done first; one becomes, then, entitled to do other actions. While doing Pûraka (inhaling), Kumbhaka (retaining) and Rechaka (exhaling) in Prâṇâyâma, meditate on the Deity stated duly. In the evening time meditate on the Bhagavatî Sandhyâ Devî thus:—The name of the then Gâyatrî Devî is Sarasvatî. She is old, of black colour, wearing ordinary clothes; in her hands are seen conch shell, disc, club and lotus. On Her feet the anklets are making sweet tinkling sounds; on Her loins there is the golden thread; decked with various ornaments. She is sitting on Garuḍa. On Her head the invaluable jewel crown is seen; on Her neck, the necklaces of stars; Her forehead is shining with a brilliant lustre emitting from the pearl and jewel Tâtamka ornaments. She has put on yellow clothes; Her nature is eternal knowledge and ever-bliss. She is uttering Sâma Veda. She resides in the Heavens and daily She goes in the path of the Sun. I invoke the Devî from the Solar Orb. O Nârada! Meditate on the Devî thus and perform the Sandhyâ. Then perform the Mârjanam by the mantra "Âpohiṣṭhâ and next by the mantra

"Agnis'cha mâ manyus'cha." The remaining actions are the same as before. Next, repeat the Gâyatrî and offer, with a pure heart, the offering of Arghya to the Sun for the satisfaction of Nârâyaṇa. While offering this Arghya, keep the two legs level and similar and take water in folded palms and meditating on the Devatâ within the Solar Orb, throw it towards Him. The fool that offers Sûryârghya in the water, out of ignorance, disregarding the injunctions of the Śrutis, will have to perform Prâyas'chitta for that sin. Next, worship the Sun by the Sûrya mantra. Then taking one's seat, meditate on the Devî and repeat the Gâyatrî. One thousand times or five hundred times the Gâyatrî is to be repeated. The worship, etc., in the evening is the same as in the morning. Now I am speaking of the Tarpaṇam in the Evening Sandhyâ. Hear. Vas'iṣṭha is the Riṣi of the aforesaid Sarasvatî. Viṣṇu in the form of Sarasvatî is the Devatâ; Gâyatrî is the Chhanda; its application is in the Evening Sandhyâ Tarpaṇam. Now the Tarpaṇam of the Sandhyânga (the adjunct of Sandhyâ) runs as follows:—

"Om Svaḥ Puruṣam Tarpayâmi."
"Om Sâmavedam tarpayâmi."
"Om Sûryamaṇḍalam tarpayâmi."
"Om Hiraṇyagarbham tarpayâmi."
"Om Paramâtmânam tarpayâmi."
"Om Sarasvatîm tarpayâmi."
"Om Devamâtaram tarpayâmi."
"Om Samkritim tarpayâmi."
"Om Vriddhâm Sandhyâm tarpayâmi."
"Om Viṣṇu rûpinîm Uṣasîm tarpayâmi."
"Om Nirmrijîm tarpayâmi."
"Om Sarvasiddhi kâriṇîm tarpayâmi."
"Om Sarvamantrâ dhipatikâm tarpayâmi."
"Om Bhurbhuvaḥ Svaḥ Puruṣam tarpayâmi."

Thus perform the Vaidik Tarpaṇam. O Nârada! Thus have been described the rules of the sin destroying evening Sandhyâ. By this evening Sandhyâ, all sorts of pains and afflictions and diseases are removed. And ultimately the Mokṣa is obtained. What more than this that you should know this Sandhyâ Bandanam as the principal thing amongst the good conduct and right ways of living. Therefore Śrî Bhagavatî fructifies all the desires of the Bhaktas who perform this Sandhyâ Vandanam.

Here ends the Twentieth Chapter of the Eleventh Book on the description of Brahma Yajña, Sandhyâs, etc., in the Mahâpurânam Śrî Mad Devî Bhâgavatam of 18,000 verses by Maharṣi Veda Vyâsa.

CHAPTER XXI.

1-55. Nârâyaṇa said:—Now I shall speak of the Gâyatrî-puras'charaṇam. Hear. By its performance all the desires are obtained and all the sins are destroyed. On the tops of mountains, on the banks of the rivers, on the roots of Bel trees, on the edges of tanks, within the enclosures of the cows (cow-stalls), in temples, on the root of As'vattha trees, in gardens, in the Tulasî groves, in the Puṇya Kṣetrams (holy places), before one's Guru, or wherever the mind feels exalted and cheerful, and gets strength, the Puras'charaṇamse if performed, lead to a speedy success. Before commencing, the Puras'charaṇam of a mantra (the Puras'charaṇam means repetition of the name of a deity or of a mantra attended with burnt offerings, oblations, etc.,) first Prâyas'chitta (penance) is done in the shape of repeating one million times the Gâyatrî with the Vyârhitis. In any Vaidic Karma or in making Puras'charaṇam of the mantra of the Devatâs Nrisiṇha, Sûrya, Varâha, etc., the first thing done is to repeat the Gâyatrî. Without the japam of Gâyatrî, no action is attended with success. The reason is this:—Every Brâhmaṇa is a Sâkta (a follower of Śakti); he cannot be a Vaiṣṇava or Śaiva; for he is the worshipper of the Prime Force Vedamâtâ Gâyatrî. Therefore obtain first the Grace of one's own Iṣṭa Devatâ Gâyatrî by Her Japam. Then worship the other Deities.

Thus one should purify one's jâpya mantra (the mantra that is to be repeated) by first repeating one million times the Gâyatrî; then one is to commence Puras'charaṇam. Again before purifying the mantra, one is to purify one's Âtman (Self). In this purification of one's Âtman three lakh times, in case of inability, one lakh times Gâyatrî is to be repeated Without one's Âtman's purification, the Japam, Homa and other actions all become useless. This is specially noted in the Vedas. By Tapas (e. g. Japam, Chândrâyaṇa and Vrata, (asceticism) mortify your body. By offering Tarpaṇam (peace-offerings) to the Fathers and the Devas, one can get self purification. If you want to get the Heavens and if you want to become great, practise Tapasyâ. There is no other way. (Tapasyâ is the intent calling of the Mother, That Call which penetrates through and through the

Brahmâṇḍa. The Kṣattriyas should cross difficulties and dangers by force of arms; the Vais'yas, by wealth; the Sûdras, by serving the twice born; and the Brâhmaṇas should cross difficulties and dangers, by Tapasyâ, Homa, Japam, etc. So the Brâhmanas should always be cheerful and in prompt readiness to do Tapasyâ. Of all sorts of tapasyâs, mortifying the body by observing vows and fastings is the best. So say the Riṣis. (This mortification of the body gives self-reliance and self intuition more surely and speedily than all the other studies and other practices.) The Brâhmaṇas should purify themselves by following duly Krichhra Chândrâyaṇa vratas, etc,. O Nârada! Now I am speaking of the purification of food. Hear. The following four occupations of the Brâhmanas are the best:—Ayâchita, (without begging or asking for anything), Unchha, (the gathering in of handfuls of the corn left by the reapers), Śukla (the maintenance derived by a Brâhmaṇa from other Brâhmaṇas; a pure mode of life). And Bhikṣû (begging). Whether according to the Tantras or according to the Vedas, the food obtained by the above four means is pure. What is earned by Bhikṣâ (begging) is divided into four parts:—one part is given to the Brâhmaṇas; the second part is given to the cows; the third part is given to the guests, the fourth part is to be taken by him and his wife. Whatever is fixed for taking (swallowing) mouthfuls of food, that is to be taken on a tray or a platter. First throw a little cow-urine over that and count duly the number of mouthfuls. The mouthfuls are to be of the size of an egg; the householders are to take eight such mouthfuls and the Vânaprasthîs are to take four such mouthfuls. The Brahmachârins can sprinkle their food with cow-urine nine times, six times, or three times as they like; while sprinkling, the fingers are to remain intact. The Gâyatrî is to be repeated also. The food offered by a thief, Chândâla, Kṣattriya or Vais'ya is very inferior. The food of a Śûdra, or the companion with a Śûdra or taking food in the same line with a Śûdra leads one to suffer in the terrible hells as long as there are the Sun and Moon. The Puras'charaṇam of Gâyatrî is repeating this twenty four lakh times (i. e. as many lakh times as there are syllables in the Gâyatrî). But, according to Vis'vâmitra, repeating thirty two lakh times is the Puras'charaṇam of Gâyatrî. As the body becomes useless when the soul leaves the body, so the mantra without Puras'charaṇam is useless. The Puras'charṇam is prohibited in the months of Jyaiṣṭha, Âṣâḍha, Pauṣa and Mala (dirty) months. Also on Tuesday, Saturday; in the Vyatîpâta and Vaidhriti Yogas; also in Aṣṭamî (eighth), Navamî (ninth), Ṣaṣṭhî (sixth), Chaturthî (fourth) Trayodos'i (thirteenth), Chaturdasî (fourteenth) and Amâvâsyâ (New Moon), Tithis (lunar days); in the evening twilight and in the night); while the star Bharaṇi, Krittikâ, Ârdrâ, As'leṣâ, Jyeṣṭhâ, Dhaniṣṭhâ, Śravaṇâ, or the Janma nakṣatra (Birth time star) is with the Moon; while the signs Meṣa, Karkaṭa, Tulâ, Kumbha, and Makara are the Lagnas (signs in the ascendant). When the moon and the stars are auspicious, especially in the bright fortnight, the Puras'charaṇam performed, gives the Mantra Siddhi. First of all repeat Svasti vâchan and perform duly the Nândi mukha Śraddha and give food and clothing to the Brâhmaṇas. Take the permission of the Brâhmaṇas and begin the Puras'charaṇam. Where the Śiva Lingam exists, facing west, or in any Śiva temple, commence repeating the mantra. The other Śiva Kṣettrams are :—Kas'i, Kedâra, Mahâ Kâla, Śrî Kṣettra, and Tryamvakam. These five are the Great Kṣettrams, known widely on this earth, for the fructification and the siddhis of the Mantras. At all other places than these, the Kurma Chakra is to be drawn according to the principles of the Tantra. And then they will be fit for Puras'charaṇam. The number of times that the Puras'charaṇam (the repeating of the mantra) is done on the first day, the same number is to be continued every day until completion; not greater nor less than that and also no intermission or stoppage should occur in the interval.

The repeating of the Mantra is to be commenced in the morning and should be done up to mid-day. While doing this, the mind is to be kept free from other subjects, and it is to be kept pure; one is to meditate on one's own Deity and on the meaning of the mantra and one should be particularly careful that no inaccuracies nor omissions should occur in the Gâyatri, Chhandas and in the repetition of the Mantra. One tenth of the total number of Puras'charaṇams that are repeated is to be used for the Homa purpose. The Charu is to be prepared with ghee, til, the Bel leaves, flowers, java grain, honey and sugar; all mixed, are to be offered as oblations to the fire in the Homa. Then the success in the Mantra comes, (*i. e.*, mantra siddhi is obtained or the Mantra becomes manifested). After the Puras'charaṇam one should do properly the daily and occasional dutis and worship the Gâyatrî that brings in dharma, wealth, objects of desire and liberation. There is nothing superior an object of worship to this Gâyatrî, whether in this world or in the next. The devotee, engaged in the Puras'charaṇam, should eat moderately, observe silence, bathe thrice in the three Sandhyâ times, should be engaged in worshipping one's Deity, should not be unmindful and should not do any other work. He is to remain, while in water, to repeat the Gâyatri three lakhs of times. In case the devotee repeats the mantra for achieving success in any other desired work (kâmya karma), then he should willingly stick to it until the desired success is attained. Now is being told how to get success in ordinary Kâmya karmas. When the sun is rising, repeat the Puras'charaṇam mantra daily thousand times. Then one's life will be lengthened, no disease will occur, and wealth and prosperity will be obtained. If it be done this way, success is surely attained within three months, six months or at the end of one year. If the Homa (offering oblations to the fire) be offered one lakh times with lotuses besmeared with ghee (clarified butter), Mokṣa (liberation) is attained. If, before the Mantra-Siddhi, or the success in realising the Mantra, is attained, one performs Japam or Homam for Kâmya Siddhi (to get certain desires) or mokṣa, then all his actions become useless. If any body performs twenty-five lakh Homas by curd and milk, he gets success (Siddhi) in this very birth. So all the Maharṣis say. By this the same result is attained that is got by the aforesaid means, (*i. e.* by the eight-limbed Yoga, whereby the Yogîs become perfect.

He will attain Siddhi if he be devoted to his Guru and keep himself under restraint for six months only (*i. e.* practise Samyama) as regards taking food etc., whether he be incapable or his mind be attached to other sensual objects. One should drink Pañcha gavya (cow-urine, cow-dung, milk, curd, ghee) one day, fast one-day, take Brâhmaṇa's food one day and be mindful in repeating the Gâyatrî. First bathe in the Ganges or in other sacred places and while in water repeat one hundred Gâyatrîs. If one drinks water on which one hundred Gâyatrîs are repeated, one is freed from all one's sins. He gets the fruit of performing the Krichhra vrata, the Chândrâyaṇa vrata and others. Be he a Ks'attriya King, or a Brâhmaṇa, if he is to remain in his own house, hold Âs'rama and be engaged in performing Tapasyâ then he will be certainly freed of all his sins. Be he a house holder or a Brahmachârî or Vânaprasthî, he should perform sacrifices, etc., according to his Adhikâra (or his rights) and he will get fruits according to his desires. The Sâgnik man (who keeps the Holy Fire) and other persons of good conduct and of learning and of good education should perform actions as prescribed in the Vedas and Smritis with a desire to attain Mokṣa. Thus one should eat fruits and vegetables and water or take eight mouthfuls of Bhikṣânna (the food got by begging). If the Puras'charaṇam be performed this way, then the Mantra Siddhi is obtained. O Nârada ! If the Puras'charaṇam be done with the mantra thus, his poverty is removed entirely. What more shall I say than this that if any body hears this simply, his merits get increased and he attains great success.

Here ends the Twenty First Chapter of the Eleventh Book on Gâyatrî Puras'charaṇam in the Mahâpurâṇam Śrî Mad Devî Bhâga vatam of 18,000 verses by Maharṣi Veda Vyâsa.

CHAPTER XXII.

1-45. Nârâyana said :—"O Nârada! In connection with this Puras'charaṇam it comes now to my memory about the rules concerning the Vais'va Deva worship. Hear. * (An offering made to the Vis'vadevâs; an offering to all deities (made by presenting oblations to fire before meals). The five yajñas are the following :—(1) The Devayajña, (2) Brahma yajña, (3) Bhuta yajña, (4) Pitri yajña, and (5) Manuṣya yajña. Fireplace, the pair of stone pestles, brooms (for sweeping, etc.), sieves and other house-hold things of the sort, wooden mortars (used for cleansing grains from husk) and water-jars, these five are the sources of evils inasmuch as they are the means of killing. So to free one's self from the above sins, one is to sacrifice before the Vais'vadeva. Never offer oblations of Vais'vadeva on hearths, on any iron vessel, on the ground or on broken tiles. They are to be offered in any sacrificial pit (Kuṇḍa) or on any sacrificial altar. Do not fire the hearth by fanning with hands, with winnowing baskets, or with holy deer skin, etc., but you can do so by blowing by your mouth. For the mouth is the origin of fire. If the fire be ignited by clothes, one is liable to get desease; if by winnowing baskets, then less of wealth comes; if by hands, one's death ensues. But if it be done by blowing, then one's success comes. (There is the danger of catching fire.)

One should sacrifice with curd, ghee fruits, roots and vegetables, and water and in their absence with fuel, grass, etc., or with any other substances soaked with ghee, curd, Pâyasa or lastly with water. But never with oil or with salty substances. If one performs the Homa with dry or stale substances, one is attacked with leprosy; if any body performs Homa with leavings of other food he becomes subdued by his enemy; if one does so with rude and harsh substances, he becomes poor and if one does with salty substances, he meets with a downward course, gets degraded in position and honour. You can offer oblations to Vais'vadeva with burning coals and ashes from the north side of the fire of the hearth after the preparation of the meals. But you should never offer sacrifices with salty things. The illiterate Brâhmaṇa who eats before offering oblations to Vais'va-Deva goes headlong downwards into the Kâla Sûtra hell. Whatever food that you are intending to prepare, whether they be vegetables, leaves, roots or fruits, offer oblations to Vais'vadeva with that. If, before the Homa be performed of Vais'vadeva, any Brâhmachârî comes, then take off, for the Homa, first something; and then give to the beggar and satisfy him and tell him to be off. For the Brahmachârî mendicant can remove any defects that may occur to Vais'vadeva but Vais'vadeva is unable to remove any defects that may occur regarding the mendicant Brahmachârî. Both the Paramahansa or Brahmachârî mendicant are the masters of the prepared food (Pakkânna); so when any body takes one's food without giving to any of these two, if they happen to come there, he will have to make the Châṇdrâyaṇa (religious or expiatory penance regulated by the moon's age, that is, waxing or waning). O Nârada! After the offering given to Vais'vanara, one is to offer Go-grâsa, that is, mouthfuls of food to the cows. Hear now how that is done. The mother Surabhi, the beloved of Viṣṇu, is always stationed in the region of Viṣṇu (Viṣṇu-pada); so O Surabhi! I am offering you mouthfuls of food. Accept it. "Salutation to the cows" saying this, one is to worship the cows and offer food to them. Hereby Surabhi, the Mother of the cows, becomes pleased. After this, one is to wait outside for a period that is taken to milch a cow, whether any guests are coming. For if any guest goes back disappointed from any house without any food, he takes away all the puṇyams (merits) of the house-holder and gives him back his own sin. The house-holder is to support mother, father, Guru, brother, son, servants, dependants, guests, those that have come, and Agni (Fire). Knowing all these, he who does not perform the functions of the house-hold is reckoned as fallen from his Dharma both in this world and in the next. The poor house-holder gets the same fruit by performing these five Mahâ jajñas that a rich Brâhmaṇa gets by performing the Soma Yajña. O Best of the Munis! Now I am talking of the Prânâgni Hotra or about taking food, knowing the rules of which makes a man free from birth, old age and death and from all sorts of sins. He who takes his food according to proper rules, is freed of the threefold debts, delivers his twentyone generations from the hells, obtains the fruits of all the Yajñas and goes unhampered to all the regions of the righteous. Think of the belly as Araṇi or the piece of wood for kindling the fire (by attrition), think of the mind as the churning rod, and think of the wind as the rope, and then kindle the fire, residing in the belly: the eyes are to be considered as the sacrificer, (the

A'ddharyu), and consider fire in the belly as the result of churning. In this fire of the belly, one is to offer oblations for the satisfaction of Prâna, etc., the five deities. First of all offer oblations to the Prâna Vâyu with food taken by the forefinger, middlefinger and thumb; next offer oblations to the Apâna Vâyu with the thumb, middlefinger and the nameles (anâmâ) finger; next offer oblations to the Vyâna Vâyu (breath) with the thumb, nameless finger and the little finger; next offer oblations to the Udâna Vâyu with the thumb, forefinger and the little finger and lastly offer oblations to the Samâna Vâyu with food taken by all the fingers. At the same time repeat respectively the mantras:—

"Om Prâṇâya Svâhâ,"
"Om Apânâya Svâhâ,"
"Om Samânâya Svâhâ,"
"Om Udânâya Svâhâ,"
"Om Vyânâya Svâhâ,"

Within the mouth, there is the Âhavanîya fire; within the heart, there is the Gârhapatya fire; in the navel, there is the Dhakṣiṇâgni fire; below the navel, there is the Sabhyâgni fire and below that there is the Âvasathyâgni fire. Think thus. Next consider the Speech as the Hotâ, the Prâṇa as the Udgâthâ, the eyes as the Addharyu, the mind as the Brahmâ, the ears as the Hotâ and the keeper of the Agni, the Ahamkâra (egoism) as beast (Pas'u), Om Kâra as water, the Buddhi (intellect) of the house-holder as the legal wife, the heart as the sacrificial altar, the hairs and pores as the Kus'a grass, and the two hands as the sacrificial ladles and spoons (Sruk and Sruva.) Then think of the colour of the Prâṇa mantra as golden the fire of hunger as the Riṣi (seer), Sûrya (the sun) as Devatâ, the chhandas as Gâyatrî and Prânâya Svâhâ as the Mantra uttered; also repeat "Idamâdityadevâya namaḥ" and offer oblations to the Prâṇa. The colour of the Apâna mantra is milkwhite. Śraddhâgni is the Riṣi, the Moon is the Devatâ, Uṣṇik is the chhandas, and "Apânâya Svâhâ," "Idam Somâya na namah" are the mantras. The colour of the Vyâna mantra is red like red lotuses; the fire Deity Hutâsana is the Riṣi, the fire is the Devatâ; Anuṣṭup is the chhandas, "Vyânâya Svâhâ and Idamagnaye na namah" are the mantras. The colour of the Udâna mantra is like that of the worm Indra Gopa; fire is the Riṣi; Vâyu is the Devatâ, Brihatî is the chhandas; "Udânâya Svâhâ" and "Idam Vâyave na namah" are the mantras. The colour of the Samâna mantra is like lightning; Agni is the Riṣi; Parjanya (the rains, water) is the Devatâ; Paukti is the chhanda; "Samânâya

Svâhâ" and "Idam Parjanyâya na namaḥ" are the mantras. O Nârada! Thus offering the five oblations to the five breaths, next offer oblations to the Âtman; the Bhiṣaṇa Vahṇi is the Riṣi; the Gâyatrî is the chhanda; the Self is the Devatâ; "Âtmane Svâhâ," and "Idamâtmane na namaḥ" are the mantras. O Nârada! He who knows this Homa of Prâṇâgnihotra attains the state of Brahma. Thus I have spoken to you in brief the rules of the Prâṇâgni hotra Homa.

Here ends the Twenty-Second Chapter of the Eleventh Book on the rules of Vais'vadeva in the Mahâpurâṇam Śrî Mad Devî Bhâgavatam of 18,000 verses by Maharṣi Veda Vyâsa.

CHAPTER XXIII.

1-20. Nârâyana said:—"The best Sâdhaka, then uttering after his meals, the mantra "Amritâpidhânamasi. "O Water-nectar! Let Thou be the covering to the food that I have taken), should make Âchaman (sip one Gaṇḍuṣa water) and distribute the remnant food (the leavings) to those who take the leavings. "Let the servants and maid-servants of our family that expect the leavings of food be satisfied with what leavings I give to them'' "Let those inhabitants of the Raurava hell or other unholy places who have remained there for a Padma or Arbuda years and want to drink water, be satisfied with this water that I offer to them and let this water bring unending happiness to them". Repeating the above two mantras let the house-holder distribute the leavings of food to the servants and the water to those who want water respectively. Then opening the knot of the Pavitra (a ring of Kus'a grass worn on the fourth finger on certain religious occasions), let him throw this on the square maṇḍalam on the ground. The Brâhmaṇa that throws this Kus'a grass on the vessel (Pâtra) is said to defile the row of Brâhmaṇas, taking their food. The Brâhmaṇa that has not yet washed his face after taking the food, on touching another such Brâhmaṇa or a dog or a Śûdra, should fast one day and then drink Pañchagabya and thus purify himself. And in case the Uchchiṣṭa Brâhmin (who has not washed his mouth and hands after meals) be touched by another Brâhmin, (who is not Uchchiṣṭa, then simply bathing will purify him. By offering this Ekâhuti (oblation once) according to rules mentioned above, one obtains the fruit of performing ten million sacrifices; and by offering this oblation five times one gets the endless fruit of performing fifty million sacrifices, and if one feeds such a man who knows well how to do this Prâṇâgnihoma, then he as well as he whom he feeds both derive full benefits and they ultimately go to heaven. The Brâhmaṇa acquires while taking each of his mouthful of food the fruit of eating Pañchagavya, who takes his food duly with the holy Pavitra Kus'a grass tied on his finger. During the three times of worship, the devotee is to do his daily Japam, Tarpaṇam and Homa and he should feed the Brâhmins. Thus the five limbed Puras'charaṇa is completely done. The religious man should sleep on a low bedding (lie on the ground); he is to control his senses and anger; he is to eat moderately, the things that are light, sweet and good; he is to be humble, peaceful and calm. He is to bathe thrice daily and not to hold any unholy conversation with any woman, a Sûdra, one who is fallen, without any initiation, and who is an atheist; as well he should not speak in a language spoken by the châṇḍâlas. One is to bow down before him who is in the act of performing the Japam, Homa and worship, etc; one is not to talk with him. Never by deed, mind or word, on all occasions never speak about sexual intercourses; nor hold any contact with such people. For the relinquishment of this subject is called Brahmacharyam (continence) of the kings as well as of the householders. But one should go to one's legal wife during the night time after her menstruation duly according to the rules of the Śâstras; the Brahmacharyam is not thereby destroyed. Man can not repay the three fold debts and he cannot aspire for mokṣa without procreating sons or without doing the duties of the house-holders, as prescribed by the Śâstras. An attempt to do so becomes entirely fruitless like the breast on the neck of a goat. Rather it drags one downwards. So the Śrutis say. So let yourself be free first from the debts due to the Devas, the debts due to the Riṣis and the debts due to the Pitris Make sacrifices first and then be free from the Deva's debt. Hold Brahmacharyam and be free from the Riṣis' debt. Offer til and water; that is, do Śrâddhas and tarpaṇams and be free from the debt due to the Pitris. Then do readily practise your own Varṇâs'rama Dharma.

21-33. One is to practise Krichchra chândrâyana Vrata and to take for his food, milk, fruits, roots and vegetables, Haviṣyânnam and food obtained by begging so that one may become sinless. One is to make japam for Puras'charaṇam. One is to avoid salt, salty or alkaline substances, acid, garlic, turnips, eating in Kâmsa vessels, chewing betels, eating twice, putting on impure clothings, the intoxicating things and the unsâstric nocturnal japam; also one is not to waste one's time over blaming and trying to find faults with the relatives, playing at dice, or talking at random with one's wife (so that evil effects may arise). One is to spend one's time in worshipping the Devas, reciting the hymns of praise, and studying the Śâstras. One is to sleep on the ground, practise Brahmacharyam, and the vow of silence, bathe thrice, not practise anything which befits the Śûdras only. One is to worship everyday make charities duly and be always happy, recitestotras daily do occasional Deva worships, have faith in one's Guru and Deva. These twelve rules are to ensure success to the devotee who does Puras'charaṇam. One is to daily praise the Sun, with one's face turned towards Him, do japam before Him; or one is to worship one's own Deity in front of fire or the image of any god, and do japam simultaneously. The devotee who practises Puras'charaṇam is to bathe, worship, do japam, meditate, practise Homa, Tarpaṇam, is to have no desires and to surrender all fruits to one's own desired Deity, etc. These are necessarily to be observed by him. Therefore while doing japam, Homa, etc., the devotee's mind is to remain always pleasant and satisfied. One should be ready to practise tapasyâ, to see the Śâstras and be merciful to all the beings. As asceticism leads one to to heaven and to the attainment of one's desires, therefore know this that all the powers come to an ascetic. An ascetic can cause another's death (mâraṇ); he can injure others, cure diseases and kill all. Whatever the several Risis wanted from the Devî Gâyatrî and to that end made Puras'charanam and worshipped Her, they obtained from Her all those things. O Nârada! I will speak of Śânti Karmas etc., in a future chapter. Here I will speak of those rules, etc., that are to be observed in Puras'charaṇam in as much as they play the principal part to success.

First of all shave yourself and have your hairs and nails, etc., cut off and bathe and be pure. Then perform the Prâjâpatya prâyas'chitta for one's peace and purification and next do the puras'charaṇam of the Gâyâtrî. Do not speak the whole day and night. Keep your thoughts pure. If words are to be spoken, speak only what you take as true. First recite Mahâvyâhriti and then the Sâvitrî mantra with Praṇava prefixed. Then recite the sin-destroying mantra "Âpohiṣṭhâ, etc.," and Svasti matî Sûkta and "Pâvamânî Sûkta." In every action, in its beginning and at its end one is to understand the necessity of doing the Japam, why and what for one is doing that.

One is to repeat the Praṇava, the three Vyârhitis and Sâvitrî ayuta times or one thousand times or one hundred times or ten times. Then offer with water, the peace offerings (tarpaṇam) to the Âchârya, Riṣi, Chhandas, and the Devas. Being engaged in action, do not speak any impure language of the Mlechchhas or talk with any Śûdra or any bad person. Do not talk with wife in the period of menstruation, with one who has fallen, with the low-class person, with any hater of the Devas and the Brâhmaṇas, Âchâryas and Gurus, with those who blame the fathers and mothers; nor shew any disrespect to anybody. Thus I have spoken in due order about all the rules of Krichchhra vrata. Now I will speak of the rules of the Prâjâpatya Krichchhra, Sântapana, Parâka Krichchhra, and Chândrâyaṇa.

43-54. One becomes freed of all the sins, if one performs the above five Chândrâyaṇas. By the performance of the Tapta Krichchhra, all sins are burnt off in an instant. By the performance of the three Chândrâyaṇas the people get purified and go to the Brahma Loka. By doing eight Chândrâyaṇas, one sees face to face one's Devatâ, ready to grant boons. With ten Chândrâyaṇas, one gets the knowledge of the Vedas and one acquires all what one wants.

In the observance of the Krichchhra Prâjâpatya Vrata, one has to take food once in midday for three days, once in the evening for three days, and for the next three days whatever one gets without asking anything from any body. For the next three days one is not to take any thing at all and go on with one's work. These twelve day's work constitutes the **Prâjâpatya Vrata.**

Now about the rules of the Śântapana Vrata. On the preceding day one has got to eat food consisting of the mixture of cow urine, cow-dung milk, curd, ghee and the water of the Kus'a grass; the day following he is to fast. These two days' work constitutes the Sântapana Vrata.

Now about the Ati Krichchhra vrata. For the first three days, one is to eat one mouthful of food a day and for the next three days one is to fast. This is the AtiKrichchhra vrata. This vrata repeated three times is called Mahâ Sântapana vrata. *Note.*—According to the opinion of Yama, the fifteen days' work constitutes Mahâ Śântapana. For the three days one has to eat cow-urine; for the next three days, cow-dung, for the next three days, curd; for the next three days milk; and for the next three days one has to take ghee. Then one becomes pure. This is called the all sin-destroying Mahâ Śântapan Vrata. Now I am speaking of the nature of the Tapta Krichchhra Vrata.

The Tapta Krichchhra vrata is carried out for the twelve days. For the first three days, one has to drink hot water; for the next three days, hot milk; for the next three days, the hot ghee and for the next three days, air only. Everyday one has to bathe once only under the above rules, and remain self-controlled. If one drinks water simply everyday under the above conditions, that is called the Prâjâpatya vrata.

To remain without any food for twelve days according to rules is called the Parâka Krichchhra vrata. By this vrata, all sins are destroyed.

Now about the rules of taking food in the Chândrâyana vrata. In the dark fortnight one will have to decraase one mouthful of food every day and in the bright fortnight one will have to increase one mouthful every day and one has to fast completely on the Amâvasyâ (new moon) day. One has to bathe thrice daily during every Sandhyâ time. This is known as the Chândrâyana Vrata.

In the Śis'u Chândrâyana Vrata one will have to take four monthfuls of food in the mid-day and four mouthfuls in the evening. In the Yati Chândrâyana one has to take eight mouthfuls in the mid-day and to control his passions.

55. These abovementioned vratas are observed by the Rudras, Âdityas' Vasus, and Marnts ; and they are enjoying thereby their full safety.

Each of the above vratas purifies the seven Dhâtus of the body in seven nights simply! First skin, then blood, then flesh, bones, sinews, marrows and semen are purified. There is no doubt in this. Thus purifying the Âtman by the above vratas, one is to do religious actions. The work done by such a purified man is sure to be met with succees. First control the senses, be pure and do good actions. Then all your desires will be undoubtedly fructified. Fast for three nights, without doing any actions and see the result. (You will not do anything and you want self control ! Is this a child's play ?) Perform for three days the nocturnal vratas. Then proceed with your desired duties. If one works according to these methods, one gets the fruits of Pursâ'charanam. O Nârada ! By the Purâs'charanam of Śrî Gâyatrî Devî all desires are fulfilled and all sins are destroyed. Before doing Purâs'charanam purify your body by performing the above vratas Then you will get all your desires completely fulfilled. O Nârada ! Thus I have spoken to you of the secret rules of Puras'charanam. Never disclose this to any other body. For it is recognised equivalent to the Vedas.

Here ends the Twenty-third Chapter of the Eleventh Book on the Tapta Krichchhra vrata and others in the Mahâ Purânam Śrî Mad Devî Bhâgavatam of 18,000 verses by Maharṣi Veda Vyâsa.

CHAPTER XXIV.

1. Nârada said:—" O Bhagavan ! Thou art the ocean of mercy ; kindly speak out to me in brief all the things and the duties to be observed and applied in the Śânti Karmas (the peace bringing acts) of Gâyatrî.

2-20. Nârâyaṇa said :—" O Nârada ! The question asked by you is esoteric. Never divulge this to a wicked person or any hypocrite. It is to be kept secret. While doing this Śânti Karma, the Brâhmaṇas are to perform the Homas with fuel soaked in milk (Payaḥ). If the fuel of the S'amî tree be offered in Homa ceremony, then diseases caused by planets are cured. If the Homa be performed with wet As'vaththa or Udumbara or other kṣîra trees, the diseases caused by demons and hob-goblins are cured. If one offers Tarpaṇam with one palmful of water, repeating the mantra "Sûryam Tarpaymi namaḥ", the pending evils are also averted and troubles are ceased. The repetition of the Gâyatrî mantra with knees immersed in water averts all evils. The repetition of Gâyrtrî with body immersed in water upto the throat, averts the danger of life ; and the same with whole body immersed grants all success. This is the best of all the Śânti karmas, the acts that bring health, wealth happiness and peace. While performing Homa, light with the fuel of Kṣîravrikṣa (the trees that emit milky juice); place Pañchagavya in a vessel made of gold, silver, copper or wood of kṣîra trees, or in the vessels made of earth, without any knot or crack ; utter the Gâyatrî mantra and offer one thousand homaṣ. Sprinkle with water at every offering, touching the Pañchagavya with Kus'a grass, thousand times. Then offer the sacrifices there where calamities or nuisances are seen and meditate on the Highest Devatâ. Thus all the magic spells used by other persons for a malevolent purpose will be rendered nugatory. Bring under your control any Deva yoni, Bhûte Yoni, or Pis'âcha Yoni that causes you troubles ; then they will quit the house, village, city, way, even that kingdom. Now hear how they are brought under control. Prepare a sacrificial altar with sand, draw a square on it, place a Sûla (spear) in its centre and plaster with Aṣṭagandha. For the sake of converting all the evils, repeat Gâyatrî mantra thousand times and impregnate it with the mantra, dig the ground and place or bury the Sûla under it. Place on the level ground or sthaṇḍila a jar or Navaphala, a fruit made of gold, silver, or copper or a newly made earther jar and enclose it with thread. Then have the sacred waters brought from the several Tirthas by the Brâhmiṇs and fill the jar, repeating the Gâyatrî Mantra. Put within this jar the twigs, then of Cardamom tree, sandal tree, karpûra tree, jâtî, aparâjitâ. Saha Devî, Pâṭala ,Mallikâ flower, Bel leaves, rice, barley, Til, mustard, as'-vattha, and udumbara trees and throw them within the jar. (The Kṣîra trees are As'vaththa, Udumbara, Plakṣa, and Nyagrodha) Doing all these, prepare one Kus'a Kurcha made of twenty seven Kus'a grass in the form of a braid of hair, round one end of a straight rod and tied in a knot and place it there. Then take your bath and repeat the Gâyatrî mantra over it one thousand times with your whole mind fully concentrated. Then the Veda knowing Brâhmaṇas would recite the Saura mantra and sprinkle the man attacked by the demon with water and make him drink also the water saturated with the mantra and bathe him also with that. Then that person will be dispossessed of the devil and be happy. Even when the man, (possessed by a devil) is going to die, he gets his life again if he be made to drink this water saturated with this mantra and have his bath with that. So a wise King must do this, with a desire to have a long life; and after he is sprinkled with this mantra-charged water he is to give one hundred cows to the Brâhmaṇas as the Dakṣiṇâ.

21-44. The Dakṣiṇa is to be given according to one's might ; and specially what gives satisfaction to the Brâhmaṇas. If one be terrified by a Devil or so or by the mischievous magic spells of others, one is to sit on Saturday under an As'vattha tree and repeat one hundred Gâyatris. For the cure of all diseases, if one has to perform the Mrityunjaya Homa, one will have to do Homa with the Galancha creeper, soaked in milk and deducting the knots thereof. For the pacification of fever, mango leaves soaked with milk ought to be used in the Homa ceremony. The wasting diseases are cured if Homa be performed with the leaves of the Vacha (वच) soaked in milk ; phthisis or consumption is cured if Homa be performed with curd, milk and ghee Again, if offerings be given to the Solar Deity and if Pâyasânnam be given to Him and if this be given to the consumptive patient, his disease will be cured. Again, on the Amâvasyâ tithi (new moon day) if Homa be performed with Soma creeper (excluding the knot joints) soaked in milk, then consumption will be cured. If Homa be made with the flowers of the S'amkhya tree, then leprosy is cured ; if the Homa be done with the seed of Apâmârga, the Mrigis or the hysteric and epileptic fits are cured. So if Homa be performed with the fuel of Kṣîra trees, lunacy is cured ; if, with the fuel of udumbara, meha (spermatorrhea) is cured ; if with sugarcane juice, gonorrhea is cured ; if with curd, milk and ghee or with the ghee of Kapilâ cow, the homa be performed, the Masûrikâ disease or smallpox will be cured, and if Homa be performed with the fuels of Udumbara, Vaṭa, and As'vatha be performed, then the diseases of cows, elephants and horses are cured. If the trouble be caused by many ants and ant-hills (Madhu Valmîka) then perform the Homa ceremony with the fuel of Samî tree one hundred times and with the food prepared of ghee one hundred times and offer sacrifices with the rest of the food; then the above troubles will cease. If there be a earth quake or if there be seen flashes of lightnings, then homa is to be performed with the fuel of Vana Vetasa and the whole kingdom will be happy. If you surcharge any piece of iron with Gâyatrî mantra repeated hundred times and if you throw it in any direction then no fear will arise from that quarter out of fire, air, or any other enemy. If one be imprisoned, and if he repeats the Gâyatrî mantrally, he will be liberated from the prison. If you touch the man possessed by a devil, disease or mortification and sorrow with the Kus'a grass and repeat the Gâyatrî mantra, and thus charge him with Divine electricity, that man will be liberated from the fear caused thereby. If you make the man possessed by devils, etc., drink the water charged with the Gâyatrî mantra or if you cast on his body the ashes charged with hundred Gâyatrîs or tie those ashes on his head repeating the Gâyatrî mantra, he will be instantly freed of all diseases and will live for one hundred years in happiness. In case a man is unable to do fully all these himself, he can get all these done by other Brâhmaṇas and pay Daṣkiṇâ (fees) to them duly for the same.

O Narada! Now I will tell you how nourishment and wealth are attained.

Wealth is attained if the Homa be performed with red lotus or fresh Jâtî flower or with the Śâli rice or with the fuel of Bel trees, leaves flowers, fruits or roots or with any portions thereof.

If for one week the oblations be offered with fuel of Bel tree mixed with Pâyasa or with ghee one hundred times, then Lakṣmî Devî will surely be attained.

If the Homa be performed with Lâja (fried rice) mixed with curd, milk, and ghee, the daughter will be obtained.

If for one week, the Homa be performed with red lotus, then gold is obtained. If the Târpaṇam (peace offering) be offered to the Sun, then the treasures, gold hidden under the water, are obtained. If the Homa be performed with food (Anna) then Anna is obtained; if Homa be perfomed with rice, then rice is obtained.

45-5. If Homa be performed with calfdung, dried and powdered, then animals are obtained. If Homa be performed with Priyangu, Pâyasa or ghee then the progeny is obtained.

If the oblations of Pâyasânna be offered to the Solar Deity and if the Prasâdam (remnant) be given to one's wife under menstruation to eat, then excellent sons will be obtained. If the Homa be performed with the fuel of wet pointed Kṣîra trees, then longevity is attained. If Homa be performed with the fuel of the Palâs'a tree, pointed and wet and mixed with curd, milk, and ghee for one hundred times consecutively, then longevity and gold are attained. If the Homa be performed with Durbâ grass, milk, honey or ghee, one hundred times, then longevity and golden lotus are obtained. If for one week the Homa ceremony be performed with the fuel of Śamî tree mixed with food milk or ghee one hundred times of each or if for one week the Homa be performed with the fuel of Nyagrodha tree and afterwards one hundred Homas be made with Pâyasânna, the fear of unnatural death is removed.

52-60. That man can conquer death who can remain for one week living on milk only and who performs during that time hundreds, and hundreds of Homas and repeats the Gâyatrî, controlling his speech. If anybody can fast three nights and control his speech and repeat Gâyatrî he gets himself freed from the hands of Death; or totally immersed in water if he repeats Gâyatrî, he will be saved from the impending danger of death. If anybody repeats the Gâyatrî mantra for one month, taking his seat under a Bel tree or performs Homa with Bel fruit, root or leaves, he gets kingdoms. (Know all the Mantrams are electric in their effects). Similarly if anybody performs Homa with one hundred lotuses, he gets a foeless kingdom. So one becomes the lord of a village if one performs Homa with Yavâgu (barley gruel) and Sâlidhânya. If the Homa be performed with the fuel of Asvaththa tree, victory in battle is ensured and if the Homa be performed with the fuel of Âkanda tree, then victory everywhere is ensured. If one hundred Homas be performed extending a week with Vetasa tree's leaves or fruits, dipped in milk and mixed with Pâyasa, the rainfall is ensured. Similarly if anybody repeats Gâyatrî for one week with his body upto navel immersed in water, the rain fall is ensured; on the contary if the Homa be performed with ashes in water, then the cessation of heavy rainfall is ensured. The Homa with the fuel of Palâsa gives Brahmateja; Homa with the flowers of Palâsa gives everything desired. Homa with milk or drinking Brâhmarasa, charged with mantra, increases the intellect; and the Homa with ghee gives Buddhi (medhâ) (intelligence).

61-69. Homa with flowers gives good smell; Homa with thread gives cloth; Homa with salt and honey mixed or Bel flowers gives one power to control anything and everything that is desired. If anybody bathes everyday immersed completely within water and sprinkles water on his body, he becomes cured of diseases and he becomes very healthy. If any Brâhmaṇa does these things for others, he becomes also no doubt healthy. If anybody wants to increase his life period he should practise good deeds and repeat Gâyatrî thousand times daily for one month. Thus his longevity will be increased. Two months' such practice gives long life and perpetual health; three month's such practice will give life, health, and wealth, four months such practice gives longevity, wealth, fame, women, sons, etc., five months such practice gives longevity, health, wealth, wife, sons and learning. So one should repeat this as many months in proportion to the number of his desires and he would get them. Again any Brâhmaṇa who stands on one leg without holding any other thing and raises both his hands and daily repeats three hundred Gâyatrîs for one month, gets all his desires fulfilled. And if he repeats one thousand one hundred Gâyatrîs, there is nothing in this world that is not met and attained with success. Controlling the Prâṇa (inhaling) and Apâna (exhaling) Vâyu (breath), he who repeats daily three hundred Gâyatrîs to the Devî, his highest desires are satisfied.

70 77. Vis'vâmitra Riṣi says :—Standing on one leg, with both hands raised and controlling Vâyu he who repeats daily one hundred Gâyatrîs for one month, gets all his desires fulfilled. Similarly with three hundred or thousand repeatings, all things are attained. Submerged under water, if one repeats Gâyatrîs as many times as mentioned above, he gets every thing. If, for one year, with hands uplifted and without holding any thing, anyone stands on one leg, controls one's breath and repeats Gayâtrî mantra three hundred times or thousand times, eating Haviṣyânnam only in the night time, he becomes a Riṣi (Seer). This thing repeated two years gives infallible speech; three years gives knowledge of the present, past and future; four years will enable one to see face to fece the Solar God; five years will give the eight Siddhis, lightness, etc., six years will enable one to assume forms as he desires; seven years gives immortality; nine years gives Manuhood; ten years gives Indrahood; eleven years gives Brahmâ-hood; and twelve years gives the state of Parama Brahma.

78-90. O Nârada! By these practices of Tapasyâs you and other Riṣis have been able to conquer the three Lokas (regions). Some ate only vegetables; some fruits; some, roots; some simply water; some, ghee; some, Somarasa; whereas some others ate only charu and did tapasyâ. Some Riṣis practised this great Tapasyâ by eating very little for a fortnight only. Some ate food, only what they got by begging during the day; and some ate only Haviṣyânna. Nârada! Now hear the rules for the purification and expiation of sins. For the expiation of the sin incurred in stealing gold, one is to repeat three thousand Gâyatrîs (daily) for one month ; then the sin will be destroyed. By this act also the sins incurred by drinking or by going to one's Guru's wife are destroyed. Vis'vâmitra Riṣi says:—The sin incurred by killing a Brâhmaṇa (Brahmahatyâ) is destroyed if one erects a shed in a forest and, living there, repeats three thousand Gâyatrîs daily for one month. Those Brâhmaṇas that have committed the Great Sins (*i. e.* Mahâpâtakas), become free, if they repeat one thousand Gâyatrîs daily, submerged under water, for twelve successive days. By controlling speech and by practising Prâṇâyâma, if one repeats three thousand Gâyatrîs daily for one month, one will be free from the Mahâpâtakas. If one practises one thousand Prâṇâyâmas repeating the Gâyatrî, one becomes freed also of Brahmahatyâ. If one draws upwards the Praâa and Apâna Vâyus six times, repeating the Gâyatrî with collected mind, this destroys all the sins and it is called all-sin destroying Prâṇâyâma. If one practises this Prâṇâyâma one thousand times for one month, the lord of the earth becomes freed of all sins. If any Brâhmaṇa incurs the sin of killing a cow, for twelve days he is to repeat three thousand Gâyatrîs daily for expiation. Similarly the repetition of ten thousand Gâyatrîs removes the sin of going to those not fit to be gone into, eating the uneatables, stealing and killing and this act brings in peace. All sins are destroysd by performing one hundred Prâṇâyâmas with Gâyatrî. Again if there be a mixture of various sins, one will have to live in the forest for one month and repeat one thousand Gâyatrîs or practise fasting and repeat three thousand Gâyatrîs ; thus all sins will be destroyed.

91-100. To repeat Gâyatrî twenty-four thousand times is equal to performing the Krichchhra vrata and to repeat sixty four thousand Gâyatrîs duly is equal to performing the Chândrâyṇa. If anybody repeats, in the morning and evening Sandhyâ times, the merit giving Gâyatrî one hundred times, with Prâṇâyâma, all his sins are destroyed. So, submerged under water, if one repeats the Gâyatrî Devî, meditating Her in the Sun, one hundred times daily, one's all the sins are fully destroyed. O Nârada ! Thus I have described to you all about averting or destroying the evils and the purification of various sins. All this is secret. Keep it carefully concealed. Never divulge this. Whoever divulges this will bring his own ruin. I have spoken to you, in brief, all about Sadâchâra (right way of living). If anybody practises this duly, according to rules, Śrî Mahâmâyâ Durgâ Devî becomes pleased with him. If anybody wants to have both enjoyment and liberation, he is to practise all these daily, as well as the occasional, and Kâmya (desired) duties duly according to rules. It is stated in all the Śâstras, that this Âchâra (right way of living) is the foremost and the chief Dharma, the Deity of which is the Supreme Mother Herself. O Nârada ! That man who practises duly this Âchâra is, in this world, holy, happy and blessed. This I speak to you truly. If anybody desires to get the Devî Bhagavatî's Grace, he should first of all set himself at once to practise this Sadâchâra. He who hears this gets wealth and great happiness. There is no doubt in this. Now speak what more you want to hear.

Here ends the Twenty fourth Chapter of the Eleventh Book on Sadâchâra in the Mahâpurâṇam Śrî Mad Devî Bhâgavatam of 18,000 verses by Maharṣi Veda Vyâsa. The Eleventh Book Completed.

[Here ends the Eleventh Book.]

THE TWELFTH BOOK.

CHAPTER I.

1-7. Nârada said:—"O Deva! The rules of Sadâchâra (right ways of living) and the all-sin-destroying unequalled Glories of the Devî Bhagavatî have been described by Thee. And I, too, have heard the nectar of the Glories of the Devî from Thy lotus mouth. The Chândrâyaṇa and other Vratas, described by Thee, are very difficult to practise. So they are impracticable with the ordinary persons. Therefore, O Lord! Kindly describe those actions which can easily be carried out by common persons, at the same time, the Devî's Grace and Siddhis can be obtained by those practices. Again what thou hast described about the Gâyatrî in connection with Sadâchâra, kindly say which are the chief and foremost as well as those that are more meritorious. O Best of the Munis! Thou hast told that there are the twenty-four syllables in the Gâyatrî. Kindly describe now their Riṣis, Chhandas, Devatâs and other things that should be known regarding them and thus satisfy my longings.

8-27. Śrî Nârâyaṇa said:—"O Nârada! The twice-born would have done what they ought to do if they be engaged in repeating their Gâyatrî only, whether they be able or not able to practise the Chândrâyaṇa and the other vratas. Whichever Brâhmiṇ repeats the Gây atrî three thousand times and offers Arghya to the Sun in the three Sandhyâ times, the Devas worship him; what to speak of other ordinary persons! Whether he practises Nyâsa or not, if anybody sincerely repeats the Gâyatrî Devî, Whose Nature is Existence, Intelligence, and Bliss and meditates on Her, even if he attains siddhi in one syllable even, then. as a result of that, he can vie with the best of the Brâhmaṇas, the Moon, and the Sun; nay, with Brahmâ, Viṣṇu, and Mahes'vara even! O Nârada! Now I will tell in due order the Riṣis, Chhandas, and the Devatâs of the twenty-four syllables of the Gâyatrî. The Riṣis, in due order, are (1) Vâma-Deva, (2) Attri, (3) Vas'iṣṭha, (4) Śukra, (5) Kaṇva, (6) Parâs'ara, (7) the very fiery Vis'vâmitra, (8) Kapila, (9) Śaunaka, (10) Yâjñavalkya, (11) Bharadvâja, (12) the ascetic Jamadagni, (13) Gautama, (14) Mudgala, (15) Vedavyâsa, (16) Lomas'a, (17) Agastya, (18) Kaus'ika, (19) Vatsya, (20) Pulastya, (21) Mâṇḍuka, (22) the ascetic in chief Durvâsâ (23) Nârada and (24) Kas'yapa.

Now about the chhandas:—(1) Gâyatrî, (2) Uṣṇik, (3) Anuṣṭup, (4) Brihatî, (5) Pankti, (6) Triṣṇup, (7) Jagatî, (8) Atijagatî, (9) Śakkarî, (10) Ati Śakkarî, (11) Dhriti, (12 Ati Dhriti, (13) Virâṭ, (14) Prastârapankti, (15) Kṛiti, (16) Prâkriti, (17) Âkriti, (18) Vikṛiti, (19) Samkṛiti, (20) Akṣarapankti, (21) Bhuḥ, (22) Bhuvaḥ, (23) Svaḥ (24) and Jyotiṣmatî. The Devatâs of the several letters in due order, are:—(1) Agni, (2) Prajâpati, (3) Soma, (4) Îs'âna, (5) Savitâ, (6) Âditya, (7) Brihaspati, (8) Maitrâvaruṇa, (9) Bhagadeva, (10) Aryamâ, (1.) Gaṇes'a, (12) Tvaṣṭrâ, (13 Pûṣâ, (14) Indrâgnî, (15) Vâyu, (16) Vâmadeva, (17) Maitrâ varuṇi (18) Vis'vadeva, (19) Mâtrikâ, (20) Viṣṇu, (21) Vasu, (22) Rudra Deva, (23) Kuvera, and (24) the twin As'vinî Kumâras. O Nârada! Thus I have described to you about the the Devatâs of the twenty-four syllables. The hearing of this destroys all sins and yields the full results of repeating the mantra Gâyatrî. (*Note*:—The Devatâs, mentioned in the Gâyatrî Brahma Kalpa are different from those mentioned here.)

Here ends the first Chapter of the Twelfth Book on the description of Gâyatrî in the Mahâpurâṇam Śrî Mad Devî Bhâgavatam of 18,000 verses by Maharṣi Veda Vyâsa.

CHPATER II.

1-18. Nârâyaṇa said:—"O Nârada! O Great Muni! Now hear which are the Śaktis in due order of the twenty-four syllables of the Gâyatri Devî:—

(1) Vâma Devî, (2) Priyâ, (3) Satyâ, (4) Vis'vâ, (5) Bhadravilâsinî, (6) Prabhâ Vatî, (7) Jayâ, (8) Śântâ, (9) Kântâ, (1) Durgâ, (11) Sarasvatî, (12) Vidrumâ, (13) Vis'âle'sâ, (14) Vyâpinî, (15) Vimalâ, (16) Tamopahâriṇî, (17) Sûkṣmâ, (18) Vis'vayoni, (19) Jayâ, (20) Vas'â, (21) Padmâlayâ, (22) Parâs'obhâ, (23) Bhadrâ, (24) and Tripadâ.

Now hear the respective colours of the several syllables of the Gâyatrî Devî:—(1) like Champaka and Atasî flowers, (2) like Vidruma, (3) like crystal, (4) like lotus; (5) like the Rising Sun; (6) white like conchshell; (7) white like Kuṇḍa flower; (8) like Prabâla and lotus leaves; (9) like Padmarâga, (10) like Indranîlamaṇi; (11) like pearls; (12) like Saffron; (13) like the black collyrium of the eye; (14) red; (15) like the Vaidûrya maṇi; (16) like Kṣaudra; (Champaka tree, honey, water.) (17) like turmeric; (18) like Kuṇḍa flower; and the milk (19) like the rays of the Sun; (20) like the tail of the bird Śuka; (21) like Śatapatra; (22) like Ketakî flower; (23) like Mallikâ flower; (24) like Karavîra flower. Now about their Tattvas:—(1) earth; (2) water; (3) fire; (4) air; (5) Âkâs'a, (ether); (6) smell; (7) taste; (8) form; (9) sound; (10)

touch ; (11) male generative organ ; (12) anus ; (13) legs, (14) hands ; (15) speech ; (16) Prâṇa (vital breath) ; (17) tongue ; (18) eyes ; (19) skin ; (20) ears ; (21) Prâṇa (up going breath) ; (22) Apâna ; (23) Vyâna, (24) Sâmâna.

Now about the Mudrâs of the syllables:—(1) Sammukha ; (2) Sampuṭa ; (3) Vitata ; (4) Vistṛita ; (5) Dvimukha, (6) Trimukha ; (7) Chaturmukha ; (8) Pañchamukha ; (9) Ṣaṇmukha ; (10) Adhomukha ; (11) Vyâpakânjali ; (12) Śakaṭa; (13) Yamapâs'a ; (14) Grathita ; (15) Sanmukhon mukha ; (16) Vilamba; (17) Muṣṭika; (18) Matsya; (19) Kûrma; (20) Varâhaka; (21) Simhâkrânta, (22) Mahâkrânta; (23) Mudgara, and (24) Pallava.

The Mahâmudrâs of the fourth foot of Gâyâtrî are (1) Trisúlayonî ; (2) Surabhi ; (3) Akṣa mâlâ ; (4) Liṇga; and (5) Ambuja. O Nârada ! Thus I have described to you all about the Mudrâs, etc., of the several syllables of the Gâyatrî. If during Japam, one thinks all these and at the same time repeats, all his sins are destroyed and his wealth gets increase and the fame attends on him.

Here ends the Second Chapter of the Twelfth Book on the description of the Śaktis, etc., of the syllables of Gâyatrî in the Mahâpurâṇam Śrî Mad Devî Bhâgavatam of 18,000 Verses by Maharṣi Veda Vyâsa.

CHAPTER III.

1-3. Nârada spoke :—" O Bhagavan ! Thou art the Lord of this world ; Thou canst shew favour and disfavour both ; Thou art specially versed in the sixty-four Kalâs (arts of learning) ; Thou art the chief of the Yogis. I therefore ask Thee to solve a doubt of mine. By what Puṇyam a man can become free from all his sins and limitations and he can realise and become of the nature of Brahma. O Lord ! And what are duly the Riṣis, Chhandas, Devatâs, Dhyân, and Nyâsa, etc., of this meritorious act ? I want to hear.

4-25. Nârâyaṇa said :—" O Nârada ! There is but one and the only one way to this and though that is very secret, I will disclose that to you. It is the Gâyatrî-Kavacha. It can destroy all sins. Therefore to recite or to hold it on one's body enables the man to become free from all his sins and to get all his desires fulfilled and he gets the Sâyuya Mukti with the Devî (be merged in the Devî-Body). Now hear the Riṣis, Chhandas, etc., of this Kavacha :—Brahmâ, Viṣṇu and Mahes'vara are the Riṣis ; the Rik, Yajus, Sâma and Atharna Vedas are the Chhandas ; the Paramâ Kalâ Gâyatrî of the nature of Brahma is the Devatâ ; " Tat " in Gâyatrî is the Vîja ; " Bharga " is the Śakti ; and " Dhîyah " is the Kîlaka ; and its viniyoga (application) is in getting the Mokṣa (liberation). With the first four syllables touch the heart ; with the next three letters touch the head; with the next four letters touch the tuft on the crown of the head; with the next three letters on the Kavacha; with the next four letters on the eyes and with the last four letters make the Nyâsa, all over the body repeating "Astrâya Phaṭ." O Nârada! Hear now the Dhyânam of Gâyatrî, that grants all desires. The Gâyatrî Devî has five faces; one of which is of white colour; and the other four is of pearl, Vidruma, golden, and Nîlakântamaṇi colour respectively. Each face has got three eyes; on the head there is a crown of jewels and the digit of the Moon is shining there. Her body is composed of the twenty-four tattvas. She has ten hands:— On the top right and left hands there are two lotuses; lower down, there are disc and conch shell; lower down, there are rope and skull; lower down, there are noose and goad; and on the bottom hands right and left she is making signs of "No fear" and "ready to grant boons." Thus meditating on Śrî Gâyatrî, one is to recite the Kavacha thus:—Let the Gâyatrî Devî protect my front; Sâvitrî Devî protect my right; the Sandhyâ Devî, my back and the Devî Sarasvatî, my left. Let my Mother Pârvatî Devî protect my quarters. Let Jalas'âyinî protect the southeast; Yâtudhâna Bhayankarî protect my South-west; Pavamâna-vilâsinî my north-west; Rudrarûpiṇî Rudrâṇî protect my north-east. Let Brahmâṇî protect my top and Vaiṣṇavî protect my nether regions. Let the word "Tat" in the Gâyatrî protect my legs; "Savituh" protect my Knees; "Vareṇyam," protect my loins; "Bhargah," my navel. Let "Devasya" protect my heart; "Dhîmahî" protect my neck; "Dhiyah," protect my eyes; "Yah," protect my forehead; "Naḥ" protect my head; and "Prachodayât" protect the tuft on the crown of my head.

Again let the "Tat" of the twenty-four syllabled Gâyatrî protect my head; "Sa," protect my forehead; "Vi" protect my eyes; "Tu" my cheeks; "Va," protect my nostrils; "Re;" my mouth; "ṇi" protect my upper lip; "Yaḥ" protect my lower lip; "Bha" within my face; "rgo," protect my cheeks; "De," my throat; "Va" my shoulders; "Sya" my right hand; "Dhî" my navel; "ma," my heart, "Hi," my belly; "Dhî," my navel; "Yo" my loins; Yo, my anus; "naḥ," my thighs, "Pra." my Knees; "Cho" my shanks "Da" my heels; "Yâ" my legs; and let "at" protect all my sides. O Nârada! This divine Kavacha of the Devî Gâyatrî can baffle hundreds and thousands of obstructions and evils; can grant sixty-four Kalâs and liberation. By the glory of this Kavacha, man can become free from all evils and can attain the state of Brahma. Moreover whoever reads or hears this acquires the fruits of making a gift of a thousand cows.

Here ends the Third Chapter of the Twelfth Book on the description of the Kavacha of Śrî Gâyatrî Devî in the Mahâpurâṇam Śrî Mad Devî Bhâgavatam of 18,000 verses by Maharṣi Veda Vyâsa.

CHAPTER IV.

1-2. Nârada said:—"O Bhagavan! I have heard from you all about the Kavacha and the Mantra of Śrî Gâyatrî. O Deva Deva! O Thou, the Knower of the present, the past, and the future! Now tell about the Hridaya, the highest, the interior or esoteric Essence of the Gâyatrî, holding which, if one repeats the Gâyatrî, he acquires all the puṇyam (merits). I am desirous to hear this.

3-8. Nârayana said:—"O Nârada! This subject on the Hridaya of Gâyatrî is explicitly written in the Atharva Veda. Now I will speak on that, the great secret, in detail. Listen. First, consider the Gâyatrî, the Devî, the Mother of the Vedas as of a Cosmic Form (Virâṭrupâ) and meditate all the Devas as residing on Her Body. Now in as much as the Piṇḍa and Brahmâṇḍa are similar, consider yourself as of the form of the Devî and meditate within yourself on the Devatâs, thus:—The Pundits, the Knowers of the Vedas, say this:—He is not yet fit to worship the Deva and he is not an Adhikârî as yet who has not been able to make himself a Deva; therefore to establish the knowledge of the oneness of the Deva and himself, he is to meditate the Devas within his body, thus:—

O Nârada! Now I will speak on the Hridaya of Gâyatrî, knowing which every man becomes able to become all the Devas. Listen. The Riṣi of this Gâyatrî Hridaya is Nârâyaṇa; the Chhandas is Gâyatrî; and Śrî Parames'varî Gâyatrî is the Devatâ. Perform the Nyâsa of this as mentioned before and taking your seat in a lonely place, meditate intently on the Devî with your heart and head well collected. Now I am speaking of the Arthanyâsa. Hear. Meditate on the Devatâ Dyau on your head; the twin As'vins on the rows of the teeth; the two Sandhyâs on your upper and lower lips; the Agni, Fire, within your mouth; Sarasvatî, on the tongue; Brihaspati on the neck; the eight Vasus on the two breasts; the Vâyus, on the two arms; the Paryanya Deva on the heart; Âkâs'a, on the belly; Antarîkṣam (the middle space) on the navel; Indra and Agni, on the loins; Prajâpati, the condensed form, as it were, of Vijnâna, on the hip joints; the Kailâs'a and the Malaya mountains on the two thighs; the Visvedevâs on the two knees; Vis'vâmitra on the shanks; the Sun's northern and southern paths, the Uttarâyana and Dakṣiṇâyana on the anus; the Pitris on the thighs; the Earth on the legs; the Vanaspati on the fingers and toes; the Riṣis on the hairs of the body; the Muhûrtas on the nails; the planets on the bones; the Ritus (seasons) on the blood and flesh; the Samvatsaras on the Nimiṣa (twinkling of eye) the Sun and the Moon on the day and night respectively. Thinking thus, repeat "I take refuge of the Divine Holy Gâyatrî, the Chief and most Excellent One, the Thousand eyed" and I take refuge wholly unto Her.

Then repeat "I bow down to Tat savitur vareṇyam," "I bow down to the Rising Sun on the East," "I bow down to the Morning Âditya," "I bow down to the Gâyatrî, residing in the Morning Sun" and I bow down to all. "O Nârada! Whoever recites this Gâyatrî Hridaya in the morning finds all the sins committed in the night all destroyed! Whoever recites this in the evening gets his sins of the day all destroyed! Whoever recites this in the evening and in the morning can rest assured to have become free of sins; he gets the fruits of all the Tîrthas; he is acquainted with all the Devas; he is saved if he has spoken anything that ought not to have been spoken; if he has eaten anything that is not fit to be eaten; if he has chewn and sucked anything that ought not to have been chewn and sucked; if he has done any thing that ought not to have been done and if he has accepted hundreds and thousands of gifts that ought never to have been accepted.

The sins incurred by eating with the others in a line cannot touch him. If he speaks lies, he will not be touched by the sins thereof; even if a non-Brahmachârî recites this, he will become a Brahmachârî. O Nârada! What more shall I say to you of the results of Gâyatrî Hridaya than this:—that whoever will study this, will acquire the fruits of performing thousand sacrifices and repeating the Gâyatrî sixty thousand times. In fact, he will get Siddhi by this. The Brâhmaṇa, who daily reads this in the morning will be freed of all the sins and go upwards to the Brahma (Loka) and is glorified there. This has been uttered by Bhagavân Nârâyaṇa Himself.

Here ends the Fourth Chapter of the Twelfth Book on Gâyatrî Hridaya in the Mahâpurâṇam Śrî mad Devî Bhâgavatam of 18,000 verses by Maharṣi Veda Vyâsa.

CHAPTER V.

1. Nârada said :—"O All knowing One ! Thou showest Thy grace to Thy devotees ! Thou hast described this sin-destroying Gâyatrî Hridaya. Now describe Her Stava (hymn of praise).

2-29. Nârâyaṇa said :—"O World-Mother ! O Thou, favouring Thy devotees ! O Thou, the Prime Force, O Omnipresent ! Infinite ! Śrî Sandhye; I bow down to Thee. Thou art the Sandhyâ ; Thou art the Gâyatrî, Sâvitrî and Sarasvatî ; Thou art Brâhmî, Vaiṣṇavî and Raudrî and Thou art red, white, and black (the colours of Gâyatrî, Sâvitrî and Sarasvatî that Thou assumest respectively. O Bhagavatî ! Thou art always meditated by the Munis as young in the morning, full of youth in the mid-day, and aged in the evening. I bow down to Thee. Thou art seen by the Tapasvis (ascetics) as Brahmâṇî, riding on Hamsa (swan), Sarasvatî riding on Garuda, and Sâvitrî riding on Bull. Thou art seen within by the ascetics as manifesting the Rigveda (in the form of Sâvitrî) in this world, as manifesting Yayurveda in the middle space (antarikṣam) and as manifesting Sâmaveda everywhere in the Rudra loka, thus roaming in the three worlds. I bow down to Thee. O Devî ! Thou art Rudrâṇî in the Rudra loka, Vaiṣṇavî in the Viṣṇu loka, and Brahmâṇî in the Brahma loka ; thus Thou shewest Thy favour to the Immortals. O Devî ! Thou art the Mother delighting the seven Riṣis (of the Great Bear) ; Thou art Mâyâ. Thou grantest great many boons to Thy Bhaktas. Thou art sprung from the eyes and hands, tears and perspiration of Śiva and Śivâ. Thou art the Mother of delights, Durgâ Devî, recited by the following ten names:— Vareṇyâ, Varadâ, Variṣṭhâ, Varavarninî, Gariṣṭhâ, Varâhâ, Varârohâ, Nîlagangâ, Sandhyâ and Bhoga Mokṣadâ. Thou art the Bhâgirathî (the river Ganges) in this world ; the Bhogavatî in the Pâtâla ; and the Mandâkinî (the milky way) in the Heavens. Thou art in this world (Bhur loka) the all-enduring Prithvî (earth) ; Thou art the Vâyu Śakti (air power) in the middle space (Bhubhar loka) ; Thou art the energy (the ocean of Tejas) in the Heavens (Svar loka) ; Thou art the Great Siddhi in the Mahar loka ; Thou art Janâ in the Janar loka ; Thou art Tapasvinî in the Tapar loka ; Thou art Truth (True Speech) in the Satya lokam. Thou art Kamalâ in Viṣṇu loka ; Gâyatrî in Brahma loka ; and the other half of Hara as Gaurî in the Rudra loka. O Devî ! Thou art sung as Prakriti.—"Aham"-"Om-Mahat" tattva and beyond that the Highest Sarva

Brahma rûpiṇî and Sâmyâvasthâ Prakriti. Thou art the Parâ Śakti; Thou art the Paramâ Śakti; O Devî! Thou art the Tri-Śakti:—the Ichchhâ Śakti (the will power), the Kriyâ Śakti (power of action) and the Jñâna Śakti (the force of knowledge). Thou art the Gangâ, Yamunâ, Vipâs'â, Sarasvatî, Sarayu, Devikâ, Sindhu; Narmadâ, Îrâvatî, Godâvarî, Śatadru; Kâverî, Kaus'ikî, Chandra Bhâgâ, Vitastâ, Gaṇḍakî, Tapinî, Karatoyâ, Gomatî, and Vetravatî and other rivers; Thou art the Iḍâ, Pingalâ, and Suṣumnâ nerves; Thou art Gândhârî, Hastajihvâ, Pûṣâ, Apûṣâ, Alambuṣâ, Kuhû, Śankhinî, Prâṇavâhinî and other nerves in the body; O Devî! Thou art the vital power in the lotus of the heart; Thou art Svapna nâikâ in the throat; Thou art Sadâdhârâ in the palate; and Thou art the Vindumâlinî Śakti in the pituitari space between the eyebrows.

Thou art the Kuṇḍalinî in the Mûlâdhâra (sacral plexus), the Vyâpinî extending upto the roots of the hairs; Thou art Madhyâsanâ on the crown of the head, and Thou art Manonmanî in the Brahmarandhra. O Devî! What need there is in stating these? Suffice it to say that whatever there is seen in this universe, all art Thou; therefore, O Śrî Sandhyâ Devî! I bow down to Thee. O Nârada! Thus I have spoken to you about the Gâyatrî-Stotra that gives all successes, destroys all sins, and yields all merits. He who reads this in the Sandhyâ times, with all attention, will get sons if he has no sons, will get wealth if he has no wealth. There is no doubt in this. Whoever reads this Stotra, gets the fruits of all Tîrthas, all Tapasyâs, all gifts, all sacrifices and all Yogas. He enjoys happiness in this world and finally gets the Mokṣa. The Munis who are engaged in Tapasyâs read this Stotra. While bathing, if one reads this, merged under water, acquires the fruits of his being merged in the Sandhyâ. O Nârada! I speak this verily, verily, verily, unto you that there is no trace of any doubt in this statement. Whoever will hear with devotion this Sandhyâ stotra, the nectar-like thing, will be freed from all sins.

Here ends the Fifth Chapter of the Twelfth Book on the Gâyatrî Stotra in the Mahâpurâṇam Śrî Mad Devî Bhâgavatam of 18,000 verses by Maharṣi Veda Vyâsa.

CHAPTER VI.

1-3. Nârada said:—"O Bhagavan! O All-knowing One! O Thou versed in all the Śâstras! I have heard from Thy mouth all the secrets of Śrutis and Smritis. Now I ask Thee, O Deva! How can the knowledge of that Veda Vidyâ (Learning) be obtained by which all sins are rooted out and destroyed, how is Brahmajñânam obtained and how can Mokṣa be obtained? How can death be conquered and how can the best results be obtained in this world and in the next. O Lotus-eyed One! Thou ought'st to describe fully all these to me.

4-9. Nârâyaṇa said:—"O Nârada! O Highly Learned One! Sâdhu! Sâdhu! You have now put a nice question indeed! Now I will describe one thousand and eight names of the Gâyatrî Devî. Listen attentively. These all sin-destroying auspicious names were composed by Brahmâ and first recited by Him. Its Riṣi is Brahmâ; the Chhandas is Anuṣṭup; the Devatâ is Gâyatrî; its Vîja is Halavarṇa (consonants) and its Śakti is Svaravarṇa (vowels). Perform the Anga Nyâsa and the Kara Nyâsa by the Mâtrikâ varṇas (that is, by the fifty syllables). Now hear its Dhyânam, that will do good to the Sâdhakas (the practisers). [*N. B.*—Amga Nyâsa—Touching the limbs of the body with the hand accompanied by appropriate Mantras. Kara Nyâsa—assignment of the various parts of fingers and hand to different deities which is usually accompanied with prayers and corresponding gesticulations.] I worship the Kumârî (virgin) Gâyatrî Devî, the Lotus-eyed One, riding on the Swan (the Prâṇas), and seated on a lotus (creation); Who is three-eyed and of a red colour; and Who is bright and decorated with gems and jewels of red, white, green, blue, yellow and other variegated colours; Who is holding in Her hands Kuṇḍikâ, the rosary, lotus and making signs as if ready to grant the desired boons and on whose neck is suspended the garland of red flowers. I worship the Devî Gâyatrî. *Note.*—The colours are the various emotions and feelings.

10-16. Now I will recite the one thousand and eight names of the Gâyatrî, beginning with the syllable "a" and going on a, â, i, î, etc., in due order of the alphabets. Listen! Her ways and actions cannot be comprehended by intellect (Buddhi); She is therefore Achintya Lakṣaṇâ; She is Avyaktâ (unmanifested; unspeakable); She is Arthamâtrimahes'varî, (because She is the Controller of Brahmâ, etc.); She is Amritârnava madhyasthâ, Ajitâ and Aparâjitâ. Thou art Aṇimâdiguṇâdhârâ, Arka maṇḍalasamsthitâ, Ajarâ, Ajâ, Aparâ, Adharmâ (she has no dharma, caste, etc.), Akṣasûtradharâ, Adharâ; Akârâdikṣakârântâ (beginning with the syllable "a" and ending with the syllable "kṣa", thus comprising the fifty syllables), Ariṣaḍvargabhedinî (destroying the five passions), Anjanâdripratîkâs'â, Anjanâdrinivâsinî, Aditi, Ajapâ, Avidyâ, Aravindanibhekṣaṇâ, Antarvahiḥsthitâ, Avidyâdhvamsinî, and Antarâtmikâ. Thou art Ajâ, Ajamukhâvâsâ (residing in the mouth of Brahmâ), Aravindanibhânanâ, (Vyanjanavarnâtmikâ, therefore called) Ardhamâtrâ, Arthadânajnâ (because She grants all the Puruṣârthas.

Arimaṇḍalamarddinî, Asuraghnî, Amâvâsyâ, Alakṣighnî, Antyajârchitâ. Thus end Her names beginning with "A". Now the names with

"Â" Thou art Âdi Lakṣmî, Âdi Śakti, Âkriti, Âyatânanâ, Âdityapadavîchârâ, Âdityaparisevitâ, Âchâryâ, Âvartanâ; Âchârâ, and Âdi Mûrti nivâsinî.

17-18. Thou art Âgneyî, Âmarî, Âdyâ, Ârâdhyâ, Âsanasthitâ, Âdhâra nilayâ (seated in the Mulâdhâra), Âdhârâ (the Refuge of all), and Âkâs'ânta nivâsinî (of the nature of Aham tattva; Thou art Âdyâkṣara samâyuktâ, Ântarâkâs'arûpinî, Âdityamaṇḍalagatâ, Ântaradhvântanâs'inî, (i. e. destroyer of the Moha of Jîvas). Then come the names beginning with "I."

19-25. Thou art Indirâ, Iṣṭadâ, Iṣṭâ Indîvaranivekṣaṇâ, Irâvatî, Indrapadâ, Indrâṇî, Indurûpiṇî, Ikṣukodaṇḍasamyuktâ, Iṣusandhânakâriṇî, Indranîlasamâkârâ, Iḍâpiṅgalarûpiṇî, Indrâkṣî, Îs'varî, Devî Îhâtrayavivarjitâ. Thou art Umâ, Uṣâ, Uḍunibhâ, Urvârukaphalânanâ, Uḍuprabhâ, Uḍumatî, Uḍupâ, Uḍumadhyagâ, Ûrdha, Ûrdhakes'î, Ûrdhâdhogatibhedinî, Ûrdhavâhupriyâ, Ûrmimâlâvâggranthadâyinî, Thou art Ṛita, Ṛiṣi, Ṛitumatî, (the Creatrix of the world) Ṛiṣidevanamaskritâ, Ṛigvedâ, Ṛiṇabartrî, Ṛiṣimaṇḍala chârinî, Ṛiddhidâ, Ṛijumârgasthâ, Ṛijudharmâ, Ṛijupradâ, Ṛigvedanilayâ, Ṛijvî, Lupta dharma pravartinî, Lûtârivarasam bhûtâ, Lûtâdiviṣahâriṇî.

26-30. Thou art Ekâkṣarâ, Ekamâtrâ, Ekâ, Ekaikaniṣṭhitâ, Aindrî, Airâvatârûḍhâ, Aihikâmuṣmikapradâ, Omkârâ, Oṣadhî, Otâ, Otaprotanivâsinî, Aurbbâ, Auṣadhasampannâ, Aupâsanaphalapradâ, Aṇḍamadhyasthitâ, Aḥkâramanurûpiṇî. (Visargarûpiṇî).

Thus end the names beginning with vowels.

Now begin the names beginning with consonants.

Thou art Kâtyâyanî, Kâlarâtri, Kâmâkṣî, Kâmasundarî, Kamalâ, Kâminî, Kântâ, Kâmadâ, Kâlakaṇṭhinî, Karikumbha stana bharâ, Karavîra Suvâsinî, Kalyaṇî, Kuṇḍalavatî, Kurukṣetranivâsinî, Kuruvinda dalâkârâ, Kuṇḍalî, and Kumudâlayâ.

31-32. Thou art Kâlajhibhâ, Karâlâsyâ, Kâlikâ, Kâlarûpiṇî, Kâmanîyaguṇâ, Kânti, Kalâdhârâ, Kumudvatî, Kaus'ikî, Kamalâ kârâ, Kâmachâraprabhanjinî. Thou art Kaumarî, Karuṇâpângî, Kakubantâ (as presiding over all the quarters), and Karipriyâ.

33-37. Thou art Kes'arî, Kes'avanutâ, Kadamba Kus'umapriyâ, Kâlindî, Kâlikâ, Kâñchî, Kalas'odbhavasamstutâ. Thou art Kâmamâtâ, Kratumatî, Kâmarûpâ, Kripâvatî, Kumârî, Kuṇḍa nilayâ, Kirâtî, Kîravâhanâ, Kaikeyî, Kokilâlâpâ, Ketakî Kusumapriyâ, Kamaṇḍaludharâ, Kâlî, Karmanirmûlakâriṇî, Kalahansagati, Kakṣâ, Krita Kautukamangalâ, Kastûrîtilakâ, Kamrâ, Karîndra Gamanâ, Kuhû, Karpûralepanâ, Kriṣṇâ, Kapilâ, Kuharâs'rayâ, Kûṭasthâ, Kudharâ, Kamrâ. Kukṣisthâkhilav'ṣṭapâ.

Thus end the names with Ka.

Now come those with Kha.

38-62. Thou art Khaḍga Kheṭadharâ, Kharbbâ, Khecharî, Khaga-
vâhanâ, Khaṭṭânga dhâriṇî, Khyâtâ, Khagarâjoparisthitâ, Khalaghnî,
Khaṇḍitajarâ, Khaḍâkṣyûnapradâyinî, Khaṇḍendu tilakâ.

Thou art Gangâ, Gaṇes'a guhapújita, Gâyatrî, Gomatî, Gîtâ,
Gândhârî, Gûnalolupâ, Gautamî, Gâminî, Gâdhâ, Gandharvâpsara-
sevitâ, Govinda charaṇâ krâṇtâ, Guṇatraya vibhâbitâ, Gandharvî,
Gahvarî, Gotrâ, Giris'â, Gahanâ, Gamî, Guhâvâsâ, Guṇavatî (of
good qualities), Gurupâpapraṇâs'inî, Gurbbî, Guṇavatî (of the three
guṇas), Guhyâ, Goptavyâ, Guṇadâyinî, Girijâ, Guhyamâtangî, Garu-
daḍhvajavallabhâ, Garvâpahâriṇî, Godâ (grating Heaven), Gokulas-
thâ, Gadâdharâ, Gokarṇanilayâ saktâ, and Guhyamaṇḍala vartinî,

Now the names with "Gha". Thou art Gharmadâ, Ghanadâ, Ghaṇṭâ,
Ghora Dânava marddinî, Ghriṇî mantra mayî (of the Surya
mantra, Ghriṇi is to shine). Ghoṣâ, Ghanasampâtadâyinî, Ghaṇṭâra-
vapriyâ, Ghrûṇâ, Ghriṇisantuṣṭikâriṇî. (giving pleasure to the Sun), Gha-
nârimaṇḍalâ, Ghúrṇâ, Ghritâchî, Ghaṇavegiṇî, Gñânadhâtumayî, Thou art
Charchâ, Charchitâ, Châruhâsinî, Chaṭulâ, Chandikâ, Chitrâ, Chitramâl-
yavi bhûṣitâ, Chaturbhujâ. Châru dantâ, Châturî, Charitapradâ, Chûlikâ,
Chitravastrântâ, Chaṇḍramah Karṇa Kuṇḍalâ, Chandrahâsâ, Châru
dâtrî, Chakorî, Ghandrahâsinî, Chendrikâ, Chandradhâtrî, Chaurî,
Chorâ, Chaṇḍikâ, Chanchadvâgvâdinî, Chaudrachûḍâ, Choravinâs'inî,
Châruchandana liptâṇgî, Chanchachchâmaravijitâ, Chârumadhyâ,
Chârugati, Chandilâ, Chandrarúpiṇî, Châruhoma priyâ, Chârvâ, Charitâ,
Chakrabâhukâ, Chandramaṇḍalamadhyasthâ, Chandramaṇḍala Darpaṇâ,
Chakravâkastanî, Cheṣṭâ, Chitrâ, Châruvilâsinî, Chitsvarûpâ; Chand-
avatî, Chandramâ, Chandanapriyâ, Chodayitrî (as impelling the Jîvas
always to actions). Chiraprajnâ, Châtakâ, Châruhetukî, Thou art
Chhatrayâtâ, Chhatradharâ, Chhâyâ, Chhandhahparichchhadâ, Chhâyâ
Devî, Chhidranakhâ, Chhannendriyavisarpiṇî, Chhandonuṣṭuppratiṣ-
ṭhântâ, Chhidropadrava bhedinî, Chhedâ, Chhatres'varî, Chhinnâ,
Chhurikâ, and Chhedanpriyâ. Thou art Jananî, Janmarahitâ,
Jâtaveda, Jaganmayî, Jâhnavî, Jaṭilâ. Jatrî, (Jetrî) Jarâmaraṇa varjitâ,
Jambu dvîpa vatî, Jvâlâ, Jayantî, Jalas'âlinî, Jitendrîyâ, Jitakrodhâ,
Jitâmitrâ, Jagatpriyâ, Jâtarûpamayî, Jihvâ, Jânakî, Jagatî, Jaṭâ (Jayâ)
Janitrî, Jahnutanayâ, Jagattrayahitaiṣinî, Jvâlamulî, Japavatî, Jvara
ghnî, Jitaviṣṭapâ, Jitâkrântamayî, Jvâlâ, Jâgratî, Jvaradevatâ. Jva-
lantî, Jaladâ, Jyeṣṭhâ, Jyâghoṣâ sphoṭa dinmukhî, Jambbinî, Jrimbhaṇâ,
Jrimbhâ,Jvalanmâṇikya Kuṇḍalâ. Jhinjhikâ, Jhaṇanirghoṣâ, Jhanjhâ

Mâruta veginî, Jhallakîvâdya kus'alâ, Ṇrûpâ, Ṇbhujâ, Ṭaṇka bhedinî, Tanka bâṇasamâyuktâ, Tankinî, Taṇka bhedinî, Tankîgaṇakṛitâghoṣâ, Taṇkanîya mahorasâ, Taṇkâra Kâriṇî, Ṭha ṭha s'avdaninâdinî.

63-80. Now come the names beginning with "Ḍa" They are :— "Ḍâmarî, Ḍâkinî, Ḍimbhâ, Ḍuṇḍamâraikanirjitâ, Ḍâmarîtantramârgasthâ, Ḍamḍaḍamarunâdinî, Ḍiṇḍiravasahâ, Ḍimbhalasat krîḍâparâyaṇâ (dancing with joy in battles). Then Ḍhuṇḍhi vighnes'a jananî, Dhakkâ hastâ, Dhilivrajâ (followed by Śiva gaṇas), Nityajnânâ, Nirupamâ, Nirguṇâ and Narmadâ river. Now:—Triguṇâ, Tripadâ, Tantrî, Tulasî, Taruṇâ, Taru, Trivikramapadâ krâṇtâ, Tû rîyapadagâminî, Taruṇâ ditya samkas'â, Tâmasî, Tuhinâ, Turâ, Trikâlajñâna Sampannâ, Trivalî, Trilochanâ, Tri Śakti, Tripurâ, Tungâ, Turangavadanâ, Timingilagilâ, Tîbrâ, Trisrotâ, Tâmasâdinî, Tantra mantravis'eṣajñâ, Tanumadhyâ, Triviṣṭapâ, Trisandhyâ, Tristanî, Toṣâsamsthâ, Tâlapratâpinî, Tâṭankinî, Tuṣârâbhâ, Tuhinâchala vâsinî, Tantujâlasamâyuktâ, Târahârâ valipriyâ, Tilahomapriyâ, Tîrthâ, Tamâla kusumâ kriti, Târakâ, Triyutâ, Tanvî, Tris'am kuparivâritâ, Talodarî, Tirobhâṣâ, Tâṭamka priyavâdinî, Trijaṭâ, Tittirî, Tṛiṣṇâ, Tribidhâ, Taruṇâ kritî, Tapta kânchanasamkâs'â, Tapta kâñchaṇa bhûṣanâ, Traiyambakâ, Trivargâ, Trikâlajñânadâyinî, Tarpaṇâ, Triptidâ, Tṛiptâ, Tâmasî, Tumvarustutâ, Târkṣyasthâ, Triguṇâkârâ, Tribhangî, Tanuvallarî, Thâtkârî, Thâravâ, Thântâ, Dohinî, Dînavatsalâ, Dânavânta karî, Durgâ, Durgâsuranivahriṇî, Devarîti, Divârâtri, Draupadî, Dundubhisvanâ, Devayânî, Durâvâsâ, Dâridrya bhedinî, Divâ, Dâmodarapriyâ, Dîptâ, Digvâsâ, Digvimohinî, Daṇḍa kâraṇya nilayâ, Daṇḍinî, Deva pûjitâ, Deva vandyâ, Diviṣâdâ, Dveṣiṇî, Dânavâ kṛiti, Dînanâ thastutâ, Dîkṣâ, Daivatâ disvarupiṇî, Dhâtṛi, Dhanurdharâ

Dhenur Dhâriṇî, Dharmachâriṇî, Dhurandharâ, Dharâdhârâ, Dhanadâ, Dhânya dohinî, Dharmas'îlâ, Dhanâdhyakṣâ, Dhanurvedavis'âradâ, Dhriti, Dhanyâ, Dhritapadâ, Dharmarâjapriyâ, Dhruvâ, Dhûmâvatî, Dhûmakes'î Dharmas'âstraprakâs'inî.

81-98. Nandâ, Nandapriyâ, Nidrâ, Nrinutâ, Nandanâtmikâ, Narmmadâ Nalinî, Nîlâ, Nîlakaṇṭhasamâs'rayâ, Rudrâṇî, Nârâyaṇapriyâ, Nityâ, Nirmmalâ, Nirguṇâ, Nidhi, Nirâdhârâ, Nirupamâ, Nityas'uddhâ, Nirañjanâ, Nâdabindu Kalâtîtâ, Nâdavindu Kalâtmikâ, Nrisimhinî, Nagadharâ, Nripanâga vibhûṣitâ, Naraka Kles'anâs'inî, Nârâyaṇapado dbhavâ, Niravadyâ, Nirâkârâ, Nâradapriyakâriṇî, Nânâjyotiḥ, Nidhidâ, Nirmalâtmikâ, Navasûtradharâ, Nîti, Nirupa drava kâriṇî, Nandajâ, Navaratnâḍhyâ, Naimiṣâraṇya vâsinî, Navanîtapriya, Nârî, Nîla jîmûta nisvanâ, Nimeṣiṇî, Nadîrûpâ, Nîlagrîvâ, Nis'is'varî, Nâmâvalî, Nis'umbhaghnî, Nâgaloka nivâsinî, Navajâmbû nadaprakhyâ, Nâgalokâ

dhidevatâ, Nûpûrâ Krântacharaṇâ, Narachitta pramodinî, Nimagnâ rakta nayanâ, Nirghâta-sama-nisvanâ, Nandanodyâ nanilayâ, Nirvyu hoparichâriṇî.

90-107. Pârvatî, Paramodârâ, Parabrahmâtmikâ, Parâ, Pañchkos'a-vinirmuktâ, Pañchapâtaka-nâs'inî, Para chitta vidhânajñâ, Panchikâ, Pañcharûpiṇî, Pûrṇimâ, Paramâ Prîti, Paratejaḥ prakâs'inî, Purâṇî. Paurṇṣî, Puṇyâ, Puṇḍarî kanibhekṣaṇâ, Pâtâla tala nirmmagnâ, Prîtâ, Prîtivivardhinî, Pâvanî, Pâda sahitâ, Pes'alâ, Pavanâs'inî Prajâpati, Paris'rântâ, Parvatastana maṇḍalâ, Padmapriyâ, Padmasamsthâ, Padmâkṣî, Padmasambhavâ, Padmapatrâ, Padmapadâ, Padminî, Priyabhâṣiṇî, Pas'upâs'a vinirmuktâ, Purandhrî, Puravâsinî, Puṣkalâ, Puruṣâ, Parbbâ, Pârijâta Kusumapriyâ, Pativratâ, Pativratâ, Pavitrângî, Puṣpahâsa parâyaṇâ, Prajñâvatîsutâ, Pautrî, Putrapûjyâ, Payasvinî, Pattipâs'adharâ, Pankti, Pitrilokapradâyinî, Purânî, Puṇyas'ila, Praṇatârti vinâs'inî, Pradyumnajananî, Puṣṭâ, Pitâmahaparigrahâ, Puṇḍarîkapuravâsâ, Puṇḍarîkasamânanâ, Prithujanghâ, Prithubhujâ, Prithupâdâ, Prithûdarî, Pravâlas'obhâ, Pingâkṣî, Pîtavâsâh, Prachâpalâ, Prasavâ, Puṣtidâ, Puṇyâ, Pratiṣṭhâ, Praṇavâ, Pati, Pañchavarnâ, Panchavâṇî, Pañchikâ, Panjarasthitâ, Paramâyâ, Parajyotiḥ, Paraprîti, Parâgati, Parâkâṣṭhâ, Pares'anî, Pâvanî, Pâvaka Dyutî, Puṇyabhadrâ, Parichchhedyâ, Puṣpahâsâ, Prithûdarâ, Pîtângî, Pîtavasanâ Pîtas'ayâ, Pis'âchinî, Pîtakriyâ, Pis'âchaghnî, Pâṭalâkṣî, Paṭukriyâ, Pañchabhakṣapriyâchârâ, Putanâ prâṇaghâtinî, Punnâgavanamadhyasthâ, Puṇyatîrthaniṣevitâ, Panchângî, Parâs'akti, Paramâlhâda kâriṇî, Puṣpakâṇḍasthitâ, Pûṣâ, Poṣitâkhila-viṣṭapâ, Pânapriyâ, Pañchas'ikhâ, Pannagoparis'âyinî, Panchamâtrât-mikâ, Prithvî, Pathikâ, Prithudohinî, Purâṇanyâyamîmâṅsâ, Pâṭalî, Puṣpagandhinî, Puṇyaprajâ, Pâradâtrî, Paramârgaikagocharâ, Pravâlas'obhâ, Pûrṇâs'â, Praṇavâ, Pallabodarî.

108-149. Phalinî, Phaladâ, Phalgu, Phutkârî, Phalakâkritî, Phaṇindra bhogas'ayanâ, Phaṇimaṇḍalamaṇḍitâ, Bâlabâlâ, Bahumatâ, Bâlâtapanibhâms'ukâ, Balabhadrapriyâ, Vandyâ, Baḍavâ, Buddhisamstutâ, Bandîdevî, Bilavatî, Baḍis'aghinî, Balipriyâ, Bândhavî, Bodhitâ, Buddhirbandhûkakusumapriyâ, Bâla bhânuprabhâkârâ, Brâhmî, Brâhmaṇa devatâ, Brihaspatistutâ, Briudâ, Brindâvana vihâriṇî, Bâlâkinî, Bilâhârâ, Bilavasâ Bahûdakâ, Bahunetrâ, Bahupadâ, Bahukarṇâvatamsikâ, Bahubâhuyutâ, Bîjarûpinî, Bahurûpiṇî, Binduṇâdakalâtîtâ, Bindunâdasvarûpiṇî, Baddhagodhângulitrâṇâ, Badaryâs'ramavâsinî, Brindârakâ, Brihatskandhâ, Brihatî, Bâṇapâtinî, Brindâdhyakṣâ, Bahunutâ, Vanitâ, Bahuvikramâ, Baddhapadmâsanâsînâ, Bilvapatratalasthitâ, Bodhidrumanijâvâsâ, Badisthâ, Bindu darpaṇâ, Bâlâ, Vâṇâsanavatî, Baḍavânalaveginî, Brahmâṇḍa bahirantasthâ, Brahmakankaṇasûtriṇî, Bhavânî, Bhîṣaṇavatî, Bhâvinî, Bhayahârinî, Bhadrakâlî, Bhujangâkṣî, Bhâratî, Bhâratâs'ayâ, Bhairavî, Bhîṣaṇâkârâ, Bhûtidâ, Bhutimâlinî, Bhâminî, Bhoganiratâ, Bhadradâ, Bhûrivikramâ, Bhûtavâsâ, Bhrigulatâ, Bhârgavî, Bhûsurârchitâ, Bhâgîrathî, Bhogavatî, Bhavanasthâ, Bhiṣagvarâ, Bhâminî, Bhoginî, Bhâṣâ, Bhavânî, Bhûridakṣiṇâ, Bhargâtmikâ, Bhîmavatî, Bhavabandhavimochinî, Bhajanîyâ, Bhûtadhâtrî-ranjitâ, Bhuvanes'varî, Bhujangavalayâ, Bhîmâ, Bheruṇḍâ, Bhâgadheyinî; Thou art Mâtâ, Mâyâ, Madhumatî, Madhujihavâ, Manupriyâ, Mahâdevî, Mahâbhâgîâ, Mâlini, Mînalochanâ, Mâyâtîtâ, Madhumatî, Madhumânsâ, Madhudravâ, Mânavî, Madhusambhûtâ, Mithilâpuravâsinî, Madhukaiṭabhasamhartrî, Medinî, Meghamâlinî, Mandodarî, Mahâ Mâyâ, Maithilî, Masriṇapriyâ, Mahâ Lakṣmî, Mahâ Kâlî, Mahâ Kaṇyâ, Mahes'varî, Mâhendrî, Merutanayâ Mandârakusumârchitâ, Manjumanjîracharaṇâ, Mokṣadâ, Manjubhâṣiṇî, Madhuradrâviṇî, Mudrâ, Malayâ, Malayânvitâ, Medhâ, Marakatas'yâmâ, Mâgadhî, Menakâtmajâ, Mahâmârî, Mahâvîrâ, Mahâs'yâmâ, Manustutâ, Mâtrikâ, Mihirâbhâsâ, Mukundapada Vikramâ, Mûlâdhârasthitâ, Mugdhâ, Maṇipûranivâsinî, Mrigâkṣî, Mahiṣârûḍhâ, Mahiṣâsuramardinî, Thou art Yogâsanâ, Yogagamyâ, Yogâ, Yauvanakâs'rayâ, Yauvanî, Yuddhamadhyasthâ, Yamunâ, Yugâdhariṇî, Yakṣiṇî, Yogayuktâ, Yakṣarâjaprasûtinî, Yâtrâ, Yâna bidhânajñâ, Yaduvaṇs'asamudbhavâ, Yakârâdi-Ha Kârântâ, (all ântaḥstha varṇas), Yâjuṣî, Yajña rûpiṇî, Yâminî, Yoganiratâ, Yâtudhâna, bhayamkarî, Rukmiṇî, Ramaṇî, Râmâ, Revaṭî, Reṇukâ, Ratî, Raudrî, Raudrapriyâkârâ Râma mâtâ, Ratipriyâ, Rohiṇî, Râjyadâ, Revâ, Rasâ, Râjîvalochanâ, Râkes'î, Rûpasampannâ, Ratnasimhâsanasthitâ, Raktamâlyâmbaradharâ, Raktagandhânu lepanâ, Râja hamsa samârûḍhâ, Rambhâ, Raktavalipriyâ, Ramaṇîyayugâdhârâ, Râjitâkhilabhûtalâ, Rurucharmaparidhânâ, Rathinî, Ratnamâlikâ, Roges'î, Rogas'amanî, Râvinî, Romaharṣiṇî, Râmachandra padâ Krântâ, Râvaṇachchhedakâriṇî, Ratnavastra parichchhinvâ, Rathasthâ, Rukma bhûṣaṇâ, Lajjâdhidevatâ, Lolâ, Lalitâ, Lingadhâriṇî. Lakṣmî, Lolâ, Luptaviṣâ, Lokinî, Lokavis'rutâ, Lajjâ, Lambodarî, Lalanâ, Lokadhâriṇî Varadâ, Vanditâ, Vidyâ, Vaiṣṇavî, Vimalâkriti, Vârâhî, Virajâ, Varṣâ, Varalakṣmî, Vilâsinî, Vinatâ, Vyomamadhyasthâ, Vârijâsanasamsthitâ, Vâruṇî, Veṇusambhutâ, Vîtihotrâ, Virûpiṇî, Vâyumaṇḍalamadhyasthâ, Viṣṇurûpâ, Vidhikriyâ, Viṣṇupatnî, Viṣṇumatî, Vis'âlâkṣî, Vasundharâ, Vâmadevapriyâ, Velâ, Vajriṇî, Vasudohinî, Vedâkṣaraparîtâmgî, Vâjapeyaphalapradâ, Vâsavî, Vâmajananî, Vaikuṇṭhanilayâ, Varâ, Vyâsapriyâ, Varmadharâ, Vâlmîkiparisevitâ,

Thou art Śakambharî, Śivâ, Śantâ. Śaradâ, Śaraṇâgati, Śâtodarî, Śubhâchârâ, Śumbhâsuramardinî, Śobhâbatî, Śivâkârâ, Śamkarârdhas'arîriṇî, Śoṇâ, (red), Śubhâs'ayâ, Śubhrâ, Śiraḥsandhânakâriṇî, Śarâvatî, Śarânandâ, Śarajjyotsnâ, Śubhânanâ, Śarabhâ, Śûlinî, Śuddhâ, Śabarî. Śukavâhanâ, Śrîmatî, Śridharânandâ, Śravaṇânandadâyinî, Śarvâṇî, Śarbbarîvandyâ, Ṣaḍbhâṣâ, Ṣaḍritupriyâ, Ṣaḍâdhârasthitâdevî, Ṣaṇmukhapriyakâriṇî, Ṣaḍamgarûpasumati, Ṣurâsuranamaṣkṛitâ.

150-155. Thou art Sarasvatî, Sadâdhârâ, Sarvamangalakâriṇî, Sâmagânapriyâ, Sûkṣmâ, Sâvitrî, Sâmasambhavâ, Sarvavâsâ, Sadânandâ, Sustanî, Sâgarâmbarâ, Sarvais'yaryapriyâ, Siddhi, Sâdhubandhuparâkramâ, Saptarṣimaṇḍalagatâ, Somamaṇḍalavâsinî, Sarvajñâ, Sândrakaruṇâ, Samânâdhikavarjitâ, Sarvottungâ, Sangahînâ, Sadguṇâ, Sakaleṣṭadâ, Saraghâ (bee), Sûryatanayâ, Sukes'î, Somasamhati, Hiraṇyavarṇâ, Hariṇî, Hrîmkârî, Hamsavâhinî, Kṣaumavastraparîtângî, Kṣîrâbdhitanayâ, Kṣamâ, Gâyatrî, Sâvitrî, Pârvatî, Sarasvatî, Vedagarbhâ, Varârohâ, Śrî Gâyatrî, and Parâmvikâ.

156-159. O Nârâda! Thus I have described to you one thousand (and eight) names of Gâyatrî, ; the hearing of which yields merits and destroys all sins and gives all prosperity and wealth. Specially in the Aṣṭamîtithi (eighth lunar day) if after one's meditation (dhyânam) worship, Homa, and japam, one recites this in company with the Brâhmaṇas, one gets all sorts of satisfactions. These one thousand and eight names of the Gâyatrî ought not to be given to anybody indiscriminately. Speak this out to him only who is very devoted, who is a Brâhmaṇa, and who is an obedient disciple. Even if any devotee, fallen from the observances of Âchârâ (right way of living), be a great friend, still do not disclose this to him.

160-165. In whatever house, these names are kept written, no cause of fear can creep in there and Lakṣmî, the Goddess of wealth, though unsteady, remains steady in that house.

This great secret yields merits to persons, gives wealth to the poor, yields mokṣa to those who are desirous of it, and grants all desires. If anybody reads this, he gets cured of his diseases, and becomes freed from bondages and imprisonment. All the Great Sins, for example, murdering Brâhmaṇas, drinking wine, stealing gold, going to the wife of one's Guru, taking gifts from bad persons, and eating the uneatables, all are destroyed, yea, verily destroyed! O Nârada! Thus I have recited to you this Great Secret. All persons get, indeed, united with Brahma (Brahama sâyujya) by this. True. True. True. There is not the least trace of doubt here.

Here ends the Sixth Chapter of the Twelfth Book on the one thousand and eight names of the Gâyatrî in the Mahâpurâṇam Śrî Mad Devî Bhâgavatam of 18,000 verses by Maharṛi Veda Vyâsa.

CHAPTER VII.

1-3. Nârada said :—I have heard the one thousand names or nâma stotras equivalent in its fruits to S'rî Gâyatrî, highly potent in making a good fortune and tending to a splendid increase of the wealth and prosperity. Now I want to hear about how initiations in Mantrams are performed, without which nobody, be he a Brâhmiṇ, a Kṣattriya, a Vais'ya or a Śûdra, is entitled to have the Devî Mantra. O Lord! Kindly describe the ordinary (Sâmânya) and the special (vis'eṣa) rules thereof.

4-41. Nârâyaṇa said :—"O Nârada! Listen. I am now telling you about the rules of initiation (Dîkṣâ) of the disciples, pure in heart. When they are initiated, they become entitled then and not before that, to worship the Devas, the Fire and the Guru. That method of instruction, and religious act and ceremony is called the Dîkṣâ (initiation) by which the Divine Knowledge is imparted; and at once flashes in the heart and mind of the initiated that Knowledge and all his sins are then destroyed. So the Pundits of the Vedas and the Tantras say. (The Divine Knowledge is like lightning, fire, arising and permeating the body, mind, and spirit.) This Dîkṣâ ought to be taken by all means. This gives excellent merits and pure results. Both the Guru and the Śiṣya (disciple) ought to be very pure and true. (This is the first essential requisite. Then the results are instantaneous). First of of all, the Guru is to perform all the morning duties, he is to take his bath and perform his Sandhyâ Vandanams. He is to return home from the banks of the river with his Kamaṇḍalu and observe maunam (silence). Then, in order to give Dîkṣâ, he is to enter into the assigned room (Yâga Maṇḍapa) and take his seat on an Âsana that is excellent and calculated to please all. He is to perform Âchamana and do Prâṇâyâma. Then he should take water in his Arghya vessel and putting scents and flowers in that, charge that water with Phaṭkâra mantra (that is, condense electricity, Spirit in that). Then uttering the Phaṭ mantra, he is to sprinkle the water on the doorways of the worshiproom and begin his Poojâ. Firstly, on the top of the door at one end invoke the Deity Gaṇanâthâ by His mantra, at the other end invoke Sarasvatî by Her mantra, and at the middle, invoke Lakṣmî Devî by Her mantra duly and worship them with flowers. Then, on the right side worship Gangâ and Bighnes'a; and on the left side worship Kṣettrapâla and Yamunâ, the daughter of the Sun. Similarly, on the bottom of the door, worship the Astra Devatâ by the

Phaṭ mantra. Then consider the whole Maṇḍapa as inspired with the presence of the Devî, and see the whole place as pervaded by Her through and through. Then, repeat the Phaṭ mantra and destroy the Celestial obstacles as well as those from the middle space (Antarîkṣa); strike the ground thrice with the left heel and thus destroy the Terrene obstacles. Then touching the left branch on the left side of the choukâṭ, put the right foot forward and enter into the Maṇḍapa. Then instal the Śânti Kumbha (the peace jar) and offer the ordinary Arghya (Sâmânyârgha). Next worship the Vâstunâtha and Padmayoni with flowers and Âtapa rice and the Arghya water, on the south-west and then purify the Pancha Gavya. Next sprinkle all the Maṇḍapa and the entrance gate with that Arghya water. And, while sprinkling with Arghya water, consider the whole space right through as inspired with the presence of the Devî and repeat the Mûla Mantra with devotion and sprinkle with Phaṭ mantra. The Kartâ, then, uttering the mantra "Phaṭ," is to drive away all the evils from the Maṇḍapa and uttering the mantra "Hûm" sprinkle water, all around, thus pacifying the atmosphere and bringing peace into the hearts of all present.

Then burn the Dhûpa incense inside and scatter Vikira (water, sandal-paste, yava, ashes, Durba grass with roots, and Âtapa rice). Then collect all these rice, etc., again with a broom made of Kus'a grass to the north east corner of the Maṇḍapa; making the Sankalap and uttering Svasti vâchana (invocation of good), distribute and satisfy the poor and orphans with fooding, clothing and money. Then he should bow down to his own Guru and take his seat humbly on the soft Âsanam allotted to him with his face eastwards and meditate on the Deity (Iṣṭa Deva) of the mantra that is to be imparted to the disciple. After meditating thus, he is to do the Bhûta s'uddhi (purification of elements) and perform Nyâsa, etc., of the Deya mantra (the mantra that is to be imparted to the disciple) according to the rules stated below:—*i. e.* the Riṣi on the head; the chhandas in the mouth, the Iṣṭa Devatâ in the heart, Bîja on the anus and Śakti Nyâsa on the two legs. Then he is to make sound thrice by the clap of his palm and thus thwart off all the evils of the earth and the middle space and then make digbandhan (tieing up the quarters) by the mudrâ chhoṭikâ three times (snapping the thumb and forefinger together). Then perform the Prâṇâyâma with the Mûla mantra of the would-be-Iṣṭa-Devatâ and do the Mâtrikâ Nyâsa in one's own body, thus:—"Om Am namaḥ s'irasi, Om Âm namah on the face, Om Im namah on the right eye, Om Îmnamah on the left eye, and so on, assign all the letters duly to their respective places. Then perform the Karânga nyâsa on the fingers and the Ṣaḍanga nyâsâ thus:—Speak:—Om Hridayâya namah, touching on the heart, utter Om Śirase svâhâ, touching the head; Om

S'ikhâyai Vaṣat, touching the tuft; Om Kavachâya Hum, touching on the Kavacha, "Om netratrayâya Vauṣaṭ, touching the eye, and "Om Astrâya Phaṭ" touching both the sides of the hand, the palm and its back. Then finish the Nayâsa by doing the Varṇanyâsa of the Mûla mantra in those places that are said in the cognate kalpas. (*i. e.* throat, heart, arms, legs, etc).

O Nârada! Next consider within your body the seat of an auspicious Âsana (a seat) and make the Nyâsa of Dharma on the right side, Jñânaṃ on the left side, of Vairâgyam (dispassion) on the left thigh, prosperity and wealth on the right thigh, of non-Dharma in the mouth and of Non-Jñânaṃ on the left side, Avairâgyam (passion) on the navel, and poverty on the right side, Then think of the feet of the Âsana (the body) as Dharma, etc, and all the limbs as Adharna (non-Dharma.) In the middle of the Âsana (body) *i.e.*, in the heart consider Ananta Deva as a gentle bed and on that a pure lotus representing this universe of five elements. Then make Nyâsa of the Sun, Moon, and Fire on this lotus and think the Sun as composed of twelve Kalâs (digits,) the Moon composed of sixteen Kalâs (digits) and the Fire as composed of ten Kalâs. Over this make Nyâsa of Sattva, Raja and Tamo Guṇas, Âtmâ, Antarâtmâ, Paramâtmâ and Jñânâtmâ and then think of this as his Iṣṭa's altar where the devotee is to meditate on his Iṣṭa Devatâ, the Highest Mother. Nyâsa-assignment of the various parts of the body to different deities which is usually accompanied with prayers and corresponding gesticulations. Next the devotee is to perform the mental worship of the Deya Mantra Devatâ according to the rules of his own Kalpa; next he is to show all the Mudrâs stated in the Kalpa for the satisfaction of the Deva. The Devas become very pleased when all these Mudrâs are shown to them.

42-46. O Nârada! Now, on one's left side, erect an hectagon; inside it a circular figure; inside this again a square and then draw within that square a triangle and over it show the Śankha Mudrâ.

After finishing the Poojâ of the Six Deities at the six corners of the hectagon, Fire, etc., take the tripod of the Śankha (conch-shell) and sprinkling it with Phaṭ mantra, place it within the triangle.

Utter, then, the Mantra "Maṃ Vahniman dalâya Das'a Kalâtmane Amuka Devyâ Arghyapâtrasthânâya namaḥ" and thus worshipping the Śânkhya vessel place it within the maṇḍala. Then worship in the Śankha pâtra, the ten Kalâs of Fire, beginning from the East,.then south-east and so on. Sprinkle the Śankha, conchshell, with the Mûla Mantra and meditating on it, place the Śankha (conch shell) on the tripod. Repeating the mantra "Am Sûrya maṇḍalâya Dvâdas'akalâtmane Amukodevyâ

Arghyapâtrâya namaḥ" worship in the Arghyapâtra Śankha, sprinkle water in the Śankha with the Mantra Sam Śankhya namaḥ." Worship in due order the twelve Kalâs of the Sun Tapinî, Tâpinî, Dhûmrâ, etc., utter the fifty syllables of the Mâtrikâ in an inverse order (*i.e.*, beginning (See the Sâradâ Tilaka) with Kṣaṃ, Haṃ, Ṣaṃ, Sam, Śaṃ etc.,) and repeating the Mûla Mantra also in an inverse order, fill the Śankha, three-fourths, with water. Next perform in it the Nyâsa of Chandrakalâ and uttering the Mantra " Uṃ Soma maṇḍalâya Ṣoḍas'akalâtmane Amukadevatâyâ Arghyâmritâya namaḥ, worship in this conchshell. Next with Ankus'a mudrâ, invoke all the tîrthas there, repeating the Mantra " Gange Cha Yamune chaiva, etc., and repeat eight times the Mûla Mantra (the basic Mantra)

Then perform the Ṣaḍaṃga Nyâsa in the water and with the Mantra. " Hridâ namaḥ, etc., worship and, repeating eight times the Mûla Mantra, cover it with Matsyamundrâ.

Next place on the right side of the Śankha, the Prokṣaṇî Pâtra (the Kus'â vessel from which water is taken for sprinkling) and put a little water in it. By this water sprinkle and purify all the articles of worship as well as one's own body and consider one's Âtman as pure and holy.

57-81. After doing works thus far the until Vis'eṣârghya is placed, the devotee should erect Sarvato bhadra maṇḍala within the altar and put the Śâli rice within its pericarp, Next spread Kus'a grass on that Maṇḍala and put on one Kurcha, looking well and auspicious within it, made of twenty-seven Kus'a grass knotted with Venyagra granthi. Worship here the Âdhâra Śakti, Prakriti, Kûrma, Śeṣa, Kṣamâ, Sudhâsindhu, Maṇimaṇḍala, Kalpa vrikṣa and Iṣṭa devatâ and the Pîṭha. (Durgâ Devî yoga pîṭhâya namah). Then have an entire kumbha (waterjâr) having no defect, wash it inside with Phaṭ mantra, and encircle it with the red thread thrice as symbolising the three Guṇas.

Place within this jar the Nava ratna (nine jewels) with Kurcha and worshipping it with scents and flowers put them in the jar repeating the Praṇava, and place that on the Pîṭha (seat). Next consider the Pîṭha and Kumbha (waterjar) as one and the same and pour waters from the Tîrthas, repeating in an inverse order the Mâtrikâ Varṇas (from Kṣa to Ka) and fill it, thinking of the Iṣṭa Deva and repeating the basic mantra, put the new and fresh twigs (Pallavas) of As'vattha, Panasa and mango trees, etc., in the jar and cover its mouth and place over it fruits, rice, and chaṣaka (honey) and wrap it with two red clothes. Then perform the Prâṇa-Pratiṣṭhâ and invoke the Spirit of the Devî by the Prâṇasthâpana Mantra and show the Mudrâs, Âvâhana, etc., and thus satisfy the Devî. Then do the Ṣoḍas'opachâra Pûjâ of the Devî after meditating on the Parames'varî according to the rules of the Kalpa. First offer "welcome" in front of the Devî and then duly offer the Pâdya, Arghya, Âchamanîya water, Madhuparka, and oils, etc., for the bath. Then offer nice red silken clothes and various jewels, ornaments; repeating the Mâtrikâ syllables electrified with the Deya Mantra, worship the whole body of the Devî with scents and flowers. Next offer to the Devî the sweet scent of Kâlâguru mixed with camphor and the Kâs'mîri sandalpaste mixed with Kastûrî and various nice scented flowers, for example, the Kunda flowers, etc.. Then offer the Dhûpa prepared from Aguru, Guggula, Us'îra, sandalpaste, sugar, and honey and know that the Dhûpa is very pleasing to the Devî. Next offer various lights and offerings of fruits, vegetables and fooding. Be particular to sprinkle everything with the water of the Kosâ, thus purifying, before it is offered to the Devî. Then complete the Anga Pûjâ and the Âvarana-pûjâ of the Devî, then perform the duty of Vais'vadeva. On the right side of the Devî erect an altar (sthandila) six feet square and instal Agni (Fire) there. Invoke there the Deity, thinking of Her Form and worship Her with scents and flowers. Then with the Vyâhriti Mantra with Svâhâ prefixed and Mûla (Deya) Mantra perform the Homa ceremony with oblations, charu and ghee, twenty five times. Next perform Homa again with Vyârhiti. Next worship the Devî with scents, etc., and consider the Devî and Pîtha Devatâ as one and the same. Then take leave of (visarjana) the Agni (Fire). Offer valis (sacrifices) all round to the Pârs'vadas of the Devî with the remnant charu of the Homa.

Now again worship the Devî with five offerings and offer betel, umbrella, châmara and others and repeat the Mûla mantra thousand times. After finishing the Japam, place Karkarî (a water-jar with small holes at the bottom, as in a sieve) on the rice in the north-eastern corner and invoke the Devî there and worship Her. Uttering the mantra "Raksa Raksa" moisten the place with water coming out of Karkarî, and repeat the Phat mantra. After re-worshipping the Devî, place Karkarî in due position. Thus the Guru finishes the Adhivâsa (foregoing) ceremony and takes his meals with the disciple and sleeps that night on that altar.

82-106. O Nârada! Now I am describing briefly about the Homa Kunda (a round hole in the ground consecrated to the Deity) and the Samskâra ceremony of the Sthandila (the sacrificial altar). Uttering, first, the Mûla Mantra, see, fix your gaze on the Kunda; then sprinkle it with water and the Phat mantra and drive away the evil-spirits from there. Then with mantra "Hum" again sprinkle it with water.

Then draw within it three lines Prâgagra and Udagagra (on the eastern and northern sides). Sprinkling it with water and the Praṇava, worship within the Pîṭha, utterring the mantras from Âdhâra Śaktaye namaḥ to Amuka Devî Yoga Pîṭhâya namaḥ. Invoke, in that Pîtha, the Highest One, Who is Śiva Śivâ with all one-ness of heart and worship Her with scents and offerings. Then think for a moment the Devî as having taken bath and as one with Śankara. Bring then fire in a vessel and taking a flaming piece thereof throw that in the south-west corner. Then purifying it by the gaze and quitting the portions of Kravyâdaḥ, impart the Chaitanya by "Raṃ," the Vahnivîja repeat "Oṃ" over it seven times. Shew, then, the Dhenumudrâ and protect it by Phaṭ Kâra and cover, veil, it with the mantra "Huṃ." Then turn the fire, thus worshipped with sandalpaste, etc., thrice over the Kuṇḍa and with both the knees on the ground and repeating the Praṇava, consider the Agni as the Vîrya of Śiva and throw it on the yoni of the Devî in the Pîṭha. Then offer Âchamana, etc., to the Deva and the Devî and worship. Then light the flame with the mantra "Chit Pingala Hana Hana Daha Daha Pacha Pacha Sarvajñâ Jñapaya Svâhâ" Then utter the stotra to the Agni Deva with great love, repeating the mantra "Agnim Prajvalitam vande Jâtavedam Hutâs'anaṃ suvarṇa varṇamamalaṃ samiddham Visvatomukhaṃ." Then perform the Ṣaḍaṃganyâsa to the Agni Deva "Om Sahasrârchchiṣe namaḥ, Oṃ Svasti Pûrṇâya Svâhâ," Oṃ Uttiṣṭha puruṣâya vaṣaṭ," "Oṃ Dhûma vyâpine Huṃ Oṃ Sapta Jihvâya vauṣat" "Oṃ Dhanur dharâya Phaṭ." Repeating the above six mantras, perform the Nyâsa on the heart, etc., the six places. Now meditate on the Agni as of a golden colour, three-eyed, seated on a lotus and holding in His four hands signs of granting boons, Śakti, Svastika and sign of "no fear"; also meditate on Agni, as the seat of the greatest auspiciousness. Then moisten the Kuṇḍa on the top of the belt (mekhalâ) with water. Next spread the Kus'a grass all around and draw the Agni yantra over it, i. e., triangle, hectagon, circle, eight-petalled figure and Bhûpura; rather have this drawing before the Agnisthâpanâ. Now meditate this only. Then, within the Yantra, recite "Vais'vânara Jâtaveda Lohitâkṣa sarvakarmâṇi Sâdhaya Svâhâ" and worship Agni. Then worship in the centre and in the hectagon at the corners worship the Saptajihvâ (seven tongues Hiraṇya, Gaganâ, Raktâ, Kriṣṇâ, Suprabhâ, Bahurûpâ, Atiraktikâ and next worship within the pericarp of the lotus the Anga Devatâs. Then recite the following mantras within the eight petals:—"Oṃ Agnaye Jâtavedase namaḥ," "Oṃ Agnaye Saptajihvâya namaḥ," "Oṃ Agnaye Havyavâhanâya namaḥ," Oṃ Agnaye As'vodarajâya namaḥ," "Oṃ Agnaye Vais'vânarâya namaḥ," "Oṃ Agnaye Kaumâra tejase namaḥ," "Oṃ Agnaye Vis'vamukhâya namaḥ," "Oṃ Agnaye Devamukhâya namaḥ" and considering the forms to hold Śakti and Svastik, worship them. Then consider Indra and the other Lokapâlas (Regents of the several quarters) situated in the east, south-east, and so-on together with their weapons, the thunderbolt and the other weapons, and thus worship them.

107-134. O Nârada! Next purify the sacrificial ladles, etc., sruk, sruva, etc., and ghee; then, taking ghee by sruva, go on with the Homa ceremony. Divide the ghee of the Âjyasthâlî (the vessel in which the ghee for the Homa purposes is kept) in three parts: take ghee from the right side and saying "Oṃ Agnaye Svâhâ" offer oblations on the right eye of the Agni; take ghee from the left side and saying "Oṃ Somâya Svâhâ offer oblations on the left eye of the Agni; take ghee from the centre and saying, "Oṃ Agnîṣomâbhyâṃ Svâhâ, offer oblations on the central eye of the Agni. Take ghee again from the right side and saying "Oṃ Agnaye Sviṣṭakṛite Svâhâ" offer oblations to the mouth of the Agni. Then the devotee is to repeat "Oṃ Bhuḥ Svâhâ," "Oṃ Bhuvaḥ Svâhâ," "Oṃ Svaḥ Svâhâ" and offer thrice the oblations; next he is to offer oblations thrice with the Agni mantra. After this, O Muni! for impregnation and each of the ten Saṃskâras, natal-ceremony, tonsure, etc., he is to repeat the Praṇava Mantra and offer the eight oblations of ghee on each occasion. Now hear of the tenfold Saṃskâras:—(1) Inpregnation, (2) Puṃsavan (a ceremony performed as soon as a woman perceives the foetus to be quick), (3) Sîmantonnayana (a ceremony observed by women in the fourth, sixth or the eighth month of pregnancy), (4) Jâta Karma (ceremony at the birth of a child), (5) Nâmakaraṇa, (naming the child), (6) Niṣkrâmaṇa (a ceremony performed when a new-born child is first taken out of the house into the open air (usually in the fourth month), (7) Annaprâs'ana (when the rice is put in the mouth of the child), (8) Chûḍâkaraṇa (the ceremony of the first tonsure, (9) Upanayana (holding the sacrificial thread; (10) Godâna and Udvâha (gift of cows and marriage). These are stated in the Vedas. Next worship Śiva Pârvatî, the Father and the Mother of Agni and take leave of them. Next in the name of Agni, offer five Samidhas (fuel) soaked in ghee and offer one oblation of ghee to each of the Âvaraṇa Devatâs.

Then take the ghee by the Śruk and covering it with the Śruva, offer ten oblations to Agni, and Mahâ Gaṇes'a with mantras ending in Vauṣaṭ.

(The Mahâ Ganes'a mantras run as follows :—(1) Oṃ, Oṃ Svâhâ (2) Oṃ Śrîṃ Svâhâ, (3) Oṃ Śrîṃ Hrîṃ Svâhâ, (4) Oṃ Srîṃ, Hrîm Klîṃ Svâhâ, (5) Oṃ Śrîṃ Hrîṃ Klîṃ Glauṃ Svâhâ, (6) Oṃ Śrîṃ Hrîm Klîṃ Glauṃ Gaṃ Svâhâ, (7) Oṃ Śrîṃ Hrîṃ Klîṃ, Glauṃ ityantaḥ Gaṃ Gaṇapataye Svâhâ, (8) Oṃ Vara Varada ityantaḥ Svâhâ, (9) Sarvajanaṃ me Vas'aṃ ityanto Svâhâ and (10) Ânaya Svâhâ ityantaḥ.

Next perform in the Agni the Pîṭha Pûjâ and meditate on the Deya Iṣṭadeva and worship him. Next offer twenty-five oblations to his face, repeating the Mûla Mantra. Then think of that and Agni Deva as one and the same, and then again as one with Âtman. Then offer oblations to each of the Ṣadaṃga Devatâs separately. Then search for the Nâḍis (veins) of Vahṇi and Iṣta Devatâ and offer twenty one oblations. Then offer oblations to each of the two Devatâs separately. Next offer one thousand and eight oblations to the Iṣṭa Deva with Til soaked in ghee or with the materials enumerated in the Kalpa. O Muni ! Thus finishing the Homa ceremony, consider that the Iṣṭa Deva (the Devî), Agni and the Âvaraṇa Deities are all satisfied. Then, by the command of the Guru, the disciple is to take his bath and perform his Sandhyâ, etc., and put on new clothes (cloth and chadar) and golden ornaments. He is to come then, to the Kuṇḍa with Kamaṇḍalu in his hand and with a pure heart. He is to bow down to the elders and superiors seated in the assembly and take his seat in his Âsana. Śrî Guru Deva then would look at the disciple with kind eyes and think the Chaitanya of the disciple within his own (the Guru's) body. Then the Guru Deva would perform the Homa and look at the disciple with a divine gaze, so that the disciple becomes pure-hearted and able to get the favours of the Devas. Thus the Guru must purify all the Adhvas (the passages) of the body of the disciple.

Then the Guru is to touch respectively the feet, generative organ, navel, heart, forehead, and the head of the disciple with Kûrcha (a bundle of Kus'a grass) and til soaked in ghee, in his left hand and offer at each touch eight oblations, repeating the mantra "Om adya Śiṣyasya Kalâdhvânaṃ Śodhayâmi Svâhâ," "etc., Thus the Guru would purify Kalâdhva (in the feet) Tattvâdhva (in the generative organ), Bhûvanâdhva (in the navel), Varṇâdhva (in the heart), Padâdhva (in the forehead) and Mantrâdhva (on the head), the six Adhvâs and think these all to be dissolved in Brahma (Brahmalîna).

135-155. Then, again, the Guru would think all these to be re-born from Brahma and transfer the Chaitanya of the disciple that was in him to the disciple. Then the Guru must offer Pûrṇâhuti and consider the Iṣta Devatâ, placed in the fire by the visarjana mantra for the Homa purposes, as entered into the water-jar. He is to perform again the Vyârhiti Homa and offer all the Amgâhutis (oblations to all the limbs) of the fire and take leave of the fire withdrawing the Deity from the jar, into his own body. Uttering then the Vauṣaṭ Mantra he would tie the eyes of the disciple with a piece of cloth and would bring him from the Kuṇḍa to the maṇḍala and make the disciple offer puṣpâñjali (flowers in his palm) to the Iṣta deva. Then he would take away the bandage or piece of cloth from his eyes and ask him to take his seat in the seat Kusâsana. Thus the Guru, after havi ng purified the elements of the body of the disciple and performed the Nyâsa of the Deya Mantra, would make the disciple sit in another maṇḍala. Then he would touch the head of the disciple with the twigs (Pallavas) of the Kuṇḍa and repeat the Mâtrikâ Mantra and make him have his bath with the water of the jar which is considered as the sea t of the Iṣta Deva. Then, for the protection of the disciple, he would sprinkle (abhiṣeka) him with the water of the Vardhani vessel placed already in the north-east corner. Then the disciple would get up and put on the pair of new clothes and besmear his whole body with ashes and sit close by the Guru. When the merciful Guru would consider that the Śiva Śakti has now passed out of his own body and that Divine Force, the Devî, has entered into the body of the disciple *i. e.* charged the disciple with the pass. Thinking now the disciple and the Devatâ to be one and the same, the Guru would now worship the disciple with flowers and scents. The Guru would then place his right hand on the head of the disciple and repeat clearly in his right ear the Mahâ Mantra of the Mahâ Devî. The disciple is to repeat also the Mahâ Mantra one hundred and eight times and fall prostrate on the ground before the Guru and thus bow down to the Guru, whom the disciple now thinks as the incarnate of the Deva.

The disciple, the devotee of the Guru, would now give as a Dakṣiṇâ all his wealth and property for his whole life to the Guru. Then he would give Dakṣiṇâ to the priests and make charities to the virgins, the Brâhmaṇas, the poor and the destitute and the orphans. Here he is not to be miserly in any way in the expenditure. O Nârada! Thus the disciple would consider himself blessed and he would daily remain engaged in repeating the Mahâ Mantra. Thus I have described to you above the most excellent Dîkṣâ. Thinking all these, you are to remain ever engaged in worshipping the lotus feet of the Great Devî. There is no Dharma higher than this in this world for the Brâhmaṇas. The followers of the Vedas would impart this Mantra according to the rules stated respectively in their own Grihya Sûtras; and the Tântrikas would also do the same according to their own Tantras. The Vaidiks should not follow the Tantra rules and the Tântriks are not to follow the Vaidik rules. Thus all the Śâstras say. And this is the Sanâtan Creed. Nârâyaṇa said :—" O Nârada! I have described all about the ordinary Dîkṣâ that you questioned me. Now the essence in brief is this that you would remain always merged in worshipping the Parâ Śakti, the Highest Force, the Mahâ Devî. What more shall I say than this that I have got the highest pleasure and the Nirvâna, the peace, that passeth all understanding, from my daily worshipping That Lotus Feet duly. Vedavyâsa said :—" O Mahârâja! O Janamejayan! After having said this Dîkṣâtattva, the highest Yogî Bhagavân Nârâyaṇa, meditated by the Yogis, closed his eyes and remained merged in Samâdhi, in the meditation of the Lotus Feet of the Devî.

Knowing this Highest Tattva, Nârada, the chief of the Riṣis, bowed down at the feet of the Great Guru Nârâyaṇa and went away immediately to perform the tapasyâ so that he also might see the Mahâ Devî.

Here ends the Seventh Chapter of the Twelfth Book on the Dîkṣâvidhi or on the rules of Initiation in the Mahâpurâṇam Śrî Mad Devî Bhâgavatam of 18,000 verses by Maharṣi Veda Vyâsa.

CHAPTER. VIII.

1-8. Janamejya spoke to Veda Vyâsa:—O Bhagavan! Thou art the knower of all the Dharmas and Thou art the chief, the crown of the Pundits, knowing all the Śâstras. Now I ask Thee how is it that the twice-born have ceased to worship the Highest S'akti, the Gâyatrîand they now worship the other Devatâs, on the face of the distinct command in the S'rutis that the worship of the Gâyatrî is nityâ, that is, daily to be done at all times, especially during the three Sandhyâ times, by all those that are twice-born ?

In this world some are the devotees of Viṣṇu, some, the followers of Gaṇapati, some are Kâpâlikas, some follow the doctrines prevalent in China; some are the followers of Buddha or Chârvâka; some of them again wear the barks of trees and others roam naked. So various persons are seen having no trace of faith in the Vedas.

O Brâhmana! What is the real cause underlying secretly here in this! Kindly mention this to me. Again there are seen many men, well versed in various metaphysics and logic, our B. A's and M. A'sbut then, again, they have no faith in the Vedaș. How is this? No body wants anything ominous to him consciously. But how is it that thes so-called learned men are fully aware and yet they are wonderfully void of any trace of faith in the Vedas? Kindly mention the cause underlying this, O Thou! The foremost of the knowers of the Vedas!

There is, again, another question:—Thou hadst described before the glories of Maṇidvîpa, the highest and the best place of the Devî. Now I want to hear how is that Dvîpa greater than the great. Satisfy this servant of thine by describing these. If the Guru be pleased, he reveals even the greatest and the highest esoteric secret to his disciple.

9-10. Sûta spoke:—Hearing the words of the King Janamejaya, the Bhagavân Veda Vyâsa began to answer the questions in due order. The hearing of this increases the faith of the twice-born in the Vedas.

11-30. Vyâsa said:—Well has this been asked by you, O King! in due time and in an appropriate moment. You are intelligent and it seems that you have got the faith in the Vedas. I now answer. Listen. In ancient days, the Asuras, maddened with pride, fought against the Devas for one hundred years. The war was very extraordinary and remarkable. In this great war various weapons were used, variegated with numerous Mâyâs or ingenious devices. It tended to destroy the whole world. By the mercy of the Highest and the Most Exalted Śakti, the Daityas were overcome by the Devas in that Great War. And they quitted the Heavens and the Earth and went to the nether regions, the Pâtâla. The Devas were all delighted and began to dwell on their own prowesses and became proud. They began to say:—"Why shall not victory be ours. Why are not our glories great? We are by far the best! Where are the Daityas? They are devils, powerless. We are the causes of creation, preservation and destruction. We all are glorious,! Oh! What can be said before us in favour of the Asuras, the devils? Thus, not knowing the Highest Śakti, the Devas were deluded. At this moment, seeing this plight of the Devas, the World Mother took pity on the Devas and, to favour them, O king! She appeared before them in the form of the Most Worshipful, the Great Holy Light. It was resplendent like ten million Suns, and cool as well like ten million Moons. It was brilliant and dazzling like ten million lightning flashes, without hands and feet, and exceedingly beautiful! Never was this witnessed before! Seing this Extraordinary Beautiful Lovely Light, the Devas were taken aback; they spoke amongst themselves, thus:—"What is this! What is this!" Is this the work of the Daityas or some other great Mâyâ (Magic) played by them or is it the work of another for creating the surprise of the Devas! O King! Then they all assembled together and decided to approach towards that Adorable

Light and to ask It what It was. They, then, would determine its strength and decide what to do afterwards. Thus, coming to this ultimate conclusion, Indra called Agni and said :—" O Agni! You are the mouth-piece of the Devas. Therefore do you go first and ascertain distinctly what this Light is. Hearing thus the words of Indra, Agni elated by his own prowess, set out immediately from the place and went to that Light. Seeing Agni coming, the Light addressed him thus:—" Who are you? What is your strength? State this before Me." At this Agni replied:—" I am Agni. All the yajñas, ordained in the Vedas are performed through me. The power of burning everything in this universe resides in me." Then that adorable Light took up a straw of grass and said:—" O Agni! If you can burn everything in this universe, then do you burn this trifling straw." Agni tried his best to burn the straw but he could not burn it. He got ashamed and fast went back to the Devas. Asked by the Devas, Agni told them everything and said:—O Devas! Know verily that the pride cherished by us that we are supreme, is entirely false."

31-50 Indra then asked Vâyu (wind) and said:—" O Vâyu! You are dwelling in this universe, through and through; by your efforts, all are moving; therefore you are the Prâṇa of all; it is possible that all forces are concentrated within you. Go and ascertain what is this Light? Verily I do not see any other person here than you who can ascertain this great adorable Light. Hearing these commendable words of Indra, Vâyu felt himself elated and went at once to that place where was that Light. Seeing the Vâyu, the Light, the Yakṣa, (the demi-god, the Spirit asked in a gentle language Who are you? What strength is there in you? Speak out all these to me." At this, Vâyu spoke arrogantly " I am Mâtarisvan, I am Vâyu; about my strength, I can move anything and I hold every thing. It is through the strength of mine, that this universe is, and is alive and brisk with movements and works. That Highest Mass of Light then replied:—" O Vâyu! Move this straw that lies before you, and if you cannot, quit your pride and go back to Indra ashamed." At this Vâyu tried all his might but, alas! He could not move the straw a bit from that place!

Vâyu then gave up his pride and returned to the Devas and spoke to them all about the Yakṣa (a sort of demi-god; a ghost) O Devas! Our pride is vain, In no way can we be able to ascertain the nature of that Light. It seems that that Holy Light, adorable by all, is extraordinary. Then all the Devas spoke with one voice to Indra:—

"When You are the King of the Devas, better go yourself and ascertain the reality of Its Nature." Indra, then, with great pride, went himself to the Light; the Light, too, began to disappear gradually from the place, and ultimately vanished from Indra's sight. When Indra found that he could not even speak to That Light, he became greatly ashamed and began to conceive of his own nothing-ness. He thought thus:—"I wo'nt go back to the Devas. What shall I say to them? Never will I disclose to them my inferiority; one is better to die than do this. One's self-honour is the only treasure of the great and honourable. If honour is gone, what use, then, is there in living? O King! Then Indra, the Lord of Devas, quitted his pride and took refuge unto That Great Light which exhibited, ere long, such a glorious character. At this moment, a celestial voice was heard from the Heavens:—"O Indra! Go on now and do the japam, the reciting of the Mâyâ Vîja Mantra, the basic Mantra of Mâyâ. All your troubles will, then, be over." Hearing this celestial voice, Indra began to repeat the Mâyâ Vîja, the Seed Mantra of Mâyâ, with rapt concentration and without any food.

51-61. Then on the ninth lunar day of the month of Chaitra when the Sun entered the meridian, suddenly there appeared in that place a Great Mass of Light as was seen before. Indra saw, then, within that Mass of Light, a Virgin Form in full youth. The lustre from Her body was like that of ten million Rising Suns; and the colour was rosy red like a full-blown Javâ flower. On Her forehead was shining the digit of the Moon; Her breasts were full, and, though veiled under the cloth, they looked very beautiful. She was holding noose and a goad in Her two hands and Her other two hands indicated signs of favour and fearlessness.

Her body was decked with various ornaments and it looked auspicious and exceedingly lovely; nowhere can be seen a woman beautiful like Her. She was like a Kalpa Vrikṣa (celestial tree yielding all desires); she was three eyed and Her braid of hair was encircled with Mâlatî garlands. She was praised on Her four sides by the Four Vedas, Incarnate, in their respective Forms. The brilliancy of Her teeth shed lustre on the ground as if ornamented with Padmarâga jewels. Her face looked smiling. Her clothing was red and Her body was covered with sandalpaste. She was the Cause of all causes. Oh! She was all Full of Mercy. O King Janamejaya! Thus Indra saw, then, the Umâ Pârvatî Mahes'varî Bhagavatî and the hairs of his body stood on ends with ecstacy. His eyes were filled with tears of love and deep devotion and he immediately fell prostrate before the feet of the Devî. Indra sang various hymns to Her and praised Her. He became very glad and asked Her "O Fair One! Art Thou that Great Mass of Light? If this be, kindly state the cause of Thy appearance." O King! Hearing this, the Bhagavatî replied.

62-83. This My Form is Brahma, the Cause of all causes, the Seat of Mâyâ, the Witness of all, infallible and free from all defects or blemishes. What all the Vedas and Upaniṣadas try to establish, what ought to be obtained, as declared by all the rules of austerity, and for which the Brâhmaṇas practise Brahmacharyam, I am all that. I have told you about that Brahma, of the nature of the Great Holy Light. The sages declare that That Brahman is revealed by "Om" and "Hrîm", the two Vîjas (mystic syllables) that are My two first and foremost Mantras wherein I remain hidden. I create this universe with My two parts (in My two aspects); therefore My Vîja mantra is two. "Om" Vîja is denominated as Sachchidânanda (everlasting existence, intelligence and bliss) and "Hrîm" Vîja is Mâyâ Prakriti, the Undifferentiated Consciousness, made manifest. Know, then, That Mâyâ as the Highest Ŝakti and know Me as that Omnipotent Goddess at present revealed before your eyes. As moon-light is not different from the Moon, so this Mâyâ S'akti in the state of equilibrium is not different from Me (The powerful man and the power he wields are not different. They are verily one and the same.) During Pralaya (the Great Latency period), this Mâyâ lies latent in Me, without there being any difference. Again at the time of creation, this Mâyâ appears as the fructification of the Karmas of the Jîvas. When this Mâyâ is potential and exists latent in Me, when Mâyâ is Antarmukhi, it is called Unmanifested ;and when the Mâyâ becomes Kinetic, when the Mâyâ is Bahirmukhi, when She is in an active Kinetic state, it is said to be Manifested. There is no origin or beginning of this Mâyâ. Mâyâ is of the nature of Brahma in a state of equilibrium. But, during the beginning of the creation, Her form consisting of the several Guṇas appears, when Mâyâ is Bahir Mukhî, She becomes Tamas, in Her Unmanifested state. O Indra! For this reason Her state of abstraction, and becoming introspective, this is Her Antarmukhî state; it is known as Mâyâ and Her looking outward is Her Bahirmukhî state; it is denominated by Tamas and the other guṇas. From this comes Sattva and then Rajas and Brahmâ, Viṣṇu and Mahes'a are of the nature of the three guṇas. Brahmâ has the Rajo guṇa in Him preponderating; in Viṣṇu, the Sattva guṇa prepond er ates and in Mahes'a, the Cause of all Causes, is said to reside the Tamo guṇa. Brahmâ is known as of the Gross Body; Viṣṇu is known as of the Subtle Body; and Rudra is known as of the Causal Body and I am known as Turîyâ, transcending the Guṇas.

This Turîya Form of Mine is called the state of equilibrium of the Guṇas. It is the Inner Controller of all. Beyond this there is another state of Mine which is called the Formless Brahma (Brahman having no Forms). Know, verily, that my Forms are two, (2) as they are with or without attributes (Saguṇa or Nirguṇa). That which is beyond Mâyâ and the Mâyic qualities is called Nirguṇâ (without Prâkritic attributes) and that which is within Mâyâ is called Saguna. O Indra! After creating this universe, I enter within that as the Inner Controller of all and it is I that impel all the Jivas always to their due efforts and actions. Know, verily, that It is I that engage Brahmâ, Viṣṇu and Rudra, the causes of the several works of creation, preservation and destruction of this universe; (they are performing their functions by My Command). Through the terror from Me the wind blows; through my terror, the Sun moves in the sky; through My terror, Indra, Agni, and Yama do their respective duties. I am the Best and Superior to all. All fear Me. Through My Grace you have obtained victory in the battle. Know, verily, that it is I that make you all dance like inert wooden dolls as My mere instruments. You are merely My functions. I am the Integral Whole. I give sometimes victory to you and sometimes victory to the Daityas; Yea, I do everything as I will, keeping My independence duly and, according to the Karmas, justly Oh! You, all, have forgotten me through your pride and sheer non-sense. You have been carried deep into dire delusion by your vain egoism. And know now that to favour you, this My Adorable Light has issued suddenly. Hence forth banish ever from your heart all your vain boastings and idle pratings. Take refuge wholly unto Me with all your head, heart and soul, unto My Sachchidânanda Form and be safe. (At times the Devas forget and so fall into troubles).

84-93. Vyâsa said:—Thus saying, the Mûla Pakriti, the Great Devî, the Goddess of the Universe, vanished from their sight. The Devas, on the other hand, began to praise Her then and there, with rapt devotion. Since that day, all the Devas quitted their pride and engaged themselves in worshipping the Devî devotedly. They worshipped the Gâyatrî Devî daily during the three Sandhyâ times and performed various Yajñas and thus they worshipped Bhagavatî daily. Thus, in the Satya Yuga, every body engaged themselves in repeating the Mantra Gâyatrî and worshipped the Goddess indwelling in the Praṇava and Hrîṇkâra. So, See now for yourself, that the worship of Viṣṇu or Śiva or initiation in the Viṣṇu Mantra or in the Śiva Mantra are not mentioned anywhere in the Vedes as to be done always and for ever. (They are done for a while and not required any more when the objects are fulfilled only the worship of Gayatrî is always compulsory, to be done at all times, as mentioned in the Vedas. O King! If a Brâhmaṇa does not worship the Gâyatrî, know, then, for certain, that in every way, he is sure to go down lower and lower. There is no doubt in this. A Brâhmiṇ is not to wait, no never, to do any other thing; he will have all his desires fulfilled if he worships only the Devî Gâyatrî. Bhagavân Manu says that a Brâhmiṇ, whether he does any other thing or not, can be saved if he worships only the Divine Mother Gâyatrî. (This worshipping the Gâyatrî is the highest, greatest, and most difficult of all the works in this universe). If any devotee of Śiva or Viṣṇu or of any other Deity worships his desired Deity without repeating the Gâyatrî, he is sure to suffer the torments of hell. (But this age of Kali deludes the people and draws away their minds from reciting this Gâyatrî save a few of them.) O King! For this reason, in the Satya Yuga, all the Brâhmaṇas kept themselves fully engaged in worshipping the Gâyatrî and the lotus feet of the Devî Bhagavatî.

Here ends the Eighth Chapter in the Twelfth Book on the appearance of the Highest Śakti in the Mahâpurâṇam Śrî Mad Devî Bhâgavatam of 18,000 verses by Maharṣi Veda Vyâsa.

CHAPTER IX.

1-20. Vyâsa said: "O King Janamejaya! Once on a time, on account of an evil turn of Fate, (Karma) of the human beings, Indra did not rain on this earth for fifteen years. Owing to want of rain, the famine appeared horribly; and almost all the beings lost their lives. No one could count in every house the number of the dead persons. Out of hunger the people began to eat horses; some began to eat bears and pigs, some began to eat the dead bodies while some others carried on any how their lives. The people were so much distressed with hunger that the mother did not refrain from eating her baby child and the husband did not refrain from eating his wife. O King! The Brâhmaṇas then united and after due discussion, came to the conclusion that that they would go to the hermit Gautama who would be able to remove their distress. So all of them wanted to go quickly to the hermitage of the Muni Gautama. They began to say:— "We hear that there is no famine in the hermitage of Gautama. Various persons are running there from various quarters." Thus coming to a conclusion, the Brâhmaṇas went to the Gautama's Âs'rama with their cows, servants and relations. Some went from the east; some from the south; some, from the west, and some from the north. Thus from various quarters the people flocked there. Seeing the Brâhmaṇas coming there, the Riṣi Gautama bowed down to them and gave them a cordial welcome and served them with seats, etc. When all took their seats and became calm and quiet, Gautama enquired about their welfare and the cause of their arrival. They described everything about the dire famine and their own states and expressed their deep regret. Seeing them very much distressed, the Muni gave them word not to have any fear; he said :—" I am to-day become blessed by the arrival of the great ascetics and honourable persons like you. I am your servant. You consider all my houses as yours. Be quite comfortable. Bear no uneasiness. When your servant is alive, what fear do your entertain and whom do you fear? When the demerits are transformed into good merits by your mere sight, and when you have blessed my house with the dust of your holy feet, then who is more blessed than me? O Vipras! Kindly perform your Sandhyâs, and Japams and rest here at ease. Vyâsa said :—" O King Janamejaya! Thus consoling the Brâhmaṇas, the Riṣi Gautama began to worship the Gâyatrî Devî with rapt devotional trance. " O Devî Gâyatrî! Obeisance to Thee! Thou art the Great Vidyâ, the Mother of the Vedas, Higher than the Highest; Thou art Vyârhiti represented by the Mantra " Om Bhur Bhuvaḥ Svaḥ ;" O Mother! Thou art the state of equilibrium *i. e.*, the Turîya; Thou art of of the Form of Hrîm; Thou art Svâhâ and Svadhâ; Thou grantest the desires of the Bhaktas. Thou art the Witness of the three states, Jâgrat (waking), Svapna (dreaming) and Suṣupti (deep sleep). Thou art the Turîyâ and Sachchidânanda Brahma. O Devî! Thou residest in the Solar Orb and appearest as a ruddy girl in the morning, an youthful maiden at noon and a black old woman in the evening. O Devî! Obeisance to Thee! Now shew favour on us at this severe famine time when all the beings are well nigh on the way to destruction.

21-40. Thus praised and worshipped, the World-Mother appeared and gave to the Riṣi one vessel (cup) full to the brim by which every one can be fed and nourished. The Mother told the Muni :—" This full vessel, given by me to you will yield whatever you wish.'

Thus saying, the Devî Gâyatrî, Higher than the Highest, vanished. Then, according to the wish of the Muni, came out from that cup, mountains of cooked rice, various curries and sweetmeats, lots of grass and fodder, silken clothings, varrious ornaments and various articles and vessels for sacrificial purposes. In fact whatever the Muni Gautama wished, that came out of the brimful cup, given by the Devî Gâyatrî. Then the Muni Gautama called the other Munis that came there and gave them wealth, grains, clothings, ornaments, and the sacrificial ladles and spoons and cows and buffaloes for the sacrificial purposes. The

Munis then assembled and performed various yajñas. The place all round, then flourished and became so much prosperous that it looked like a second heaven. In fact whatever fair and beautiful there exist in the Trilokas, all came from the brimful cup given by the Devî Gâyatrî. At this time the Munis, with sandalpaste all over on their bodies, and decorated with very bright ornaments looked like the gods and their wives looked like goddesses. Daily utsabs began to be held in in the Âs'rama of Gautama. Nowhere were seen any diseases or dacoities and there was no fear from any such things. Gradually the Âs'rama's boundary extended to one hundred Yojanas (4 hundred miles) Hearing this greatness of Gautama, many persons came there from various quarters. And the Muni Gautama, too, gave them words "cast away fear" and fed them. The Devas, on the other hand, became very much satisfied by the various Yajnas and extolled the Muni's greatness. So much so, that the famous Indra the Lord of the Devas, came in the midst of the assembly and extolled his greatness, thus :—"This Gautama has fulfilled all our wishes and has verily become a Kalpa Vrikṣa (celestial tree yielding all desires). If this man had not done such things, in this hard famine time, we would not have got the Havih offered in sacrifices and the prospect of our lives would have been at stake." O King Janamejaya ! Thus the Muni Gautama fed and nourished for twelve years all the Munis like his sons and that place came to be recognised as the chief centre (the Head Quarters) of the Gâyatrî Devî. Even to-day, all the Munis perform with devotion the Puraṣacharaṇams and worship thrice the Bhagavatî Gâyatrî Devî Even to-day the Devî is there seen as a girl in the morning, as a youthful maiden at noon, as an old woman in the evening. Then, once on a time, Nârada, of best conduct, came there playing on his great lute and singing in tune the highest glories of Gâyatrî and took his seat in the assembly of the Munis.

42-62. Seeing the tranquil hearted Nârada coming there, Gautama and the other Munis received him duly and worshipped him with the Pâdya and Arghya. In course of conversation he began to describe the glories of Gautama and said :—"O Best of Munis ! I have heard from the mouth of Indra, in the assembly of the Devas, your glories as to your supporting and feeding the pure-hearted Munis and I have come to see you. By the Grace of Śrî Bhagavatî Gâyatrî Devî, you have now become blessed. There is no doubt in this. Thus saying, the Devarṣi Nârada entered into the temple of the Devî Gâyatrî and with eyes, gladdened by love, saw the Devî there and offered due hymns in praise of Her and then ascended to the Heavens. Here, on the other hand, the Brâhmaṇas that were fed by Gautama, became jealous at so much honour offered to Gautama and tried their best so that no further honour be paid to him. They further settled not to stay any longer in his Âs'rama, when the next good harvest season comes. (Thus his glories will wane). O King! Some days passed when good rains fell and there was an abundance of crops everywhere and the famine ended. Hearing this, all the Brâhmiṇs united, Alas! O King! to curse the Riṣi Gautama. Oh! Their fathers and mothers are blessed in whom do not arise such feelings of jealousy! This all is the wonderful play of the powerful Time; it cannot be expressed by any person. O King! These Brâhmiṇs created, by Mâyâ, an aged cow, who was to die and pushed her in the sacrificial hall of the Muni Gautama at the time of the Homa ceremony. Seeing that cow entering into the enclosure where the Homa was being performed, Gautama cried out "Hoom Hoom" when the cow fell there and died. And the other Brâhmaṇas instantly cried out "Look! Look! The wicked Gautama has killed the cow." Seeing this inconceivable event, Gautama was greatly nonplussed and, completing his Homa ceremony, entered into Samâdhi and began to think the cause of it. Then, coming to know that this has been concocted by the Mâyâ of the Brâhmiṇs, he became angry like Rudra at the time of dissolution; his eyes were reddened and he cursed the Riṣis, thus :—Oh vile Brâhmiṇs! When you are ready to cause mischief to me unjustly then let you be averse to meditate and do the japam of the Devî Gâyatrî, the Mother of the Vedas. "For your this act, never you will be eager to perform any Vedic sacrificial acts or any action concerning thereof. There is no doubt in this. You will be always averse to the mantra of Śiva or the Tantra of Śiva. You will be always averse to Mûla Prakriti Śrî Devî, to Her Dhyânam, mantra, to any conversation regarding Her; to the visiting of Her place or Temple, to do worship and other ceremonies to Her, to see the Grand Festivals of the Devî, to singing the names and glories of the Devî, to sit before the Devî and to adore Her.

61-81. O vile Brâhmaṇas! You will be always averse to see the festivals of Śiva, to worship Śiva, to Rudrâkṣa, to the Bel leaves, and to the holy Bhaṣma (ashes). You will be wholly indifferent to practise the right ways of living as presented in the Vedas and Smritis, to preserve your conduct good and to observe the path of knowledge to Advaita Jnânam, to practise restraint of senses and continence, to the daily practices of Sandhyâ Bandanam, to performing the Agnihotra ceremonies, to the study of the Vedas according to one's own Śâkhâ or to the daily studies thereof as to teach those things or to give, as gifts, cows, etc., or to perform the Śrâddhas of the fathers, etc., or to perform Krichchra Chândrâyaṇa and other penances. O Vile Brâhmaṇas! As you are ready to do these mean things, you will have to suffer for this that you will desist from worshipping the Most

Adorable Śrî Bhagavatî Devî and that you will worship the other Devas with faith and devotion and hold on your bodies S'amkha, Chakra and other signs. You will follow the Kâpâlikas, Bauddha Śâstras and other heretics. You will sell your father, mother, brothers, sisters, sons and daughters and even your wives too!

You will sell the Vedas, Tîrthas, and your Dharma. You will not feel ashamed in any way to sell all these. You will certainly have faith in Kâpâilka and Bauddha opinions, Pâñcharâtras and Kâma S'âstras. O vile Brâhmaṇs! You will not hesitate to go to your mother, daughters or sisters and you will always be licentious with others' wives and spend your time in that. This is not to you only but to the women and men all that will come in your families. Let the Gâyatrî Devî be always indignant with you and let you all go in the end to the Andha Kûpa hells, etc. Vyâsa said:—" O Janamejaya! Thus taking the water symbolising the true rules and laws of creation, and cursing the Brâhmaṇas, the Muni Gautama went hastily to see the Gâyatrî Devî and, on arriving at the temple there bowed down to Her. The Devî, too, became surprised to see their actions. O King! Even to day Her Lotus Face looks similarly astonished!

82-90. Then the Gâyatrî Devî told Gautama with amazement:—" O Gautama! The venom of the snake does not become less if you feed the serpents with milk; so never mind all these things; the Karmas take their peculiar turns; it is hard to say when will happen what things. Now be peaceful. Do not be sorry. Hearing these words of the Devî, Gautama bowed down to Her and went thence to his own âs'rama. Here, on the other hand, the Brâhmaṇas forgot everything due to the curse of Gautama, of the Vedas and the Gâyatrî Mantra. They then began to look at this event with wonder as unique and extraordinary. All united they afterwards repented and going before Gautama, fell prostrate at his feet. But they could not speak any word out of shame. Only they said frequently:—" Be pleased, be pleased with us." When all the assembly of the Brâhmaṇas prayed to him for favour and grace, the Muni Gautama took pity on them and replied. My word will never turn out false. You will have to remain in Kûmbhîpâka hell upto the time when S'rî Krişṇa will take his incarnation. Then you will be born in the earth in the Kali age and whatever I have uttered will exactly come unto you. And if you are in earnest to avert my curse then go and worship the Lotus Feet of S'ri Gâyatrî Devî. The is no other remedy.

91-100. Vyâsa said:—Thus dismissing the Brâhmaṇas, Gautama Muni thought that all these occurred as a result of Prârabdha Karma and he became calm and quiet. For this reason, after Śrî Kriṣṇa Mahâraja ascended to the Heavens, when the Kalî age came, those cursed Brâhmaṇas got out of the Kumbhîpâka hell and took their births in this earth as Brâhmiṇs, devoid of the three Sandhyâs, devoid of the devotion to Gâyatrî, devoid of faith in the Vedas, advocating the heretics' opinion and unwilling to perform Agnihotra and other relegious sacrifices and duties and they were devoid of Svadhâ and Svâhâ. They forgot entirely the Unmanifested Mûla Prakriti Bhagavatî. Some of them began to mark on their bodies various heretical signs *e. g.*, Taptamûdrâ, etc.; some became Kâpâ likas; some became Kaulas; some Bauddhas and some Jainas. Many of them, though learned, became lewd and addicted to other's wives and engaged themselves in vain and bad disputations. For these, they will have to go again surely to the Kumbhîpâka hell. So O King! Worship with your heart and soul Śri Bhagavatî Parames'varî Devî. The worship of Viṣṇu or Śiva is not constant (to be done everyday); only the worship of Śakti is to be constantly performed. For this reason whoever does not worship Śakti is sure to fall. Thus I have answered all your questions. Now I shall describe the highest and most beautiful place, Maṇidvîpa of the Primal Force Bhagavatî, the Deliverer from this bondage of world. Listen.

Here ends the Ninth Chapter of the Twelfth Book on the cause of Śraddhâ in other Devas than the Devî Gâyatrî in the Mahâpurâṇam Śrî Mad Devî Bhâgavatam of 18,000 verses by Maharṣi Veda Vyâsa.

CHAPTER X.

1-20. Vyâsa said:—" O King Janamejaya! What is known in the Śrutis, in the Subâla Upaniṣada, as the Sarvaloka over the Brahmaloka, that is Maṇidvîpa. Here the Devî resides. This region is superior to all the other regions. Hence it is named "Sarvaloka." The Devî built this place of yore according to Her will. In the very beginning, the Devî Mûla Prakriti Bhagavatî built this place for Her residence, superior to Kailâs'a, Vaikuṇṭha and Goloka. Verily no other place in this universe can stand before it. Hence it is called Maṇidvîpa or Sarvaloka as superior to all the Lokas. This Maṇidvîpa is situated at the top of all the regions, and resembles an umbrella. Its shadow falls on the Brahmâṇḍa and destroys the pains and sufferings of this world. Surrounding this Maṇidvîpa exists an ocean called the Sudhâ Samudra, many yojanas wide and many yojanas deep. Many waves arise in it due to winds. Various fishes and conches and other aquatic animals play and here the beach is full of clear sand like gems. The sea-shores are kept always cool by the splashes of the waves of water striking the beach. Various ships decked with various nice flags are plying to and fro. Various trees bearing gems are adorning the beach. Across this ocean, there is an iron enclosure, very long and seven yojanas wide, very high so as to block the Heavens. Within this enclosure wall the military guards skilled in war and furnished with various weapons are running gladly to and fro. There are four gateways or entrances; at every gate there are hundreds of guards and various hosts of the devotees of the Devî. Whenever any Deva comes to pay a visit to the Jagadîs'varî, their Vâhanas (carriers) and retinue are stopped here. O King! This place is being resounded with the chimings of the bells of hundreds of chariots of the Devas and the neighings of their horses and the sounds of their hoofs. The Devîs walk here and there with canes in their hands and they are chiding at intervals the attendants of the Devas. This place is so noisy that no one can hear clearly another's word. Here are seen thousands of houses adorned with trees of gems and jewels and tanks filled with plenty of tasteful good sweet waters. O King! After this there is a second enclosure wall, very big and built of white copper metal (an amalgam of zinc or tin and copper); it is so very high that it almost touches the Heavens. It is hundred times more brilliant than the preceding enclosure wall; there are many principal entrance gates and various trees here. What to speak of the trees there more than this that all the trees that are found in this universe are found there and they bear always flowers, fruits and new leaves! All the quarters are scented with their sweet fragrance!

21-40. O King! Now hear, in brief, the names of some of the trees that are found in abundance there:—Panasa, Vakula, Lodhra, Karṇikâra, Śins'apa, Deodâra, Kânchanâra, mango, Sumeru, Likucha, Hingula, Elâ, Labanga, Kaṭ fruit tree, Pâṭala, Muchukunda, Tâla, Tamâla, Sâla, Kankola, Nâgabhadra, Punnâga, Pîlu, Sâlvaka, Karpûra, As'vakarṇa, Hastikarṇa, Tâlaparṇa, Pomegranate, Gaṇikâ, Bandhujîva, Jamvîra, Kuruṇḍaka, Châmpeya, Bandhujîva, Kanakavrikṣa, Kâlâguru, (usually coiled all over with cobrâs, very black poisonous snakes) Sandaltree, Datetree, Yûthikâ, Ṭâlaparṇi, Sugercane, Kṣîra-tree,

Khadira, Bhallâtaka, Ruchaka, Kuṭaja, Bel tree and others, the Talasi and Mallikâ and other forest plants. The place is interspersed with vorious forests and gardens. At intervals there are wells, tanks, etc., adding very much to the beauty of the place. The cuckoos are perching on every tree and they are cooing sweetly, the bees are drinking the honey and humming all around, the trees are emitting juices and sweet fragrance all around. The trees are are casting cool nice shadows. The trees of all seasons are seen here; on the tops of these are sitting pigeons, parrots, female birds of the Mayanâ species and other birds of various other species. There are seen rivers flowing at intervals carrying many juicy liquids. The Flamingoes, swans' and other aquatic animals are playing in them. The breeze is stealing away the perfumes of flowers and carrying it all around. The deer are following this breeze. The wild mad peacocks are dancing with madness and the whole place looks very nice, lovely and charming. Next this Kâmsya enclosure comes the third enclosure wall of copper. It is square shaped and seven yojanas high. Wthin this are forests cf Kalpavrikṣas, bearing golden leaves and flowers and fruits like gems. Their perfumes spread ten yojanas and gladden things all around. The king of the seasons preserves always this place. The kings' seat is made of flowers; his umbrella is of flowers; ornaments made of flowers; he drinks the honey of the flowers; and, with rolling eyes, he lives here always with his two wives named Madhu Śrî and Mâdhava Śrî. The two wives of Spring have their faces always smiling. They play with bunches of flowers. This forest is very pleasant. Oh! The honey of the flowers is seen here in abundance. The perfumes of the full blown flowers spread to a distance of ten yojanas. The Gandharbbas, the musicians, live here with their wives.

41-60. The places round this are filled with the beauties of the spring and with the cooing of cuckoos. No doubt this place intensifies the desires of the amorous persons! O King! Next comes the enclosure wall, made of lead. Its height is seven yojanas. Within this enclosure there is the garden of the Santânaka tree. The fragrance of its flowers extends to ten yojanas. The flowers look like gold and are always in full bloom. Its fruits are very sweet. They seem to be imbued with nectar drops. In this garden resides always the Summer Season with his two wives Śukra Śrî and Śuchi Śrî. The inhabitants of this place always remain under trees; otherwise they will be scorched by summer rays. Various Siddhas and Devas inhabit this place. The female sensualists here get their bodies all anointed with sandal paste and all decked with flowers garlands and they stalk to and fro with fans in their hands. There is water to be found here very cool and refreshing. And owing to heat all the people here use this water. Next to this lead enclosure comes the wall made of brass, the fifth enclosure wall. It is seven yojanas long. In the centre is situated the garden of Hari Chandana trees. Its ruler is the Rainy Season.

The lightnings are his auburn eyes; the clouds are his armour, the thunder is his voice and the rainbow is his arrow. Surrounded by his hosts he rains incessantly. He has twelve wives :—(1) Nabhah Śrî, (2) Nabhahsya Śrî, (3) Svarasya, (4) Rasyasâlinî, (5) Ambâ, (6) Dulâ, (7) Niratni, (8) Abhramantî, (9) Megha Yantikâ, (10) Varṣayantî, (11) Chivuṇikâ, and (12) Vâridhârâ (some say Madamattâ. All the trees here are always seen with new leaves and entwined with new creepers. The whole site is covered all over with fresh green leaves and twigs. The rivers here always flow full and the current is strong, indeed ! The tanks here are very dirty like the minds of worldly persons attached to worldly things. The devotees of the Devî, the Siddhas and the Devas and those that consecrated in their life times tanks, wells, and reservoirs for the satisfaction of the Devas dwell here with their wives. O King ! Next to this brass enclosure comes, the sixth enclosure wall made of five fold irons. It is seven yojanas long. In the centre is situated the Garden of Mandâra trees. This garden is beautified by various creepers, flowers and leaves. The Autumn season lives here with his two wives Iṣalakṣmî and Ûrjalakṣmî and he is the ruler. Various Siddha persons dwell here with their wives, well clothed. O King ! Next to this comes the seventh enclosure wall, seven yojanas long and built of silver.

61-80. In the centre is situated the garden of Pârijâta trees. They are filled with bunches of flowers. The fragrance of these Pârijâtas extend upto the ten Yojanas and gladden all the things all around. Those who are the Devî Bhaktas and who do the works of the Devî are delighted with this fragrance. The Hemanta (Dewy) season is the Regent of this place. He lives here with his two wives Saha Śrî and Sahasya Srî and with his hosts. Those who are of a loving nature are pleased hereby. Those who have become perfect by performing the Vratas of the Devî live here also. O King ! Next to this silver, there comes the eighth enclosure wall built of molten gold. It is seven Yojanas long. In the centre there is the garden of the Kadamba tree. The trees are always covered with fruits and flowers and the honey is coming out always from the trees from all the sides. The devotees of the Devî drink this honey always and feel intense delight ; the Dewy Season is the Regent of this place. He resides here with his two wives Tapah Śrî and Tapasyâ Śrî and his various hosts, and enjoys gladly various objects of enjoyments. Those who had made various gifts for the Devi's satisfaction, those great Siddha Puruṣas live here with their wives and relatives very gladly in various enjoyments. O King! Next to this golden enclosure wall comes the ninth enclosure made of red Kum Kum like (saffron) Puṣparâga gems. The ground inside this enclosure, the ditches or the basins for water dug round their roots are all built of Puṣparâga gems. Next to this wall there are other enclosure walls built of various other gems and jewels; the sites, forests, trees, flowers birds, rivers, tanks, lotuses, maṇḍapas (halls) and their pillars are all built respectively of those gems. Only this is to be remembered that those coming nearer and nearer to the centre are one lakh times more brilliant than the ones receding from them. This is the general rule observed in the construction of these enclosures and the articles contained therein. Here the Regents of the several quarters, the Dikpâlas, representing the sum total of the several Dikpâlas of every Brahmâṇḍa and their guardians reside. On the eastern quarter is situated the Amarâvatî city. Here the high-peaked mountains exist and various trees are seen. Indra, the Lord of the Devas, dwells here. Whatever beauty exists in the separate Heavens in the several places, one thousand times, rather more than that, exists in the Heaven of this cosmic Indra, the thousand-eyed, here. Here Indra mounting on the elephant Airâvata, with thunderbolt in his hand, lives with Śachî Devî and other immortal ladies and with the hosts of the Deva forces.

On the Agni (south-eastern) corner is the city of Agni. This represents the sum total of the several cities of Agni in different Brahmâṇḍas.

81-100. Here resides the Agni Deva very gladly with his two wives Svâhâ and Svadhâ and with his Vâhana and the other Devas. On the south is situated the city of Yama, the God of Death. Here lives Dharma Râja with rod in his hand and with Chitragupta and several other hosts. On the south-westen corner is the place of the Râkṣasas. Here resides Nirriti with his axe in his hand and with his wife and other Râkṣasas. On the west is the city of Varuṇa. Here Varuṇa râja resides with his wife Vâruṇî and intoxicated with the drink of Vâruṇî honey; his weapon is the noose, his Vâhana is the King of fishes and his subjects are the aquatic animals. On the north-western corner dwells Vâyudeva. Here Pavana Deva lives with his wife and with the Yogis perfect in the practice of Prâṇâyâma. He holds a flag in his hand.

His Vâhana is deer and his family consists of the fortynine Vâyus. On the north resides the Yakṣas. The corpulent King of the Yakṣas, Kuvera, lives here with his Śaktis Vriddhi and Riddhi, and in possession of various gems and jewels. His generals Maṇibhadra, Purṇa bhadra, Maṇimân, Maṇikandhara, Maṇibhûṣa, Manisragvî, Maṇikarmukadhârî, etc, live here. On the north eastern corner is situated the Rudra loka, decked with invaluable gems. Here dwells the Rudra Deva, On His back is kept the arrow-case and he holds a bow in his left hand. He looks very angry and his eyes are red with anger. There are other Rudras like him with bows and spears and other weapons, surrounding him. The faces of some of them are distorted; some are very horrible indeed! fire is coming out from the mouths of some others. Some have ten hands; some have hundred hands and some have thousand hands; some have ten feet; some have ten heads whereas some others have three eyes. Those who roam in the intermediate spaces between the heaven and earth, those who move on the earth, or the Rudras mentioned in the Rudrâdhyâya all live here. O King! Îsâna, the Regent of the north eastern quarter lives here with Bhadrakâlî and other Mâtrigaṇas, with Koṭis and Koṭis of Rudrâṇîs and with Ḍâmarîs and Vîra Bhadras and various other Śaktis. On his neck there is a garland of skulls, on his hand there is a ring of snakes; he wears a tiger skin; his upper clothing is a tiger skin and his body is smeared with the ashes of the dead. He sounds frequently his Ḍamaru; this sound reverberates on all sides, he makes big laughs called Aṭṭahâsya, reverberating through the heavens. He remains always surrounded with Pramathas and Bhûtas; they live here.

Here ends the Tenth Chapter of the Twelfth Book on the description of Maṇi Dvîpa in the Mahapurâṇam Śrî Mad Devî Bhâgavatam of 18,000 verses by Maharṣi Veda Vyâsa.

CHAPTER XI.

1-30. Vyâsa said:—"O King Janamejaya! Next to this Puṣparâga maṇi enclosure wall comes the tenth enclosure wall, made of Padmarâga maṇi, red like the red Kunkuma and the Rising Sun. It is ten yojanas high. All its ground, entrance gates and temples and arbours are all made of Padmarâga maṇi. Within this reside the sixtyfour Kalâs or Sub-Śaktis adorned with various ornaments and holding weapons in their hands. Each of them has a separate Loka (region) allotted and within this Loka he has got his own formidable weapons, Vâhanas, families and their leaders or Governors. O King! Now hear the names of the sixtyfour Kalâs:—They are:—Pingalâkṣî, Vis'âlâkṣî, Samriddhi, Vriddhi, Śraddhâ, Svâhâ, Svadhâ, Mâyâ, Sañgñâ, Vasundharâ, Trilokadhâtrî, Sâvitrî, Gâyatrî, Tridas'es'varî, Surûpâ, Bahurûpâ, Skandamâtâ, Achyutapriyâ, Vimalâ, Amalâ, Aruṇî, Âruṇî, Prakriti, Vikriti, Sriṣṭi, Sthiti, Saṃrhiti, Sandhyâ, Mâtâ, Satî, Hamsî, Mardikâ, Vajrikâ, Parâ, Devamâtâ, Bhagavatî, Devakî, Kamalâsanâ, Trimukhî, Saptamukhî, Surâsura vimardinî, Lamboṣṭhî, Ûrdhakes'î, Bahusîrṣâ, Vrikodarî Ratharekhâh-vayâ, Śas'irekâ, Gaganavegâ, Pavanavegâ, Bhuvanapâlâ, Madanâturâ, Anangâ, Anangamathanâ, Anangamekhalâ, Anangakusumâ, Visvarûpâ, Surâdikâ, Kṣayaṃkarî, Akṣyobhyâ, Satyavâdinî, Bahurûpâ, Śuchivratâ, Udârâ and Vâgiṣ'î. These are the sixtyfour Kalâs. All of them have got luminous faces and long Lolling tongues. Fire is always coming out from the faces of all of them. The eyes of all of them are red with anger. They are uttering:—We will drink all the water and thus dry up the oceans; we will annihilate fire, we will stop the flow of air and control it, To-day we will devour the whole universe and so forth. All of them have got bows and arrows in their hands; all are eager to fight. The four quarters are being reverberated with the clashing of their teeth. The hairs on their heads are all tawny and they stand upwards. Each of them has one hundred Akṣauhiṇî forces under them. O King! What more to say than this that each of them has got power to destroy one lakh Brahmâṇḍas; and their one hundred Akṣauhiṇî forces also can do the same. There is nothing that is not impracticable with them. What they cannot do cannot be conceived by mind nor can be uttered in speech. All the war materials exist within their enclosures. Chariots, horses, elephants, weapons, and forces all are unlimited. All the war materials are ready at all times and in abundance. Next comes the eleventh enclosure wall built of Gomedamaṇi. It is ten Yojanas high. Its colour is like the newly blown Javâ flower. All the ground, trees, tanks, houses, pillars, birds and all other things are all red and built of Gomedamaṇi. Here dwell the thirty-two Mahâ Śaktis adorned with various ornaments made of Gomedamaṇi and furnished with various weapons. They are always eager to fight. Their eyes are always red with anger; their faces are like Pis'âchas and their hands are like chakras (discs). "Pierce him" "Beat him," "Cut him," "Tear him asunder," "Burn him down," are the words constantly uttered by them. The inhabitants of the place always worship them. Each of them has ten Akṣauhiṇî forces. These are inordinately powerful. It is impossible to describe that. It seems that each S'akti can easily destroy one lâkh Brahmâṇḍas.

Innumerable chariots, elephants, horses, etc., and other vâhanas are here. Verily all the war materials of the Devî Bhagavatî are seen in this Go-meda-maṇi enclosure.

31-51. Now I am mentioning the auspicious, sindestroying names of these Śaktis:—Vidyâ, Hrî, Puṣṭi, Prajñâ, Sinî vâlî, Kuhû, Rudrâ, Viryâ, Prabhâ, Nandâ, Poṣaṇî, Riddhidâ, Śubhâ, Kâlarâtri, Mahârâtri, Bhadra Kâlî, Kapardinî, Vikriti, Daṇḍi,, Muṇḍinî, Sendukhaṇḍâ, Śikhaṇḍinî, Nis'umbha s'umbha mathanî, Mahiṣâsura marddinî, Indrâṇî, Rudrâṇî, Śankarârdha sarîriṇî, Nârî, Nârâyaṇî Tris'ûlinî, Pâlinî, Ambikâ, and Hlâdinî. (See the Dakṣiṇâ Mûrti Samhitâ and other Tantras.)

35. Never there is any chance that they will be defeated any where. Hence if all those Śaktis get angry at any time, this Brahmâṇḍa ceases to exist. Next to this Go-meda enclosure comes the enclosure made of diamonds. It is ten yojanas high; on all sides there are the entrance gates; the doors are hinged there with nice mechanisms. Nice new diamond trees exist here. All the roads, royal roads, trees, and the spaces for watering their roots, tanks, wells, reservoirs, Sâranga and other musical instruments are all made of diamonds. Here dwells Śrî Bhuvanes'varî Devî with Her attendants. O King! Each of them has a lakh attendants. All of them are proud of their beauty Some of them are holding fans in their hands; some are holding cups for drinking water; some, betelnuts; some are holding umbrellas; some chowries; some are holding various clothings; some flowers; some, looking glasses; some, saffrons; some collyrium, whereas some others are holding Sindûra (red lead). Some are ready to do the painting works; some are anxious to champoo the feet; some are eager to make Her wear ornaments; some are anxious to put garlands of flowers on Her neck. All of them are skilled in various arts of enjoyments and they are all young. To gain the Grace of the Devî, they consider the whole universe as trifling. Now I shall mention to you the names of the attendants of the Devî, proud of their possessing lots of amorous gestures and postures. Listen. They are:—Anangarûpâ, Anangamadanâ, Madanâturâ, Bhuvanavegâ, Bhuvanapâlikâ, Sarvas'is'ira, Anangavedanâ, Anangamekhalâ, these are the Eight Sakhis. Each of them is as fair as Vidyullatâ. Each is adorned with, various ornaments and skilled in all actions. When they walk to and fro with canes and rods in their hands in the service of the Devî, they look as if the lightning flashes glimmer on all sides.

52-71 On the outer portion of the enclosure wall on the eight sides are situated the dwelling houses of these eight Sakhîs and they are always full of various vâhanas and weapons. Next to this enclosure of diamond comes the thirteenth enclosure wall made of Vaidûrya maṇi, Its height is ten yojanas. There are entrance gates and doorways on the four sides. The court inside, the houses, the bigroads, wells, tanks, ponds, rivers and even the sands are all made of Vaidûrya maṇi. On the eight sides reside the eight Mâtrikâș Brâhmî, etc., with their hosts. These Mâtrikâs represent the sum-total of the individual Mâtrikâs in every Brahmâṇḍa Now hear their names:—(1) Brâhmî, (2) Mâhes'varî, (3) Kaumârî, (4) Vaiṣṇavî, (5) Vârâhî, (6) Indrâṇî, (7)Châmuṇḍâ, and (8) MahâLakṣmî.

Their forms are like those of Brahmâ and Rudra and others. They are always engaged in doing good to the Universe and reside here with their own Vâhanas and weapons.

60-61. At the four gates, the various Vâhanas of Bhagavatî remain always fully equipped. Somewhere there are Koṭis and Koṭis of elephants. At some places there are Koṭis and Koṭis of horses ; at others there are camps, houses, at others there are swans, lions; at others there are Garuḍas; at other places there are peacocks, bulls and various other beings all fully equipped and arranged in due order. Similarly the above mentioned animals are yoked to Koṭis and Koṭis of chariots ; there are coachmen (syces) ; at some places flags are fluttering high on them so as to reach the heavens and thus they are adding beauty. At other places the aerial cars are arranged in rows, countless, with various sounding instruments in them, with flags soaring high in the Heavens and endowed with various ensigns and emblems. O King ! Next to this Vaidûrya enclosure, comes the fourteenth enclosure wall built of Indranîlamani; its height is ten Yojanas. The court inside, houses, roads, wells, tanks and reservoirs, etc., all arebuilt of Indranîlamaṇi. There is here a lotus consisting of sixteen petals extending to many Yojanas in width and shining like a second Svdars'ana Chakra. On these sixteen petals reside the sixteen Śaktis of Bhagavatî, with their hosts. Now I am mentioning the names of these, Hear :—Karâlî Vikârâlî, Umâ, Sarasvatî, Śrî, Durgâ, Ûṣâ, Lakṣmî, Śruti, Smriti, Dhriti, Śraddhâ, Medhâ, Mati, Kânti, and Âryâ. These are the 16 Śaktis. They all are dark blue, of the colour of the fresh rain-cloud ; They wield in their hands axes and shields. It seems they are ever eager to fight. O King ! These Śaktis are the Rulers of all the separate Śaktis of the other Brahmâṇḍas. These are the forces of Śrî Devî.

72-90. Being strengthened by the Devî's strength , these are always surrounded by various chariots and forces, various other Śaktis follow them. If they like, they can cause great agitation in the whole universe. Had I thousand faces, I would not have been able to describe what an amount of strength they weild. Now I describe the fifteenth enclosure wall :—Listen. Next to this Indranîlmani enclosure, comes the enclosure made of pearls (muktâ), very wide and ten Yojanas high. The court inside, its space, trees, all are built of pearls. Within this enclosure there is a lotus with eight petals, all of pearls. On these petals reside the eight Śaktis, the advisers and ministers of the Devî. Their appearances, weapons, dresses, enjoyments, everything is like those of Śrî Devî. Their duty is to inform the Devî of what is going on in the Brahmâṇḍas. They are skilled in all sciences and arts and clever in all actions. They are very clever, skilful and clever in knowing beforehand the desires and intentions of Śrî Devî and they perform those things accordingly. Each one of them has many other Śaktis who also live here. By their Jnâna Śakti they know all the news concerning the Jîvas in every Brahmâṇḍa. Now I mention the names of these eight Śakhis. Listen. Anangakusumâ, Anangakusumâturâ, Anangamadanâ, Ananga madanâturâ, Bhuvanapâla Gaganavegâ, Śas'irekhâ, and Gaganarekhâ. These are the eight Śakhis. They look red like the Rising Sun ; and in their four hands they hold noose, goad, and signs of granting boons and "no fear." At every instant they inform Śrî Devî of All the Events of the Brahmâṇḍa. Next to this comes the sixteenth enclosure wall made of emerald (marakata) ; it is ten Yojañas high ; the court inside, its space, and houses and everything are built of emeralds (marakata mani). Here exist all the good objects of enjoyments. This is hexagonal, of the Yantra shape. And at every corner reside the Devas. On the eastern corner resides the four-faced Brahmâ ; he lives with Gâyatrî Devî ; he holds Kamandalu, rosary, signs indicating " no fear" and Daṇḍa (rod). The Devî Gâyatrî is also decorated with these. Here all the Vedas, Smṛitis, the Purâṇas, and various weapons exist incarnate in their respective forms. All the Avatâras of Brahmâ, Gâyatrî, and Vyâhritis that exist in this Brahmâṇḍa, all live here. On the south-west corner Mahâ Viṣṇu lives with Sâvitrî ; He holds conch shell, disc, club, and lotus. Sâvitrî has got also all these. The Avatâras of Viṣṇu that exist in every Brahmâṇḍa Matsya, Kurma, etc., and all the Avatâras of Sâvitrî that exist in every universe, all dwell in this place. On the north western corner exists Mahâ Rudra with Sarasvatî. Both of them hold in their hands Paras'u, rosary, signs granting boons and " no fear."

91-110. All the Avatâras of Rudra and Pârvatî (Gaurî, etc.) facing south that exist in all the Brahmâṇḍas, dwell here.

All the chief Âgamas, sixtyfour in number and all the other Tantras reside here, incarnate in their due forms. On the south-eastern corner, the Lord of wealth, Kuvera, of Bhagavatî, surrounded by roads and shops resides here with Mahâ Lakṣmî and his hosts holding the jar of jewels (Maṇi Karaṇḍikâ). On the western corner exists always Madana with Rati, holding noose, goad. bow and arrow. All his amorous attendants reside here, incarnate in their forms. On the north-eastern corner resides always the great hero Gaṇes'a, the Remover of obstacles, holding noose and goad and with his Puṣṭi Devî. O King! All the Vibhûtis (manifestations) of Gaṇes'a that exist in all the universes reside here. What more to say than this, that Brahmâ and the other Devas and Devîs here represent the sum-total of all the Brahmâs and the Devas and the Devîs that exist in all the Brahmâṇḍas. These all worship Śrî Bhagavatî, remaining in their own spheres respectively. O King! Next come the seventeenth enclosure wall made of Prabâla. It is red like saffron and it is one hundred Yojanas high. As before, the court inside, the ground and the houses all are made of Prabâla. The goddesses of the five elements, Hrillekhâ, Gaganâ, Raktâ, Karâlikâ, and Mahochchhuṣmâ reside here. The colours and lustres of the bodies of the goddesses resemble those of the elements over which they preside respectively All of them are proud of their youth and hold in their four hands noose, goad and signs granting boons and "no fear." They are dressed like S'rî Devî and reside here always. Next to this comes the eighteenth enclosure wall built of Navaratna (the nine jewels). It is many yojanas wide. This enclosure wall is superior to all others and it is higher also. On the four sides there exist innumerable houses, tanks, reservoirs, all built of Navaratna; these belong to the Devîs, the presiding Deities of Âmnâyas (that which is to be studied or learnt by heart; the Vedas). The ten Mahâ Vidyâ s Kâlî, Târâ, etc., of S'rî Devî and the Mahâbhedâs, that is, their all the Avatâras all dwell here with their respective Âvaraṇas, Vâhanas and ornaments. All the Avatâras of S'rî Devî for the killing of the Daityas and for showing favour to the devotees live here. They are Pâs'âṃkus'es'varî, Bhuvanes'varî, Bhairavî, Kapâla Bhuvanes'varî, Aṃkus'a Bhuvanes'varî, Pramâda bhuvanes'varî, S'rî Krodha Bhuvanes'varî, Tripuṭâs'vârûḍhâ, Nityaklinnâ, Annapurnâ, Tvaritâ, and the other avatâras of Bhuvanes'varî, and Kâlî, Târâ and the other Mahâvidyâs are known as Mahâvidyâs. They live here with their Âvaraṇa Devatâs, Vâhanas, and ornaments respectively. (*Note*:—The Âvaraṇa Deities are the attendant Deities). Here live also the seven Koṭis of Devîs presiding over the Mahâ Mantras, all brilliant and fair like the Koṭi Suns. O King! Next to this enclosure wall comes the chief and crowning palace of S'rî Devî, built o

Chintâmaṇi gems. All the articles within this are built of Chintâmaṇi gems. Within this palace are seen hundreds and thousands of pillars. Some of these pillars are built of Sûryakântamaṇi, some are built of Chandrakânta maṇî, and some are built of Vidyutkânta maṇi. O King! The lustre and brilliance of these pillars is so strong that no articles within this palace are visible to the eye. (*Note*:—The face of the Goddes Kâlî is so bright that it appears like a shadow, *i. e.* black).

Here ends the Eleventh Chapter on the description of the enclosure walls built of Padmarâga maṇi, etc., of the Maṇi Dvîpa in the Mahâpurâṇam S'rî Mad Devî Bhâgavatam of 18,000 verses by Maharṣi Veda Vyâsa.

CHAPTER XII.

1-17. Vyâsa said:—"O King Janamejaya! The Ratnagriha, above mentioned, is the Central, the Chief and the Crowning Place of Mûlâ Prakriti. (The nine jewels are:—(1) Muktâ, (2) Mâṇikya, (3) Vaidûrya, (4) Gomeda, (5) Vajra, (6) Vidruma, (7) Padmarâga, (8) Marakata, and (9) Nîla). This is situated in the centre of all the enclosures. Within this there are the four Maṇḍapas *i. e.*, halls built of one thousand (*i.e.*, innumerable) pillars. These are the S'rîngâra Maṇḍapa, Mukti Maṇḍapa, Jñâna Maṇḍapa and Ekânta Maṇḍapa; on the top there are canopies of various colours; within are many scented articles scented by the Dhûpas, etc. The brilliance of each of these is like that of one Koṭi Suns. On all sides of these four Maṇḍapas there are nice groups of gardens of Kâs'mîra, Mallikâ, and Kunda flowers. Various scents, and scented articles, for example, of musk, etc., are fully arranged in due order. There is a very big lotus tank here; the steps leading to it are built of jewels. Its water is nectar, on it are innumerable full-blown lotuses and the bees are humming always over them. Many birds, swans, Kâraṇḍavas, etc., are swimming to and fro. The sweet scents of lotuses are playing all round. In fact, the whole Maṇidvipa is perfumed with various scented things. Within the Sriṅgâra Maṇḍapa, the Devî Bhagavatî is situated in the centre on an Âsana (seat) and She hears the songs sung in tune by the other Devis along with the other Devas. Similarly sitting on the Mukti Maṇḍapa, She frees the Jîvas from the bondages of the world. Sitting on the Jñâna Maṇḍapa, She gives instructions on Jñâna, and sitting on the fourth Ekânta Maṇḍapa, She consults with Her ministers, the Sakhis, Ananga Kusuma, etc, on the creation, preservation, etc., of the universe. O King! Now I shall describe about the main, Khâs, room of S'rî Devî. Listen. The Khâs Mahal palace of the Devî Bhagavatî is named Śrî Chintâmaṇi Griha. Within this is placed the raised platform, the dais and sofa whereon the Devî taketh Her honourable seat. The ten S'akti-tattvas form the staircases. The four legs are (1) Brahmâ, (2) Viṣṇu, (3) Rudra, and (4) Mahes'vara. Sadâs'iva forms the upper covering plank. Over this Śrî Bhuvanes'vara Mahâ Deva or the Supreme Architect of the Universe is reigning. Now hear something about this Bhuvanes'vara. Before creation while intending to sport, the Devî Bhagavatî divided Her Body into two parts and from the right part created Bhuvanes'vara. He has five faces and each face has three eyes. He has four hands and He is holding in each hand deer, signs indicating do not fear, axe, and signs granting boons. He looks sixteen years old. The lustre of of His Body is more beautiful then Koṭi Kandarpas and more fiery than thousand Suns; and at the same-time cool like Koṭi Suns. His colour is crystal white, and on His left lap S'rî Bhuvanes'varî Devî is always sitting.

18-29. On the hip of Śrî Bhuvanes'varî, is shining the girdle with small tinkling bells, built of various jewels; the ornaments on the arms are made of burnished gold studded with Vaidûryamaṇis; the Tâṭanka ornaments on Her ears are very beautiful like Śrîchakra and they enhance very much the beauty of Her lotus face. The beauty of Her forehead vies with, or defies the Moon of the eighth bright lunar day. Her lips challenge the fully ripened Bimba fruits. Her face is shining with the Tilaka mark made of musk and saffron. The divine crown on Her head is beautified with the Sun and Moon made of jewels; the nose ornaments are like the star Venus and built of transparent gems, looking exceedingly beautiful and shedding charming lustre all around. The neck is decorated with necklaces built of gems and jewels. Her breasts are nicely decorated with camphor and saffron. Her neck is shining like a conchshell decorated with artistic designs. Her teeth look like fully ripe pomegranate fruits. On Her head is shining the jewel crown. Her lotus face is beautified with alakâ as if these are mad bees. Her navel is beautiful like the whirls in the river Bhâgirathî; Her fingers are decorated with jewel rings; She has three eyes like lotus leaves; the lustre of Her body is bright like Padmarâgamaṇi cut and carved and sharpened on stone. The bracelets are adorned with jewel tinkling bells; Her neck ornaments and medals are studded with gems and jewels. Her hands are resplendent with the lustre of the jewels on the fingers; the braid of hair on Her head is wreathed with a garland of Mallikâ flowers; Her bodice (short jacket) is studded with various jewels.

30-45. O King! Śrî Devî is slightly bent down with the weight of Her very high hard breasts. She has four hands and She is holding noose, goad and signs granting boons and "fear, do not." The all-beautiful all merciful Devî is full of love gestures and beauties. Her voice is sweeter than that of lute; the lustre of Her body is like Koṭis and Koṭis of Suns and

Moons if they rise simultaneously on the sky. The Sakhis, attendants, the Devas and the Devîs surround Her on all sides. Ichchâ Śakti, Jnâna Śakti, and Kriyâ Śakti all are present always before the Devî. Lajjâ, Tuṣṭi, Puṣṭi, Kîrti, Kânti, Kṣamâ, Dayâ, Buddhi, Medhâ, Smriti, and Lakṣmî are always seen here incarnate in their due Forms. The nine Pîṭha Śaktis, Jayâ, Vijayâ, Ajitâ, Aparâjitâ, Nityâ, Vilâsinî, Dogdhrî, Aghorâ, and Mangalâ reside here always and are in the service of the Devî Bhuvanes'varî. On the side of the Devî are the two oceans of treasures; from these streams of Navaratna, gold, and seven Dhâtus (elements) go out and assume the forms of rivers and fall into the ocean Sudhâ Sindhu. Because such a Devî Bhuvanes'varî, resplendent with all powers and prosperities, sits on the left lap of Bhuvanes'vara, that He has, no doubt acquired His omnipotence. O King! Now I will describe the dimensions of the Chintâmaṇi Griha. Listen. It is one thousand Yojanas wide; its centre is very big; the rooms situated further and further are twice those preceding them. It lies in Antarîkṣa (the intervening space) without any support. At the times of dissolution and creation it contracts and expands like a cloth. The lustre of this Chintâmani Griha is comparatively far more bright and beautiful than that of other enclosure walls. Srî Devî Bhagavatî dwells always in this place. O King! All the great Bhaktas of the Devî in every Brahmâṇḍa, in the Devaloka, in Nâgaloka, in the world of men or in any other loka, all those that were engaged in the meditation of the Devî in the sacred places of the Devî and died there, they all come here and reside with the Devî in great joy and festivity.

46-59. On all sides rivers are flowing; some of ghee, some of milk, curd, honey, nectar, pomegranate juice, jambu juice, and some of mango juice, sugarcane juices are flowing on all sides. The trees here yield fruits according to one's desires and the wells and tanks yield water also as people desire. Never is there any want felt here of anything. Never are seen here diseases, sorrow, old age, decripitude, anxiety, anger jealousy, and envy and other lower ideas. All the inhabitants of this place are full of youth and look like one thousand Suns. All enjoy with their wives and they worship Śrî Bhuvanes'varî. Some have attained Sâlokya, some Sâmîpya, some Sârûpya and some have attained Sârṣṭi and pass their days in highest comfort. The Devas that are in every Brahmâṇḍa all live here and worship Śrî Devî. The seven Koṭi Mahâ Mantras and Mahâ Vidyâs here assume forms and worship the Mahâ Mâyâ Śrî Bhagavatî, Who is of the nature of Brahma. O King! Thus I have described to you all about this Maṇidvipa. The lustre of Sun, Moon and Koṭis and Koṭîs of lightnings cannot be one Koṭieth of one Koṭi part of Its lustre. At some places the lustre is like Vidrumamaṇi; some places are illumined like the lustre of Marakata Maṇi; some, like Sûrya Kânta maṇi and some places are rendered brilliant like Koṭis and Koṭis of lightnings. The light at some places is like Sindûra; at some places like Indranîlamaṇi; at some places, like Mâṇikya, and at some places like diamond. Some places are blazing like the conflagration of fire; and some places look like molten gold; some places seem filled with the lustre of Chandrakântamaṇi, and some places look brilliant like Sûryakântamaṇi.

60-73. The mountains here are all built of gems and jewels; the entrance gates and enclosures are built of gems and jewels; the trees and their leaves all are of gems; in fact all that exist here are all of gems and jewels. At some places numbers of peacocks are dancing; at some places cuckoos are captivating the minds of persons by cooing in the fifth tune and at others doves and pigeons and parrots are making sweet cackling sounds. Lakhs and lakhs of tanks are there with their pure crystal-like waters.—The Red lotuses have blown fully and enhanced the beauty of the place. The captivating scents of these lotuses extend to a distance one hundred Yojanas all round and gladden the minds of people. The leaves are rustling with gentle breeze. The whole sky overhead is radiant with the lustre of Chintâmaṇi gems and jewels. All the sides are illuminated with the brilliancy of the gems and jewels. O King! These jewels act like lamps. And the sweet scented trees emit their fragrance and it is transmitted by breeze all around. Thus these trees serve the purpose of dhûp (scent). The rays of these gems pierce through the openings of the jewel screens on the houses and fall on the mirrors inside, thus causing a nice brilliant appearance that captivates the mind and causes confusion. O King! And what shall I say of this place, more than this, that all the powers, and wealth, all the love sentiments, all the dress suited to amorous interviews, all the splendours, fire, energy, beauty and brilliance, the omniscience, the indomitable strength, all the excellent qualities and all mercy and kindness are present here! The All Comprehending Bliss and the Brahmânanda can always be witnessed here! O King! Thus I have described to you about the Maṇidvîpa, the most exalted place of the Devî Bhagavatî. At Her remembrance all the sins are instantly destroyed. The more so, if a man remembers the Devî and about this place at the time of death, He surely goes there. O King! He who daily reads the five Chapters *i. e.*, from the eighth to this twelfth chapter, is surely untouched by any obstacles due to the Bhûtas, Pretas and Pis'âchas. Especially, the recitation of this at the time of building a new house and at the time of Vâstuyâga ensures all good and auspiciousness.

Here ends the Twelfth Chapter of the Twelfth Book on the description of MaṇiDvîpa in the Mahâpurâṇam S'rî Mad Devî Bhâgavatam of 18,000 verses dy Maharṣi Veda Vyâsa.

CHAPTER XIII.

1-4. Vyâsa said:—"O King Janamejaya! Thus I have answered all your nice querries; also what Nârâyaṇa spoke to the highsouled Nârada is also said by me. He who hears this greatly wonderful Purâṇam S'rî Devî Bhâgavatam certainly becomes dear to the Devî and all his actions become fructified with success. Now as regards your mental distress, how you prevent any evil falling to your late father in his future life, I advice you to do the Yajña in the name of Bhagavatî; and certainly your father will be saved. And you also better take the Most Excellent Mantra of the Mahâ Devî duly, according to rules; and your human life will then be crowned with success; (your life will be saved; thus you as well as your father will be saved).

5-12. Sûta said:—"O Riṣis! Hearing thus, the King asked Vyâsa Deva to initiate in the Great Devî Mantra and thus to become his Guru. He was then initiated duly according to rules with the Great Mantra of Bhagavatî united with Praṇava. When the Navarâtra period arrived, he called Dhaumya and other Brâhmaṇas and performed the Navarâtra Vrata so very dear to the Devî, according to his state. At this time for the satisfaction of the Devî, he caused this Devî Bhagavata Purâṇa to be read by the Brâhmaṇas and fed innumerable Brâhmaṇas and Kumârîs (virgins) and gave in charity lots of things to the poor, orphans, and the Brâhmiṇ boys and thus finished the Vrata. O Riṣis! Thus completing the Devîjajña, while the King was sitting on his seat, the fiery Devarṣi Nârada came there from above playing with his lute. Seeing him there, all on a sudden, the King got up, and paid due respects to him by asking him to take his seat, with other necessary things. When the Devarṣi became relieved of his labour of journey, the King asked him about his welfare and then enquired into the cause of his coming there.

13-19. O Devarṣi! "Whence and what for are you now coming? By your arrival here I am become blessed and feel that my Lord has come to me; now what can I serve to you; kindly command and oblige. Hearing this, the Devarṣi Nârada said:—"O King! Today I saw in the Devaloka a very wonderful event. I wanted eagerly to inform that to you. Hence I have come here. Your father met with a bad turn of fate for his bad action. I saw to-day he assumed a divine form and he was going on a chariot. The Devas were praising him and the Apsarâs were encircling him. It seemed he was going in that dress to the Maṇi Dvipa. O King! You performed the Navarâtra Vrata and read the Devî Bhâgavata; it seems, as a result of that, your father has now been rewarded with such a noble and good turn of fate. Now you have become blessed and your actions have borne fruits. You have delivered your father from the hell and so you have become an ornament in your family. To-day your name and fame have extended to the Devaloka.

20-30. Sûta said:—O Riṣis! Hearing these words from the mouth of Nârada, the King Janamejaya became very much happy and delighted and fell prostrate at the feet of Vyâsa Deva of glorious deeds and said:— O Best of Munis! By Thy Grace, to-day I have become blessed. Now what return can I pay to Thee save bowing down to Thee. I pray that Thou dost shew such favours to me ever and anon. "O Riṣis! Hearing these words of the King Janamejaya, Vâdarâyaṇa Veda Vyâsa blessed him and spoke to him in sweet words:—" O King! Now leave all other actions. Read always the Devî Bhâgavata and worship the Lotus Feet of S'rî Devî. Leave off all laziness and now perform the Devî Jajña with great eclât. And you will surely be able to cross this bondage of the world. True there are various Purâṇas, the Viṣṇu Purâṇa, the S'iva Purâṇa, but those cannot compare with one sixteenth of this Devî Bhâgavatam. In fact, this Purâṇa is the Essence of all the Purâṇas How can the other Purâṇas be compared with this, wherein is estabilsh ed the Devî Mûlâ Prakriti? Reading this Purâṇa from the beginning to the end yields the result of reading the Vedas. So the wise persons should try their best to study it always. Thus saying to Janamejaya, Veda Vyâsa departed. Then the pure minded Dhaumya and the other Brâhmaṇas highly praised the Devî Bhâgavatam and went to their desired places. And the King Janamejaya, on the other hand, began to read and hear always the Devî Bhâgavatam and spent his days happily in governing his kingdom.

Here end the Thirteenth Chapter of the Twelfth Book on the description of Janamejaya's Devî Yajña in the Mahâ Purâṇam S'rî Mad Devî Bhâgavatam of 18000 verses by Maharṣi Veda Vyâsa.

CHAPTER XIV.

1-17. Sûta said:—" O Riṣis! In days of yore, from the Lotus Face of the Devî Bhagavatî came out S'rî Mad Bhâgavatam in the form of half a Śloka, as the decided conclusion of the Vedas. About what She gave instructions to Viṣṇu, sleeping on a leaf of a Banyan tree, that same thing, the seed of the S'rî Mad Bhâgavata, Brahmâ Himself expanded into one hundred Koṭi s'lokas. Then, Veda Vyâsa, in order to teach his own son Śuka Deva, condensed them into eighteen thousand s'lokas, in Twelve Books and named it S'rî Mad Devî Bhâgavatam, the present volume. That voluminous book comprising one hundred Koṭi s'lokas compiled by Brahmâ are still extant in the Deva loka. There is no Purâṇa like the Devî Bhâgavatam, so merit-giving, holy and capable to destroy all the sins. The reading of every line yields the fruits of performing many As'vamedha sacrifices. Human beings addicted to wordly affairs will get the merit of giving lands to the Brâhmaṇas and they will enjoy also all the pleasures of the world and in the end will go to the region of the Devî, if they can hear, after they have fasted and controlled their passions, the recitation of this Purâṇam from the mouth of a Paurâṇik Brâhmaṇa, who has been worshipped and given clothings and ornaments and is considered as a second Veda Vyâsa. Or, if any body writes the whole of the Devî Bhâgavatam with his own hand or gets it written by a writer from the beginning to the end and gives to a Paurâṇik Brâhmin the book placed in a box of the form of a lion made up of gold and a cow yielding milk with her calf with gold as his sacrificial fee; or if he feeds as many Brâhmaṇas as there are the number of chapters of the Devî Bhâgavatam and worship as many Kumârîs (virgin girls) with saffron, sandalpaste and ornaments and feeds them with Pâysânna, he gets the merits of giving lands and enjoys all the pleasures of the world and goes in the end to the region of the Devî. He has no want of any thing who daily hears with rapt devotion this Devî Bhâgavatam. One who has no wealth gets abundance of wealth, those who are students get knowledge, one who has no sons, gets sons if one hears this Devî Bhâgavatam with true devotion. A barren woman, or one who bears still-born children or whose offsprings never live long or who bears only a single child, gets all her defects removed, if she hears this Devî Bhâgavatam. with a steadfast devotion. The house where this Purâṇa is worshipped, Lakṣmî and Sarasvatî dwell there, leaving their animosities towards each other. By the influence of this Devî Bhâgavatam the Dâkinîs, Vetâlas, Râkṣases, and other ghosts can not cast a glance even on its devotee. If any body gets fever and if the Śrî Devî Bhâgavatam be read touching him with a concentrated attention, all the complaints disappear. By reading this Bhâgavatam, one hundred times even more difficult than the severe disease pthisis is cured.

18-20. If after performing the Sandhyâ, one reads only one chapter of this Bhâgavatam with a collected mind, he soon acquires the Real Knowledge. O Muni Śaunaka! While going to read this Bhâgavatam, first examine omens and then read. I have spoken already on this subject. If during the S'âradîya Pûjâ (the autumnal Dûrgâ Pûjâ), at the

Navarâtra period, one reads with devotion this Bhagavatam, the Devî Bhagvatî becames greatly pleased and awards him results more than his desires.

21-31. During the Navarâtrî period all can read well this book for the satisfaction of his Iṣṭa Deva (his own deity) whether be be a Vaiṣṇava, S'aiva, Saura, Gâṇapatya or a S'âkta. All can read this for the satisfaction of Lakṣmî, Umâ and other Śaktiṣ. The Vaidik Brâhmaṇas are to recite this daily for the satisfaction of the Devî Gâ yatrî. This Purâṇam is not contradictory to any sectarian belief. The reason of this being that to whatever deity he pays his worship, he must worship some S'akti or other, this is stated every where. So for the satisfaction of one's own S'akti, all can read this, without contradicting each other. Never any woman nor any S'udra is to read this herself or himself, even out of ignorance ; rather they should hear this from the mouth of a Brâhmaṇa. This is the rule of the S'âstras. (The vibrations and the consequent results would be truer then.) O Riṣis ! What more to say on this book than this, that this Purâṇam is the most excellent of all and yields great merits. It is the essence of the Vedaṣ. This I tell you with great certainty. There is not the least doubt in this. Reading or hearing this yields results equivalent to reading or hearing the Vedas. I now bow to the Devî of the nature of Hrîṃ and established by Gâyatrî, of the nature of Everlasting Existence, Intelligence and Bliss, Who stimulates our activities to the understanding of various subjects. Thus hearing the excellent words of Sûta, the great Paurâṇik, all the Munis of Naimiṣâraṇya worshipped him specially and as the result of hearing this Purâṇam glady became the servants of the Lotus Feet of the Devî and they attained the Highest Rest. The Munis expressed their humility and gratitude to Sûta frequently and bowed down to him again and again. And they said:—" O Sûta ! It is you that have saved us from this ocean of world." Thus (the great Bhâgavata) Sûta, the bee drinking the honey of the Lotus Feet of the Devî, recited before the assemblage of the best of the Munis this Pûraṇam from the beginning to the end, the Secret of all the Nigamas and full of the Glories of the Devî Bhagavatî. After this the Riṣis bowed down to him and he blessed and honoured them.

Then he went away to his desired place. Here the Devî Bhâgavatam ends and is fully completed.

THE END.

Here ends the Fourteenth Chapter of the Twelfth Book on the recitation of the fruits of this Purâṇam in the Mahâ Purâṇam Śrî Mad Devî Bhâgavatam of 18,000 verses by Maharṣi Veda Vyâsa.

Here ends as well the Full Treatise, Śrî Mad Devî Bhâgavatam.
Oṃ. Oṃ. Oṃ. Oṃ Tat Sat. Oṃ. Hari Oṃ.

Milton Keynes UK
Ingram Content Group UK Ltd.
UKHW021003101023
430299UK00006B/394